The HarperCollins GUIDE TO WRITING

NANCY SOMMERS
LINDA SIMON
Harvard University

The HarperCollins

GUIDE TO WRITING

with Sourcebook

HarperCollins*CollegePublishers*

For
Rachel, Alexandra, and Aaron

Senior Acquisitions Editor: Jane Kinney
Project Editor: Melonie Parnes
Design Supervisor: Heather A. Ziegler
Text Design: Jan Kessner
Cover Design: Heather A. Ziegler
Cover Illustration: Victoria Kahn
Production Administrators: Linda Murray/Valerie Sawyer
Compositor: Ruttle, Shaw & Wetherill, Inc.
Printer and Binder: R.R. Donnelley & Sons Company
Cover Printer: The Lehigh Press, Inc.

Library of Congress Cataloging-in-Publication Data

Sommers, Nancy I.
The HarperCollins guide to writing : with sourcebook / Nancy Sommers, Linda Simon.
p. cm.
Includes index.
ISBN 0-673-38637-6
1. Authorship. I. Simon, Linda, —. II. Title.
PN151.S63 1993
808′.042—dc20
92-25270
CIP

93 94 95 9 8 7 6 5 4 3 2

Brief Contents

Detailed Contents

CHAPTER 7 *Questioning Sources* 141

CHAPTER 8 *Arguing a Position* 171

Preface

The HarperCollins Guide to Writing is a book about the ways writers write and the work they produce. Writers, whether student or professional, seem always to be in the midst of a conversation: they're always listening to a number of voices as they formulate their own ideas. In this book, we've tried to capture the essence of those conversations, some actual, some imagined. We've tried to give students a sense of just how such conversations lead to good writing.

We've created part of that conversational context by including in *The HarperCollins Guide to Writing* a "Sourcebook of Readings" about a variety of topics: individual identity, morality and authority, and education. When students write about these issues, they have a chance to join conversations already begun by other writers. The *Guide* shows students how to enter these conversations on their own authority, how to ask questions and revise questions as they consider either the evidence they find in these selections or in additional sources they gather during their own searches.

ORGANIZATION

The HarperCollins Guide to Writing is actually three books in one—a rhetoric, a reader, and a handbook—a complete writing course. All of the tools necessary for your composition course are organized as follows:

Part One "Creating an Essay"
Part Two "Purposes for Writing"
Part Three "The Research Essay"
Part Four "A Sourcebook of Readings"
Part Five "Handbook"

Part One shows students what an essay is, how it is created, planned, drafted, and revised. This is the section where we introduce students to the process of writing, a process of working through a piece of writing draft by draft. We show students the nature of the task and the likely rewards. We also show students that there is no simple "right" way to go about composing an essay. Students can compare early drafts with final drafts to see the value of drafting and revising.

Part Two contains four chapters: questioning experience (Chapter 6), questioning sources (Chapter 7), arguing a position (Chapter 8), and analyzing texts (Chapter 9). Chapter 6 connects with the section in the Sourcebook on questioning identities; Chapter 7 with the section on questioning issues of authority and morality; Chapter 8 with the section on questioning ways of learning; and Chapter 9 with all three sections of the Sourcebook.

The entire book converses with itself—reexamining earlier materials in light of later ones—just as writers do in composing. The book has a sequenced organization. Part Two loops back to use materials from Part One, but both parts simultaneously look forward and use parts of the Sourcebook. Chapter 7 on questioning and annotating sources and Chapter 9 on analyzing texts prepare students for the focus on research in Part Three.

PHILOSOPHY

The HarperCollins Guide to Writing suggests that a course about writing should be a course about reading. We show students how to read sources, how to ask questions, how to annotate the text, how to have a conversation with it, and how to speak back to printed sources. These are the kind of strategies that help students become better readers as well as writers. The questioning spirit of the writer needs to be the questioning spirit of the reader.

The HarperCollins Guide to Writing moves students from writing about personal experience to questioning sources to arguing and analyzing texts. We encourage students not to leave behind their own observations and ideas as they read and study other authorities. We encourage them as well to be present in their own writing. We want students to write essays that are both personal and authoritative, both scholarly and reflective.

You will find, as you look through this book, that the words *questioning, reflecting,* and *exploring* recur frequently. We consider the act of questioning central to the writing process. Throughout the book, we show students how questioning can help them choose a topic, focus their essay, and revise their writing. We show students the kinds of questions that writers ask about their own drafts, and the kinds of questions readers ask. We offer students strategies for questioning the sources that they use in thinking about their topics. We show how questioning lies at the heart of planning and revising essays. But *The HarperCollins Guide to Writing* does not stop with questioning; it goes on to show students how those questions lead to reflection and how reflection leads naturally to further exploration, additional reading, and more questions.

WRITING OPPORTUNITIES

In every chapter of *The HarperCollins Guide to Writing* we have created opportunities for students to reflect on their sources, to record their ideas in a journal or notebook, to write informally—through letters, response essays—and questions—to professional writers and to their peers. We want to give students confidence in their own ability to respond to other writers, to think about ideas, and to develop ideas of their own. We have taught writing for fifteen years, and semester after semester we have seen students subordinate themselves to secondary source material, intimidated by the voices of "experts." Yet when they write about their own lives, they write with confidence. As soon as they turn their attention to other sources, they too often defer to the voice of the academy and write in the persona of "everystudent" to an audience they think of as "everyteacher." We want students to write naturally, with confidence, about ideas of their own. We want them to join the company of the experts, knowing full well that they too have something important to say.

USING SOURCES

We have written *The HarperCollins Guide to Writing* to help students understand the ways in which sources enrich and complicate their thinking about a topic. We want students to understand how to use their own experiences as primary source material that can be questioned and analyzed. Similarly, we want students to know how to use the words and ideas of other writers as touchstones for their own work.

We want students to learn how to question, analyze, and speak back to printed sources. Time and time again in this book, we'll ask students to take their place beside other writers. When they learn about questioning sources (Chapter 7), students work in the company of writers and thinkers such as Joan Didion, Ruth Macklin, Stanley Milgram, George Orwell, and others (professional and student) who are questioning issues of authority and morality. When they learn about arguing (Chapter 8), for example, they work in the company of writers and thinkers such as Carol Gilligan, June Jordan, Theodore Sizer, Claude Steele, and others (professional and student) whose essays appear in the "Sourcebook of Readings." Thus, students are not being asked to write essays or create arguments in a vacuum as if they were the first people ever to question issues of authority, morality, and learning. Instead they're asked to join an ongoing conversation. By joining that conversation, they learn how to establish common ground with other writers—how to find controversies, paradoxes, questions left unanswered—as they develop their own position.

A SOURCEBOOK OF READINGS

The "Sourcebook of Readings" is a balanced collection of essays that includes primary and secondary sources, student and professional essays, personal, argumentative, and analytical essays—a range of multicultural readings that can be used in a variety of ways. The essays were chosen because they are lively, provocative, and, of course, well-written. They serve as catalysts for students. They encourage students to read, to get involved, to be engaged, to take ideas seriously.

STUDENT WRITING

The HarperCollins Guide to Writing celebrates student writing and gives it the respect and attention it deserves. There are 25 student essays published in the *Guide.* In almost every chapter there is a case study of a student writer at work. We watch as the student explores, asks questions, seeks and uses advice, and becomes part of the conversation as the writing unfolds. Every chapter of the book emphasizes the importance of collaboration with peers and teachers and the importance of using primary and secondary sources. We show students how to become peer readers and how to listen to the written and oral conversations about their drafts.

Our goal in writing and publishing *The HarperCollins Guide to Writing* is to encourage students to experiment with language, structure, and ideas and to take an active role in analyzing and interpreting the issues we present in this rhetoric. Somewhere along the way, sooner rather than later, we want students to see themselves not as students completing writing assignments, but as writers claiming authority for their own ideas.

ACKNOWLEDGMENTS

A big rhetoric such as *The HarperCollins Guide to Writing* is truly a collaborative writing project. Our students have challenged us and offered us valuable insights into their writing processes. Our colleagues have offered us their wisdom and knowledgeable suggestions. We are deeply indebted to the sustaining conversations over the last fifteen years with our students and colleagues.

Specifically, we would like to thank our colleagues David Gewanter and Myra McLarey who tested our book in their classrooms and offered us numerous suggestions for strengthening the book. Our colleagues, friends, and family members Elsie Adler, Stephen Donatelli, Joan Feinberg, Gordon Harvey, Erica Hiersteiner, Charles Mary Kubricht, Jenny Lewis, Donald McQuade, Nancy Perry, Linda Roseman, Mimi Schwartz and Louise, Walter, and Ronald Sommers encouraged us and offered us their enthusiasm for our project. Richard Marius has created the spirited and lively writing community in which we work and has consistently offered us his support. Pat Hoy, a wise teacher, generously read chapter after chapter, giving each chapter the kind of close and rigorous reading we needed. His discerning criticism and his instincts for teaching have deeply enriched this book.

Our editor at HarperCollins, Jane Kinney, graciously and professionally guided this book into print. We have benefited from the advice and support of Laurie Likoff, Marissa L'heureux, and Ann Stypuloski. And we are especially grateful to Melonie Parnes, our project editor, who helped us through the labyrinth of production.

We would also like to thank our reviewers who advised us throughout the writing of this book and whose expertise and detailed responses made this a better book. We gratefully acknowledge the valuable contributions of: Katherine H. Adams, Loyola University; Ken Autry, Francis Marion College; Wendy Bishop, Florida State University; Deborah L. Coxwell, Florida State University; Carol Klimick Cyganowski, DePaul University; Carol David, Iowa State University; John A. R. Dick, University of Texas at El Paso; Lisa Ede, Oregon State University; Theresa Enos, University of Arizona; Mike Hennessy, Southwest Texas State University; James L. Hill, Albany State College; Elaine Hughes, Nassau Community College; David A. Jolliffe, University of Illinois at Chicago; David Mair, University of Oklahoma; Lisa J. McClure, Southern Illinois University at Carbondale; Christina Murphy, Texas Christian University; Twila Yates Papay, Rollins College; Nell Ann Pickett, Hinds Community College; Karen Rodis, Dartmouth College; David R. Russell, Iowa State University; Charles Schuster, University of Milwaukee at Wisconsin; Bob Schwegler, University of Rhode Island; Louise Smith, University of Massachusetts; Kurt Spellmeyer, Rutgers University; Johnny E. Tolliver, Norfolk State University; and Richard J. Zbaracki, Iowa State University.

We dedicate this book to our children—Rachel and Alexandra

Sommers-Hays and Aaron Simon—who learned to live with grace and good humor as we wrote this book, and who reminded us day after day about the pleasures of writing.

Nancy Sommers
Linda Simon

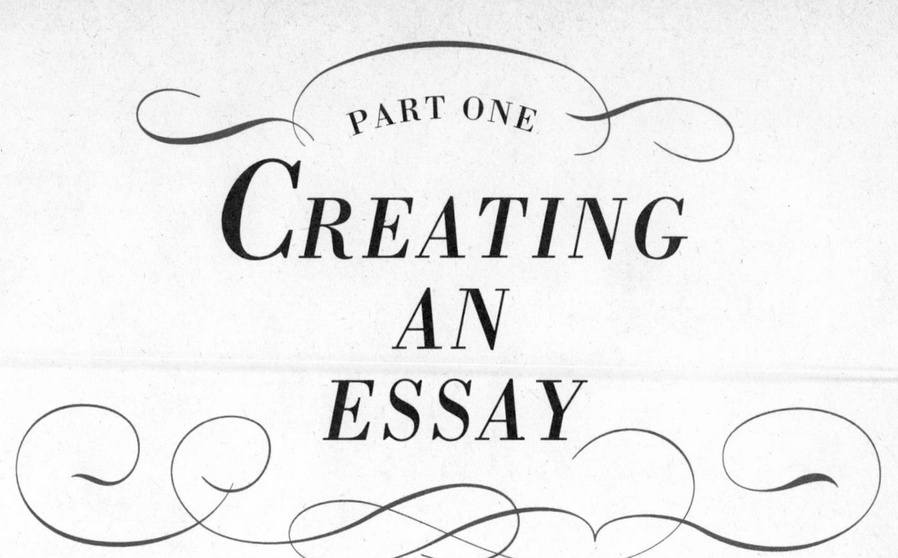

PART ONE

CREATING AN ESSAY

CHAPTER 1

A Word or Two About Writing

There is something you find interesting, for a reason hard to explain. It is hard to explain because you have never read it on any page; there you begin.

—Annie Dillard

This is a book about writing, a book about the ways writers write and the work they produce. More specifically, this book is about writing college essays. In almost every academic discipline, essays are an important way of communicating ideas and expressing reasoned opinions. While teaching you how to develop your own ideas and how to organize your thoughts, this book will show you what good essays have in common. Your essays will develop out of a context of thinking, reading, talking, and investigating. They may very well begin with a glimmer of curiosity, with something, as writer Annie Dillard puts it, that you find interesting.

You become involved in the process of writing when you begin to ask questions, when you discuss ideas with classmates or friends, when you respond to ideas by writing in a journal or notebook, when you take a long walk and think about how to express your conviction about an issue. You are involved in writing when you sit in a quiet corner of the library and read an article that seems related to a topic you are thinking about, and when you allow that article to take you down a new path, causing you to revise and modify your conviction.

Writers, thinkers, and scholars seem always to be in the midst of a conversation: They're always listening to a number of voices as they formulate their own ideas. We've created part of that context for you by including a Sourcebook of Readings about a variety of topics: morality and authority, education, and individual identity. When you write about these issues, you'll have a chance to join conversations already begun by other writers. We want you to discover that you can enter these conversations on your own authority, ask questions and revise questions as you consider evidence that you find on your own or from other writers whose work appears in this book. These writers expect you to speak up; they don't expect you to sit in silence and reproduce their words, or to subordinate your experiences to theirs. They, like you, were once students attempting to find a language to give voice to their experiences and ideas. They invite you to speak back to them, to use their words as catalysts or touchstones for your own thinking, and to take your turn in the conversation.

We will be encouraging you to write exploratory, argumentative, and analytical essays that show your questioning, ruminating mind at work—essays that are both scholarly and authoritative, essays that invite a conversation with readers. The range of essays in this book suggests a wide variety of topics, approaches, and styles that can make an essay successful. You need do no more at the outset than enter willingly into the conversation, alert to new possibilities, new ways of seeing, new ways of expressing your hard-earned conviction. The purpose of this book is to help you succeed in writing college essays—but more important, to welcome you to the community of writers and scholars.

THREE PREMISES ABOUT WRITING

All Students Have the Ability to Be Successful Writers

Students often enter a composition course with different writing experiences and different assessments of themselves as writers. "If you watched me writing," one student said, "You'd see someone staring at a blank piece of paper for a very long time." "You'd see someone covering sheet after sheet with notes, boxes, and arrows," said another student. "And somehow, from all that mess, I finally find out what it is I really have to say." While each of these students has a particular way to begin a writing assignment, neither one has the "right answer" or "the correct method." Writing, like speaking, walking, dancing, or playing a musical instrument, reflects who you are. This book will help you build upon the skills you already have as a writer and experiment with new strategies for planning and writing college essays.

Writing Is Not a Mysterious Process

Sometimes even people who write well do not explain well what happens when they write. Professional authors sometimes perpetuate the idea that writing is a mystical experience available only to a privileged few. Writing is a craft you can master; practice will indeed help you write better. Writing is not something that you are born knowing how to do, but neither are most of the other skills that we develop as we mature.

Writing Is a Creative and Empowering Experience

Often, the term *creative writing* makes students think about poetry or fiction, literary forms that invite readers into an invented world of characters and happenings that exist only in the mind of one particular writer. But writing nonfiction, including college essays, is no less creative.

When we enter the England of Jane Austen or the America of Zora Neale Hurston we make new discoveries about those cultures and about ourselves. When we enter the England of historian A. L. Rowse or the America of historian Barbara Tuchman, we are also privileged to make new discoveries. These discoveries come not from reading about invented worlds, but from reading about reality, as it is recreated, analyzed, and interpreted by other writers.

The essays you will create in college reflect your judgments, interpretations, and beliefs. You bring to your writing a diversity of experiences that informs your thinking. The way you make friends, the way you dress, spend money, behave at a job interview, the choices you make daily, all reflect the way you see yourself as an individual. When you read a poem or short story, when you look at a painting or listen to music, when you confront a controversial issue or learn about an historical event, your responses are colored by who you are. Honest reactions, thoughtful and candid responses, form the basis of your writing and shape the conversation and connections you create with other texts and other writers.

If you look around the classroom, the cafeteria, or the student center, you'll notice the differences among students that reflect important cultural and ethnic diversity. The differences you see are apparent, too, in the writings you each produce. The samples of student writing included in this book demonstrate that there is really no "right" way to fulfill a writing assignment, but a number of ways depending on who you are, how you define your purpose for writing, and how you support your assertions.

Writing, besides giving you an opportunity to express yourself in words and ideas, places you in a powerful position. In many daily interactions, you influence other people through your use of words: The note you post on the bulletin board in your dormitory or the message you leave on your friend's answering machine may affect another person's plans for the day. When you help to draft a petition for a change in campus policy, even when you offer your opinion of a movie or restaurant, you are influencing other people through your use of language. An essay, because it is a piece of writing addressed to more than one reader, gives you an opportunity to influence the ideas and even the lives of a large audience.

When you write, you say to your readers, "Listen to me. Don't be distracted. Don't put this essay down. Just follow along, and by the end of the piece you may begin to see things in a different way." You don't need to write the Declaration of Independence to exert power over your readers. All writers assert their authority as soon as they create a text for others to read. Throughout this book, you'll learn ways in which you can establish your own authority as a writer.

Opportunities for Reflecting

1. This chapter began with a quotation from writer Annie Dillard. Dillard tells us: "There is something you find interesting, for a reason hard to explain. It is hard to explain because you have never read it on any page; there you begin."

We will be encouraging you throughout this book to begin asking questions about those topics that engage your curiosity and imagination. What topics interest you right now? What do you want to find out more about?

In your journal or notebook, begin reflecting and asking questions about two topics that interest you. See where your questions lead you.

2. Various writers have described the reasons they write. Patricia Hampl, whose essay "Memory and Imagination" can be found on page 306 of the Sourcebook, tells us, "I write in order to find out what I know." George Orwell, in an essay entitled "Why I Write," offers four reasons for writing: sheer egoism, aesthetic enthusiasm, historical impulse, and political impulse. Think about why you write and what pleases you about what you have written. You have probably written one piece—a letter, a note, or an essay—in which you have emphatically said to your readers, "Listen to me; don't put this writing down; see it my way."

In your journal, describe something that you have written that has made a difference to you and your intended readers. How has this piece of writing taught you something about your power and authority as a writer?

Opportunities for Exploring Connections

Here are three short passages from essays you will find in the Sourcebook. Write a page or two of response to these passages by questioning them and letting your own experiences speak back to the writers of these passages; use their words as catalysts or touchstones for your own thinking. Do you, for instance, agree with Theodore Sizer that school is like a job? Can you think of another analogy that better describes for you what school is like? How do you respond to Margaret Mead's opening question, "Is war a biological necessity, a sociological inevitability, or just a bad invention?" Or, for instance, what is your response to Paul Theroux's bold statement "The whole idea of manhood in America is pitiful, in my opinion."

Your questions and responses to these passages will help you explore your own thinking about these topics. Exchange your writing with your classmates. What do you learn about reading and writing from hearing these different responses?

From "What High School Is"

Theodore Sizer

School is to be like a job: you start in the morning and end in the afternoon, five days a week. You don't get much of a lunch hour, so you go home early, unless you are an athlete or are involved in some special school or extracurricular activity. School is conceived of as the children's workplace, and it takes young people off parents' hands and out of the labor market during prime-time work hours. Not surprisingly, many students see going to school as little more than a dogged necessity. They perceive the day-to-day routine, a Minnesota study reports, as one of "boredom and lethargy." One of the students summarizes: School is "boring, restless, tiresome, puts ya to sleep, tedious, monotonous, pain in the neck."

From "Warfare: An Invention—Not a Biological Necessity"

Margaret Mead

Is war a biological necessity, a sociological inevitability or just a bad invention? Those who argue for the first view endow man with such pugnacious instincts that some outlet in aggressive behavior is necessary if man is to reach full human stature. It was this point of view which lay back of William James's famous essay, "The Moral Equivalent of War," in which he tried to retain the warlike virtues and channel them in new directions. A similar point of view has lain back of the Soviet Union's attempt to make competition between groups rather than between individuals. A basic, competitive, aggressive, warring human nature is assumed, and those who wish to outlaw war or outlaw competitiveness merely try to find new and less socially destructive ways in which these biologically given aspects of man's nature can find expression. Then there are those who take the second view: warfare is the inevitable concomitant of the development of the state, the struggle for land and natural resources of class societies springing, not from the nature of man, but from the nature of history. War is nevertheless inevitable unless we change our social system and outlaw classes, the struggle for power, and possessions; and in the event of our success warfare would disappear, as a symptom vanishes when the disease is cured.

One may hold a compromise position between these two extremes; one may claim that all aggression springs from the frustration of man's biologically determined drives and that, since all forms of culture are frustrating, it is certain each new generation will be aggressive and the aggression will find its natural and inevitable expression in race war, class war, nationalistic war, and so on.

From "Being a Man"

Paul Theroux

I have always disliked being a man. The whole idea of manhood in America is pitiful, in my opinion. This version of masculinity is a little like having to wear an ill-fitting coat for one's entire life (by contrast, I imagine femininity to be an oppressive sense of nakedness). Even the expression "Be a man!" strikes me as insulting and abusive. It means: Be stupid, be unfeeling, obedient, soldierly and stop thinking. Man means "manly"—how can you think about men without considering the terrible ambition of manliness? And yet it is part of every man's life. It is a hideous and crippilng lie; it not only insists on difference and connives at superiority, it is also by its very nature destructive—emotionally damaging and socially harmful.

WRITING ESSAYS

The essays that you write in college may take many forms. You may be asked to write an in-class essay in response to questions on an exam; you may be asked to write a 20-page research paper based on many sources. In a poetry class, you may be asked to write an essay based on a close reading of a single poem. In a psychology class, you may be asked to write a review of current studies about a given subject. These writings, generated by many different assignments, might be labeled with various names across the disciplines, but they actually have much in common; they are all forms of the essay.

Essays Have a Clear, Well-Defined Focus

The focus of an essay is sometimes called a *thesis* or an *organizing idea.* This organizing idea is different from a *topic.* For example, a writer may be interested in the topic of violence on television. That topic may generate many questions: How does violence on television affect young children? Should violence on television be regulated more strictly than it is? How does violence on television affect a viewer's perception of reality? What is the relationship between violence on television and actual occurrences of crime? Any one of those questions will help the writer find a focus for an essay. The answer to the question becomes the organizing idea for the essay.

Essays Are Intended for More Than One Reader

Some forms of written communication are informal and private, reflecting a special relationship between writer and reader. You might easily write a three-page letter to a friend you haven't seen in some time, but the letter, most likely, will not be an essay. Instead, it will be a compilation of news and thoughts and reflections, a personal monologue. You may begin by writing about mutual friends, move to happenings at school, then, possibly, end with your thoughts about the movies you've seen in the past months. Because you know your reader, you may not have to explain many references to people, places, and even ideas in the letter.

A college essay, however, is not intended merely for one reader, a person who knows the writer well. Instead, it will be read by many people—your instructor and classmates, for example—most of whom do not know you at all. This distance between you and your readers makes it necessary for you to explain precisely what you mean. You cannot assume that readers will share your context, ascribe the same meaning to words, or even agree with your general premises. A college essay must consider the needs of many readers.

Essays Have a Logical Structure

Letters tend to resemble an individual's stream of consciousness. When you write to a friend, you can be as quirky and illogical as you want to be. Writing about your part-time job might lead you to remember a film you once saw together; writing about a class might lead you to speculate about your future career plans. Because you are writing to someone who knows you and understands the context of your experiences, often you do not have to include the kind of background information that you would provide for a stranger. But when you write an essay, you are addressing someone who does not know you and your way of thinking; you need to allow your reader to follow your ideas logically, to understand how one idea leads to the next, to see clearly how your ideas are supported by evidence.

There is no single model for organizing ideas in an essay. Although essays need to be logical, each essay has its own appropriate logical structure. In the next chapter, you will have a chance to read two essays on a similar theme, but two essays with very different organizing structures. Both writers could have chosen any number of different kinds of structures for their essays, as long as readers could follow the logic of their thinking.

An essay has a *beginning,* where the focus or organizing idea is introduced; a *middle,* where that idea is developed in as many paragraphs as necessary; and an *end,* where the significance of the idea is emphasized or placed into a larger context. There is no prescribed length for any part of an essay. Sometimes, for example, the beginning may be one or two sentences, sometimes, several pages.

Essays Are Reflections of Serious Thinking

In the preceding paragraphs, we've described essays as nouns, as something on paper that results from thinking and writing. But *essay* is also a verb, meaning to try or to attempt. When you *essay* an idea, you try it out to see if it is supportable or controversial, to see what kind of response it evokes in your reader or yourself. Essays involve tries—false starts, wrong turns, bold careenings, cautious trackings, thoughtful side trips—tries that lead you to insights and ideas. Essays never offer the last word on a subject; they keep the conversation going.

Although the tone of some essays may be light, playful, even humorous, essays reflect genuine engagement with ideas. An essay is the chronicle of an intellectual journey, reflecting a conversation with ideas that comes from your own experiences or from other thinkers. Throughout this book, we will repeat several key words that we think are important in the writing of an essay: *questioning, analyzing,* and *arguing.* These words require that you do more than locate new information about a topic to serve as a basis for your essay. These words ask you to think and reflect.

Many college students report that much of their undergraduate education takes place in lecture halls or in large classes. Lecture classes, although they serve many important functions, often encourage passivity and the feeling that you are moving from class to class in what writer

Theodore Sizer calls "an academic supermarket." Talking about issues in discussion groups is one way of engaging actively in learning; writing, of course, is another. When you write you impose order and structure on ideas; you see patterns emerge from the mass of information that comes through reading and listening. Writing is an important way of making connections, weighing contradictory evidence, and developing your own point of view.

Opportunities for Exchanging Ideas

1. We have offered you four different characteristics of good essays—they have a clear, well-defined focus; they are intended for more than one reader; they have a logical structure; and they are a reflection of serious thinking. Working in small groups, select two essays from the Sourcebook to read and discuss. What do these essays have in common? What other criteria can you develop to describe their common features? Why would a reader want to read these essays? What questions do these essayists seem to be asking?

2. How is an essay different from a news report? Find two newspaper reports and bring them to class. What is the purpose of each report? Do the reporters want to create a dialogue with their readers? Are the reporters asking their readers to think about the situation with them? What would be needed to turn each report into an essay? Discuss these questions with your classmates.

WRITING FOR ASSIGNMENTS

Much of your writing will be assigned by your instructors. But much of the writing that professional writers do also is assigned—by magazine and newspaper editors or by employers—and must meet standards set by someone else. Whether the reward for a good piece of writing is an A or a paycheck and publication, that writing still must meet outside approval. Writing for an assignment does not mean that your writing needs to be inauthentic or dishonest; it does not mean that your writing cannot reflect your own personality and interests; it does not mean that you abdicate authority over the work. Your writing is *yours*, necessarily and inevitably.

Many students, nevertheless, say they feel frustrated by what they see as the limitations imposed on them by assignments. "When I first got to college," one senior said, "I kept asking myself, 'What does he want? What does he want?' Whenever I got an assignment, it drove me crazy. I spent more time, I think, trying to psych out the teacher than I did planning my paper. Then, when I was a junior, my government professor asked me, 'What do *you* want?' And it was the first time I ever thought that my paper could mean something to me. We talked about the assignment—we were supposed to examine states' rights during the Roosevelt administration—and he asked me what I had read that bothered me. Well, that was a new way for me to think about an assignment. What *bothered* me? What didn't satisfy me? What didn't make sense? I found a topic and from then on, whenever I had a paper to write, instead of asking, 'What does he want?' I'd ask myself those three questions. Soon I began to feel that my papers belonged to me, not to my professors, even when I was writing on an assigned topic."

Even when professional writers are completing an assignment, they write because they want to find something out for themselves, not for someone else. Of course they hope that others will be interested, but they trust themselves to make their writing so interesting that it will attract readers. They consider their readers' background; they ask themselves what information readers will need to understand the point of the piece. But while those questions help to shape the writing, they don't provide the writer's motivation. Every writer who feels joy and accomplishment from writing does so because the writing itself is a reflection of discovery.

When instructors in various disciplines are asked why they give writing assignments, they often identify two reasons: first, to test knowledge, and second, to extend the course beyond the boundaries of class time and assigned readings. They expect that you will have learned enough from the course to provide a background for writing in an informed way. They want to make sure that you understand the key issues of the course. But the element of testing is only a small part of the reason for assigning essays. More important, instructors hope that you will find something in the course that excites you. They want you to bring your own experiences to bear on the course material and to make the course your own.

In the academic community, scholars try to listen with generosity. While they may not agree with each other's analysis or position, they grant one another the authority to take a particular point of view. That authority is granted to you as a student, as you explore new courses of study and learn to use more and more complex sources. The point of view that you take needs to be substantiated by your sources, yet it need not be a view that no one has ever thought of before. Originality, after all, is an intimidating concept for any writer. Honesty is a much more useful term, and it is a term that will be recalled often in this book.

College students are often required to complete writing tasks most professional writers would find difficult. As you move from class to class, subject to subject, you are asked to write as an experimental psychologist one day, as an art historian another day, and as a marine biologist the next day. As a writer, you will have to assume an authority that may feel uncomfortable at first. "I remember when I wrote my first psychology paper," one student recalled, "I kept thinking, 'who am I to say anything about this topic.' I thought I had to read everything written by everyone who ever thought about the topic."

You are the writer. In assigning writing, your instructors are interested in you: how you think, what you think. They hope you will express your opinions directly. "The feminine sensibility of the early twentieth century may be understood graphically through a reading of Edith Wharton's *The House of Mirth*" is a timid and circuitous way of saying, "When I read Edith Wharton's *The House of Mirth* I understood something about what it meant to be a woman in the early twentieth century."

Your instructors expect that your opinions will be supported by strong details or strong evidence. If you are reading a poem, for example, your interpretation needs to be grounded in the evidence of the text. An opinion that cannot be defended by evidence, however passionately it is stated, simply will not persuade your readers. Your instructors hope, too, that your work will reflect genuine interest and engagement in a subject.

USING A TEXTBOOK

This textbook offers you a chance to examine the process of creating an essay, particularly the kind of essay that you will write in many of your college courses. No textbook can answer all questions, solve all writing problems, address all concerns. No textbook can make writing quick and easy: Writing is a task that requires concentration and perseverance. No textbook can enable you to write an A paper every time you sit down at the typewriter or computer.

But nearly all writers find that when they think about their writing, their own work becomes more fluent and accomplished. When we learn what alternatives and strategies are open to us, we can break out of patterns that make our writing boring and unsatisfying. When we practice writing, we improve. We believe that using this book will help you become a better writer.

We hope that you will experiment in your own way with language and structure and take an active role in analyzing and interpreting what we offer you. Somewhere along the way, sooner rather than later, you will begin to see yourself not only as a student completing writing assignments but also as a writer.

Opportunities for Writing

1. All of us at some time in our lives have made a discovery that changed us. The discovery may have been something tangible—a book, a song, or a work of art, for example—or it may have been an idea. Think of a discovery you have made. What did this discovery reveal about you? In a brief essay, describe this discovery and your response to it.

Exchange descriptions with your classmates. Find out from your readers what more they need to know about the discovery. What further details do they need in order to understand the significance of the discovery for you? Revise your essay using the questions and suggestions from your classmates.

2. Read the following passage from Paula Gunn Allen's essay "Where I Come from Is Like This." What do you find interesting in the passage? What might Gunn Allen mean, for instance, when she writes, "The oral tradition is vital; it heals itself and the tribal web by adapting to the flow of the present while never relinquishing its connection to the past." Have a conversation with Gunn Allen in your journal as you reflect on the meaning of her passage.

Since the coming of the Anglo-Europeans beginning in the fifteenth century, the fragile web of identity that long held tribal people secure has gradually been weakened and torn. But the oral tradition has prevented the complete destruction of the web, the ultimate disruption of tribal ways. The oral tradition is vital; it heals itself and the tribal web by adapting to the flow of the present while never relinquishing its connection to the past. Its adaptability has always been required, as many generations have experienced. Certainly the modern American Indian woman bears slight resemblance to her forebears—at least on superficial examination—but she is still a tribal woman in her deepest being. Her tribal sense of relationship to all that is continues to flourish. And though she is at times beset by her knowledge of the enormous gap between the life she lives and the life she was raised to live, and while she adapts her mind and being to the circumstances of her present life, she does so in tribal ways, mending the tears in the web of being from which she takes her existence as she goes.

My mother told me stories all the time, though I often did not recognize them as that. My mother told me stories about cooking and childbearing; she told me stories about menstruation and pregnancy; she told me stories about gods and heroes, about fairies and elves, about goddesses and spirits; she told me stories about the land and the sky, about cats and dogs, about snakes and spiders; she told me stories about climbing trees and exploring the mesas; she told me stories about going to dances and getting married; she told me stories about dressing and undressing, about sleeping and waking; she told me stories about herself, about her mother, about her grandmother. She told me stories about grieving and laughing, about thinking and doing; she told me stories about school and about people; about darning and mending; she told me stories about turquoise and about gold; she told me European stories and Laguna stories; she told me Catholic stories and Presbyterian stories; she told me city stories and country stories; she told me political stories and religious stories. She told me stories about living and stories about dying. And in all of those stories she told me who I was, who I was supposed to be, whom I came from, and who would follow me. In this way she taught me the meaning of the words she said, that all life is a circle and everything has a place within it. That's what she said and what she showed me in the things she did and the way she lives.

Now read the following passage from Joan Didion's essay "On Morality." Use Gunn Allen's passage as a point of departure for thinking and writing about Didion's passage. How can these two passages talk to each other? How would Gunn Allen, for instance, respond to Didion's claim, "For better or worse, we are what we learned as children." What kind of "morality" do you imagine Gunn Allen learned from her mother's stories? Look for connections between these two passages. Write a brief essay in which you explore an idea that connects these two passages.

As it happens I am in Death Valley, in a room at the Enterprise Motel and Trailer Park, and it is July, and it is hot. In fact it is 119°. I cannot seem to make the air conditioner work, but there is a small refrigerator, and I can wrap ice cubes in a towel and hold them against the small of my back. With the help of the ice cubes I have been trying to think, because *The American Scholar* asked me to, in some abstract way about "morality," a word I distrust more very day, but my mind veers inflexibly toward the particular. 1

Here are some particulars. At midnight last night, on the road in from Las Vegas to Death Valley Junction, a car hit a shoulder and turned over. The driver, very young and apparently drunk, was killed instantly. His girl was found alive but bleeding internally, deep in shock. I talked this afternoon to the nurse who had driven the girl to the nearest doctor, 185 miles across the floor of the Valley and three ranges of lethal mountain road. The nurse explained that her husband, a talc miner, had stayed on the highway with the boy's body until the coroner could get over the mountains from 2

Bishop, at dawn today. "You can't just leave a body on the highway," she said, "It's immoral."

It was one instance in which I did not distrust the word, because she meant something quite specific. She meant that if a body is left alone for even a few minutes on the desert, the coyotes close in and eat the flesh. Whether or not a corpse is torn apart by coyotes may seem only a sentimental consideration, but of course it is more: one of the promises we make to one another is that we will try to retrieve our casualties, try not to abandon our dead to the coyotes. If we have been taught to keep our promises—if, in the simplest terms, our upbringing is good enough—we stay with the body, or have bad dreams. 3

I am talking, of course, about the kind of social code that is sometimes called, usually pejoratively, "wagon-train morality." In fact that is precisely what it is. For better or worse, we are what we learned as children: my own childhood was illuminated by graphic litanies of the grief awaiting those who failed in their loyalties to each other. The Donner-Reed Party, starving in the Sierra snows, all the ephemera of civilization gone save that one vestigial taboo, the provision that no one should eat his own blood kin. The Jayhawkers, who quarreled and separated not far from where I am tonight. Some of them died in the Funerals and some of them died down near Badwater and most of the rest of them died in the Panamints. A woman who got through gave the Valley its name. Some might say that the Jayhawkers were killed by the desert summer, and the Donner Party by the mountain winter, by circumstances beyond control; we were taught instead that they had somewhere abdicated their responsibilities, somehow breached their primary loyalties, or they would not have found themselves helpless in the mountain winter or the desert summer, would not have given way to acrimony, would not have deserted one another, would not have *failed.* In brief, we heard such stories as cautionary tales, and they still suggest the only kind of "morality" that seems to me to have any but the most potentially mendacious meaning. 4

Opportunities for Exchanging Ideas

The following student essay "Site Y" was written by Michael Stern, a college freshman. As you read Stern's essay, consider the following questions: What is Stern curious about? What questions does he seem to be asking in his essay? What arguments does he make? What information do you find persuasive? What kinds of sources is he using? Locate specific passages that you find particularly effective. Locate passages where you would want to begin a conversation with Stern. Discuss Stern's essay with your classmates.

Site Y

Michael Stern

There stands in central New Mexico a great mesa, which rips 1000 feet up from the desert floor, daring us to remember that it exists only because the earth around it wore away. Men today call it the Los Alamos mesa, but such names do not stick for long. Even the Anasazi Indians died out up there, leaving behind only pueblo ruins and pictograms of salamanders. 1

Nature erodes and creates in a single process, and civilizations, like trees and mesas, develop this way. Our cities grow and link like patches of fuzz in a petrie dish, and the scattered instances in which the process is perverted compose the most painful sections of our history books. The United States has had the honor of participating in several such corruptions, not only in the immolation of Dresden and the dissection of Berlin, but also through the act of establishing, where there had been none before, a city atop the Los Alamos mesa. 2

In 1942 it became clear the United States might be able to build a new sort of bomb, an atomic bomb, of unprecedented power. The technology involved would be so advanced and the moral questions so divisive that any citizen not directly involved in the design of the weapon was considered a potential enemy. There was no place to house such a project, and the government decided that it was futile to try modifying existing labs to fit the security requirements. An entirely new kind of community was needed, an integrated series of labs, homes and stores completely isolated from the outside world. 3

Dr. Robert Oppenheimer chose the location atop the Los Alamos mesa; he had gone horseback riding there as a child and remembered the beauty of the area. It is a lovely place, and well-secured by vertical mesa walls; the south end provides the best rock climbing for hundreds of miles around. The army had the first labs and housing completed within six months and the scientists and technicians have been arriving constantly since. 4

They maintained a secrecy so extreme that it has become legendary. Wives who came to Los Alamos were not told of what their husbands were building until after the bombs were dropped in 1945. Newspaper reporters then, scurrying to complete articles on the construction of the bomb, found that they knew nothing about the installations they were supposed to cover, and many chose to write instead about the secrecy itself. The *New York Times*, for one, believed that the project was kept a secret even from those who worked there: 5

> A second town was built for reasons of isolation and security on a New Mexico Mesa. . . .
>
> None of the people, who came to the developments from homes all the way from Maine to California, had the slightest idea of what they were making in the gigantic Government plant they saw around them. . . .'

The *Denver Post*, on the other hand, suggested that it had known all along:

> The government has protected its Los Alamos bomb project west and north of here, with such extreme secrecy that it has almost wiped the community off the map. . . .
>
> Reporters were never given an opportunity to visit the project. But the public knew there was something hidden in the hills and conjectured privately over whether it was turning out gas, rockets, jet propulsion, pilotless planes, death rays—or atomic energy.

Some time ago, the army ceded control of the laboratory to the regents 6
of the University of California, and the new management has relaxed security. The road from Santa Fe was widened a few years ago, but when I worked there in 1988 it was a 15 mile traffic jam by 7:30 as employees who can't live at night in the isolation of the Mesa tried to get to work on time. Clearance badges are so ubiquitous that they're easily ignored, and for red badge employees like I was, security checks are nominal. A few Tech Areas remain off limits, of course. I went jogging once beneath the bridge that connects Diamond Drive to the labs, and came too close to some secure installation. Automatic searchlights thudded on and tracked me until I was blinded and could not see the soldiers with automatic rifles which popular rumors said would be lining up behind the fence. I backed off and when I had passed some critical threshold, the lights shut themselves off and I jogged away.

The woman I shared an office with later said that it was probably a 7
plutonium lab. This was the popular interpretation for all the Tech Areas with the weird numbers that most of us had never seen.

Given the paucity of information about the town, papers in the forties 8
had little choice but to print exactly what the government told them. What the government said, in this case, was that the town was normal. It was secret, but normal. The *Times* went a bit overboard on this point:

> The War department today described life there as not unlike that of any other American community. A "town council" of eight elected

> members serves in an advisory capacity, meeting with representatives of the project and Col. Gerald B. Tyler, commander of the army post stationed there. A school board oversees the operation of an accredited elementary school and high school. There is even a nursery school for the benefit of housewives who work on the project.
>
> While the community is isolated, there is plenty of opportunity for recreation and entertainment. Among the facilities is a nine-hole golf course, built by volunteer labor.

Why did the Department of War present the town so? Los Alamos is not a normal community and never has been. Deprived of its evolution and history, it has no place in its environment. It is an aberration, filled with PhDs from California and Massachusetts who arrived to do their bit for national defense and haven't yet gotten out.

Scientists arriving in Los Alamos are presented with a quandary: each day of their employment may draw closer the end of the world. There are two "easy" solutions to the moral questions this raises: to point to the virtue of the weapons as a deterrent against foreign tyranny, or to ignore the fact that the research plays any role in a larger drama. Enrico Fermi founded the second school, begging others not to bother him with politics on the grounds that the bomb was "beautiful physics." In recent years, faith in the evil of the Soviet Union has waned and the "foreign threat" argument has become less tenable; increasing numbers of scientists follow the other path, ignoring the connections between their work and the outside world. The few involved in weapons development who recognized the impact of their work but chose to remain in Los Alamos anyway become cynical and cavalier. The old head of X division keeps the shell of the Fat Man prototype in his backyard, for use as a barbecue and a birdbath. 9

People have accused the Los Alamos scientists of blindness for forty-five years. The classic response, offered by Robert Oppenheimer after the destruction of Hiroshima and Nagasaki, is that scientists exist to explore the world and stretch the limits of knowledge, without judging that knowledge. The ability to split atoms would have been realized with or without the Manhattan Project: "If you are a scientist, you can not control such a thing" (Rhodes, 761). 10

But these arguments are not enough. Oppie would have us believe that scientists are supposed to sit in laboratories and churn out formulae, bombs and VCRs, but not ever *think* about their work once it leaves the lab. He justifies the production of any gun, any bomb, any nerve gas, and the use of these weapons as well. Oppenheimer is wrong; bombs are not built in Los Alamos because they have to be built somewhere. Bombs are built in Los Alamos because a society was planted there in which it is possible to ignore moral obligations and never see connections between your life 11 and the outside world. On August 6, 1988 nobody in Los Alamos put out peace lanterns.

It is the nature of the town to have no memory; for those designing doomsday, it makes little sense but to live for the present. Of the 7000 scientists in Los Alamos today, half, or almost half are working on military projects. Only they know the details of their assignments, but they certainly include laser research, development of explosives and missile guidance systems. Even my group, which was ostensibly not-military, was working on SDI and WWIII air defense simulation. A laboratory health and safety official once bragged to me that Los Alamos knew more about handling toxic waste than anybody else because we had *invented* most kinds of toxic waste. At the time, there were 20,000 gallons of radioactive PCBs in a parking lot about three miles from where I worked. They couldn't find a place to dump them. 12

Such conspiracy creates a sense of community, and the trappings of suburbia fit easily onto this shell. The illusion presented by our government in 1945 has by now been synthesized, with the depressing conclusion that though we could end man's tenure on this planet tomorrow, the scientists responsible still think they're living in "Leave it to Beaver." Cities were never meant to be installed; such haste can only produce aberrations. For all the picket fences and school plays and little churches scattered along 9th Street, Los Alamos remains out of place, a tumor on the Mesa. 13

Note

[1] It should probably be noted that Los Alamos's first ski run was built by George Kistiakowsky, the Manhattan Project's explosives expert and Harvard chemistry professor, who wired a hillside with C4 and blew off all the trees.

Works Cited

"Blind Girl Saw First Bomb Test 120 Miles Away." *Denver Post* (August 6, 1945):1.

"Material for Atomic Bomb Assembled at Pasco Plant." *Denver Post* (August 6, 1945):1.

Rhodes, Richard. *The Making of the Atomic Bomb.* New York: Simon & Schuster, 1986.

Walz, Jay. "Atomic Bombs Made in Three Hidden Cities." *New York Times* (August 7, 1945):1.

Wilson, Jane and Serber, Charlotte, ed. *Standing By and Making Do: Women of Wartime Los Alamos,* Los Alamos: Los Alamos Historical Society, 1988.

CHAPTER 2

Two Writers at Work: The Making of an Essay

I hope my essay reflects how important Black American history is and how little the public knows about it. I wanted to help my readers understand why racism is still a problem and why they should be more sensitive to Black culture.

—Miriam Thaggert, college freshman

In this chapter, you will have a chance to look at two essays written for a college composition course, Miriam Thaggert's "Double Vision" and Marc Beauboeuf's "A Word." In writing these essays, both Miriam and Marc were faced with the challenges that confront many beginning writers: Given considerable freedom in choosing a topic, what should they write about? What assumptions could they make about their readers? What effect did they want to have on their readers? How could they achieve that effect? How should they organize an essay? What expectations did their instructors have about college writing?

As you look closely at the process that Miriam followed in writing her essay, and as you read drafts and revisions of some paragraphs, you'll see how Miriam made connections among the ideas she discovered along the way. You'll see the kinds of questions that she asked and the kinds of sources that she chose to help her answer those questions. Her essay reflects many choices and decisions. When you read Marc's essay, you'll see how another student, writing on a similar topic, made different choices and decisions, responding to different questions and sources.

In Chapter 1, we presented the idea that an essay needs to fulfill four criteria:

1. Essays have a clear, well-defined focus.
2. Essays are intended for more than one reader.
3. Essays have a logical structure.
4. Essays are reflections of serious thinking.

Throughout this book, we'll develop these criteria, explaining more fully how you find a focus, communicate with readers, and organize ideas. We'll be working with you as you write your own essays in response to the various assignments and writing opportunities throughout the book.

To start, we will look at the work of two college freshmen as they approach their first writing assignment. By observing the writing process as a whole, you can follow the *thinking* that underlies the creation of an essay.

Both Miriam and Marc were asked to reflect on a personal experience that had a significant impact on their lives. We'll see how they chose their topic, asked questions about their experiences, and gained some perspective on their own work as they worked through drafts and made decisions about revising.

A WRITER AT WORK: MIRIAM THAGGERT

Choosing a Topic

Miriam had a fairly easy time choosing a topic because she was able to identify one particular experience in her life as more important than others. In Chapter 3, we'll discuss ways to generate ideas when they do not come as easily as they did here, for Miriam.

"I knew from past experiences that the only good essays I write are on subjects that I feel strongly about," Miriam told us. "Even when I get a specific assignment for a course, I need to find a way to put myself into it. And I do have strong feelings about my own heritage and culture. Therefore, it was fairly easy to select a topic." At first, Miriam's topic consisted of three words: racism, identity, and history. As she herself realized, that topic was too large to discuss adequately in one essay. She knew she had to limit her focus, and she began by considering the sources available to her.

This process of limiting a focus and considering sources took Miriam several days. Like many other freshmen, Miriam often found herself thinking about her life at home. These memories seemed to offer material that could become part of her writing. She would mull over ideas about her assignment as she walked to classes, talked with her friends, or did her laundry. She kept notes of possible sources.

First among those sources were Miriam's own experiences as a child growing up in rural southwest Louisiana, in a town called Abbeville. "It's an area," she described, "steeped in the traditions of the old Confederacy, and the bayous still whisper of the ill-fated escapes of the slaves. Abbeville, in particular, is Cajun land, where in the fall, festivals of every kind celebrate the Southern way of life; and families are reunited over crawfish, jambalaya and gumbo." Within that context, Miriam first encountered racism and first heard the word *nigger*. "Traditions die hard in the South," she said, "and racism is one of the oldest customs in that region."

Besides her personal memories, Miriam also thought about what she had read, both inside and outside of school. She remembered her first encounter with the Constitution of the United States, and her feelings when she read the phrase "all men are created equal." And she remembered her strong reaction to W. E. B. Du Bois' book *The Souls of Black Folk*, where she encountered the phrase *double-consciousness*, words that somehow seemed to express her own feeling about being a black American.

If Miriam's assignment had asked her to find additional sources, she might have drawn upon diaries, autobiographies, or letters of black

Americans. She might also have used historical or sociological studies to provide additional information. But because she was asked to use personal experiences as her sources, she decided to focus her topic by writing about the development of her own consciousness as a black American.

Asking Questions

Once you have a topic, you need to find ways to explore it. Questioning, as we'll discuss in more detail throughout this book, helps you make important discoveries. In Chapter 6, for instance, you'll have a chance to question your own experiences; in Chapter 7, you'll see ways in which you can question outside sources, including the readings in this book.

Thinking about her own experiences as a child growing up in Louisiana led Miriam to formulate some questions:

- What does it mean to me to be a black American?
- Why did I think *nigger* was a bad word?
- How does our environment teach us to be racists?
- How do children learn so easily about racism?

These questions, in turn, led her back to thinking about her experiences not as just memories, but as sources for an essay. "The hardest part of writing this essay," she told us, "was choosing that one idea or thought or experience that would adequately express my feelings." To sort through her experiences, she decided to draw a diagram that would give some order to many jumbled details. Her diagram consisted of nothing more than several boxes, each one headed by a label that identified a particular experience. In each box, Miriam jotted down words to remind her of details about the experience and feelings that the experience evoked in her. Finally, she decided to write about the time a classmate called her a "nigger" because she saw from her diagram that she could detail that experience most fully. She titled her first draft "The Lesson." Here is how it began:

The Lesson

To be Black is not just to be a color. It is to possess an attitude, a feeling. Being Black is knowing and understanding your history and having pride in that history. This fact is not innate in every

African-American, and I myself didn't learn it all at once. The lesson started when I heard one word, the first time I was called a "nigger."

The lesson began, appropriately enough, at school, while I was waiting for my mom to pick me up. I was sitting among a crowd of other students, who were either waiting for their own parents or their buses to bring them home. To pass the time until I made my final escape from school, I decided to play pick-up sticks with two other girls in the third grade. The three of us played two games and I won both times. This was disturbing for one girl, Angela, who seemed to be accustomed to winning. According to her, I couldn't have won on my own merits. I was cheating, she thought. My efforts to convince her of my innocence were in vain, since she had her own thoughts about why I had won.

"Nigger!" she cried. "Get away from me!"

Becoming a Reader

Revising your drafts depends on your ability to shift from being a writer to being a reader. What impact does your essay have on your readers? What do you want your readers to think or feel in response to your words? In Chapter 5, we'll offer you many strategies for revising. All of those strategies invite you to consider your work from a reader's point of view.

Miriam knew that many of her readers never experienced racism directly. While they might be aware of racism as a social problem, and even have strong feelings about its injustice, reading an essay about a child who was called a "nigger" would not immediately generate in them the kind of response that Miriam herself had.

When she read her draft with her readers in mind, she found that her own view of it changed. The scene seemed too sentimental, and even too stereotyped. Her readers might feel sorry for the little girl, but how would they understand Miriam's feeling of anger, how would they understand how that event changed her consciousness?

When Miriam shifted her role from writer to reader, she felt dissatisfied and also a bit frustrated. She could see what was wrong with her draft, but she didn't know how to improve it. She reread her draft several times in the few days after she wrote it, and each time she liked it less. For a moment, she thought about throwing the whole thing away and beginning again. But no other experience seemed as interesting to her as the one she had written about. She felt that this experience was a kind of puzzle that needed deciphering. What, she asked herself, did it really mean?

Since questions had helped her to focus her draft in the first place, Miriam decided to think about the questions that were generated by her draft. What was important about that experience that kept her so interested in it? Why did she think about it so often? Why did she remember it so vividly?

Gradually, as Miriam thought about the experience and her draft, she developed some new questions about her topic, questions that were more specific and focused than the broad, general questions she asked initially. Instead of asking what it means to be a black American, Miriam decided that she really wanted to know how a black American develops a sense of separateness from the rest of American culture. Instead of asking how our environment teaches us to be racists, she wanted to know how our culture defines insiders and outsiders.

These new questions urged her to move beyond the single event she was reporting and to place that event in a larger context. In thinking about that context, Miriam was drawn back to her own memories. What specific events in her life, she asked herself, might help readers understand her experience as a black American? As Miriam sifted through many memories, she began to make connections between experiences that she had considered separate and distinct. She decided that one experience in particular—an incident in a high school history class—could serve well to enlarge the context of her essay.

She also began to think, again, about the term *double-consciousness.* "One of the most influential books in my life has been Du Bois' book *The Souls of Black Folk.* I wanted to understand what Du Bois meant. Mostly, I wanted to understand what 'double-consciousness' meant to me and how I feel when the topic turns to racism and every white person looks at me. I think that 'double-consciousness' is a good term to express how I feel about racism, about being called 'nigger,' and about being the only Black person in my history class." Du Bois, whose book she had read long before, now became a strong voice in helping Miriam shape her ideas. Du Bois had helped her to find a phrase that could describe the kind of experiences that she, Du Bois, and many other black Americans shared.

Here is the beginning of Miriam's second draft:

W. E. B. Du Bois called it "double-consciousness," the feeling of "always looking at oneself through the eyes of others. . . .

One ever feels his twoness—an American, a Negro." Of course, this is a legitimate grievance for any minority, racial or religious, in America. The duality of being one thing while striving to hold on to the ideals of another is difficult when you recognize that those ideals are not wholly correct. As an African-American, I have felt the force and the complexity of Du Bois' words.

In my American history class, I listened to a lecture on the founding of that great document, a symbol of freedom and democracy everywhere, the United States Constitution. The three-fifths compromise, the article that allowed the states to count the slaves three-fifths of a white person, was mentioned in passing, and I became attentive. The fact that a person could be considered three-fifths of another was disturbing in itself. That none of the "great founding fathers" thought this compromise was wrong made me equally upset. I could feel the anger in my heart boiling, rising up and foaming over the brim of self-control.

When Miriam evaluated her draft as a reader rather than as a writer, her decisions about what to include changed. The first revision of her draft, besides allowing her to think about Du Bois' use of *double-consciousness,* also taught her a new meaning of the term: Writers themselves develop a double-consciousness in the way they perceive their work. They shift from writer, to reader, to writer, each time looking at their words in a new way. They learn to see their work through the eyes of others, readers who bring to the essay their own experiences, assumptions, and ideas. Miriam's new consciousness of the impact of her draft led her to make some major changes.

Once Miriam expanded her sources to include another experience and Du Bois' book, she found that she wrote the second draft more quickly than the first.

Engaging Readers

Essays are written to be read by other people. Many professional writers show their work to colleagues, editors, or friends before their work is published. Responses from such readers often help shape the final draft. In a classroom, you have a community of writers who can serve as responsive readers for your work. In Chapter 5, we'll offer many suggestions for peer review. Miriam had the benefit of such review as she worked on her essay.

Besides her own developing consciousness in reading her work, Miriam had the response of other readers: her instructor and classmates. These readers helped her ask questions about the text that she was producing. When Miriam wrote that she found over 100 years of black American history "missing" from the pages of her high school textbook, one reader asked how learning "an edited version of truth" affected her. Another asked if Miriam thought that our culture always edited its history; what else might be missing from the textbooks that we read in high school? Furthermore, does each individual edit and revise his or her own history? A few readers asked Miriam to include more details about her history class and also to give some more background about herself.

Miriam asked some of her readers specific questions about their reactions. What did they think her purpose was in writing the essay? Did they feel uncomfortable reading any part of it? Did they understand her anger? What assumptions did they have, before they read the essay, about the meaning of the term *double-consciousness?* From their replies, Miriam was able to think about the impact of her words and what changes she would make as she revised.

After listening to her readers and considering their comments, Miriam wrote and revised two more drafts. She wrote the first revision quickly, but she was not fully satisfied with it. She seemed to hear all her readers' voices as she wrote, and she tried to respond to everyone's suggestions. In her second revision, however, Miriam was able to weigh the suggestions. Sometimes, her readers' suggestions substantially improved the draft; but sometimes she just didn't like the results and followed her own responses. Here is her final draft:

Double Vision

Miriam Thaggert

W. E. B. Du Bois called it "double-consciousness": the feeling of "always looking at oneself through the eyes of others. . . . One ever feels his two-ness, an American, a Negro; two souls, two thoughts, two unreconciled strivings; two warring ideals in one dark body whose dogged strength alone keeps it from being torn asunder." It's the duality of being one thing while striving to hold on to the ideals of another even when you recognize that those ideals are not wholly correct. History is inevitably connected to double-consciousness, for as the old analogy goes, a person without knowledge of himself is like a tree without roots: nothing to draw upon 1 for the strength to live. I have two histories, one which denies the significance of the other, and the struggle I endure is a frustrating attempt to unite the two. Double-consciousness affects all minorities in America, but I believe it is different for each person. There is a history that merges people together, but a unique perception of double-consciousness distinguishes the individual.

My own history lesson occurred the first time I was called a nigger and 2
began, appropriately enough, at school while I was waiting for my mom to pick me up. I decided to play pick up sticks with a group of girls, and I won the few games we played. This was disturbing for one girl, Angela, who seemed to be accustomed to winning. According to her, I couldn't have won on my own merits. I was cheating, she thought, which of course, I denied. My efforts to convince her of my innocence were in vain, since she seemed to have her own idea about why I had won.

"Nigger!" she cried. "Get away from me!"

The word came as a jolt and paralyzed my throat. I was tempted to 3
launch an attack, but I thought it would be safer to flee. I did get away from her, crying as I left. Fortunately, my mom arrived within a few minutes.

When I got into the car, my mother looked at my face and asked what 4
was wrong. I told her what Angela said. Her immediate response was to ask, "Where is she?"

I attempted to dry my eyes and pointed her out. The car door opened 5
with a force and slammed shut. "Stay in the car," Mom said. I looked up in interest, my distress forgotten in childlike curiosity about what my mother would do.

I saw Mom walk up to the girl and point to the car. I ducked down as 6
the girl looked over in my direction. When I came up, Mom had the girl by the shoulders and was shaking her back and forth.

"Don't you ever call my daughter a nigger again! Do you hear me? Do 7
you hear?" Amazingly, no one felt it was necessary to rescue the girl from my mother's grip.

Later at home in the kitchen, my mom stood before me with her hands 8
on her hips. "Tell me," she said, "what does the word 'nigger' mean?"

I looked at the floor and thought. It suddenly occurred to me that I had 9
no idea what the word meant. I searched my brain, looking for an incident in which I had heard someone say it. I tried to see where and when I had heard that awful word before, but I couldn't. No one, within the hearing range of my eight year old ears had ever uttered the word. But why, then, did I react to that one word instantly, so violently, as if the word was familiar, but unspeakable, to my young lips?

"It's a bad person," I managed.

"Bad in what way?"

"It's a person who is bad and mean and evil in every way."

"Are you a nigger?"

"No."

Here my mother got on her knees before me and gently took my small hands in her much larger ones. Softly, she questioned, "Then, Miriam, baby, why did you cry?" 10

That was a good question. I didn't know. My mom's question remained unanswered. 11

"All right," she sighed. She got up, pulled a chair next to me, and sat down. "It's time you learn something about yourself." And there at the kitchen table, Mom proceeded to tell me about white and Black folks. I learned that I had a history that went further than the day I was born and a heritage that was a golden link between two distant continents. I realized that to be Black is not just to be a color. It is to have an attitude, a feeling. And now when I hear the word "nigger," I am amazed at how such a small and simple word can contain so much violence and racism, yet also summon intense self-respect in my certain and unquavering knowledge of what I am and what I am not. 12

As I grew up, my knowledge of myself also increased, and I became more conscious of my Blackness. I began to see the world with different eyes. When I passed another Black person on the street, I instinctively found myself exchanging a nod with that person to acknowledge our common past and kinship, a glance to acknowledge our existence. Most Americans look at their past history to find their heroes. But my history compels me to look at the present, at the brother or sister sitting next to me, to see what a real hero, a survivor, looks like. Then I remember that most Americans don't see this, and at that moment, Du Bois' double-consciousness sets in. I inevitably compare myself to the person others see, and I become acutely aware of two separate souls occupying one being. 13

But it was good that my mother told me about that history, for I never learned it anywhere else. Over 100 years of Black history were "missing" from the pages of my American history textbook. In my American history class, I listened to a lecture on the three-fifths compromise, a compromise that allowed Blacks to be counted as three-fifths of a white man. Though I was passively sitting in my desk, I could feel the anger in my heart boiling, rising up and foaming over the brim of self-control as I thought about the obvious exclusion of Blacks not only from the rights of the Constitution, but even from a carefully edited history. History can remember the three-fifths compromise, but then disregards the memoir describing the sweat that made the South and the sacrifices that built a country. How could I be expected to learn a history that denied my rights, my person, even my existence? The history my mother told me about did not exist. The history that shaped my culture did not exist. My history—me! I did not exist! With this troubling thought, I saw that Du Bois was right. My two separate souls, Black and American, each with their own history, would remain unreconciled. 14

My discomfort deepened when I realized that everyone was staring at me, the sole Black person in the class. I could feel everyone's eyes, and I was unprepared for the riveted gaze of my peers. Why did everyone feel a need to watch my expression, wondering how I would react to the fact that it was once possible for the U.S. government to consider me unequal to a white person? Their line of vision reached me as an onslaught of 1000 pins, each needling me to expose some form of shame or denigration. If only they knew about the wonders that existed before the missionaries came, if only they knew about the contributions. But even if they did know, would they understand my anger? I tried to deal with the unwelcoming glare as best as possible and raised my chin up a little higher and straightened my spine, forcing both feet to make contact with the floor, an effort to stop their nervous twitching. Somehow, I survived the hour. Now, looking back, I wonder if that surveillance really did occur. Did I merit a whole class's stare, or was my double-consciousness taking over? 15

This, really, is the essence of being Black in America, of contending with double-consciousness. Not just knowing who you are and where you came from, but trying to endure society's surveillance. Not just learning your history, but surviving life in a society that doesn't know and understand it. This, for me, is Du Bois' double-consciousness. It is a feeling that is as much a part of Blacks as the history that made them. The history of the Black man is the history of this strife, of reconciling these two selves. Unknown, unacknowledged perhaps, but history nonetheless. 16

Du Bois described it as a "peculiar sensation," and that really is the only apt way to describe it, a feeling as if you're always on the outside, always living on the periphery of what everyone else around you calls life, of looking into a world, instead of examining the wonders inside, of feeling the conscious barrier that separates one world, and the single, solitary existence of another. This is a peculiar sensation, yet one that is all too familiar to me. This is my double-consciousness. 17

Opportunities for Exchanging Ideas

1. Discuss Miriam's essay with your classmates. What do you like about this essay? What does Miriam do to hold your interest and attention? Try to define as a group what it is about the essay that you find compelling and memorable. Locate specific details and passages that you consider especially effective.

2. In writing her third draft, Miriam's challenge was to figure out how to connect her two experiences with her reading of Du Bois. She wrote her introduction this way:

When I remember the first time I heard "nigger," I am amazed at how such a small and simple word can contain so much violence and racism, yet also summon intense self-respect in my certain and unquavering knowledge of what I am and what I am not. W. E. B. Du Bois called it "double-consciousness": the feeling of "always looking at oneself through the eyes of others. . . . One ever feels his twoness, an American, a Negro." The duality of being one thing while striving to hold on to the ideals of another is difficult when you recognize that those ideals are not wholly correct. As an African-American, I have felt the force of Du Bois' words. There are these two selves, but isn't there a third? One telling you that you're neither? A voice dictating what you know is correct, but becoming inaudible compared to the scream of society, shouting what is and what is not acceptable? The struggle I endure is one I believe all minorities face: How to reconcile those two warring ideals into one body, and in such a way without having to justify or explain your actions? The first time I heard one word, the first time I was called a nigger, planted the seeds of Black consciousness which would inevitably be nourished in the fertile ground of pride-Black-pride and sparked my realization of just what double-consciousness meant.

Compare this introduction with Miriam's final-draft introduction on page 29. How would you describe the difference? Does the final introduction more successfully help Miriam to focus her essay? Could you and your classmates create yet another introduction that you think would combine the best of each of these paragraphs?

Opportunities for Reflecting and Exploring Connections

1. W. E. B. Du Bois' words served as a touchstone for Miriam's thinking. The following excerpt from Du Bois' book, *The Souls of Black Folk,* gives you the words that inspired Miriam:

It is a peculiar sensation, this double-consciousness, this sense of always looking at one's self through the eyes of others, of measuring one's soul by the tape of a world that looks on in amused contempt and pity. One ever feels his twoness,—an American, a Negro; two souls, two thoughts, two unreconciled strivings; two warring ideals in one dark body, whose dogged strength alone keeps it from being torn asunder.

The history of the American Negro is the history of this strife—this longing to attain self-conscious manhood, to merge his double self into a better and truer self. In this merging he wishes neither of the older selves to be lost. He would not Africanize America, for America has too much to teach the world and Africa. He would not bleach his Negro soul in a flood of white Americanism, for he knows that Negro blood has a message for the world. He simply wishes to make it possible for a man to be both a Negro and an American, without being cursed and spit upon by his fellows, without having the doors of Opportunity closed roughly in his face.

What does the term *double-consciousness* mean to you? Can you think of experiences in which you looked at your self through the eyes of others and measured your soul "by the tape of a world that looks on in amused contempt and pity"? Reflect in your journal on the term *double-consciousness.* Use Du Bois' words as a touchstone for your thinking.

2. Du Bois' words had a powerful influence on Miriam's thinking. What have you read—a book, quotation, story, poem, news report, for example—that has had a similar influence on you? Why has this reading stayed with you? Use your journal to reflect and consider the impact of a writer's words on your developing self.

3. In your journal, describe some personal experiences that have become permanent parts of your memory, experiences you cannot forget. Did they involve something you said or did, something you saw or heard, something that happened to you or you wished could have happened? Try to figure out for yourself why these experiences linger in your memory.

Do you see any ideas that connect these experiences with the reflections that you described in the previous exercise? What questions do you want to ask about these connections?

A WRITER AT WORK: MARC BEAUBOEUF

Like Miriam Thaggert, Marc Beauboeuf, a college freshman, was asked to write an essay based on personal experiences. Marc developed a theme similar to Miriam's. His essay, of course, is different, reflecting the way he focused his ideas, the sources upon which he drew, his assumptions about his readers, and his aims in affecting his readers' thinking. Although you won't be following Marc's writing process in as much detail as Miriam's, you'll have a chance to see some differences in the way these two writers worked.

Marc's first draft, like Miriam's, recorded an experience that has stayed with him long after it occurred.

The word stalled in the hot, humid air of the playground. It could not quite cross the space between us. It was not yet accepted, it was still under consideration.

"Nigger?" I didn't fully understand the word but I sensed it was bad. However, that feeling was enough to force it out of limbo. The implication was clear and thus the label was allowed to continue its passage from mouth to ear.

The face across from mine was pale, pudgy, a little grimy as are most playground faces, and obviously angry. As the first syllable left his mouth the left side of his upper lip slithered into a sneer stretching his nostril wide. Both lids narrowed to cracks shadowing his green eyes, and I caught a glimpse of his small crooked baby teeth. At the second syllable the curve of the lip slowly receded but his eyes opened wider allowing a view of the hate behind them. As the final R crawled off his tongue his eyes suddenly opened wide and the hate in them flashed intensely for a second and then almost immediately dissipated.

It was as if he had suddenly heard what he had said. But I had seen the word take possession of him, contorting his features, feeding off the anger that had made him say it and then gaining a life of its own like a wizard's rune. Then the word stopped, caught in the gulf between speaker and listener, waiting to be understood, waiting for my comprehension to provide a connection so that it could enter me.

As I accepted it my blood began to rush to my head. My fingers tingled as I clenched them into fists and my jaw clamped tight. Large tears formed in my eyes, blinding me. My heart began to thump rapidly, forcefully, creating a pounding in my ears. The word reverberated in my skull, becoming a chant, a litany of hatred indifferent to race.

Unable to diffuse the explosion within me I lashed out with my whole body. Fists, arms, legs, feet, all trying to release the bile that was poisoning me. I couldn't stop; when I had let the word enter me I had allowed it to possess me as it had him.

Finally a teacher pulled me off him and we stared unbelieving at each other, unable to comprehend the power of that word. But secretly we each blamed it for what it had done to us.

Asking Questions

One word loomed so powerfully for Marc that it dominated his thinking and his first draft. When he reread his draft, he decided to write his reactions in a notebook. By recording his reactions, Marc gave himself a chance to consider their implications for future drafts of his essay. His reflections show his thinking and talking on paper as he tries to find a focus for his essay. Here are Marc's notebook entries:

There is a relationship between speaker and listener that is derived from who speaks first. Had I not understood or sensed what the boy meant when he said "nigger," the word simply would have died for lack of a place to live. It's as if the word when traveling through the air is in a medium where it can't survive. The word must be understood and accepted in the mind of the listener for it to live and thus cause a reaction, positive or negative. If the word is misunderstood, or not understood at all, it is rejected and thus dies.

The word "nigger" is one of those words that carries such a strong negative connotation that I immediately recognized it as bad. It is the kind of word that is so powerful in the emotions it generates on both sides that the reaction we both had was awe, as we saw what it did to each of us.

That was the first time that I had heard the word spoken, and obviously it was the first time it was spoken to me out of hatred. My reaction was completely honest in that I truly acted what I felt. My thoughts upon the word were nonexistent until afterwards, when I asked my parents for a clear definition.

As Marc reread his notebook reflections, he discovered a pattern to his reflections and to the questions he seemed to be asking about his experience:

- What did I really understand about the word the first time that I heard it?
- How does a word get a negative connotation; after all, it's just letters that come together to make a sound?
- Am I really interested in writing about the power of words or about race? What did the experience come to mean in my life? Was it a lesson about race or about language?

Engaging Readers

Before Marc wrote a second draft, he decided he wanted some reactions from his readers. He had a group conference with four classmates to ask them what they thought the essay was about. What did reading about his experience mean to them?

Marc's readers thought that the image he created was powerful, and several suggested that he tell more about the other boy. What was the context for the insult? What had happened?

Marc understood from these comments that he needed to say more about the event, but he still wasn't sure what to write. He had many memories of the experience, but somehow they seemed irrelevant. They would help to expand the length of the essay, but not its meaning.

Two students, however, made comments that Marc found especially helpful. One student said, "At the beginning of your draft, right in the second paragraph, you put in something that's confusing to me. I don't understand what you mean when you say that some 'feeling was enough to force the word out of limbo.' Wouldn't you have *heard* the word no matter what feeling you had?"

The other student said that Marc seemed to be making some distinction between being physically assaulted and verbally assaulted. "What is it that words can do?" she asked. "If the other boy had hit you instead of calling you a name, would the experience have been the same? What connection are you trying to make between the power of words and this racist experience?"

These suggestions helped Marc think about the impact of his experience on his readers. Again, he turned to his notebook to work out some of his ideas. Here are two paragraphs that resulted from several days of thinking:

A spoken word has its own power. The other boy tried to put a spell on me with that word. He succeeded because it was the first time I had heard the word, or rather because it was the first time the word was directed at me with such anger. Now, when I hear the word, it has much less impact. There's something special about the first time a word is used in that way.

Sometimes blacks call other blacks niggers. Yet the impact is totally different from when a white uses it against a black person. That's because when whites use it they are lumping all blacks together, refusing to see that the person they are insulting is a separate human being.

While Marc was working on this essay, everything he read became relevant as a possible source to help him generate or clarify some ideas. In reading for another course, he came upon an essay by James Baldwin that contained the phrase *ironic tenacity*—a phrase Baldwin used to describe a black American's ability to feel triumph and despair at the same time. Marc was interested in this term because it seemed to describe the feeling that he had, sometimes, when he himself used the word *nigger* as a joking putdown among his black friends. He hated the word, but at the same time using it himself gave him a feeling of power: It was *his* word, and if he owned it, he took power away from people who would use it against him.

As you read the final draft of Marc's essay, you'll see evidence of many moments of reflection. Marc worked through several drafts to revise his thinking and clarify his ideas for himself and his readers. And, in some ways, Marc knows he is still not finished with this particular subject.

A Word

Marc Beauboeuf

The word stalled in the hot, humid air of the playground. It could not quite 1
cross the space between us. It was not yet accepted, it was under consideration.

The face across from mine was pale, pudgy, a little grimy as are most 2 playground faces, and obviously angry. I watched the contortion of the face before me, the details rooting themselves in my memory. The first syllable left his mouth, pulling the left side of his upper lip into a sneer that stretched his nostril wide. Both lids narrowed to cracks, intensifying his green eyes, and I caught a glimpse of small, crooked baby teeth. At the second syllable the curve of the lip receded, as if in slow motion, but his eyes opened wider. As the final R crawled off his tongue the eyes suddenly opened wide and hate in them flashed and then almost immediately dissipated.

It was as if he had suddenly heard what he had said. But I had seen the word take possession of him, warping his features, feeding off the anger that had made him speak it and then gaining a life of its own, like a talisman. The emotion filled the word with venom, making it expand until it was distended, ready to explode. Venom extracted from hundreds of years of the white man's fear and the black man's hatred of himself. 3

But the word stopped, caught in the gulf between speaker and listener, waiting to be understood, waiting for my comprehension to provide a connection so that it could enter me. A word forces a relationship between speaker and listener. Its power is derived from both. It's as if a word traveling through the air is in a medium where it can't survive. A word must be internalized in the mind of the listener for it to cause a reaction, positive or negative. If the word is not understood, it is rejected and dies. 4

But both of us knew the word was evil, even though I was hearing it, and he was speaking it, for the first time. He knew it was the best way to hurt me and I knew I had been struck hard. This knowledge was somehow conferred on us by our society, by parents and teachers. Possibly he heard the word first from an older sibling, and gathered its power from context—even though he had been taught never to say it, just I had been taught that I should never hear it. Somehow he knew he could hurt me and I knew to be hurt, to be a victim, unarmed and naked—and to feel powerless. He was white: the overseer, the master, the slave trader, and even the well-intentioned liberal. The slave trader or owner could take the black man's freedom away, but the "nigger lover" had to give it back. The Man giveth and He taketh away. 5

A spoken word is a spell with its own life and power. He was the white wizard seeking to destroy me with his most powerful spell—but a spell that could only be used once, because each time it is repeated it loses effectiveness. A word-spell wanes as we become adults, partly because we stop listening; as we get used to hearing words, we are desensitized to their emotional impact. Partly, too, the impact diffuses as a word's contexts multiply. Since that day I have heard the word in so many different contexts and with so many different inflections, that I have become less sensitive to it. 6

I have even incorporated it into my vocabulary. And the first time 7 another black called me a nigger I did not respond at all like I did on the playground. I laughed; we both laughed. James Baldwin has described the black man's ability to feel triumph and despair at the same time as "ironic tenacity." In this spirit we laughed, ironically and tenaciously. We were diluting the word, in effect drinking the very venom that hurt us and reveling in its flavor.

This is why blacks enjoy calling other blacks niggers. Sometimes the 8
word is said out of a sense of superiority over another black, but more often it is spoken as a powerful bond, an almost tangible sense of commonality that transcends any individuality that could be insulted. For blacks are not individuals: whites do not view blacks as individuals; blacks do not view blacks as individuals. We are faceless except for our color, our identities are invisible in our blackness. We *do* see whites as individuals, however. We see whites and judge whites by the same standards with which they judge each other. We are not blinded by whiteness; rather it illuminates. Whites are Katherine, Ethan, John, or Mary. Their identities are clear so they are judged as individuals, and insulted as individuals. To call Ethan a name is to call only Ethan that name, the entire white race is not indicted. But the commonality of blacks results in their being insulted as a group. To call one black a nigger is to call all blacks niggers. But while a black that calls me a nigger is a nigger too, and we ascend together to joyfully rejoice in our blackness, a white calling me a nigger ascends as I descend, turning my blackness into a dungeon.

This sameness among blacks, however strongly it is felt, is not overtly 9
recognized and thus confusing. It is not recognized that blacks, because of it, must always fight a battle within themselves to establish an identity. At a young age, blacks realize that they are different from whites,and so they feel a pressing need to form a bond with other blacks, a bond based on hiding together in the dark shell of their skin. This bond affords comfort, but at a great cost. I am Marc, but I am forced to see my blackness as larger than that, as inescapable. When I am called a nigger I lose myself. I am forced to link myself with hundreds of years of subjugation, demoralization, fear and hatred and anger. No matter what I have accomplished, no matter how far I have tried to develop the qualities that make me stand as an individual, self-preserving, entity, I am again forced to crawl through my own filth as my ancestors did in the dark hold of a trader's ship.

The white skin is clean, in fact translucent; it allows the single, separate 10
person within to shine through and be judged, fairly or unfairly. When blacks are judged, that judgment is always unfair insofar as they are judged as black. Their skin is opaque, causing the person inside to grow stunted for lack of light, choked by the weeds of self-doubt, caught between the overpowering sense of belonging to other blacks and the self-consuming desire to burst forth as an individual.

"Nigger!"

I didn't understand the word but I sensed it was bad, and that was enough to force it out of limbo, to let it continue its passage from mouth to ear. As I stood, stripped of my singularity, my blood rushed to my head. My fingers tingled as I clenched them into fists, and my jaw clamped tight. Large tears formed in my eyes, blinding me. My heart began to thump, pounding in my ears. The word reverberated in my skull, becoming a chant, a litany of hatred amplified by history. The ancient stripping of self I sensed, and the ancient powerlessness in the face ot it, fed my anger. I lashed out with my whole body. Fists, arms, legs, feet, all trying to release the bile that was poisoning me. I couldn't stop; when I let the word enter me I allowed it to possess me as it had him. 11

Finally a teacher pulled me off him and we stared angrily at each other, disbelieving the power of that word, but secretly blaming it for what it had done to us.

Opportunities for Exchanging Ideas

1. Marc tells his readers the story of what happened to him one hot day on a playground. He begins his essay with these words: "The word stalled in the hot, humid air of the playground. It could not quite cross the space between us. It was not yet accepted, it was under consideration." Yet not until the eleventh paragraph do we finally hear the word, do we finally know what *it* explicitly refers to. The word stops in midair as Marc reflects on the meaning and power of one word.

Discuss with your classmates Marc's essay. Why, for instance, does Marc keep the word in midair and delay his readers from knowing what the word is? What kind of dramatic effect does this delay create for you? How does he use the delay to reflect on the meaning of the experience?

2. Instead of simply writing, "Someone stood across from me on the playground," Marc uses vivid details to create a powerful picture. He writes, "The face across from mine was pale, pudgy, a little grimy as are most playground faces, and obviously angry." Look closely at Marc's use of details. Discuss with your classmates which details you find especially effective and engaging. How do these details work together to support and develop Marc's ideas?

Opportunities for Exploring Connections

1. How does Marc express his double-consciousness? Imagine a conversation between Marc and Miriam? How might Marc respond to Miriam's essay? How might she respond to his? Describe this conversation in your journal. Then enter the conversation yourself. How do you respond to Miriam and Marc's essays? How do your experiences speak to theirs?

2. Read Paula Gunn Allen's essay "Where I Come from Is Like This" on page 295 of the Sourcebook. How does Allen express her double-consciousness?

Opportunities for Writing

1. Imagine that you are an editor for a national magazine. The editor in chief says there is room to publish only one essay and you must choose between Marc's and Miriam's. Make your choice, giving your reasons and evidence in detail, along with whatever suggestions for improvements that you might have for each writer.

You'll want to consider the ideas in each essay and the way they are handled: the organization of each essay, particular passages or sentences or words that seem to you especially effective or weak (you will certainly want to quote the occasional phrase or passage). Is the essay clear at every point? Do some aspects of it need developing? Do you see other ideas that could be developed, other directions for the essayist to go? Which essay best holds the reader's attention, and how does it do it?

Write a letter or memo to the editor in chief. Remember, you are writing this letter or memo to a person you know well. Write at least two pages.

2. In your journal you have been reflecting and exploring the meaning of several important experiences in your life. Reread these reflections to see what ideas connect these various experiences. What questions do you seem to be asking about these experiences?

Shape these experiences into an essay by finding the idea that connects these separate experiences. Use concrete and vivid details to convey the power of your experiences.

3. Marc Beauboeuf writes: "A word forces a relationship between speaker and listener. Its power is derived from both." What names have you been called? What labels have been applied to you? How have these names or labels helped you define your identity? What have you learned about the power of the spoken word?

Reflect on these questions in your journal. Let your experiences and reflections lead you to an idea you could develop in an essay. Try out your idea on some of your classmates. See what engages them about your idea. Listen to the questions and concerns they can offer you.

Write an essay in which you use your personal experiences to develop your ideas about the power of words.

CHAPTER 3

Getting Started

You can tell by the way I am staring into space that the writing assignment is one I am unprepared for. My motionless state gives the impression of someone deep in meditation, reaching my inner soul for that inspiration that will result in a Pulitzer Prize or at least an A. After several moments I lift my pen and begin to write. Behold, it is not the masterpiece I am hoping for, but simply my name. It is slow progress, but progress nonetheless. Remember, I tell myself, it is the slow and steady tortoise that won the race.

—Craig Chilton, college freshman

If someone came into my room while I was trying to write, I would probably kick them out. Assuming, however, that this person was invisible and silent, this is what he or she would see: Julie is sitting in front of her brand-new Macintosh. She is probably dressed in grubby sweats—maybe her father's old sweatshirt. When she types something, she does it in spurts, meaning that she will think for quite a while and then type a paragraph furiously into the computer. Every now and then she will get up, perhaps go into the lounge to see who's there, or just dance around to whatever music she has playing.

—Julie Cotler, college freshman

For most of us, the hardest part of writing is getting started. We sit, pen in hand or at our computer keyboard, wondering whether we will be able to find enough words to cover the blank page or the blank screen. We create diversions: listening to music, sharpening our pencils, making phone calls, organizing our tape collection—anything to avoid setting words on paper.

Getting started seems so hard because some writers think they must know exactly what they are going to say before they begin. They have learned, somewhere along the way to college, that a first paragraph should grab the reader's attention, and they sit awaiting that paragraph to emerge from their imaginations. "I wait," one freshman told us, "for an idea that will be perfect, say the right thing, fit the assignment, sound brilliant and original, and will come across my computer screen in perfectly formed sentences and paragraphs."

Of course, those perfectly formed sentences and paragraphs do not appear. Instead, the writer forces herself to create a sentence, then unhappily strikes it out, crumples up the paper or deletes it from the computer screen, mumbles to herself "this isn't what I want to say," and begins again and again. As the crumpled paper piles up, such writers lose confidence in their own ability to communicate. They have nothing to say, they decide. They might as well play video games in the student lounge; and they do.

The next time they sit down to write, often just hours before their paper is due, they feel even worse. Every word they write glares from the page as evidence that others can judge. Sometimes it is not a lack of ideas that keeps writers from writing. They may have plenty of ideas; they may be convinced that their ideas are interesting; but committing those ideas to paper makes the writer vulnerable.

Throughout this chapter, you will encounter some strategies for getting started, strategies that will make the task easier. Yet even after reading this chapter and this book, even after years of practice at writing, you still may feel moments of anxiety when you begin to write. You're not alone.

Opportunities for Reflecting and Exchanging Ideas

1. If someone walked into your room and observed you trying to get started writing, what would this person see? Describe yourself. Exchange descriptions with your classmates. What do you learn about the process of getting started from hearing these various descriptions?

2. Think about your own writing process and answer these questions in your journal. Discuss your answers with your classmates:

- What are your earliest memories of writing?
- What is the easiest thing for you to do when you write?
- What is the hardest aspect of writing for you?
- What special habits do you have when you write?

THAT BLANK SHEET OF PAPER AND YOU

> If someone walked into my room and observed me trying to get started writing, this person would see me alternately staring into space while sitting with my legs bent to my chest and pacing back and forth around the room. There may possibly be a sheet of (usually blank) paper on a table or desk nearby, presumably on which to make notes. This situation could go on for several hours, even for a short paper, while I brainstorm and think of topics. I might have my hands on my head or be covering my eyes in a sign of frustration or with a look of "Help. How am I ever going to write this paper?"
>
> —Sanjiv Kinkhabwala, college freshman

Students have different ways of describing those first moments of writing an essay, but one experience is common for all writers: the blank computer screen, the blank sheet of paper.

The way you approach writing depends on how you can answer one question: Whose blank sheet of paper is it, your instructor's or yours?

If the blank sheet of paper belongs to the instructor, the person handing out an assignment and doling out a grade, you may stare at it as if it contains a message written in invisible ink. If you only stare hard enough, you imagine, the "right" essay might appear. That essay is the one in the reader's mind, the one against which all other efforts will be judged, the quintessential "A paper." You see the process of getting ideas on paper as something mysterious and magical. You aspire not so much to write what is in your own mind, but what is in your reader's.

If the blank sheet of paper belongs to you, however, the process is different. Whatever will appear on that paper will *be* you, the writer, reflected in words, in images, in details. The rhythm of the prose will echo the way you speak, and even the way you move. "Writing, for me, is performance," one college freshman wrote. "But it is a higher kind of performance, for it can be persuasive, it can change someone's thinking."

In Chapter 2, when Miriam Thaggert admitted that her most successful essays were those that reflected her own interests and feelings, she spoke for many students. The common theme of all your writing will be your beliefs, your judgments. Even when you are writing about a story you have read or a painting you have seen, even when you are discussing a political issue or grappling with an ethical question, you bring your judgments into your writing. The details you present to your reader, the evidence you mount to support your opinions—all these are reflections of who you are.

Opportunities for Exchanging Ideas

On page 410 of the Sourcebook you will find an essay entitled "Responsibility not Authority" by Lara Herrington. Read this student essay and discuss it with your classmates. How does the essay reflect Lara's interests and judgments? How does she show up in the essay as a writer? Identify particular passages and details that show Lara's personal presence in her essay.

THE WRITING PROCESS

Most processes that end in the production of some *thing* are linear: You begin at one point, move through certain steps, and end at another point. But writing, although it may end in the production of an essay, is not a straightforward, linear process. You will find yourself asking and reasking questions, making choices, and discovering new sources or new insights that may significantly change what and how you write. Writing is *recursive,* a process that circles back upon itself.

Choosing a Topic

The process begins when you decide on a **topic,** sometimes on your own, sometimes in response to an assignment. A topic is the subject for the essay; a topic defines the boundaries within which you are going to inquire. When you choose one topic, you eliminate other possibilities. A writer interested in the problem of homelessness, for example, will not be writing about acid rain or space exploration.

Asking Questions

Once you have a topic, you begin to ask questions about it, trying to find a focus for an essay. If you choose to write about homelessness, what is it about this topic that interests you? Do you want to know what social services are available for homeless people in your area? Do you want to know what changes in housing demographics caused an increase of homelessness in one particular city? Do you want to investigate the problems faced by one homeless family? Or are you interested in giving an overview of the problem during a specific period of time? These questions, and others, questions that you do not already have answers to, help you move from topic to focus.

Finding a Focus

From the many questions that you generated, a few will seem more interesting or more appropriate for the essay you are assigned to write. Sometimes, you can choose questions on the basis of what material is available to you: If you do not have access to social workers, you may decide not to choose a question that depends on interviews or observations. If your community has a homeless shelter, you may decide to choose a question that requires visits and conversations with both workers and families who have stayed there.

As you look at your questions, you may see that several of them are related. Answering these questions may help you present a coherent discussion about your topic.

Sometimes, you will find that those questions that seem to lead you astray are really the ones that lead you to the heart of an issue. Your questions about homelessness may urge you to consider issues about urban planning, about your community's budget problems, or even about the plight of one particular homeless family.

Writing a Draft

Drafting helps you understand your own thinking and develop your organizing idea. A first draft may lack important details, but it gives you a chance to think through your ideas and to present them, in a logical, albeit rough, form for the first time. Patricia Hampl, whose essay "Memory and Imagination" appears on pages 306–316 of the Sourcebook, says that she tries "to let pretty much anything happen in a first draft."

> For me, writing a first draft is a little like meeting someone for the first time. I come away with a wary acquaintanceship, but the real friendship

> (if any) and genuine intimacy—that's all down the road. Intimacy with a piece of writing, as with a person, comes from paying attention to the revelations it is capable of giving, not by imposing my own preconceived notions.

Students who use computers find that this technology is especially helpful at the drafting stage. "Before word processors," one student told us, "I used to first write a whole draft by hand, then change things around, then type it, then edit it and retype it. Since I type faster than I can write, I like to do a draft on the word processor. When I start thinking quickly, I want to get my ideas down as fast as I can."

Drafting on a word processor allows you to move ideas around as you write. You can delete whole sentences or paragraphs, move passages around, and make notes to yourself by highlighting passages in bold or underlined print.

Becoming a Reader

Paying attention to your writing, as Patricia Hampl advises, comes from reading it carefully. Once you have rewritten your first draft, *you become the reader*—a reader who is reflective, skeptical, and interested. As you evaluate your draft, you may think of ways to make your organizing idea more compelling for other readers. New questions may arise for you, and they may require more thinking or research.

Engaging Other Readers

When others read your essay, they may help you clarify your purpose, consider the assumptions that other people have about your topic, and ask new questions. Engaging other readers and listening to their responses helps you understand the effect of your ideas. You learn the extent to which you have created a *common ground* that links you with your readers.

Revising

Revising results in a new draft in which you ask new questions, rethink your organizing idea, and reevaluate your goals. When you write, you explore, and you may end up surprised at finding new connections or understanding something that you did not know before. Writing is a process of questioning, responding, discovering, and revising that ends only when a writer decides the writing is complete—if not forever, at least for now.

In the remainder of this chapter, we'll look at the beginning of this process, when all you have is a topic, a blank sheet of paper, and a due date circled on your calendar.

STRATEGIES FOR DEVELOPING IDEAS

Before you can begin asking questions to find a focus for your essay, you need to find out what you already know. From your own experiences, from books and articles you have read, from television programs and films, from conversations you have had, what ideas do you have about your topic? What interests you? What do you want to learn? The strategies you'll read about in the following pages have helped students get ideas down on paper, not in the form of an essay, but in an informal way, as a place to start.

Journals

Throughout this book, we encourage you to keep a journal as a way to learn how to reflect and explore ideas. A journal is a private place to respond to experiences, observations, or readings; it can become a storehouse of rich material. You can fill your journal with long reflections about whatever topic you are considering for an essay; or you might want to use your journal to remind yourself of questions you have about those subjects that interest you. Here is the way one student described his journal:

> Well, usually when I'm writing an essay about a subject, I don't see my essay right away like a light bulb above my head, but I feel interested. I have a bunch of peripheral interests that all touch upon the topic I've been given but don't really hit the spot. The journal has shown me a way of finding something in those little racings in my mind that can turn into an interesting essay—some theme or set of themes—something that links things together. Also, when I'm trying desperately to work on an essay that isn't quite what I'm interested in, I always want to make digressions. Well, in my journal I can write all those digressions right out and settle down, or, more often, discover that the side issues and the digressions are what I really want to talk about.

Keeping a journal helps you develop the habit of reflecting on paper about your reading and thinking, making you more attentive to conversations and observations. A journal allows you to keep and remember what might have been lost otherwise.

Although many students keep a notebook as a journal, others find it useful to record their ideas in a computer file—sometimes with its own private password. "While I'm thinking about a paper," one student said, "I enter my ideas into a file that reads almost like a diary. I find it really easy to access ideas by using the Search function of the word processing program. I just look for a word that I know I've used in a few places, and it's easy to find those entries. It's about a million times neater than the notes and scraps of paper that used to be all over my desk."

Double-Entry Journals

A double-entry journal is part of your regular journal and is a way to create a conversation with yourself about your own reflections, observations, and readings. On the right side of the page, you record your thoughts, notes, quotations, and passages from reading. On the left side, you begin a conversation with these ideas. For instance, on the right side you might copy three paragraphs from a reading that interests or puzzles you. On the left side, you begin a conversation with yourself about these paragraphs. You might begin by asking: what are these paragraphs about? Why do they interest me? What connections do I see with other texts? What words or details seem particularly important and worth thinking about? You might use the left side as a way to find common ground with another writer or to find contradictions and paradoxes in the writer's thinking. A double-entry journal offers you an opportunity to enlarge and expand your thinking by beginning a conversation between yourself and other writers. Such conversations lead you to creating your own source—your essay.

Brainstorming

When you **brainstorm,** you quickly jot down, as haphazardly as necessary, words and phrases that might later lead you to a focused idea for an essay. The words and phrases come both from your sources—details noted from memories or from texts—and from responses to those sources. Brainstorming frees you from the requirement that ideas, while they are being discovered or explored, need to be logical, ordered, neat, and correct. From the mass of material generated during a brainstorming session (or several sessions), you can then hunt for the ideas that seem most promising for your essay.

Freewriting

Freewriting may look like an essay, but it isn't. Instead, it's a record of your thinking, unedited. Freewriting may produce long pages of prose. Everything you know about your topic, all your ideas, are free to come pouring out onto the page. When those ideas are just spinning in your mind, it sometimes feels as if they will never get into any shape or order. But many students find that once their ideas are down on paper, once they can actually see them, they can make some sense of them. They can order them more logically.

Students who freewrite on the computer agree that sometimes they can get ideas down much faster than if they write in longhand. When they return to their freewritten draft, they can move passages around, delete passages that they don't want, and develop ideas that need expanding.

Solitary Reflection

When we asked some students to talk about ways of getting started, some of them responded that they just sit and think. "If someone saw me trying to start a piece of writing," one student said, "he would see my lying down on my bed with a pencil and paper, talking to myself." Some students told us that they take a long walk. Some find that ideas come to them while jogging, or making popcorn, or exercising. Being alone, free from distractions, and even far from your desk, can give you the time and space you need to think creatively.

Talking

Sometimes talking about your topic helps. When other people question you about your sources, when they ask you to explain your ideas, you may find yourself clarifying important points. If something seems to be missing in an argument, if you don't think your reader will be able to follow your logic, you might try talking through your ideas with a friend, classmate, or instructor. Talking through ideas gives you concrete proof about what is interesting or not. When one student was writing an essay about anorexia, she spent some time explaining the causes of the disease to one of her roommates. When her listener did not understand something, she found that she had to clarify her terms and her thinking. By the time she sat down to write her essay, she had a strong sense of what information her readers would need. Such preliminary tries at telling a story or putting forth an argument serve as oral "first drafts."

Sitting at a desk and putting words on paper can be a solitary, isolated pursuit. But that is only part of what you do when you write. As a writer, you'll find it helpful to talk about your work, listen to suggestions, respond to questions, and ask for help.

Through conversations and collaboration with friends, instructors, colleagues, or editors, you will begin to see the importance of your ideas, to understand connections, and to anticipate questions your readers might have about your topic. And when a reader says, "That's really an interesting idea," you will begin to develop confidence in your abilities to be a successful writer.

Opportunities for Reflecting

1. Take your journal to a cafeteria, laundromat, grocery store, bus station, library, gym, or some such place and observe people. What are they doing, wearing, talking about? What rituals do you observe? Record your observations for three days. What surprises you about your journal notes? Read through your notes and see what connections you make. What patterns do you discover? Develop two ideas that could lead to a focus for an essay?

2. Reread Lara Herrington's essay "Responsibility not Authority" on page 410 of the Sourcebook. Create a double-entry journal by copying three paragraphs from this essay that interest you. On the left side, begin a conversation with these ideas. Why do these paragraphs interest you? What words or details seem particularly important and worth thinking about? You might want to find common ground with Herrington or find the contradictions and paradoxes in her thinking.

3. Find a photograph of yourself from five to ten years ago. Think about what you were doing when that photograph was taken. What kind of person were you then? How does the photograph reflect who you were? How are you different now? In your journal, brainstorm or freewrite on these questions. Find an idea that could be used to focus an essay you would write.

Opportunities for Exchanging Ideas

1. Look at these advertisements. When do you think they appeared in popular magazines? What details support your guess? What are the differences between them? The similarities? What were they advertising? What do the ads suggest about our culture then and now? Brainstorm these questions with your classmates. Then, brainstorm together to find ideas that could focus an essay comparing two or more advertisements.

(*Text continued on p. 57.*)

Are You Keeping Up With Your Husband?

ARE you still the attractive, alert, up-to-date woman he married? Are you keeping up with the interesting things in life as he is, or are you devoting all your time, strength and thought to housework?

The busiest man in office, shop or profession manages to have time to meet people and progresses mentally as he succeeds financially. But many a wife, intending to help her husband, gets along without many household aids, and thus is forced to confine her activity to the narrow sphere of housework. This is false economy from the financial standpoint, and wrong from the standpoint of companionship.

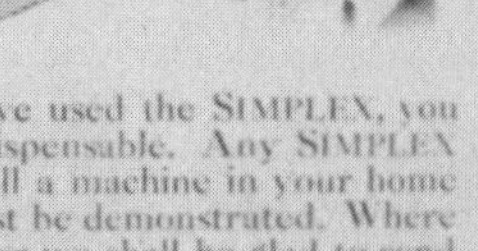

Hand ironing is tiring and aging work, which can and should be eliminated. The SIMPLEX Ironer will do your entire ironing in an hour or two instead of your spending a whole day at it. The hours gained can be put to more profitable and enjoyable use.

Once you have used the SIMPLEX, you will find it indispensable. Any SIMPLEX dealer will install a machine in your home where it can best be demonstrated. Where there is no dealer we shall be glad to send a SIMPLEX on approval.

Send for our book "Clean Linen in Abundance" and our illustrated story "Aunt Eliza from Boston" which tells of the joy the SIMPLEX brought into one home.

Our Service Department will plan and arrange your home laundry—no obligation.

AMERICAN IRONING MACHINE CO., 503, 168 N. Michigan Ave., CHICAGO

We also make Ironing Machines for the Small or Hand Laundry, Hotel, Institution, etc. Write for catalog.

Every Woman Admires a Tall Man
If you are short, you will appreciate the unpleasant and humiliating position of the little man in the above illustration. But you are probably unaware that it is no longer necessary to be short and uncomfortable.
The Cartilage Company, of Rochester, N. Y., is the owner of a method whereby any one can add from two to three inches to his stature It is called the "Cartilage System" because it is based upon a scientific and physiological method of expanding the cartilage, all of which is clearly and fully explained in a booklet entitled "How to Grow Tall," which is yours for the asking.
The Cartilage system builds up the entire body harmoniously. It not only increases the height, but its use means better health, more nerve force, increased bodily development and longer life. Its use necessitates no drugs, no internal treating, no operation, no hard work, no big expense. Your height can be increased, no matter what your age or sex may be, and this can be done at home without the knowledge of others. This new and original method of increasing one's height has received the enthusiastic endorsement of physicians and instructors in physical culture. If you would like to add to your height, so as to be able to see in a crowd, walk without embarrassment with those who are tall, and enjoy the other advantages of proper height, you should write at once for a copy of our free booklet "How to Grow Tall." It tells you how to accomplish these results quickly, surely, and permanently. Nothing is left unexplained. After you read it, your only wonder will be "Why did not some one think of it before?" Write to-day.
THE CARTILAGE COMPANY, 74 P, Unity Building, ROCHESTER, N. Y.

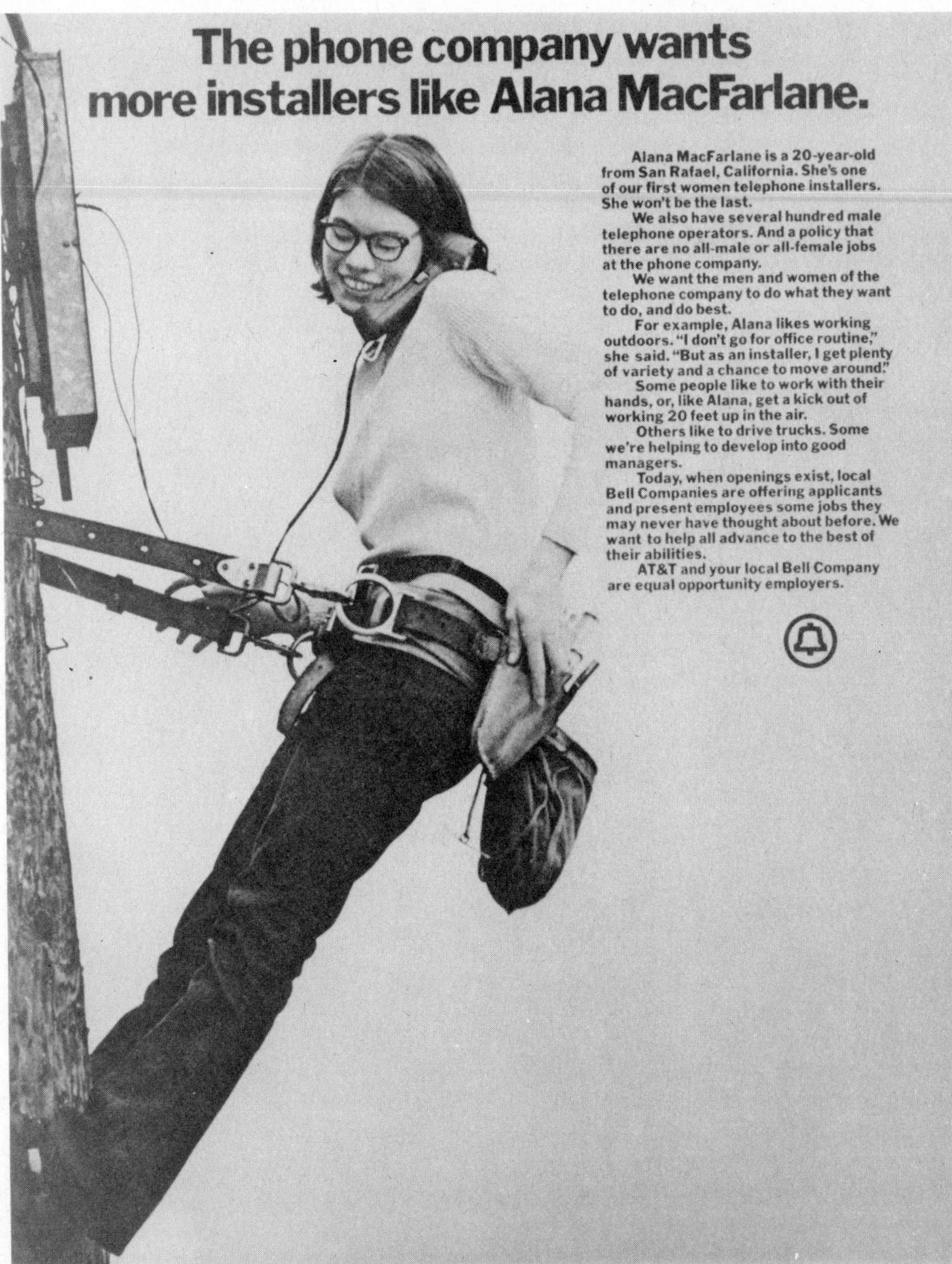
The phone company wants more installers like Alana MacFarlane.
Alana MacFarlane is a 20-year-old from San Rafael, California. She's one of our first women telephone installers. She won't be the last.
We also have several hundred male telephone operators. And a policy that there are no all-male or all-female jobs at the phone company.
We want the men and women of the telephone company to do what they want to do, and do best.
For example, Alana likes working outdoors. "I don't go for office routine," she said. "But as an installer, I get plenty of variety and a chance to move around."
Some people like to work with their hands, or, like Alana, get a kick out of working 20 feet up in the air.
Others like to drive trucks. Some we're helping to develop into good managers.
Today, when openings exist, local Bell Companies are offering applicants and present employees some jobs they may never have thought about before. We want to help all advance to the best of their abilities.
AT&T and your local Bell Company are equal opportunity employers.

When Crusher Lizowski talks about being a homemaker, you listen.

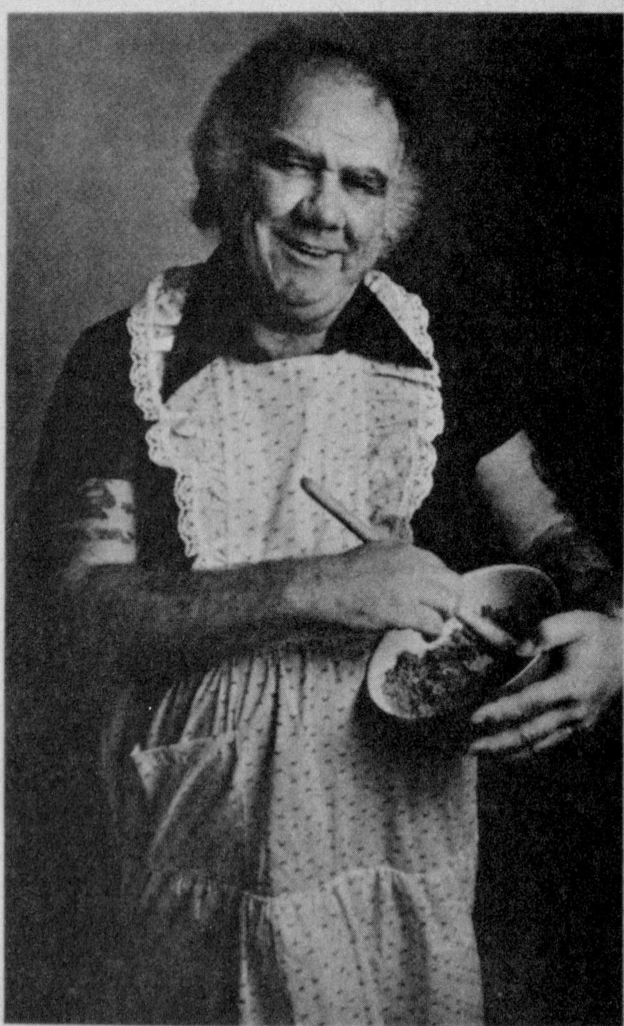

"I like to cook, and I think I'm pretty good at it. My specialty is Japanese dishes. Sushi, tempura, teriyaki, shabu-shabu.

"When I'm not on the road, I do most of the cooking around our house. I'm even teaching my oldest son how to cook.

"My wife and I feel that making a home is sharing. Equally. In the drudgery. In the fun. In everything. Especially in the important things like the care and guidance of our children and in establishing values in our home.

"The point is, I don't believe in the old stereotype about being the lord and master around the house while the little woman raises the kids and cooks the meals.

"I don't see anything unusual in that. Nobody kids me when I put on an apron. Not in front of me at least.

"Being a homemaker is, after all, being an adult. Learning how to manage your life.

"Learning how to give. And how to give yourself to the people you love.

"Another thing I'm into is macrame. I'm learning how to make belts and plant hangers.

"Nobody kids me about that either."

This message about homemaking is brought to you as a public service by Future Homemakers of America and this publication. For more information, write: Future Homemakers of America, 2010 Massachusetts Ave. NW, Washington, DC 20036.

HOMEMAKING
The most misunderstood profession.

2. In the following report, we look behind the scenes at *Newsweek* to see how one staff writer, Melinda Beck, describes her strategies for getting started and overcoming the terror of the blank page. What do you learn from Beck's description of herself? How do her strategies for getting started compare with yours? Discuss Beck's report with your classmates.

Getting Started at *Newsweek*

Melinda Beck

There's nothing more daunting than facing a blank sheet of paper or an empty VDT screen. I've been a writer at *Newsweek* for more than six years and it never gets any easier. That's why I've developed a means of filling up those empty spaces before I begin writing seriously. Here's how my system works: 1

Once I get a story assignment. I read as much information as I can about the topic, taking notes religiously. Some writers I know keep their "notes" mentally. But I find I have a headstart on the writing if I've written things down, putting the facts and ideas into my words as I go. Soon, I find that my notes are arranging themselves into categories and subthemes. These eventually become the building blocks of my story. I also jot down any colorful words or nice turns-of-phrase that occur to me so I'll remember to use them later, and I keep an eye out for any interesting bits of color or drama that I might want to use at the beginning or the end. 2

When I'm through collecting information, I put my notes aside, mentally take two giant steps back and try to sum up the main point of my story in a single phrase. If I can't do that, it's usually a danger sign that I don't know what I'm trying to say and need to think about it further. 3

Depending on the type of story I'm writing, it may be that my core idea provides the perfect opening sentence. This is classic newspaper journalism, with the "news" stated very simply in the lead. *Newsweek's* style is a little different. Usually, we'll start with an interesting detail or insight or dramatic scene that illustrates the main point of the story. We don't try to tell the whole story in the lead, merely pique the reader's interest so he will read further. That opening scene may take up the entire first paragraph, but I generally work in my central theme fairly soon after that, often as the "topic sentence" of the second paragraph. This immediately alerts the 4 reader to what the story is about and focuses my own thinking for what will come next.

Once I've written the lead and made my main point, I'm half-way home. I go back to my notes and usually find that the rest of the story shapes itself. In part, it's a process of elimination. I ask myself, what's the most important point I want to make,and the next and the next? Are there any big "buts" or qualifiers I should include? Where do I want to end? Some writers find that their ideas are flowing so fast at this point that they can compose right on the typewriter or VDT screen. I like to outline my subthemes on paper first, and fill in the specifics as I go back through my notes. Writing is something like putting a jigsaw puzzle together, I've found, and it helps to know what the picture should look like. . . . 5

One last thing: I don't expect to write polished prose the first time through, and that relieves some of the initial pressure. Once I get to the VDT screen, I rap out a first draft very quickly. It's usually a woolly mammoth full of disjointed sentences, rotten grammar, leaps in logic and typos, but it gives me something to work with, rather than an empty screen. The second (and third and fourth) times through, I'll smooth out the rough edges—even rearrange whole ideas. With every sentence, I ask myself, can I say this more colorfully, more clearly or more succinctly? 6

All this is a laborious process. It takes time and patience. But it gets me over those horrible getting-started blues. 7

Opportunities for Writing

1. Write a portrait of yourself as a writer. Use either first or third person depending on the tone and purpose of your portrait.

2. Go to the library and find the *New York Times* or your local paper for the date of your own birth. From your reading of that day's edition, choose an article that relates in any way to your own life. For example:

- An article about race riots might prompt a reflection on racial tensions in your own life or school and how they resemble or do not resemble the confrontations in the article.
- A column on fashion might prompt a look through your own closet to describe changes and similarities between the significance in our culture's thinking about clothes then and now.
- An article on the draft lottery might prompt you to write of a family member's experience during the Vietnam era and how that affected your own political upbringing.

Copy passages of the newspaper article in your journal and use the double-entry method. Ask yourself why the article is important to you? What does it suggest about you; your life; decisions, people, or personal objects that have been important to you? How might your life have been different had this event not happened? Create a conversation between yourself and the words of the article.

Write an essay in which you summarize the article briefly and then describe your response to it. Your essay will reflect your thoughts and your judgments.

CHAPTER 4

Developing a First Draft

The strategies you use to help you get started generate notes, underlinings, lists, questions, and many ideas buzzing in your mind. A draft is the first opportunity you have to get your ideas down in a logical and coherent structure. A first draft is often called a *discovery draft* because it allows you to examine your ideas for patterns and connections. From those patterns and connections you are able to discover an *organizing idea* that gives your draft a logical order.

Simply put, a discovery draft helps you identify precisely what your essay is about. By the time you start your draft, of course, you already have identified your topic, have thought about it, and have taken notes about what you want to include in your essay. If someone asked, "What are you writing about?" you could answer by referring to your topic. By the time you have completed your draft, your response can be more precise: You know the particular question that you want to answer and the particular point of view you want to put forth.

As writer and educator Wayne Booth reminds us, the word *idea* has many different meanings. A person can have an idea for a shortcut to the beach or an idea of how solar panels collect energy. But these meanings of the word are different from its meaning in writing. *An idea is an expression of thought that reflects interpretation.* When you write, you'll put forth ideas about your topic and discuss those ideas throughout your essay, supporting your ideas with evidence from various sources.

An idea is different from a fact. If a question can yield more than one response, those responses are *ideas.* If you ask, "What is the cube root of 27?" only one response is possible. That response is a fact, not an idea. If you ask, "When did James Baldwin write *Go Tell It on the Mountain,*" the response will be a fact. It is a fact that the newspaper *USA Today* has been commercially successful. If you ask why it has been so successful, you need to come up with some ideas to provide an answer. You might get those ideas from examining articles in the newspaper and drawing conclusions about why they are appealing. You might ask readers of the newspaper why they read it. You might compare the newspaper with others that are available to get a sense of its commercial strengths.

An idea also is different from an *expression of feeling*. If someone asks you, "How did you like *Go Tell It on the Mountain*?" your response ("I liked it") is an expression of feeling, not an idea. You may want to write about your responses to a person, an event, or a work of art or literature. Responses which rely on evidence from sources to support them are ideas. If your topic is *Go Tell It on the Mountain,* for example, you might ask how Baldwin elicits an emotional response in his readers. Your expression of feeling about the book then becomes useful for you as you analyze strategies that Baldwin used to get you to like his book. Your question necessarily would generate ideas. If you wrote down some of those ideas, you'd begin to see a pattern emerge. Several ideas might be subsumed under one idea. That idea, which could serve to focus and organize your essay, would be your *organizing idea.*

An idea, as Wayne Booth put it, is always connected to other ideas, always has the capacity to generate other ideas, and always can yield more than one argument or position. Because good questions generate so many ideas, writing a first draft often seems complicated. Sometimes you may feel that if you don't choose the "right" organizing idea, your essay will be a failure.

There is no "right" organizing idea, however, for most essays. The questions that you ask may be answered in a variety of ways. By experimenting, revising, and reworking your ideas, you'll find a way of organizing your essay that you feel is effective. Sometimes, you'll begin writing with a tentative organizing idea that you have found by making an outline, brainstorming, freewriting, or talking about your ideas with other people. You may begin your first draft with one idea that seems to organize your essay logically and then, as you think and write, you'll discover ways to change or modify that idea to make it clearer and more precise. New information may change the way you think about an issue; new questions will occur to you to help you refine and redefine your focus.

The process of drafting involves focusing on a question or issue that you want to write about, selecting material from personal or outside sources, thinking about the needs of your readers, and organizing your ideas. As you write, you'll find yourself going back and forth among these tasks: You decide that your readers need more information, and you go back to your sources; you discover some interesting new sources, and you refocus your original question; you take a new perspective on your topic and find that you need to reorganize your ideas. Writing is a continual process of decision making and evaluation.

In this chapter you'll see how Jessica Yellin moved from ideas through discovery draft as she thought about the issue of sexism and language. Her experience can show you some of the strategies that writers find helpful as they work through their drafts.

Opportunities for Exchanging Ideas

The following list offers some topics that are too broad for an essay. Brainstorm with your classmates until you've found three facts for each topic. Ask some *why* questions about each fact and see how your questions can generate ideas. Let your ideas generate other ideas.

- Education
- Peer pressure
- Sexism and language
- Censorship

Opportunities for Reflecting

Take a topic you are curious about or one you are currently planning to write about. Brainstorm to find four or five facts about this topic. Ask questions about each fact and see how your questions generate more questions and, in turn, generate ideas.

FOCUSING ON YOUR TOPIC

Writing is a process of making decisions. When you choose one word, you close off the possibility of using another word.When you choose certain details to describe a scene, you select those details from all others that might have been included. Any piece of writing, even a thousand-page volume, is the result of choices of inclusion and exclusion. These choices are made throughout the writing process. The words you choose in your first draft may be changed significantly by the time you begin writing your final draft. Details you decided to delete from your first draft may make their way into a later draft.

The first major decision that you make in writing involves choosing your topic. Focusing on a writing topic means that you will not write about other topics at this time. Focusing on one question means that you will not answer other questions that you might ask about an issue. Focusing means that you have decided on the limits of your inquiry.

You may be interested, for example, in writing an essay about environmental problems. If you decide to focus on the topic of the greenhouse effect, you limit your inquiry so that you will not be writing about acid rain, hazardous waste, or water pollution. As you think about the topic of the greenhouse effect, you may come up with many questions that you could address in an essay. How do scientists define this phenomenon? What controversy exists among scientists about the greenhouse effect? Why does this controversy exist? If you are persuaded that the greenhouse effect is a legitimate claim, what recommendations for environmental change would you make? How might these changes affect the environment? As you choose the questions you will answer, you eliminate those questions that are not relevant to your particular inquiry.

How do you make the choices you need to make when focusing an essay? Sometimes, your focus will be defined for you. In a course on environmental planning, for example, your instructor may ask you to read *Discordant Harmonies: A New Ecology for the Twenty-first Century* by biologist Daniel Botkin and evaluate the evidence that Botkin presents to support his thesis. Often, however, you will have to define your own focus.

Here are some questions to ask yourself as you narrow your focus:

1. What issue, question, or problem interests me? When you write about something important to you, you are likely to sustain your interest and energy throughout the writing of an essay. If you keep a journal or notebook, you may want to write down ideas that come to you as you talk with other people, read newspapers and magazines, see films, watch television, or simply look around you. What questions would you like to pursue—now or in the future? What issues do you think are important? Keeping an ongoing list of ideas can be a useful resource as you write essays in college.

In Chapter 2, you read two essays by students writing about an issue that touched their lives directly. Other students might be interested in such issues as the environment, AIDS, education, drugs and alcohol, or career choices. You may find yourself wondering about a large question: How will daily life change in the next century? In writing an essay, of course, you will have to find ways to limit your inquiry so that you are exploring only part of this question. You may decide to look at a specific technological change: video telephones, for example, or increased use of home computers in personal banking; you may decide to look at a change in a social institution such as the family; you may decide to focus on changes in the way we might receive health care.

Sometimes, however, you begin with a question that already is specific and limited. What efforts might improve the relationship between ethnic groups in your home community, for example; or, what are some advantages to bilingual education for young children? These questions are not answered simply; they cannot be answered by turning to only one source; they require some interpretation and analysis of your own. For these reasons, they may be provocative questions to serve as the basis for an essay.

2. **What sources can help me think about this issue, answer questions, or pose solutions to a problem?** Are these sources available to me? Do I have sufficient time to use them adequately?

Sometimes you will think of questions that are interesting and important but that require extensive research into materials that are not readily available in your college library or in your community. It is better to write about such questions later, when you have more time to commit to this effort, than to consider them superficially now. Many sources are available to you—beginning with your own experiences—that can be valuable in examining a wide variety of issues.

Suppose, for example, you decided to write about the issue of bilingual education. Sources available for this project might include:

- Essays and articles in professional journals of education
- Studies about the effects of bilingualism on future achievement in school
- Interviews with educators of young children
- Interviews with educators of teachers
- Interviews with students who studied in bilingual classrooms
- Textbooks and materials used in bilingual classrooms

These sources would help you formulate specific questions about bilingual education and provide evidence to support your conclusions. You need to allot enough time to read, conduct interviews, and examine your sources before you begin to write. As you consider sources, consider also the time you have to complete your assignment.

3. **Can I consider this issue adequately in the length of essay that I am to write?** If your instructor asks you to write an essay of five to eight pages, you need to limit your focus to a question that does not require 20 pages—or a 300-page volume—for an adequate consideration.

The issue of AIDS, for example, has generated scores of books and articles. What can you write about AIDS in five to eight pages? Asking a limited question about the issue gives you a chance to do substantive research and real thinking; a question that is too large can only result in a superficial essay. You might, then, ask about the effectiveness of AIDS education in a local high school. You might ask about changes in hospital procedures among health care workers in your school infirmary or a local hospital as a result of AIDS. Such questions can help you explore a manageable part of a large topic.

4. Will I have a chance to do more than summarize information from my own experiences or from outside sources? Will I have a chance to interpret these sources and to come to my own conclusion?

There are two kinds of questions that you can ask about any issue or topic: questions that can be answered by gathering information from other people who have done research on your topic and by reporting those people's conclusions, and questions that can be answered by drawing conclusions or making interpretations on your own. When you make interpretations of your own, you generate your own ideas. In the Sourcebook, for example, you'll find an essay by Theodore Sizer about high schools. If you wanted to ask questions about high school education, you might read this essay and report Sizer's conclusions. If you reported Sizer's conclusions, you would be conveying his ideas, rather than your own, to your readers. On the other hand, you might visit several high schools, interview some students, recall your own high school experiences, and draw conclusions on your own. Sizer might very well be a source for your conclusions, but you would not be simply reporting information that you learned from his essay. You would be putting forth your own interpretations and your own ideas.

Opportunities for Reflecting

1. We have offered you four questions to ask yourself as you find a focus:

- What issue, question, or problem interests me?
- What sources can help me think about this issue?
- Can I consider this issue adequately in the length of essay I am to write?
- Can I do more than summarize information from my own experiences or from outside sources?

Ask these questions about the topic you are currently considering for your next essay.

A WRITER AT WORK: JESSICA YELLIN

In the next pages, you'll follow Jessica Yellin as she drafts an essay for her composition class. Jessica's experience will show you the kind of decisions that writers make as they move from idea to discovery draft.

Choosing a Topic

When Jessica Yellin first began to think about a topic for an essay, she thought she would write about rap music because something about the lyrics she was hearing disturbed her. She didn't count herself among those people who think tapes should be rated the way films are, but she was concerned about the violent language and images in many of the rap songs and wondered if they encouraged violent behavior. As she listened to these songs on the radio, she tried to imagine the ways other listeners might respond to the words.

Jessica's initial interest in a topic, then, came from feeling *disturbed* and *concerned*. Those are the feelings that many professional writers rely upon when they choose topics for their own writing. In the Sourcebook, for example, you'll find an essay by David Owen, who questioned the correlation between Scholastic Aptitude Tests and intelligence. He was disturbed by the explanations he read about the value of the SAT, and he decided to do some research so that he could draw his own conclusions. You will also find an essay by Joan Didion, who expresses her dissatisfaction with conventional definitions of morality and formulates in their place definitions of her own. And you'll find an essay by Paul Theroux, who disagreed with the way society commonly characterizes masculinity and who wanted to argue for a broader perspective. These writers had feelings that generated questions; questions lead the writers to sources of information; and information helped them formulate their own ideas.

Whenever you come up with a topic that you want to write about, you need to think about what your responsibilities will include in order to answer questions about your topic. Jessica knew that she could find the lyrics to many rap songs, but she was afraid that her essay merely would convey her observations that some of the language contained violent images. She would be conveying a fact—rap songs contain violent language—rather than developing ideas. If she were a sociologist or psychologist, she might be able to go further and question teenagers who listen to rap music about their behavior or their values. But she had no way of doing such a study on her own. She might be able to write about her impressions and feelings, but she would have no persuasive support for any ideas. Although Jessica remained interested in the possible connection between rap music and violence, she just didn't see a way to turn her impressions into an essay.

Jessica's initial discouragement was typical of many students' experiences in choosing a topic: There's a good topic, but not enough resources to generate ideas. When this discouragement sets in, it's useful to think about related questions. What questions, Jessica asked herself, could she answer with the resources she had available?

Jessica realized that in asking about the lyrics to rap songs, she was asking about the power of words to influence people. How do words affect behavior? Perhaps, she thought, she could find some way of answering that question.

Jessica's thinking about the power of words began to make its way into her conversations with friends. For the next few days, she found herself talking with them about the way words we hear in advertisements, political speeches, and even in everyday language affect how we think about ourselves and other people. One of her roommates, who was reading George Orwell's "Politics and the English Language," contributed some interesting ideas about the way politicians manipulate language to try to make other people see reality through the politicians' eyes. It seemed to Jessica that this manipulation happened outside of politics too. More and more, her conversations with friends focused on gender. "I found myself getting into arguments about my use of *she* instead of *he* to mean *just anyone*," Jessica said. "Some of my friends think it sounds really affected. They said that *she* stands out, but *he* is just conventional. Many of my friends think it's just not important to use *he* when you mean a man *or* a woman. They told me that using *she* doesn't change the way anyone thinks about men and women. But I'm not so sure about that."

Jessica decided that if she wanted to write about the power of words, she might begin by focusing on words related to gender. How do these words reflect the reality of relationships between men and women? How do these words affect the way that men and women see themselves or think about themselves and one another? With these questions in mind, Jessica saw that her own experiences, observations, and conversations would be good sources of information. She remembered an essay she had read in high school that, she said, "never left me." The essay was Adrienne Rich's "On Taking Women Students Seriously," and Jessica saw that many of Rich's ideas about "He-Man grammar" could help her formulate her own ideas about language and gender.

Here again, Jessica chose a topic that both disturbed and concerned her. This time, however, she believed that she had adequate resources to consider the question she was asking.

Discovering Guiding Questions

How do words affect the way that men and women think about themselves and one another? Jessica's question gave her the initial focus for her essay. That question led her to think about her own experiences, to listen to conversations in a new way, to talk about these issues with friends, and to be alert to books and articles that might be relevant to her topic. Jessica's first responsibility in confronting this question was to limit the words she wanted to think about. What words did she think were especially powerful?

Although the English language does not assign gender to words, Jessica easily thought of many words that carry connotations of being masculine or feminine. But Jessica kept returning to the two words that recurred in her conversations: *he* and *she.* When we use *he* to mean both male and female, she thought, we are sending a message that says *he* is dominant in our culture, while *she* is less important. At first Jessica simply wanted to focus on *he* and *she* for her essay, but after a bit more thought, she decided to think about the effect of the words *humankind* and *mankind* on herself and her friends. The dictionary, Jessica explained, defines *mankind* as meaning *humankind.* How does that equivalency make women feel? How does it make men feel? Even if *humankind* came into common usage, would it make any difference?

These questions became Jessica's first *guiding questions,* helping her think concretely about her topic. Guiding questions often change as you think, read, talk with people, and explore sources. Guiding questions are important in helping you direct your inquiry and refine your focus.

Exploring Sources

Throughout the drafting process, Jessica kept a notebook in which she recorded her ideas, took notes on readings, and set up a preliminary plan for her first draft. Some students find it more efficient to keep such notes in a computer file; later, when they access their notes for use in a draft, they use the Search function of their word processing program to locate keywords in the file. Although Jessica decided to keep her notes on paper, the process she used can serve as a model for other systems of note keeping.

On one page of her notebook, Jessica set out her tentative goals:

I plan to argue in favor of the widespread adoption of the word *humankind* in place of *mankind* and for the use of gender-related pronouns (*he, she, him, her*) that agree with the author's gender. And perhaps I'll argue for the adoption of a new pronoun that is neither male nor female, but all inclusive.

I'm going to argue that writing needs to be precise and that we need to include women in our writing. Since *womankind* only refers to the female gender, *mankind* similarly refers to the male gender, although in popular usage, *mankind* is said to include both women and men. I will argue that such male-oriented language excludes women.

Women have fought for legal, economic, and political rights; now we should be brought into the language more fully, and finally recognized as a full member of the human race.

After a few days, Jessica's notebook contained numerous pages of entries—ideas that popped into her mind, passages from readings, and her reflections about various conversations or observations. Because this project was not intended to be based heavily on outside sources, Jessica did not need to do the kind of research that you will have a chance to read about in Chapters 10 to 12. Instead, Jessica referred to some articles that she had read before, such as the essay by Adrienne Rich, some essays that she had heard about in other courses, and some books that her friends had mentioned to her.

Here are a few entries from her notebook that will give you an idea of the kinds of sources Jessica explored:

In Spanish class today: teacher cannot find English equivalent for the man in the town who carries everyone's keys; therefore we all doubt that such a man exists.

"Unlike Welsh, Breton, Swahili, or Amharic, that is, languages of minority or colonized groups, there is no mother tongue, no genderlect spoken by the female population in a society, which differs significantly from the dominated language."

Elaine Showalter, "Feminist Criticism in the Wilderness" <u>Writing and Sexual Difference</u>, p. 22.

women's rights rally in Los Angeles: don't forget speaker who wanted to spell women—WOMYN

conversation with Gina: why is a woman who heads a committee called "chairman"; does it matter if you call her "chairperson"

"The content of education itself validates men even as it invalidates women. Its very message is that men have been the shapers and thinkers of the world, and that this is only natural."
Adrienne Rich, "On Taking Women Students Seriously"

Elaine Pagels thinks that women have been written out of history since the earliest times. There's an earlier version of the Bible in which God creates women first!!!!!

Shaping an Idea

Every time Jessica made an entry in her notebook, she reread the other notes she had made. After reading the entries many times, she saw how some entries contained ideas that were similar to others. As she began to sort the entries into groups that addressed some common themes, she decided to highlight these groups in different ways—using colored highlighters, stars, underlinings, or other annotations. If she were keeping her notes in a computer file, she could easily shift entries around using the Move function of her word processing program. By shifting entries, she could keep similar ideas under appropriate headings in the file.

Sorting through the entries helped Jessica to recognize *patterns* among her notes. Some notes, for example, were evidence of her growing consciousness that the English language was biased toward men. Jessica found that she had three illustrations of this bias: from a high school class, from a women's rally she once attended, and from an art lecture she went to with her mother.

These illustrations, she thought, could help her present a *context* for her question about the relationship between language and gender. Her readers, after all, would ask: Where did the question come from? Why did Jessica think about this question? What did the question mean to her? Why is the question important for readers?

Jessica noticed that some notebook entries would help her *define the issue* that she was presenting. She also had entries that showed how her own thinking changed as she examined some sources and thought about her question. These notes could help her explain her solution to the problem or her answer to the question.

As she noticed patterns, Jessica saw a plan emerge. Instead of having a few notebook pages filled with quotes, reflections, and reminders, Jessica now had a notebook where passages were highlighted in different ways (colored pens, highlighter, brackets, for example) to indicate that they were related to one another. Jessica had begun to shape her ideas into a draft.

Planning an Essay

Some writers rely on the kind of outlines they learned to make in grade school. Such an outline details the structure of paragraph clusters by indicating *the general topic of the paragraphs* (shown by a roman numeral), *the topic of supporting paragraphs* (shown by a capital letter), and *the supporting details within the paragraph* (shown by the arabic numerals). Here is an example of one section from this kind of outline:

I. Early experiences with gender bias in language

- **A.** High school
  - **1.** Changing spelling of *woman*
  - **2.** Women's studies course
  - **3.** Art lecture

Making such an outline, however, assumes that you have ideas well organized at the start. Often, ideas come together as you write. You may not know, before you begin your essay, just how each paragraph will be organized.

Some writers, therefore, prefer to make a working plan by drafting a diagram of blocks or circles with ideas noted within the different shapes. An example of such a diagram is shown on page 72. Here, you need to know generally which ideas relate to which other ideas, but the order is not as rigid as in a numerical outline. A diagram outline helps you organize the shape of your first draft, while still allowing you a chance to add or delete information.

Because Jessica had coded her notebook entries before she began to write, she decided to use a simple list outline. She divided her ideas into three sections: *presenting the problem, explaining why it is important, suggesting a solution.* Within each section heading, Jessica wrote a few words or ideas that reminded her of the notebook entries she wanted to incorporate into her essay. Her outline, in the end, was a personal record of the evolution of her thinking.

Presenting the problem

high school

women's rally

art lecture with Mom

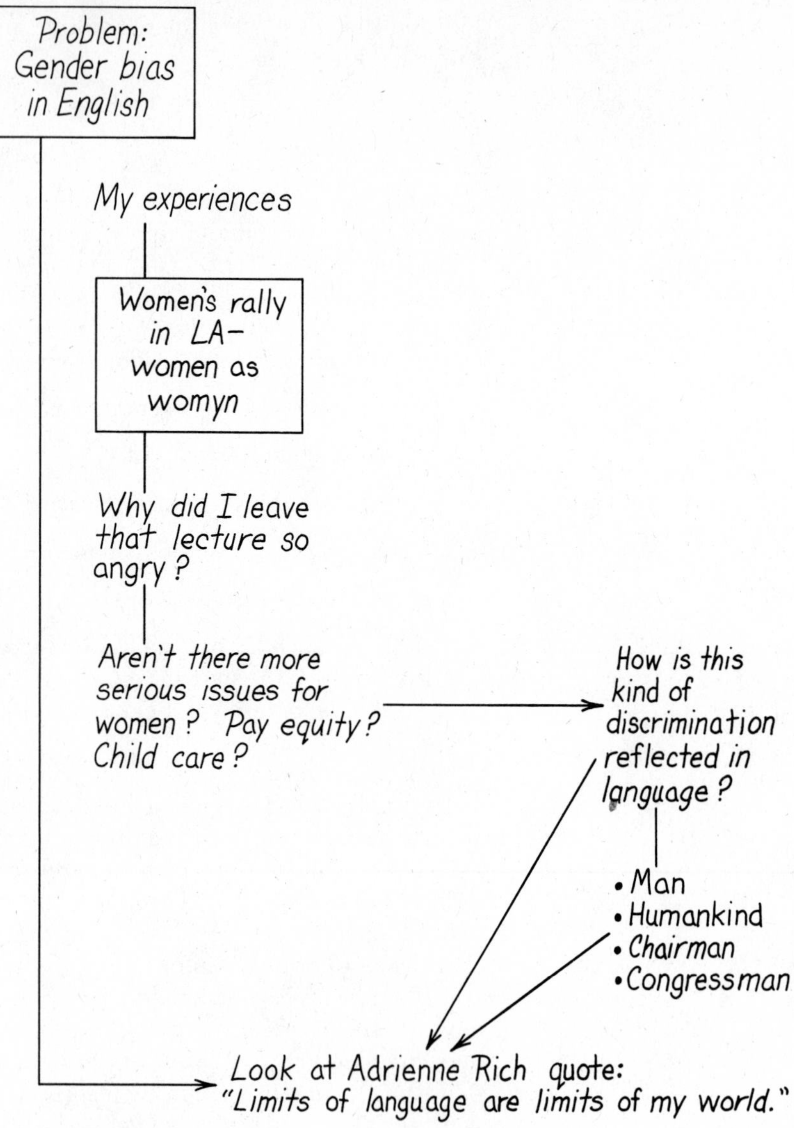
Problem:
Gender bias
in English
My experiences
Women's rally
in LA–
women as
womyn
Why did I leave
that lecture so
angry?
Aren't there more
serious issues for
women? Pay equity?
Child care?
How is this
kind of
discrimination
reflected in
language?
• Man
• Humankind
• Chairman
• Congressman
Look at Adrienne Rich quote:
"Limits of language are limits of my world."

Explaining importance
politics/power
women written out of history
Spanish teacher

Solutions
changing language for each individual
which words are important to change

Jessica's simple list outline gave her a direction and served as a guide for writing her first draft.

Formulating an Organizing Idea

Whenever you write, you bring together many ideas about your topic. One idea, however, serves to focus the examples, illustrations, and explanations that you include in your essay. That idea is the *organizing idea.* Your organizing idea responds to the question that generated your thinking, reading, talking, and observing. Depending on your purpose in writing, your organizing idea may indicate your position on an issue, summarize your argument, express your analysis of an event or a text: Your organizing idea always reflects your own interpretation.

In Chapter 2, we saw how Miriam Thaggert's essay reflects her goal of explaining her experience of double-consciousness. In the first paragraph, she reveals the organizing idea that focuses her essay:

> Double-consciousness affects all minorities in America, but I believe it is different for each person. There is a history that merges people together, but a unique perception of double-consciousness distinguishes the individual.

An organizing idea lets the reader know what to expect from the rest of the essay. Here, you expect that Miriam will discuss the concept of double-consciousness, and you expect that she will explain, by examples and illustrations, what her own experience has been.

When Jessica tried to define her organizing idea, she returned to her original questions. How are gender and language related? How do the words we use affect the way we see one another as individuals? After making notes in her journal, after thinking about the questions and talking with others, Jessica was ready to venture a statement that could serve as her tentative organizing idea:

> Language is our means of communicating with one another and therefore the basis of our relationships and communities. By altering language to fully include women, in very subtle ways, women may come to be perceived and treated in every sense as full members of our society.

With that tentative organizing idea to guide her, Jessica began to write the first draft of her essay.

Developing a First Draft

Like most writers, Jessica felt that sitting down at her computer was an uncertain undertaking. She had many ideas in her mind and many notes on the pages before her. She had an outline reflecting her decision to begin her essay with some examples of ways in which language is biased toward males. But still, the computer screen appeared threateningly blank. As she glanced at her notes, she was taken with one quotation by feminist scholar Elaine Showalter, whose essay Jessica had read in a book required for a women's studies course. The quotation seemed so elegant and concise that Jessica decided to begin with it and follow with a statement of her organizing idea.

Here is Jessica's first attempt to write her introductory paragraph:

> "Unlike Welsh, Breton, Swahili, or Amharic, that is, languages of minority or colonized groups, there is no mother tongue, no genderlect spoken by the female population in society, which differs significantly from the dominated language," wrote Elaine Showalter in an essay on feminist criticism. Language is our means of communicating with one another and therefore the basis of our relationships and communities. By altering language to fully include women, in a very subtle way, women may come to be perceived and treated in every sense as full members of our society. As Adrienne Rich wrote, "The content of education itself validates men even as it invalidates women. Its very message is that men have been the shapers and thinkers of the world, and that this is only natural."

After writing the first paragraph, Jessica stopped and referred to her outline. She had planned to present the problem, and in a sense Showalter and Rich did that for her. But she had decided, also, to use examples from her own experiences, and suddenly it seemed a big leap from the first paragraph she just drafted to Jessica in high school. She wondered what kind of transition would make that leap possible. She felt stuck.

As she reread the first paragraph, she realized that despite her preparation for writing, she had reverted to a familiar strategy of beginning her essays by relying on experts to provide ideas. Perhaps she would use Showalter sometime in her essay; and perhaps she would refer to an essay by Adrienne Rich. But Jessica knew that she had her own strong material to show why the question of gender and language mattered to her. She decided to try again, this time relying on her own experiences to give authority to her writing.

Here, then, is Jessica's draft:

Speaking in Tongues

Jessica Yellin

"To be a fine writer, one must appreciate the power of language." This is an English teacher's favorite sentence; at least, I can't recall an English teacher who did not type it neatly on a class assignment sheet several times a year. It was one of those affected and hackneyed statements that was expected to explain itself, and was therefore never actually discussed in class. Since I received high enough marks on my high school papers, I assumed that my "appreciation of the power of language," was acceptable and that seemed to be enough.

My first meaningful introduction to the "power of language" occurred at a rally for women's rights in Los Angeles that highlighted the not-so-subtle chauvinism in the English language. I was surprised to discover that the rally was not going to offer plans for the reintroduction of the Equal Rights Amendment or a call to elect more women to political office. Instead, the day's key speech was on gender bias in the English language. When the rally began, the speaker at the podium read aloud the words on a sign above the podium: "Spell it with a Y: WOMYN." Turning to the audience she shouted, "And why not spell it with a y? We must break away from the male bias in our language. So many of our words are based on a male model—their, her, they, she all have the word he in them; son is the base of person; lad is the base of lady; and man is the base of both human and woman. Now is the time for us to reclaim our language! We do not need men to define ourselves; we can stand on our own. That is why I say: Spell it with a Y!"

"Pathetic," was my only thought. "These women sound like man-hating radical freaks." I left that lecture fuming. To me, the speakers at the event were working against women. They were not being pragmatic. It seemed so simple: If these people just devoted the same energy to enlightening the police force about the prevalence and seriousness of rape; to opening homes for battered women; to introducing pay equity legislation in Congress; to electing female politicians to government office; to improving national child care; to removing books with a sexist bias from the reading lists of preschools—then they would impact the lives of women, and they would be making a contribution to society. But screeching about a y here or a son there would only succeed in alienating the moderates without helping a single female.

And so I was stubbornly convinced for most of my high school years. However, in my senior year of high school, I became more and more aware of the gender bias in our language, and I suddenly found myself endorsing the same argument which those "radical" women had articulated. At the time I was taking a women's studies course that acquainted me with the history and status of women in the United States, and I was becoming conscious of the chauvinism in our "modern, liberated" society. Stories such as a classmate's account of a Los Angeles judge who told her mother—who was six months pregnant—that it was "indecent" for a pregnant woman to be seen in public convinced me that women are not always accepted as equals in our society; the more I read, the more I recognized the discrimination against women in my world, and the more I became aware of the ways in which this chauvinism is reflected in our language.

Toward the middle of my senior year, my mom invited me to join her for an art lecture at a museum. The lecture, which was about Degas' paintings, was sponsored by a group largely run by women. Before the lecture began, an elegant and serious-looking woman stood at the podium, placed her half-glasses on her nose and began the introduction of officers and thank-yous that precede such events.

"Would each woman stand when named, and please hold all applause until everyone is standing," she said in a clipped voice.

"Event chairman, Amanda Arlington; Finance Committee Chairman, Joyce Harrelson; Ombudsman, Lynn Peters." As she made the introductions, chairman after chairman stood, each wearing a skirt or a dress, high heels, boots, or flats—each clearly female. The scene struck me as ludicrous. How could this woman be introducing her peers as men? It was crazy.

Thoughts that once seemed radical and offensive to me now were bubbling in my mind. During the car ride home, I tried to understand why I was so disturbed by the word chairman, or why it struck me as so blatantly incorrect. I reasoned that the purpose of language is to communicate with one another, to express ourselves, to define our feelings, our thoughts, and our environment. Therefore, words serve as labels for the feelings, objects, and miscellany that we share in our lives; words are meaningless without the correlating reality that they define. If we were taught that spleen is really the name for the color green, the properties of green would not be at all different, we simply would call them by a different name. Therefore, the word green is insignificant; we have simply named it so that we can communicate with one another.

Like many other languages, English is riddled with a male bias. We say, "Mankind evolved from a primordial soup billions of years ago." We hear that "American businessmen understand the power of money." Our elected officials are officially referred to as our CongressMEN, The Constitution holds that all

MEN are created equal, and MANkind is the word most used to define our species. "So, that's tradition," many people will argue. "These words evolved from a patriarchal society; since men were the most powerful people at the time English was evolving, all the chairpeople and Congresspeople really were men. Now we understand that these words include women, but we can't go around changing them or everyone will be confused."

I say archaic traditions can be changed. Women weren't allowed to vote until 1920. Is that a tradition we should have retained? Should Americans have continued slavery since, after all, it was a traditional practice?

Throughout the course of human civilization, women have been written out of history. For example, as Elaine Pagels tells us in her book Adam, Eve, and the Serpent, the earliest versions of the Bible tell an alternative creation story in which God creates woman before man, but we do not learn of this story. Adrienne Rich, in her essay "On Taking Women Students Seriously," tells us that women like Ethel Smyth, an early suffragist; Anne Askew, a woman burned and tortured to death several centuries ago for her political activism; and Jane Harrison, an antipatriarchal anthropologist, are passed over and forgotten. Similarly, woman are still not included in the Constitution as having civil rights; we are not guaranteed equal pay for equal work; we lose the right to control our reproductive organs when we are placed in jail. However, none of this is ultimately surprising, since women are excluded in the one variable that defines our society more than any other—our language.

In "On Taking Women Students Seriously," Rich proclaims, "The limits of my language are the limits of my world." Since we are trained to explain, analyze, and understand only that which we can define, our thoughts, our work, and our society are controlled by the language we use for definitions.

Several weeks ago my Spanish teacher was explaining the meaning of a Spanish word for which she could not recall the English equivalent. The word referred to a man who held all of the keys to the houses in certain neighborhoods of Spanish towns, so that residents could leave their houses without their keys and call him to open their doors when they returned home.

Everyone in the class became very disturbed after this explanation. "What do you mean?" we asked our professor. "One man had everyone's keys? Do you mean he was a locksmith? Or maybe you mean a landlord? Janitor? Superintendent? No, you must mean something else. He couldn't possibly have everyone's keys . . . there's no such thing!" Because the word for *el sereno* does not exist in English, we could not accept the fact that such a person existed at all.

Our language defines our reality. In the classroom, language reflects what Adrienne Rich calls "He-Man grammar": "The student should test himself on the above questions"; "The poet is representative. He stands among partial men for the complete man." While each of these passages is intended to include me, I do not identify with their male subjects. I am continually and unconsciously receiving the message that male is the norm, but while I am many things—student, daughter, friend, sister, thinker—I am not a man.

When I arrived home after the lecture at the museum, I found my parents' thousand-page dictionary and looked up the word woman. The first definition read, "Not of the male sex; the female human being as distinguished from the man." Here, too, women were defined in terms of a male standard, as non-men. From that day forward I decided to alter my language, to replace mankind with humankind, man with human, and the abstract he with she, for my experience is a female experience, and the world is made up of women and men. In my opinion, we both deserve a mention in our language. I am changing my language because I believe that changes start small. We cannot pass legislation decreeing changes in language. Language evolves through use. We do not have to start spelling women with a y, but I think that it is about time we started including her in our language.

Opportunities for Exchanging Ideas

1. Discuss Jessica's draft with your classmates. What is her organizing idea? Do you find this idea interesting and compelling? What kind of sources does she use to support her idea? What advice might you give her to strengthen this idea? Indicate passages in the draft where you have questions or concerns about her idea and the sources she uses.

2. Jessica had some trouble drafting her introduction. She abandoned her first introduction because it relied too heavily upon quotations from Elaine Showalter and Adrienne Rich. Look closely at her second introduction. Does this introduction successfully introduce the essay? Does the introduction pull you into the world of the essay? What advice might you give Jessica about her introduction?

3. How would you describe Jessica's tone? Do you find her tone offensive, engaging, adequate, and so on? What advice might you give Jessica about her tone?

4. Jessica entitled this draft "Speaking in Tongues." Comment on the effectiveness of this title.

5. Write a letter to Jessica summarizing your response to her draft and offering her detailed suggestions for revising "Speaking in Tongues."

Opportunities for Drafting

Develop a plan for the essay you are currently drafting. As you think about your plan, look for patterns in your notes. What do these patterns reveal to you? How do your guiding questions reflect your interest in your topic? Consider how your guiding questions are important to you and to your readers. How does your organizing idea reflect your interpretation of your topic? Write a draft of your essay.

CHAPTER 5

Responding and Revising

When you first start writing—and I think it's true for a lot of beginning writers—you're scared to death that if you don't get that sentence right that minute it's never going to show up again. And it isn't. But it doesn't matter—another one will, and it'll probably be better. And I don't mind writing badly for a couple of days because I know I can fix it—and fix it again and again and again, and it will be better. . . . Because the best part of it all, the absolutely delicious part, is finishing it and then doing it over . . . I rewrite a lot, over and over again, so that it looks like I never did. I try to make it look like I never touched it, and that takes a lot of time and a lot of sweat.

—Toni Morrison, "The Site of Memory"

I always throw away the first draft. Starting an essay is like starting up a car that has not been used for a long time. The first time you take it for a spin, the muck that has collected in the tailpipe may cause the car to backfire. But once the hot fumes from the engine have burnt away the debris, the car will ride more smoothly. My first thoughts for an essay are usually like the muck clogging up the tailpipe: Once I've swept them out of my head and onto paper, I can throw them into the garbage can and restart with a clear head. My first attempt to write this description now enjoys the company of three old cereal boxes and a banana peel in my garbage can. The advantage to working this way is that I assume that my first draft might be garbage, so I rarely suffer from the writer's block of those who feel that they must write well from the start.

—Adam Fisher, college freshman

The printed page does not reveal how it was created. When writing reads smoothly and logically, we assume that the writing must have flowed smoothly from the writer's pen or keyboard. We, as readers, do not see the crumpled-up paper, the deleted lines on the computer screens, the starts and stops, the scratch-outs and drafts, the private decisions and conversations that went on in the writer's mind to produce such writing. For when a piece of writing is successful, we do not see the seams; the writing carries us along so that we are not concerned with the writer's process.

Edgar Allan Poe, in his essay "The Philosophy of Composition," suggested that "authorial vanity" might be the reason writers don't want to show the ways they put their work together. Most writers, Poe claimed, "would positively shudder at letting the public take a peep behind the scenes, at the elaborate and vacillating crudities of thought—at the true purposes seized only at the last moment—at the cautious selections and rejections—at the painful erasures." Yet from writers who have allowed us to take a look behind the scenes to see their drafts, we see how necessary it is to write multiple drafts: necessary, because fully developed ideas are the result of questioning, thinking, and writing draft after draft.

Revising begins with writers asking questions about their drafts and working against the illusion of being finished. Drafts are attempts, approximations, trial runs; they are not finished essays. You can begin tentatively and end definitively; no one needs to see this journey, nor the detours of thought and purpose. Writing offers you this possibility of revising, of changing your mind, rethinking your questions, clarifying your organizing idea. In speaking, you are not always so fortunate. If you want to erase what you have said, you cannot do it without showing the eraser itself. You must say: "Oh, what I meant to say was . . ." or "Excuse me, I expressed myself badly . . ." Speech, in many ways, is irreversible. All you can do in speaking is to tack on another utterance; you can never retract what you have said. In writing, though, no one needs to see your eraser.

Sometimes we all struggle so hard to write a draft that when it has what looks like a beginning, middle, and end, we want to believe that we are almost finished. A good objective in revising is never to fall in love with what you have written in a first draft and not to place too much emphasis too early on writing a polished draft. Many student writers often equate revision with remedial work, punishment for writing poorly and for not getting it right the first time. They suppose that if they were only better writers, if they had a larger vocabulary, or if they knew more about their subject, they would not have to revise. The need to revise is not a sign of failure; it is an opportunity: It is, as the writer Toni Morrison tells us, "the delicious part" of creating a piece of prose.

UNDERSTANDING REVISION

To revise means, literally, *to see again,* to obtain a new vision. This definition may sound slightly mystical to you and raise questions in your mind: How will I obtain this "new vision"; how will I *see* my writing in any way other than the way I saw it the first time? When getting started, you choose between alternatives—between one topic and another, between different ideas and different ways of organizing them, and between different sources of information. Your writing, when you are first getting started, exists as a series of parts and pieces that you will weave together during the drafting stage. Although you have been changing your ideas and revising your questions from the moment you got started, it is not until you have a completed first draft that you can begin to see how all the pieces fit together to form a whole essay. Revision is a *reenvisioning of the whole* that is possible only after the first draft is written.

In this chapter we will talk about revising the essay as a whole, seeing how a writer's guiding questions and organizing idea are interrelated; how sources and strategies are used most effectively. This kind of revision involves revising *globally*: that is, rethinking your questions, clarifying your organizing idea, reorganizing paragraphs, replacing supporting details with material from other sources.

Many students are so used to thinking of revision as correcting or proofreading that they focus first on word- or sentence-level changes, searching for the precise word or the most descriptive phrase, deleting or rearranging sentences, checking grammar and punctuation for correctness. Later in this book we will consider sentence-level revision, what one writer called "the realm of the final inch." As you will see in this chapter, however, revising first involves looking at the larger realm of the whole essay.

The following introductory paragraph from a draft of a student essay illustrates the need to look globally at the whole essay before correcting or proofreading.

Each year, Americans spend more than ten billion dollars in the diet industry. This booming industry, as it surely is one, includes appetite suppressant pills with names like Dexatrim and Acutrim, powdered liquid meals like Slim-Fast and the Cambridge Diet, and best-selling diet books written by all kinds of people from doctors and nutrition experts to the woman who's willing to tell you how she lost hundreds of pounds her own way. The simple size and extent of the diet industry reveals an even more widely promoted and insidious perception of the idea that thin is desirable and fat is ugly. A study of the diet industry conducted at the State University of New York at Stony Brook found that the mass media plays an important role in reinforcing the perception that thin is in. In the rush to achieve an unrealistic standard of slimness, many Americans are engaging in harmful and risky dieting habits that ultimately may not work.

What is this paragraph about? The writer probably began the paragraph with the general purpose of discussing the growth of the diet industry. He changed direction, though, and began to discuss the causes and culprits of this growth and the harmful effects of risky dieting habits. The paragraph exists as a series of statements about the diet industry with each sentence taking the writer in a different direction.

The paragraph will not be improved if the writer begins revising by wanting to correct or proofread, by asking himself, "Is my first sentence too clichéd? Is the phrase, 'as it surely is' too wordy?" Or, "Have I repeated the words 'the diet industry' too many times?" Since his focus is unclear, the entire paragraph needs to change dramatically. The paragraph cannot be revised in isolation, only in the context of the whole essay. The writer needs to see how this paragraph fits with his organizing idea, how it helps him consider the questions he is trying to explore, and to decide which direction he will pursue.

Revising—both on the global and the sentence level—allows you to learn from your writing what it is that you want to say. Your first drafts are discovery drafts, showing you a direction and helping you clarify your ideas. When you revise, you often will discover that a draft does not express those ideas accurately, that, in fact, your intentions have changed, and you have become aware of other ways of developing your topic. Sometimes you may decide to take from your draft one word, image, sentence, or quotation, and begin anew.

Drafts often look impenetrable when you see your own words, not exactly etched in stone, but at least neatly printed on the page, staring back at you. *Where do you begin? How do you read your own drafts? What are the clues that will help you know what to change? What are the questions to ask yourself or your readers about your drafts?* These are the questions that we will explore in this chapter.

Opportunities for Reflecting

1. How do *you* revise? What is easy for you to do when you revise? What is difficult? If someone walked into your room and observed you revising, what would this person see? Reflect on these questions in your journal.

2. Look carefully at a piece of writing you are currently revising. How do you decide what needs to be revised? What clues in your own draft suggest to you the need to make changes? What do the conversations sound like in your head as you are revising? Reflect on these questions in your journal.

Opportunities for Exchanging Ideas

Here are some definitions of *revising* from student and professional writers. How do these definitions compare to your own description of your revising process? What are the revision concerns of these writers? Discuss these definitions with your classmates. Also discuss what you understand to be the similarities and differences between the groups.

Student writers

When I revise I just review every word and make sure that everything is worded right. I see if I am rambling; I see if I can put a better word in or leave one out. Usually when I read what I have written, I say to myself, "that word is so bland or so trite," and then I go and get my thesaurus.

I don't really rewrite because I only write one draft and the changes I make are made on top of that draft. The changes I make are usually marking out words and putting different ones in.

I call revising slashing and throwing out. I throw things out of my writing and say they don't work. I like to write like Fitzgerald did by inspiration, and if I feel inspired then I don't need to slash and throw much out.

Professional writers

Rewriting means on one level, finding the argument, and on another level, language changes to make the argument more effective. Most of the time I feel as if I can go on rewriting forever. There is always one part of a piece of writing that I could keep revising. It is always difficult to know at what point to abandon a piece of writing. I like the idea that a piece of writing is never finished, just abandoned.

> Revising means taking apart what I have written and putting it back together again. I ask major questions of my ideas, respond to those questions, and think of proportion and structure. I find out which ideas can be developed and which should be dropped. I am constantly chiseling and changing as I revise.
>
> My cardinal rule in revising is never to fall in love with what I have written in a first or second draft. An idea, sentence, or even a phrase that looks catchy, I don't trust. I like to give myself as much time as possible between drafts. I am much more in love with something after I have written it than I am a day or two later. It is much easier to change anything with time.

BETWEEN THE DRAFTS

Something has to happen between drafts—some new way of seeing, thinking, or questioning—or else writers are stuck doing mop and broom work: polishing, cleaning, and fixing. The next two sections offer you strategies for *reading as a writer* and *engaging readers in peer review*—revising strategies to help you learn from your drafts what you want to say.

Reading as a Writer

When you revise you become both writer and reader, shifting your role back and forth, listening and reading your own words. Who is this reader you have become? Someone who is a collaborator, an ally, a devil's advocate, a helpful critic who keeps asking you questions. In reading your own drafts, you need to read not only what is on the page, but also, and sometimes more important, what is not on the page—what your draft still needs in order to achieve its intended purpose with its intended audience. This means reading your draft with an eye toward other choices and possibilities: a different set of questions, a different organizing idea, a different organization, or perhaps, a different tone. Every rereading raises the possibility of change and of making new decisions. Your drafts represent work in progress.

In rereading your text you are beginning to rethink your ideas and explain your writing to yourself. We all often read into our writing what we intended to say, not what is on the page. If you doubt the important connection between reading and revising, see how uneasy you would feel if you could not read what you have written. Or try, as one British research team did, to write with a worn-out pen, using carbon paper so that you can't read while you write, but can later on see what you have written. You will quickly see how important reading is to maintain control of what you are writing and thinking. Here are some strategies to help you read as a writer:

Read Aloud Writers need to hear their own writing. Your eye might not catch what is repetitious, boring, clunky, or unclear, but your ear will. As you read aloud, you should circle what doesn't sound right to you. Keep asking yourself: Who is the voice of this essay? Does this essay sound like me?

Read and Reread Revising requires several readings of a draft, each with a different emphasis. Read first to learn from your writing what you are trying to say. Then read to evaluate your guiding questions, organizing idea, sources, and organization. Read later drafts, carefully and closely, to strengthen paragraphs, sentences, and diction. Annotate your draft each time you reread your writing with questions and comments to guide your revisions.

Read for Strengths Read your drafts to see where you have been successful and to see what surprises or interests you about what you have written. You might find an idea, an example, or a tone emerging that you had not expected. Circle, underline, or annotate what surprises or interests you about what you have written. These surprises might lead you in a different direction, or they might help you focus and achieve clarity.

Read for Discrepancies Read your drafts to see if there is a gap between what you want to say and what you are actually saying. Look for the lack of clarity, the vagueness, the repetition of ideas. Find what your essay still needs.

Allow for Time to Pass Sometimes time helps. We are less in love with what we have written after the ink is dry and we feel somewhat distant from what we wrote. Time and distance often bring the fresh perspective that we need to reenvision our drafts.

Opportunities for Reflecting

1. Read, reread, and reread again the draft you are currently revising or an essay you already consider finished. Does the essay sound like you? As you read, ask yourself questions about your draft. Use them as

clues to understand how to revise your draft. Write comments in your journal about what interests and surprises you in your draft. How does your draft work as a whole? How do all the paragraphs work together? Where are the discrepancies between what you intended to write and what you actually wrote?

2. If possible, allow two days to pass between reading your drafts. How does the passing of time influence your reading? What do you see two days later that you didn't see right away? What changes would you make now that you wouldn't have made two days ago? Reflect on these questions in your journal.

A Writer at Work: Reading as a Writer

In a freshman composition class, Rita Morelli was given the broad assignment to explain some aspect of learning or schooling that interested her. As an avid rock climber, Rita was curious about why she learned to rock climb so easily, whereas so many other subjects she was taught in school never stayed with her. In her journal, she spent some time reflecting on the differences between learning inside and outside of school. In a small-group discussion, her peers offered her the idea of contrasting the way she learned to rock climb with the way she learned a specific school subject. Rita focused her first draft with these guiding questions:

- Why do I learn so easily outside of school?
- What was it about the way I learned to rock climb that made rock climbing so appealing to me?
- What was it about the way I was taught geography in seventh grade that made it so impossible to learn or remember anything?

As she read and reread her draft, Rita shifted her role back and forth from writer to reader, beginning to see her draft through the eyes of her readers. "What do they know about my subject; what do they need to know?" she asked herself. Readers, she knew, ask questions such as: What is the idea of this essay? What is the writer trying to say?

Rita circled what she liked and what surprised her about her draft. She liked the way she described rock climbing in the first two paragraphs but wondered if the first paragraph was too long and if her readers needed to know somewhere in that first paragraph what her essay would be about. She began to make notes in the margins, asking herself questions, creating a conversation between herself as writer and reader.

She learned something about her draft from roughly outlining each paragraph, writing a one-sentence summary of the paragraph in the margins, and asking herself: *What is this paragraph about? Does this paragraph need further development? What am I trying to say here?* Here is Rita's draft with her notes to herself.

Ropes and Geography

Paragraph #1 → my first rock-climbing class

I took my first rock-climbing class when I was 15. I can't remember exactly what inspired me to take the class offered by Cal Adventures, nor whether it was even my idea to begin with, but in any case I enrolled for a beginning "Rock I" seminar. On the planned weekend the teachers brought us (the students) to Indian Rock, the local crag, and within a half an hour we were climbing. When I think back about what I learned in that class I realize it wasn't much. I did not learn how to set up ropes or about how to make a safe anchor. What I learned certainly didn't make me even a remotely competent climber. However, in my mind, the class was great. It left me with a feeling of what climbing is all about. I got a glimpse of the beauty of climbing—of the intense concentration a sheer granite wall demands. Although Indian Rock is only 200 feet high, I got a glimpse of the tremendous satisfaction in getting to the top. It was this feeling the class left me with that has carried me up thousands of feet in the Grand Tetons, that has forced me to bivouac on a narrow ledge in Yosemite, that has led me to some of the best times in my life.

I like this sentence →

Is this paragraph too long?

I like the way I said this. →

Paragraph #2
↓
Learned the skills of rock climbing naturally from that first class.

Is this paragraph too general? Should I show more specifically what I learned?

During the past three years I've learned the skills necessary to become a competent rock climber. I learned them with a friend, often the hard way, often the dangerous way. I remember we once arrived home battered and bloody, but knowing in a very personal meaningful sort of way that the rappel knot must go on the vertical part of the rock. The details and skills we learned all followed naturally from catching that glimpse of the true nature of rock climbing in my beginners' class.

Paragraph #3
↓
Learned the essence of rock climbing—that's what is important

I like my details here →

What does glimpse mean to me?

Can I make this statement about all subjects?

The class did not even try to teach those details. I did not learn about how carribeaners must be opposite and opposed or about what makes a good belay stance. I did not learn any of the skills one actually needs to rock climb. Yet I don't think being drilled countless times about the efficiency of tying a butterfly knot instead of an overhand knot and other such information would have done anything but scared me away from climbing at that beginning stage. It is the initial glimpse of the essence of rock climbing that gets one up cliffs, not the knowledge of certain concepts and facts. [I think this is true for any subject.]

Paragraph #4
↓
Never learned geography

I learned absolutely nothing from my seventh grade geography class. We called the teacher Ditto Daily because of the immense quantities of smudgy handouts she was so fond of. Everyday she would hand out purple mimeographed copies of a map, a list of capitals, or some other quantity of information. Every two weeks there would be a test which would consist of writing down worldly facts or differences between cultures. We learned a great deal of worthwhile facts, but the class was a dead end. When it was over I promptly forgot everything and didn't touch geography again.

I think old Ditto Daily tried the impossible. She tried to teach us the ropes before she taught us rock climbing. She tried to teach us the details—the carribeaners, the location of a country and the culture of another, not the essence of the subject—the beauty of rock climbing, whatever she found so wonderful about geography. Surely the information of where countries are will naturally follow if students are given a glimpse at what being in an exotic land is all about, just as how my rock skills followed from catching that glimpse of the nature of rock climbing. If Ditto Daily wanted to teach us details and facts, that's great, just as how I wouldn't object to more instruction on how to climb safely, but she should only do so after showing the beauty of living in other countries. Let us have classes that hint at the essence of subjects. The facts, the details, the knowledge that teaches a climber in spirit to become a compent climber will all come naturally with time if we only hint at the won-

I could have learned about mountains in a geography class. I need to show the difference in learning about mountains from smudgy dittos vs. learning about them from sleeping on a ledge.

I like the way I bring them together - But what is the essence of geography?

Is this my organizing idea?

Paragraph #5 → Difference between rock climbing and geography the details vs. the essence

too general

Does this paragraph come as a surprise to a reader?

?

Here's what I need to say more about

I keep repeating the word essence - but do I show and explain what I mean by this word?

derful mysteries, beauty, and satisfaction our subjects have to offer. I need to show more about the wonderful power of learning the mysteries of a subject

Constructing a rough outline of each paragraph in the margins of her draft gave Rita an easy way between the drafts to see the shape and structure of her emerging essay. She realized from her rough outline that her first three paragraphs were entirely about rock climbing, that her fourth paragraph was about geography, and her fifth paragraph brought the two together. Outlining her draft helped her to see that her readers would probably be surprised about the introduction of geography in the fourth paragraph after three solid paragraphs about rock climbing.

Rita's guiding questions helped her write her first draft, but as she reread her draft she began to see new questions emerging, more specific questions. Her draft itself produced new questions, and she revised her guiding questions. Instead of asking: Why do I learn so easily outside of school? or, Why did I learn rock climbing and not geography? she asked, What does it mean to learn the ropes before rock climbing, the details before the essence? What happens to learning when teachers mistake the technical aspects of the subject for the beauty and mystery of it? She learned from her draft that she wasn't really interested in exploring the differences between learning inside and outside of school. Instead, from her revised questions, Rita began to see an organizing idea emerging, an idea that surprised and pleased her. She wanted to explain the importance of not mistaking the technical aspects of the subject for the essence. When we learn a subject, Rita wanted to say, whether it is inside or outside of school, we need to learn the beauty and mystery of it first. Rock climbing was a good illustration of an experience in which she learned the beauty and mystery first; geography, which she never learned, was a good illustration of an experience in which the teacher mistook the technical aspects for the essence.

Before revising her next draft, Rita had some specific questions she wanted to talk about with her peers and her instructor. She wanted to know:

- Does it come as a surprise that I bring up geography in the fourth paragraph? Should I introduce my organizing idea in my opening paragraphs?

- Do I repeat the idea in the first three paragraphs about getting a glimpse of a subject without really developing what I mean?
- If I am going to use rock climbing as such a pivotal example, do I need to give a more detailed description of what I learned on the first day?
- Can I really speak about all subjects from my two examples? Have I earned the right to generalize?
- Should I include another example from school, chemistry, for instance, to show how it is possible to learn the beauty and mystery of a subject inside of school?

Opportunities for Exchanging Ideas

All rough drafts are filled with possibilities and different directions. Rita's draft illustrates the challenges and opportunities of revising.

How would you respond to Rita's draft and her questions? Reread her draft with her comments and questions in mind. Write a letter to Rita in which you address each of her questions. Help her think about her own questions, and offer her your suggestions for revising.

Discuss your letter with your classmates. Consider the similarities and differences in the ways various classmates respond to Rita's draft. What can you learn about revising from these different responses?

Opportunities for Revising

1. Reread the draft you are currently revising. Outline each paragraph and write a one- or two-sentence summary of the paragraph. Ask yourself: *What is this paragraph about? How does this paragraph develop and expand my organizing idea? Does the paragraph need further development?* What do you learn about your organizing idea from constructing this rough outline? What do you learn about the structure and emphasis in your draft that you will want to change?

2. Exchange drafts with a classmate. Ask your classmate to read your draft and write a one- or two-sentence summary of your paragraphs. Compare your classmate's summaries with your own.

ENGAGING READERS: PEER REVIEW

Becoming your own reader, trusting your own judgments, knowing what questions to ask yourself as you revise—these are all important "writerly skills" to develop. Equally important is developing the skill of working with other writers and learning how to invite their responses and engage those writers in a conversation about your drafts. Revising—like getting started and drafting—need not be a solitary activity. Working with your peers either one-on-one, in a small group, or with your entire class gives you the most immediate sense of a real, living, breathing, thinking audience.

The purpose of peer review is to let you know how well you have expressed your ideas. Your readers can help you revise by letting you see your draft in a way that you might not be able to see by yourself. They will tell you what they find engaging about your draft, what they find new and interesting, memorable, and persuasive. They can tell you if your guiding questions and organizing idea are clear or where they become confused and need more explanation. Hearing your readers question the purpose of a particular paragraph, for instance, can be a clue that you might be taking unnecessary detours from your organizing idea or, in fact, that this detour should be followed in the next draft to see where it could lead you.

In peer review, it *is* the written and oral conversations about your draft that matter; you will hear these conversations, between the drafts, as you reread and revise. Hearing your peers respond to your work, writer to writer, hearing what made them laugh, applaud, cry out for more, will suggest to you the strengths of your own draft. Peers need to see their role as fellow writers, allies, and not as critics who attack or destroy the draft. It is not the peer's job to take over the direction or responsibility for revising the draft. Nor is it your role in peer review to defend your work. You, the writer, are always in charge of deciding which responses and comments to use from the conversation about your work.

How to Comment

You will learn a great deal about writing from having your work read by your peers and also from the opportunity to be on the other side as a peer reviewer. How do peer reviewers work? They work by remembering that all writers need readers who are interested, curious, and encouraging; readers who want to understand the writer's purpose; readers who will offer thoughtful and respectful comments. What does a helpful comment look like?

The most helpful comments are specific ones. Of course, you will be happy to know that your readers "liked" your draft or that they "really could understand" what your draft is about. Such comments provide positive encouragement, but they don't give you specific direction. Be as concrete, direct, and straightforward as you can when you comment on the drafts of your peers. Comments such as "I liked the first example you used in your opening paragraph, but your second example in that paragraph seems to contradict your first example" gives you a specific problem to think about in revising. Equally helpful are comments phrased as questions.

How to begin? Read your peer's draft once to get a sense of the whole piece. Then, comment on the global, larger issues first:

- ➤ Does the draft have a clear organizing idea? What do you think this idea is? Can you summarize the idea in two or three sentences?
- ➤ Is the writer asking interesting questions? What are these questions? How do these questions engage you as a reader?
- ➤ Does the draft give you a sense of discovery? Or does it exist simply to present a set of ready-made conclusions?
- ➤ How do the specific details or examples support and develop the writer's organizing idea?

These are general questions to guide you in reading a rough draft. No one checklist of questions will work for each assignment because checklists by their very nature are too general. The best set of questions are the specific ones you develop to match the different expectations and requirements of each assignment. As you read a draft, write comments in the margins about the specific ideas, paragraphs, or sentences that deserve comments. If you are confused or if you think the writer is repetitious, show the writer where in the draft this occurs. Likewise, if you think a particular example or a piece of evidence is effective, show the writer how this effect is created.

After you have written your comments in the margins, write a letter to your peer giving your overall response. Start with the strengths of the draft. Offer the writer a close and careful reading of his or her draft, giving specific suggestions for revising, and encouraging the writer's efforts.

How to Receive Peer Response

Peer response presents opportunities and challenges for writers. Receiving a multitude of responses and questions can propel your thinking, giving you the encouragement and direction for revising. On the other hand, receiving what you perceive to be negative, idiosyncratic, or contradictory responses can be discouraging and confusing. Remember that your peers are not criticizing *you*; try not to be defensive or argumentative. The responses given to you are not commands or prescriptions. They are comments that are meant to be interpreted and used by you to learn about the ways different readers respond to your work.

All comments thoughtfully given deserve your attention and respect, but you need not blindly accept them. When a reader comments, "I don't know what your essay is about," ask your reader specific questions: "Where in my draft are you confused?" Always translate your readers' suggestions into your own language. Guide the conversation about your draft by asking *why* and *where* questions. For instance, "Why doesn't this example seem persuasive to you?" Or, "Where do you think this quotation would be the most effective?" "Where in the draft am I being repetitious?" Talk directly with your peers about both the specific questions they are asking and the ones you are asking about your draft.

After a peer review, it is often helpful to let some time pass between receiving comments and revising your draft. Let the comments sort themselves out as you review the conversation and reread your peers' responses. A useful strategy between drafts is to write notes to yourself, looking for a pattern in the various comments you received, and developing a plan for revising.

A Writer at Work: Working with Peers

Writers often have different styles of revising. Some, like Rita Morelli, try to set down their ideas from the start, engaging their readers at an early stage in their revising process. Other writers may not feel comfortable doing so. Some writers, like Ari Shapiro, whose writing we will look at next, prefer to set down their ideas in their notebooks or journals, where they can consider them privately and wait until they have written a second draft before they ask for peer review.

Ari Shapiro's assignment was to remember two or three important experiences in his life and to find a connecting idea embedded in these separate experiences that he could explore. In his journal, Ari first wrote about an experience from seventh grade when he and his father went to a bookstore called Seven Rays. At the time Ari could not understand why anyone would shop at a bookstore like Seven Rays where strawberry incense was usually burning and where they sold tarot cards and books about transcendental meditation. Ari's father was irritated with his lack of appreciation of the store and told him, "You are a good kid, but you are too damned logical—too logical to appreciate the emotional side of life."

Ari also brainstormed in his journal about his experience of becoming a part-time Hebrew teacher. He had tried hard as a beginning teacher to imitate the behaviors of his favorite teachers. His efforts failed one day when he was trying to teach the Hebrew word for love, *ahava*. All his attempts to logically understand the behaviors of his former teachers could not help him when one student disrupted the class and refused to believe that Ari, as a teacher, understood what love meant.

These journal entries gave Ari a good place to begin. He developed these guiding questions to focus his draft:

- What does logic mean to me now? What did being logical mean to me as a seventh grader?
- Why did my dad say I was "too damned logical"?
- What did I learn about being too logical from my experience as a Hebrew school teacher?
- What is the other side of logical that I always seem to be struggling against?

After reading and rereading his rough draft, Ari wrote a second draft that he felt was ready for peer review. Here is Ari's draft with one peer reader's comments in the margins and the letters he received from all his peer readers summarizing their responses.

Logic

This is a great beginning

You use the word logic or logical a lot. Why so many times? A reader will not be puzzled if you use the word logic less and your details more.

I was not born logical. When I was a baby I bit my dad whenever he tried to give me a bath. I love him. It wasn't logical to bite him. You don't hurt the people you love. You don't bite the hand that feeds you. I know that now, because I'm logical. Somewhere along the line, I got logic. My teachers and my parents were quite intent on giving it to me, and I took to it well. Learning language was my first step towards logic. Making sounds into coherent words and sentences bearing ripe ideas requires tremendous logical reasoning. Every once and a while my dad plays the cassette

This sounds like you are showing off

recording of my first words: "hamburger" and "aurora borealis." Dad taught me to say his name, and I became a student. In the fourth grade somebody thought I was logical and placed me in the Gifted and Talented program. Eight years later some college admissions officers agreed, and now I'm a college student here.

Being a student is a privileged position. Protected from the dangers of the outside world, students are exposed to its ideas. Most of the important ideas that we learn in school follow a system of logical. The theorems of mathematics, the hypotheses of the natural and social sciences, and the syntax of language are all logical ideas that we spend years, even lifetimes, learning. Those who have mastered logic or at least can convince others that they have done so, may become teachers. They assume the burden of passing logic on to its next generation of victims.

Do you intend to sound so logical and so certain here?

In my senior year of high school I became a part-time Hebrew school teacher. Feeling that I had a grave responsibility to the children, I took the job seriously. I approached each class with a logically and thoughtfully constructed lesson plan, modeled after the lessons of the best teachers I ever had. On October 19th, 1988, my lesson was going well. The class was working on the word "ahava"—love. Lin-

This is good—here you show yourself being logical by developing a lesson plan to teach the word "love"

guistically, "ahava" is an interesting word because it contains two silent consonants. The silent consonant is a tough concept for English speakers to grasp, because in English all of the consonants make sounds, at least most of the time. The kids were working hard at "ahava." I floated among them, helping them out, joking with them, making eye contact and assuring them that they were having fun. After 45 minutes we stopped for a game of Hebrew seven-up. Avi Blackmore won.

Do we need all these details? All this background?

Avi Blackmore was tall and thin. He picked his nose in class and seemed not to care. I always found myself watching him. Sometimes when I called on him in class he would pretend he had not heard me. Other times he would respond curtly with the right answer. He was unfriendly toward the other kids and oblivious to his surroundings. He stared out the window a lot and liked to play with his hands. I scolded him once for elevating his middle finger. He did not understand why that upset me. He smiled at me a lot, and looked at me and though he never said much I felt we understood each other.

Why is the steam and heat so important? Show us

That particular Sunday he came up to me and said, "Ari, please help me understand this. It is hot in here, but it is not boiling hot and anyway there is no water here to boil. Still, I can see steam rising all around me and I can't see anymore and I do not know whether I will be able to keep breathing much longer." There was absolutely no steam in the room.

Show us

I invited Avi to go outside for some cool, fresh air.

"It is the same out there," he told me, rushing, panting. "It is the same everywhere."

"Avi," I said slowly, "I don't understand." I forced a smile that came out as a mocking grin.

"You are not my teacher," Avi screamed at me. "You are just a fake and you don't care and you don't have 'ahava' for me and even if I die you will be happy because there will be one less kid picking his nose in your stupid class!"

Not exactly clear what this experience helped you to understand

I had been logical with Avi. I had reasoned with him calmly. There was no steam at all in the room and I could not understand what he was reacting to. I did not know how to deal with him. We lost contact and he felt betrayed, abandoned, angry. My logic could not handle his feelings and I was baffled.

Good transition between experiences

When I was about Avi's age I was very logical, or so my dad said. In the seventh grade, or maybe the summer before eighth grade, my father and I went to Seven Rays bookstore on the corner of Westcott Street and Pearl Avenue. Seven Rays is not a conventional bookstore. I had always called it a hippie bookstore. Strawberry incense was always burning at Seven Rays, and new age music hovered in its smoke. I could never tell whether the person behind the counter was a man or a woman. A tea kettle was always whistling. I do not recall anyone ever actually drinking tea. I could never tell whether the other customers were teenagers or 40-year-olds who never outgrew their faded jeans. The bookshelves were wooden: not metal, and certainly not plastic. They sold crystals and herbs at Seven Rays, and tarot cards and books about transcendental meditation and Buddhism and eating wild berries with chopsticks. A display of pipes seemed incongruous among all the health food stuff. The futons and Persian rugs at Seven Rays were not the kind you could get at department stores. At Seven Rays they carried the genuine article, no designer imitations.

this doesn't sound like your language

In seventh grade, or maybe during the summer before eighth, I thought Seven Rays was weird. I much preferred Economy Books, where they sold normal stuff, like Nancy Drew books and mechanical pencils and magazines about personal computers and golf.

Dad and I had an argument over the relative merits of

the two bookstores. I said there was nothing in Seven Rays that anyone ever *really* needed. And everything is overpriced there, not like at Economy Bookstore where you can get stuff with pink tags at 33 1/3 percent off. Dad told me I was a smart kid, a good reader, good in school, and patient and kind to my friends and my little sister. He even told me I was a good lacrosse player, which was a lie. And he told me I was too damned logical.

He said, "Ari, you are too damned logical."

this is great how you bring your ideas together at this point.

I didn't understand. He was the one who taught me to be logical. He taught me to talk and was so proud when I learned to say "hamburger." He helped me with my math homework. I remember trying to decide whether to stay overnight at my best friend Travis's house and he told me to decide by weighing the pros and cons of each alternative. How contradictory it was that the man who was my mentor in logic should tell *me* that *I* am too logical.

this is really good!

Well, Dad was right. I am only beginning to see that now, but he saw it then. He said it would be something with which I would have to struggle. With Avi, my logic made me mad. All I wanted to do was figure out what was wrong, help him feel better. I couldn't because logic got in the way. I was not born with logic, but I got it. Avi never did, and that kept me from understanding him. I struggled with that. Jessica taught me that struggle is good.

Jessica is one of those athletes people call a natural. People say runners like her have a gift from God. Jessica dropped out of the first cross-country race senior year. It hurt too much; she couldn't keep running. Afterwards she went away somewhere, maybe into the woods, maybe to be by herself. I don't know because I didn't see her go, but I knew how she was feeling. She fell from God's grace that day, and she was upset. I knew she would rise again, and so did she, but that did not make it any easier. "We all have to struggle sometimes," she said later, "with the things that keep us running."

this is not clear
- *Who is Jessica?*
- *What have you learned from her?*
- *How has she showed you something about struggling?*

My struggle is with logic. I never dropped out of a cross-country race. The object of entering a race is finishing it, so where is the logic in dropping out? But, I wish I had dropped my logic with Avi Blackmore. He proved to me that logic does not always lead to answers. The aspect of human personality that the word "ahava" really represents, the aspect that Seven Rays bookstore attracts, is the aspect that Avi Blackmore understands. I am struggling to appreciate it. Struggling makes me angry, because it is hard and sometimes I fail and I don't like to fail. Jessica showed me

You keep repeating the word struggle.

that struggling is good and worthwhile, but I still don't like to do it. That's not very logical, is it? Ah—maybe there's hope for me. ← this doesn't sound very honest.

Ari: I really like your draft.
- Can you do more with the idea of struggling?
- What is your struggle against? → against feeling? → against love's lack of logic?

TO: Ari
FROM: Tanya

Your draft is clear and interesting. Your idea—I think—is that living by a code of cold logic can prove emotionally limiting and can close you off from many of life's adventures. This is a great idea and makes for good reading.

From the moment I began reading your draft I wanted to know what YOU mean by the word "logic." What is logic to you? You repeat the words "logic" and "logical" so many times that it really bothered me as a reader. Is logic a lack of creativity, a paralyzing need to always be correct, a refusal to allow emotions to influence your life? Is it what we learn in school as opposed to all those bits of wisdom we gain through experience? What do you mean when you say, "Now, I am logical"?

Your Jessica story seems out of place. I am not sure who

she is or why she taught you something important. I suggest you give us more background on Jessica or simply cut her out.

This is certainly a strong draft.

Tanya

TO: Ari
FROM: Paul

This draft reads very smoothly and the ideas are well connected. My biggest problem in understanding your idea had to do with Jessica. I don't see how she showed you that struggling is worthwhile, even though she said that "we all have to struggle sometimes." Give us more details and explain how she showed you the value of this struggle.

I also am not sure that the Hebrew school example is clear. Do you want to make a case for the superiority of emotion, of love, of "ahava" in this example? Or do you want to show the problem of trying to explain emotional reactions with logic?

Hope these few questions and my comments show you how much I enjoyed your draft.

Paul

TO: Ari
FROM: Miriam

I really enjoyed reading your draft. You captured the sometimes confusing, sometimes unpleasant nature of logic. Your draft makes me wonder if logic is really logical and comprehensible. When do we need logic and when do we not? How do we know the difference? Thanks for making me think about these questions.

I like your introduction, but I wonder if you are overstating your organizing idea. Couldn't you just let your details work for you without always stating your purpose for including them?

I love your dialogue, especially hearing your dad say to you that you are "too damned logical."

I like your description of Seven Rays, and it made me think of a similar bookstore in New Orleans. I don't really understand the meaning of the Hebrew school example. Is "ahava" all that important to the general idea of your essay? Also, I would like to know more about Jessica? Why does she just run in and run out of your draft?

Your conclusion is really effective. You do a good job of bringing these various experiences together so we understand their connections.

Miriam

Ari was greatly encouraged after receiving these responses. He learned about his own draft, but also he learned that many of the questions he had about writing this assignment were those shared by his peers. Working with his peers made him feel less alone.

Ari read the comments he received and found a common pattern to the responses. When he met with Tanya, Paul, and Miriam he asked them specific questions about their comments. Specifically, he wanted to know:

- How can I show the tension, my struggle, between logic and feeling without using the word *logic* so many times?
- What more do you want to know about Jessica?
- Do you see how the various experiences are connected and how each one develops my organizing idea?

The conversation about his draft, the various comments and responses he received, gave Ari a new way of seeing his draft. He revised his guiding questions and revised his essay. Here is Ari's final draft:

Logic?

Ari Shapiro

I was not born logical. When I was a baby I bit my dad whenever he tried to give me a bath. I loved him. It wasn't logical to bite him. You don't hurt the people you love. You don't bite the hand that feeds you. I know that now, because now I am logical. Biting Dad was not reasonable. As I grew up, I learned logic. My teachers and my parents were intent on teaching it to me, and I took to it well. Learning language was my first step towards 1 logic. Making sounds into coherent words and words into sentences bearing ripe ideas demands tremendous reasoning. Every once and a while my dad plays the cassette recording of my first words: "hamburger" and "aurora borealis." Later, Dad taught me to say his name, and I became a student.

For me, being a student is a privileged position. Protected from the dangers of the outside world, I am exposed to its ideas. Most of the ideas that I've learned in school follow a system of logic. The theorems of mathematics, the hypotheses of the natural and social sciences, and the syntax of language are all logical ideas. Erving Goffman, for example, explained human behavior using the theater as an analogy. He said people assume roles in society. They surround themselves with props to convey the image of their character, and act as society expects their character to act. Their biggest fear is behaving out of character and shattering the illusion for their audience. Goffman calls his system a dramaturgical analysis. Shakespeare said that all the world is a stage and all the people are players. Goffman agreed. His logic explains behavior accurately and predicts it beautifully. I work hard to learn logic and find its beauty. Good teachers master the logic of their fields. They assume the burden of passing logic on to the next generation of students. 2

Last year, I became a part-time Hebrew school teacher. I felt that I had a dire responsibility to the children. I took the job seriously. I approached each class with a clear and thoughtfully constructed lesson plan, modeled after the lessons of the best teachers I ever had. On October 19th, 1988, my lesson was going well. The class was working on the word "ahava"—love. Linguistically, "ahava" is an interesting word because it contains two silent consonants. The silent consonant is a tough concept for English speakers to grasp, because in English all of the consonants make sounds, most of the time. The kids were working hard at "ahava." I floated among them, helping them out, joking with them and assuring them that they were having fun. After 45 minutes we stopped for a game of Hebrew seven-up. Avi Blackmore won. 3

Avi Blackmore was tall and thin. He picked his nose in class and seemed not to care. I always found myself watching him. Sometimes when I called on him in class he would pretend he had not heard me. Other times he would respond curtly with the right answer. He was unfriendly toward the other kids and oblivious to his surroundings. He stared out the window a lot and liked to play with his hands. I scolded him once for elevating his middle finger. He didn't understand why that upset me. He smiled at me a lot and looked at me, and though he never said much, I felt we understood each other. 4

That particular Sunday he came up to me and said, "Ari, please help me understand this. It is hot in here, but it is not boiling hot and anyway 5 there is no water here to boil. Still, I can see steam rising all around me and I can't see anymore and I do not know whether I will be able to keep breathing much longer." There was absolutely no steam in the room, so I dismissed his concern. Goffman would say that he was deviating from his role as a rational student and acting the part of the irrational child.

I invited Avi to go outside for some cool, fresh air. 6

"It is the same out there," he told me, rushing, panting. "It is the same 7
everywhere."

"Avi," I said, "I don't understand." I forced a smile that came out as a 8
mocking grin.

"You are not my teacher," Avi screamed at me. "You are just a fake and 9
you don't care and you don't have 'ahava' for me and even if I die you will be happy because there will be one less kid picking his nose in your stupid class!"

I had been logical with Avi. I had reasoned with him calmly. There was 10
no steam at all in the room and I could not understand what he was reacting to. He was lost in a world of emotion. The steam represented something for him, some feeling that logic kept me from understanding. Maybe he was isolated or scared or maybe he was trying to hide behind his steam, and wanted me to hide with him. I don't know. He wanted me to help him through the steam, but I couldn't even see it. My dramaturgical analysis could not comprehend his feelings. He felt betrayed, abandoned, angry.

When I was about Avi's age I was very logical, or so my dad said. In 11
the seventh grade, or maybe during the summer before eighth grade, my father and I went to Seven Rays bookstore on the corner of Westcott Street and Pearl Avenue. Seven Rays was not a conventional bookstore. I had always called it a hippie bookstore. Strawberry incense was always burning at Seven Rays, and new age music hovered in its smoke. I could never tell whether the person behind the counter was a man or a woman. A tea kettle was constantly whistling, but I don't recall anyone ever actually drinking tea. I could never tell whether the other customers were teenagers or 40-year-olds who never outgrew their faded jeans. The bookshelves were wooden: not metal, and certainly not plastic. They sold crystals and herbs at Seven Rays, and tarot cards and books about transcendental meditation and Buddhism and eating wild berries with chopsticks. A display of pipes seemed incongruous among all the health food stuff. The futons and Persian rugs at Seven Rays were not the kind you could get at department stores. At Seven Rays they carried the genuine article.

In seventh grade, or maybe during the summer before eighth, I 12
thought Seven Rays was weird. I much preferred Economy Books. Economy Books was in the mall. They sold normal stuff, like Nancy Drew books

and mechanical pencils and magazines about personal computers and golf. The guy behind the counter pushed buttons on the cash register while a security guard watched for shoplifting. Food and drink were prohibited in Economy Books, and there was absolutely no smoking.

Dad and I had an argument over the relative merits of the two bookstores. I said there was nothing in Seven Rays that anyone ever *really* needed. And everything is overpriced there, not like at Economy Bookstore where you can get stuff with pink tags at 33⅓ percent off. Dad told me I was a smart kid, a good reader, good in school, and patient and kind to my friends and my little sister. He even told me I was a good lacrosse player, which was a lie. And he told me I was too damned logical. 13

He said, "Ari, you are too damned logical." 14

I didn't understand. He taught me to talk and was so proud when I learned to say "hamburger." He helped me with my math homework. I remember trying to decide whether to stay overnight at my best friend Travis's house and he told me to decide by weighing the pros and cons of each alternative. How contradictory it was that the man who was my mentor in logic should tell *me* that *I* am too logical. 15

Well, Dad was right. I am only beginning to see that now, but he saw it then. He said I would have to struggle with it. With Avi, my logic made me mad. I cared about Avi as teachers care about students. I wanted to figure out what was wrong with him and make it better. I couldn't, because logic kept me from entering his emotional world. I was not born with logic, but I learned it. Avi never did, and that kept me from understanding him. I struggled with that. 16

Jessica taught me that struggle is good. I don't remember when or how I met Jessica. I've known her so long now that it doesn't really matter. When I think of Jessica, I see her dirty blond, ratty hair covering at least three-quarters of her face. I see a smile and hear a hearty, gutteral laugh, an honest laugh. Jessica and I have always been friends. 17

She called me one night last summer. She had seen me teaching my little sister how to ride a bike. I ran up and down Ramsey Avenue holding tightly to the seat of her bike, trying to keep 60 pounds of terrified child upright. My arm throbbed from holding the bike up. Sometimes, when I felt she had her balance, I'd let go. She was on her own. She'd sail gloriously for a moment then fall, crying. Sweaty, I'd give her a hug and tell her she was all right, tell her she could do it. She finally rode around the whole block alone, and I smiled silent consonants at her. We laughed with joy and danced in the middle of the street. Jessica had seen all that from her window. She said it was beautiful. 18

She said, "Ari, that was the most beautiful thing I've ever seen." 19

Jessica and I ran together last summer. We were training buddies. I 20 am an average runner. Jessica is a natural. She runs with grace and ease. People say runners like her have a gift from God. After all of our training, and despite her gift, Jessica dropped out of the first cross-country race senior year. It hurt too much; she couldn't keep running. Determination, desire, and will could not make the pain go away. She felt her body telling her to stop and, although she could have won the race, she listened. Afterwards she went away somewhere, maybe into the woods, to be by herself. I don't know because I didn't see her go, but I saw tear stains on her cheeks when she came back. Her body had not listened to her will, and she hated herself for it. She understood what had happened, accepted it, and cried. It never happened again. She has finished every race since. "We all have to struggle sometimes," she said later, "with the things that keep us running."

My struggle is against my logic. I never dropped out of a cross-country 21
race. The object of entering a race is finishing it, so where is the logic in dropping out? But, I wish I had dropped my logic with Avi Blackmore so that I could have entered his emotional, antilogical world. He proved to me that logic does not always lead to answers. The aspect of human personality that the word "ahava" really represents, the aspect that Seven Rays bookstore attracts, is the aspect in which Avi Blackmore was lost. He floundered in the extreme emotional world that Seven Rays represents. I am struggling to appreciate it. Struggling makes me angry, because it is hard and sometimes I fail and I don't like to fail. I wish I was innocent enough to laugh about it and try again, like my sister on her bike. I know I have to keep struggling. Jessica showed me that struggling is good and worthwhile, but I still don't like to do it. That's not very logical, is it?

Opportunities for Exchanging Ideas

Read Ari's final draft carefully. Identify specific changes he has made. How do these changes strengthen his essay? How did his peers' comments help him to develop his ideas more fully? Discuss these questions with your classmates.

Opportunities for Writing and Revising

1. Work with a peer group on the draft you are revising. Develop a set of questions to guide the conversation about your draft. Use your peers' suggestions to help you revise.

2. Some writer once said that writing is never finished, just abandoned. Look through your journal or abandoned drafts and find some

reflection, observation, or introduction that you began and then abandoned. What possibilities for development do you see in this piece of writing now that you might not have seen before? Create a conversation between yourself as writer and reader as you consider possibilities for revising. Continue this conversation with your peers.

3. The following draft from a student writer presents interesting revision possibilities. This student's assignment was to offer his interpretation of a fairy tale. Read this draft together with your peer group. What do you as a group see as the strengths of this draft? What questions does the writer seem to be asking? What is his organizing idea? How do all the paragraphs fit together to develop this idea? Annotate the draft, commenting, asking questions of the writer, and offering specific suggestions for revising. Summarize your responses and suggestions in a letter to the writer.

Well-Dressed Monsters

One of the most common ways parents try to turn their children into "perfect" humans is by reading them stories such as "Red Riding Hood"; stories that teach all the values necessary to lead a good life. Just as how Red Riding Hood learned to "never wander off in the forest again" and to never follow beautiful flowers to nowhere in particular, children learn to be focused and productive. Children also learn to always obey the wise words of their elders from Red Riding Hood, who, after much erring, "knew now that she must listen to her mother." Another lesson of life the story teaches is to never trust strangers, for when the innocent Red Riding Hood met the wolf in the forest she "did not know that he was a wicked animal and so she was not at all afraid of him." Because she so foolishly trusted a stranger she was led astray and eventually eaten. Children learn here, as well in the evil forests of Snow White, and in Jack and the Beanstalk when the ogress (who was not stingy) trusted Jack and was thus taken advantage of, that all strangers and forests are wicked. Indeed most fairy tales seem to breed this "perfect" person—one who is highly focused and productive, one who distrusts strangers and forests, and one who worships the word of his/her elders.

Well, I met some of these "perfect" humans a few days ago, and it got me thinking about just how great these people actually are. I was skipping down the street in the best of spirits, and I came across two kids with bookbags who looked like they might have been in third grade. I was in a real good mood, and as I passed them I shouted "Hi!", and gave them a big sincere smile. They immediately turned their eyes down, didn't answer, and put a damper on my mood. They had obviously been told countless times by their parents, by stories they were read, not to talk to strangers, and so they obeyingly regarded me with utmost suspicion. It seems so sad that we teach our children not to trust strangers. I wonder how we can ever expect to achieve world peace if the habit of Americans is, when they meet foreigners, to distrust them, and assume that they cannot teach us or do us any good. This concept that the stranger is wicked makes it impossible to deal with the Russians. I'm not saying that every child should jump up and throw themselves onto each potential kidnapper, only that for the preservation of the whole world we need to trust strangers more, and certainly not think of them as wicked. In this case, it seems like fairy tales have way overtaught the value of distrusting strangers. I looked around to see what other "perfect" humans I could find.

I ran into some people in suits. These businessmen were the epitome of the focused and productive. They executed their labors with practiced efficiency. Never would they fall for the evil words of the wolf, as Red Riding Hood did, "Look at all the flowers, Red Riding Hood. Why don't you look about you? I think you do not even hear the birds sing. You are just as solemn as if you were going to school, but everything is so gay out here in the woods." This is, though, a brilliant comment. The wolf is saying that we should never get so caught up in what we are doing that we miss all the beauty around us. He offers an eye-opener for the narrow-minded businessmen, if they would stop being so productive for just one second, by showing them just how wonderful the forest is. Something they will probably never notice because they think of the forest as a kind of stranger, a place full of monsters to hurry through, not to get to know. I know from personal experience, like the wolf, and unlike what the fairy tales try so hard to teach, that the forest is a friendly stranger who's worth meeting and wandering through. I know, too, that often the best thing in life is to follow one beautiful flower to the next, to see what surprise nature throws out, and not to plan on getting anything done at all. I feel tremendously sorry for the businessman who firmly believes from childhood readings in being focused and productive, and that forests are dark and full of monsters.

Unfortunately the values these stories teach our children are engraved quite deeply because they also teach them to worship the words of their elders, and not to question and challenge everything that is told to them. I see fairy tales as breeding, not perfect humans, but monsters, who can't think for themselves, but instead believe what their elders say, what the stories teach. Monsters who have learned the lessons of distrusting strangers and being productive far too well.

Revising and Word Processing

Word processing makes revising easy, but it cannot do the real work of reading and reseeing your drafts. A computer cannot make decisions for you. It can't tell you what your organizing idea is or how to revise your guiding questions. It cannot tell you if an example is persuasive or if your readers, like Ari Shapiro's readers, need more information about a specific example.

Word processing does give you the opportunity of printing draft after draft, relieving you of the tedious time-consuming task of retyping or recopying your words. This is a great savings in time and effort and makes it easier for you to give multiple copies of your drafts to your peers.

Here are some tasks that a word processor can perform:

1. *Delete or remove material.* If you have information in one paragraph that does not belong there, you can delete this material altogether, or you can move it to an appropriate place in the essay. You can also delete entire paragraphs and create new ones in their place.

2. *Insert material.* If you have a paragraph with an idea that needs more development, you can add this material where it belongs. You can create a paragraph to serve as a transition between two existing paragraphs. You can expand your introduction by adding new details to introduce your organizing idea.

(continued)

3. *Change words or phrases.* You can change single words, or you can identify a word and change that word each time it is used in the essay.

4. *Move paragraphs.* You can reorder your essay to make it more logical to your reader. You may find that you discover the real point of the essay when you come to the conclusion of your first draft. You can move this paragraph and revise it as a new introduction.

5. *Save a text for later revision.* A word processor gives you the ability to write a draft, save it, and recall it when you are ready to revise. That way, you do not have to type a draft and retype it again and again as you make changes. You may decide to revise on the computer screen, or to print out a hard copy and revise on paper.

PART TWO

PURPOSES FOR WRITING

CHAPTER 6

Questioning Personal Experience

I am forced to admit that memoir is not a matter of transcription, that memory itself is not a warehouse of finished stories, not a static gallery of framed pictures. . . . It still comes as a shock to realize that I don't write about what I know: I write in order to find out what I know.

—Patricia Hampl, "Memory and Imagination"

Life does not begin with college. You enter with memories, experiences, stories of your own. You do not go to your classes as a blank slate, to be filled with information from Colonial American History, Psychology of Adolescence, or Economics and Marketing. Yet, often, students consider it inappropriate to bring the facts of their lives into the classroom and especially into their writing. They seem hesitant to connect their academic experiences with the common events of childhood and adolescence, of the working world and daily life. Yet those daily experiences can be the material that essays are made of. Your personal experiences can serve as important sources for your writing.

In this chapter, we will ask you to remember your experiences and to reflect on their significance. As Patricia Hampl tells us, writing about personal experiences requires more than merely recording events. By questioning your own experiences, you see that they have not ended. They still have importance for you; they still are alive; they still are worth thinking about. When you explore those experiences, you begin to understand the personal trajectory of your own life, and you begin to see the forces that have shaped you. In writing about those experiences, you learn what they mean to you, and you can use them to clarify your ideas and influence your readers.

The ways in which you will find yourself responding to Colonial American History, Psychology of Adolescence, and Economics and Marketing reflect all that has shaped you: your family and community, ethnic heritage, economic status, educational opportunities, and the time and place in which you find yourself. Many of the disciplines that you will study in college are the results of scholarly efforts to understand the way people think, feel, and behave. Not only psychology and sociology, but literature, history, economics, and communications are, fundamentally, about people: people like you.

Reflecting on your own experiences will help you to enter the worlds of these disciplines as an active participant rather than as a passive observer. What does Freud say in his works about the human personality, and what does he say to you? What does James Baldwin say in his novels and essays, and what does he say that relates to your life? What does Karl Marx say in his treatises about economics, and what does he say that helps you understand your experiences as a worker?

Each thinker whose works you read in college has emerged from a particular historical, cultural, and social context. You, too, have been shaped by a context. By exploring your own experiences, you can better understand how your experiences affect the way you read, respond to, and write about ideas.

Opportunities for Reflecting

1. Paula Gunn Allen writes about the stories her mother told her: "My mother told me stories about cooking and childbearing; she told me stories about menstruation and pregnancy; she told me stories about gods and heroes, about fairies and elves, about goddesses and spirits . . . And in all those stories she told me who I was, who I was supposed to be, whom I came from, and who would follow me." Take some time to reflect and remember some stories a parent or relative told you that helped you know who you are and who you are supposed to be. Tell some of these stories in your journal. How did these stories help you understand something about yourself?

2. Read Minh Dang's essay "Voicing the Monster" on page 333 of the Sourcebook. What is Minh's organizing idea? What does she seem to be questioning in this essay? Identify passages in Minh's essay where she is reflecting. How do her reflections connect you, the reader, to her experiences? How has Minh shown up in her writing? How do her words, sentence rhythms, and reflections reveal the voice of the writer?

Opportunities for Exchanging Ideas

Read Paula Gunn Allen's essay "Where I Come From Is Like This" on page 295 of the Sourcebook or Brent Staples's essay "Black Men and Public Space" on page 317 of the Sourcebook. What are these writers trying to understand about their experiences? How have their identities been shaped by issues of race, class, and gender? To what extent do your own experiences influence your reading of these essays? How do these writers' reflections help you understand something about yourself and your own experiences? Discuss Gunn Allen's or Staples's essay with your classmates.

QUESTIONING PERSONAL EXPERIENCES

Memory can be a rich source of information when you write. Memories, though, work in unpredictable, seemingly unsystematic ways. "It is a funny thing what the brain will do with memories," wrote anthropologist Loren Eiseley, "and how it will treasure them and finally bring them into odd juxtapositions with other things." You do not record the events of your life on blank tapes and retrieve them faithfully transcribed. You are likely to rewrite memories, so that events you wish had occurred differently or events that never happened are shaped to serve your needs and dreams. As you move away in time from a particular event, you are able to see that event in the context of all your other experiences. This context shapes the way you remember the event and discover its meaning.

Many experiences may result in conflicting feelings or in feelings that you wish you didn't have. Sometimes you may be tempted to reduce your emotions to absolutes, good or bad; to sentimentalize your family; or to recreate a harmonious time when the tea kettle whistled and grandparents rocked peacefully on a shady veranda. Sometimes you may be tempted to force a "moral" onto your story to underscore what you learned from an experience. As you'll see when you read personal experience essays in this chapter and in the Sourcebook, such essays do not need happy endings or uplifting messages to be effective. It takes courage to admit uncertainty, anger, or anxiety, or to try to understand people from their own perspectives.

Writing about personal experiences invites you to go beyond the summary of the experience and to ask what that experience means. Writing allows you to connect fragmentary experiences of your life. When novelist Toni Morrison decided to write about her father and grandmother, she soon realized that her subject, really, was herself. "[T]hese people are my access to me," she said. "They are my entrance into my own interior life. Which is why the images that float around them—the remains, so to speak, at the archaeological site—surface first, and they surface so vividly and so compellingly that I acknowledge them as my route to a reconstruction of a world . . . and to the revelation of a kind of truth."

The archaeological site that forms the source for personal experience essays is not composed only of personal memories. As you'll see when you read and write personal experience essays, novels and poems, films and music, conversations and observations—all these sources have a place in such an essay.

Opportunities for Exchanging Ideas

We have offered you a variety of personal experience essays in the Sourcebook to show you the wide range of experiences and strategies available to you. Read two of the student essays in the Sourcebook section "Questioning Identities" and discuss the following questions with your classmates: What are the writers trying to understand about their experiences? How do the various experiences the writers offer work together within the same essay? What idea connects these different experiences? How do the writers introduce their idea? Mark words, sentences, and passages that you find particularly effective.

Opportunities for Reflecting

1. If you could have a conversation with any of the student writers whose essays are printed in the Sourcebook section "Questioning Identities," what questions would you like to ask them about their essays? What connections did you make between their experiences and your own? How did the writer help you think about your own experiences? Reflect on these questions in your journal.

2. Personal experience essays focus on people, places, and events that have had significance in a writer's life. In your journal, make a list of five people, five places, and five events that you think are important. What do these items have in common? Have you located a particular time in your life, a place where you have lived, or a set of relationships that is especially important to you? Select one person, place, or event that you would most like to think about as a source for an essay and write two pages of reflections in your journal.

FROM ANECDOTE TO ESSAY

A personal experience essay offers more than a record of an experience. The details that you include in your essay serve to illustrate or explain an *organizing idea.* When Rita Morelli wrote about rock climbing in her essay that appears in Chapter 5, she wanted to do more than describe the physical efforts involved in the activity: She used her personal experience to write about ways people learn. When Marc Beauboeuf wrote "A Word," the essay that appears in Chapter 2, he wanted to do more than tell readers about his encounter with a racist epithet: He used his personal experience to explore the issue of the power of language. Anecdotes, then, serve as *evidence* in a personal experience essay; they help your reader understand your organizing idea.

In the next few paragraphs, you'll read about an experience that the writer Phyllis Theroux had when she was a child. What is the significance of this experience? What is Theroux's organizing idea?

> When I was ten years old, I stepped into my first sailboat alone. It was a small, one-passenger dinghy, hardly more than a walnut shell with a board nailed across the middle, and as I grasped the tiller and observed how the breeze filled up the sail, drawing the boat gently away from the dock, I marveled at how easy a thing sailing was. I was wrong.
>
> After the boat had gotten a fair distance away from the dock, the wind picked up force, the mast snapped to attention, and the sail was suddenly

> full of dangerous ideas that set the boat racing well ahead of my ability to control it. I tugged at the sheet rope, which, in my inexperience, I thought would rein the boat back, like a horse. The boat responded by bucking sideways at a frightening angle to the water, an angle I tried to correct by tugging on the sheet rope even harder and leaning away from the gunwale, which was about to take on the lagoon. Nothing worked. We were, I saw, going to capsize. In desperation I tossed the sheet rope away, dove for the bottom of the boat, and waited for the end.
>
> The decision, born of total inexpertise, turned out to be the correct nautical judgment. The boat, now free of restraints, instantly swung into the wind, righted itself, and when I looked up from my cowardly crouch, the sail was flapping idly against the mast, waiting for a real captain to sail the boat home.

The anecdote that Theroux tells is exciting in itself. She makes sure that you know, from the very first sentence, that she had this experience as a 10-year-old child: Your identification with this child is important if you are to become engaged in the drama of the event. As soon as the wind picks up force, your feeling of terror and helplessness increases, just as it did for the young girl.

Theroux offers vivid descriptions throughout the essay. Such phrases as "the mast snapped to attention" and "the sail was suddenly full of dangerous ideas" not only convey the physical setting but also the tension inherent in the event. By animating inanimate objects, Theroux creates a scene in which she, as a young girl, was fighting more than mere sailcloth and rope. When she tells you that the boat bucked like a horse, she invests it with a will of its own. The struggle, then, becomes a contest of wills.

Still, even if you acknowledge Theroux's talent at writing and her ability to create a dramatic scene, this anecdote does not yet yield its significance. When you read it, you wonder why Theroux is writing about it. What did the experience mean to her? What can the experience mean to you? Only by questioning the details of the event does its meaning become evident.

These details may be listed as follows:

1. A 10-year-old girl is alone on a sailboat.
2. Near the dock, sailing is easy.
3. At sea, sailing is dangerous.
4. A first intuitive response fails.
5. A second intuitive response succeeds.

Theroux did not learn to sail that day. She did learn, however, that new situations sometimes pose challenges for which she might be unprepared. She learned that nature, which she considered benign, can be dangerous and threatening. She learned that she could not always trust her intuition. She learned that she needed to think of alternatives when faced with possible failure.

These conclusions go beyond applicability to a sailing situation and might be illuminating for any of her readers. Here is her next paragraph, where she tells her readers what she learned:

> That afternoon I learned the first rule of sailing, respect for the wind. I also gained a rudimentary understanding of how power of any kind operates. The trick in sailing (as in writing or living) lies in knowing what is possible under the circumstances. Circumstances are the raw material for any voyage, and as I tacked clumsily back and forth across the invisible line of my vision toward the dock, I learned that somewhere between absolute control of, and absolute surrender to, circumstances lies the way home.

In this paragraph, Theroux places her anecdote in a context by showing how it matured her. A story about sailing becomes an illustration for an organizing idea about learning and about negotiating a risky world.

Opportunities for Exchanging Ideas

Read Senta Wong's essay "The Nude" on page 348 of the Sourcebook. Identify the anecdotes Senta uses. How does she use each one as evidence? What is she trying to understand from each experience? How do her various experiences work together to create a context for her essay? What is the organizing idea that connects these different experiences and reflections? Discuss Senta's essay and these questions with your classmates.

STRATEGIES FOR QUESTIONING PERSONAL EXPERIENCE

You begin with a memory, with an image in your mind of a person, place, or event. In Chapter 2, you saw how Miriam Thaggert and Marc Beauboeuf each began with a memory of a childhood incident that had stayed with them long after it happened. To write an essay about that memory, however, you have to transform it, to create it in words for your reader, and to explain its meaning, first to yourself and then to your readers. The meaning of your experiences may not be obvious at the significance of experiences as you consider them at different times of your life.

In the following pages, you'll encounter strategies that can help you move from memory to essay.

Creating an Anecdote

Writing about personal experience depends on the vividness of details. The characters, the action, and the setting all need to be made clear and interesting to your readers. Writers focusing on personal experience often use description, narration, and dialogue as they recreate a scene.

In creating an anecdote, you may find it helpful to think of the five questions that reporters ask themselves when they cover a news event:

Who?
What?
When?
Where?
Why?

These questions can help you recall the important details of your experience. Your anecdote, or simple retelling of the experience, may be one paragraph or several pages. You may add or delete details later, but your first rendering of your personal experience should be as complete, accurate, and vivid as you can make it.

In her essay "Memory and Imagination," Patricia Hampl offers an anecdote about her first piano lesson with Sister Olive Marie. The first 12 paragraphs were written separately and served later as the basis for the whole essay. Read the first 12 paragraphs, noting the details that Hampl gives to make her experience vivid.

When I was seven, my father, who played the violin on Sundays with a nicely tortured flair which we considered artistic, led me by the hand down a long, unlit corridor in St. Luke's School basement, a sort of tunnel that ended in a room full of pianos. There many little girls and a single sad boy were playing truly tortured scales and arpeggios in a mash of troubled sound. My father gave me over to Sister Olive Marie, who did look remarkably like an olive. 1

Her oily face gleamed as if it had just been rolled out of a can and laid 2 on the white plate of her broad, spotless wimple. She was a small, plump woman; her body and the small window of her face seemed to interpret the entire alphabet of olive: her face was a sallow green olive placed upon the jumbo ripe olive of her black habit. I trusted her instantly and smiled, glad to have my hand placed in the hand of a woman who made sense, who provided the satisfaction of being what she was: an Olive who looked like an olive.

My father left me to discover the piano with Sister Olive Marie so that 3
one day I would join him in mutually tortured piano-violin duets for the edificaton of my mother and brother who sat at the table meditatively spooning in the last of their pineapple sherbet until their part was called for: they put down their spoons and clapped while we bowed, while the sweet ice in their bowls melted, while the music melted, and we all melted a little into each other for a moment.

But first Sister Olive must do her work. I was shown middle C, which 4
Sister seemed to think terribly important. I stared at middle C and then glanced away for a second. When my eye returned, middle C was gone, its slim finger lost in the complicated grasp of the keyboard. Sister Olive struck it again, finding it with laughable ease. She emphasized the importance of middle C, its central position, a sort of North Star of sound. I remember thinking, "Middle C is the belly button of the piano," an insight whose originality and accuracy stunned me with pride. For the first time in my life I was astonished by metaphor. I hesitated to tell the kindly Olive for some reason; apparently I understood a true metaphor is a risky business, revealing of the self. In fact, I have never, until this moment of writing it down, told my first metaphor to anyone.

Sunlight flooded the room; the pianos, all black, gleamed. Sister Olive, 5
dressed in the colors of the keyboard, gleamed; middle C shimmered with meaning and I resolved never—never—to forget its location: it was the center of the world.

Then Sister Olive, who had had to show me middle C twice but who 6
seemed to have drawn no bad conclusions about me anyway, got up and went to the windows on the opposite wall. She pulled the shades down, one after the other. The sun was too bright, she said. She sneezed as she stood at the windows with the sun shedding its glare over her. She sneezed and sneezed, crazy little convulsive sneezes, one after another, as helpless as if she had the hiccups.

"The sun makes me sneeze," she said when the fit was over and she 7
was back at the piano. This was odd, too odd to grasp in the mind. I associated sneezing with colds, and colds with rain, fog, snow and bad weather. The sun, however, had caused Sister Olive to sneeze in this wild way, Sister Olive who gleamed benignly, and who was so certain of the location of the center of the world. The universe wobbled a bit and became

unreliable. Things were not, after all, necessarily what they seemed. Appearance deceived: here was the sun acting totally out of character, hurling this women into sneezes. a woman so mild that she was named, so it seemed, for a bland object on a relish tray.

I was given a red book, the first Thompson book, and told to play the first piece over and over at one of the black pianos where the other children were crashing away. This, I was told, was called practicing. It sounded alluringly adult, practicing. The piece itself consisted mainly of middle C, and I excelled, thrilled by my savvy at being able to locate that central note amidst the cunning camouflage of all the other white keys before me. Thrilled too by the shiny red book that gleamed, as the pianos did, as Sister Olive did, as my eager eyes probably did. I sat at the formidable machine of the piano and got to know middle C intimately, preparing to be as tortured as I could manage one day soon with my father's violin at my side. 8

But at the moment Mary Katherine Reilly was at my side, playing something at least two or three lessons more sophisticated than my piece. I believe she even struck a chord. I glanced at her from the peasantry of single notes, shy, ready to pay homage. She turned toward me, stopped playing, and sized me up. 9

Sized me up and found a person ready to be dominated. Without introduction she said, "My grandfather invented the collapsible opera hat." 10

I nodded, I acquiesced, I was hers. With that little stroke it was decided between us—that she should be the leader, and I the sidekick. My job was admiration. Even when she added, "But he didn't make a penny from it. He didn't have a patent"—even then, I knew and she knew that this was not an admission of powerlessness, but the easy candor of a master, of one who can afford a weakness or two. 11

With the clairvoyance of all fated relationships based on dominance and submission, it was decided in advance: that when the time came for us to play duets, I should always play second piano, that I should spend my allowance to buy her the Twinkies she craved but was not allowed to have, that finally, I should let her copy from my test paper, and when confronted by our teacher, confess with convincing hysteria that it was I, I who had cheated, who had reached above myself to steal what clearly belonged to the rightful heir of the inventor of the collapsible opera hat. . . . 12

Opportunities for Exchanging Ideas

Look closely at the first 12 paragraphs of Hampl's essay "Memory and Imagination." What do we learn about this piano lesson? Look at the details that Hampl uses to describe Sister Olive Marie and Mary Katherine Reilly. What details do you find particularly effective and memorable? How do the details reflect what Hampl wants her readers to understand about the significance of the piano lesson? Discuss these questions with your classmates.

Annotating Your Anecdote

Once you have written an anecdote about your experience, you have the beginning of a personal experience essay. Annotating your anecdote lets you ask questions about the meaning of the experience. Why do you remember this experience? That is what Hampl asks in paragraph 14 of her essay, when she admits that she doesn't know why she remembers this particular fragment of her past.

Annotating your writing allows you to approach your anecdote as a reader and to question your own decisions about what you included or omitted from your description. You might underline or highlight words or passages, write comments or notes in the margin, ask yourself questions or jot down reminders. You may use your journal to reflect upon particular passages in your anecdote. When you annotate your writing, you have a specific task in mind: *expanding and elaborating the anecdote to make its meaning accessible to your readers.*

As Hampl makes clear, the details that she chose for her description are "not merely information, not flat facts." These details help readers understand the meaning of the experience. Meaning, Hampl tells us, "is not 'attached' to the detail by the memoirist; meaning is revealed." As Hampl reread her description, she noted that the red music book, for example, became a *symbol* for an idea: evidence of her childhood longing and disappointment.

Hampl annotated her description within the rest of her essay. Here are her comments, for example, on paragraphs 8 through 12:

. . . .

As for Mary Katherine Reilly. She didn't even go to grade school with me (and her name isn't Mary Katherine Reilly—but I made that change on purpose). I met her in Girl Scouts and only went to school with her later, in high school. Our relationship was not really one of leader and follower; I played first piano most of the time in duets. She certainly never copied anything from a test paper of mine: she was a better student, and cheating just wasn't a possibility with her. Though her grandfather (or someone in her family) did invent the collapsible opera hat and I remember that she was proud of that fact, she didn't tell me this news as a deft move in a childish power play. 19

> So, what was I doing in this brief memoir? Is it simply an example of 20
> the curious relation a fiction writer has to the material of her own life? Maybe. That may have some value in itself. But to tell the truth (if anyone still believes me capable of telling the truth), I wasn't writing fiction. I was writing memoir—or was trying to. My desire was to be accurate. I wished to embody the myth of memoir: to write as an act of dutiful transcription. . . . .
>
> I really did feel, for instance, that Mary Katherine Reilly was far superior 34
> to me. She was smarter, funnier, more wonderful in every way—that's how I saw it. Our friendship (or she herself) did not require that I become her vassal, yet perhaps in my heart that was something I wanted: I wanted a way to express my feeling of admiration. I suppose I waited until this memoir to begin to find the way.

As you can see from these paragraphs, Hampl was aware that she might have distorted her experiences, and she was interested in finding out why she wrote about them as she did. She annotated those passages of her anecdote that bothered her, that urged her to think more about the experience, to ask more questions. She used her initial recollection as a means to gain deeper understanding of her experience.

Opportunities for Reflecting

1. You have been reflecting in your journal about various personal experiences. Choose one of these experiences and write an anecdote about it. Create the characters, the scene, and some dialogue as a way of developing the significance of this experience.

2. Use your journal to annotate those passages of your anecdote that disturb you, intrigue you, urge you to think more about the meaning of the experience. Note, also, where you think a reader might need more details about the experience. Do you notice places where you left out information? Why do you think this omission occurred? Do you notice places where you may have distorted the reality of the experience? In what ways? Why?

3. Let your annotations help you expand and elaborate the significance of this experience. For instance, have you thought about this experience in different ways at different times in your life? What have these various ways of understanding shown you about this experience and about your evolving self?

Questioning

"If I approach writing from memory with the assumption that I know what I wish to say, I assume that intentionality is running the show," Hampl tells us in paragraph 28 of her essay. "Things are not that simple." Hampl, like many writers, is a strong proponent of the first draft: letting go, creating a text that can be revised later, giving memory and imagination a chance to speak. Back in control, later, the writer can question that text, shape it, illuminate its meaning. The piano lesson description, she says, is a first draft "because I haven't yet gotten to know it, haven't given it a chance to tell me anything."

In order for a draft to tell you anything, you need to ask it questions. Questioning, then, can be a useful strategy in writing an essay based on personal experience. What kinds of questions might you ask about your draft? Here are some questions paraphrased from Hampl's essay:

1. Why do I remember this story in particular?

2. What details can I verify? What details might be invented? Why did I invent these details?

3. What am I doing in this memoir?

4. What purpose does the anecdote about Mary Katherine Reilly serve?

5. What purpose does the red piano book serve?

6. What other experiences have influenced the way I remember this one?

7. What do I want my reader to understand about this experience?

These questions helped Hampl find the meaning of the experience and convey that meaning to her readers.

Opportunities for Reflecting

1. What kind of questions do you want to ask about the experiences you have been writing about in your journal? You might ask some of the questions we imagined Hampl asked. For instance: Why do I remember this experience? What details might be invented? Why did I invent these details? What purpose do my various anecdotes serve? Reflect on these questions in your journal.

2. Think of other experiences that are connected in some way with the experiences you have been reflecting about. In your journal, describe these other experiences and allow your imagination to connect these seemingly separate experiences. What do they have in common? What threads do they connect for you? How might they have influenced each other?

Expanding the Context

"Naturally," Hampl writes, "I've had a lot of experiences since I packed away that one from the basement of St. Luke's School; that piano lesson has been effaced by waves of feeling for other moments and episodes." In writing about any memory, you cannot recall that experience as it was lived, only as you remember it in the context of all your other experiences. Like Hampl, you can then explore "the mysterious relationship between all the images [you] could round up" and all the feelings those images evoke. "Stalking the relationship, seeking the congruence between stored image and hidden emotion—that's the real job of memoir."

When you turn your description into a personal experience essay, you may well decide to expand the context of that experience by adding details of related experiences, of readings, of conversations or observations. Miriam Thaggert, whose essay "Double Vision" you read in Chapter 2, conveyed the meaning of her experience by expanding the context to include her reading of W. E. B. Du Bois. Marc Beauboeuf helped to convey the meaning of his experience by bringing in his reading of James Baldwin. Ari Shapiro, in his essay "Logic?" which appears in Chapter 5, referred to his reading of sociologist Erving Goffman.

You may decide to expand the context for one experience by relating that experience to another, or to several others; by bringing experiences together, you help the reader see consistencies and patterns, and you illuminate the essay's organizing idea.

A STUDENT WRITER AT WORK: THE STORY OF AN ESSAY

Let's look at Leon Yen's essay "No Name" to see how one student expanded the context of a single event by using other personal experiences as sources.

The basis for Leon's essay was a single memory:

When I first entered elementary school in the States, I went by many names. One day I might call myself John, another day Steve, Kevin, so on, and so on. My teacher didn't care, really. She just thought I was kind of queer and liked to play this identity game that kids like to play sometimes. To her I was number eleven in her roll book, and so I called myself Eleven. My classmates never got used to that. One day this bully cornered me during recess and demanded to know my name.

"Eleven," I answered him.

"No, stupid! You can't have a number for a name," he yelled at me. "What is your REAL name?"

I told him I didn't have one. He badgered me and twisted my arm. Finally I relented and said that I had had a name before, but that it was dead, and so it didn't matter anymore.

"What is your old name, then," he insisted.

"Shih-Wei," I said flatly, unconvinced that the name belonged to me.

Hearing my gibberish, he burst out, "What kind of name is that? That's not a name; I've never heard of it. Why can't you have a normal name like the rest of us. Get a real name! Will ya?"

When Leon questioned the description that he had written, he realized that the event was not an isolated occurrence in his life, but part of a pattern in his evolving search for an identity, both personal and cultural. He began to think of other occasions when telling his name to people had been difficult, or when he wished that he felt more assimilated into the culture into which his parents had brought him. Although he had only called himself Eleven for a short time in elementary school, he remembered another time—a much longer time—when he identified with another number, this time Sixteen, his number on his high school's water polo team.

When I was in high school I was eager to distinguish myself, to establish my name, so to say. I was awed by the seniors who played water polo and absorbed by the spectacle when they came back from their conquest bathed in all their glory. For these same grandiose dreams I also played water polo.

I was number sixteen on the team. But even though I tried very hard to be a good water polo player, I always remained a normal Sixteen compared to the other studs on the team. Everyday, practice before dawn, practice after school. No weekends, no spring break, no summer vacation. For two years, Sixteen hoped that he could start someday. Still, Sixteen would be in second string. It wasn't really Sixteen's fault or anybody's fault; it's just that he had played for all the wrong reasons. Sixteen thought that water polo was an easy means to a glorious end. He didn't count on the competition, much less defeat. Out of pride, he stuck with the team, thinking that he was sure to have his day. He waited and waited. One day Sixteen couldn't wait any longer. He broke down in the middle of a game and felt his whole world crumbling in on him. The funny thing was that Sixteen didn't get played in the game; Sixteen had been sitting on the icy bench for the past three quarters or, for all that matter, the past two years. What happened was that Sixteen suddenly felt bone-chilling, got up, ran into the locker room, and took a long hot shower that never quite eased the numbness or the emptiness within him.

As Leon wrote about this second memory, he noticed connections to the first experience that he had not seen before. "To make a name for yourself" was an idiom that took on a new meaning for Leon because he felt so uncomfortable with his own name. On the one hand, he wanted to prove himself as someone admirable, someone his peers would like; on the other hand, he wanted to fit in with the group. By calling himself Eleven, he took his place in the class list; he belonged among the other students. He had a specific place in the school community. When he called himself Sixteen, he wanted to excel, to be extraordinary.

When Leon reread his two anecdotes, he came up with a list of questions that helped him to think about how the two pieces were related:

1. How is a name related to a person's identity?
2. In what ways do people distinguish themselves in a group? What

ways feel safe—that is, ways that ensure you'll have friends and get along with people? What ways feel dangerous—that is, ways that cut you off from other people?

3. What kinds of names do people give themselves in their lives—not only nicknames, but titles, names of roles they have, names they use only in special situations, like work or sports?

4. When did I first feel that it was all right to use my real name? When did I stop hiding behind other names?

These questions helped Leon to think about a structure for his essay. By connecting his first anecdote with another, by placing these two anecdotes together, he found that he had more to say about the issue of naming and identity.

Leon worked on his essay by taking notes in his journal, writing a first draft, receiving peer response, and revising. Here is Leon Yen's final draft:

ONAMAEWA
(What is your name?)

Leon Yen

A person's name is a person's identity. I lost mine when I immigrated to this foreign land; I have been searching for it ever since. Throughout the years I have adopted others to use as my own, only to find myself enmeshed with their reality and going around in a circle, gradually returning to the starting point, a point where I should have been. I never thought I would be able to find myself again. 1

When I first entered elementary school in the States, I went by many names. One day I might call myself John, another day Steve, Kevin, so on, and so on. My teacher didn't care, really. She just thought I was kind of queer and liked to play this identity game that kids like to play sometimes. To her I was number eleven in her roll book, and so I called myself Eleven. My classmates never got used to that. One day this bully cornered me during recess and demanded to know my name. 2

"Eleven," I answered him. 3

"No, stupid! You can't have a number for a name," he yelled at me. "What is your REAL name?" 4

I told him I didn't have one. He badgered me and twisted my arm. 5

Finally I relented and said that I had had a name before, but that it was dead, and so it didn't matter anymore.

"What is your old name then," he insisted. 6

"Shih-Wei," I said flatly, unconvinced that the name belonged to me. 7

Hearing my gibberish, he burst out, "What kind of a name is that? 8
That's not a name; I've never heard of it. Why can't you have a normal name like the rest of us. Get a real name! Will ya?"

I did. 9

When I was in high school I was eager to distinguish myself, to establish 10
my name, so to say. I was awed by the seniors who played water polo and absorbed by the spectacle when they came back from their conquest bathed in all their glory. For these same grandiose dreams I also played water polo.

I was number sixteen on the team. But even though I tried very hard 11
to be a good water polo player, I always remained a normal Sixteen compared to the other studs on the team. Everyday, practice before dawn, practice after school. No weekends, no spring break, no summer vacation. For two years, Sixteen hoped that he could start someday. Still, Sixteen would be in second string. It wasn't really Sixteen's fault or anybody's fault; it's just that he had played for all the wrong reasons. Sixteen thought that water polo was an easy means to a glorious end. He didn't count on the competition, much less defeat. Out of pride, he stuck with the team, thinking that he was sure to have his day. He waited and waited and waited. One day Sixteen couldn't wait any longer. He broke down in the middle of a game and felt his whole world crumbling in on him. The funny thing was that Sixteen didn't get played in the game; Sixteen had been sitting on the icy bench for the past three quarters or, for all that matter, the past two years. What happened was that Sixteen suddenly felt bone-chilling, got up, ran into the locker room, and took a long hot shower that never quite eased the numbness or the emptiness within him. As though the dream that had shaped and sustained him for these past two years had been consumed and spent, he felt like a dry husk, burnt out, his reality crumbling in. And like an old man, he was shaking. It was Sixteen's debut into the world.

Mid-July summer in the subterranean city of Tokyo was unbearable. 12
The heat and humidity outside were magnified tenfold underground, but I didn't mind that really. It was the facelessness of the crowd that killed me; they reminded me of my own anonymity. As I tiptoed on the deck of the Ginza Station with the mob of rush-hour people enveloping me, I grew nervous; wiping my face and my neck with a towel became a preoccupation. I sweat too much. A heightened uneasiness emanated from the mob like a breathing heat wave. It was intimidating, but then none of us had any choice but to suffer each other. It seemed as though the train and the

mob had a mind of their own, and yet they never seemed to understand each other. Nor did they understand me.

A gush of cool air. A sign of relief. Then the rail and the whole underground structure hummed, echoed, and rattled. Three-two-one. The train roared into the station with unfailing punctuality. 13

"Three rows! Three rows," the conductor yelled as the mob, antlike, split neatly into three columns and filed into the tin can while the hired hands tackled and shoved the last few, unfortunate ones through the threshold of the boxcar so that the door would engage and close. 14

The boxcar thundered through the subterranean world amidst the illuminating lights shooting by like a meteor shower. Out of boredom I decided to check out the crowd around me. Stacked against my right hip stood a student in his hideous, black uniform. I couldn't understand the name sewn on his shirt, only the ID number 724. Somehow, this 724 managed to grab on to a seat and read and sweat at the same time in this cramped, overheated world. Cramming for college exams, I presumed. He reminded me of Sixteen. Sixteen thought that the way to distinguish himself in this world was to conquer himself, the competition, and the system. Perhaps 724 had been told that getting into Tokyo University would be his ticket to success with the promise of a solid, steady job upon graduation. However, neither Sixteen nor 724 had intended on being reduced to a statistic. 15

In front of me stood a thin, gaunt businessman in his thirties. Sweat had formed a crescent under his armpit, but the man stared mindlessly out of the window at the shooting stars, oblivious to his surrounding and sealed in his own private world. He seemed like someone who had conquered the odds and had carved out his turf in the world. And yet he was forlorn, perhaps troubled by some remote possibility that he might have found happiness if he had been a carpenter instead of a manager, or perhaps upon reflection he might have asked himself, "Is this all worth it?" Sixteen asked himself the same questions when he was taking that long hot shower in the locker room. Could it be a case of mid-life crisis? I didn't know. I was only a kid with no name. Somehow I had this urge to get 724 and this sweaty man together; perhaps the sparks from the dry husks of this man could cause an inflammation in the mind of 724. But alas, I didn't speak Japanese. 16

I was so busy trying to steady myself and looking in front of me that I almost stumbled on someone behind me. I turned around and there was this short, old woman dressed in her kimono with a baby strapped at her back. Her face looked wrinkled like a raisin's skin, old and haggard except for those two tiny beads that shone with kindness and equanimity. Even with the weight of the baby she withstood the push and shove of the mob; even in this unbearable heat she was serene and unruffled in her thick 17 kimono. As my fascination with this old woman grew, I realized that if I stretched my ears I could hear her humming an ancient lullaby, her lone voice crisp and clear against the thundering metallic roar. Mo-mo-ta-ro . . .

I had heard of that voice somewhere in my past when I still had my 18
name. That melancholic tune lingered round and round in my head like a voice leading me out of this subterranean darkness until suddenly I realized that of all these people, she was the only person who had told me her name. To me her stamina in the midst of this faceless, sweaty crowd could only come from the strength of her character; her lone voice wrote a signature in my heart. Her lullaby defined her identity, her immortality in that cramped space and time. I realized at that moment that I had a name all along, except that I had abandoned it in search of something more grandiose. At eleven I was unsure of who I was. At sixteen I was too eager to live someone else's reality, adopting for myself a clay cast to mold into even if it didn't fit me. I wasn't meant to be Eleven or John or Steve, much less Sixteen, 724, the sweaty man, or the old woman. I was meant to be only myself, like the old woman was herself. Some people told me that if I traveled far enough I would meet myself eventually. That was why I went to Japan in the first place. And I did see what I had set out to see, what I wanted to see, and what I needed to see. I saw myself in the reflection of the old woman, and it came as a shock because I had always thought I would see myself in the crowd. I didn't believe in miracles, but she had awakened me. Her lullaby still rings in my ear, louder even than the metallic roar of the subway.

Opportunities for Exchanging Ideas

1. How do Leon Yen's various anecdotes work together to help you understand the significance of his idea? How does the organization of Leon's essay help convey his idea? Look closely at the last paragraphs of Leon's essay. How does he tie together all the details of his essay? Discuss Leon's essay and these questions with your classmates.

2. Read Alice Walker's essay "Beauty: When the Other Dancer Is the Self" on page 322 of the Sourcebook. Identify the many different anecdotes that Walker describes. How do these various anecdotes work together? How do they help Walker understand the significance of her eye injury? What is Walker's organizing idea? Discuss Walker's essay and these questions with your classmates.

Opportunities for Reflecting

Leon Yen's first anecdote led him to remember another, related experience. Using your anecdotes, and your annotations and questions, write another anecdote about a related experience. What ideas do these anecdotes have in common? What is their common theme? What will a reader know about your experiences by reading these anecdotes together? Reflect on these questions in your journal.

PRESENTING PERSONAL EXPERIENCES

Leon Yen and Alice Walker present their experiences by juxtaposing anecdotes. Leon presents these anecdotes in the past tense, remembering them from his perspective as an adult. He begins his essay by introducing a problem: his own search for identity. Readers know, then, after the first paragraph, that the anecdotes will explain how Leon confronted this problem and perhaps solved it.

Alice Walker presents anecdotes in the present tense, as if she is recording them as she experiences them. Throughout the essay, she comments about these anecdotes in the past tense as if she were an adult reading her own diary or journal entries. By writing in the present tense, she conveys a sense of immediacy to her readers; by commenting in the past tense, she shows her readers how she is reflecting on her experiences at a much later time.

Walker does not follow the strict chronological order that Leon does. Although she begins her essay with an anecdote about something that occurred when she was 2½, she then moves back and forth between adulthood and childhood. This movement helps her readers see how the central event—the injury to her eye—took on different meanings at different times of her life, and how later experiences caused her to return to question and explore her memory of the injury.

The structure of a personal experience essay can be as varied as the anecdotes on which the essays are based. There is no prescription for form. All personal experience essays, though, must have a clear and interesting organizing idea and vivid and detailed anecdotes to illuminate that idea for readers. The structure you choose will depend on your organizing idea, your anecdotes, your audience, and your purpose in writing. The various personal experience essays you have read in this chapter have shown you the wide range of strategies writers use to question and explore personal experience.

Opportunities for Writing

In the following sequence you are being asked to question and explore your experiences and to find connections between experiences that you might have previously considered separate and distinct. From these questions and the conversations they engender, you will develop an idea to explore in your essay.

> Locating touchstones—the red music book, the olive Olive, my father's violin playing—is deeply satisfying. Who knows why? Perhaps we all sense that we can't grasp the whole truth and nothing but the truth of our experience. Just can't be done. What can be achieved, however, is a version of its swirling, changing wholeness. A memoirist must acquiesce to selectivity, like any artist. The version we dare to write is the only truth, the only relationship we can have with the past. Refuse to write your life and you have no life. At least, that is the stern view of the memoirist.
>
> —Patricia Hampl, *"Memory and Imagination"*

1. Look closely at the various experiences and anecdotes you have been reflecting about in your journal. Take one or two that look most promising or begin again by retrieving an experience from your memory and reconstructing it. It might help you to think of this memory as an image, a visual record of what happened. Recreate these experiences. Make them vivid and immediate. Use dialogue. Select details that will orient your reader. Put your reader on the scene. Make your reader understand why these experiences linger in your memory.

2. This writing exercise builds upon the previous one. Its purpose is to identify and describe some outside text. This text can be a book, a quotation, a story, a song, a painting, or a photograph that has had a powerful influence upon you.

First, describe your text in such a way that your readers can also appreciate it. Use quotes if necessary, or create a word picture of your text.

Then ask yourself why this text has stayed with you. Do you see any ideas that connect this text with the experiences and anecdotes you have been reflecting upon and remembering in your journal? Take some time to think about these connections.

Reread all the various experiences you have written about. What questions do you want to ask now about these experiences? Let your questions help you explore connections between experiences that you might have previously considered separate and distinct.

3. This writing exercise builds upon the previous two. Its purpose is to help you discover an *organizing idea.* It is an exercise in making relevant, imaginative connections between lived experience and an outside text—an exercise that will lead to an essay.

As you reflected on why these experiences and text stayed with you, the experiences and text may at first have had no apparent connection to each other—in fact, they may seem odd in conjunction with each other. But simply because they are both important to you, they "comment" in an interesting way upon each other—and that can give rise to a new idea. Use the experiences and text as a touchstone for your thinking. Try out one or two organizing ideas that you see embedded in everything you have been thinking about.

4. You started this sequence by recreating a memory. Then you reflected on a text that has special meaning to you, exploring the possible reasons why. Finally, you have asked questions about what connects them, giving rise to an organizing idea—an idea based upon your questioning of your personal experiences.

Your opportunity now is to shape those reflections into an essay. *The purpose of this essay is to explore one of the ideas you discovered.* The writing exercises and journal reflections will serve as evidence for this essay, or they may trigger other memories, or cause you to recall other sources that will help you develop your organizing idea.

Questioning Experience: Questions for Peer Review

1. What is the writer's organizing idea? How does the writer introduce this idea? How does the writer develop and expand this idea? Mark words, sentences, and passages that you find particularly effective in conveying the writer's organizing idea.

2. How does the organization of the draft convey the writer's idea? How does the writer move from anecdote to anecdote? From description to reflection and back again? Is there anything about the organization that you would suggest changing?

3. Where in the draft is the writer reflecting? Are there places in the draft where you want more reflection from the writer?

4. How has the writer shown up in the draft? How do the writer's words, sentence rhythms, reflections reveal the voice and judgments of the writer?

5. How does the writer's introduction pull you into the world of the essay? After reading the entire draft, is there anything confusing or distracting about the introduction?

(continued)

6. How does the writer's conclusion pull together the entire essay? Should the conclusion be more effective? If so, in what ways?

Annotate the writer's draft by commenting on its strengths and weaknesses. Ask the writer questions. Write a letter in which you offer your honest, careful, and generous comments and suggestions for revising.

CHAPTER 7

Questioning Sources

Whenever you share ideas with other people, you rarely refer only to your personal experiences. You may recall something you read in last week's *Time* magazine or yesterday's college newspaper; you may refer to a television program or film; you may quote a book you are reading, or you may relate information from a friend, relative, classmate, or co-worker. All of those sources enrich and enlarge the ideas that come to you from your own experiences.

Most people accumulate sources haphazardly, without a specific plan. You happen to read an article about the greenhouse effect in a newspaper, and you happen to remember the article when you talk to a friend one hot summer's day. Reading the article gives you information that you did not have before and helps you discuss the greenhouse effect with specific facts and examples. Instead of complaining about the heat, you can offer scientific evidence about why the greenhouse effect is occurring.

Although you may encounter some sources accidentally, sometimes you may actively pursue sources because of a special interest—in computers, for example, or jazz—that leads you to read specialized books and articles, to talk with experts in the field (a computer programmer or a jazz trumpeter), or even to make research expeditions (to a computer display or a nightclub). These sources help deepen your knowledge.

USING SOURCES

Most college writing depends on sources beyond personal experience. Sometimes you will find these sources on your own; other times you will be directed by class assignments or readings. Using sources effectively requires that you do more than excerpt passages and appropriate them in your essay. If you only assemble sources, you are expecting those sources to substitute for your own ideas. A quotation from a newspaper editorial will not take the place of your own analysis of a political situation; a quotation from a literary critic will not take the place of your own analysis of a poem or short story. In the early years of the century, some artists experimented with collage, pasting bits of newspapers and magazines onto their paintings. These scraps of texts substituted for the artist's own drawings of newspapers and magazines. When writing an essay, you must do more than create a collage of sources.

The sources that you find may enrich your own ideas, but they cannot substitute for them. This chapter will help you to think about the use of sources and will offer you strategies for questioning sources and incorporating them into your writing.

You will have many opportunities to use a variety of sources as you respond to writing assignments in different classes. Sources are not limited to books and articles. You may decide to conduct interviews for an oral history project, to take notes at a government meeting in your community, to distribute a questionnaire to your classmates. You may look at paintings, listen to music, watch films. All these sources can provide evidence to support your ideas.

Most often, though, you will be using written texts. In a literature course, you may write about a poem by Emily Dickinson or read criticism of that poem by Cynthia Griffin Wolff. In a history course, you may examine a speech by John F. Kennedy or refer to a study of Kennedy by Arthur Schlesinger. In a psychology course, you may read a research report about dreaming in the *Journal of Psychology*, Freud's *Interpretation of Dreams*, or Peter Gay's biography of Freud.

In Chapter 4, you read an essay about sexist language by Jessica Yellin, a college freshman. As Jessica tells us, her awareness of sexist language first began in high school, when she attended a rally for women's rights and was exhorted by a speaker to change the spelling of *women* to *womyn*, to avoid the "male" ending. Jessica begins her essay by describing her reaction to this speaker, and she goes on to reflect on other personal experiences that made her aware of the relationship between language and sexism.

In writing the essay, however, Jessica did not limit herself to thinking only about personal experiences. She was able to broaden her explorations by looking beyond the boundaries of her own life to other sources: a scholarly study of early religion by Elaine Pagels and an essay by the feminist poet Adrienne Rich. These sources allowed Jessica to reflect on the ways that other people have been thinking about the topic that interested her.

Opportunities for Reflecting

Think about a topic you are interested in writing about. Reflect in your journal by listing some sources outside of your own experience that would help you think about this topic. Don't limit your potential sources to print material. Consider interviews, surveys, and other frequently overlooked sources.

Opportunities for Exchanging Ideas

The following list contains many different kinds of sources. Beside each source, indicate one topic for which this source might help you ask questions and develop ideas. An interview with the writer Stephen King, for example, might serve as a source for an essay about horror stories, about the relationship between a writer and his or her audience, or about the process of writing fiction. What other topics might make this source useful? Discuss your answers with your classmates.

- Diaries of pioneer women
- Steven Spielberg's film *E.T.*
- A survey on the increasing number of homeless families in five major U.S. cities
- Etiquette books from the 1890s
- Statistics on reading test scores in the Chicago public schools
- The latest issue of *Time* magazine
- A biography of Martin Luther King, Jr.

KINDS OF SOURCES

No matter what topic you are exploring, you will encounter two kinds of sources: primary sources and secondary sources.

Primary Sources

Primary sources often are called "original" sources because they do not contain within them someone else's interpretation of the material. Primary sources may include court records, census figures, political speeches, laws and statutes, maps, and diaries. The letter of a Civil War soldier, reporting his experiences to his mother, is a primary source. Lincoln's "Gettysburg Address" is a primary source. Both of these sources might be used by someone writing an essay about the Civil War. That essay might in turn become a secondary source for another writer.

Picasso's *Man with a Guitar* or Beethoven's Fifth Symphony are primary sources; an art historian's essay about Picasso's painting or a music critic's assessment of Beethoven's composition is a secondary source.

A short story by Eudora Welty is a primary source. You, as a writer, might examine the plot, or the characters, or Welty's use of dialogue. Your own reading of the story leads to your interpretation. A letter by Eudora Welty to her editor, explaining the origins of that story, is also a primary source. You, as a writer, can give your own opinions about the letter, can draw your own conclusions about Welty's motivations and aims, and can make connections between the letter and the story to which it refers. You would be using the letter as a primary source. But if a literary critic wrote an essay about Welty examining one of her stories or describing one of her letters, that essay would be a secondary source for you as a writer.

Secondary Sources

Secondary sources are materials that offer interpretation or analysis of primary sources. The historian E. E. Morison, writing a biography about Theodore Roosevelt, is creating a secondary source when he offers interpretations and conclusions based on his research. You, as a reader, are not likely to have access to Morison's primary sources—Roosevelt's letters, for example—when you read the biography. If you use Morison's biography as a source for your own essay about Theodore Roosevelt, you will be able to develop your ideas from a larger pool of material than you could if you worked only from the primary sources available in your college library. You need to remember, however, that when you use Morison's book as a source, you are reading someone else's interpretation of primary sources.

This interpretation often can be helpful. The writer of a secondary source is likely to have done extensive research and to have collected information from primary sources. Secondary sources can help you to understand primary material within its context. Morison's interpretation of Roosevelt, for example, resulted from long years of research and writing. His insights might help you to ask questions, see connections, or consider material in new and important ways.

Understanding the difference between primary and secondary sources is important for college writers. Primary sources pose a challenge: They ask you to draw your own conclusions about what they mean and what significance they have. Secondary sources too often seem to offer ready-made conclusions, allowing you simply to borrow ideas from other authors—experts, scholars, researchers, or critics—without evaluating those ideas.

Opportunities for Exchanging Ideas

Read Tracy Grikscheit's essay "All His Vital Organs Lay in a Pan Beside His Head" on page 406 and Ayano Kato's essay "a moral person" on page 417 of the Sourcebook. Identify the primary and secondary sources each writer uses. In small groups, discuss how these sources work together to enlarge and enrich the scope of the essays.

HOW TO USE SOURCES

Sources provide details to illustrate, explain, confirm, or expand your own ideas. Your ideas, however, must be the basis for your essay. Sources can help you think about those ideas in new ways, but they cannot substitute for your thinking.

Sometimes, beginning writers feel inhibited in the presence of experts. You may have your opinions about sexist language, for example, but when you read the work of a scholar like Elaine Pagels or a feminist like Adrienne Rich, you may feel more comfortable if they make statements *for* you, rather than help you support your own ideas. Let's look at a paragraph from Jessica Yellin's draft in which she uses sources to support her own ideas:

Throughout the course of human civilization, women have been written out of history. For example, as Elaine Pagels tells us in her book *Adam, Eve, and the Serpent,* the earliest versions of the Bible tell an alternative creation story in which God creates women before man, but we do not learn of this story. Adrienne Rich, in her essay "On Taking Women Students Seriously," tells us that women like Ethel Smyth, an early suffragist; Anne Askew, a woman burned and tortured to death several centuries ago for political activism; and Jane Harrison, an antipatriarchal anthropologist, are passed over and forgotten. Similarly, women are still not included in the Constitution as having civil rights; we are not guaranteed equal pay for equal work; we lose the right to control our reproductive organs when we are placed in jail. However, none of this is ultimately surprising, since women are excluded in the one variable that defines our society more than any other—our language.

As you see in this paragraph, Jessica found examples in both of her sources to support her own idea: Women have been excluded from our history and from our language. Before she read Pagels, Jessica's familiarity with women's exclusion from history went back only as far as the suffrage movement of the early twentieth century. From reading about this period, Jessica had an idea about how ardently women had fought to be included in the historical process by campaigning for the right to vote. Using Pagels as a source, however, allowed Jessica to support her idea with information about women at a much earlier period.

Reading Adrienne Rich gave Jessica some information about women with whom Jessica had not been familiar, including Ethel Smyth, Anne Askew, and Jane Harrison, who fought for a place in their culture and were punished or ignored. These examples strengthened Jessica's assertion and helped move her argument chronologically to the present time, where her own observations and experiences serve as sources.

STRATEGIES FOR EXPLORING SOURCES

In the next few pages, you'll find an essay by Lewis Thomas, a physician and writer with wide-ranging interests. In "The Iks," Thomas considers the culture and behavior of a small African tribe, as reported by one anthropologist. Thomas's essay will serve as the basis for looking at strategies you can use when you encounter sources in your college work.

The Iks

Lewis Thomas

The small tribe of Iks, formerly nomadic hunters and gatherers in the mountain valleys of northern Uganda, have become celebrities, literary symbols for the ultimate fate of disheartened, heartless mankind at large. Two disastrously conclusive things happened to them: the government decided to have a national park, so they were compelled by law to give up hunting in the valleys and become farmers on poor hillside soil, and then they were visited for two years by an anthropologist who detested them and wrote a book about them. 1

The message of the book is that the Iks have transformed themselves into an irreversibly disagreeable collection of unattached, brutish creatures, totally selfish and loveless, in response to the dismantling of their traditional culture. Moreover, this is what the rest of us are like in our inner selves, and we will all turn into Iks when the structure of our society comes all unhinged. 2

The argument rests, of course, on certain assumptions about the core of human beings, and is necessarily speculative. You have to agree in advance that man is fundamentally a bad lot, out for himself alone, displaying such graces as affection and compassion only as learned habits. If you take this view, the story of the Iks can be used to confirm it. These people seem to be living together, clustered in small, dense villages, but they are really solitary, unrelated individuals with no evident use for each other. They talk, but only to make ill-tempered demands and cold refusals. They share nothing. They never sing. They turn the children out to forage as soon as they can walk, and desert the elders to starve whenever they can, and the foraging children snatch food from the mouths of the helpless elders. It is a mean society. 3

They breed without love or even casual regard. They defecate on each other's doorsteps. They watch their neighbors for signs of misfortune, and only then do they laugh. In the book they do a lot of laughing, having so much bad luck. Several times they even laughed at the anthropologist, who found this especially repellent (one senses, between the lines, that the scholar is not himself the world's luckiest man). Worse, they took him into the family, snatched his food, defecated on his doorstep, and hooted dislike at him. They gave him two bad years. 4

It is a depressing book. If, as he suggests, there is only Ikness at the center of each of us, our sole hope for hanging on to the name of humanity will be in endlessly mending the structure of our society, and it is changing so quickly and completely that we may never find the threads in time. Meanwhile, left to ourselves alone, solitary, we will become the same joyless, zestless, untouching lone animals. 5

But this may be too narrow a view. For one thing, the Iks are extraordinary. They are absolutely astonishing, in fact. The anthropologist has never seen people like them anywhere, nor have I. You'd think, if they were simply examples of the common essence of mankind, they'd seem more recognizable. Instead, they are bizarre, anomalous. I have known my share of peculiar, difficult, nervous, grabby peope, but I've never encountered any genuinely, consistently detestable human beings in all my life. The Iks sound more like abnormalities, maladies. 6

I cannot accept it. I do not believe that the Iks are representative of isolated, revealed man, unobscured by social habits. I believe their behavior is something extra, something laid on. This unremitting, compulsive repellence is a kind of complicated ritual. They must have learned to act this way; they copied it, somehow. 7

I have a theory, then. The Iks have gone crazy. 8

The solitary Ik, isolated in the ruins of an exploded culture, has built a new defense for himself. If you live in an unworkable society you can make up one of your own, and this is what the Iks have done. Each Ik has become a group, a one-man tribe on its own, a constituency. 9

Now everything falls into place. This is why they do seem, after all, vaguely familiar to all of us. We've seen them before. This is precisely the way groups of one size or another, ranging from committees to nations, behave. It is, of course, this aspect of humanity that has lagged behind the rest of evolution, and this is why the Ik seems so primitive. In his absolute selfishness, his incapacity to give anything away, no matter what, he is a successful committee. When he stands at the door of his hut, shouting insults at his neighbors in a loud harangue, he is city addressing another city. 10

Cities have all the Ik characteristics. They defecate on doorsteps, in rivers and lakes, their own or anyone else's. They leave rubbish. They detest all neighboring cities, give nothing away. They even build institutions for deserting elders out of sight. 11

Nations are the most Iklike of all. No wonder the Iks seem familiar. For total greed, rapacity, heartlessness, and irresponsibility there is nothing to match a nation. Nations, by law, are solitary, self-centered, withdrawn into themselves. There is no such thing as affection between nations, and certainly no nation ever loved another. They bawl insults from their doorsteps, defecate into whole oceans, snatch all the food, survive by detestation, take joy in the bad luck of others, celebrate the death of others, live for the death of others. 12

That's it, and I shall stop worrying about the book. It does not signify that man is a sparse, inhuman thing at his center. He's all right. It only says what we've always known and never had enough time to worry about, that we haven't yet learned how to stay human when assembled in masses. The Ik, in his despair, is acting out this failure, and perhaps we should pay closer attention. Nations have themselves become too frightening to think about, but we might learn some things by watching these people. 13

To use sources effectively, you need to take an active role in reading and responding. The strategies described in the following pages will help you use sources to shape your ideas, make connections, and develop your own opinions.

Summarizing Your Sources

What is your source about? **Summarizing**—extracting important ideas and information and putting those ideas in your own words—gives you a chance to test your understanding of the material you are considering. Sometimes—when you read a text, listen to a lecture, or even look at a painting—certain details may distract you from finding the central ideas. In writing a summary, you separate supporting details from the main points.

A summary may be one paragraph or, if you are summarizing a long piece of writing, several pages. A summary condenses the original work and, therefore, highlights the most important ideas.

Let's look at one paragraph from Thomas's essay and try to separate the central ideas from the supporting details:

> Cities have all the Ik characteristics. They defecate on doorsteps, in rivers and lakes, their own or anyone else's. They leave rubbish. They detest all neighboring cities, give nothing away. They even build institutions for deserting elders out of sight.

In this paragraph, Thomas gives many supporting details for one main idea: *Cities have Ik characteristics*. That main idea belongs in your summary. The supporting details—about polluting rivers and lakes, leaving rubbish, and ignoring the needs of the elderly—do not belong in your summary.

One strategy for writing a summary of a text is first to make an outline of each paragraph, restating the main point of the paragraph in one sentence. Then, as you reassemble your sentences, edit out those that are not important in conveying the meaning of the text. Provide your own transitions so that sentences follow one another logically. Your summary need not follow the organization of the text precisely. Organize your sentences so that your summary is clear and coherent.

Opportunities for Writing

Write a summary of Thomas's essay, "The Iks," using the strategy we just explained. How does your summary help you to understand Thomas's ideas? Compare your summary with the summaries of two or three classmates. Describe the similarities and differences between the various summaries. How do you account for any differences?

Opportunities for Exchanging Ideas

Look closely at the structure and content of your summary. Discuss with your classmates how a summary is different from an essay.

Annotating the Text

As you read Thomas's essay for the first time, you learned what he thinks about the Iks and their relationship to our own society. After one reading, you should have a general impression of what the essay is about; after writing your summary, you should be even more confident about your understanding of his main points. But to use sources effectively in your own writing, you need to go beyond understanding or summarizing the source; you need to respond to the source with your own ideas.

Responding to a source requires more active engagement than simply reading. When you respond to a source, you test the ideas in that source against your own experiences, observations, and other readings. You ask the source how the ideas it presents can help you to think about a topic you may be studying or writing about. You respond to the person who created the source as a human being, as if you were engaging in a conversation.

When you have a conversation with someone, you don't expect the other person to conduct a monologue to which you will listen passively. You know that a conversation means the sharing of ideas: Even if the other person is telling you about experiences that are unfamiliar to you, you will try to find a way to participate in the conversation by asking questions or by commenting about ways in which the conversation affects you. Your participation enriches the conversation for you. When you respond to a text by asking questions and making comments, you can enrich your encounter with the text.

One way of responding is by annotating the text. Some writers underline or highlight words or passages that interest them. Others scribble notes in the margins. Still others keep a double-entry notebook or journal, where they copy phrases or passages on one side and write their own comments on the other side.

Annotating the text allows you to begin a conversation with the author. For example, Thomas is telling us something about the Iks. Why? What interests him? What is his purpose in writing? As a reader, what bothers you about his ideas? What intrigues you? Where do you want more information? What questions does Thomas leave unanswered? Following, you'll see a few paragraphs of Thomas's essay with one student's annotations. As you compare the text with the annotations, think about the student's responses. What ideas interest this student?

The Iks

Lewis Thomas

Who are the Iks? Are they a real tribe?

The small tribe of Iks, formerly nomadic hunters and gatherers in the mountain valleys of northern Uganda, have become celebrities, literary symbols for the ultimate fate of disheartened, heartless mankind 1 at large. Two disastrously conclusive things happened to them: the government decided to have a national park, so they were compelled by law to give up hunting in the valleys and become farmers on poor hillside soil, and then they were visited for two years by an anthropologist who detested them and wrote a book about them.

2 The message of the book is that the Iks have transformed themselves into an irreversibly disagreeable collection of unattached, brutish creatures, totally selfish and loveless, in response to the dismantling of their traditional culture. Moreover, this is what the rest of us are like in our inner selves, and we will all turn into Iks when the structure of our society comes all unhinged.

→ Who did the Iks learn this behavior from?
→ Were the Iks "totally selfish and loveless" before their culture was taken away from them?

3 The argument rests, of course, on certain assumptions about the core of human beings, and is necessarily speculative. You have to agree in advance that man is fundamentally a bad lot, out for himself alone, displaying such graces as affection and compassion only as learned habits. If you take this view, the story of the Iks can be used to confirm it. These people seem to be living together, clustered in small, dense villages, but they are really solitary, unrelated individuals with no evident use for each other. They talk, but only to make ill-tempered demands and cold refusals. They share nothing. They never sing. They turn the children out to forage as soon as they can walk, and desert the elders to starve whenever they can, and the foraging children snatch food from the mouths of the helpless elders. It is a mean society.

I don't want to agree with this.

→ I would not want the Iks to make moral judgments about me. I wouldn't want anyone to force me off my land.

They breed without love or even casual regard. They defecate 4
on each other's doorsteps. They watch their neighbors for signs of misfortune, and only then do they laugh. In the book they do a lot of laughing, having so much bad luck. Several times they even laughed at the anthropologist, who found this especially repellent (one senses, between the lines, that the scholar is not himself the world's luckiest man). Worse, they took him into the family, snatched his food, defecated on his doorstep, and hooted dislike at him. They gave him two bad years.

It is a depressing book. If, as he suggests, there is only Ikness at 5
the center of each of us, our sole hope for hanging on to the name of humanity will be in endlessly mending the structure of our society, and it is changing so quickly and completely that we may never find the threads in time. Meanwhile, left to ourselves alone, solitary, we will become the same joyless, zestless, untouching lone animals.

Of course, they are "joyless"—they lost their land.

But this may be too narrow a view. For one thing, the Iks are 6
extraordinary. They are absolutely astonishing, in fact. The anthropologist has never seen people like them anywhere, nor have I. You'd think, if they were simply examples of the common essence of mankind, they'd seem more recognizable. Instead, they are bizarre, anomalous. I have known my share of peculiar, difficult, nervous, grabby people, but I've never encountered any genuinely, consistently detestable human beings in all my life. The Iks sound more like abnormalities, maladies.

I cannot accept it. I do not believe that the Iks are representative of isolated, revealed man, unobscured by social habits. I believe their behavior is something extra, something laid on. This unremitting, compulsive repellence is a kind of complicated ritual. They must have learned to act this way; they copied it, somehow. 7

I have a theory, then. The Iks have gone crazy. 8

→ Reading about the Iks makes me think about Native Americans who have seen their culture dismantled. Native Americans have been displaced in an Iklike fashion to government-defined reservations. When freedom is taken away from people, do they exhibit behaviors that seem "crazy"? "Crazy" is more likely a natural human outcry for freedom and self-determination that is alive in all of us, including the Iks.

The Iks do not dirty their neighbors' porches out of anger. They do it as a show of autonomy and independence. Deep down we are all Iks. That which is life-sustaining in us is the Ik, the restless animal that knows only how to survive.

Opportunities for Reflecting

1. Look closely at this example. What ideas do you see emerging from the student's annotations and his double-entry notebook? How is this student questioning Thomas? What questions does Thomas leave unanswered? Do you disagree with anything the student has written? Which of his questions interests you? Which questions might you develop into an essay? Reflect on these questions in your journal.

2. Select a few paragraphs from Thomas's essay. Annotate the essay or use your journal to respond to these paragraphs. Why did you choose them? What ideas interest you? Compare your summary with your annotations. How do your annotations allow you to go beyond Thomas's ideas and develop your own? How do your annotations allow you to begin a conversation with Thomas? Reflect on these questions in your journal.

Questioning Your Source Material

A good source will allow you to move beyond the information it provides. It should lead you to ask questions of your own about the material it presents. You'll find that you ask many questions among your responses as you annotate the text or keep a double-entry notebook. Listing these questions may lead you to think of more. When we asked some students to write questions about Thomas's essay, they came up with these:

1. What can we learn from the Iks? What lesson do the Iks teach us?
2. What is keeping our society "hinged" so that we are not Iks?
3. What is so bad about the Iks that Thomas concludes that they must be crazy?
4. How does behavior between nations differ from behavior between individuals?
5. How does behavior among individuals change as people mature?
6. Is all behavior learned?
7. What can a person do who lives in an unworkable society?
8. How do crowded cities dehumanize people?
9. Are the Iks happy?
10. How does group pressure change a person's behavior?

11. Who is the anthropologist who wrote about the Iks? Why might he have a particular point of view about them?

12. What does it mean to be an Ik? Are we all Iks?

Like annotating the text or keeping a double-entry notebook, asking questions reflects a thoughtful reading of the essay. The students who came up with these questions had moved beyond the information that Thomas presented and were able to ask: *What does this information mean to me? Why is it important to me? Where can this essay lead me in my own thinking?* Writing out questions allows you to see connections and to explore patterns.

Opportunities for Reflecting

1. Read Stanley Milgram's essay "The Perils of Obedience" on page 378 and Joan Didion's essay "On Morality" on page 353 of the Sourcebook. After you have read the essays once, reread them and annotate the texts. Ask questions of Milgram and Didion. Ask yourself: What are these essays about? What engages you about these essays? How do Milgram and Didion make you think about something that connects with your own experience?

2. Identify what you consider to be important passages of Milgram's and Didion's essays. Copy three passages from each essay into your journal. Ask questions: What intrigues you about Milgram's and Didion's ideas? What bothers you? What questions do Milgram and Didion leave unanswered? What connections do you see between the questions you wanted to ask Thomas and the questions you want to ask Milgram and Didion?

Engaging the Author

Often, when students use sources they fix their attention on the ideas and information provided in the source, forgetting the writer who offered those ideas. Annotating the text is one way of engaging in a conversation. Writing directly to the author is another way of engaging in a conversation. As you look at the annotations you made in response to your source and as you evaluate your questions, ask yourself what ideas seem most interesting to you? Which questions do you want to pursue? Which questions would you like to ask the author? What responses would you like to share?

Composing a letter to the writer of a source provides an informal, conversational way of clarifying and organizing your ideas, responses, and questions. Such a letter serves well as an early draft of an essay and gives you an opportunity to begin exploring the ideas presented by your source. After reading "The Iks," Paul Scocca, a college freshman, wrote the following letter to Lewis Thomas. As you read it, you'll discover the particular interest that Paul has in "The Iks." To what extent does Paul touch on questions that you, too, wonder about? How does his response to the source differ from yours? What interests him?

Dear Mr. Thomas:

"The Iks" is an interesting essay about human nature. You raise a number of questions in my mind, and I wonder if I could share some of them with you.

First of all, do you really accept the anthropologist's work at face value? How extreme was the portrait that the anthropologist painted? Do you believe that portrait, or did you just take it to make your own points about human nature? Suppose the Iks are not as bad as the anthropologist made them seem? Would that have changed your essay at all?

Your description of the behavior of people in groups touches on something that I have wondered about myself. How are nations like individuals? You describe nations as being like the Iks, showing inhumanity in relationships with others. You say that normal human interaction is different from the way nations act. In international relations, though, nations do seem to share some behavior traits with individual humans. Arrogance, bullying, patronizing, hypocrisy, selfishness, and conspiracy are not alien traits to our society. This range of behaviors does not seem anywhere nearly as extreme and weird as that of the Iks, as related in your essay.

It really seems to me that nations behave like kids on a playground. The biggest ones force the littler ones to submit to their authority, and they feud over the social order. They band together in cliques, excluding others to increase their stature. When I see the Arab nations colluding, I see the "guys wearing brown leather belts" club from my nursery school. Nations are very insecure about the prospect of losing face, just like children entering the new world of social interaction. Kids and nations both don't know all the rules of the world in which they have to interact. So their range of actions is limited to those that are easily understood by all parties involved and that let each party keep a sense of independence.

Children, of course, eventually grow up and learn the more sophisticated rules by which normal humans interact in society. The question is, how and when will nations do the same? Is it possible for the nations of the world to grow up and treat each other like civilized people? I don't want to believe that the picture you present of nations is really true.

Paul Scocca

In his letter, Paul reflects on the implications of Thomas's ideas. How, he asks Thomas, does individual behavior differ from the behavior of such groups as nations? Paul is not satisfied with Thomas's conclusions. He is bothered by some of the assertions that Thomas makes. He is ready to move beyond this one source to find out what others think about this issue and to discover how new ideas affect his thinking.

Opportunities for Writing

Select one of the essays that you have read from the Sourcebook section, "Questioning Issues of Authority and Morality." Ask yourself: What ideas seem most interesting in this essay? Which questions do I want to pursue? Which questions do I want to ask the essayist? What responses would I like to offer? Write a letter to the essayist. Engage the essayist in a conversation.

Opportunities for Exchanging Ideas

Before writing her essay "a moral person," Ayano Kato wrote a letter to George Orwell, whose essay "Shooting an Elephant" helped her to formulate and clarify her own ideas. In her letter, she questions Orwell and connects her questioning of Orwell to her reading of Joan Didion's essay "On Morality" and Stanley Milgram's essay "The Perils of Obedience."

Read Orwell's essay on page 390 of the Sourcebook. Then read Ayano's letter to Orwell. What questions is Ayano asking Orwell? How does she create a conversation between Orwell, Didion, Milgram and herself? How does her letter help her pose questions and explore these sources? How do you respond to Ayano's questioning of Orwell? Discuss Ayano's letter and these questions with your classmates.

Dear George,

I read your essay "Shooting an Elephant," and I find that many points on morality that you raise draw my attention. I find myself asking questions, both of you and your opinions, and of the Burmese and their actions.

You focus upon your own actions and decisions, and on your thoughts on imperialist governments. I find myself asking questions not only on these points, but also on others, such as the Burmese crowd. What are their moral codes? They retaliate against British rule and display their contempt in petty ways, tripping you on the football field, and spitting on women. I find this cowardly. And especially the Buddhist priests, those whom I would expect the most moral and orderly conduct from. And of the elephant, you state that "it was a bit of fun to them." But the elephant is a threat to the village, and one of the natives has been crushed to death. To you, it is certainly an important ordeal, and it should be to them, too. But instead, they "watch. . . as they would watch a conjurer about to perform a trick"; this is all that it is worth to them. And they are anxious for the meat, not caring at all about the owner of the elephant. All they have is self-interest. Surely they are not a moral people.

You claim in your essay that you were "all for the Burmese and all against their oppressors, the British." But were you at that point aware of the petty and loose morality of the natives? You saw the faults of the imperialist government, but did you see those of the Burmese other than the direct discomfort you experienced? Would you still have been on the natives' side if you had realized this? This leads me to think about the nature of morality. The imperialist government was "bad," and so it made sense to oppose them. But the natives were not entirely "good." And so is it right to side with them? Are moral decisions made on relative terms? But who can make a judgment on who is "better" or "worse"? Didion claims that no one can, for "what could be more arrogant than to claim the primacy of personal conscience?"

You were "stuck between [your] hatred of the empire [you] served and [your] rage against the evil-spirited beasts," but what if you did not dislike the natives as you did then . . . would you still have tried to impress them in the same way? Would you have felt even more pressured, to condescendingly "prove" your power to the lowly natives? Or on the contrary, would you have felt more comfortable with your own judgment and position not to be moved by the crowd's expectations?

And what if you did not hate imperialism and condemn your country as you did then? Would you have still gone through the same moral dilemma, and found your interests at conflict? Perhaps you would not have felt as uncomfortable with the natives if you were sure of your authority. And if this were the case, then can one really say that all imperialist governments are fated as puppets, to be controlled by invisible strings against their will? For it is a question of a moral dilemma; does the situation arise if the dilemma does not?

This raises the question of ignorance and realization. The other Europeans in your essay, especially the younger officials, have obviously not considered the moral implication of such actions. You have. And yet you chose to go against what one would assume to be the "morally just" action. My experience was identical; I knew too what I should have done. But out of selfishness, I chose what I knew to be "morally wrong." Does it make us worse people, because we knowingly chose the unjust path? Or does it make us better off because we are at least conscious of our wrong decisions and have thought about their consequences?

Your sentence "The people expected it of me, and I had got to do it" reminds me of Milgram's essay. Some of the subjects in his experiment felt pressured not to let the experimenter down, to "hurt his feelings," because the experimenter was in a position of psychological authority, just as the natives were, controlling your moves. I, too, felt that way. I felt apologetic and extremely guilty toward the little boy, and yet I had to join in with my friends because it was expected of me. You describe the enormous pressure you felt as "two thousand wills pressing [you] forward, irresistibly." But what was pressing me along? Ultimately, it was my need to belong, supported by my circle of friends and the taunting older boys. But their voices came from inside me. I pressured myself. If I were to give external pressure as a reason for my actions, Milgram would no doubt call this an act of hiding from responsibility. The subjects in his essay hid in the experimenter's authority, rubbing all responsibility on him even though moral responsibilities lay on them just as much. I too would be doing this if I were to lay all blame on others. But is this not exactly what you are doing? You claim that it was your situation and the circumstances that pushed you toward your actions. You give the British government and overall the Burmese crowd as excuses. But the ultimate decision came from you and you alone. Your use of the word "irresistibly" confirms this. And you also constantly try to justify your reasons for not killing the elephant in a material sense. "Besides, there was the beast's owner to be considered." Why do your moral judgments not suffice? And on the opposite stand, you try to justify having shot the elephant; "Besides, legally I had done the right thing." You are hiding behind the authority of the legal system, hiding from moral responsibility.

At the end, you show your guilt; "I felt that I had got to put an end to that dreadful noise," you say. And by trying to put the elephant out of its misery, are you not trying to escape, to "redeem" yourself? I did the same thing, by hoping and praying that the little boy would not hear my words, just as some of Milgram's subjects did too, by touching the lever "gingerly."

One large question that comes to my mind is the strength of morality. First of all, you claim that "When a white man turns tyrant it is his own freedom that he destroys . . . For it is the condition of his rule that he shall spend his life in trying to impress the 'natives,' and so in every crisis he has got to do what the 'natives' expect of him." But where does morality fit in here? Is it of lesser consequence? And at the end, you are "glad that the coolie had been killed'' for selfish reasons, to protect yourself in the legal light. What is the moral justification for this? Are morals in reality so weak that one can block them out underneath other things such as the fear of ridicule or the fear of punishment? Or is it that they are things of such grave consequence that we are tempted to hide from morals and moral responsibility? Many such questions come to mind as I read your essay.

Sincerely,
A Kato
A. Kato

Expanding the Context

Looking at other sources allows you to consider ideas in new contexts. "The Iks" brings up questions about morality and authority: How do people learn to act "civilized"? What is the difference between the way individuals behave and the way nations behave?

You may look at many different kinds of sources to help you think about these questions, including studies by sociologists, psychologists, and anthropologists. Such secondary sources could provide you with a broad overview of the issues you want to consider. You also may turn to primary sources, such as actual testimonies of individuals who were faced with moral dilemmas or who questioned their obedience to authority.

How you respond to these additional sources will depend on the questions that focus your reading. If you look again at the list of questions on page 154, you'll see ways of moving in many directions from your first source, Thomas's essay. For example, if you ask, "Is all behavior learned?" you may find yourself reading works by E. O. Wilson, a sociobiologist; B. F. Skinner, a behaviorial psychologist; or John Dewey, a philosopher and educator. Although you will come upon much new information in these works, your reading will be guided by your own question: What can these writers tell you about the causes of human behavior?

If you ask the question, "How does group pressure change a person's behavior?" you may find yourself reading works by Carol Gilligan, Stanley Milgram, or Hannah Arendt. Both your choice of sources and the ideas that you find in these sources will be affected by the questions that you ask.

As you gather sources about a topic, you may find that writers disagree with or contradict one another. In the Sourcebook section "Questioning Issues of Authority and Morality," for example, you will find differing views on such ideas as individual responsibility toward others or innate human aggression. It is your job, then, to weigh the evidence that each writer gives you to support his or her own ideas. How persuasive are their arguments? How are they drawing their conclusions? Which sources do you find most credible? A writer who presents a position that you basically do not agree with still can offer you new ways of thinking about your questions.

"When I have my own questions in mind," one student told us, "it's much easier to take notes. Sometimes it's like reading with 3-D glasses: The ideas that I want to connect with just seem to jump up at me. But when I don't have those questions in my mind, I get distracted by a lot of information that's really interesting, but not really relevant."

The questions that you ask may change in small or even large ways as you encounter additional sources. "Ten Sweet Potatoes," an essay by college freshman Makkalearn Em, a native Cambodian, is a primary source that considers, in its own way, some of the issues brought up in Lewis Thomas's "The Iks." Read this essay with your questions in mind. How does "Ten Sweet Potatoes" help you think about your questions? How does it change your thinking?

Here is Makkalearn's essay:

Ten Sweet Potatoes

Makkalearn Em

Cambodia, 1978. The Communist Khmer Rouge continued its program of forced starvation into the third year. Located in the midst of bamboo, palm trees, oaks, and various thorny underbrushes, my little village had its share of forced starvation. I am not certain how old I was. I might have been nine or ten, but time was not of any immediate concern to me or anyone else. Hunger and indiscriminate governmental executions narrowed our concern to survival. Death from malnutrition no longer caused any surprise, and we learned not to question sudden disappearances. 1

Prolonged starvation started to break down my body. My skin turned sickly yellow; my body became a skeleton with thin, loose skin hanging over it. My whole body always trembled, and I felt perpetually exhausted. I had to take special efforts to perform such basic acts as walking or standing up. 2

Hunger became my shadow. At one point when I had malaria and 3 thought that I was going to die, I started from the realization that my first regret was not being able to eat the sweet potatoes that were going to be planted in the future.

Now it was fall, the season when the government tightened its already meager food ration. I ate young, bitter leaves, tough, stringy bark, and tasteless tree sap, but I still felt insatiable. Sometimes I asked myself why feces could not serve as food. It was originally food, and nothing about it changed except that it smelled rotten. 4

Small private plots of various crops helped us survive through such times. Although my family had a plot of sweet potatoes in the back yard, they had not fully grown yet. My family did not have much experience in farming because my father was a teacher before the Communist regime. My neighbor, on the other hand, had about six rows of ripe sweet potatoes, some cherry peppers, eggplant trees, and some cucumbers in his yard. This food supplemented the inadequate government ration. 5

Because the government intentionally induced starvation, stealing government food was acceptable in the community. My father and I stole government watermelons behind our tiny wooden thatched-roof hut. At night we would silently slip to the edge of our back yard and crawl to the watermelon patch, rip the melons from their stalks, and crawl back with the melons on our stomachs. 6

Stealing from one another, on the other hand, was taboo. Once, the wife of a respected teacher stole a hen from her neighbor, and she was seen committing the crime. Although no one reported her to the authorities, she was silently ostracized. Her case provided a compelling reason to avert me from even harboring any notion of stealing my neighbor's sweet potatoes. In addition to running the risk of being humiliated by everyone, I would break the moral code established by the community. Throughout my young life I had been taught to be a good boy, not to steal, to be honest, and to keep a good family name. Furthermore, stealing from my neighbor was wrong because he and his family were starving too. 7

Yet the constant hunger tempted me to steal those sweet potatoes. Passing almost every day by his potato patch on a small footpath along the side of my back yard made the temptation even worse. And wanting to save our unripe potatoes for later, I decided to steal his potatoes. 8

The neighbor's potato patch, separated by a thin row of small, five-foot trees, was only twelve inches away from the path. I chose a spot near the edge of the forest as a base of operations and a nearby elm as a hiding place for the potatoes. I was biding my time, waiting for the most favorable moment. One evening all the adults were still working and my two brothers and sister were in our tiny wooden hut. The evening was perfect for theft, and quietly I slipped to the chosen spot. I first checked to make sure no one was around; then, my heart pounding wildly, my mouth drying up, my 9 body trembling, my palms sweating, I sprinted to the potato patch, my little feet squishing into the soft, fertile soil. I dug both hands into one of the potato rows, grabbed the potatoes underneath the soil, pulled them out, and ripped them from their vines; hugging the ten potatoes with both hands against my stomach, I ran to the elm, leaving behind torn vines and holes in the potato row.

In five minutes I had successfully looted ten potatoes, not daring to steal more for fear of getting caught. Still breathing hard from running, my first reaction was triumph, like the feeling after winning a hard-won race. I hastily dug with my right hand a small hole near the base of the old elm and placed the potatoes inside, covering them with dry, brown, dead leaves. After calming down, I returned to my hut, talking to my brothers and sister as if nothing out of the ordinary had happened. 10

That night, squatting in a circle on the wooden floor, all six of us had our usual dinner: a small bowl of watery rice porridge and watery fish soup with a few vegetables floating around. Only the clinking sound of the spoons against the bowls interrupted the silence. Even in the face of my family's suffering, I kept the potatoes all to myself. The one who suffered the most was my youngest brother, Makkasen. Four years old, Makkasen had a disproportionately huge stomach, arms and legs skinny as stilts, and a large head with deep, hollow eyes. His skin hung flabbily on his bony frame. He looked like one of the Ethiopian children who simply wasted away for lack of food. Yet I did not want to share the potatoes with my parents, sister, and brothers, not even with little Makkasen. During the dinner, all I could think of was how best to get away and roast the stolen potatoes that evening. 11

Late in the evening after dinner, I sneaked out, taking with me an ember from home. I headed for the elm, took off my dirty, ragged shirt, and wrapped the potatoes in it. Carrying the ember in one hand and the potatoes in the other, I entered the thickest part of the forest behind my hut. I built a small crackling fire and roasted all ten potatoes in it. The potatoes popped as they expanded. They emitted an aroma like warm home-made bread. Even before they were fully cooked I started eating them one by one, leaving those not yet eaten in the fire. Relishing the warmth of the fire, I engrossed myself in eating the potatoes; so content did I feel that I could not think about anyone else. For the moment, no one else existed. 12

When I returned home that evening, my family received me in silence. I betrayed no sign of wrongdoing. Although Makkasen's specter made me feel cruel, I still felt happy. For once, I felt full and satisfied. 13

The next morning I greeted my neighbor as if I had done him no wrong. Innocently and enthusiastically I chatted with him. I told him that everyone in my family was well and asked about his family's health. He 14 replied that his family was also well. Never did he mention that his potatoes were missing. Because he gave the appearance of a deep understanding of human nature, I was afraid that he would know that I stole his potatoes. Each second I prayed that he would leave me. I felt dizzy, but I mustered enough strength to hide it. When he finally left, I was relieved.

I broke all my most important values by stealing. Harming others is 15
instinctively repulsive to me; yet I harmed my neighbor and his family. They never gave me any reason to dislike them. On the contrary, they were friendly and undemanding. All the lessons about being a good boy and keeping a good family name had no immediacy; hunger did. By crossing the invisible barrier set up by others and myself, I had those sweet potatoes which made me much happier, at least for a while. So hungry was I that the community standards and my ethics seemed out of place.

This experience led me to believe that values exist only to structure 16
individual behavior during times of normalcy when basic needs are met. In an extreme situation, values break down, and the instinct for survival dominates. When a few years ago the survivors of the plane crash in the Andes ate their dead companions to keep themselves alive, I sympathized with them rather than judging them. I feel very reluctant to throw away any food at the Freshman Cafeteria, always forcing myself to eat all that I take, even though I am full. When I do throw away food, I feel bad.

My stealing the potatoes from my neighbor was a wrongful, pathetic 17
act. My not telling it to anybody indicated how wrong I thought it was. As far as I know, no one knew of my crime until now. It has been a constant reminder of how far one can go for self-preservation.

Opportunities for Writing

As you reread Makkalearn's essay, respond to it in the same way that you did with "The Iks": annotating the text and asking questions. Write a letter to Makkalearn about the issues his essay brings up for you. Tell him about a time in your life when you thought about the consequences of breaking the moral code of a community.

Opportunities for Reflecting

Read Shirley Jackson's story "The Lottery" on page 357 or William Carlos Williams's story "The Use of Force" on page 396 of the Sourcebook. Explore the story you have selected by asking questions and annotating the text. How do your questions help you understand the story? Copy passages from one story into your journal.

Opportunities for Exchanging Ideas

How might Lewis Thomas respond to Makkalearn's essay? How might Makkalearn respond to Thomas? What ideas do these writers have in common? Where do they differ? In what ways does Makkalearn's essay expand the context of Thomas's essay? How does Makkalearn help you think about morality and authority? Discuss these questions with your classmates.

Making Connections

Using sources means more than merely compiling information and quotations; you need to make connections between ideas offered in various sources. *Making connections means seeing patterns or themes in one source that are echoed in other sources.* On the surface, Thomas seems to be writing only about an obscure African tribe, and Makkalearn Em seems to be writing about an experience that is unique to his life. Only when you think about these two essays in context can you begin to see ideas or themes that the two writers have in common. As a reader, you create the bridge between these two sources. That bridge of ideas can find its expression in your own essay.

When you write an essay, you yourself create a new source that offers your interpretation and analysis of other sources. Through the process of summarizing, annotating, questioning, and engaging other writers, you will be able to find the ideas that interest you, find patterns among ideas, and find evidence to support those ideas.

In this chapter, you read an essay by Lewis Thomas, responding to the ideas that he found in a study by an anthropologist. Thomas's essay, "The Iks," then became a source for Paul Scocca as he considered questions about morality and authority. He began reading with some questions already formulated, just from his own experience. But "The Iks" inspired other questions and helped Paul think about the ideas that really interested him.

You saw how Jessica Yellin expanded her own experience at a rally for women's rights by reading sources by other writers on related issues. Both Elaine Pagels and Adrienne Rich gave Jessica a new way to think about her experiences. Neither writer told Jessica what to think; neither told her what the rally should mean to her. But their ideas complicated Jessica's thinking and led her to formulate new ideas of her own.

The readings in the Sourcebook of this text offer you groups of related essays on several themes. These essays will serve as primary and secondary sources for your own writing as you question issues of authority and morality. As you think about, plan, and write your essays, the strategies discussed in this chapter will help you to engage in a lively conversation with your sources.

Opportunities for Exploring Connections

Read Lara Harrington's essay "Responsibility Not Authority" on page 410 or Amir Goldkorn's essay "Why Bother with Morality" on page 400 of the Sourcebook. How have these writers created a conversation between the various sources they are questioning? How might their essays become a source for you to explore and question? Discuss these questions and one of these essays with your classmates.

Opportunities for Writing

In the following sequences you are being asked to question and explore issues about individual morality and group authority. From these questions and the conversations they engender, you will develop an idea to explore in your essay.

Sequence 1

1. Makkalearn Em writes, "values exist only to structure individual behavior during times of normalcy when basic needs are met. In an extreme situation, values break down, and the instinct for survival dominates." Do you agree with Makkalearn's conclusion? *Under what conditions is it right to break the moral code of the community?* Think about your own experiences and let your experiences speak to Makkalearn's. Let your experiences and your reading of Makkalearn's essay lead you to ask questions. Write your questions and reflections in your journal.

2. Reread Shirley Jackson's story "The Lottery" on page 357 of the Sourcebook. Annotate Jackson's story. How does Jackson help you to think about the ideas in Makkalearn Em's essay and the ideas you have been thinking about all through this chapter? List questions in your journal that Jackson's story brings up for you. Try to find connections between all the questions you have been asking.

3. Reread Stanley Milgram's essay "The Perils of Obedience" on page 378 of the Sourcebook. Create a conversation between Em, Jackson, and yourself responding to Milgram's experiment and his conclusions. How, for instance, do you respond to Milgram's statement: "The essence of obedience is that a person comes to view himself as the instrument for carrying out another person's wishes and he therefore no longer regards himself as responsible for his actions." Let your questions and comments set the tone of the conversation. Find common ground between the writers, but also find paradoxes and questions left unanswered.

4. You have been asking questions, reflecting, and complicating your own thinking. Your sources have enriched your thinking and taken you beyond your own experiences and observations. Now is your opportunity to create a new source, your own essay, your bridge between all the sources that have enriched your thinking.

You have many written exercises that are preliminary drafts for you. Through the process of annotating, questioning, and engaging other writers you have found the ideas that interest you and the patterns among ideas. Write an essay exploring the idea that interests you about individual morality and group authority. Use your sources as necessary to support your idea.

Sequence 2

1. Think about one or two moments from your past when you found yourself in a moral dilemma. Play those moments against one another, trying to locate the real source of your conflict. Were those occasions when your own values clashed with group values? Were those moments when you were trying to do the right thing? Or were they moments in which you questioned your moral obligation to tell the truth or to protect someone? How did you resolve your problem? Looking back on those moments from a new vantage point, how do you assess your actions? Can you imagine a different resolution? Did you know then what you were doing?

Let these questions and others of your choosing shape your reflections. Let the questions help you think your way through your dilemma. Reflect on these questions in your journal.

2. Read Ruth Macklin's essay "Applying Moral Principles" on page 364 of the Sourcebook. Macklin asks questions about medical ethics. Is it ethically permissible, Macklin asks, to allow some infants to die, rather than make every effort to preserve their lives? Or, how do we resolve the moral tension between respect for human life and the need to reduce pain and suffering?

Write a summary of Macklin's essay. Reduce your summary to four or five sentences. Annotate Macklin's essay. Mark sentences and passages that strike you as interesting. Keep a running commentary or response beside each passage. Copy two or three passages into your journal. Let the passages generate more questions for you. What connections can you find between the situations you described in the previous exercise and the questions that engaged you in reading Macklin's essay?

3. Select one of the essays from the Sourcebook section "Questioning

Issues of Authority and Morality." What intrigues you about this author's ideas? What questions is he or she asking? What questions are left unanswered? Write a letter to the author of this essay. Show the author the various connections you have found between his or her essay and the ideas in the various essays and stories you have been reading for this assignment. Of course, feel free to bring in any other sources that help you explore your idea. Making connections means seeing patterns or themes in one source that are echoed in other sources. Your task here is to create a conversation in your letter between the various writers and yourself. Find common ground between writers, but also find paradoxes and questions left unanswered.

4. You have been asking questions, reflecting, and complicating your own thinking. Your sources have enriched your thinking and taken you beyond your own experiences and observations. Now is your opportunity to create a new source, your own essay, your bridge between all the sources that have enriched your thinking.

Write an essay exploring the ideas about individual morality and group authority that all your questions and explorations have been leading you to. Use your sources as necessary to support your ideas.

Questioning Sources: Questions for Peer Review

1. What is the writer's organizing idea? How does the writer introduce this idea? How does the writer develop and expand this idea? Mark words, sentences, and passages in the writer's draft that you find particularly effective in conveying his or her idea.

2. How does the writer question sources? What questions does the writer seem to be asking of each source? Does the writer get inside the source and show you that he or she really knows this source? Does the writer reveal something interesting and surprising about the source? How does the writer use the source to develop his or her own idea?

3. How does the writer introduce and create a context for his or her sources? Do you feel as if the writer is dropping these sources into the essay for decoration? Or, do the sources help the writer to think about the questions being posed?

4. Where in the essay is the writer reflecting and trying to make sense of the sources he or she is questioning? Are there other places in the essay where you want more reflection from the writer? Mark those places.

5. Where in the essay has the writer said anything that is confusing or unclear to you? Show the writer where you think he or she needs more details or examples.

(*continued*)

6. How has the writer shown up in the essay? How do his or her words and sentence rhythms reveal the voice of the writer?

7. How does the writer's introduction pull you into the world of the essay? After reading the entire draft, is there anything confusing or unnecessary about the introduction? Is there anything you might suggest adding?

8. How does the writer's conclusion pull together the entire essay? How might the conclusion be more effective?

Annotate the writer's draft by commenting on its strengths and weaknesses. Ask the writer questions. Write a letter in which you offer your honest, careful, and generous comments and suggestions for revising.

CHAPTER 8

Arguing a Position

When we use the word in everyday conversation, *argument* implies contentiousness or disagreements. An argumentative person seems always to be looking for a fight. But when we apply the word to college writing, it has a different meaning. In exploring sources, including your own experiences, you will draw conclusions and come to opinions that allow you to take a position on any number of issues. Your essays, then, will be *argumentative.* An argumentative essay does not have to be about a controversial subject: It does need to be a reasoned, well-supported defense of your opinions.

You may be asked to write argumentative essays in response to many college assignments. If you have had assignments in the past asking you to defend your views on abortion, affirmative action laws, or capital punishment, you may be surprised to find now that you are expected to take a position on the interpretation of a poem or the artistic intentions of a sculptor or on the significance of a poll taken during the last presidential election.

In much of the writing that you do in college, you will present your own opinions and conclusions based on your questioning and exploring of sources. Your sources will help you support your opinions by providing evidence. In an argumentative essay, you say to your readers, "Here is my position, here is how I have thought through the issue, here is the evidence I've found, here is my response to other people's positions about the issue, here is why readers might want to agree with me."

You read about strategies for questioning sources in Chapter 7. In this chapter, you'll see how those strategies can be used to produce an argumentative essay. You'll see ways in which an argumentative essay can be structured, and you'll have a chance to consider the kinds of arguments that are effective in persuading readers.

In Chapter 7, you focused on the issue of morality and authority as you practiced questioning and responding to sources. In this chapter, you'll be focusing on the topic of education, drawing upon some selections from the Sourcebook. There you'll find essays about testing, high school life, the place of black English in schools, the contexts in which people learn, and women's educational experiences. These sources will provide you with evidence to support your argument.

KINDS OF ARGUMENTS

No matter what position you may take on an issue, there are two basic ways of structuring your argument: *inductive* or *deductive.* Whatever structure you use, however, your argumentative essay will contain four basic elements:

1. A *claim*, or the position that you put forth
2. *Evidence*, or the details that support your claim
3. *Definitions of terms*, so that you and your reader share an understanding of the terms that you use in presenting your claim and your evidence
4. *Consideration of counterarguments*, or opposing claims, to show your reader why these are weak and your claim is strong

Inductive Arguments

An **inductive argument** begins with observations of particular details that lead you to make a generalization. Later in this chapter, on page 175, you will read an essay by K. C. Cole about women in science. Cole observed that few physicists are women, saw examples of how female students are discouraged from learning science, and read about gender bias in the sciences. She concluded, therefore, that women are not welcome in scientific disciplines. She was moving from observation of particulars to a generalization.

The strength of an inductive argument, then, rests on the particular examples that you use to make your generalization. If Cole had used only her personal experience to argue that women are not welcome in scientific disciplines, her readers might have questioned her conclusions. After all, she might have had a few biased teachers, or she may have not studied hard and caused her own failure, or she may have chosen to take courses for which she was not prepared.

Because Cole drew upon a variety of sources—readings, interviews, her own observations, and personal experiences of other people—her readers are more likely to be persuaded that her conclusion is valid.

Many arguments that you make daily are based on inductive reasoning. You are likely to see patterns in your experiences, and those patterns lead you to draw conclusions. In Cole's essay, you'll read about one woman who used inductive reasoning to conclude that science has "macho mores."

When you do research using sources, you also look for patterns that lead you to draw conclusions. Cole found agreement in many different kinds of sources; that agreement supported her argument.

Deductive Arguments

A **deductive argument** relies on the truth of related premises to point to a conclusion. The basic structure of a deductive argument contains three parts:

1. A major premise
2. A minor premise
3. A conclusion

If the major premise is true,
and the minor premise is true,
then the conclusion will follow logically.

In the Sourcebook section "Questioning Issues of Authority and Morality," you'll find an essay on medical ethics by Ruth Macklin. That essay brings up the question of medical intervention for newborn babies with severe birth defects. You might use the following deductive argument in support of medical intervention:

Major Premise: Killing is wrong.
Minor Premise: Withholding medical care can kill the patient.
Conclusion: Withholding medical care is wrong.

This argument is *valid* because the conclusion follows logically from the major and minor premises. However, you may argue against medical intervention if you disagree with either the major or minor premise. You may decide, for example, that in certain cases killing is not wrong. Or you may decide that withholding medical care does not actively kill the patient, but instead does not intervene to save the patient.

On page 179, you will read an essay by journalist Tom Wicker that questions the right of school administrators to censor student newspapers. Wicker used deductive reasoning to structure his argument.

Major Premise: Freedom of speech is guaranteed in this country by the Bill of Rights.

Minor Premise: One high school principal denied this right to students.

Conclusion: This principal acted unconstitutionally.

Both inductive and deductive reasoning can produce successful arguments. Both kinds of arguments depend on evidence, and an argument is only as strong as that evidence.

RELYING ON EVIDENCE

Effective arguing depends on the kinds of evidence you present to your readers. That evidence depends on the sources available and on the argumentative strategies you have learned. A student writing about works of literature may decide to use only those works as sources, while a student proposing a ban on automobiles in major cities may decide to cite statistics on pollution, to interview transportation experts, to read articles in journals on city planning, and to observe traffic patterns.

Personal anecdotes may help you set up a context for your argument and, in some cases, be an important source of evidence. But other sources often need to be brought to your work to widen the context and provide support for your position.

In writing an argument, be sure you have distinguished between primary and secondary sources. What evidence comes from firsthand experiences or observations? How reliable are these sources? If you interview people, what interests might they have in promoting a certain point of view? What information comes from sources that already have been interpreted? If you cite statistics or reproduce tables, where do these come from? How reliable are these sources? How up-to-date are they? These are the kind of questions you need to ask yourself as you evaluate your evidence.

In the essay that follows, K. C. Cole, a science writer, asks why there are so few women in scientific careers. She bases her argument on her own experience and several primary and secondary sources. As you read the article, notice the kinds of sources that Cole uses to provide evidence for her argument.

Women and Science

K. C. Cole

I know few other women who do what I do. What I do is write about science, mainly physics. And to do that, I spend a lot of time reading about science, talking to scientists, and struggling to understand physics. In fact, most of the women (and men) I know think me quite queer for actually liking physics. "How can you write about that stuff?" they ask, always somewhat askance. "I could never understand that in a million years." Or more simply, "I hate science." 1

I didn't realize what an odd creature a woman interested in physics was until a few years ago when a science magazine sent me to Johns Hopkins University in Baltimore for a conference on an electrical phenomenon known as the Hall effect. We sat in a huge lecture hall and listened as physicists talked about things engineers didn't understand and engineers talked about things physicists didn't understand. What *I* didn't understand was why, out of several hundred young students of physics and engineering in the room, less than a handful were women. 2

Sometime later, I found myself at the California Institute of Technology reporting on the search for the origins of the universe. I interviewed physicist after physicist, man after man. I asked one young administrator why none of the physicists were women. And he answered: "I don't know, but I suppose it must be something innate. My seven-year-old daughter doesn't seem to be much interested in science." 3

It was with that experience fresh in my mind that I attended a conference in Cambridge, Mass., on science literacy, or rather the worrisome lack of it in this country today. We three women—a science teacher, a young chemist, and myself—sat surrounded by a company of august men. The chemist, I think, first tentatively raised the issue of science illiteracy in women. It seemed like an obvious point. After all, everyone had agreed over and over again that scientific knowledge these days was a key factor in economic power. But as soon as she made the point, it became clear that we women had committed a grievous social error. Our genders were suddenly showing; we had interrupted the serious talk with a subject unforgivably silly. 4

For the first time, I stopped being puzzled about why there weren't any women in science and began to be angry. Because if science is a search for answers to fundamental questions then it hardly seems frivolous to find out why women are excluded. Never mind the economic consequences. 5

A lot of the reasons women are excluded are spelled out by the Massachusetts Institute of Technology experimental physicist Vera Kistiakowsky in a recent article in *Physics Today* called, "Women in Physics: Unnecessary, Injurious and Out of Place?" The title was taken from a nineteenth-century essay written in opposition to the appointment of a female mathematician to a professorship at the University of Stockholm. "As decidedly as two and two make four," a woman in mathematics is a "monstrosity," concluded the writer of the essay. 6

Dr. Kistiakowsky went on to discuss the factors that make women in science today, if not monstrosities, at least oddities. Contrary to much popular opinion, one of those is *not* an innate difference in the scientific ability of boys and girls. But early conditioning does play a stubborn and subtle role. A recent "Nova" program, "The Pinks and the Blues," documented how girls and boys are treated differently from birth—the boys always encouraged in more physical kinds of play, more active explorations of their environments. Sheila Tobias, in her book, *Math Anxiety*, showed how the games boys play help them to develop an intuitive understanding of speed, motion, and mass. 7

The main sorting out of the girls from the boys in science seems to happen in junior high school. As a friend who teaches in a science museum said, "By the time we get to electricity, the boys already have had some experience with it. But it's unfamiliar to the girls." Science books draw on boys' experiences. "The examples are all about throwing a baseball at such and such a speed," said my stepdaughter, who barely escaped being a science drop-out. 8

The most obvious reason there are not many more women in science is that women are discriminated against as a class, in promotions, salaries and hirings, a conclusion reached by a recent analysis by the National Academy of Sciences. 9

Finally, said Dr. Kistiakowsky, women are simply made to feel out of place in science. Her conclusion was supported by a Ford Foundation study by Lynn H. Fox on the problems of women in mathematics. When students were asked to choose among six reasons accounting for girls' lack of interest in math, the girls rated this statement second: "Men do not want girls in the mathematical occupations." 10

A friend of mine remembers winning a Bronxwide mathematics competition in the second grade. Her friends—both boys and girls—warned her that she shouldn't be good at math: "You'll never find a boy who likes you." My friend continued nevertheless to excel in math and science, won many awards during her years at the Bronx High School of Science, and then earned a full scholarship to Harvard. After one year of Harvard science, she decided to major in English. 11

When I asked her why, she mentioned what she called the "macho mores" of science. "It would have been O.K. if I'd had someone to talk to," she said. "But the rules of comportment were such that you never admitted you didn't understand. I later realized that even the boys didn't get everything clearly right away. You had to stick with it until it had time to sink in. But for the boys, there was a payoff in suffering through the hard times, and a kind of punishment—a shame—if they didn't. For the girls it was O.K. not to get it, and the only payoff for sticking it out was that you'd be considered a freak." 12

Science is undeniably hard. Often, it can seem quite boring. It is unfortunately too often presented as laws to be memorized instead of mysteries to be explored. It is too often kept a secret that science, like art, takes a well-developed esthetic sense. Women aren't the only ones who say, "I hate science." 13

That's why everyone who goes into science needs a little help from friends. For the past ten years, I have been getting more than a little help from a friend who is a physicist. But my stepdaughter—who earned the highest grades ever recorded in her California high school on the math Scholastic Aptitude Test—flunked calculus in her first year at Harvard. When my friend the physicist heard about it, he said "Harvard should be ashamed of itself." 14

What he meant was that she needed that little extra encouragement that makes all the difference. Instead, she got that little extra discouragement that makes all the difference. 15

"In the first place, all the math teachers are men," she explained. "In the second place, when I met a boy I liked and told him I was taking chemistry, he immediately said: 'Oh, you're one of those science types.' In the third place, it's just a kind of social thing. The math clubs are full of boys and you don't feel comfortable joining." 16

In other words, she was made to feel unnecessary and out of place. 17

A few months ago, I accompanied a male colleague from the science museum where I sometimes work to a lunch of the history of science faculty at the University of California. I was the only woman there, and my presence for the most part was obviously and rudely ignored. I was so surprised and hurt by this that I made an extra effort to speak knowledgeably and well. At the end of the lunch, one of the professors turned to me in all seriousness and said: "Well, K. C., what do the women think of Carl Sagan?" I replied that I had no idea what "the women" thought about anything. But now I know what I should have said: I should have told him that his comment was unnecessary, injurious, and out of place. 18

Cole's own experiences—attending conferences and talking with other scientists—did not provide her with strong enough evidence from which to draw a conclusion. Because she had many unanswered questions about the issue that interested her, she was led to outside sources:

- An article by Vera Kistiakowsky, an experimental physicist
- A *Nova* program on gender differences
- A book, *Math Anxiety*, by Sheila Tobias
- A conversation with a friend who teaches in a science museum
- A study done by the National Academy of Sciences
- A study done by the Ford Foundation
- A conversation with a friend who won a math prize in second grade
- Conversations with her stepdaughter

These sources provided her with enough evidence to formulate a strong argument: Women are discouraged from pursuing an interest in science both by male scientists within the field and by social conventions that stereotype women scientists as strange beings.

Opportunities for Exchanging Ideas

1. Discuss Cole's essay and the sources she used. Identify the evidence that Cole derives from each source to support her argument.

2. Discuss which sources are strongest in this essay? Where do you think Cole gets her best support? What evidence is most persuasive? Why? How does she integrate the sources so that they work together to support her argument?

CONSIDERING YOUR READERS: ASSUMPTIONS AND COUNTER-ARGUMENTS

In taking a stand, you hope to persuade readers that your subject is important and your position is valid and substantiated. Because readers may or may not be informed about the particular issue on which you decide to take a stand, you need to consider how much background information to supply for your audience. Readers may approach an issue with opinions, ideas, and even misconceptions. Anticipating those opinions can help you consider **counterarguments** to your position. Counterarguments need not weaken your position. In fact, bringing these counterarguments into your essay and showing your readers why they are weak will serve to strengthen your own position.

You need to consider your audience both to win support and to structure an argument. Readers need a reason to think that the issue is important to them, that they have an investment in reading the essay. You do not want to alienate readers by appearing angry, supercilious, or arrogant, no matter how passionate you may be about your position.

The essay that follows was written by Tom Wicker, a journalist on the staff of the *New York Times*. Wicker read reports about a dispute over freedom of speech at a St. Louis high school. The principal, attempting to protect the privacy of some students and their families, stopped the publication of articles on divorce and teenage pregnancies that were to appear in the school's student newspaper. The newspaper staff sued, and the Supreme Court, when it heard the case on appeal, upheld the principal's position. Reports on the case caused Wicker to ask some questions about the issue of free speech and education:

- What lesson did school officials teach students in this dispute?
- What pedagogical concerns might justify censorship?
- How did the Court's decision about this dispute reflect the value that America supposedly puts on open debate?
- Under what circumstances, if any, should student speech be limited?

Wicker's questions required him to think about the provisions of the First Amendment and about his own work as a journalist. He also reread the reports that had appeared about the case, and he even read a copy of the Court transcript made when the case was heard.

These sources helped Wicker formulate his own opinion about the issue and write an argumentative essay that appeared as an editorial in the *New York Times*. As you read the following essay, think about the assumptions that Wicker thought his readers might hold.

The Wrong Lesson

Tom Wicker

The Supreme Court, as Justice William J. Brennan Jr. wrote in dissent, taught "young men and women" the wrong civics lesson when it upheld the right of a principal to impose prior restraint on a student newspaper. 1

So it did, and that damaging lesson may well be absorbed far beyond the corridors of high school.

Most specifically, the Court's 5-to-3 decision in the Hazelwood school case may now be invoked in efforts to limit freedom of expression in student publications, theatrical presentations and the like at state universities. Despite the differences in high schools and colleges, it's hard to see why the rationale of the decision—that public education officials may censor an activity "reasonably related to legitimate pedagogical concerns"—could not be cited by university administrators. 2

What, moreover, are "legitimate pedagogical concerns"? Justice Byron R. White's opinion for the majority went so far as to say that schools could legitimately censor expression that might "associate the school with any position other than neutrality on matters of public controversy." What kind of support is that for the supposedly American values of robust debate and the "marketplace" of ideas? 3

Besides, the Hazelwood principal did far more than dissociate his school from articles to which he objected in its student newspaper. He quashed the printing of two pages of the paper, effectively silencing speech—not just in the two articles to which he objected, but in four others on the pages. The Court found this action "not unreasonable," owing to the nature of his objections to the two articles, to the fact that the student publication, in the Court's view, was not a "public forum" and that its contents were a "legitimate pedagogical" matter over which the principal had jurisdiction. 4

In so finding, the Court nevertheless upheld a "prior restraint"—the prevention of publication of something someone finds offensive. In the Pentagon Papers case and others, prior restraints have been held unconstitutional except in the most exceptional cases. Now the Court not only holds that prior restraint may be imposed almost routinely on student publications: but it adds substance to the view that in some cases, for some forms of expression, prior restraint is constitutional after all. 5

A high school newspaper partially financed by the school board, and which is published as part of the curriculum, may not be technically, as Justice White insisted, a "public forum." But it may be the only forum the students have: if school officials can censor it, student rights of expression previously established by the Supreme Court have been limited. If student speech is not fully protected by the First Amendment, are there other classes of citizens who might be so limited? 6

The decision well may drive some students to "underground" publications—and to the logical conclusion that what schools teach about free speech is not what schools practice. Isn't *that* a legitimate pedagogical concern? 7

The Hazelwood principal's reasons for objecting to the articles in ques- 8 tion seem reasonable—he thought one might violate some students' privacy and that the other was unfair to a person mentioned in it. But whatever his good intentions, he had open to him other remedies than prior restraint.

It's not even clear why he couldn't have insisted upon changes he thought necessary. Page proofs were shown to him on May 10: publication was not scheduled until May 13. 9

But if there really was no time for editing, the principal could have specified his objections and warned against future violations. In addition, to prevent future problems, he could have ordered a change in procedure to make sure he had adequate time to read page proofs and work out agreed-upon changes with the student editors. Perhaps a stronger, or a better understood, set of rules for publication could have been worked out to prevent future conflicts. 10

All of these possible courses of action, it will be objected, would have resulted in publication of the articles to which the principal objected. But some expressions will always be found offensive or unjustifiable or incorrect by some in the audience; and it is inherent in a free press that privacy will sometimes be violated, not always necessarily, and that some stories may be unfair. 11

If such excesses could be prevented by authority, the press, in the nature of the case, would not be free. The Hazelwood lesson is that some authorities can prevent some publications. As Justice Brennan observed, that's the wrong lesson. 12

When Wicker wrote his argument, he was aware that some of his readers might disagree with him and take a position supporting the school's administration and the Supreme Court. He anticipated these opinions when he first asked the question "What are legitimate pedagogical concerns?" In paragraphs 8 and 10, he directly confronts some counterarguments:

- The principal's objections (the articles would violate privacy) seem reasonable.
- Any action other than censorship would have resulted in the publication of the articles in question.

To the first counterargument, Wicker responds by suggesting that the principal, even if one agrees with his objections, had other courses of action open to him. He could have insisted upon editorial changes; if there was no time for these changes, he could have changed editorial procedure so that he had time to work with the student editors on future issues.

To the second counterargument, Wicker responds that publication of the articles would have been the lesser of two evils: Censorship is worse than invasion of privacy. Freedom of the press for a society has a higher priority than freedom of any individual to privacy.

Wicker's readers may come away from his essay still not agreeing with him. But they cannot say that he ignores their point of view. Whenever you formulate an argument, you strengthen your position by considering other views.

Opportunities for Exchanging Ideas

1. Read "How They Write the SAT" on page 459 of the Sourcebook. What is Owen's argument in this essay? What evidence does he use to support his argument? What counterarguments does he present? Can you think of additional counterarguments to offer Owen? Discuss Owen's essays and these questions with your classmates.

2. Consider the following claims. Working in small groups, offer as many counterarguments to these claims as you can think of. See if your classmates can offer counterarguments to your counterarguments.

Claim: To become educated, one should stay away from schools.

Claim: Intelligence can accurately be measured by standardized tests.

Claim: Colleges treat students as if they were merely empty vessels waiting to be filled with teacherly facts.

Opportunities for Reflecting

1. One of the clichés we often hear about learning is that "Experience is the best teacher." Brainstorm in your journal and write five other clichés about learning and education. Select two of these clichés and explore their meaning. What questions would you want to ask about these clichés? What terms would you want to define? Offer counterarguments to these clichés.

2. Explore in your journal two claims about learning that you might want to argue in an essay. What terms will you have to define? Develop as many counterarguments to your own claims as you can. What kinds of sources might you use to support these claims? What kind of evidence would be most persuasive?

FLAWS IN REASONING

Whether your argument is organized inductively or deductively, your reasoning can be weakened by *logical fallacies,* or flaws in your logic. In an inductive argument, for example, you simply may not have enough particular examples to warrant a generalization. In the last chapter, you read Lewis Thomas's essay on "The Iks," concerning a society from which he drew generalizations about the nature of authority and morality. The Iks themselves offer only one example of social structure and behavior. In attacking Thomas's argument, then, you might well accuse him of making an unwarranted generalization.

Following are some common fallacies that can result in a weakened argument.

Begging the Question

If you assume that the question being argued has already been proven, you are begging—or avoiding—the question. You might argue, for example, that only countries with strong human rights records should be given American aid. This argument assumes, however, that you have already proven what constitutes a strong human rights record. Such assumptions leave you open to attack by your readers and weaken a position with which they might otherwise agree.

Non Sequitur

Non sequitur means "it does not follow"; that is, a premise does not logically lead to a conclusion. If you argue that people should be allowed to drink at age 18 because they can vote at age 18, you are offering a *non sequitur:* there is no evident relationship—such as cause and effect—between voting and drinking.

Ad Hominem Argument

In an *ad hominem* argument, you attack a person rather than the issue about which you are taking a position. An argument criticizing Ezra Pound's poetry, for example, might be weakened if you attack Pound for engaging in treason during World War II, unless you find a way to show how his political views affected the quality of his writing.

Faulty Use of Authority

Experts can be found to bolster almost any position that you may choose to take. Who are these experts? How can you evaluate their credentials?

Upon whose authority are you relying? Merely quoting an expert does not give you, the writer, authority to take a position. When you rely on experts, you need to show in your essay why an experts' opinion is worth considering.

Either/Or

Students sometimes choose "prepackaged" topics for argument papers—capital punishment, for example, or nuclear disarmament—because they believe that there are only two sides to the issue and lack confidence in considering complexities. When you take a position, you are not required to demolish all other alternatives; rather, you have to provide a logical argument for your conclusions, taking into consideration possible counterarguments.

The premise on which you base your argument does not have to be construed as an either/or statement. "If we don't build nuclear power plants, we will be dependent on Middle Eastern oil," for example, is an either/or statement that a reader could attack. We can develop other kinds of energy sources, or we can explore other sources of oil, or we can change our patterns of fuel consumption. Since these alternatives are available to us, an either/or statement is not valid.

Oversimplification

Like the either/or fallacy, oversimplification fails to consider complexities. If you argue that increased low-cost housing will eradicate homelessness, you are oversimplifying a complex issue by failing to consider other factors—such as unemployment, lack of job training facilities, cutbacks in mental health facilities—that also affect the problem of homelessness. Your argument would be stronger if you made a more modest assertion about the relationship between the availability of low-cost housing and the problem of homelessness.

STRATEGIES FOR CREATING AN ARGUMENT

An argument begins with questions, and those questions may come from your own experiences. Let's explore some issues in education along with Russell Thompson, a college freshmen who was asked to write a brief essay recalling an early educational experience. Here's what Russell wrote:

Russell in Numberland

Russell Thompson

On the first day of kindergarten, I and my fellow students sat in a large circle and memorized each other's names. On the second, we colored in pretty little drawings of house and home. On the third day of kindergarten we conducted standardized testing routines to determine our placement in the class. The way it worked was very simple. You simply stood in front of the teacher and recited numbers as high as you could go. One, two, three, . . . thirteen, fourteen, . . . twenty-one, . . . thirty-five, . . . forty-nine, . . . sixty-three, . . . uh, . . . uh, . . . bang, you're dead.

In some sense the implications were terrifying. Suppose that these numbers were the years left that you had to live? Suppose they determined your average salary over the ages twenty-one to thirty? Suppose you could only have as many girlfriends as you could count? In a move that seemed deliberately malicious, too, my teacher posted big signs stretching across one wall that advertised the number to which you could count. Each student then had a little card which was hung under the proper number. Those students on the right were good; fate smiled upon them. Those on the left, however, were destined to work at McDonald's for all perpetuity.

And then I was tested, and my score came up . . . sixty. Which meant that I was branded . . . average. You have to understand me. No kid thinks that he is average until third grade, when test scores start coming in hot and heavy. Before that, he basks in his parents' loving admiration and it never occurs to him to compare himself to others.

That night I tossed and turned, sleepless in bed until dawn, when I got up with a cold resolve and a mind bent on fierce vengeance. I studied. I memorized the respectable cardinals and the honorable ordinals, and then all the unflinching numerals and their corresponding symbols. And then to top it off, I learned *ROMAN* numerals. And on the next day in class I kicked the living bejesus out of everyone else, even my best friend.

It wasn't so hard. I could do it again if I had to. But that's not the point, because to the far right of the classroom is a sign that states 213 under which hangs a card that says Russell Thompson. (That was as far as I got before the teacher got bored.)

Russell asks many questions in his second paragraph, but the real question that underlies this essay is this: How do we measure intelligence? Looking back at his experience in kindergarten, Russell sees that counting up to 60 on the third day of school was not an accurate measure of his intelligence; after all, he went home and memorized numbers so that by the next day he could count beyond 213. He had proven to himself and his teacher that he was not merely "average."

Why, though, should his teacher want to measure his intelligence? To what extent could such measurement predict how well Russell would do in school? And even if his teacher wanted such information, do any tests accurately measure intelligence? What *is* intelligence, anyway? Russell could not answer these questions from his personal experience alone, but when he was assigned to write an argumentative essay, his experience in Numberland suggested a topic for him: He decided to explore the issue of measuring intelligence.

In the following pages, you'll trace Russell's work as he located sources to help him consider the issue of measuring intelligence; read, annotated, and questioned those sources; kept a journal reflecting on his readings and ideas, and focused on the position he decided to defend.

Beginning with a Source

Russell's latest experience with testing had been the Scholastic Aptitude Test, or SAT, a test that many high school seniors take as part of the college application process. Because he had personal experience with this test, he was interested in David Owen's essay "How They Write the SAT." Russell might have found Owen's essay in several ways: by looking up the topic of testing, intelligence, or educational measurement in the *Reader's Guide to Periodical Literature*, for example, or by seeing the essay cited in the bibliography of a book on educational measurement. In Chapter 10, "Directing the Search," you'll have a chance to consider more fully the process of locating sources. For now, let's look at Owen's essay to see how Russell can use it to think about his topic.

Opportunities for Reflecting

1. Russell copied the following passages from Owen's essay "How They Write the SAT" into his journal. In your journal, respond with questions and comments to these passages or passages of your own choosing. Where do these passages lead you in your thinking? How do they help you question ways of learning?

> Understanding how the test-makers think is one of the keys both to doing well on ETS tests and to penetrating the mystique in which the company cloaks its work. Despite ETS's claims to the contrary, its tests are written by people who tend to think in certain predictable ways.
>
> But, of course, in taking a test like this, the student has to suppress his sometimes powerful urge to respond according to his own sense of what is right. He has to remember that the "best" answer—which is what ETS always asks for, even on math and science tests—isn't necessarily a good answer, or even a correct one. He has to realize that the ETS answer will be something drab, humorless, and plodding. . . . Thus bright students sometimes have trouble on ETS tests, because they see possibilities that ETS's question-writers missed. The advice traditionally given to such students is to take the test quickly and without thinking too hard.
>
> ETS calls delta a measure of "difficulty," but this definition is circular. A question is hard if few people answer it correctly, easy if many do. But since delta refers to no standard beyond the item itself, it makes no distinction between one body of subject matter and another. Nor does it distinguish between knowledge and good luck.

Questioning Sources

When Russell responded to these passages, he came up with many questions about measuring intelligence. He decided to list those questions so that he could get a sense of how to proceed as he looked at other sources. Here are his questions:

- How does a mass test like the SAT differ from the kind of tests we get all through school?
- How does school teach test taking?
- What role does testing have in schools? Was my own experience typical?
- Why do colleges even require the SAT? What purpose does it serve?

Russell decided that before he read any more about testing, he would pay a visit to the guidance counselor at the high school nearest to his college. The guidance counselor, busy though he was, agreed to see Russell for half an hour one morning. Russell went to the interview prepared with several questions:

- How are tests used in your high school? What is the purpose of testing?
- How consistent are test scores for individual students?
- What does your high school do to prepare students for the SAT?
- How well does the SAT measure a student's ability to do college work?
- Do tests really measure intelligence and knowledge?

As he talked with the guidance counselor, Russell found himself comparing his own high school experiences with what the guidance counselor was telling him. Here are the notes that Russell took during the interview:

—High schools test for motivation and retention
—Students not motivated to work unless they know they'll have a test at the end of the week
—Would I work without tests? I told him it would depend on the subject
—Tests allow for standardization of curriculum, control of what teachers are teaching
—Students usually are pretty consistent: B student, A student, etc.
—SAT just one measurement; other factors considered
—Makes distinction between testing skills and achievement and testing intelligence and aptitude
—Skills and achievement can be tested
—Recommends Sizer—Says it sounds like my own experience

The guidance counselor defended testing as something that was educationally sound and necessary. He said that students probably would not be motivated to work as hard if they did not anticipate frequent assessments of their learning. Also, tests let students know where they were strong and where they needed to work harder.

Russell had not thought about testing as a service to students, but he began to consider his own high school experience in the light of this idea. Would he have worked as hard if he were not rewarded with a good grade on a test? Did the spirit of competition really work in his favor?

The guidance counselor seemed confused when Russell asked about measuring intelligence. What did Russell mean by intelligence? Did he mean ability to learn? Or did he mean measuring what information had been learned? What did Russell mean by knowledge? A body of information within a discipline (like knowledge of chemistry)? Or some kind of general intuition about the world? When Russell found himself unable to answer these questions, he knew that he would have to *define his terms* before he could organize his argument.

The guidance counselor left Russell with the suggestion to read a book by Theodore Sizer, an educator who studied high schools and wrote *Horace's Compromise: The Dilemma of the American High School.* Sizer's book, he said, seemed close to Russell's own high school experience.

Opportunities for Reflecting

1. Read "What High School Is," a selection from *Horace's Compromise,* on page 467 of the Sourcebook. Write a summary of Sizer's essay in your journal.

2. In your journal, copy passages from Sizer's essay that you find particularly interesting. What do these passages mean to you? How do they relate to the kinds of experiences that you had in high school? What assumptions is Sizer making about education? Argue with and against Sizer's ideas.

Making Connections

Now Russell had four sources to help him think about the issue of measuring intelligence: his own experiences, an essay by David Owen, a book by Theodore Sizer, and an interview with a high school guidance counselor. In his journal, Russell had his reflections on some passages from Owen, a summary of Sizer's main points, and notes from his interview. As he looked through his material, he began to formulate a preliminary argument in his mind. He decided to write down some ideas.

Tests are useful to measure achievement, but not real knowledge and not creativity. Students learn to take tests throughout high school. These help to standardize what students learn. But in the end tests measure the ability to take tests. Real knowledge is something different. What is real knowledge? I know what it isn't: It isn't memorizing facts and separating ideas from other ideas. It has something to do with putting ideas together, and being able to come up with new ideas, ones that you aren't taught, but that you think of in response to what happens to you in the world.

Expanding the Context

Russell's question—What is real knowledge?—stood out for him in the passage that he wrote. When the guidance counselor had asked him the same question, he couldn't answer. But without some definition of knowledge, he knew he couldn't make a successful argument about what tests can or cannot measure. He couldn't assume that he and his readers would share a definition of knowledge.

Russell spent some time in the library one morning and came up with a fifth source, an essay by Loren Eiseley, an anthropologist and a poet, who wrote about a special kind of learning that he encountered from unexpected teachers. Eiseley's essay helped Russell to think about the whole idea of knowledge.

Opportunities for Reflecting

1. Read Loren Eiseley's essay "The Hidden Teacher" on page 423 of the Sourcebook. Annotate Eiseley's text as you read it. What is Eiseley's argument? What does Eiseley learn from the spider? How do Eiseley's other examples of hidden teachers expand and complicate what he has learned from the spider? Reflect on these questions in your journal.

2. Eiseley writes that he "once received an unexpected lesson from a spider." Write a letter to Eiseley telling him about some unexpected lessons and hidden teachers in your life. What lessons did you learn?

Opportunities for Exploring Connections

1. Imagine a conversation between Eiseley and Sizer. What ideas about learning do they share? How would Eiseley respond to Sizer's observations about high school education? How would Sizer respond

to Eiseley's ideas about hidden teachers? Discuss these questions with your classmates.

2. Read June Jordan's essay "Nobody Mean More to Me Than You and the Future Life of Willie Jordan" on page 445 of the Sourcebook and Claude Steele's essay "Race and the Schooling of Black Americans" on page 477 of the Sourcebook. How would Steele respond to Jordan's essay? How would Jordan respond to Steele's essay? Imagine a conversation between Jordan and Steele. Discuss with your classmates the connections you find between Jordan's and Steele's essays.

Supporting a Claim

After he thought about his five sources, Russell felt that he was ready to begin writing an argumentative essay about the issue of measuring intelligence. He believed that there was a difference between acquiring information and acquiring knowledge. Information can be tested; knowledge cannot be tested. These ideas formed the basis for his argument.

Russell's plan for his essay included the four major components of an argument.

- A claim
- Evidence to support the claim
- Definition of key terms
- Consideration of counterarguments

Russell's claim, that information can be tested, but knowledge cannot, was the conclusion that he drew after considering five sources and reflecting on the connections between them. His evidence came from his own experiences, his conversation with a high school guidance counselor, the research that David Owen conducted for his article about the SAT, Theodore Sizer's study of American high schools, and Loren Eiseley's essay about learning in contexts outside of traditional schools. Most of his sources agreed with one another about the purpose of testing and the difference between testing information and knowledge. But when Russell interviewed the guidance counselor, he came away with some ideas about counterarguments that could be leveled against his own claim. He also came away from that interview with a clear idea about the key terms that he had to define.

Engaging Readers

When you create an argumentative essay, your aim is to directly affect your reader's thinking about a particular issue. Sometimes you may be urging reform. But just as often, you may urge readers to think about an issue in a new way, to realize that an issue they may have considered not controversial is, in fact, something about which individuals can argue and debate.

Your particular focus will be clarified when you consider your purpose and the needs of your readers. K. C. Cole, for example, published her essay in the "Hers" column of the *New York Times,* where women writers are invited to air their opinions about many issues. These writers frequently take a feminist point of view. How might Cole's essay be received if she read it to physicists at a scientific conference?

After you have completed a draft of an argument essay, your peer readers may help you evaluate your assumptions and your reasoning. Here are some questions that you may want to ask of readers:

Questions for Peer Readers

- Do you understand why I am arguing about this issue? Do you understand the context for this essay?
- Is my position clear early in the essay?
- Have I clearly distinguished any points I want to make?
- Do I have strong evidence to support those points? What sources have I used to build my argument? To what experts do I refer? Are these experts persuasive?
- Are there any stated or unstated assumptions that weaken the argument?
- Is my argument free from flaws in reasoning?
- Have I considered any counterarguments?
- Is my argument organized logically?
- Is it technically correct?

Russell asked these questions of peer readers after he had completed a first draft of his essay. He went through two more drafts before he was satisfied with the result. The essay that follows shows Russell's progress from his first piece of writing, "Russell in Numberland," through the thinking, reading, and writing that resulted in a coherent argument.

What Do Tests Test?

Russell Thompson

On the first day of kindergarten, I and my fellow students sat in a large circle and memorized each other's names. On the second, we colored in pretty little drawings of house and home. On the third day of kindergarten we conducted standardized testing routines to determine our placement in the class. The way it worked was simple: You stood in front of the teacher and counted as high as you could. Then the teacher put your name under a number posted on big signs that hung from left to right across the room. Those students on the right were good; fate smiled upon them. Those on the left, however, were destined to work at McDonald's for all perpetuity. 1

The third day of kindergarten was the first time I was tested, but not the last. Since then I have been tested on my ability to memorize fifteen spelling words a week from grades one through six; the capitals of each state in the United States; the imports and exports of each African nation; and the abbreviation of each element in the periodic table. 2

I have taken midterms, finals, pretests and retests. I have had pop quizzes and take-home exams. I even have been tested on my ability to broad jump and do push-ups. I have never taken a course in which I was not tested, and I must admit that I usually do fairly well on these tests. I admit also that I am a very poor speller (thank spell-check for this essay); have no idea what the capital of Ohio, Montana, or Alabama is; could probably not even name each African nation, let alone their imports and exports; and have no recollection of the elements, except for a few, such as oxygen and hydrogen and, mysteriously, lead. I have learned, however, how to take tests. That ability, in my view, is all that tests measure. Tests do not measure real knowledge. 3

Real knowledge is something different from the facts I learn to pass tests. I don't remember state capitals or the abbreviations of elements because this information doesn't have anything to do with the way I live my life each day. To pass the test of daily living, I need another kind of knowledge. I need to know how to get along with people. I need to know some survival skills, such as how to recognize danger and how to find my way around in a strange city. When I have to earn my own living, I will need some professional skills for whatever career I choose. Most important, though, I need to have a sense of values: What's important in life, what purpose does my life have, how can I make some contribution to the world? This kind of knowledge cannot reveal itself through a test. 4

Tests, as David Owen writes in his essay about the Scholastic Aptitude 5
Test, "are written by people who tend to think in certain predictable ways." That, it seems to me, is the reason why tests don't reflect real knowledge. Real knowledge is the ability to respond to unpredictable circumstances. It's the ability to invent a solution to a problem that you've never seen before because you can put ideas together in new ways.

Students who do well on tests learn how to anticipate a predictable 6
kind of thinking. Multiple choice tests, like the SAT, are of course easier to predict than an open-ended essay examination. As Owen shows, the correct answer on a standardized test is usually "drab, humorless, and plodding." If the student wants to think creatively, he's bound to get it wrong.

Tests like the SAT are well prepared for by high schools. Rote, repetition, 7
and memorization are the tasks students do in many courses, from languages to math to science. Theodore Sizer describes a biology class in which students are told that they will be tested on the names of several laboratory specimens that are set out in the classroom. The students apparently have no interest in the specimens other than their use to help them pass the test. Next period, a French test is returned and each question and answer reviewed for most of the period. There will be another test the next day.

As Sizer notes, there is little opportunity for students to put all this 8
information in any context, to pull it all together in any way. We learn biology as separate from math or literature, and English as separate from French or biology. We never learn that there are ideas that cross these disciplines. We never really learn about ideas at all. How would they be tested?

Instead, we have to memorize "facts." "The subjects come at a student 9
. . . in random order," Sizer tells us, "a kaleidoscope of worlds: algebraic formulae to poetry to French verbs to Ping-Pong to the War of Spanish Succession, all before lunch. Pupils are to pick up these things. Tests measure whether the picking up has been successful." We need to question Sizer's use of the word *successful* here. I and many of my classmates could manage to "pick up these things" for a short time, and the tests measured this ability. But the tests did not measure what we really learned, if we define learning in a broader way.

Schools defend tests as a way to standardize curriculum and motivate 10
students. Would students in biology really care about laboratory work if they didn't have a test to measure what they know or don't know? Maybe not, if my own experience is typical. But why should they care? Tests defend a curriculum that in itself may need to be reformed. Tests defend the segregation of subjects, but students live in the real world and know that economics, history, math, literature, and science come together in many

ways. You only have to read the daily newspaper to see connections. Only in school are things separated from each other and from life.

In his essay "The Hidden Teacher," Loren Eiseley argues that there is something more to knowledge than just knowing facts, and that there is another kind of learning, one that transcends and makes sense of all our other experience. This other type of learning comes through what he calls the hidden teacher. This hidden teacher can occur in unexpected places: in fields or woods, in a shopping center, or even in dreams. This teacher helps us to understand ourselves in relation to our world. 11

Eiseley would not deny the importance of traditional education or conclude that it is all useless. But learning "facts," such as Sizer shows us occurs in high school, accomplishes little if it only points a person inward. Most conventional fact-knowledge is learned from conventional teachers, Eiseley says, but the transcendent insights that make sense of all these disparate facts can come only by grace of a natural revelation. 12

The kind of knowledge that Eiseley is writing about cannot be tested. When I first read Eiseley's essay, I found it difficult to understand what he really meant by knowledge, because he seemed to be describing a mystical or even religious experience in his encounter with spiders, oceans, and galaxies. Eiseley, unlike the people who write the SAT, does not think in predictable ways. When I read his anecdote about encountering a spider and learning from it, I thought he meant that true knowledge was a kind of epiphany that made everything suddenly clear in a moment of happy revelation. 13

As I reconsidered what he said, however, I saw that he meant something quite different. Learning does not happen passively. Instead, learning must be a process that builds upon itself where each new bit of information is seen to complicate and comment on what came before. Only by reflection and effort does real knowledge come. Every time we "get" a joke, for example, we have made some connection between two ideas that we held as entirely separate or incongruous, and that are now related, even if the relation is absurd. 14

As Sizer illustrates in his essay, high school is a place where barriers are erected between ideas that are labeled as "subjects." But real learning is the breaking down of such barriers to discover what ideas have in common. Eiseley sends us out into the world to ask questions of what we see and encounter. He tells us that just as a spider perceives, wrongly, that it is the center of its small world, we humans tend to think that as well, and therefore are limited in what we can understand. Testing only reinforces the idea that there is one way to learn, and one body of information to master. It does not reflect creative thinking, the ability to put ideas together in new ways, or the ability to have a thought that no one has ever had before. 15

Testing, as I have experienced it, only tells me what I can remember for a short time, sometimes even so short as overnight. It does not reflect my ability to consider what Eiseley calls the "formidable riddles" of life. It does not reflect my real knowledge.

Opportunities for Exchanging Ideas

1. Discuss Russell's essay in class. What is his claim? What kind of evidence does he present to support his claim? How persuasive is his evidence? What counterarguments does he present? What strategies does he use to engage his readers?

2. In small groups, discuss how you would argue against Russell's argument and what counterarguments you could present to him.

3. Read Rachel Manalili's essay "Learning the Alphabet" on page 500 and David Gray's essay "Dulcis Est Sapientia" on page 491 of the Sourcebook. What arguments about learning are these students making? What kind of evidence do they offer to support their argument? Do they define their terms? What counterarguments could you present to them to refute their arguments? Discuss these questions and these essays with your classmates.

Opportunities for Writing

In the following sequence you are being asked to think and explore the very general question of *what it means to learn,* and from these explorations develop a position about learning and education that you can argue.

1. Begin by describing a time in your life when you felt you really learned something. Make this description vivid; make it immediate. Give your readers a sense of why this experience was so important to you.

Then, reflect and describe a time in your life when you really wanted to learn something, but didn't or couldn't for whatever reasons. Develop this experience so that your readers know why it continues to stay with you.

Next, read these descriptions together and explore the connections that you see. What thought-provoking ideas reside beneath the surface details you remembered and selected? How do these two descriptions connect and comment on each other? What ideas do you see in your own descriptions that will help you think about the nature of learning?

2. Select one of the essays from the Sourcebook section "Questioning Ways of Learning." What is the argument in this essay? What is the writer's position? What evidence does the writer use to support his or her argument? Select key sentences and passages that show the writer's thinking. Write a counterargument to the argument in this essay.

3. Select two of the essays about learning from the Sourcebook. Create a conversation between any two of these writers and yourself. You are the leading figure in this conversation. As you write, let your questions and comments set the tone. Let your experiences speak to their ideas. The goal of this conversation is not only to find common ground with these writers but also to find controversies, paradoxes, and questions left unanswered. What terms do you need to define? What counterarguments would these writers offer to you? In writing your conversation, you should feel comfortable quoting these writers, allowing them to use their own words, and letting them talk for themselves when necessary.

4. Now it is time to write an argumentative essay in which you take a stand and support your position. You have been thinking and exploring your own ideas about learning and education. The various sources you have read have helped you define, clarify, and expand your thinking. The previous exercises and reflections will serve you well as preliminary drafts of your thinking. Write your argumentative essay supporting your ideas about learning. Use sources to support and expand your ideas. Remember to define your terms and consider the necessary counterarguments.

Arguing a Position: Questions for Peer Review

1. What is the writer's organizing idea? Summarize for the writer what you think this organizing idea is. How does the writer introduce this idea? How does the writer develop and expand this idea? Mark words, sentences, and passages that you find particularly effective in conveying the writer's idea.

2. Does the writer offer effective and persuasive evidence to support his or her argument? Indicate what pieces of evidence seem particularly strong and what pieces could be strengthened. Does the writer integrate sources so that they work together to support his or her argument?

3. What assumptions is the writer making? Are there any stated or unstated assumptions that weaken the argument?

(continued)

4. Has the writer considered the necessary counterarguments? Offer the writer some counterarguments that he or she might not have considered.

5. Read carefully and see if you notice any flaws in the writer's reasoning. Does the writer overgeneralize or beg the question?

6. Is the writer's argument organized logically? Can you suggest any changes in the organization?

7. Where in the essay has the writer said anything that is confusing or unclear to you? Show the writer where you think more details are needed.

8. How has the writer shown up in the essay? How do words and sentence rhythms reveal the voice of the writer?

9. How does the introduction pull you into the writer's argument? After reading the entire draft, is there anything confusing or unnecessary about the introduction? Is there anything you might suggest adding or deleting?

10. How does the writer's conclusion pull together the entire essay? How might the conclusion be more effective?

Annotate the writer's draft by commenting on its strengths and weaknesses. Ask the writer questions. Write a letter in which you offer your honest, careful, and generous comments and suggestions for revising.

CHAPTER 9

Analyzing Texts

You may be familiar with the word *text*, meaning a body of printed words: a poem, short story, novel, or essay. Lincoln's "Gettysburg Address" is a text, and so are the lyrics to the latest top-ten single. But in the world of scholarship, a text can refer to pictorial or graphic material: photographs, cartoons, paintings, and films. A text may even be an object: a piece of sculpture, perhaps, or a building. A text can be summarized—you can describe its properties and tell what it is about; and a text can be analyzed—its elements may be broken down and examined so that you can offer some interpretation about its meaning or significance.

When you offer that interpretation, you are, of course, taking a position or putting forth an argument. Analysis is not an end in itself; when you write an analytical essay, you really are writing an argumentative essay. But analysis poses some special challenges for the writer. In this chapter, we'll consider some of those challenges and look at strategies that you can use to meet them.

WHAT ANALYSIS MEANS

In all disciplines, you will have to analyze texts, responding to them intellectually, emotionally, and sometimes aesthetically. Analysis helps you see how a text evokes those responses.

Sometimes you may resist the idea of analyzing a text, believing that analysis interferes with or dilutes your first intense reaction. Analysis may seem dry and intellectualized, while emotional responses feel exciting and authentic. But analysis also can be satisfying because it allows you to experience a text on yet another level. It allows you to go beyond a superficial reading of a text and to explore the sources for your feelings and responses. Analysis does not lead you away from your intuitive responses, but asks that you trust your intuitions and interests as you formulate questions about texts.

When you first look at a text, it may appear to be daunting and impenetrable. If it is written text, it appears as a self-contained unit of words that conveys meaning. Once you understand that meaning—that is, once you can summarize or paraphrase the text—what else can you say about it? What kinds of questions can you pose about a text after you have asked "What does it mean?" What about a text can you possibly analyze? Let's look at a short text, a poem by Adrienne Rich, and see what analysis means.

Power

Living   in the earth-deposits   of our history

Today a backhoe divulged   out of a crumbling flank of earth
one bottle   amber   perfect   a hundred-year old
cure for fever   or melancholy   a tonic
for living on this earth   in the winters of this climate

Today I was reading about Marie Curie:
she must have known she suffered   from radiation sickness
her body bombarded for years   by the element
she had purified
It seems she denied to the end
the source of the cataracts on her eyes
the cracked and suppurating skin   of her finger-ends
till she could no longer hold   a test-tube or pencil

She died   a famous woman   denying
her wounds
denying
her wounds   came   from the same source as her power

When you first read this poem, you come away with a general sense of its meaning: the beginning of the poem tells you about the unearthing of a hundred-year-old bottle; the rest of the poem reflects on Marie Curie's radiation sickness. Analysis, however, asks you to go beyond this general summary to ask specific questions about the theme of the poem and about how the poem conveys its meaning.

What Is the Text About?

Any text tells you about something. When someone asks, "What is the movie about?" or "What is the novel about?" you know that you are being asked to recount the plot. When someone asks, "What is that painting about?" you know you are being asked to tell what the subject of the painting is. What is Adrienne Rich's poem about?

Its title tells you that it is about power, a word that carries many connotations. Reading the poem carefully will reveal to you why Adrienne Rich chose this particular title for her poem. When you read a text carefully, you might find yourself stopping after each unit of thought—sometimes one sentence, sometimes several sentences; because a poem is a special kind of literary text that contains lines and stanzas rather than sentences, you may read several lines before coming to the end of a unit of thought. Reading a text carefully line by line is called *close reading*. Paraphrasing these lines helps you to make sense of the meaning of the text.

Rich divides her poem into units of thought that are not punctuated in conventional ways. Instead of punctuation, she separates ideas by using spaces between groups of words, and she separates related lines by putting spaces between them.

The opening line of the poem serves to set up the context for the rest of the poem. The first word, *living,* can be a verb form (present participle or gerund) or an adjective: What effect does each part of speech have on the meaning of the line? Rich refers to *our history.* What is this history to which she refers: each one's personal history, or a common history that all humans share?

The next four lines complete a unit of thought. An object was found buried in the "earth-deposits" that are mentioned in the first line. Rich tells us that the bottle contained a tonic that could cure fever or melancholy. The last two stanzas of the poem refer to Marie Curie, the Polish-French chemist whose work with radioactivity won her two Nobel Prizes. Curie suffered from ailments caused by her work with radiation. Her power as a scientist resulted from these discoveries; but these discoveries also resulted in her death.

In this poem, Rich unearths two "artifacts" from our past: a bottle and a famous scientist. By writing a summary paraphrasing this poem, you can begin to unearth Rich's meaning. Here is one student's summary of "Power."

In her poem, Adrienne Rich thinks about power. She looks at two images from the past: a hundred year old bottle that contained some patent medicine, and Marie Curie, whose work with radiation caused her death. Rich tells us that the medicine was taken for common ailments such as fever or depression. She

> says that such medicines were taken for the problems we encounter in our daily lives. Marie Curie discovered radiation, which is a more powerful agent than patent medicines. Radiation caused many serious ailments in Curie, and eventually caused her death. Curie could not admit, however, that the same thing that gave her power as a scientist was the agent that was killing her.

This student's summary reflects her close reading of the poem. She includes those details that she thinks are most important to answer the question, "What is this poem about?"

What Is the Meaning?

Discovering what a text is about is not the same as discovering what point the text is trying to make. The point, or *meaning*, of the text is sometimes harder to discover.

Recounting the plot of a film doesn't usually convey the point of the film. A film may be about the Vietnam War; it may recount battles and the tedium of the soldiers' lives. But the filmmaker's point may be to communicate the idea of the senselessness of war. The point, or meaning, of the text is something that you, as a viewer, need to figure out.

In the Sourcebook you'll find a short story by William Carlos Williams about a physician's encounter with a little girl who turns out to have diphtheria. Williams' purpose in writing the story was not merely to document an event, but to make a point. When you, as a reader, conclude what that point is, you've begun to analyze the story.

Your conclusion about the meaning of a text will depend on your own background and experiences. A text is a place where writer and reader meet, bringing to the text their assumptions, values, and interests. How a text affects you, what it communicates to you, depends on who you are.

When trying to find the meaning of a text, you'll find it useful to ask some of these questions:

1. What is the problem or question that motivates the author?

2. From what context is the author writing?

3. What assumptions does the author bring to the text? What assumptions does the author make about his or her readers?

4. What argument is the author putting forth?

5. Are there contradictions in the text? If so, why are they there? How do they affect your understanding of the main point of the text?

6. What evidence does the author use to support his or her assertions? What effect does that evidence have on you?

7. What is the key moment or passage in the text? What makes it so important? How does this part of the text relate to the rest of the work?

8. What does this text say about the way people behave or about the forces that affect people? What is the author's point of view about people?

9. Is there anything about the text that disturbs you or makes you uncomfortable? In what ways can you explain this feeling?

10. How does the text speak to your own experience? Has anything happened to you that might support or qualify the ideas that are presented in the text?

These questions can help you understand the message that the author of the text wants to convey to readers or viewers.

After you summarize any text, go back to the text with questions that you think may help you discover its meaning. Keeping a double-entry notebook or making notes in a journal will help you to organize responses as you reread the text. One student reread Adrienne Rich's poem, stopping after each unit of thought, and came up with the following questions:

1. What does Rich mean by "our history": Does she mean each one's personal history, or the history of the human race, or both?
2. What kind of "cure" was in the bottle? I read once that patent medicines contained mostly alcohol. How was alcohol used as a cure for fevers and depression? Maybe its ability to cure really was in the heads of the people who used it. They wanted it to be a cure and so it was. They gave the medicine whatever power it had.
3. Marie Curie discovered radiation, which is used as a cure for cancer. She became really famous because of it. She wasn't able to admit that the same source that gave her so much power as a

scientist could be the thing that was destroying her. Maybe Rich is saying that something we think is powerful can also be destructive?

How Does the Text Communicate?

Adrienne Rich's poem is a text with a special form. It has 17 lines of different length, broken up into four stanzas, one of which is only one line long. Many lines are interrupted by spaces. There is no punctuation. The poem is narrated by a speaker who refers to itself as "I" and seems to be speaking directly to the reader.

When you analyze a text, you need to ask yourself how the structure or language of the text is significant in conveying the meaning. Does the fact that Rich's poem has 17 lines help her to make her point? Does the lack of punctuation help convey the meaning? How does the particular language that Rich uses—her choice of verbs, nouns, and adjectives—help us understand what the poem is about?

When you are examining ways in which a text communicates, you might ask these questions:

1. What is the basic form or structure of this text? Can you relate this text to other texts that you have read before?

2. How does the structure relate to the meaning of the text?

3. How can you account for recurring images, ideas, words, or situations in the text? What relationship do these items have to the meaning of the text?

4. Do any words, images, or sentence patterns disturb you or seem strange to you? Why?

5. Are there words that carry with them *connotations,* or meanings beyond the dictionary definition? How do these connotations affect your understanding of the meaning of the text?

One student reading Rich's poem became interested in the way Rich used spaces to introduce an unexpected use of language. In the second line, she has a backhoe *divulging* something. *Divulge* usually means to reveal a secret, but backhoes do not have that capacity. They can dig things up but not tell us what the things are. Still, the space after the word *divulged* makes us think about how unusual the word is in the context of the poem.

The word *tonic* ends line 4, leaving us with the expectation that we will discover another ailment for the medicine in the bottle. But line 5 tells us that the tonic was a remedy for *living on this earth.* Living is not ordinarily considered to be an ailment, like fever or melancholy, and because Rich begins a line with this phrase, she emphasizes its importance.

Although this student noticed something interesting about Rich's poem, merely writing about Rich's use of spacing is not enough to provide an analysis. Commenting on spacing is useful only if it helps readers understand how the text communicates its meaning. How, this student must ask, does Rich's use of spacing help her to convey her ideas about power? How can observations about language or structure be placed in the context of what the poem means?

Here are a few paragraphs from a draft that Tanya Jordan wrote as she tried to relate her observations about structure to her thoughts about "Power."

In "Power," Adrienne Rich tells us that we ourselves give power to things that affect us. A hundred years ago, we might use patent medicines to cure fevers or depression. But since these medicines were really mostly alcohol, they got their power from our own desire to be cured.

Sometimes we want something to be powerful and therefore will not admit that the force can be destructive, too. Marie Curie was killed by the radiation that she discovered, but she could not admit that this force could be deadly because it was the source of so much of her power.

One way Rich shows that our minds influence our expectations is the way she structures the poem. For example, she uses a word that has a certain connotation, then surprises us by following that word with a phrase that changes its meaning. Our expectations are not met, and we are startled. In line 2, for example, the word *divulged* means *revealed secrets.* But Rich tells us that it was a backhoe, a machine, that divulged something; and it divulged not a secret, but an old amber bottle. Similarly, when she tells us that the bottle contained a tonic, we expect that in the next line we will find out what the tonic was supposed to cure. Then she tells us that the tonic was "for living on this earth." Again, she is showing us that what we anticipate affects our reading of the poem.

Opportunities for Exchanging Ideas

1. Reread Adrienne Rich's poem "Power" on page 200. What problem or question do you think intrigues Rich? What argument is she putting forth about power? What is for you the key moment or passage in this text? What questions do you want to ask about this poem? Discuss Rich's poem and these questions with your classmates.

2. A text is a place where writer and reader meet, bringing to the text their assumptions, values, and interests. Reread Tanya Jordan's draft on page 205. What assumptions and interests is Tanya bringing to her reading of Rich's poem? What questions might you want to ask Tanya? How might you want to argue with her analysis? How might you want to extend it? Discuss Tanya's draft and these questions with your classmates.

STRATEGIES FOR QUESTIONING TEXTS

In the following pages, you'll find questions to ask when analyzing specific kinds of texts: nonfiction, fiction or drama, poetry, and art. These questions can help you to discover *what the text is about, what its meaning is, and how it communicates to readers.*

Analyzing Nonfiction

In a government course, you may read The Declaration of Independence. In a history course, you may read Thomas Paine's *Common Sense.* In a psychology course, you may read Freud's *Interpretation of Dreams.* You may summarize the main points of each of these texts, but you also may go beyond a summary to focus on a key passage and discuss its importance to the rest of the text. You may examine ways that the author's social and economic status, religious beliefs, or philosophical background informed the text. You may point out contradictions in the text that disturb you. These methods of analysis will enable you to discuss the text and enhance its meaning for you and your readers.

Throughout this textbook, as you read about ways to create, revise, and respond to essays, you are learning how to analyze works of nonfiction. Here are some questions you may consider for analyzing nonfiction:

1. Meaning

   - What is this text about?
   - What is the author's central point?

- Where does the author express the organizing idea of the text?
- What problem or question does the author consider?

2. Audience
   - Who is the author addressing?
   - What is the relationship between the author and the reader?
   - What assumptions does the author make about the reader?

3. Purpose
   - Why has the author created this text?
   - To what extent does the author want to change the reader's way of thinking or acting?

4. Style
   - What is the author's tone in this text? Casual? Conversational? Didactic? Distant? How does the tone relate to the meaning of the text?
   - What words, phrases, or images recur throughout this text? How are these important in conveying the meaning or fulfilling the author's purpose?
   - What strategies—description, narration, and dialogue, for example—does the author use in this text? How do these strategies help to convey the meaning of the text?

Analyzing Fiction or Drama

In an American literature course, you may be asked to analyze a short story by Willa Cather, a novel by Richard Wright, a play by Eugene O'Neill. What are the ways that you can analyze these works?

No analysis can focus on everything in a single text. Your readers will not expect you to comment on plot, setting, characters, theme, and style in a single essay. Yet any of these items may interest you as you write an analysis. As you read and reread a work of fiction or drama, think about ways in which you are responding to that work. What seems important to you? Are you drawn to a particular character? Does one scene seem especially powerful? Are you interested in a problem that the author presents to the characters? Are you interested in ways that the author has created a realistic sense of place or time? Your initial responses will serve as a guide in focusing an analysis.

Here are some questions you may consider as you analyze fiction or drama:

1. Plot

   - What is the story told in this text?
   - What happens?
   - How are events arranged?
   - How are events related to one another?
   - What are the most significant events? Why are they significant?

2. Characters

   - Who are the *protagonists*, or main characters, in this text?
   - What personality traits do they exhibit?
   - What happens to them? Do they change? If so, how?
   - How do the characters relate to one another?
   - To what extent are the characters realistic? Stereotypical?
   - What do the characters learn?
   - How do the characters confront their problems or conflicts?
   - How does the author make you care about the characters?

3. Setting

   - Where does the action take place?
   - What is the social, cultural, and historical context for the story?
   - To what extent is setting important in this text?
   - How does the setting relate to the plot?
   - How does the setting affect the characters?
   - How does the author create a sense of place? Of time? Of social context?

4. Point of view

   - Who is narrating the story?
   - Does the narrator have an *omniscient*, or complete, point of view, knowing everything about every character? Or does the narrator have a limited point of view? How does the narrator affect the telling of the story?
   - How reliable is the narrator?
   - How objective is the narrator?
   - What is the narrator's relation to the author?
   - What is the narrator's tone: serious, flippant, angry, ironic . . . ?

5. Meaning
   - What is the central idea of this text?
   - What problems does the author present in the text?
   - What issues does the author consider?
   - How does the text communicate the meaning? What elements—plot, characters, setting, dialogue, narration—are most important in setting forth the meaning?

6. Style
   - What particular stylistic strategies do you notice about this text: word choice, imagery, sentence structure? Why are they significant?
   - How does the author's style help you to understand the story or respond to the meaning?
   - What images recur throughout the text? How are they important?

Analyzing Poetry

In a course on modern poetry, you may encounter a poem by Nikki Giovanni or William Carlos Williams. You may examine the structure of that poem; you may focus on Williams' choice of imagery, or you may decide to look at recurring elements in the poem. You may place the poem in the context of other works by Williams or by some of his contemporaries. You may compare the poem that he wrote with others of a similar theme. All these tasks ask you to go beyond a summary or *close reading* of the poem, where you are aiming to understand *what* the text tells us. Analysis tells you *how* the text works.

Here are some elements you may decide to explore as you analyze a poem:

1. Voice
   - Who is the speaker in the poem? Is it the poet or someone else?
   - What is the speaker's point of view?
   - To whom is the speaker addressing this poem?

2. Meaning
   - What is the main idea of the poem?
   - What point does the poet want to make?
   - What problem or issue is the poet addressing?

3. Form
    - Does the poem fit into a prescribed form, such as sonnet, ode, elegy, haiku? If so, to what extent does it conform to the requirements of this form of poetry?
    - Does the poem have stanzas? How do the stanzas help to develop the meaning?
    - How do variations in form (length of stanzas or lines and breaks in lines, for example) relate to the meaning of the poem?
4. Sound
    - How do the sounds of the poem convey the meaning?
    - What sounds are important in this poem? Which are repeated or emphasized? Why?
    - Does the poem rhyme? Is rhyme significant in this poem? If so, why?
5. Meter
    - Does the poem have a regular meter?
    - What is the effect of the meter on your response to the poem?
    - How does the meter help to convey meaning?
6. Language
    - What particular words, phrases, or figures of speech are significant in this poem?
    - How does the language used by the poet help to convey the meaning of the poem?
    - What images recur? Why?
    - How does the poet use *similes* and *metaphors*, two kinds of analogy.
    - To what extent does the poet use language symbolically: that is, words or images will stand for other ideas? How does this symbolism help to convey the meaning of the poem?

Analyzing Works of Art

In an art history course, you may examine Picasso's *Guernica*. You may have a strong response to this violent and graphic painting. Why? What causes this kind of response? You may decide to analyze the *formal* elements in the painting—looking at line, shape, color, and texture—to see how these elements work to produce an effect. You may decide to place the painting in historical context or in the context of Picasso's other works. You may decide to look at other works of art with a theme of social protest.

Here are some elements that you may decide to look at if you are analyzing a work of art:

1. Context
   - When and where was this work created?
   - What purpose did it serve?
   - To what audience is this work addressed?
   - Who was the creator of this work? What biographical information helps you to understand this work?
2. Subject
   - What kind of work is this (for example, portrait, landscape, statue, monument, frieze, urn)?
   - What is the subject of the work?
   - What medium did the creator use?
   - What size is the work?
3. Composition
   - What is the effect of light in this work?
   - What is the effect of color?
   - What is the effect of space and arrangement?
   - What is the creator's angle of vision?
4. Meaning
   - What effect does this work have on you?
   - What elements of design, color, medium, or form evoke this effect?

Opportunity for Reflecting

Select one of the essays in the Sourcebook. Read the essay carefully and closely. Use your journal to answer the questions on pages 206–207 for analyzing nonfiction. Let these questions lead you to asking questions of your own. What puzzles you about this essay?

Opportunity for Writing

Keith Carter, an East Texas photographer, tells his viewers that he is interested in anything that glows—images that seem to have an inner light. On a wall in his darkroom in Beaumont, Texas, Carter has tacked the following saying: "Try to make pictures that are something rather than about something and try to make images that are wise rather than clever."*

Look closely at the photograph by Carter shown on page 213. What do you see? What kind of image has Carter created? What effect does the photograph have upon you? What elements of design create this effect? See how the questions on pages 209–210 for analyzing works of art can help you think about the meaning of this photograph. What are the multiple meanings that the photograph embodies? Write a brief analysis of this photograph.

STRATEGIES FOR ANALYZING TEXTS

The purpose of writing an analytical essay is not to prove to your readers that you have read the text attentively or looked at a work of art carefully, but to illuminate the text, to place the text in a context, and to communicate your discoveries about the text.

You already may have experience analyzing texts in a casual way. Whenever you read a political cartoon, for example, you have to place that text within a context or you could not understand it. If you have not read news reports about the event or situation that is being satirized, the cartoon would not convey its meaning to you. You are bringing to that text, the cartoon, a background that enhances its meaning.

The term *enhancement* may, in fact, more accurately describe the process of writing about texts than the term *analysis*. When you enhance a text, you explain it, you may find a subtext, you may bring background information to bear upon the text, you may compare it with other texts, you may place it within a context, you may use the text to prove a larger thesis. You may dissect it and examine one part of it: a single character from a novel or the climactic scene from a play, perhaps. When you ask questions about the text, the answers you find enlarge your understanding.

* *Texas Monthly*, January 1992, Vol. 20, Issue 1.

George Washington by Keith Carter.

In Chapter 7, you learned some strategies for questioning sources. Those strategies will be useful in analyzing texts, and we will look at them again in this chapter.

At first, when you approach a text, you may feel that it is an offering made by an artist or writer for you to admire. But texts invite your active participation in order to understand them fully. Analyzing does not destroy the integrity of a text; it makes the text richer.

Summarizing the Text

No matter what text you are going to analyze, it's a good strategy to begin by summarizing. Sometimes texts are hard to understand, and simply deciding what they are about is a difficult task. When you look at a painting by Salvador Dalí or Pablo Picasso, describing that painting may help you come to some understanding about its subject or theme. Describing a work of art involves summarizing its details. When you read a short story by Flannery O'Connor or a play by William Shakespeare, summarizing that work helps you to focus on the main characters and the basic plot.

With short texts such as poems, your summary may be longer than the text itself because you will have to fill in information. Here, for example, is a three-line poem by Matsu Basho, a seventeenth century Japanese poet, followed by one student's summary:

Old pond
leap-splash
a frog.

Summary:
In the silence of still water comes a sudden splash that disturbs the pond's unbroken mirrorlike surface. Ripples move in widening circles that slowly subside until once again tranquility reigns.

The student extends the image of the three elliptical lines so that they form a prose description of the basic action of the poem. This summary, however, is only the first step to a real analysis. An analysis usually includes a summary—you do want your reader to know what you are referring to—but it goes beyond it.

Here is historian Roland Marchand in *Advertising the American*

Dream looking at advertisements that depict small-town America. First, he must give us a *summary* of a typical advertisement:

> Almost invariably, the idealized village contained a single spire that towered above the other buildings. In most cases, this spire was identifiable a a church steeple. In other cases, it was sufficiently indistinct to have been either a steeple or the spire of a town hall. In nearly every case, the houses of the town were grouped close together, with the steeple or spire roughly in the center. Almost never did another prominent building appear—except in close-up illustrations of the main street with its bank, general store, and perhaps a gas station and movie theater.

That summary merely conveys information given by the text. The details that Marchand includes here help the reader to visualize the advertisement, to see what Marchand sees. Marchand can use this summary as a reference when he begins to analyze and interpret the advertisement.

Opportunities for Writing and Exchanging Ideas

In the following pages, you'll find "Four Appointments with the Discus Thrower," an essay by Richard Selzer, a contemporary essayist who also happens to be a surgeon. In this essay, Selzer explores the relationship he had with one particular patient. Read Selzer's essay.

Four Appointments with the Discus Thrower

Richard Selzer

One

I spy on my patients. Ought not a doctor to observe his patients by any means and from any stance, that he might the more fully assemble the evidence? So I stand in the doorways of hospital rooms and gaze. Oh, it is not all that furtive an act. Those in bed need only look up in order to discover me. But they never do. 1

From the doorway of Room 542, the man in the bed seems deeply tanned. Blue eyes and close-cropped white hair give him the appearance of vigor and good health. But I know that his skin is not brown from the sun. It is rusted, rather, in the last stage of containing the vile repose within. And the blue eyes are frosted, looking inward like the windows of a snowbound cottage. This man is blind. This man is also legless—the right leg 2 missing from midthigh down, the left from just below the knee. It gives him the look of an ornamental tree, roots and branches pruned to the purpose that the thing should suggest a great tree but be the dwarfed facsimile thereof.

Propped on pillows, he cups his right thigh in both hands. Now and 3
then, he shakes his head as though acknowledging the intensity of his suffering. In all of this, he makes no sound. Is he mute as well as blind?

If he is in pain, why do I not see it in his face? Why is the mouth not 4
opened for shrieking? The eyes not spun skyward? Where are tears? He appears to be waiting for something, something that a blind man cannot watch for, but for which he is no less alert. He is listening.

The room in which he dwells is empty of all possessions—the get-well 5
cards, the small private caches of food, the day-old flowers, the slippers—all the usual kickshaws of the sickroom. There is only a bed, a chair, a nightstand, and a tray on wheels that can be swung across his lap for meals. It is a wild island upon which he has been cast. It is Room 542.

Two

"What time is it?" he asks. 6

"Three o'clock." 7

"Morning or afternoon?" 8

"Afternoon." 9

He is silent. There is nothing else he wants to know. Only that another 10
block of time has passed.

"How are you?" I say. 11

"Who is it?" he asks. 12

"It's the doctor. How do you feel?" 13

He does not answer right away. 14

"Feel?" he says. 15

"I hope you feel better," I say. 16

I press the button at the side of the bed. 17

"Down you go," I say. 18

"Yes, down," he says. 19

He falls back upon the bed awkwardly. His stumps, unweighted by 20
legs and feet, rise in the air, presenting themselves. I unwrap the bandages from the stumps, and begin to cut away the black scabs and the dead glazed fat with scissors and forceps. A shard of white bone comes loose. I pick it away. I wash the wounds with disinfectant and redress the stumps. All this while, he does not speak. What is he thinking behind those lids that do not blink? Is he remembering the burry prickle of love? A time when he was whole? Does he dream of feet? Of when his body was not a rotting log?

He lies solid and inert. In spite of everything, he remains beautiful, as though he were a sailor standing athwart a slanting deck. 21

"Anything more I can do for you?" I ask. 22

For a long moment he is silent. 23

"Yes," he says at last and without the least irony, "you can bring me a pair of shoes." 24

In the corridor, the head nurse is waiting for me. 25

"We have to do something about him," she says. "Every morning he orders scrambled eggs for breakfast, and instead of eating them, he picks up the plate and throws it against the wall." 26

"Throws his plate?" 27

"Nasty. That's what he is. No wonder his family doesn't come to visit. They probably can't stand him any more than we can." 28

She is waiting for me to do something. 29

"Well?" 30

"We'll see," I say. 31

Three

The next morning, I am waiting in the corridor when the kitchen delivers his breakfast. I watch the aide place the tray on the stand and swing it across his lap. She presses the button to raise the head of the bed. Then she leaves. 32

In this time, which he has somehow identified as morning, the man reaches to find the rim of the tray, then on to find the dome of the covered dish. He lifts off the cover and places it on the stand. He fingers across the plate until he probes the eggs. He lifts the plate in both of his hands, sets it on the palm of his right hand, centers it, balances it. He hefts it up and down slightly, getting the feel of it. Abruptly, he draws back his right arm as far as he can. 33

There is the crack of the plate breaking against the wall at the foot of his bed and the small wet sound of the scrambled eggs dropping to the floor. Just so does this man break his fast. 34

And then he laughs. It is a sound you have never heard. It is something new under the sun. 35

Out in the corridor the eyes of the head nurse narrow. 36

"Laughed, did he?" 37

She writes something down on her clipboard. 38

A second aide arrives, brings a second breakfast tray, puts it on the nightstand out of his reach. She looks over at me, shaking her head and making her mouth go. I see that we are to be accomplices. 39

"I've got to feed you," she says to the man. 40

"Oh, no you don't," the man says. 41

"Oh, yes I do," the aide says, "after what you just did. Nurse says so." 42

"Get me my shoes," the man says. 43

"Here's oatmeal," the aide says. "Open." And she touches the spoon 44
to his lower lip.

"I ordered scrambled eggs," says the man. 45

"That's right," the aide says. 46

I step forward. 47

"Is there anything I can do?" I say. 48

"Who are you?" the man asks. 49

Four

In the evening, I go once more to that ward to make my rounds. The 50
head nurse reports to me that Room 542 is deceased. She has discovered this quite by accident, she says. No, there had been no sound. Nothing. It's a blessing, she says.

I go into his room, a spy looking for secrets. He is still there in his bed. 51
His face is relaxed, grave, dignified, as the faces of the newly dead are. After a while, I turn to leave. My gaze sweeps the wall at the foot of the bed, and I see the place where it has been repeatedly washed, where the wall looks very clean and very white in contrast to the rest, which is dirty and gray.

---

1. Write a summary of "Four Appointments with the Discus Thrower" in no more than one page, using the strategies for summarizing that you learned in Chapter 7. How does your summary help you to understand the main idea of the essay? Compare your summary with the summaries of two of your classmates. How are they similar? How are they different?
2. Revise your summary by reducing your one page to a paragraph. Compare your paragraphs with those of your classmates.

Annotating the Text

Many texts are both elusive and allusive. They are *elusive* because they may hint at meanings that are not obvious or straightforward. Writers may use strategies such as metaphor or analogy that require interpretation. If the meaning of a text seems to elude you, annotating that text may help you to locate the parts that you need to think about.

Texts can also be *allusive;* that is, writers can refer to ideas, other texts, or cultural phenomena that they assume the reader will, but sometimes does not, share. Consider, for example, the following poem by William Carlos Williams.

Landscape with the Fall of Icarus

According to Brueghel
when Icarus fell
it was spring

a farmer was plowing
his field
the whole pageantry

of the year was
awake tingling
near

the edge of the sea
concerned
with itself
sweating in the sun
that melted
the wings' wax

unsignificantly
off the coast
there was

a splash quite unnoticed
this was
Icarus drowning

In this poem, Williams alludes to a painting by the Dutch painter Pieter Brueghel, *Landscape with the Fall of Icarus,* depicting the myth of Icarus, the boy who flew too close to the sun while wearing wings made of wax. The heat of the sun melted the wings, and Icarus drowned, punished for his folly. The painting takes a particular point of view about the myth by making the landscape and peasant figures more central than Icarus himself, who is seen only in a corner of the painting.

Unless you know these allusions to the myth and the painting about Icarus, you may not understand the full meaning of the poem.

Annotating the text where you perceive allusions helps you to know how much information you need to find out about a text in order to understand it.

Some texts, even if they appear to be straightforward, may elicit questions. You may wonder why the author chose to include certain details: What response are you supposed to have to those details? You may wonder why the author structured the text in a certain way: How does the structure affect the way you read and understand the text? You may wonder why the narrator takes a certain tone of voice: What relationship is the narrator trying to establish with the reader? Annotating a text can help you to question an author's choices and articulate your responses.

Here is one student's annotation of the first two paragraphs of Selzer's essay "Four Appointments with the Discus Thrower."

"Ought not a doctor"—What rights and privileges does a doctor have? What is Selzer telling us about this doctor and patient?

Why does a doctor need to spy? Selzer seems to want to tell us that doctors know a lot of secrets. What kind of evidence is Selzer looking for?

I spy on my patients. Ought not a doctor to observe his patients by any 1
means and from any stance, that he might the more fully assemble the evidence? So I stand in the doorways of hospital rooms and gaze. Oh, it is not all that furtive an act. Those in bed need only look up in order to discover me. But they never do.

From the doorway of Room 542, the man in the bed seems deeply 2
tanned. Blue eyes and close-cropped white hair give him the appearance of vigor and good health. But I know that his skin is not brown from the sun. It is rusted, rather, in the last stage of containing the vile repose within. And the blue eyes are frosted, looking inward like the windows of a snowbound cottage. This man is blind. This man is also legless—the right leg missing from midthigh down, the left from just below the knee. It gives him the look of an ornamental tree, roots and branches pruned to the purpose that the thing should suggest a great tree but be the dwarfed facsimile thereof.

Why does Selzer call him "the man in the bed"? Does the patient have a name? Ought not a doctor know his patient's name?

Look at the language and images Selzer uses to describe the patient. The patient's eyes are frosted—he looks like an ornamental tree—his skin is not suntanned, but brown from sickness. So Selzer deliberately contrasting images of health and the outdoors with the hospital room? What do these images say about the patient?

These annotations reflect places in the text that seemed particularly interesting, disturbing, or puzzling to the student. Annotations help you to formulate questions about the text that will aid you in discovering its meaning.

Opportunities for Reflecting

Reread "Four Appointments with the Discus Thrower." In your journal or in the margins of the text, annotate the whole essay. What about this story puzzles you? What questions do you have? What responses do you have to the information that Selzer presents to you? What responses do you have to the structure of the essay?

Questioning the Text

When you read a literary or artistic text, you may ask questions about the text that will help you to deepen your understanding of it. In Williams' poem, "Landscape with the Fall of Icarus," for example, you may wonder why the poet chose to use such short lines, why he chose three-line stanzas, why he did not use any punctuation. You may question his choice of words: *pageantry*, for example, or *tingling*. You may wonder who or what, in lines 11 and 12, is "concerned / with itself."

Questioning allows you to focus on specific parts of the text to see how they work in themselves and how they relate to the whole text.

The questions about analyzing fiction, nonfiction, poetry, and art on pages 206–211 suggest ways of exploring different kinds of texts. Your summaries and annotations will suggest additional questions specific to the text you are considering.

Here, for example, are some questions that one student asked about "Landscape with the Fall of Icarus."

1. What does Williams want us to feel in response to this poem?
2. What kinds of images does the poem contain? What effect do these images have?
3. Why is this landscape seen in the spring?
4. Why does Williams use many words that convey the idea of awakening?
5. Why does Williams break his stanzas where he does? How do these breaks affect our reading of the poem?

These questions helped the student to focus on ways that the text communicates its meaning to readers.

Opportunities for Reflecting

1. Reread the questions about analyzing nonfiction on pages 206–207. These questions will suggest some specific ways of thinking about essays. Your own summary and annotations of "Four Appointments with the Discus Thrower" will offer you a direction for your questions.

Use your journal to reflect and ask questions about "Four Appointments with the Discus Thrower." Let your questions lead you to specific passages that you want to read more closely and carefully.

2. Find a passage in Selzer's essay that you think holds the key to the meaning of the essay. Copy this passage in your journal. Ask yourself: How do I know that this passage reveals the meaning of the essay? How does this passage depend on other elements in the essay to give it depth and richness? Reflect on the meaning of this passage within the context of the entire essay.

Engaging the Author

In one of her poems, Emily Dickinson proclaims that she writes "a letter to the world" when she writes poetry. Anyone who creates a text sends it to a world of readers who may respond to it in very different ways. Your annotations and questions reflect your own responses to the text and can serve as a beginning to a conversation with the author. Engaging the author of the text is a useful strategy for helping you to define and focus your own responses to the particular work. Here is one student's letter to William Carlos Williams, responding to "Landscape with the Fall of Icarus."

Dear Mr. Williams:

I did not know about the myth of Icarus when I first was assigned your poem, but I don't think you necessarily need too many details of the myth to understand your meaning. The whole poem, after all, is not about Icarus, so much as it is about one painting about Icarus. I haven't ever seen this painting by Brueghel, and although I get an idea about it from your poem, I think I'd like to see a reproduction of it to know what it is you were looking at or thinking of as you wrote. Brueghel's painting, you tell us, looks at the myth in a special way.

The first three lines of your poem form a single sentence that would read as prose, "According to Brueghel, when Icarus fell it was spring." The main part of the sentence tells us that it was spring. The fact that Icarus fell is almost like an aside; it is incidental, and so you put it in a dependent clause, in the middle of the sentence, the part that is emphasized least.

The rest of the poem concerns the landscape, and it is only in the last stanza that we find out about "a splash" that was Icarus falling into the water. I think it's unusual to describe someone's drowning as a "splash," which seems to be a word reserved for playing around at the pool, but I think that you chose that word deliberately to show us how little Icarus's death meant to the world.

If Icarus was the subject of a myth, then he must have been a god or someone who was important to the culture. It is sad that his death would be so insignificant, and I wonder if you are commenting about the irrelevance of Greek myths to our modern world, or about something more—about the ways in which we ignore or forget about tragedies. You seem to be saying that Icarus died in vain, and he is just one example of many who die in vain.

I think you are saying that the world goes on without really caring about a tragedy. Right now, someone may be dying who is as important as Icarus, and I don't know anything about it. Even if I find out on the news tonight, I'm bound to forget quickly.

Sincerely,

Maria Picanso

A letter to the author helps you to formulate your responses more fully than when you were making annotations and questions. Your annotations and questions were intended for only one reader: yourself. But a letter is intended for another reader; therefore, a letter requires you to explain your ideas, to make them clear, and to make logical connections between them.

Opportunities for Writing and Exchanging Ideas

Write a letter to Richard Selzer. Tell Selzer that you have just read his essay "Four Appointments with the Discus Thrower" and need to ask him some questions. Use your letter to engage the author and define and focus your own responses to the story. Discuss your letter with your classmates.

Expanding the Context

When you look at texts that are related to the material you are analyzing, you can consider ideas and strategies in new contexts. You may look at other texts that focus on the same subject or theme, or you may look at other texts created by the same person. You may read critical texts, the works of other writers who have commented on the text you are analyzing. You may consult historical accounts or sources to help you place your text in the context of time and place.

Your questions about the text you are analyzing will help you to choose sources that can expand the context of your analysis. If you are interested in Williams' use of visual imagery, for example, you may decide to read other poems by Williams to see whether and how such imagery appears elsewhere. If you are interested in the transition of painting to poem, you might want to read other poems that have derived their theme from a painting.

Often, *compare or contrast* is an effective way of expanding the context for analyzing a text. When you compare, you discuss similarities and differences between related texts. When you contrast, you discuss only differences between related texts. The word *related* is important when you decide to compare or contrast. While you could compare Williams' poem about Icarus with a Shakespearean love sonnet, you would find few points of comparison between the two texts because they are so different in terms of style, theme, purpose, and language. You might observe some superficial similarities because both texts are poems, but such observations would not help you to analyze Williams' poem or support an argument about that poem. You might be able to contrast the two texts, but your points of contrast would not likely help you to support an argument about Williams' poem. If, however, you compared Williams' poem with another poem by Williams, by a poet who uses similar strategies, or by a poet writing about a similar theme, you might find ways to enhance your understanding of Williams' poem.

The purpose of compare or contrast is not to record your observations about similarities or differences, but to use these observations as evidence for your argument about the text. In considering "Landscape with the Fall of Icarus," then, you might well turn to the Brueghel painting itself as a text with which to compare Williams' poem. Or you might decide to look at another poem written in response to Brueghel's painting, such as W. H. Auden's "Musée des Beaux Arts." That poem follows.

Musée des Beaux Arts

About suffering they were never wrong,
The Old Masters: how well they understood
Its human position; how it takes place
While someone else is eating or opening a window or just walking
dully along;
How, when the aged are reverently, passionately waiting
For the miraculous birth, there always must be
Children who did not specially want it to happen, skating
On a pond at the edge of the wood:
They never forgot
That even the dreadful martyrdom must run its course
Anyhow in a corner, some untidy spot
Where the dogs go on with their doggy life and the torturer's horse
Scratches its behind on a tree.

In Brueghel's *Icarus,* for instance: how everything turns away
Quite leisurely from the disaster; the plowman may
Have heard the splash, the forsaken cry,
But for him it was not an important failure, the sun shone
As it had to on the white legs disappearing into the green
Water; and the expensive delicate ship that must have seen
Something amazing, a boy falling out of the sky,
Had somewhere to get to and sailed calmly on.

If you decide to write a comparison essay using Williams' and Auden's poems, you can organize that essay in two ways: making a text-by-text comparison or making a point-by-point comparison. The questions you ask about the texts and the position you decide to argue about the texts will determine which way of organizing will be most effective.

Any comparison essay begins with an organizing idea that tells the reader why you are comparing the texts and what point you want to make about the texts. A text-by-text comparison then discusses each text separately, focusing on similar points in each discussion. If you examine theme, language, and imagery in one text, you will then examine theme, language, and imagery in the other text.

A point-by-point comparison organizes the essay according to the points of comparison, discussing both texts in a paragraph or cluster of paragraphs devoted to a single point. For example, if you are discussing theme, you will focus on both the Williams poem and the Auden poem in that discussion. Then, you may move on to discuss imagery, again focusing on both poems in that discussion.

As you examine another text, you may discover new ways of thinking about the text you are analyzing. Or your questions may change as you encounter other texts. After reading, annotating, and questioning Williams' poem, one student looked at Auden's poem as a way of expanding the context for analysis. Here are some reflections from that student's journal:

Both William Carlos Williams and W. H. Auden use a painting by Brueghel as a source for their poems about the Greek myth of Icarus. But Williams seems interested in giving his readers a sense of the energy of the painting. He uses verbs mostly: plowing, tingling, sweating, melted, drowning. Since the poem is so spare, these verbs really stand out. You can see the painting in your mind, but mainly you get a sense of the activity within it. Icarus's drowning is just dropped into the last line, so it doesn't have any more significance than the other activity in the painting. Williams lets the reader figure out the relationship between Icarus and the rest of the scene. He doesn't come right out and tell you that it's sad or wrong that no one noticed his drowning.

But Auden presents a kind of argument in his poem. He tells you right off, in the first lines, that suffering has a small place in our lives. So the painting becomes just one example of people ignoring suffering. But the main point of the poem is not this one painting. The point is that time and time again suffering and tragedy are just another daily occurrence. There are many more words in Auden's poem—adjectives and adverbs, especially—that make it seem as if Auden is talking to us, as if he were standing in front of the painting, but not really looking at it the way Williams looks at it.

Such reflecting can help you to find points of comparison between two texts. Here, the student found the following points of comparison:

1. Purpose
   - Williams wants us to feel the energy in the painting.
   - Auden wants to present an argument, using the painting as an example.
2. Language
   - Williams relies mostly on verbs.
   - Auden uses adverbs and adjectives to help explain his ideas.
3. Form
   - Williams uses a spare form of seven, three-line stanzas, making the reader fill in information.
   - Auden writes in sentences, more conversationally, in two stanzas that work like two paragraphs: one gives the thesis, the other supports it with an example.

With even a rough outline, you can then go on to structure a comparison essay, discussing each poem separately, or discussing both poems point by point.

Opportunities for Reflecting

Compare Selzer's "Four Appointments with the Discus Thrower" on page 215 with William Carlos Williams' "The Use of Force" on page 396 of the Sourcebook. How can Williams' story enhance your understanding of Selzer's essay? How can you use Williams to expand the context of your analysis? Use your journal to write the comparison and reflect on these questions.

Engaging the Reader

Texts are incomplete without a reader, viewer, or observer. These individuals collaborate with the creator of the text to give the text meaning. When you analyze a text, therefore, you are helping to complete the experience of making the text intellectually alive. Readers come to analytical essays hoping for illumination and insight that will enrich *their* interaction with the text. What can you tell your readers that will help them go beyond a superficial understanding of the text?

Some texts—a well-known fairy tale, for example, or a popular film—may be familiar to your readers. But more often, the text you analyze will be something your readers have not read, seen, or heard.

Your reader, then, needs a clear idea of what the text is about. If it is a story, what is the basic plot and who are the characters? If it is a painting, what does it look like? If it is a poem, what is its theme? Your summary of the text cannot include every detail, but it should highlight those details that your reader needs to follow your analysis.

Your reader also needs to understand how you are setting about to analyze a text. Besides giving a close reading, what are you bringing to the text that can enhance it for yourself and your readers?

When you write an essay analyzing a text, you are presenting your reader with two texts: the text that is your subject and the text that is your essay. Everything that you have learned about writing an essay—establishing a clear organizing idea, organizing arguments logically, offering substantial evidence—applies to your analysis of a text.

Opportunities for Exchanging Ideas

Brandt Kwiram, a student writer, wrote the following essay, "The Patient Doctor," for his composition course. Read Brandt's essay. What questions does Brandt seem to be asking about Selzer's essay? What is Brandt's organizing idea? How does his idea reveal an understanding of the text that goes beyond a summary? How might you want to argue or extend his analysis? How has Brandt shown you, the reader, what he considers to be key moments or passages in Selzer's essay? Discuss these questions and Brandt's essay with your classmates.

The Patient Doctor

Brandt Kwiram

A short, delicate portrait of a patient—this is the first impression one has of Dr. Richard Selzer's essay "Four Appointments with the Discus Thrower." Selzer's persona is an inquisitive physician, looking in on his patient, who is a blind man lacking legs, seriously ill and about to die. The doctor describes his encounters with him before and after his death. This patient, known only as "Room 542," would be an ordinary, if unusually unfortunate sufferer, were it not for his odd habit of throwing his breakfast plate at the wall every morning. 1

Selzer is a subtle presence in his portait; as in a story, his meaning isn't obvious. There is not a line of the direct argument and exposition of idea 2 that one expects from an essay; there is only description of the patient and a record of the doctor's conversations with him. Selzer never emerges to deliver a speech or jab an idea home. The entrances into the essay's meaning are the doctor's words themselves, starting with his references to himself as a "spy," a man "looking for secrets," and the criminal undertone of the piece. It becomes clear that the doctor is commenting upon the crimes being committed against 542, upon the indignities Room 542 is enduring and the strength of his character. But Room 542 is not, ultimately, the subject of the submerged meaning in the essay; the doctor is the subject. The doctor is judge, jury, and executioner in his essay, and he returns a verdict of guilty against himself.

"I spy on my patients," our physician confesses in the first sentence of the essay, "by any means and from any stance" (27). Actually his spying isn't sinister; he simply stands in the doorways of rooms and gazes. Room 542, the object of his attention, has blue eyes and short white hair; he looks well tanned and healthy. But the doctor knows that "his skin is not brown from the sun. It is rusted, rather, in the last stage of containing the vile repose within." And his blue eyes are "frosted" with blindness, able only to look inward. Half of each leg is missing. The doctor imagines him in great pain, yet 542 gives no indication of agony. He makes no sound, only shakes his head occasionally. 3

542 is entirely helpless. He cannot tell by himself whether it is day or night, who is in the room with him, what will happen next. He cannot walk or move about by himself; he has only the use of his arms. He requires nurses to bring him his food. Despite the man's deformities and sicknesses, to the doctor, 542 "remains beautiful, as though he were a sailor standing athwart a slanting deck" (29). The doctor likens him repeatedly to a tree, a tree whose roots and branches have been "pruned . . . that the thing should suggest a great tree but be the dwarfed facsimile thereof" (27). He is a tree whose flowering and blooming appendages have been removed, leaving only the stumps. In his room there are no pictures from friends or family, no flowers or gifts. He is alone, beautiful, dying, helpless. 4

The physician's colleagues are not as sympathetic to 542. The head nurse, in particular, does not like him. She tells the doctor something must be done about 542. She describes how every morning he orders scrambled eggs for breakfast and then hurls his plate at the wall. "Nasty. That's what he is," the nurse concludes. "His family probably can't stand him any more than we can" (29). The doctor, intrigued, comes to watch the next morning, as an aide places the breakfast tray before the man and leaves. 542, upon finding the plate of eggs with his fingers, carefully sets it on the palm of his right hand, hefts it, and lets fly. He breaks his fast by breaking his plate. Then he laughs, a laugh the physician wonderingly describes as "something new under the sun." The head nurse, hearing his laugh, writes 5 something down on her clipboard. A peeved second aide arrives with a second plate; she is going to have to feed 542 by hand. Looking at the physician, the aide is "making her mouth go." The doctor observes that they "are to be accomplices."

Until this point there has been no indication of the purpose of the criminal imagery, no indication of what crimes the doctor might be committing. But by referring to himself as an "accomplice," he creates a crime and victim. This man whom the aide is going to feed by hand has control only over his breakfast. In breaking his plate every morning, 542 is exercising his independence as a living being, a being capable of rebellion and free will. Indeed, twice in the essay 542 asks that his shoes be brought to him. His shoes represent his autonomy, his ability to walk and move by himself. Thus it is a point of honor that he throw his plate. Feeding him by hand strips him of the last thing he can do himself, reducing him to an utterly dependent creature. 6

But the essay is not simply a description of a lone rebel fighting faceless flunkies. The nurses are actively criminal; there is also a passive criminal act on the physician's part. He is standing by, watching, not getting involved, doing nothing to prevent the crime from being committed. Finally he steps forward and asks if there is anything he can do. In his capacity as spy and observer, the man who, as 542's doctor, should hold ultimate power, stands by and lets the crime happen. 7

He is not given a chance to redeem himself. That afternoon the man dies, an event the head nurse calls "a blessing." The physician goes to the man's room a last time, a "spy looking for secrets" (31). The man is grave and dignified in death. As he is turning to go, the doctor sees the spot on the wall where it has been repeatedly washed after being decorated with eggs. It is, he says, "very clean and very white in contrast to the rest, which is dirty and gray." For Selzer, we understand, the man is a white spot in the midst of a dirty gray bureaucracy. He is a vigorous living being, a discus thrower, a vital force. He is alive, and his living is too irritating for the nurses, who mark his behavior down on clipboards, who are cogs in a machine. The nurses want him to die a quiet death. They want him to accept the conditions of his existence and part from them peacefully. They hate him for his refusal. 8

The doctor makes it clear he does not ally himself with the nurses. He conveys this in details, such as his description of the aide "making her mouth go." And unlike them he is fascinated by Room 542 and what he does. But he does not explain his fascination, and we are left to decipher it from the clues he has left in his language. Why is Selzer spying? To what end is he "gathering evidence"? Someone must be guilty. 542 is not the guilty party; he has earned the doctor's praise. The nurses are peripheral figures, not central players. The only character left worthy of all the evi- 9 dence-gathering is the doctor himself. He must be guilty, by his own admission. But what, aside from the minor passive crime above, could constitute his guilt?

The first clue he gives is in the title. There are four numbered sections to the essay, corresponding to the "four appointments with the discus thrower." The discus thrower is officially the patient, yet it is the doctor who has four appointments in Room 542. Somehow the doctor wants 542 to help him. The character holding healing power is apparently not the doctor but the patient. A second clue lies in the doctor's speculation about the man's mental state, especially in parts one and two of the essay. He asks, "what is he thinking behind those lids that do not blink?" (29). He wonders if 542 is recalling "the burry prickle of love," or perhaps a time of health, "a time when his body was not a rotting log." He is curious; he itches to know what 542 is thinking and feeling, what it is like to be him. 10

A third clue is in the doctor's question, "Is there anything I can do?" He asks this twice in his essay. Although he doesn't actually do anything for the man outside of his duties as a doctor, he asks if he can assume a more active role. He seems to want to help, but not badly enough to act decisively. He is unsure of himself, whether he can actually do anything for the inimitable 542. He also isn't sure if he actually wants to become anything more than a spectator. 11

With great self-consciousness the physician has set up the scene and now hides behind it, waiting to be discovered, waiting for someone to unravel the mystery and point a finger at him. For in the essay the least sick individual is Room 542. Room 542 is the most alive of them all. The doctor is living off him, living through him, using him as a drug. Or, to return to the metaphor in the title, he watches 542 like a child watches a star athlete on television in awe, the sports figure clothed in mystery. How wonderful it must be to be a star! What mysterious force propels him? 12

The doctor, it appears, is a weary man. He lives out his life in the halls and rooms of a dirty gray hospital, spending his time inspecting and tending the sick and dying. He does not often have contact with people other than the ill or those who service them. His is a confined life, a limited life, a life of watching people give up and die. But instead of trying to break out of his shell and routine, he resorts to spying. He assembles evidence that others are alive, that they are more alive than he; the spectacle of a virtually powerless person struggling so spectacularly draws him like a moth to a flame. As Selzer sees it, Room 542 is trying to teach the peeping doctor something about how to live. 13

The doctor must speculate about what 542 is thinking and feeling because he, as someone living off the energy of others, needs more than just an image of rebellion and strength. He needs to feel a part of that life, that he is an accomplice of the man who is criminally breaking his plate 14 every morning. If Room 542 is an outlaw, living excitingly and dangerously from his hospital bed, the doctor wants to be his sidekick, to watch with pounding heart the desperado transgress, without getting too near the danger, without taking the risk of daring action in his own life. The more evidence "against" 542 he gathers, the more he can feel a part of 542's life, the closer to him he feels.

15 But finally, the physician is ambivalent about the part he is playing and the way he is living. He realizes what he is doing; he is attracted by the secret thrills of voyeurism, and also repulsed by his own lack of vitality. In asking, "Is there anything I can do," he is expressing his desire to become an active being, a being who understands what needs to be done and can do it; he is also indicating his own indecision about how active he wants to be. Instead of saying "I'm going to do something," he asks a question, which leaves him a passive escape route. Instead of living in and for himself, he lives off his patients, or at least those who still haven't given up. The white spot on the wall is the doctor's romanticization of Room 542's struggle and strength; it is his idolization of the champion discus thrower. In symbolic terms, when 542 asks for his shoes, the doctor cannot give them to him because he possesses none of his own.

16 What at first glance looks like a portrait and at second glance reads like an elegy to a man who fought the system is, finally, a confession. The physician, Selzer somewhere behind him, is telling us of the way he lives, the way, perhaps, some of us live, through movie stars or athletes, feeding ourselves from tabloids or sports pages. The doctor never comes out and delivers his own prognosis; we must look for it in his word choice and the repetition of questions, in his attitudes toward people and the images he uses. Behind it all the voyeur is hiding, waiting in guilty excitement for someone to read his essay and recognize him as the criminal. At some emotional level, he wants to be identified as guilty. That too would give him a thrill.

Works Cited

"Four Appointments with the Discus Thrower." In *Confessions of a Knife*. New York: Morrow, 1979. 27–31.

Opportunities for Writing

1. Select one of the essays in the Sourcebook. Reread the questions about analyzing nonfiction on pages 206–207, and let these questions suggest ways to explore the essay you have selected to analyze.

Summarize the text; annotate it; ask questions of the text; engage the author of the text. Let your summary, annotations, and questions lead you to define and focus your analysis. Let your explorations take you beyond the text you are analyzing to a second or third essay, either by the same writer or a different writer. Use these additional essays to expand the context for your analysis. Write an analytical essay about the essays you have selected.

2. Read Shirley Jackson's "The Lottery" on page 357 of the Sourcebook and William Carlos Williams' "The Use of Force" on page 396 of the Sourcebook. Choose one of these stories to analyze. Reread the questions about analyzing fiction on pages 208–209, and let them guide you through your analysis.

Summarize the story; annotate it; ask questions of the text; engage the author of the story. Let your summary, annotations, and questions lead you to define and focus your analysis. Let your explorations take you to one of the essays in the Sourcebook section on questioning issues of authority and morality. Use this essay to help you expand the context for your analysis. Write an analytical essay.

3. You have worked closely with Richard Selzer's essay "Four Appointments with a Discus Thrower." In the following pages you will find another essay by Selzer, "The Masked Marvel's Last Toehold." After you read this essay by Selzer, summarize the text. Annotate it; ask questions of the text. Find the key passages and moments in this essay. What points of comparison do you find between the two essays? What puzzles you about these two texts? What idea connects Selzer's essays? What assumptions is Selzer making in both essays? How does "The Masked Marvel's Last Toehold" help you to enhance your understanding of "Four Appointments with the Discus Thrower"?

Develop an organizing idea to focus your analysis of these two texts. Write an analytical essay comparing the two Selzer essays.

The Masked Marvel's Last Toehold

Richard Selzer

Morning rounds

On the fifth floor of the hospital, in the west wing, I know that a man is sitting up in his bed, waiting for me. Elihu Koontz is seventy-five, and he 1 is diabetic. It is two weeks since I amputated his left leg just below the knee. I walk down the corridor, but I do not go straight into his room. Instead, I pause in the doorway. He is not yet aware of my presence, but gazes down at the place in the bed where his leg used to be, and where now there is the collapsed leg of his pajamas. He is totally absorbed, like an athlete appraising the details of his body. What is he thinking, I wonder. Is he dreaming the outline of his toes? Does he see there his foot's incandescent ghost? Could he be angry? Feel that I have taken from him something for which he yearns now with all his heart? Has he forgotten so soon the pain? It was a pain so great as to set him apart from all other men, in a red-hot place where he had no kith or kin. What of those black gorilla toes and the soupy mess that was his heel? I watch him from the doorway. It is a kind of spying, I know.

Save for a white fringe open at the front, Elihu Koontz is bald. The hair has grown too long and is wilted. He wears it as one would wear a day-old laurel wreath. He is naked to the waist, so that I can see his breasts. They are the breasts of Buddha, inverted triangles from which the nipples swing, dark as garnets. 2

I have seen enough. I step into the room, and he sees that I am there. 3

"How did the night go, Elihu?" 4

He looks at me for a long moment. "Shut the door," he says. 5

I do, and move to the side of the bed. He takes my left hand in both of his, gazes at it, turns it over, then back, fondling, at last holding it up to his cheek. I do not withdraw from this loving. After a while he relinquishes my hand, and looks up at me. 6

"How is the pain" I ask. 7

He does not answer, but continues to look at me in silence. I know at once that he has made a decision. 8

"Ever hear of The Masked Marvel?" He says this in a low voice, almost a whisper. 9

"What?" 10

"The Masked Marvel," he says. "You never heard of him?" 11

"No." 12

He clucks his tongue. He is exasperated. 13

All at once there is a recollection. It is dim, distant, but coming near. 14

"Do you mean the wrestler?" 15

Eagerly, he nods, and the breasts bob. How gnomish he looks, oval as the huge helpless egg of some outlandish lizard. He has very long arms, which, now and then, he unfurls to reach for things—a carafe of water, a get-well card. He gazes up at me, urging. He *wants* me to remember. 16

"Well . . . yes," I say. I am straining backward in time. "I saw him wrestle in Toronto long ago." 17

"Ha!" He smiles. "You saw *me*." And his index finger, held rigid and upright, bounces in the air. 18

The man has said something shocking, unacceptable. It must be challenged. 19

"You?" I am trying to smile. 20

Again that jab of the finger. "You saw *me*." 21

"No," I say. But even then, something about Elihu Koontz, those prolonged arms, the shape of his head, the sudden agility with which he leans from his bed to get a large brown envelope from his nightstand, something is forcing me toward a memory. He rummages through his papers, old newspaper clippings, photographs, and I remember . . . 22

It is almost forty years ago. I am ten years old. I have been sent to Toronto to spend the summer with relatives. Uncle Max has bought two tickets to the wrestling match. He is taking me that night. 23

"He isn't allowed," says Aunt Sarah to me. Uncle Max has angina. 24

"He gets too excited," she says. 25

"I wish you wouldn't go, Max," she says. 26

"You mind your own business," he says. 27

And we go. Out into the warm Canadian evening. I am not only abroad, I am abroad in the *evening!* I have never been taken out in the evening. I am terribly excited. The trolleys, the lights, the horns. It is a bazaar. At the Maple Leaf Gardens, we sit high and near the center. The vast arena is dark except for the brilliance of the ring at the bottom. 28

It begins. 29

The wrestlers circle. They grapple. They are all haunch and paunch. I am shocked by their ugliness, but I do not show it. Uncle Max is exhilarated. He leans forward, his eyes unblinking, on his face a look of enormous happiness. One after the other, a pair of wrestlers enter the ring. The two men join, twist, jerk, tug, bend, yank, and throw. Then they leave and are replaced by another pair. At last it is the main event. "The Angel vs. The Masked Marvel." 30

On the cover of the program notes, there is a picture of The Angel hanging from the limb of a tree, a noose of thick rope around his neck. The Angel hangs just so for an hour every day, it is explained, to strengthen his neck. The Masked Marvel's trademark is a black stocking cap with holes for the eyes and mouth. He is never seen without it, states the program. No one knows who The Masked Marvel really is! 31

"Good," says Uncle Max. "Now you'll see something." He is fidgeting, waiting for them to appear. They come down separate aisles, climb into the ring from opposite sides. I have never seen anything like them. It is The Angel's neck that first captures the eye. The shaved nape rises in twin columns to puff into the white hood of a sloped and bosselated skull that is too small. As though, strangled by the sinews of that neck, the skull had long since withered and shrunk. The thing about The Angel is the absence of any mystery in his body. It is simply *there*. A monosyllabic announcement. 32

A grunt. One looks and knows everything at once, the fat thighs, the gigantic buttocks, the great spine from which hang knotted ropes and pale aprons of beef. And that prehistoric head. He is all of a single hideous piece, The Angel is. No detachables.

The Masked Marvel seems dwarfish. His fingers dangle kneeward. His 33
short legs are slightly bowed as if under the weight of the cask they are forced to heft about. He has breasts that swing when he moves! I have never seen such breasts on a man before.

There is a sudden ungraceful movement, and they close upon one 34
another. The Angel stoops and hugs The Marvel about the waist, locking his hands behind The Marvel's back. Now he straightens and lifts The Marvel as though he were uprooting a tree. Thus he holds him, then stoops again, thrusts one hand through The Marvel's crotch, and with the other grabs him by the neck. He rears and . . . The Marvel is aloft! For a long moment, The Angel stands as though deciding where to make the toss. Then throws. Was that board or bone that splintered there? Again and again, The Angel hurls himself upon the body of The Masked Marvel.

Now The Angel rises over the fallen Marvel, picks up one foot in both 35
of his hands, and twists the toes downward. It is far beyond the tensile strength of mere ligament, mere cartilage. The Masked Marvel does not hide his agony, but pounds and slaps the floor with his hand, now and then reaching up toward The Angel in an attitude of supplication. I have never seen such suffering. And all the while his black mask rolls from side to side, the mouth pulled to a tight slit through which issues an endless hiss that I can hear from where I sit. All at once, I hear a shouting close by.

"Break it off! Tear off a leg and throw it up here!" 36

It is Uncle Max. Even in the darkness I can see that he is gray. A band 37
of sweat stands upon his upper lip. He is on his feet now, panting, one fist pressed at his chest, the other raised warlike toward the ring. For the first time I begin to think that something terrible might happen here. Aunt Sarah was right.

"Sit down, Uncle Max," I say. "Take a pill, please." 38

He reaches for the pillbox, gropes, and swallows without taking his 39
gaze from the wrestlers. I wait for him to sit down.

"That's not fair," I say, "twisting his toes like that." 40

"It's the toehold," he explains. 41

"But it's not *fair,*" I say again. The whole of the evil is laid open for me 42
to perceive. I am trembling.

And now The Angel does something unspeakable. Holding the foot 43
of The Marvel at full twist with one hand, he bends and grasps the mask where it clings to the back of The Marvel's head. And he pulls. He is going to strip it off! Lay bare an ultimate carnal mystery! Suddenly it is beyond mere physical violence. Now I am on my feet, shouting into the Maple Leaf Gardens.

"Watch out," I scream. "Stop him. Please, somebody, stop him." 44

Next to me, Uncle Max is chuckling. 45

Yet The Masked Marvel hears me, I know it. And rallies from his bed of 46
pain. Thrusting with his free heel, he strikes The Angel at the back of the knee. The Angel falls. The Masked Marvel is on top of him, pinning his shoulders to the mat. One! Two! Three! And it is over. Uncle Max is strangely still. I am gasping for breath. All this I remember as I stand at the bedside of Elihu Koontz.

Once again, I am in the operating room. It is two years since I ampu- 47
tated the left leg of Elihu Koontz. Now it is his right leg which is gangrenous. I have already scrubbed. I stand to one side wearing my gown and gloves. And . . . *I am masked.* Upon the table lies Elihu Koontz, pinned in a fierce white light. Spinal anesthesia has been administered. One of his arms is taped to a board placed at a right angle to his body. Into this arm, a needle has been placed. Fluid drips here from a bottle overhead. With his other hand, Elihu Koontz beats feebly at the side of the operating table. His head rolls from side to side. His mouth is pulled into weeping. It seems to me that I have never seen such misery.

An orderly stands at the foot of the table, holding Elihu Koontz's leg 48
aloft by the toes so that the intern can scrub the limb with antiseptic solutions. The intern paints the foot, ankle, leg, and thigh, both front and back, three times. From a corner of the room where I wait, I look down as from an amphitheater. Then I think of Uncle Max yelling, "Tear off a leg. Throw it up here." And I think that forty years later I am making the catch.

"It's not fair," I say aloud. But no one hears me. I step forward to break 49
The Masked Marvel's last toehold.

Analyzing Texts: Questions for Peer Review

1. What problem or question about the text motivates the writer?

2. How has the writer's analysis enlarged your understanding of the text? What did you learn about the text from reading the analysis? What assumptions is the writer making about the text?

3. Has the writer given you enough summary of the text to create a context for his or her analysis?

4. How has the writer shown you the key moments, passages, or details of the text?

5. What is the writer's organizing idea? Is this idea interesting and compelling?

6. How can you argue with the writer's analysis of this text?

7. Where in the essay has the writer said anything that is confusing or unclear to you? Show the writer where you think more details are needed.

8. How has the writer shown up in the essay? How do the words and sentence rhythms reveal the writer's voice?

9. How does the introduction pull you into the writer's analysis? Is there anything you might suggest adding or deleting?

10. How does the writer's conclusion pull together the entire essay? How might the conclusion be more effective?

Annotate the writer's draft by commenting on its strengths and weaknesses. Ask the writer questions. Write a letter in which you offer your honest, careful, and generous comments and suggestions for revising.

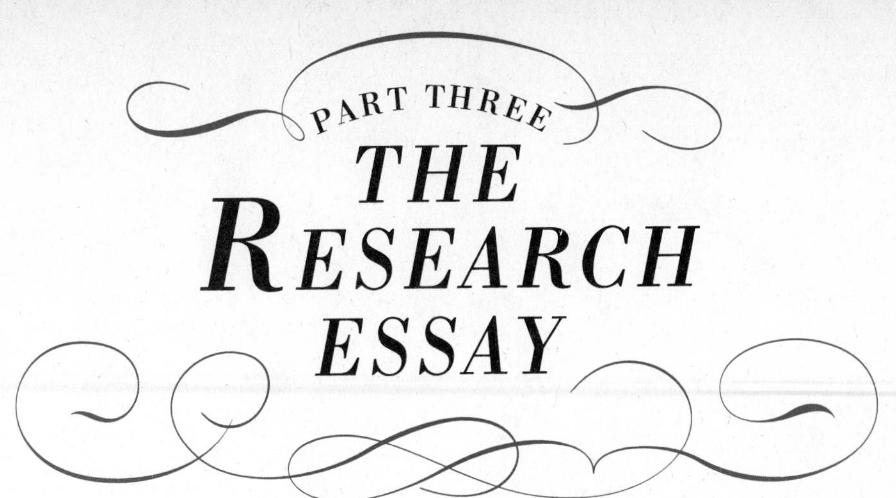

PART THREE

THE RESEARCH ESSAY

CHAPTER 10

Directing the Search

Writing a research essay allows you to gather and interpret information about a topic that interests you. Research is much like detective work: You ask questions, follow leads, pick up clues, analyze information, and draw conclusions. You have had experience in some of these activities in previous chapters where you have learned to question sources and analyze texts. These next chapters will help you engage productively in the research process.

Some students think of a research essay as a kind of test: They believe they are supposed to prove to their instructor that they have found and read a great number of sources on a certain topic. When they write, they try to incorporate many quotations into their essay and to amass a long bibliography. Most instructors, however, consider a research assignment to be a way of expanding the boundaries of their course. After all, within a semester the class can cover only so much material. Writing offers a way of individualizing the course. Through a research essay, students can pursue questions that interest them.

A research essay, then, is not a test. It is not testimony to a hunting and gathering expedition. Instead, a research essay answers questions about a topic with evidence compiled from a variety of primary and secondary sources. It is not merely a report that conveys information to readers; rather, it involves interpretation, analysis, and argumentation. In a research essay, just as in any other kind of college essay, you are expected to take a position, defend your position with supporting details, and draw conclusions.

In a modern American literature course, for example, one student, having read some well-known novels from the 1920s and 1930s, wondered how those works were first received by their intended audience. Because he was especially interested in the works of F. Scott Fitzgerald, he decided to explore the critical reception of one of Fitzgerald's novels. He thought that considering this information would help him to understand the cultural context in which the novel was written. By reading reviews of the novel that appeared right after it was published, he hoped that he would be able to get a sense of the values and expectations that readers brought to the book. From the list of required and recommended books for the course, he decided to write a research essay on the critical reception of *The Great Gatsby*. His research essay did not merely summarize these reviews for his readers, it offered his own interpretation about the common expectations and evaluations made by the reviewers.

In a course on ethics, a student decided to write a research essay on the ethical issues involved when adopted children want access to information about their biological parents. Although this topic was not directly related to course readings, the student was deeply interested in it because she herself was an adopted child. Her research led her to articles in popular journals and essays in law journals. These sources, supplemented by her own experiences, enabled her to write a research essay focusing on the ethical problems that this issue has generated. Her essay did not merely report what other people considered to be ethical issues, but offered her own interpretation about how these issues directly affect the lives of adopted children.

Essays that result from inquiries like the two just described often are longer than the kind of college essays we have been discussing elsewhere in the book. Some instructors assign research essays of 12 to 15 pages; some ask for more extended essays. As you will see later in this chapter, research essays also need to be fully documented with footnotes, endnotes, or parenthetical documentation. A research essay contains references to sources outside your own experience. These references may be in the form of quotations, paraphrased passages, or summaries of information.

A research essay is an exercise in discovery. When you are genuinely interested in your topic, when you ask good questions, when you allow yourself enough time to inquire into many sources, the process of doing research can be one of the most satisfying parts of your course work.

CHOOSING A TOPIC

A good topic for a research essay is interesting, manageable in size, and able to be researched with the sources you have available. If you know that you will be writing a research essay for a course, begin early in the semester to make notes of possible areas of interest. If you keep a journal or notebook, your questions or comments on readings and class discussions can help you generate ideas for a research essay.

Sometimes these ideas will be closely related to your course work.

In a course on film narrative, for example, you may notice that some directors are remarkably consistent in the kinds of characters they create in their films. Despite the actors cast to portray characters in their films, you may be able to identify a certain kind of hero in every John Huston film or in every Martin Scorsese film. How does a director achieve such consistency? By focusing on the work of one director, you may be able to come to some conclusions about the director's imagination. You may decide, then, to write a research essay on the portrayal of women in the films of Alfred Hitchcock.

Ideas for a research essay sometimes come from unexpected sources: a footnote in a required text or a question a classmate asks. In a critical edition of the *Adventures of Huckleberry Finn,* for example, one student found interesting the many footnotes referring to Mark Twain's letters. In these letters, it seemed, Twain reflected on the process of writing *Huckleberry Finn.* As a research project, the student decided to use Twain's letters as a primary source to examine Twain's writing process.

You may not be sure that your instructor will approve a topic that seems peripheral to the syllabus; in that case, ask. Often, you can redirect your interest to a question that falls within the boundaries of the course. An art history class, for example, had been studying the works of major modern painters—Cézanne, Picasso, Braque, Matisse—and most students were writing research essays using paintings, the writings of artists, and the works of critics as sources. One student, however, became interested in the role of art collectors as influences in the work of some of these artists. She decided to write a research essay particularly on Gertrude and Leo Stein as art collectors and the ways their purchases affected the careers of Matisse and Picasso. Her instructor approved the topic with enthusiasm even though the class discussions had not focused on collectors. She thought that the research essay would give the student an interesting context in which to think about the paintings.

One student in a marketing course had spent several summers in high school working at odd jobs in his hometown. He usually found work by posting handmade notices in local shops and libraries; but because he wanted to make himself known to a larger public, he was interested in researching more sophisticated marketing techniques. This interest led to a research essay evaluating marketing techniques used by self-employed individuals and small businesses. His research essay proved so interesting to some of his classmates, in fact, that he rewrote his findings as a feature article for the college newspaper.

These topics, because they were inspired by the real interests of the students who thought of them, resulted in satisfying research experiences.

FROM TOPIC TO QUESTION

As you have seen throughout this book, any essay needs to be focused by a question you can answer with both the time and resources available. Topics, on the other hand, sometimes are large and unwieldy. If you are taking a course in government, you might be interested in how laws affect public policy; but this topic is too large for a college research essay. How do you hone a topic into a manageable question? Researchers try to look at issues from six different angles, asking *who, what, when, where, why,* and *how.* These question words can help you find many possible subtopics. If, for example, you are interested in how the law affects public policy, you can ask:

- *What* specific law am I interested in finding out about?
- *Why* was that law created? What problem did it address?
- *When* was it created? From what historical context did it come?
- *How* did that law change public policy or behavior once it was enacted?
- *Where* did the law have significant impact?
- *Who* was involved in creating the law? Whom did the law affect?

Each question might be the focus of a research essay. Suppose you decide you are interested in the laws enacted after the creation of the Food and Drug Administration early in this century. You might ask about the impact on physicians of the regulation of patent medicines. Depending on the availability of sources, this question could serve to focus an interesting research essay within the broad topic of the law and public policy.

You might be interested, instead, in civil rights laws and their effect on schools and jobs. Which civil rights laws interest you? Where would you like to study their effect? What do you want to know? One student, a Japanese-American, found himself interested in the effect of affirmative action policy on college admission decisions. He thought that researching this topic would help him to make up his own mind about whether affirmative action laws afforded equal opportunity or caused reverse discrimination. This question allowed him to move from a broad topic to a manageable focus.

Opportunities for Reflecting

What would you like to read about if you had the time? What questions are you curious about? What issues or problems puzzle you? One student wondered if there were a finite number of area codes in the

United States and wanted to know what would happen when we run out of area codes.

Brainstorm and list some possible topics for a research essay. Ask questions about your topic. Is there a conflict or a controversy that makes this topic interesting? Begin to select a topic that is interesting and limited, one that you can adequately research with the resources available to you.

Opportunities for Exchanging Ideas

Work in small groups and present your tentative research topic and research questions to your classmates. Ask questions, seek advice, and gather ideas. Help each other narrow topics that seem unwieldy and unmanageable.

EXPLORING PRELIMINARY SOURCES

Once you have a question to focus your search, you need to assess possible sources. These sources may include:

Reference books (encyclopedias, dictionaries, indexes)
Books on the topic
Periodicals
Government documents
Pamphlets and brochures
Computer databases
Films
Recordings
Videotapes
Television and radio programs
Interviews
Questionnaires
Lectures or class notes

Of course, you will not need all these sources for every research essay that you write. For a research essay on affirmative action and college admissions, for example, you may find it appropriate to use books; periodical articles; interviews with students, admissions officers, or professors; questionnaires; and lectures. The student who decided to write a research essay about reviews of *The Great Gatsby* would rely primarily on those reviews as sources of evidence.

As you learned in Chapter 7, some of these sources will be primary sources and some secondary sources. For the topic of affirmative action and college admissions, primary sources would be an interview with a college admissions officer about the school's affirmative action policy, an editorial in a college newspaper putting forth an opinion about this policy, and the transcript of legal proceedings involving an affirmative action decision. Secondary sources might include an article in a legal journal about the impact of affirmative action on education and a book about affirmative action policy in general.

A primary source, you will remember, contains no interpretation within it. You, as the writer, analyze and interpret the source. A secondary source contains someone else's interpretation of information or evidence.

Exploring Sources in the Library

For most college research essays, library sources contain significant information. However, even a small college library seems to be a large, impenetrable space to someone who has had little experience in locating sources. Here are some basic guides to resources within the library.

The Card Catalog Whether your library's card catalog is located in oak filing cabinets or accessed on a computer terminal, you will use the same techniques for finding material. A card catalog is organized by author, title, and subject. When you are first exploring sources, the subject heading will be most useful. How, though, do you know the subject under which your topic will be listed?

Sometimes, the category of subject will be obvious. The student who decided to write an art history essay about the influence of Gertrude and Leo Stein on the work of Matisse and Picasso may be looking up entries in the following subject areas:

Stein, Gertrude
Stein, Leo
Picasso, Pablo
Matisse, Henri
Art collectors
Modern art

Sometimes, however, the subject may be elusive because it cannot be easily categorized in one area. One student, for example, wanted to write a research essay on changes in dating customs before and after World War II. How would she find information about this subject? What subject headings might help her?

For students in a quandary about the precise wording of subject headings, reference librarians can be invaluable. Reference librarians are experts in academic detective work. With special guides and years of experience, they can shorten the time that you might otherwise take in locating materials. Even if you have used other libraries successfully, the reference librarian at your college library can give you useful tips about a library with which you are unfamiliar.

Another resource can be found in a book on the subject you are researching. The student writing about dating had read the book *Intimate Matters: A History of Sexuality in America.* This book gave her some information about changes in dating, but she hoped to find other sources. Within the book itself, she found useful leads. The first lead can be found on the copyright page of any book. This page, usually the back of the title page, contains the year of publication and other copyright information. It also contains a facsimile of the Library of Congress catalog card (see page 248).

Like any catalog card, the Library of Congress catalog card contains the name of the author, the title of the book, and the publisher; it also tells you whether the book has an index and a bibliography. And, most important when you are exploring library sources, it tells you under what subject heading the book is filed. In this case, the subject heading reads:

Sex Customs—United States—History

Often a book will be listed under more than one subject heading. For example, other books on dating or courtship might be listed under:

Social Life and Customs—United States—Twentieth Century

or

Sex Education

Besides the copyright page, the bibliography notes often can guide you to other sources on the same topic. *Intimate Matters* contains a 13-page bibliography that included many books and articles the student thought might be useful. And these sources, in turn, led the student to other sources. (See page 249 for a sample page from the bibliography of *Intimate Matters.*)

A hardcover edition of this book was published in 1988 by Harper & Row, Publishers.

First PERENNIAL LIBRARY edition published 1989.

Library of Congress Cataloging-in-Publication Data

D'Emilio, John
Intimate matters.

"Perennial Library"
Bibliography: p.
Includes index.
1. Sex customs—United States—History. I. Freedman, Estelle B., 1947–. II. Title.
HQ18.U5D45 1989 306.7'0973 87-45608
ISBN 0-06-091550-1 (pbk.)

89 90 91 92 93 FG 10 9 8 7 6 5 4 3 2 1

Subject heading

Copyright page from *Intimate Matters*.

Imperialism, Culture, and Resistance." *Radical History Review* 20 (Spring–Summer 1979): 99–130.

Du Bois, W. E. B. *The Philadelphia Negro.* Reprint. Milwood, New York: Kraus-Thompson Organization, 1973.

Easterlin, Richard A. "Factors in the Decline of Farm Fertility in the United States: Some Preliminary Research Results." *Journal of American History* 63 (December 1976): 600–614.

Eckhardt, Celia Morris. *Fanny Wright: Rebel in America.* Cambridge: Harvard University Press, 1984.

Ehrenreich, Barbara. *The Hearts of Men: American Dreams and the Flight from Commitment.* Garden City, N.Y.: Anchor/Doubleday, 1983.

———; Hess, Elizabeth; and Jacobs, Gloria. *Re-Making Love: The Feminization of Sex.* Garden City, N.Y.: Anchor, 1986.

Ehrmann, Winston. *Premarital Dating Behavior.* New York: Henry Holt, 1959.

Ellis, Havelock. *Studies in the Psychology of Sex.* New York: Random House, 1936.

Epstein, Barbara. *The Politics of Domesticity: Women, Evangelism, and Temperance in Nineteenth-Century America.* Middletown, Conn.: Wesleyan University Press, 1981.

Erenberg, Lewis A. "Everybody's Doin' It: The Pre–World War I Dance Craze, the Castles and the Modern American Girl." *Feminist Studies* 3 (Fall 1975): 155–70.

———. *Steppin' Out: New York Night Life and the Transformation of American Culture, 1890–1930.* Westport, Conn.: Greenwood Press, 1981.

Ewen, Elizabeth. "City Lights: Immigrant Women and the Rise of the Movies." *Signs* 5 (Spring 1980): 45–65.

Exner, M[ax]. J. *Problems and Principles of Sex Education: A Study of 948 College Men.* New York: Association Press, 1915.

Facey, Paul, S. J. "The Legion of Decency: A Sociological Analysis of the Emergence and Development of a Social Pressure Group." Ph.D. dissertation, Fordham University, 1945.

Faderman, Lillian. *Surpassing the Love of Men: Romantic Friendship and Love Between Women from the Renaissance to the Present.* New York: William Morrow and Co., 1981.

Farley, Reynolds. *Growth of the Black Population.* Chicago: Markham Publishers, 1970.

Fass, Paula S. *The Damned and the Beautiful: American Youth in the 1920s.* New York: Oxford University Press, 1977.

Flaherty, David H. *Privacy in Colonial New England.* Charlottesville: University of Virginia Press, 1972.

Foster, Lawrence. *Religion and Sexuality: Three American Communal Experiments of the Nineteenth Century.* New York: Oxford University Press, 1981.

Foucault, Michel. *The History of Sexuality.* Trans. Robert Hurley. Vol. 1, *An Introduction.* New York: Pantheon, 1978.

Frankfort, Roberta. *Collegiate Women: Domesticity and Career in Turn-of-the-Century America.* New York: New York University Press, 1977.

Fraser, Antonia. *The Weaker Vessel: Woman's Lot in Seventeenth-Century England.* London: Weidenfeld and Nicholson, 1984.

Sample page from the 13-page bibliography of *Intimate Matters*.

Computer Searches If your library's holdings are in a computer database, you may be able to search widely for sources by using subject headings, title, author, and keywords. The keyword option on computers allows you to ask the computer to find titles of books (and articles too, if these are entered in your library's database) in which a word appropriate to your topic appears. For the student writing about changes in dating, keywords might include *dating, courtship, engagement, sex, marriage.* A computer search using the keyword option yielded sources that included:

> *Premarital Dating Behavior* (1959)
>
> *Engagement and Marriage* (1955)
>
> *Sexual Behavior in the 1970s* (1974)
>
> "Dating Becomes the Way of American Youth," *Essays in the Family and Social Change* (1983)

These sources themselves had notes and bibliographies that led the student to other sources.

Libraries often have specialized databases too. These include ERIC (Educational Resources Information Center), PSYCHINFO, SOCIAL SCISEARCH (Social Sciences Citation Index), SCISEARCH (Science Citation Index), MEDLINE (Medical Literature Analysis and Retrieval System) and NTIS (National Technical Information Service). Sometimes libraries charge a small fee for using these specialized searches.

Reference Material Sometimes you need to find some basic background material on your topic before you feel comfortable looking for sources. Your library contains many reference books that will give you overviews of a wide range of topics. These reference books include:

1. **Encyclopedias.** These range from general volumes such as the *Encyclopedia Americana* to specialized volumes on religion, philosophy, science, or other subjects.

2. **Bibliographies.** *A World Bibliography of Bibliographies* and *Bibliography Index* contain bibliographies according to subject area (see page 251). These volumes may be useful to you in beginning to look for sources. However, they will not include books or articles published after the volume was sent to press.

3. **Periodical indexes.** *The Reader's Guide to Periodical Literature* includes articles in general interest magazines, such as *Time, The Atlantic,* or *Ebony* (see page 252). More specialized indexes compile entries from

(text continued on page 254)

Discrimination in criminal justice administration
Myers, Martha A., and Talarico, Susette M. The social contexts of criminal sentencing. Springer-Verlag 1987 p197-210
Radelet, M. L. Executions of whites for crimes against blacks: exceptions to the rule? *Sociol Q* 30:542-4 Wint '89

Great Britain

Waters, Robert. Ethnic minorities and the criminal justice system. Avebury 1990 p183-92

Discrimination in education
See also
Segregation in education
Sex discrimination in education

Discrimination in employment
See also
Affirmative action programs
Age and employment
Equal pay for equal work
Sex discrimination in employment
Casper, Dale E. Employment discrimination in the public sector; recent journal articles, 1982-1989. (Public administration series, bibliography P-2830) Vance Bibls. 1990 6p
Casper, Dale E. Public regulation, rules, and policy governing employment at will; recent journal articles, 1985-1989. (Public administration series, bibliography P-2829) Vance Bibls. 1990 7p
Edelman, L. B. Legal environments and organizational governance: the expansion of due process in the American workplace. *Am J Sociol* 95:1437-40 My '90
Riccucci, Norma. Women, minorities and unions in the public sector. (Contributions in labor studies, no28) Greenwood Press 1990 incl bibl
Singer, M. S. and Sewell, C. Applicant age and selection interview decisions: effect of information exposure on age discrimination in personnel selection. *Pers Psychol* 42:152-4 Spr '89

Law and legislation
United States

Greene, Kathanne W. Affirmative action and principles of justice. (Contributions in legal studies, no53) Greenwood Press 1989 p177-81

Discrimination in housing
Goering, J. M. and Coulibably, M. Investigating public housing segregation: conceptual and methodological issues. *Urban Aff Q* 25:292-7 D '89
Saltman, Juliet. A fragile movement; the struggle for neighborhood stabilization. (Contributions in sociology, no86) Greenwood Press 1990 p435-43
Weiher, G. R. Public policy and patterns of residential segregation. *West Polit Q* 42:673-7 D '89

South Africa

Oliver-Evans, Ceridwen, and Thomas, Elmar. The abolition of influx control and related issues; a bibliography. (Saldru working paper, no72-73) Southern Africa Labour & Development Res. Unit 1988 2v

Sample entries from *Bibliographic Index* 1990.

DISARMAMENT—*cont.*

Inspection

Initial compliance costs for major arms treaties could exceed $3 billion, plus $660 million yearly [Congressional Budget Office report] J. D. Morrocco. il *Aviation Week & Space Technology* 133:74-5 N 19 '90

DISASTER RELIEF *See* Relief work

DISASTERS

See also

Brush fires
Building failures
Earthquakes
Forest fires
Hurricanes
Tornadoes

How to cope with disaster [special section] il *McCall's* 118:73-8+ O '90

The other side of Mother Nature. C. Purdy. il *Current Health 2* 17:20-1 S '90

Psychological aspects

How to cope with disaster. N. Cousins. il *McCall's* 118:73-4+ O '90

DISC BRAKES, AUTOMOBILE *See* Brakes, Automobile

DISC JOCKEYS

See also

Joyner, Tom
Payola

DISCH, THOMAS M.

about

The cardinal detoxes [drama] Reviews
The Christian Century 107:961 O 24 '90
The Nation 251:405 O 15 '90

DISCHARGE OF EMPLOYEES *See* Employees—Dismissal

DISCIPLESHIP *See* Christian life

DISCIPLINE

See also

Children—Management and training
Physicians—Discipline
School discipline

DISCIPLINE-BASED ART EDUCATION

Achieving discipline-based arts education [excerpt from Aesthetic persuasion] S. S. Kaagan. *The Education Digest* 56:55-8 D '90

DISCONNECT (TERM)

That shifty functional. W. Safire. il *The New York Times Magazine* p6 D 30 '90

DISCOUNT HOUSES (RETAIL TRADE)

See also

Burlington Coat Factory
Loehmann's, Inc.
Outlet stores
Warehouse clubs

Canada

See also

Bargain Harold's Discount Limited

DISCOVERY: THE CHILDREN'S MUSEUM (LAS VEGAS, NEV.) *See* Las Vegas Library/Discovery Museum

DISCRIMINATION

See also

Civil Rights Act of 1990
Race discrimination
Sex discrimination
United Nations. Sub-commission on Prevention of Discrimination and Protection of Minorities

Quotas. T. Matthews. il *Newsweek* 116:28-9 D 31 '90

What's really fair [affirmative action] M. Kinsley. il *Time* 136:124 N 19 '90

DISCRIMINATION IN EDUCATION

See also

Colleges and universities—Desegregation
Public schools—Desegregation
Sex discrimination in education

Fighting prejudice in education [special section; with editorial comment by Ken Schroeder] il *The Education Digest* 56:2-27 N '90

DISCRIMINATION IN EMPLOYMENT

See also

Aged—Employment
Blacks—Employment
Civil Rights Act of 1990
Equal pay for equal work
United States. Equal Employment Opportunity Commission
Women—Employment

Bennett hits the hot button [politics of quotas] E. Clift. il por *Newsweek* 116:26 D 3 '90

Hyping the 'quota' wars [effects of affirmative action] M. Cooper. il *U.S. News & World Report* 109:40-2 D 24 '90

Matsushita loses a bias suit [Quasar subsidiary in U.S.] *Newsweek* 116:47 D 24 '90

The race card [effects of the quota issue on midterm elections] F. Barnes. *The New Republic* 203:10+ D 17 '90

Race vs. rich [1992 campaign] J. Klein. il *New York* 23:16+ D 10 '90

Republicans may have found the perfect Democrat-slayer [attacking affirmative action] P. Dwyer. *Business Week* p36 D 3 '90

Reverse discrimination [male teacher, G. Schafer, denied paternity leave] P. A. Zirkel. bibl f il *Phi Delta Kappan* 72:249-50 N '90

Scientific American drops Christian writer with creation beliefs [F. Mims] K. H. Sidey. il por *Christianity Today* 34:56 N 19 '90

Testing the waters on race [quota issue] L. I. Barrett. il por *Time* 136:21-2 D 24 '90

Trial by genetics. il *Ms.* 1:30 S/O '90

India

Affirmative action, Indian-style [views of Thomas Sowell] D. Seligman. il *Fortune* 122:190 D 3 '90

Christians and the caste controversy. L. A. Lawrence. *The Christian Century* 107:1014-15 N 7 '90

Fatal fires of protest [Brahmins protest Prime Minister V. P. Singh's affirmative action policies for lower castes] E. W. Desmond. il *Time* 136:63 O 15 '90

United States

See Discrimination in employment

DISCRIMINATION IN MEDICAL CARE

Barriers to access. S. Henry. il *Modern Maturity* 33:33-6 O/N '90

DISCRIMINATION IN SPORTS

See also

Sex discrimination in sports

45 years in sports. A. Ashe. il por *Ebony* 46:100+ N '90

An act of conscience [T. Watson resigns from Kansas City Country Club to protest blackballing of H. Bloch] J. Garrity. por *Sports Illustrated* 73:110 D 10 '90

Black hockey pioneer recalls racial fight [W. O'Ree] il por *Jet* 79:48 D 3 '90

Equality begins at home [lack of black college coaches] W. F. Reed. il por *Sports Illustrated* 73:138 N 26 '90

Nuggets charged with racist hiring practices [charges brought by fired coach D. Moe] *Jet* 79:48 O 15 '90

One is not enough [racism at Shoal Creek Country Club in Alabama] E. G. Graves. il *Black Enterprise* 21:9 O '90

DISCRIMINATION IN THE THEATER

The many sins of "Miss Saigon" [exclusion of Asian American actresses] M. Suh. *Ms.* 1:63 N/D '90

DISCS, COMPACT *See* Compact discs

DISCS, VIDEO *See* Videodiscs

DISCUSSION

See also

Debates and debating
Negotiation

DISEASE MODELS, ANIMAL *See* Diseases—Animal models

DISEASE RESISTANCE *See* Immunity

DISEASES

See also

Brain—Diseases
Digestive system—Diseases
Ear—Diseases
Epidemics
Eye—Diseases and defects
Fetus—Diseases
Heart—Diseases
Heredity of disease
Immunologic diseases
Infants, Newborn—Diseases
Infection
Kidneys—Diseases
Liver—Diseases
Prostate gland—Diseases
Reproductive organs—Diseases
Respiratory organs—Diseases
Urinary organs—Diseases
Virus diseases
Women—Diseases

See also names of diseases; *also* subhead Diseases and pests under names of plants and animals

Animal models

See also

AIDS (Disease)—Animal models

Sample entries from *Reader's Guide to Periodical Literature.*

Discrimination (Psychology)
See also
Auditory discrimination
Brightness discrimination
Learning, Psychology of—Discrimination learning
Perception
Similarity (Perception)

Attentional limits on the perception and memory of visual information. J. Palmer. bibl *J Exp Psychol Hum Percept Perform* 16:332-50 My '90

Filtering by movement in visual search. P. McLeod and others. bibl *J Exp Psychol Hum Percept Perform* 17:55-64 F '91

Generalized discrimination of positive facial expressions by seven- and ten-month-old infants. P. M. Ludemann. bibl il *Child Dev* 62:55-67 F '91

Local processes in preattentive feature detection. W. F. Bacon and H. E. Egeth. bibl *J Exp Psychol Hum Percept Perform* 17:77-90 F '91

Reallocation of visual attention. R. Egly and D. Homa. bibl *J Exp Psychol Hum Percept Perform* 17:142-59 F '91

Reduction of unique noise in the psychophysics of hearing by group operating characteristic analysis. A. Taylor and others. bibl *Psychol Bull* 109:133-46 Ja '91

Risk discrimination of direct versus tangential approach by basking black iguanas (Ctenosaura similis): variation as a function of human exposure. J. Burger and M. Gochfeld. bibl *J Comp Psychol* 104:388-94 D '90

Stimulus discrimination following covert attentional orienting to an exogenous cue. J. M. Henderson. bibl *J Exp Psychol Hum Percept Perform* 17:91-106 F '91

Discrimination in criminal justice administration

Gender bias in juvenile justice handling of seriously crime-involved youths. R. Horowitz and A. E. Pottieger. bibl *J Res Crime Delinq* 28:75-100 F '91

Paternalism and the female status offender: remanding the juvenile justice double standard for desexualization. W. A. Reese, II and R. L. Curtis, Jr. *Soc Sci J* 28 no1:63-83 '91

Discrimination in education
See also
Blacks—Education—Discriminatory practices
Segregation in education

A most respectable prejudice: inequality in educational research and policy. J. Murphy. *Br J Sociol* 41:29-54 Mr '90; Discussion. 41:473-5 D '90

Discrimination in employment
See also
Affirmative action programs
Discrimination in sports
Equal pay for equal work
Mexican Americans—Employment—Discriminatory practices
Occupational segregation
United States—Minorities—Employment—Discriminatory practices
United States. Equal Employment Opportunity Commission
Women—United States—Employment—Discriminatory practices

Breaking through. *Economist* 318:29 Ja 26 '91

The impact of job applicants' facial maturity, gender, and academic achievement on hiring recommendations. L. A. Zebrowitz and others. bibl *J Appl Soc Psychol* 21:525-48 Ap 1 '91

New struggle over civil rights brings shift in strategy. J. Biskupic. *Congr Q Wkly Rep* 49:366-73 F 9 '91

Preferential hiring and the question of competence [criticism of views of George Sher] M. Philips. *J Bus Ethics* 10:161-3 F '91

Sample entries from *Social Science Index*, June 1991.

scholarly journals in particular fields. If your topic is music, art, the social sciences, the humanities, or history, for example, you will find specialized indexes that may contain important sources. Some of these indexes may be on microfilm or compact disks (see page 252).

4. Newspaper indexes. *The New York Times Index* is likely to be on your library's shelf. Other newspapers, such as the *Los Angeles Times* or the *London Times* also may be indexed in your library. Some of these indexes are on microfilm. These indexes will refer you to articles in newspapers that usually are stored on microfilm.

5. Biographical indexes. If you are looking for information about a person, current or historical, you may want to consult one of the many biographical indexes that are available. *Biography Index* will lead you to articles in journals or books. *Current Biography* selects important subjects for a biographical sketch each year. A cumulative index to these volumes may lead you to an entry on your subject. *Contemporary Authors* and the Gale series on literature contain biographical and critical overviews of writers. *Biography and Genealogy Master Index* will tell you in what encyclopedia or dictionary you will find an entry about your subject.

6. Dictionaries. *The Oxford English Dictionary* will provide you with a history of word usage for particular terms. But specialized dictionaries—for science, religion, music, philosophy—may give you more detailed information on terms related to a particular field.

7. Pamphlets. The *Vertical File Index: A Subject and Title Index to Selected Pamphlets* will tell you what pamphlets are available on your subject, and it will give you the information necessary to order them.

8. Government documents. Documents published by the U.S. government include congressional reports, statistics, and other records. The *Monthly Catalog of U.S. Government Publications,* the *Congressionl Information Service,* and the *Congressional Record* all may be useful in tracking down government documents.

9. Dissertation abstracts. Each year, brief summaries of doctoral dissertations are filed according to subject area in *Dissertation Abstracts International,* a multivolume work. A photocopy or microfilm of dissertations may be purchased from University Microfilms International or, if available, borrowed through interlibrary loan. Usually, these studies offer complete and up-to-date bibliographies of particular topics.

As you explore sources in a library, you may find yourself overwhelmed by the amount of material available on your topic. Of all the books and articles that you find, how do you know which ones are reliable? As you gain experience researching, you will learn the skills necessary to help you evaluate sources.

Opportunities for Exploring Sources

1. Use a section of your journal or start a separate research notebook to keep your notes and ideas together. Go to the library and begin exploring possible sources for your research topic. Use your library's card catalog or conduct a computer search. Look for key words that will lead you to other sources. Check bibliographies and let sources lead you to explore new sources.

2. As you begin exploring sources, pay attention to the names you encounter. Who has written a lot about your topic? Who are the authorities? The key figures? Who is controversial, respected, persuasive?

3. Explore a source you never have used before. Explore a government document, for instance, or *The Vertical File Index*—some source that is unfamiliar to you, but one that you imagine might contain important primary source information.

Begin making lists of all the possible primary and secondary sources that you will want to explore for your research project.

Evaluating Sources

If you decide to write a research essay asking why smoking has increased among teenage women in the past five years, you will find articles in many different kinds of journals. You may find an essay about smoking in *Seventeen* magazine, written by a journalist who interviewed young women smokers; you may find an article in *The New England Journal of Medicine* written by three physicians who conducted a study of teenage smokers at a large metropolitan hospital. You also may find references to smoking in books about public health policy published by Indiana University Press; you even may find discussions of smoking in a self-help book for parents of adolescents published by Doubleday. All these sources give statistics, anecdotal information about teenage women smokers, and conclusions about the cause for the increased rate. Which sources are reliable? In the following pages, you will find some guidelines to help you evaluate the publication, the author, and the content of the source.

Kind of Publication Academic presses and scholarly journals subject their articles to review. When a writer submits a manuscript, it is sent to competent scholars to judge its merits. A book published by Indiana University Press will have had this review; a book published by Doubleday is not likely to be reviewed by experts in the field. An essay in the *New England Journal of Medicine* has been reviewed; an article in *Psychology Today* usually has not.

This review process does not mean that facts and opinions are infallible. But it does mean that the book or essay is taken seriously by experts in the field. A manuscript published by a trade publisher or in a popular magazine, however, often is reviewed after publication. These reviews may help you to evaluate the merit of the work. *The Book Review Digest* excerpts and summarizes reviews from major newspapers and periodicals. You can look up a book in the volume corresponding to the year of its publication. The excerpts will lead you to the full review, where you can see how others have evaluated the book.

Status of Author Frequently, the byline of an essay or article or the jacket of a book will tell you something about the author. If you are writing about smoking and teenage women, you may ask about the medical effects of smoking. To answer that question, you may find an article written by a physician and an article written by a journalist for a Sunday news supplement to your local paper. The status of the physician may give you confidence in the information she offers; a quotation from her may carry more weight than a quotation from the journalist. On the other hand, if you are interested in first-hand accounts from teenagers about their reasons for smoking, the journalist's status may not be relevant to the usefulness of the article.

In some fields, you may not have enough information to weigh the credentials of critics, historians, or commentators. Several reference sources can help you place these writers in perspective. *Contemporary Authors* and the *Directory of American Scholars* contains biographical information about many writers in the humanities and social sciences. *Modern Scientists and Engineers* and *American Men and Women of Science* are useful for the sciences.

In some fields—literature, history, and sociology, for example—the author may carry assumptions that could affect the conclusions presented in a book or article. For instance, an author may be feminist, Marxist, socialist, or conservative. These positions may affect the author's interpretation of information. Knowing about an author's assumptions helps you evaluate a source. Sometimes you will learn of these assumptions when you research the author's reputation; often, the introduction or preface to the book will refer to the author's particular orientation.

As you research a particular topic, you are likely to find names of certain authors recurring in notes and bibliographies. Gradually, you get a sense of who is respected in the field, who has written important studies, and who is reliable.

Content Your research question is your most valuable guide to evaluating sources. What do you want to know? What source can best provide that information? What source helps you find evidence to support your own argument or analysis?

When you find a source, you need to decide how reliable it is. Besides considering the author's credentials and the kind of publication in which it appears, you will look at the evidence within the source itself. Here are some questions to guide you:

1. **Is the source based on primary or secondary sources?** If the author relied on primary sources, how extensive was the research? Some authors use interviews or eyewitness accounts as evidence: How many people were interviewed? How many witnesses gave testimony? What authority do these people have to give evidence about the topic?

For example, if you were writing a research essay asking what kinds of classes, workshops, or programs are most effective for teaching high school students about AIDS, you might find an article in *Newsweek* that refers to six high school programs throughout the country. You might also find an article in *Public Health Policy* that reports the results of a survey of five hundred high schools. The extensiveness of the research may make the *Public Health Policy* article more important for your research essay. On the other hand, if you decide to interview high school students about their reaction to AIDS education, the *Newsweek* article might be more relevant if it contained quotations from students. In that case, the *Public Health Policy* article might be less relevant if it contained only statistics and tables.

2. **If the source you have found is based on secondary sources, how original are the conclusions presented?** You need to decide whether the author is drawing conclusions based on interpretation, or whether the author is merely reporting other people's conclusions. You may want to go back to the author's secondary sources, if these are available to you, and apply the same criteria for evaluation to those sources.

3. **Do the author's conclusions follow from the evidence?** Sometimes an author may argue for a particular point of view without pre-

senting strong evidence to support that view. You may agree with the author's conclusions, but it is your responsibility to provide good evidence when you write your research essay.

As you explore and evaluate sources, you will be taking notes, asking questions of your sources, and beginning to organize your ideas. The next chapter will help you record the information that you find during the research process.

Opportunities for Evaluating Sources

1. Choose one book that you think will be important in researching your topic. Find the reviews of your book in *The Book Review Digest.* How has your book been evaluated? Are there any controversies surrounding the book? Can you find references in the reviews to other books by the same author or to important books on the same topic?

2. Your research question is your most valuable guide in evaluating the usefulness of each source. Choose one of your sources and evaluate this source by exploring the kind of publication it is and the status of the author. Look at the evidence within the source itself and ask: Is the source based on primary or secondary sources? Are the conclusions of the source original? Do the author's conclusions follow from the evidence? Write a two-page evaluation of this source.

CHAPTER 11

Recording Information

A research project often takes weeks or even months to complete. At the same time that you are working on the research project, you may have essays to write for other courses, finals to study for, and other course work to do. If you keep careful records of your research, you will find that you will be well prepared when you begin to write your research essay.

In this chapter we will follow the research process of Theodore Omachi, who wrote "Affirmative Action: Equal Opportunity or Reverse Discrimination?" as his research essay for a freshman composition course. Theodore had been interested in this topic since applying to colleges as a high school senior. He noticed that some colleges emphasized the diversity of the student population, while others did not. He remembered that some college recruiters at his high school were especially interested in strong minority students. At the time, feeling anxious about his own chances at college admissions, he could hardly sort out his responses to affirmative action. Once he entered college, however, and came to know a variety of students from many different backgrounds, he could consider the issue from a new perspective. His research essay gave him a chance to talk with students, consider many sources, and think more about the issue.

As you read this chapter, you'll have a chance to see how Theodore recorded and organized the information that he gathered as he conducted his research, and you'll see how he integrated this information into his research essay.

BASIC SUPPLIES

Whether you keep written records or ultimately enter information on computer files, you will need some basic research supplies:

Three-by-five-inch index cards for bibliography entries

A notebook, five-by-seven-inch index cards, or a file folder for taking notes

These supplies will enable you to keep your research in accessible order.

Bibliography Cards

Most researchers find it useful to enter each source they find on a three-by-five-inch index card, including all bibliographic information. It can be frustrating to write a paper and find, sometime after midnight when the library is closed, that you are missing the year of publication for one of your sources, or that you forgot to write down the page numbers for an article you decided to use.

Make sure each bibliography card contains the following information:

- Author's name
- Title of the work you are using (if you are using an article, be sure to include the title of the journal or anthology in which it appears)
- Place of publication (except for periodicals)
- Publisher's name (except for periodicals)
- Date of publication
- Inclusive page numbers for the essay, article, or other short text

Some researchers also like to make a note of the library call number for the article so that they can easily find the source again if they need to do so.

See page 261 for a sample bibliography card from Theodore's project.

Note Cards

Note cards contain quotations, paraphrased passages, summaries, or other information from your sources. Because note cards can be easily shuffled and reordered, they are a useful way of taking notes. Some researchers, however, devise their own system using a notebook and a self-made index. The following guidelines for keeping note cards may be helpful no matter what system you decide to use.

Klitgaard, Robert
Choosing Elites
New York: Basic Books, 1985

Sample bibliography card.

1. Put a heading on each note card to help you organize your information. Sometimes, you may want to use a separate card for each source (some sources may require many cards, which should be numbered consecutively); sometimes, you may want to use a subject heading for each card. If you begin your research with a preliminary outline of the different sections of your research essay, you may want to head each card with a section of your outline.

2. Indicate the source and page number for each quotation or paraphrased passage that you write on your note cards.

3. Be sure to put quotation marks around every word, phrase, or passage that comes directly from your source.

Theodore conducted some interviews with students as he gathered information for his project. The note card (page 262) shows how he recorded information from two interviews.

TAKING NOTES

With photocopying readily available in libraries, taking notes may seem a bit old-fashioned. But transcribing information from sources to note

Student Interviews

Interview with David Combs: April 9, 1991
- freshman, biochemistry major

"If I had a black chemistry professor, I'd probably get the same grade, but having a black professor might encourage me to become one."

"I am a minority student, and really it makes me want to try harder because I have something to prove to myself."

Student Interviews

Interview with Brian Ruder: April 10, 1991

"I think that the problem is that we like <u>to think</u> we deserve our intelligence."

Brian – freshman majoring in government

Theodore Omachi's notecards.

cards or computer files requires you to read a text carefully and choose the information that is relevant to your research essay. Taking notes requires more effort than simply underlining or highlighting a text; it requires you to actively think about your source. When students read a source, they often think of quoting as the only way of taking notes. As you will see, however, paraphrasing and summarizing also are useful note-taking strategies.

Quoting Sources

When you *quote,* you copy a passage exactly as it appears in a source onto your note card, place it within quotation marks, and indicate the source and page(s) on which you found it. Be sure that you have a good reason for quoting. You, as the researcher, must select the particular passage you want to quote. You do not copy entire texts, but choose only those parts that you think will be important for your research essay. Sometimes, it is difficult to choose passages to quote, especially when the author of a source writes well. You may be tempted to quote long passages, incorporate these passages into your research essay, and therefore, in effect, allow another writer to write your essay.

Here are some guidelines to help you decide when you should quote from a source.

1. The person you quote is an authority or expert on the material. When you include a quotation in your essay, your readers have a right to know why the person is being quoted. Who is this source? Why should a statement by this person be offered as evidence for your main points? In his essay on affirmative action and college admissions, Theodore included this quotation:

So if being judged on merit "means that admissions committees should take nothing into account but scores on some particular intelligence test," says Ronald Dworkin, a professor of political philosophy, "then it is arbitrary, and, in any case, contradicted by the long-standing practice" of most universities.

Here, an opinion about college admissions is offered by someone who is both an expert on political philosophy and a member of a university community.

2. **The person you quote says something remarkably well.** Students sometimes beome intimidated by professional writing because it seems so precise and smooth. Because published authors seem to write better than they do, students are tempted to quote rather than summarize and paraphrase. If you quote excessively, however, your research essay will appear to have been written by others, not by you. Still, there are times when someone else's words are exceedingly apt: "Nothing goes by luck in composition," wrote Henry David Thoreau. "It allows of no tricks. The best you can write will be the best you are."

3. **The quotation itself adds color or feeling to the essay that would be lost through paraphrasing.** Some quotations convey a vivid feeling of the speaker or writer and a vivid sense of the context from which the quotation comes. The special voice conveyed by the quotation justifies its use.

Paraphrasing Sources

When you *paraphrase,* you rephrase someone else's statement in your own words. When you paraphrase in your essay, you always cite the source in your documentation, as you will see in the next chapter. You need to refer your reader to the author of the idea you are presenting.

When you paraphrase, you need to think about a passage, understand its meaning, and translate that meaning in your own language. Paraphrasing, then, is a more active way of note taking than quoting. You need to be careful, however, to change the wording of the source completely. Here is a passage that Theodore found in one of his sources (*Shifts in Employment and Occupational Status of Black Americans in a Period of Affirmative Action,* by Julianne Malveaux):

> Affirmative action in the educational arena has made the improvement in the occupational distribution of black Americans a more possible achievement than it would have been without such educational opportunities.

If Theodore wanted to paraphrase this sentence, he might have written:

Because black Americans have been able to enter college through affirmative action policies, they are finding a greater number of job opportunities open to them.

This paraphrase is succesful because it keeps the meaning of the source but changes the language into Theodore's own natural, conversational way of writing.

Summarizing Sources

When you *summarize,* you pick out the main points of a book, article, or passage and restate these points in your own words. In effect, you are producing a condensed version of a longer piece. Here is Theodore's summary of the main argument presented by one of his sources (*Invisible Victims: White Males and the Crisis of Affirmative Action,* by Frederick Lynch):

Frederick Lynch argues that affirmative action contributes to and perpetuates the perception that minorities should find role models among their own race.

This summary, entered on his note cards, eventually made its way into Theodore's research essay.

Opportunities for Recording Information

1. How can you use quotations to add substance and persuasiveness to your writing? How can you avoid using quotations only as ornaments to decorate your writing? Reread the guidelines on pages 263–264 to help you decide when you should quote from a source. Look closely at the notes you have taken for your research project. Have you quoted long passages? Is the person you are quoting an authority? Has the person said something important? Can you analyze the quotation and offer your own thinking about the meaning of the quote? Think carefully and critically about the quotations you are recording.

2. Look closely at the material you are gathering for your research essay. Practice paraphrasing and summarizing important information from your sources.

INTEGRATING SOURCES

The quotations, paraphrased passages, and summaries that you compile on your note cards must be woven seamlessly into your essay. A research essay is not a patchwork quilt of fragmented material from other sources. It is a text, created by you, which calls upon sources as evidence for your ideas. Your words, your ideas, and your thinking must give the essay its shape and character.

Setting Up a Context

When you refer to sources in your essay, you need to give some context for the source *within* your essay, not only in footnotes, endnotes, or works cited. Let's look at a paragraph from Theodore's essay in which he includes two quotations from his sources. Notice how he makes the quotation part of his own essay.

Generalizations based on race only seem different because, as Dworkin puts it, they "have historically been motivated not by some instrumental calculation, as in the case of intelligence or age or regional distribution or athletic ability, but because of contempt for the excluded race or religion as such" (Dworkin, 301). California Court of Appeal Justice Macklin Fleming argues that affirmative action is "discrimination in favor of X [which] is automatic discrimination against Y" (Fleming, 47). But while affirmative action might allow a minority to fill a space in a college that might have gone to a Caucasian, it does so in the same way that standardized tests allow more intelligent students to fill spaces that might have gone to less intelligent students. In other words, it is not true discrimination but a useful generalization. Affirmative action does not inflict a pervasive injury on the white race as a whole; this is how it is different from prejudice.

Because Theodore already referred to Ronald Dworkin in a previous paragraph, here he need only mention Dworkin's name as identification. Earlier, Theodore gave Dworkin's full name and even included his position, as professor of political philosophy, to justify the use of a quotation by him. The quotation from Justice Fleming was the first time Fleming was cited in Theodore's paper; therefore, Theodore gave full identification of him. Even though both sources are documented in parenthetical citations and in a Works Cited list at the end of the essay, Theodore included this information so that readers, as they follow the points of the essay, know where quotations come from, why they are being cited, and what weight they carry. If Dworkin's or Fleming's ideas, for example, were put forth by a lawyer defending someone suing a university for discrimination, those ideas would have to be considered differently.

Weaving Texts Together

When you quote from another text, you must make sure that the passage makes sense within your own essay. Just as you check your own writing for grammatical errors, you need to make sure that the quoted passage remains grammatically correct when you integrate it into your essay.

Here, for example, is a passage from K. C. Cole's essay "Women and Science," which you will find in Chapter 8.

> I didn't realize what an odd creature a woman interested in physics was until a few years ago when a science magazine sent me to Johns Hopkins University in Baltimore for a conference on an electrical phenomenon known as the Hall effect. We sat in a huge lecture hall and listened as physicists talked about things engineers didn't understand and engineers talked about things physicists didn't understand. What *I* didn't understand was why, out of several hundred students of physics and engineering in the room, less than a handful were women.

One student, writing about women scientists, wanted to quote from this passage. Here is how she integrated the quotation into her essay:

Many women get their first hard look at their place in the profession when they attend a conference with their peers. "I didn't realize what an odd creature a woman in physics was," science writer K. C. Cole wrote in an essay, "until a few years ago when a science magazine sent me to Johns Hopkins University in Baltimore for a conference on an electrical phenomenon known as the Hall effect."

Here, the student broke up the quotation to tell her readers who was being quoted. As a variation from introducing each quotation by a beginning phrase, breaking up a long quotation gives an essay an easy-to-read, conversational style.

Editing Quotations

There are several ways the student could have edited the quotation if she had wanted to. She might have omitted information that was not especially relevant to her essay, still keeping the sense of the quotation. When any information is omitted from a quotation, the omission needs to be indicated by an ellipsis, a series of three dots. Here is an example of how an ellipsis is used:

Many women get their first hard look at their place in the profession when they attend a conference with their peers. "I didn't realize what an odd creature a woman in physics was," science writer K. C. Cole wrote in an essay, "until a few years ago when a science magazine sent me to . . . a conference on an electrical phenomenon known as the Hall effect."

This writer thought that the place of the conference, Johns Hopkins University, was not essential to the sense of the quotation. In the interest of conciseness, she decided to omit that information by substituting an ellipsis.

If the ellipsis comes before any punctuation, the three dots must *precede* the punctuation; ellipses do not take the place of other punctuation. Here, then, is an ellipsis at the end of a sentence:

Many women get their first hard look at their place in the profession when they attend a conference with their peers. "I didn't realize what an odd creature a woman in physics was," science writer K. C. Cole wrote in an essay, "until a few years ago when a science magazine sent me to Johns Hopkins University in Baltimore for a conference. . . ."

Notice that there are four dots at the end of this sentence: three dots are the ellipsis, meaning that part of a quoted passage has been omitted; the fourth dot is the period. If the ellipsis had occurred before a comma, you would type three dots and a comma within the quotation marks, followed by the rest of your sentence.

Sometimes, instead of omitting words from a quoted passage, you need to add words so that the quotation will make sense in your essay. Here is the way one student chose to use a sentence from Cole's essay:

> K. C. Cole, in a recent essay, wrote that she "didn't realize what an odd creature a woman interested in physics was until a few years ago when a science magazine sent [her] to Johns Hopkins University in Baltimore for a conference. . . . [Cole and others] sat in a huge lecture hall and listened as physicists talked about things engineers didn't understand and engineers talked about things physicists didn't understand."

This student added words in *brackets* so that Cole's passage would make sense in the essay. Whenever you change a quotation by adding words or phrases, you use brackets, not parentheses.

If you find yourself using ellipses and brackets often within a quoted passage, you may want to paraphrase the quotation instead. Whenever you bring sources into your essay, whether through quoting, paraphrasing, or summarizing, you want the sources to be woven easily into your own writing; you do not want them to stand out awkwardly, causing your reader to stumble or stop.

Opportunities for Integrating Sources

1. Draft a paragraph using one of the quotations you will use in your research essay. Consider these questions as you draft your paragraph: How will you introduce this quotation? How will you create a context for the quotation so that the source is woven comfortably into your writing? How will you reflect upon this quotation and show your readers what this piece of evidence means? Exchange paragraphs with your classmates.

2. Take two or three of the longer quotations you plan to use. Practice editing them.

PLAGIARISM

Most of your college writing will depend upon outside sources such as books, articles, and interviews. When you draw upon such sources in your own writing, you must acknowledge the source by proper documentation. If you do not acknowledge the source, you are, in effect, stealing material from another writer. This stealing is called *plagiarism* (the root of the word means *kidnapping*), which is a serious offense.

Plagiarism usually results from two causes:

1. Sometimes when you take notes, you may be tired or rushed. You begin to write down only some main ideas and a few phrases from your source, but soon, without realizing it, you begin to write down longer passages. When you go back to your notes, you think that the passages are your own because you have not indicated quotation marks or page numbers, and you incorporate this material into your own essay.

To avoid this inadvertent plagiarism, take notes carefully, indicating the page number from which you have taken information. Always place quotation marks around words that you copy from the source, even if it is only one word.

2. Sometimes when you take notes, you have read the source so many times that you feel you know it by heart, and when you sit down to write you can't think of any other way to present the material. Besides, you think, the writer of the source is a much better writer than you are, and you can't seem to find exactly the right words to get a point across.

To avoid plagiarizing because of faulty paraphrases, remember that a paraphrase needs to show your own ideas, not just someone else's ideas in a slightly different wording from the original. As a writer, you need to bring your own interpretation and analysis to the sources you find. You are serving as more than a compiler of other people's ideas; you are presenting your own ideas *based upon* sources, not merely reporting those sources.

Here is a passage from "Warfare: An Invention—Not a Biological Necessity" by anthropologist Margaret Mead. In this essay, Mead says that warfare

> is an invention like any other of the inventions in terms of which we order our lives, such as writing, marriage, cooking our food instead of eating it raw, trial by jury, or burial of the dead, and so on. Some of this list any one will grant are inventions: trial by jury is confined to very limited portions of the globe; we know that there are tribes that do not bury their dead but instead expose or cremate them; and we know that only part of

> the human race has had a knowledge of writing as its cultural inheritance. But, whenever a way of doing things is found universally, such as the use of fire or the practice of some form of marriage, we tend to think at once that it is not an invention at all but an attribute of humanity itself.

Here is how one student used this passage in his essay:

> We know that there are many cultures that do not have warfare, and therefore it seems that warfare *is an invention like any other of the inventions in terms of which we order our lives, such as writing, marriage, cooking our food instead of eating it raw, trial by jury, or burial of the dead.*

You can see that the italic portion comes directly from Mead's text. Therefore, this passage is *plagiarized.* It does not matter that the inventions that Mead lists could have been thought of by anyone else. It does not matter that the student learned this material from Mead, and thinks that he doesn't need to document everything that he has learned. The fact is: This material comes directly from another writer, is not placed within quotation marks, is not documented, and therefore is stolen.

Here is how another student used Mead's text:

> We know that there are many cultures that do not have warfare, and therefore warfare seems to be just another invention, much like marriage, or cooking food, or burying the dead. After all, we know that some cultures do not bury the dead. Yet whenever we find a behavior occurring universally, we think that it is not an invention, but an inevitable part of the human race.

Although this student changed some of the wording, the passage is very close to Mead's own ideas. It is not a good idea to paraphrase so closely. And certainly the paraphrase needs to be documented.

Another student used Mead's text more successfully:

> As Margaret Mead has concluded, one way of deciding whether or not a cultural behavior is an invention is seeing how pervasive

it is in other cultures. We know there are wide variations in such behavior as marriage, raising children, or division of labor by males and females, so we know that these behaviors are not the same for all humans. We know, also, that warfare does not exist in many cultures, so we can guess that it is merely an invention.

Here, the student substantially changed Mead's wording, still acknowledging Mead as the source of his point, and he added information of his own. Mead, as you remember, did not write anything about raising children or sharing work. The student brought in these ideas to expand the context of Mead's point. This passage is not plagiarized.

One way to avoid plagiarism, then, is by expanding upon the ideas you find in sources. By adding information, interpreting, or analyzing those ideas, you go beyond the information in the source. Another way to avoid plagiarism is by using a combination of summary, paraphrase, and quotation to refer to information that you found in a particular source. Here is an example of this strategy:

The case that warfare is nothing more than an invention is made strongly by the anthropologist Margaret Mead, who compares such aggressive behavior with marriage, cooking food, and burying the dead. These behaviors, like warfare, are not practiced universally, and so can justly be called an invention. Only when something is practiced universally, Mead says, do we conclude "that it is not an invention at all, but an attribute of humanity."

Here, the student is referring directly in his essay to the work of Margaret Mead. He summarizes Mead's ideas at the beginning of the paragraph. It is clear to the reader that the ideas presented are Mead's and not the author's. At the end of this passage, the author decides to paraphrase part of Mead's idea and to quote the rest. We know from the information that the student gives us that this material is from Mead. This passage is not plagiarized.

A WRITER AT WORK: THEODORE OMACHI

In the following pages you'll have a chance to read "Affirmative Action: Equal Opportunity or Reverse Discrimination?" by Theodore Omachi.

As you read, notice the evidence from sources that Theodore uses to support his assertions. Where does Theodore use primary sources? How effective are these sources in supporting Theodore's ideas? What kinds of secondary sources does he use? How do these secondary sources help Theodore to argue his point of view?

Notice, too, how Theodore integrates quotations into his own text. As a reader, you are always given enough information to know why Theodore is quoting from a certain source.

In this essay, Theodore uses the MLA (Modern Language Association) citation form, which calls for references to sources to be in parentheses within the text, and provides complete documentation of those sources in a list of Works Cited. The MLA form of citation currently is preferred for essays in the humanities and social sciences. You will find more information about forms of documentation in Chapter 12.

Affirmative Action: Equal Opportunity or Reverse Discrimination?

Theodore Omachi

When I was young, my father used to warn me about the evils of discrimination, about treating people differently because of the color of their skin or the way they look. Born in one of the relocation camps for Japanese-Americans during World War II, my father had experienced first-hand the injustice of treating people on the basis of vague generalizations, or interning all Japanese-Americans because people were afraid that some might commit treason. I grew up with the notion that race shouldn't affect our judgment or treatment of others because after all, he said, "people are people." But when I entered high school, I learned of something called affirmative action, which seemed inconsistent with this idea of judging people on their merits. To consider the race of an applicant seemed to make use of the very racism that affirmative action was fighting against. When I learned that my father supported such a policy, I decided he was a hypocrite. But lately, I have changed my mind: I think a racially conscious test for student admission to college is in fact a desirable policy that is consistent with judging people on their merits. 1

In coming to this conclusion, I had first to recognize that affirmative action is not reverse discrimination and then to see that despite its drawbacks, it is still beneficial, at least in education. The question is not whether affirmative action has any considerable disadvantages; I think it almost always does. We need to ask first whether these disadvantages violate any 2 civil rights and, second, simply whether disadvantages outweigh advantages. As Michael Sandel, a professor of political philosophy explains, "Once no individual rights [are] seen to be at stake [in affirmative action], utilitarian considerations automatically prevail" (Sandel, 165).

What right might be violated in affirmative action? The most frequently made argument, and the one that previously appealed to me, is best voiced by U.S. Supreme Court Justice Douglas, who said in his dissent of one affirmative action case, "Whatever his race, [the applicant] had a constitutional right to have his application considered on its individual merits in a racially neutral case" (*Defunis v. Odegaard,* 507). Most of us have been brought up with the idea that we should strive for excellence and that we will be rewarded for excellence. Such catch phrases as "The important thing is that you tried your hardest" have taught us that effort is truly what should count. So the practice of rewarding applicants with admission to colleges in part because they happen to be minorities, a fact over which they have no control, doesn't seem fair. 3

But what is merit anyway, and how much of the fact that we are in college is really a result of our own efforts? Many reasons why we are accepted at a college come from factors over which we have had no control. While it is true that minorities didn't choose to be minorities, it is also true that we did not choose our levels of intelligence. So if being judged on merit "means that admissions committees should take nothing into account but scores on some particular intelligence test," says Ronald Dworkin, a professor of political philosophy who considers the issue of affirmative action in his book *A Matter of Principle,* "then it is arbitrary, and, in any case, contradicted by the long-standing practice" of most universities (Dworkin, 299). If universities are allowed to weigh factors other than intelligence, such as the contribution an applicant can make to the college or society as a whole, then race seems no less valid a factor than intelligence, athletic ability, or geographic origin. Intelligence counts as a "merit" only because it will someday allow a student to better serve society. Similarly, black skin may someday enable an applicant to provide a role model for other blacks and so is no less valid a "merit." 4

Perhaps the reason we find a problem with calling race a merit is that we tend to consider much of our talent and status as deserved and, therefore, distinguish race because it is obviously undeserved. But when I personally think about why I am able to attend college, I realize that much of it could be ascribed to luck. If I hadn't been born relatively smart, or into *my* family, which provided my educational opportunities and emotional support, then I probably wouldn't be in college. Brian Ruder, a classmate of mine, summarized this argument when he said, "I think the problem is that we like *to think* we deserve our intelligence" (Ruder interview). Being a minority then is not less deserved than many other factors of college admission. 5

Opponents also think that affirmative action does not treat people as individuals but discriminates against them only because they are members of a certain race. That kind of generalization sent my father to a relocation camp. But while generalizations can be discriminatory if they are unfounded, sometimes they are necessary. After all, colleges generalize that students who get a B in a particular subject are less able than students who get an A. No one asks whether the B student had a harder instructor. Instead, the admissions committee makes a generalization. Generalizing the contributions that an applicant may make because of his [or her] race is no less valid. 6

Generalizations based on race only seem different because, as Dworkin puts it, they "have historically been motivated not by some instrumental calculation, as in the case of intelligence or age or regional distribution or athletic ability, but because of contempt for the excluded race or religion as such" (Dworkin, 301). California Court of Appeal Justice Macklin Fleming argues that affirmative action is "discrimination in favor of X [which] is automatic discrimination against Y" (Fleming, 47). But while affirmative action might allow a minority to fill a space in a college that might have gone to a Caucasian, it does so in the same way that standardized tests allow more intelligent students to fill spaces that might have gone to less intelligent students. In other words, it is not true discrimination but a useful generalization. Affirmative action does not inflict a pervasive injury on the white race as a whole; this is how it is different from prejudice. 7

While affirmative action, then, does not violate anyone's rights, we still need to look at its usefulness. The long-term goal of affirmative action is to reduce class distinction between whites and minorities and, therefore, to reduce the degree to which American society is racially conscious. The theory, according to Dworkin, is that "the United States will continue to be pervaded by racial divisions as long as the most lucrative, satisfying, and important careers remain mainly the prerogative of members of the white race" (Dworkin, 294). 8

In 1974, about two percent of medical doctors were black while blacks composed eleven percent of the general population. Without affirmative action, such numbers would not have changed and will not continue to change. Julianne Malveaux of the Rockefeller Foundation performed a statistical analysis of the effects of affirmative action in educational institutions and the workplace and concluded, "Affirmative action in the educational arena has made the improvement in the occupational distribution of black Americans a more possible achievement than it would have been without such educational opportunities. . . . If educational opportunities for black Americans decline . . ., the occupational convergence projected for the near future will be jeopardized" (Malveaux, 166). Perhaps the best example is that of the Medical School of the University of California at Davis, the defendant supporting affirmative action in the *University of California* 9

Regents v. Bakke U.S. Supreme Court case. In 1968, the first class of the medical school contained three Asians and no other minority students. This proportion changed only after a special admissions program for minority students was instituted.

An affirmative action program provides a more integrated campus, not 10
because having a campus which reflects the racial makeup of society as a whole is desirable in itself, but because association "between blacks and whites," writes Dworkin, "will decrease the degree to which whites think of blacks as a race rather than as people" (Dworkin, 295). Imagine what our perception of people of other races would be if we had no or little contact with them but learned about them only through textbooks. Upon meeting them, we would probably be too overwhelmed with the color of their skin to consider their personalities.

Affirmative action breaks down historical barriers to professions domi- 11
nated by whites by providing minority role models. Dworkin notes that affirmative action attempts to provide minority role models because "the success of whites, for now, is likely to mean little or nothing" for minorities (Dworkin, 195). However, there are those, like sociologist Frederick Lynch, who argue that affirmative action just perpetuates the idea that minorities should find role models only among their own race (Lynch, 127). To see the fallacy of this argument, we need to look at both the history of race consciousness and the future of affirmative action. We see clearly that history, not affirmative action, has been the cause of such extreme racial consciousness that minorities are much more likely to identify with people of their own race rather than another. It is too bad that such race consciousness still exists, but it does. David Combs, a black first-year college student who is planning to major in biochemistry, says that having black role models is definitely important. "If I had a black chemistry professor," says David, "I'd probably get the same grade, but having a black professor might encourage me to become one" (Combs interview).

Affirmative action does reflect race consciousness and might even per- 13
petuate it. But once minorities are brought up to equal representation and fulfill their potential, then nonracial admissions programs, whatever their consequence, can be accepted. Some day young people will be able to find role models of any race; but for now, affirmative action must make use of the race consciousness that does exist and will continue to exist, with or without affirmative action.

The advantages of affirmative action are certainly considerable, but admittedly, so are its disadvantages. Many critics of affirmative action say that the policy stigmatizes minorities. Justice Macklin Fleming summarized this argument when he wrote, "If in a given class the great majority of the black students are at the bottom of the class, this factor is bound to instill, unconsciously at least, some sense of intellectual superiority among the white students and some sense of intellectual inferiority among the black students" (Fleming, 45). To give an example, James McPherson, [a] black lawyer, poet, and literary critic, once wrote that "he and other blacks at Harvard Law School felt that 'perhaps we were not authentic law students' and that white classmates 'knew that we were not and, like certain members of the faculty, had developed paternalistic attitudes toward us' " (O'Neil, 141).

If we look at the alternative to affirmative action, this argument seems weak. If minorities are admitted under less rigorous standards than Caucasians, they may not do as well. Yet, if they were not on campus at all, campuses would be effectively segregated, and that would hardly go far in lessening the gap between races. 14

Some minority students, in fact, perform very well. David Combs says that being a minority student "makes [him] want to try harder because [he has] something to prove" to himself (Combs interview). Even at Stanford, where accepted black applicants scored an average of 310 points lower on the S.A.T., their scores did not predict their success once they were enrolled (Klitgaard, 175). 15

My father was correct in telling me that prejudice against people simply because of their physical features is evil and unjust. But affirmative action is not prejudice. While racial classifications have been used in the past for bad purposes, such classifications are not inherently bad. Affirmative action carries risks, but considering what is to be gained, those risks are certainly worth taking. Without affirmative action, integration will slow to a crawl. With it, we can find justice that was previously denied. 16

Works Cited

Combs, David. Personal interview. 9 Apr. 1991.

Defunis v. Odegaard, U.S. Supreme Court No. 82-1169. Decided 1973.

Dworkin, Ronald. *A Matter of Principle.* Cambridge: Harvard UP, 1979.

Fleming, Macklin. "The Black Quota at Yale Law School," *The Public Interest.* Spring 1970: 42–52.

Klitgaard, Robert. *Choosing Elites.* New York: Basic Books, 1985.

Lynch, Frederick. *Invisible Victims: White Males and the Crisis of Affirmative Action.* New York: Greenwood, 1989.

Malveaux, Julianne. *Shifts in Employment and Occupational Status of Black Americans in a Period of Affirmative Action.* New York: The Rockefeller Foundation, 1979.

O'Neil, Robert. *Discriminating against Discrimination.* Bloomington: Indiana UP, 1975.

Ruder, Brian. Personal Interview. 10 Apr. 1991.

Sandel, Michael J. *Liberalism and the Limits of Justice.* Cambridge, England: Cambridge UP, 1982.

Opportunities for Exchanging Ideas

1. Discuss Theodore Omachi's research essay with your classmates. Consider the following questions in your discussion: What question is Theodore asking about affirmative action? What distinctions is he trying to create? What arguments and counterarguments does he present? How does he use primary sources? Secondary sources? How effective are these various sources in supporting his arguments?

Identify specific paragraphs where you think Theodore uses evidence successfully. How does he introduce and create a context for his quotations? How does he show his readers his own reflections and analysis of these quotations? How does he summarize and paraphrase selected quotations?

2. If given the opportunity and time, Theodore would probably revise this research essay again. What suggestions would you offer him for strengthening his essay? Could you identify for him specific passages where you think the evidence could be stronger? What questions would you ask Theodore about his argument and his ideas? Discuss Theodore's essay and these questions with your classmates.

Opportunities for Writing

Write a brief proposal describing your plans for a research essay. In this proposal you will want to describe the following: your research questions, the sources you plan to use, how you are questioning and analyzing your sources, and how you will use your sources to argue your position. Exchange proposals with your classmates.

CHAPTER 12

Documentation

When you write a research essay, you are sharing with your readers the results of your investigations into a variety of sources. Part of the conversation you have with your readers occurs in *citations,* references to your sources, where you tell readers about your research process. They will learn from your citations exactly where you found evidence to support your assertions.

Many students think that references to sources are included to serve as a check on their honesty. But citations offer your readers important information about your sources. They give readers a chance to find the context of passages that you may have quoted or paraphrased. They allow readers to follow their interest in sources that are relevant to something they may be researching.

Understanding the reasons for referring to sources does not make citation any easier. Even experienced writers often refer to a documentation guide to help them cite sources correctly. Among the many guides available, the most useful for college writing are the *MLA Handbook for Writers of Research Papers,* 3rd ed. (New York: Modern Language Association, 1988) and the American Psychological Association's *Publication Manual,* 3rd. ed. (Washington: American Psychological Association, 1983).

The MLA guide offers citation information that is usually accepted in the humanities (English, history, languages, composition, philosophy). The APA guide offers citation information that is appropriate for the social sciences (psychology, sociology, anthropology). Many scientific disciplines have specific manuals for that field, which will be recommended by your instructor. When in doubt about the style of citations required for a research essay, always check with your instructor.

In the following pages, you will find the basic information that you need in order to document books and articles properly in both the MLA and APA styles. Many more examples are available in the MLA and APA manuals.

MLA CITATION STYLE

Two ways of citing sources are recommended by the Modern Language Association (MLA). You may include references in parentheses in your text, with a Works Cited list at the end of your text; or you may use footnote or endnote numbers in the text to refer your readers to citations at the bottom of the page (footnotes) or at the end of your essay (endnotes). Many instructors favor parenthetical citations. In Chapter 11, you'll notice that Theodore Omachi cited his sources in parentheses within his essay.

Parenthetical Citation

If your instructor asks you to cite using parentheses within the text, you will always have a list entitled "Works Cited" appended to your essay. When you cite in parentheses, you include as much information as your readers will need to find the complete reference in the list of Works Cited. The parenthetical citation appears at the end of a sentence in which you refer to a source. Often a parenthetical citation will follow a quotation, but sometimes, as in the following passage, a parenthetical citation will follow the material you have paraphrased or summarized.

Carol Gilligan's essay "Teaching Shakespeare's Sister" (on page 433 of the Scourcebook) contains the following passage. We have rewritten it using parenthetical citations.

At the edge of adolescence, eleven- and twelve-year-old girls observe where and when women speak and when they are silent (Brown, 62–71). As resisters, they may be especially prone to notice and question the compliance of women to male authority. One of Woolf's questions in *A Room of One's Own* is why mothers do not provide more rooms for their daughters, and why, more specifically, mothers do not endow their daughters' education with greater comfort (20–24).

The citations refer the reader to the following entries in a list of Works Cited:

Brown, Lyn Mikel. "A Problem of Vision: The Development of Voice and Relational Knowledge in Girls Ages Seven to Sixteen." *Women's Studies Quarterly* 19 (1991): 52–71.
Woolf, Virginia. *A Room of One's Own.* 1928. New York: Harcourt, 1957.

Notice that different information is given for each parenthetical citation. In the first, the reader needs to know the name of the author and the page reference because neither appears in the essay. In the second citation, readers know that Gilligan refers to an essay by Virginia Woolf, so only page numbers are needed.

Here is a paragraph from Theodore Omachi's essay, using parenthetical citations.

> Generalizations based on race only seem different because, as Dworkin puts it, they "have historically been motivated not by some instrumental calculation, as in the case of intelligence or age or regional distribution or athletic ability, but because of contempt for the excluded race or religion as such" (301). California Court of Appeal Justice Macklin Fleming argues that affirmative action is "discrimination in favor of X [which] is automatic discrimination against Y" (47).

Notice that quotation marks surround the quote that you are citing. After the quotation marks comes the reference in parentheses, followed by a period. In the second quotation, Theodore has added a word in brackets so that the quotation will make sense within his essay.

For both citations, Theodore needs only to provide the page number for the quotation. Since he named the author in the text, readers easily can find the source in his list of Works Cited. Using commonsense rules makes citation easier. If you are referring to more than one work by a single author, for example, you need to include a shortened version of the source's title within the parenthetical citation. If you are referring to an entire work, rather than to a specific page or pages, you need only to include the author's last name within the parenthetical citation.

Works Cited

A list of works that you referred to in your parenthetical citations follows the text of your essay. The list begins on a separate page. You list sources alphabetically according to the author's last name, and include all publishing information.

When you type your list of Works Cited, begin each entry at the margin and double-space both within and between each entry. Parts of each entry (author, title, publication information) are separated by a period. Subsequent lines for each source are indented five spaces. List your sources in strict alphabetical order. If a source does not have an author, alphabetize the source according to the first significant word of the title. Inclusive page numbers for any article or short work are listed, not only the page to which you may have referred in your essay.

The following are some sample entries.

Books by One Author

Dworkin, Ronald. *A Matter of Principle.* Cambridge: Harvard UP, 1979.

Books by More than One Author

Burgess, Ernest W., and Harvey J. Locke. *The Family: From Institution to Companionship.* New York: American Book, 1945.

Books by a Group or Corporate Author

American Historical Association. *Guide to Historical Literature.* New York: Macmillan, 1963.

Books with No Author Named

Dictionary of Computing. Oxford: Oxford UP, 1983.

Books with an Author and Editor (or Author and Translator)

Auden, W. H. *Selected Poems.* Ed. Edward Mendelson. New York: Vintage, 1979.

Edited Collections

Anshen, Ruth Nanda, ed. *The Family: Its Function and Destiny.* New York: Harper, 1949.

Books in Several Volumes

Gilbert, Sandra, and Susan Gubar. *No Man's Land.* 2 vols. New Haven: Yale UP, 1988.

Journal Articles

Fleming, Macklin. "The Black Quota at Yale Law School." *The Public Interest.* Spring 1970: 45–52.

Newspaper and Magazine Articles

Axthelm, Peter. "The Bear in the Tower." *Newsweek.* 12 Nov. 1979: 133–35.

Works in a Collection

Auden, W. H. "Musee de Beaux Arts." *Selected Poems.* Ed. Edward Mendelson. New York: Vintage, 1979: 79.

Government Documents

U.S. Dept. of Health, Education, and Welfare. *Minorities and Women in the Health Fields.* HRA Pub. No. 75–22. Washington: GPO, 1974: 11.

Reprints of a Book

Wilder, Thornton. *The Bridge of San Luis Rey.* 1927. New York: Washington Square, 1969.

Interviews

Combs, David. Personal interview. 9 Apr. 1991.

Films

Reynolds, Kevin, dir. *Robin Hood: Prince of Thieves.* Warner Brothers, 1991.

Lectures

Davis, Donald. Class Lecture. History 105. University of Nebraska, Lincoln, Nebraska. 23 Feb. 1990.

Notes

Footnotes and endnotes are an alternative method of citing sources. Passages that you cite are followed by a *superscript number,* that is, a number raised above the line. When you type, you simply roll the carriage one-half line up; if you use a word processing program on a computer, numbers for notes are entered automatically.

The numbers refer to consecutive notes. The first reference to a source contains complete bibliographic information:

- Name of author
- Title of source
- Place of publication

- Publisher
- Date
- Page number to which you are referring

Here is a paragraph from Theodore Omachi's essay with citations by notes.

Generalizations based on race only seem different because, as Dworkin puts it; they "have historically been motivated not by some instrumental calculation, as in the case of intelligence or age or regional distribution or athletic ability, but because of contempt for the excluded race or religion as such."[1] California Court of Appeal Justice Macklin Fleming argues that affirmative action is "discrimination in favor of X [which] is automatic discrimination against Y."[2]

The superscript numbers refer to the following notes:

[1] Ronald Dworkin, *A Matter of Principle* (Cambridge: Harvard UP, 1979) 301.

[2] Macklin Fleming, "The Black Quota at Yale Law School," *The Public Interest* Spring 1970: 47.

Indent the first line of each note five spaces, just as you would for a paragraph. Raise the note number above the line. There is no period after the note number. Use a comma between the author's name and the title of the work. Set off the place of publication, publisher, and date in parentheses. Double-space within each source and between entries.

When you cite the same work again, you need only use the author's last name and the page number to which you are referring. If Theodore had used *A Matter of Principle* a second time, the entry might read:

[3] Dworkin 302.

Notice that no punctuation is necessary here between the author's name and the page number. If, however, you are referring to an author who has written more than one book or article that you are using, you need to include the title of the work, or a short form of the title, to avoid confusion.

Often, you will be using sources that require more complicated citations. Here are some guidelines to a variety of citation forms.

Books by One Author

1. Ronald Dworkin, *A Matter of Principle* (Cambridge: Harvard UP, 1979) 294.

Books by More than One Author

2. Ernest W. Burgess and Harvey J. Locke, *The Family: From Institution to Companionship* (New York: American Book, 1945) 15.

Books by a Group of Corporate Author

3. American Historical Association, *Guide to Historical Literature* (New York: Macmillan, 1963) 135.

Books with No Author Named

4. *Dictionary of Computing* (Oxford: Oxford UP, 1983) 48.

Books with an Author and Editor (or Author and Translator)

5. W. H. Auden, *Selected Poems*, ed. Edward Mendelson (New York: Vintage, 1979) 79.

Edited Collections

6. Ruth Nanda Anshen, ed., *The Family: Its Function and Destiny* (New York: Harper, 1949) 68.

Books in Several Volumes

7. Sandra Gilbert and Susan Gubar, *No Man's Land*, 2 vols. (New Haven: Yale UP, 1988) 1: 90.

Journal Articles

8. Macklin Fleming, "The Black Quota at Yale Law School," *The Public Interest* Spring 1970: 47.

Newspaper and Magazine Articles

9. Peter Axthelm, "The Bear in the Tower," *Newsweek* 12 Nov. 1979: 133.

Works in a Collection

10. W. H. Auden, "Musee de Beaux Arts," *Selected Poems*, ed. Edward Mendelson (New York: Vintage, 1979) 79.

Government Documents

11. U.S. Dept. of Health, Education, and Welfare, *Minorities and Women in the Health Fields* HRA Pub. No. 75-22 (Washington: GPO, 1974) 11.

Reprints of a Book

12. Thornton Wilder, *The Bridge of San Luis Rey* (1927; New York: Washington Square, 1969) 75.

Interviews

13. David Combs, personal interview, 9 Apr. 1991.

Films

14. *Robin Hood: Prince of Thieves*, Kevin Reynolds, dir., Warner Brothers, 1991.

Lectures

15. Donald Davis, class lecture, History 105, University of Nebraska, Lincoln, Nebraska, 23 Feb. 1990.

Endnotes for Commentary

The function of endnotes is not limited to citation. Sometimes, you may want to make a comment to your readers that supplements or explains a point in your essay, or you may want to refer your readers to works that do not appear as citations or bibliography entries. Such comments would interrupt the flow of ideas if they appeared within the essay. Here is an example of such an endnote.

At the same time that feminist criticism has given readers a new way to look at literature, many feminist writers have been continually reassessing their point of view.[1] Since the late 1980s, we have seen more divergence and disagreement within the community of feminist scholars than we had seen in the two decades previously. It seems hardly possible that writers such as the historian Elizabeth Fox-Genovese and the journalist Sylvia Hewlett, questioning the assumptions of feminism, would have been published twenty years ago.

[1] Such works include Sheila Rowbotham's *The Past is Before Us* (Boston: Beacon, 1991) and Elizabeth Spelman's *Inessential Woman: Problems of Exclusion in Feminist Thought* (Boston: Beacon, 1988). An interesting application of a diversity of views by feminist scholars appears in *Life/Lines: Theorizing Women's Autobiography,* edited by Bella Brodski and Celeste Schenck (Ithaca; Cornell UP, 1988).

As you can see, the note here leads readers to sources beyond those referred to in the essay. With such a note, you are saying to your readers, "Here is where you can look if you are interested in this idea and would like to pursue it further."

APA CITATION STYLE

In APA (American Psychological Association) style, all citations are made within parentheses in the text, and a list of references for those citations is included at the end of the text. The parenthetical information includes the author's last name, the date of publication, and the page number to which you are referring. If you are referring to an entire work, you need not include any page numbers. When you refer specifically to the author of the source to introduce a quotation or reference, you do not have to repeat that name within the parenthetical citation.

Here is an edited version of a paragraph from Theodore Omachi's essay, written in APA citation style:

Generalizations based on race only seem different because, as one political philosopher indicates, they "have historically been motivated not by some instrumental calculation, as in the case of intelligence or age or regional distribution or athletic ability, but because of contempt for the excluded race or religion as such" (Dworkin, 1979, p. 301). California Court of Appeal Justice Macklin Fleming argues that affirmative action is "discrimination in favor of X [which] is automatic discrimination against Y" (1970, p. 47).

Notice that when the author of the quotation is not introduced by name, his or her last name appears in the citation; but when the author is introduced in the essay, the name can be omitted from the citation.

List of Sources

In APA style, the bibliography is called "References" and starts on a separate page at the end of the research essay. As in MLA style, the list is written in strict alphabetical order. The first line begins at the margin, with subsequent lines indenting three spaces. Double-space within entries and between entries.

The form in APA style is slightly different from MLA style:

Last name, Initial of first name of author. (date of publication). *Title of work.* Place of publication: Publisher.

When giving the title of a work, capitalize only the first word of the title, the first word of the subtitle, and proper names. In titles of journals, capitalize all significant words.

The following are some sample entries.

Books by One Author

Dworkin, R. (1979). *A matter of principle.* Cambridge: Harvard University Press.

Books by More than One Author

Burgess, E. W., and H. J. Locke. (1945). *The family: From institution to companionship.* New York: American Book.

Books by a Group or Corporate Author

American Historical Association. (1963). *Guide to historical literature.* New York: Macmillan.

Books with No Author Named

Dictionary of computing. (1983). Oxford: Oxford University Press.

Books with an Author and Editor (or Author and Translator)

Auden, W. H. (1979). *Selected poems*, ed. E. Mendolson. New York: Vintage Books.

Edited Collections

Anshen, R. N., ed. (1949). *The Family: Its function and destiny.* New York: Harper.

Books in Several Volumes

Gilbert, S., and S. Gubar. (1988). *No man's land.* 2 vols. New Haven: Yale University Press.

Journal Articles

Fleming, M. (1970, Spring). The black quota at Yale Law School. *The Public Interest.* pp. 45–52.

Newspaper and Magazine Articles

Axthelm, P. (1979, Nov. 12). The Bear in the Tower. *Newsweek,* pp. 133–135.

Works in a Collection

Baier, K. (1970). Responsibility and Action. In M. Brand (Ed.), *The nature of human action* (pp. 100–116). New York: Scott, Foresman.

Government Documents

U.S. Dept. Health, Education, and Welfare. (1974). *Minorities and women in the health fields.* HRA Pub. No. 75-22. Washington, D.C.: Government Printing Office.

Reprint of Books

Wilder, T. (1927, 1969). *The bridge of San Luis Rey.* New York: Washington Square Press.

Interviews

In APA style, interviews that you conduct yourself are not included in a list of references. Instead, cite the information in parentheses in your essay. Here is a sample from Theodore's essay:

It is too bad that such race consciousness still exists, but it does. David Combs, a black first-year college student who is planning to major in biochemistry, says that having black role models is definitely important. "If I had a black chemistry professor," says David, "I'd probably get the same grade, but having a black professor might encourage me to become one" (personal communication, April 9, 1991).

Opportunities for Writing Develop your research proposal into a research essay. Write your research essay. Remember that the strongest research essays include a mixture of primary and secondary sources. Remember, also, that part of the conversation you have with your readers in a research essay occurs in citations. Look closely at the conversation you have created in your citations.

The Research Essay: Questions for Peer Review

1. What research questions is the writer asking? Is it clear to a reader why these questions are interesting and important?

2. Has the writer taken a clear position in answering the research questions? Restate the writer's position for the writer.

3. Has the writer used a variety of primary and secondary sources? Show the writer which of his or her sources you find particularly effective. Has the writer overused any source? Can you suggest other sources you think the writer should consult?

4. Has the writer questioned his or her sources? Does the writer offer his or her own interpretation of these sources? Does the writer create a context for introducing the sources?

5. If you wanted to look up the writer's sources, could you easily find them in a library? Has the writer used proper documentation procedures?

6. Do the writer's conclusions follow from the evidence presented? Could you offer the writer a counterargument or counterconclusion to the evidence he or she has presented?

7. Where in the essay has the writer said anything that is confusing or unclear to you? Show the writer where you think more evidence or more analysis is needed.

8. Does the writer's introduction successfully introduce you to the research questions? Is there anything you might suggest adding or deleting?

9. How does the writer's conclusion pull together all the arguments and evidence presented? How might the conclusion be more effective?

Annotate the writer's draft by commenting on its strengths and weaknesses. Ask the writer questions. Write a letter in which you offer your honest, careful, and generous comments and suggestions for revising.

PART FOUR
A SOURCEBOOK OF READINGS

SECTION I Questioning Our Identities

Section I

Questioning Our Identities

PROFESSIONAL ESSAYS

Where I Come from Is Like This

Paula Gunn Allen

Paula Gunn Allen (b. 1939), a native of New Mexico, comes from Lebanese and Native American heritage. Poet, novelist, and essayist, she teaches Native American Studies at the University of California, Berkeley. The essay that follows appeared in The Sacred Hoop: Recovering the Feminine in American Indian Traditions *(1986). Its title conveys a sense of Allen's primary concerns: feminism, traditional folktales, and Native American culture.*

I

Modern American Indian women, like their non-Indian sisters, are deeply engaged in the struggle to redefine themselves. In their struggle they must reconcile traditional tribal definitions of women with industrial and postindustrial non-Indian definitions. Yet while these definitions seem to be more or less mutually exclusive, Indian women must somehow harmonize and integrate both in their own lives. 1

An American Indian woman is primarily defined by her tribal identity. 2 In her eyes, her destiny is necessarily that of her people, and her sense of herself as a woman is first and foremost prescribed by her tribe. The definitions of woman's roles are as diverse as tribal cultures in the Americas. In some she is devalued, in others she wields considerable power. In some she is a familial/clan adjunct, in some she is as close to autonomous as her economic circumstances and psychological traits permit. But in no tribal definitions is she perceived in the same way as are women in western industrial and postindustrial cultures.

In the west, few images of women form part of the cultural mythos, 3 and these are largely sexually charged. Among Christians, the madonna is the female prototype, and she is portrayed as essentially passive: her contribution is simply that of birthing. Little else is attributed to her and she certainly possesses few of the characteristics that are attributed to mythic figures among Indian tribes. This image is countered (rather than balanced) by the witch-goddess/whore characteristics designed to reinforce cultural beliefs about women, as well as western adversarial and dualistic perceptions of reality.

The tribes see women variously, but they do not question the power 4
of femininity. Sometimes they see women as fearful, sometimes peaceful, sometimes omnipotent and omniscient, but they never portray women as mindless, helpless, simple, or oppressed. And while the women in a given tribe, clan, or band may be all these things, the individual woman is provided with a variety of images of women from the interconnected supernatural, natural, and social worlds she lives in.

As a half-breed American Indian woman, I cast about in my mind for 5
negative images of Indian women, and I find none that are directed to Indian women alone. The negative images I do have are of Indians in general and in fact are more often of males than of females. All these images come to me from non-Indian sources, and they are always balanced by a positive image. My ideas of womanhood, passed on largely by my mother and grandmothers, Laguna Pueblo women, are about practicality, strength, reasonableness, intelligence, wit, and competence. I also remember vividly the women who came to my father's store, the women who held me and sang to me, the women at Feast Day, at Grab Days,[1] the women in the kitchen of my Cubero home, the women I grew up with; none of them appeared weak or helpless, none of them presented herself tentatively. I remember a certain reserve on those lovely brown faces; I remember the direct gaze of eyes framed by bright-colored shawls draped over their heads and cascading down their backs. I remember the clean cotton dresses and carefully pressed hand-embroidered aprons they always wore; I remember laughter and good food, especially the sweet bread and the oven bread they gave us. Nowhere in my mind is there a foolish woman, a dumb woman, a vain woman, or a plastic woman, though the Indian women I have known have shown a wide range of personal style and demeanor.

My memory includes the Navajo woman who was badly beaten by 6
her Sioux husband; but I also remember that my grandmother abandoned her Sioux husband long ago. I recall the stories about the Laguna woman beaten regularly by her husband in the presence of her children so that the children would not believe in the strength of power of femininity. And

---

[1] *Grab Days:* Laguna ritual in which women throw food and small items (like pieces of cloth) to those attending.

I remember the women who drank, who got into fights with other women and with the men, and who often won those battles. I have memories of tired women, partying women, stubborn women, sullen women, amicable women, selfish women, shy women, and aggressive women. Most of all I remember the women who laugh and scold and sit uncomplaining in the long sun on feast days and who cook wonderful food on wood stoves, in beehive mud ovens, and over open fires outdoors.

Among the images of women that come to me from various tribes as well as my own are White Buffalo Woman, who came to the Lakota long ago and brought them the religion of the Sacred Pipe which they still practice; Tinotzin the goddess who came to Juan Diego to remind him that she still walked the hills of her people and sent him with her message, her demand and her proof to the Catholic bishop in the city nearby. And from Laguna I take the images of Yellow Woman, Coyote Woman, Grandmother Spider (Spider Old Woman), who brought the light, who gave us weaving and medicine, who gave us life. Among the Keres she is known as Thought Woman who created us all and who keeps us in creation even now. I remember Iyatiku, Earth Woman, Corn Woman, who guides and counsels the people to peace and who welcomes us home when we cast off this coil of flesh as huskers cast off the leaves that wrap the corn. I remember Iyatiku's sister, Sun Woman, who held metals and cattle, pigs and sheep, highways and engines and so many things in her bundle, who went away to the east saying that one day she would return. 7

II

Since the coming of the Anglo-Europeans beginning in the fifteenth century, the fragile web of identity that long held tribal people secure has gradually been weakened and torn. But the oral tradition has prevented the complete destruction of the web, the ultimate disruption of tribal ways. The oral tradition is vital; it heals itself and the tribal web by adapting to the flow of the present while never relinquishing its connection to the past. Its adaptability has always been required, as many generations have experienced. Certainly the modern American Indian woman bears slight resemblance to her forebears—at least on superficial examination—but she is still a tribal woman in her deepest being. Her tribal sense of relationship to all that is continues to flourish. And though she is at times beset by her knowledge of the enormous gap between the life she lives and the life she was raised to live, and while she adapts her mind and being to the circumstances of her present life, she does so in tribal ways, mending the tears in the web of being from which she takes her existence as she goes. 8

My mother told me stories all the time, though I often did not recognize them as that. My mother told me stories about cooking and childbearing; 9

she told me stories about menstruation and pregnancy; she told me stories about gods and heroes, about fairies and elves, about goddesses and spirits; she told me stories about the land and the sky, about cats and dogs, about snakes and spiders; she told me stories about climbing trees and exploring the mesas; she told me stories about going to dances and getting married; she told me stories about dressing and undressing, about sleeping and waking; she told me stories about herself, about her mother, about her grandmother. She told me stories about grieving and laughing, about thinking and doing; she told me stories about school and about people; about darning and mending; she told me stories about turquoise and about gold; she told me European stories and Laguna stories; she told me Catholic stories and Presbyterian stories; she told me city stories and country stories; she told me political stories and religious stories. She told me stories about living and stories about dying. And in all of those stories she told me who I was, who I was supposed to be, whom I came from, and who would follow me. In this way she taught me the meaning of the words she said, that all life is a circle and everything has a place within it. That's what she said and what she showed me in the things she did and the way she lives.

Of course, through my formal, white, Christian education, I discovered 1
that other people had stories of their own—about women, about Indians, about fact, about reality—and I was amazed by a number of startling suppositions that others made about tribal customs and beliefs. According to the un-Indian, non-Indian view, for instance, Indians barred menstruating women from ceremonies and indeed segregated them from the rest of the people, consigning them to some space specially designed for them. This showed that Indians considered menstruating women unclean and not fit to enjoy the company of decent (nonmenstruating) people, that is, men. I was surprised and confused to hear this because my mother had taught me that white people had strange attitudes toward menstruation: they thought something was bad about it, that it meant you were sick, cursed, sinful, and weak and that you had to be very careful during that time. She taught me that menstruation was a normal occurrence, that I could go swimming or hiking or whatever else I wanted to do during my period. She actively scorned women who took to their beds, who were incapacitated by cramps, who "got the blues."

As I struggled to reconcile these very contradictory interpretations of 1
American Indians' traditional beliefs concerning menstruation, I realized that the menstrual taboos were about power, not about sin or filth. My conclusion was later borne out by some tribes' own explanations, which, as you may well imagine, came as quite a relief to me.

The truth of the matter as many Indians see it is that women who are 1
at the peak of their fecundity are believed to possess power that throws male power totally out of kilter. They emit such force that, in their presence,

any male-owned or -dominated ritual or sacred object cannot do its usual task. For instance, the Lakota say that a menstruating woman anywhere near a yuwipi man, who is a special sort of psychic, spirit-empowered healer, for a day or so before he is to do his ceremony will effectively disempower him. Conversely, among many if not most tribes, important ceremonies cannot be held without the presence of women. Sometimes the ritual woman who empowers the ceremony must be unmarried and virginal so that the power she channels is unalloyed, unweakened by sexual arousal and penetration by a male. Other ceremonies require tumescent women, others the presence of mature women who have borne children, and still others depend for empowerment on postmenopausal women. Women may be segregated from the company of the whole band or village on certain occasions, but on certain occasions men are also segregated. In short, each ritual depends on a certain balance of power, and the positions of women within the phases of womanhood are used by tribal people to empower certain rites. This does not derive from a male-dominant view; it is not a ritual observance imposed on women by men. It derives from a tribal view of reality that distinguishes tribal people from feudal and industrial people.

Among the tribes, the occult power of women, inextricably bound to 13
our hormonal life, is thought to be very great; many hold that we possess innately the blood-given power to kill—with a glance, with a step, or with a judicious mixing of menstrual blood into somebody's soup. Medicine women among the Pomo of California cannot practice until they are sufficiently mature; when they are immature, their power is diffuse and is likely to interfere with their practice until time and experience have it under control. So women of the tribes are not especially inclined to see themselves as poor helpless victims of male domination. Even in those tribes where something akin to male domination was present, women are perceived as powerful, socially, physically, and metaphysically. In times past, as in times present, women carried enormous burdens with aplomb. We were far indeed from the "weaker sex," the designation that white aristocratic sisters unhappily earned for us all.

I remember my mother moving furniture all over the house when she 14
wanted it changed. She didn't wait for my father to come home and help—she just went ahead and moved the piano, a huge upright from the old days, the couch, the refrigerator. Nobody had told her she was too weak to do such things. In imitation of her, I would delight in loading trucks at my father's store with cases of pop or fifty-pound sacks of flour. Even when I was quite small I could do it, and it gave me a belief in my own physical strength that advancing middle age can't quite erase. My mother used to tell me about the Acoma Pueblo women she had seen as a child carrying huge ollas (water pots) on their heads as they wound their way up the

tortuous stairwell carved into the face of the "Sky City" mesa, a feat I tried to imitate with books and tin buckets. ("Sky City" is the term used by the Chamber of Commerce for the mother village of Acoma, which is situated atop a high sandstone table mountain.) I was never very successful, but even the attempt reminded me that I was supposed to be strong and balanced to be a proper girl.

Of course, my mother's Laguna people are Keres Indian, reputed to be 15
the last extreme mother-right people on earth. So it is no wonder that I got notably nonwhite notions about the natural strength and prowess of women. Indeed, it is only when I am trying to get non-Indian approval, recognition, or acknowledgment that my "weak sister" emotional and intellectual ploys get the better of my tribal woman's good sense. At such times I forget that I just moved the piano or just wrote a competent paper or just completed a financial transaction satisfactorily or have supported myself and my children for most of my adult life.

Nor is my contradictory behavior atypical. Most Indian women I know 16
are in the same bicultural bind: we vacillate between being dependent and strong, self-reliant and powerless, strongly motivated and hopelessly insecure. We resolve the dilemma in various ways: some of us party all the time; some of us drink to excess; some of us travel and move around a lot; some of us land good jobs and then quit them; some of us engage in violent exchanges; some of us blow our brains out. We act in these destructive ways because we suffer from the societal conflicts caused by having to identify with two hopelessly opposed cultural definitions of women. Through this destructive dissonance we are unhappy prey to the self-disparagement common to, indeed demanded of, Indians living in the United States today. Our situation is caused by the exigencies of a history of invasion, conquest, and colonization whose searing marks are probably ineradicable. A popular bumper sticker on many Indian cars proclaims: "If You're Indian You're In," to which I always find myself adding under my breath, "Trouble."

III

No Indian can grow to any age without being informed that her people 17
were "savages" who interfered with the march of progress pursued by respectable, loving, civilized white people. We are the villains of the scenario when we are mentioned at all. We are absent from much of white history except when we are calmly, rationally, succinctly, and systematically dehumanized. On the few occasions we are noticed in any way other than as howling, bloodthirsty beings, we are acclaimed for our noble quaintness. In this definition, we are exotic curios. Our ancient arts and customs

are used to draw tourist money to state coffers, into the pocketbooks and bank accounts of scholars, and into support of the American-in-Disneyland promoters' dream.

As a Roman Catholic child I was treated to bloody tales of how the savage Indians martyred the hapless priests and missionaries who went among them in an attempt to lead them to the one true path. By the time I was through high school I had the idea that Indians were people who had benefited mightily from the advanced knowledge and superior morality of the Anglo-Europeans. At least I had, perforce, that idea to lay beside the other one that derived from my daily experience of Indian life, an idea less dehumanizing and more accurate because it came from my mother and the other Indian people who raised me. That idea was that Indians are a people who don't tell lies, who care for their children and their old people. You never see an Indian orphan, they said. You always know when you're old that someone will take care of you—one of your children will. Then they'd list the old folks who were being taken care of by this child or that. No child is ever considered illegitimate among the Indians, they said. If a girl gets pregnant, the baby is still part of the family, and the mother is too. That's what they said, and they showed me real people who lived according to those principles. 18

Of course the ravages of colonization have taken their toll; there are orphans in Indian country now, and abandoned, brutalized old folks; there are even illegitimate children, though the very concept still strikes me as absurd. There are battered children and neglected children, and there are battered wives and women who have been raped by Indian men. Proximity to the "civilizing" effects of white Christians has not improved the moral quality of life in Indian country, though each group, Indian and white, explains the situation differently. Nor is there much yet in the oral tradition that can enable us to adapt to these inhuman changes. But a force is growing in that direction, and it is helping Indian women reclaim their lives. Their power, their sense of direction and of self will soon be visible. It is the force of the women who speak and work and write, and it is formidable. 19

Through all the centuries of war and death and cultural and psychic destruction have endured the women who raise the children and tend the fires, who pass along the tales and the traditions, who weep and bury the dead, who are the dead, and who never forget. There are always the women, who make pots and weave baskets, who fashion clothes and cheer their children on at powwow, who make fry bread and piki bread, and corn soup and chili stew, who dance and sing and remember and hold within their hearts the dream of their ancient peoples—that one day the woman who thinks will speak to us again, and everywhere there will 20 be peace. Meanwhile we tell the stories and write the books and trade tales of anger and woe and stories of fun and scandal and laugh over all manner of things that happen every day. We watch and we wait.

My great-grandmother told my mother: Never forget you are Indian. 2 And my mother told me the same thing. This, then, is how I have gone about remembering, so that my children will remember too.

Casa: A Partial Remembrance of a Puerto Rican Childhood

Judith Ortiz Cofer

Judith Ortiz Cofer (b. 1952), a native of Puerto Rico, began her career as a bilingual teacher in the public schools of Palm Beach, Florida. She has since taught poetry at many colleges and universities. Her volumes of poetry include Latin Women Pray *(1980) and* Reaching for the Mainland *(1984). "My family is one of the main topics of my poetry," she says. ". . . In tracing their lives, I discover more about mine. The place of birth itself becomes a metaphor for the things we all must leave behind; the assimilation of a new culture is the coming into maturity by accepting the terms necessary for survival."*

At three or four o'clock in the afternoon, the hour of *café con leche,* the 1 women of my family gathered in Mamá's living room to speak of important things and retell familiar stories meant to be overheard by us young girls, their daughters. In Mamá's house (everyone called my grandmother Mamá) was a large parlor built by my grandfather to his wife's exact specifications so that it was always cool, facing away from the sun. The doorway was on the side of the house so no one could walk directly into her living room. First they had to take a little stroll through and around her beautiful garden where prize-winning orchids grew in the trunk of an ancient tree she had hollowed out for that purpose. This room was furnished with several mahogany rocking chairs, acquired at the births of her children, and one intricately carved rocker that had passed down to Mamá at the death of her own mother.

It was on these rockers that my mother, her sisters, and my grand- 2 mother sat on these afternoons of my childhood to tell their stories, teaching each other, and my cousin and me, what it was like to be a woman, more specifically, a Puerto Rican woman. They talked about life on the island, and life in *Los Nueva Yores,* their way of referring to the United States from New York City to California: the other pace, not home, all the same. They told real-life stories though, as I later learned, always embellishing them with a little or a lot of dramatic detail. And they told *cuentos,* the morality and cautionary tales told by the women in our family for generations: stories that became a part of my subconscious as I grew up in two worlds, the tropical island and the cold city, and that would later surface in my dreams and in my poetry.

One of these tales was about the woman who was left at the altar. 3
Mamá liked to tell that one with histrionic intensity. I remember the rise and fall of her voice, the sighs, and her constantly gesturing hands, like two birds swooping through her words. This particular story usually would come up in a conversation as a result of someone mentioning a forthcoming engagement or wedding. The first time I remember hearing it, I was sitting on the floor at Mamá's feet, pretending to read a comic book. I may have been eleven or twelve years old, at that difficult age when a girl was no longer a child who could be ordered to leave the room if the women wanted freedom to take their talk into forbidden zones, nor really old enough to be considered a part of their conclave. I could only sit quietly, pretending to be in another world, while absorbing it all in a sort of unspoken agreement of my status as silent auditor. On this day, Mamá had taken my long, tangled mane of hair into her ever-busy hands. Without looking down at me and with no interruption of her flow of words, she began braiding my hair, working at it with the quickness and determination that characterized all her actions. My mother was watching us impassively from her rocker across the room. On her lips played a little ironic smile. I would never sit still for *her* ministrations, but even then, I instinctively knew that she did not possess Mamá's matriarchal power to command and keep everyone's attention. This was never more evident than in the spell she cast when telling a story.

"It is not like it used to be when I was a girl," Mamá announced. "Then, 4
a man could leave a girl standing at the church altar with a bouquet of fresh flowers in her hands and disappear off the face of the earth. No way to track him down if he was from another town. He could be a married man, with maybe even two or three families all over the island. There was no way to know. And there were men who did this. Hombres with the devil in their flesh who would come to a pueblo, like this one, take a job at one of the haciendas, never meaning to stay, only to have a good time and to seduce the women."

The whole time she was speaking, Mamá would be weaving my hair 5
into a flat plait that required pulling apart the two sections of hair with little jerks that made my eyes water; but knowing how grandmother detested whining and *boba* (sissy) tears, as she called them, I just sat up as straight and stiff as I did at La Escuela San Jose, where the nuns enforced good posture with a flexible plastic ruler they bounced off of slumped shoulders

and heads. As Mamá's story progressed, I noticed how my young Aunt Laura lowered her eyes, refusing to meet Mamá's meaningful gaze. Laura was seventeen, in her last year of high school, and already engaged to a boy from another town who had staked his claim with a tiny diamond ring, then left for Los Nueva Yores to make his fortune. They were planning to get married in a year. Mamá had expressed serious doubts that the wedding would ever take place. In Mamá's eyes, a man set free without a legal contract was a man lost. She believed that marriage was not something men desired, but simply the price they had to pay for the privilege of children and, of course, for what no decent (synonymous with "smart") woman would give away for free.

"María La Loca was only seventeen when *it* happened to her." I listened 6
closely at the mention of this name. María was a town character, a fat middle-aged woman who lived with her old mother on the outskirts of town. She was to be seen around the pueblo delivering the meat pies the two women made for a living. The most peculiar thing about María, in my eyes, was that she walked and moved like a little girl though she had the thick body and wrinkled face of an old woman. She would swing her hips in an exaggerated, clownish way, and sometimes even hop and skip up to someone's house. She spoke to no one. Even if you asked her a question, she would just look at you and smile, showing her yellow teeth. But I had heard that if you got close enough, you could hear her humming a tune without words. The kids yelled out nasty things at her, calling her *La Loca,* and the men who hung out at the bodega playing dominoes sometimes whistled mockingly as she passed by with her funny, outlandish walk. But María seemed impervious to it all, carrying her basket of *pasteles* like a grotesque Little Red Riding Hood through the forest.

María La Loca interested me, as did all the eccentrics and crazies of our 7
pueblo. Their weirdness was a measuring stick I used in my serious quest for a definition of normal. As a Navy brat shuttling between New Jersey and the pueblo, I was constantly made to feel like an oddball by my peers, who made fun of my two-way accent: a Spanish accent when I spoke English, and when I spoke Spanish I was told that I sounded like a *Gringa.* Being the outsider had already turned my brother and me into cultural chameleons. We developed early on the ability to blend into a crowd, to sit and read quietly in a fifth story apartment building for days and days when it was too bitterly cold to play outside, or, set free, to run wild in Mamá's realm, where she took charge of our lives, releasing Mother for a while from the intense fear for our safety that our father's absences instilled in her. In order to keep us from harm when Father was away, Mother kept us under strict surveillance. She even walked us to and from Public School No. 11, which we attended during the months we lived in Paterson, New Jersey, our home base in the states. Mamá freed all three of us like pigeons

from a cage. I saw her as my liberator and my model. Her stories were parables from which to glean the *Truth.*

"María La Loca was once a beautiful girl. Everyone thought she would marry the Méndez boy." As everyone knew, Rogelio Méndez was the richest man in town. "But," Mamá continued, knitting my hair with the same intensity she was putting into her story, "this *macho* made a fool out of her and ruined her life." She paused for the effect of her use of the word "macho," which at that time had not yet become a popular epithet for an unliberated man. This word had for us the crude and comical connotation of "male of the species," stud; a *macho* was what you put in a pen to increase your stock. 8

I peeked over my comic book at my mother. She too was under Mamá's spell, smiling conspiratorially at this little swipe at men. She was safe from Mamá's contempt in this area. Married at an early age, an unspotted lamb, she had been accepted by a good family of strict Spaniards whose name was old and respected, though their fortune had been lost long before my birth. In a rocker Papá had painted sky blue sat Mamá's oldest child, Aunt Nena. Mother of three children, stepmother of two more, she was a quiet woman who liked books but had married an ignorant and abusive widower whose main interest in life was accumulating wealth. He too was in the mainland working on his dream of returning home rich and triumphant to buy the *finca* of his dreams. She was waiting for him to send for her. She would leave her children with Mamá for several years while the two of them slaved away in factories. He would one day be a rich man, and she a sadder woman. Even now her life-light was dimming. She spoke little, an aberration in Mamá's house, and she read avidly, as if storing up spiritual food for the long winters that awaited her in Los Nueva Yores without her family. But even Aunt Nena came alive to Mamá's words, rocking gently, her hands over a thick book in her lap. 9

Her daughter, my cousin Sara, played jacks by herself on the tile porch outside the room where we sat. She was a year older than I. We shared a bed and all our family's secrets. Collaborators in search of answers, Sara and I discussed everything we heard the women say, trying to fit it all together like a puzzle that, once assembled, would reveal life's mysteries to us. Though she and I still enjoyed taking part in boys' games—chase, volleyball, and even *vaqueros,* the island version of cowboys and Indians involving cap-gun battles and violent shoot-outs under the mango tree in Mamá's backyard—we loved best the quiet hours in the afternoon when the men were still at work, and the boys had gone to play serious baseball at the park. Then Mamá's house belonged only to us women. The aroma of coffee perking in the kitchen, the mesmerizing creaks and groans of the rockers, and the women telling their lives in *cuentos* are forever woven into the fabric of my imagination, braided like my hair that day I felt my 10 grandmother's hands teaching me about strength, her voice convincing me of the power of storytelling.

That day Mamá told how the beautiful María had fallen prey to a man 11 whose name was never the same in subsequent versions of the story; it was Juan one time, José, Rafael, Diego, another. We understood that neither the name nor any of the *facts* were important, only that a woman had allowed love to defeat her. Mamá put each of us in María's place by describing her wedding dress in loving detail: how she looked like a princess in her lace as she waited at the altar. Then, as Mamá approached the tragic denouement of her story, I was distracted by the sound of my Aunt Laura's violent rocking. She seemed on the verge of tears. She knew the fable was intended for her. That week she was going to have her wedding gown fitted, though no firm date had been set for the marriage. Mamá ignored Laura's obvious discomfort, digging out a ribbon from the sewing basket she kept by her rocker while describing María's long illness, "a fever that would not break for days." She spoke of a mother's despair: "that woman climbed the church steps on her knees every morning, wore only black as a *promesa* to the Holy Virgin in exchange for her daughter's health." By the time María returned home from her honeymoon with death, she was ravished, no longer young or sane. "As you can see, she is almost as old as her mother already," Mamá lamented while tying the ribbon to the ends of my hair, pulling it back with such force that I just knew I would never be able to close my eyes completely again.

"That María is getting crazier every day." Mamá's voice would take a 12 lighter tone now, expressing satisfaction, either for the perfection of my braid, or for a story well told—it was hard to tell. "You know that tune María is always humming?" Carried away by her enthusiasm, I tried to nod, but Mamá still had me pinned between her knees.

"Well, that's the wedding march." Surprising us all, Mamá sang out, 13 "Da, da, dara . . . da, da, dara." Then lifting me off the floor by my skinny shoulders, she would lead me around the room in an impromptu waltz—another session ending with the laughter of women, all of us caught up in the infectious joke of our lives.

1989

Memory and Imagination

Patricia Hampl

Patrcia Hampl (b. 1946) is a poet and autobiographer whose search for her Czechoslovakian roots took her to her family's native Prague. A Romantic

Education *(1981), the chronicle of that journey and a memoir of her youth in St. Paul, Minnesota, won a Houghton Mifflin Literary Fellowship.*

When I was seven, my father, who played the violin on Sundays with a nicely tortured flair which we considered artistic, led me by the hand down a long, unlit corridor in St. Luke's School basement, a sort of tunnel that ended in a room full of pianos. There many little girls and a single sad boy were playing truly tortured scales and arpeggios in a mash of troubled sound. My father gave me over to Sister Olive Marie, who did look remarkably like an olive. 1

Her oily face gleamed as if it had just been rolled out of a can and laid on the white plate of her broad, spotless wimple. She was a small, plump woman; her body and the small window of her face seemed to interpret the entire alphabet of olive: her face was a sallow green olive placed upon the jumbo ripe olive of her black habit. I trusted her instantly and smiled, glad to have my hand placed in the hand of a woman who made sense, who provided the satisfaction of being what she was: an Olive who looked like an olive. 2

My father left me to discover the piano with Sister Olive Marie so that one day I would join him in mutually tortured piano-violin duets for the edification of my mother and brother who sat at the table meditatively spooning in the last of their pineapple sherbet until their part was called for: they put down their spoons and clapped while we bowed, while the sweet ice in their bowls melted, while the music melted, and we all melted a little into each other for a moment. 3

But first Sister Olive must do her work. I was shown middle C, which Sister seemed to think terribly important. I stared at middle C and then glanced away for a second. When my eye returned, middle C was gone, its slim finger lost in the complicated grasp of the keyboard. Sister Olive struck it again, finding it with laughable ease. She emphasized the importance of middle C, its central position, a sort of North Star of sound. I remember thinking, "Middle C is the belly button of the piano," an insight whose originality and accuracy stunned me with pride. For the first time in my life I was astonished by metaphor. I hesitated to tell the kindly Olive for some reason; apparently I understood a true metaphor is a risky business, revealing of the self. In fact, I have never, until this moment of writing it down, told my first metaphor to anyone. 4

Sunlight flooded the room; the pianos, all black, gleamed. Sister Olive, dressed in the colors of the keyboard, gleamed; middle C shimmered with meaning and I resolved never—never—to forget its location: it was the center of the world. 5

Then Sister Olive, who had had to show me middle C twice but who seemed to have drawn no bad conclusions about me anyway, got up and 6 went to the windows on the opposite wall. She pulled the shades down, one after the other. The sun was too bright, she said. She sneezed as she stood at the windows with the sun shedding its glare over her. She sneezed and sneezed, crazy little convulsive sneezes, one after another, as helpless as if she had the hiccups.

"The sun makes me sneeze," she said when the fit was over and she 7
was back at the piano. This was odd, too odd to grasp in the mind. I associated sneezing with colds, and colds with rain, fog, snow and bad weather. The sun, however, had caused Sister Olive to sneeze in this wild way, Sister Olive who gleamed benignly and who was so certain of the location of the center of the world. The universe wobbled a bit and became unreliable. Things were not, after all, necessarily what they seemed. Appearance deceived: here was the sun acting totally out of character, hurling this woman into sneezes, a woman so mild that she was named, so it seemed, for a bland object on a relish tray.

I was given a red book, the first Thompson book, and told to play the 8
first piece over and over at one of the black pianos where the other children were crashing away. This, I was told, was called practicing. It sounded alluringly adult, practicing. The piece itself consisted mainly of middle C, and I excelled, thrilled by my savvy at being able to locate that central note amidst the cunning camouflage of all the other white keys before me. Thrilled too by the shiny red book that gleamed, as the pianos did, as Sister Olive did, as my eager eyes probably did. I sat at the formidable machine of the piano and got to know middle C intimately, preparing to be as tortured as I could manage one day soon with my father's violin at my side.

But at the moment Mary Katherine Reilly was at my side, playing some- 9
thing at least two or three lessons more sophisticated than my piece. I believe she even struck a chord. I glanced at her from the peasantry of single notes, shy, ready to pay homage. She turned toward me, stopped playing, and sized me up.

Sized me up and found a person ready to be dominated. Without 10
introduction she said, "My grandfather invented the collapsible opera hat."

I nodded, I acquiesced, I was hers. With that little stroke it was decided 11
between us—that she should be the leader, and I the sidekick. My job was admiration. Even when she added, "But he didn't make a penny from it. He didn't have a patent"—even then, I knew and she knew that this was not an admission of powerlessness, but the easy candor of a master, of one who can afford a weakness or two.

With the clairvoyance of all fated relationships based on dominance 12
and submission, it was decided in advance: that when the time came for us to play duets, I should always play second piano, that I should spend my allowance to buy her the Twinkies she craved but was not allowed to have, that finally, I should let her copy from my test paper, and when

confronted by our teacher, confess with convincing hysteria that it was I, I who had cheated, who had reached above myself to steal what clearly belonged to the rightful heir of the inventor of the collapsible opera hat. . . .

There must be a reason I remember that little story about my first piano lesson. In fact, it isn't a story, just a moment, the beginning of what could perhaps become a story. For the memoirist, more than for the fiction writer, the story seems already *there,* already accomplished and fully achieved in history ("in reality," as we naively say). For the memoirist, the writing of the story is a matter of transcription. 13

That, anyway, is the myth. But no memoirist writes for long without experiencing an unsettling disbelief about the reliability of memory, a hunch that memory is not, after all, *just* memory. I don't know why I remembered this fragment about my first piano lesson. I don't, for instance, have a single recollection of my first arithmetic lesson, the first time I studied Latin, the first time my grandmother tried to teach me to knit. Yet these things occurred too, and must have their stories. 14

It is the piano lesson that has trudged forward, clearing the haze of forgetfulness, showing itself bright with detail more than thirty years after the event. I did not choose to remember the piano lesson. It was simply there, like a book that has always been on the shelf, whether I ever read it or not, the binding and title showing as I skim across the contents of my life. On the day I wrote this fragment I happened to take that memory, not some other, from the shelf and paged through it. I found more detail, more event, perhaps a little more entertainment than I had expected, but the memory itself was there from the start. Waiting for me. 15

Or was it? When I reread what I had written just after I finished it, I realized that I had told a number of lies. I *think* it was my father who took me the first time for my piano lesson—but maybe he only took me to meet my teacher and there was no actual lesson that day. And did I even know then that he played the violin—didn't he take up his violin again much later, as a result of my piano playing, and not the reverse? And is it even remotely accurate to describe as "tortured" the musicianship of a man who began every day by belting out "Oh What a Beautiful Morning" as he shaved? 16

More: Sister Olive Marie did sneeze in the sun, but was her name Olive? As for her skin tone—I would have sworn it was olive-like; I would have been willing to spend the better part of an afternoon trying to write the exact description of imported Italian or Greek olive her face suggested: I wanted to get it right. But now, were I to write that passage over, it is her intense black eyebrows I would see, for suddenly they seem the central fact of that face, some indicative mark of her serious and patient nature. 17

But the truth is, I don't remember the woman at all. She's a sneeze in the sun and a finger touching middle C. That, at least, is steady and clear.

Worse: I didn't have the Thompson book as my piano text. I'm sure of 18
that because I remember envying children who did have this wonderful book with its pictures of children and animals printed on the pages of music.

As for Mary Katherine Reilly. She didn't even go to grade school with 19
me (and her name isn't Mary Katherine Reilly—but I made that change on purpose). I met her in Girl Scouts and only went to school with her later, in high school. Our relationship was not really one of leader and follower; I played first piano most of the time in duets. She certainly never copied anything from a test paper of mine; she was a better student, and cheating just wasn't a possibility with her. Though her grandfather (or someone in her family) did invent the collapsible opera hat and I remember that she was proud of that fact, she didn't tell me this news as a deft move in a childish power play.

So, what was I doing in this brief memoir? Is it simply an example of 20
the curious relation a fiction writer has to the material of her own life? Maybe. That may have some value in itself. But to tell the truth (if anyone still believes me capable of telling the truth), I wasn't writing fiction. I was writing memoir—or was trying to. My desire was to be accurate. I wished to embody the myth of memoir: to write as an act of dutiful transcription.

Yet clearly the work of writing narrative caused me to do something 21
very different from transcription. I am forced to admit that memoir is not a matter of transcription, that memory itself is not a warehouse of finished stories, not a static gallery of framed pictures. I must admit that I invented. But why?

Two whys: why did I invent, and then, if a memoirist must inevitably 22
invent rather than transcribe, why do I—why should anybody—write memoir at all?

I must respond to these impertinent questions because they, like the 23
bumper sticker I saw the other day commanding all who read it to QUESTION AUTHORITY, challenge my authority as a memoirist and as a witness.

It still comes as a shock to realize that I don't write about what I know: 24
I write in order to find out what I know. Is it possible to convey to a reader the enormous degree of blankness, confusion, hunch and uncertainty lurking in the act of writing? When I am the reader, not the writer, I too fall into the lovely illusion that the words before me (in a story by Mavis Gallant, an essay by Carol Bly, a memoir by M. F. K. Fisher), which *read* so inevitably, must also have been *written* exactly as they appear, rhythm and cadence, language and syntax, the powerful waves of the sentences laying themselves on the smooth beach of the page one after another faultlessly.

But here I sit before a yellow legal pad, and the long page of the 25 preceding two paragraphs is a jumble of crossed-out lines, false starts, confused order. A mess. The mess of my mind trying to find out what it wants to say. This is a writer's frantic, grabby mind, not the poised mind of a reader ready to be edified or entertained.

I sometimes think of the reader as a cat, endlessly fastidious, capable, by turns, of mordant indifference and riveted attention, luxurious, recumbent, and ever poised. Whereas the writer is absolutely a dog, panting and moping, too eager for an affectionate scratch behind the ears, lunging frantically after any old stick thrown in the distance. 26

The blankness of a new page never fails to intrigue and terrify me. Sometimes, in fact, I think my habit of writing on long yellow sheets comes from an atavistic fear of the writer's stereotypic "blank white page." At least when I begin writing, my page isn't utterly blank: at least it has a wash of color on it, even if the absence of words must finally be faced on a yellow sheet as truly as on a blank white one. Well, we all have our ways of whistling in the dark. 27

If I approach writing from memory with the assumption that I know what I wish to say, I assume that intentionality is running the show. Things are not that simple. Or perhaps writing is even more profoundly simple, more telegraphic and immediate in its choices than the grating wheels and chugging engine of logic and rational intention. The heart, the guardian of intuition with its secret, often fearful intentions, is the boss. Its commands are what a writer obeys—often without knowing it. Or, I do. 28

That's why I'm a strong adherent of the first draft. And why it's worth pausing for a moment to consider what a first draft really is. By my lights, the piano lesson memoir is a first draft. That doesn't mean it exists here exactly as I first wrote it. I like to think I've cleaned it up from the first time I put it down on paper. I've cut some adjectives here, toned down the hyperbole there, smoothed a transition, cut a repetition—that sort of housekeeperly tidying-up. But the piece remains a first draft because I haven't yet gotten to know it, haven't given it a chance to tell me anything. For me, writing a first draft is a little like meeting someone for the first time. I come away with a wary acquaintanceship, but the real friendship (if any) and genuine intimacy—that's all down the road. Intimacy with a piece of writing, as with a person, comes from paying attention to the revelations it is capable of giving, not by imposing my own preconceived notions, no matter how well-intentioned they might be. 29

I try to let pretty much anything happen in a first draft. A careful first draft is a failed first draft. That may be why there are so many inaccuracies in the piano lesson memoir: I didn't censor, I didn't judge. I kept moving. But I would not publish this piece as a memoir on its own in its present state. It isn't the "lies" in the piece that give me pause, though a reader has a right to expect a memoir to be as accurate as the writer's memory can 30 make it. No, it isn't the lies themselves that makes the piano lesson memoir a first draft and therefore "unpublishable."

The real trouble: the piece hasn't yet found its subject; it isn't yet about what it wants to be about. Note: what *it* wants, not what I want. The difference has to do with the relation a memoirist—any writer, in fact—has to unconscious or half-known intentions and impulses in composition. 31

Now that I have the fragment down on paper, I can read this little piece as a mystery which drops clues to the riddle of my feelings, like a culprit who wishes to be apprehended. My narrative self (the culprit who has invented) wishes to be discovered by my reflective self, the self who wants to understand and make sense of a half-remembered story about a nun sneezing in the sun. . . . 32

We only store in memory images of value. The value may be lost over the passage of time (I was baffled about why I remembered that sneezing nun, for example), but that's the implacable judgment of feeling: *this,* we say somewhere deep within us, is something I'm hanging on to. And of course, often we cleave to things because they possess heavy negative charges. Pain likes to be vivid. 33

Over time, the value (the feeling) and the stored memory (the image) may become estranged. Memoir seeks a permanent home for feeling and image, a habitation where they can live together in harmony. Naturally, I've had a lot of experiences since I packed away that one from the basement of St. Luke's School; that piano lesson has been effaced by waves of feeling for other moments and episodes. I persist in believing the event has value—after all, I remember it—but in writing the memoir I did not simply relive the experience. Rather, I explored the mysterious relationship between all the images I could round up and the even more impacted feelings that caused me to store the images safely away in memory. Stalking the relationship, seeking the congruence between stored image and hidden emotion—that's the real job of memoir. 34

By writing about the first piano lesson, I've come to know things I could not know otherwise. But I only know these things as a result of reading this first draft. While I was writing, I was following the images, letting the details fill the room of the page and use the furniture as they wished. I was their dutiful servant—or thought I was. In fact, I was the faithful retainer of my hidden feelings which were giving the commands. 35

I really did feel, for instance, that Mary Katherine Reilly was far superior to me. She was smarter, funnier, more wonderful in every way—that's how I saw it. Our friendship (or she herself) did not require that I become her vassal, yet perhaps in my heart that was something I wanted; I wanted a way to express my feeling of admiration. I suppose I waited until this memoir to begin to find the way. 36

Just as, in the memoir, I finally possess that red Thompson book with the barking dogs and bleating lambs and winsome children. I couldn't (and still can't) remember what my own music book was, so I grabbed the name and image of the one book I could remember. It was only in reviewing the piece after writing it that I saw my inaccuracy. In pondering this "lie," I came to see what I was up to: I was getting what I wanted. At last. 37

The truth of many circumstances and episodes in the past emerges for the memoirist through details (the red music book, the fascination with a nun's name and gleaming face), but these details are not merely information, not flat facts. Such details are not allowed to lounge. They must work. Their work is the creation of symbol. But it's more accurate to call it the *recognition* of symbol. For meaning is not "attached" to the detail by the memoirist; meaning is revealed. That's why a first draft is important. Just as the first meeting (good or bad) with someone who later becomes the beloved is important and is often reviewed for signals, meanings, omens, and indications. 38

Now I can look at that music book and see it not only as "a detail," but for what it is, how it *acts.* See it as the small red door leading straight into the dark room of my childhood longing and disappointment. That red book *becomes* the palpable evidence of that longing. In other words, it becomes symbol. There is no symbol, no life-of-the-spirit in the general or the abstract. Yet a writer wishes—indeed all of us wish—to speak about profound matters that are, like it or not, general and abstract. We wish to talk to each other about life and death, about love, despair, loss, and innocence. We sense that in order to live together we must learn to speak of peace, of history, of meaning and values. Those are a few. 39

We seek a means of exchange, a language which will renew these ancient concerns and make them wholly and pulsingly ours. Instinctively, we go to our store of private images and associations for our authority to speak of these weighty issues. We find, in our details and broken and obscured images, the language of symbol. Here memory impulsively reaches out its arms and embraces imagination. That is the resort to invention. It isn't a lie, but an act of necessity, as the innate urge to locate personal truth always is. 40

All right. Invention is inevitable. But why write memoir? Why not call it fiction and be done with all the hashing about, wondering where memory stops and imagination begins? And if memoir seeks to talk about "the big issues," about history and peace, death and love—why not leave these reflections to those with expert and scholarly knowledge? Why let the common or garden variety memoirist into the club? I'm thinking again of that bumper sticker: why Question Authority? 41

My answer, of course, is a memoirist's answer. Memoir must be written 42 because each of us must have a created version of the past. Created: that is, real, tangible, made of the stuff of a life lived in place and in history. And the down side of any created thing as well: we must live with a version that attaches us to our limitations, to the inevitable subjectivity of our points of view. We must acquiesce to our experience and our gift to transform experience into meaning and value. You tell me your story, I'll tell you my story.

If we refuse to do the work of creating this personal version of the past, 4
someone else will do it for us. That is a scary political fact. "The struggle of man against power," a character in Milan Kundera's novel *The Book of Laughter and Forgetting* says, "is the struggle of memory against forgetting." He refers to willful political forgetting, the habit of nations and those in power (Question Authority!) to deny the truth of memory in order to disarm moral and ethical power. It's an efficient way of controlling masses of people. It doesn't even require much bloodshed, as long as people are entirely willing to give over their personal memories. Whole histories can be rewritten. As Czeslaw Milosz said in his 1980 Nobel Prize lecture, the number of books published that seek to deny the existence of the Nazi death camps now exceeds one hundred.

What is remembered is what *becomes* reality. If we "forget" Auschwitz, 4
if we "forget" My Lai, what then do we remember? And what is the purpose of our remembering? If we think of memory naively, as a simple story, logged like a documentary in the archive of the mind, we miss its beauty but also its function. The beauty of memory rests in its talent for rendering detail, for paying homage to the senses, its capacity to love the particles of life, the richness and idiosyncrasy of our existence. The function of memory, on the other hand, is intensely personal and surprisingly political.

Our capacity to move forward as developing beings rests on a healthy 4
relation with the past. Psychotherapy, that widespread method of mental health, relies heavily on memory and on the ability to retrieve and organize images and events from the personal past. We carry our wounds and perhaps even worse, our capacity to wound, forward with us. If we learn not only to tell our stories but to listen to what our stories tell us—to write the first draft and then return for the second draft—we are doing the work of memoir.

Memoir is the intersection of narration and reflection, of story-telling 4
and essay-writing. It can present its story *and* reflect and consider the meaning of the story. It is a peculiarly open form, inviting broken and incomplete images, half-recollected fragments, all the mass (and mess) of detail. It offers to shape this confusion—and in shaping, of course it necessarily creates a work of art, not a legal document. But then, even legal documents are only valiant attempts to consign the truth, the whole truth and nothing but the truth to paper. Even they remain versions.

Locating touchstones—the red music book, the olive Olive, my father's violin playing—is deeply satisfying. Who knows why? Perhaps we all sense that we can't grasp the whole truth and nothing but the truth of our experience. Just can't be done. What can be achieved, however, is a version of its swirling, changing wholeness. A memoirist must acquiesce to selectivity, like any artist. The version we dare to write is the only truth, the only relationship we can have with the past. Refuse to write your life and you have no life. At least, that is the stern view of the memoirist. 47

Personal history, logged in memory, is a sort of slide projector flashing images on the wall of the mind. And there's precious little order to the slides in the rotating carousel. Beyond that confusion, who knows who is running the projector? A memoirist steps into this darkened room of flashing, unorganized images and stands blinking for a while. Maybe for a long while. But eventually, as with any attempt to tell a story, it is necessary to put something first, then something else. And so on, to the end. That's a first draft. Not necessarily the truth, not even *a* truth sometimes, but the first attempt to create a shape. 48

The first thing I usually notice at this stage of composition is the appalling inaccuracy of the piece. Witness my first piano lesson draft. Invention is screamingly evident in what I intended to be transcription. But here's the further truth: I feel no shame. In fact, it's only now that my interest in the piece truly quickens. For I can see what isn't there, what is shyly hugging the walls, hoping not to be seen. I see the filmy shape of the next draft. I see a more acute version of the episode or—this is more likely—an entirely new piece rising from the ashes of the first attempt. 49

The next draft of the piece would have to be a true re-vision, a new seeing of the materials of the first draft. Nothing merely cosmetic will do—no rouge buffing up the opening sentence, no glossy adjective to lift a sagging line, nothing to attempt covering a patch of gray writing. None of that. I can't say for sure, but my hunch is the revision would lead me to more writing about my father (why was I so impressed by that ancestral inventor of the collapsible opera hat? Did I feel I had nothing as remarkable in my own background? Did this make me feel inadequate?). I begin to think perhaps Sister Olive is less central to this business than she is in this draft. She is meant to be a moment, not a character. 50

And so I might proceed, if I were to undertake a new draft of the memoir. I begin to feel a relationship developing between a former self and me. 51

And, even more compelling, a relationship between an old world and me. Some people think of autobiographical writing as the precious occupation of a particularly self-absorbed person. Maybe, but I don't buy that. True memoir is written in an attempt to find not only a self but a world. 52

The self-absorption that seems to be the impetus and embarrassment 53 of autobiography turns into (or perhaps always was) a hunger for the world. Actually, it begins as hunger for *a* world, one gone or lost, effaced by time or a more sudden brutality. But in the act of remembering, the personal environment expands, resonates beyond itself, beyond its "subject," into the endless and tragic recollection that is history.

We look at old family photographs in which we stand next to black, boxy Fords and are wearing period costumes, and we do not gaze fascinated because there we are young again, or there we are standing, as we never will again in life, next to our mother. We stare and drift because there we are . . . historical. It is the dress, the black car that dazzle us now and draw us beyond our mother's bright arms which once caught us. We reach into the attractive impersonality of something more significant than ourselves. We write memoir, in other words. We accept the humble position of writing a version rather than "the whole truth."

I suppose I write memoir because of the radiance of the past—it draws me back and back to it. Not that the past is beautiful. In our communal memoir, in history, the death camps *are* back there. In intimate life too, the record is usually pretty mixed. "I could tell you stories . . ." people say and drift off, meaning terrible things have happened to them.

But the past is radiant. It has the light of lived life. A memoirist wishes to touch it. No one owns the past, though typically the first act of new political regimes, whether of the left or the right, is to attempt to re-write history, to grab the past and make it over so the end comes out right. So their power looks inevitable.

No one owns the past, but it is a grave error (another age would have said a grave sin) not to inhabit memory. Sometimes I think it is all we really have. But that may be a trifle melodramatic. At any rate, memory possesses authority for the fearful self in a world where it is necessary to have authority in order to Question Authority.

There may be no more pressing intellectual need in our culture than for people to become sophisticated about the function of memory. The political implications of the loss of memory are obvious. The authority of memory is a personal confirmation of selfhood. To write one's life is to live it twice, and the second living is both spiritual and historical, for a memoir reaches deep within the personality as it seeks its narrative form and also grasps the life-of-the-times as no political treatise can.

Our most ancient metaphor says life is a journey. Memoir is travel writing, then, notes taken along the way, telling how things looked and what thoughts occurred. But I cannot think of the memoirist as a tourist. This is the traveller who goes on foot, living the journey, taking on mountains, enduring deserts, marveling at the lush green places. Moving through it all faithfully, not so much a survivor with a harrowing tale to tell as a pilgrim, seeking, wondering.

Black Men and Public Space

Brent Staples

Brent Staples (b. 1951) is a journalist and writer who earned a Ph.D. in psychology from the University of Chicago. After working for the Chicago Sun Times *and other Chicago periodicals, Staples became assistant metropolitan editor of* The New York Times. *In his essay, Staples describes how he became "thoroughly familiar with the language of fear."*

My first victim was a woman—white, well dressed, probably in her early twenties. I came upon her late one evening on a deserted street in Hyde Park, a relatively affluent neighborhood in an otherwise mean, impoverished section of Chicago. As I swung onto the avenue behind her, there seemed to be a discreet, uninflammatory distance between us. Not so. She cast back a worried glance. To her, the youngish black man—a broad six feet two inches with a beard and billowing hair, both hands shoved into the pockets of a bulky military jacket—seemed menacingly close. After a few more quick glimpses, she picked up her pace and was soon running in earnest. Within seconds she disappeared into a cross street. 1

That was more than a decade ago. I was twenty-two years old, a graduate student newly arrived at the University of Chicago. It was in the echo of that terrified woman's footfalls that I first began to know the unwieldly inheritance I'd come into—the ability to alter public space in ugly ways. It was clear that she thought herself the quarry of a mugger, a rapist, or worse. Suffering a bout of insomnia, however, I was stalking sleep, not defenseless wayfarers. As a softy who is scarcely able to take a knife to a raw chicken—let alone hold one to a person's throat—I was surprised, embarrassed, and dismayed all at once. Her flight made me feel like an accomplice in tyranny. It also made it clear that I was indistinguishable from the muggers who occasionally seeped into the area from the surrounding ghetto. That first encounter, and those that followed, signified that a vast, unnerving gulf lay between nighttime pedestrians—particularly women—and me. And I soon gathered that being perceived as dangerous is a hazard in itself. I only needed to turn a corner into a dicey situation, or crowd some frightened, armed person in a foyer somewhere, or make an errant move after being pulled over by a policeman. Where fear and weapons meet—and they often do in urban America—there is always the possibility of death. 2

In that first year, my first away from my hometown, I was to become thoroughly familiar with the language of fear. At dark, shadowy intersections, I could cross in front of a car stopped at a traffic light and elicit the 3 *thunk, thunk, thunk, thunk* of the driver—black, white, male, or female—hammering down the door locks. On less traveled streets after dark, I grew accustomed to but never comfortable with people crossing to the other side of the street rather than pass me. Then there were the standard unpleasantries with policemen, doormen, bouncers, cabdrivers, and others whose business it is to screen out troublesome individuals *before* there is any nastiness.

I moved to New York nearly two years ago and I have remained an avid night walker. In central Manhattan, the near-constant crowd cover minimizes tense one-on-one street encounters. Elsewhere—in SoHo, for example, where sidewalks are narrow and tightly spaced buildings shut out the sky—things can get very taut indeed. 4

After dark, on the warrenlike streets of Brooklyn where I live, I often see women who fear the worst from me. They seem to have set their faces on neutral, and with their purse straps strung across their chests bandolier-style, they forge ahead as though bracing themselves against being tackled. I understand, of course, that the danger they perceive is not a hallucination. Women are particularly vulnerable to street violence, and young black males are drastically overrepresented among the perpetrators of that violence. Yet these truths are no solace against the kind of alienation that comes of being ever the suspect, a fearsome entity with whom pedestrians avoid making eye contact. 5

It is not altogether clear to me how I reached the ripe old age of twenty-two without being conscious of the lethality nighttime pedestrians attributed to me. Perhaps it was because in Chester, Pennsylvania, the small, angry industrial town where I came of age in the 1960s, I was scarcely noticeable against a backdrop of gang warfare, street knifings, and murders. I grew up one of the good boys, had perhaps a half-dozen fistfights. In retrospect, my shyness of combat has clear sources. 6

As a boy, I saw countless tough guys locked away; I have since buried several, too. They were babies, really—a teenage cousin, a brother of twenty-two, a childhood friend in his mid-twenties—all gone down in episodes of bravado played out in the streets. I came to doubt the virtues of intimidation early on. I chose, perhaps unconsciously, to remain a shadow—timid, but a survivor. 7

The fearsomeness mistakenly attributed to me in public places often has a perilous flavor. The most frightening of these confusions occurred in the late 1970s and early 1980s, when I worked as a journalist in Chicago. One day, rushing into the office of a magazine I was writing for with a deadline story in hand, I was mistaken for a burglar. The office manager called security and, with an ad hoc posse, pursued me through the labyrinthine halls, nearly to my editor's door. I had no way of proving who I was. I could only move briskly toward the company of someone who knew me. 8

Another time I was on assignment for a local paper and killing time before an interview. I entered a jewelry store on the city's affluent Near North Side. The proprietor excused herself and returned with an enormous red Doberman pinscher straining at the end of a leash. She stood, the dog extended toward me, silent to my questions, her eyes bulging nearly out of her head. I took a cursory look around, nodded, and bade her good night. 9

Relatively speaking, however, I never fared as badly as another black male journalist. He went to nearby Waukegan, Illinois, a couple of summers ago to work on a story about a murderer who was born there. Mistaking the reporter for the killer, police officers hauled him from his car at gunpoint and but for his press credentials would probably have tried to book him. Such episodes are not uncommon. Black men trade tales like this all the time. 10

Over the years, I learned to smother the rage I felt at so often being taken for a criminal. Not to do so would surely have led to madness. I now take precautions to make myself less threatening. I move about with care, particularly late in the evening. I give a wide berth to nervous people on subway platforms during the wee hours, particularly when I have exchanged business clothes for jeans. If I happen to be entering a building behind some people who appear skittish, I may walk by, letting them clear the lobby before I return, so as not to seem to be following them. I have been calm and extremely congenial on those rare occasions when I've been pulled over by the police. 11

And on late-evening constitutionals I employ what has proved to be an excellent tension-reducing measure: I whistle melodies from Beethoven and Vivaldi and the more popular classical composers. Even steely New Yorkers hunching toward nighttime destinations seem to relax, and occasionally they even join in the tune. Virtually everybody seems to sense that a mugger wouldn't be warbling bright, sunny selections from Vivaldi's *Four Seasons.* It is my equivalent of the cowbell that hikers wear when they know they are in bear country. 12

Being a Man

Paul Theroux

Paul Theroux (b. 1941) has taught English in Malawi, Uganda, and Singapore, as well as at the University of Virginia. He has written more than 20 works of fiction and nonfiction, including Sunrise with Seamonsters: Travels and Discoveries 1964–1984, *from which this essay was taken.*

There is a pathetic sentence in the chapter "Fetishism" in Dr. Norman Cameron's book *Personality Development and Psychopathology*. It goes, "Fetishists are nearly always men; and their commonest fetish is a woman's shoe." I cannot read that sentence without thinking that it is just one more awful thing about being a man—and perhaps it is an important thing to know about us. 1

I have always disliked being a man. The whole idea of manhood in America is pitiful, in my opinion. This version of masculinity is a little like having to wear an ill-fitting coat for one's entire life (by contrast, I imagine femininity to be an oppressive sense of nakedness). Even the expression "Be a man!" strikes me as insulting and abusive. It means: Be stupid, be unfeeling, obedient, soldierly and stop thinking. Man means "manly"—how can one think about men without considering the terrible ambition of manliness? And yet it is part of every man's life. It is a hideous and crippling lie; it not only insists on difference and connives at superiority, it is also by its very nature destructive—emotionally damaging and socially harmful. 2

The youth who is subverted, as most are, into believing in the masculine ideal is effectively separated from women and he spends the rest of his life finding women a riddle and a nuisance. Of course, there is a female version of this male affliction. It begins with mothers encouraging little girls to say (to other adults) "Do you like my new dress?" In a sense, little girls are traditionally urged to please adults with a kind of coquettishness, while boys are enjoined to behave like monkeys towards each other. The nine-year-old coquette proceeds to become womanish in a subtle power game in which she learns to be sexually indispensable, socially decorative and always alert to a man's sense of inadequacy. 3

Femininity—being lady-like—implies needing a man as witness and seducer; but masculinity celebrates the exclusive company of men. That is why it is so grotesque; and that is also why there is no manliness without inadequacy—because it denies men the natural friendship of women. 4

It is very hard to imagine any concept of manliness that does not belittle women, and it begins very early. At an age when I wanted to meet girls—let's say the treacherous years of thirteen to sixteen—I was told to take up a sport, get more fresh air, join the Boy Scouts, and I was urged not to read so much. It was the 1950s and if you asked too many questions about sex you were sent to camp—boy's camp, of course: the nightmare. Nothing is more unnatural or prison-like than a boy's camp, but if it were not for them we would have no Elks' Lodges, no pool rooms, no boxing matches, no Marines. 5

And perhaps no sports as we know them. Everyone is aware of how few in number are the athletes who behave like gentlemen. Just as high school basketball teaches you how to be a poor loser, the manly attitude towards sports seems to be little more than a recipe for creating bad marriages, social misfits, moral degenerates, sadists, latent rapists and just 6 plain louts. I regard high school sports as a drug far worse than marijuana, and it is the reason that the average tennis champion, say, is a pathetic oaf.

Any objective study would find the quest for manliness essentially right-wing, puritanical, cowardly, neurotic and fueled largely by a fear of women. It is also certainly philistine. There is no book-hater like a Little League coach. But indeed all the creative arts are obnoxious to the manly ideal, because at their best the arts are pursued by uncompetitive and essentially solitary people. It makes it very hard for a creative youngster, for any boy who expresses the desire to be alone seems to be saying that there is something wrong with him. 7

It ought to be clear by now that I have something of an objection to the way we turn boys into men. It does not surprise me that when the President of the United States has his customary weekend off he dresses like a cowboy—it is both a measure of his insecurity and his willingness to please. In many ways, American culture does little more for a man than prepare him for modeling clothes in the L. L. Bean catalogue. I take this as a personal insult because for many years I found it impossible to admit to myself that I wanted to be a writer. It was my guilty secret, because being a writer was incompatible with being a man. 8

There are people who might deny this, but that is because the American writer, typically, has been so at pains to prove his manliness that we have come to see literariness and manliness as mingled qualities. But first there was a fear that writing was not a manly profession—indeed, not a profession at all. (The paradox in American letters is that it has always been easier for a woman to write and for a man to be published.) Growing up, I had thought of sports as wasteful and humiliating, and the idea of manliness was a bore. My wanting to become a writer was not a flight from that oppressive role-playing, but I quickly saw that it was at odds with it. Everything in stereotyped manliness goes against the life of the mind. The Hemingway personality is too tedious to go into here, and in any case his exertions are well-known, but certainly it was not until this aberrant behavior was examined by feminists in the 1960s that any male writer dared question the pugnacity in Hemingway's fiction. All the bullfighting and arm wrestling and elephant shooting diminished Hemingway as a writer, but it is consistent with a prevailing attitude in American writing: one cannot be a male writer without first proving that one is a man. 9

It is normal in America for a man to be dismissive or even somewhat apologetic about being a writer. Various factors make it easier. There is a heartiness about journalism that makes it acceptable—journalism is the manliest form of American writing and, therefore, the profession the most independent-minded women seek (yes, it is an illusion, but that is my point). Fiction-writing is equated with a kind of dispirited failure and is only manly when it produces wealth—money is masculinity. So is drinking. Being a drunkard is another assertion, if misplaced, of manliness. The American 10 male writer is traditionally proud of his heavy drinking. But we are also a very literal-minded people. A man proves his manhood in America in old-fashioned ways. He kills lions, like Hemingway; or he hunts ducks, like Nathanael West; or he makes pronouncements like, "A man should carry enough knife to defend himself with," as James Jones once said to a *Life* interviewer. Or he says he can drink you under the table. But even tiny drunken William Faulkner loved to mount a horse and go fox hunting, and Jack Kerouac roistered up and down Manhattan in a lumberjack shirt (and spent every night of *The Subterraneans* with his mother in Queens). And we are familiar with the lengths to which Norman Mailer is prepared, in his endearing way, to prove that he is just as much a monster as the next man.

When the novelist John Irving was revealed as a wrestler, people took him to be a very serious writer; and even a bubble reputation like Eric *(Love Story)* Segal's was enhanced by the news that he ran the marathon in a respectable time. How surprised we would be if Joyce Carol Oates were revealed as a sumo wrestler or Joan Didion active in pumping iron. "Lives in New York City with her three children" is the typical woman writer's biographical note, for just as the male writer must prove he has achieved a sort of muscular manhood, the woman writer—or rather her publicists—must prove her motherhood.

There would be no point in saying any of this if it were not generally accepted that to be a man is somehow—even now in feminist-influenced America—a privilege. It is on the contrary an unmerciful and punishing burden. Being a man is bad enough; being manly is appalling (in this sense, women's lib has done much more for men than for women). It is the sinister silliness of men's fashions, and a clubby attitude in the arts. It is the subversion of good students. It is the so-called "Dress Code" of the Ritz-Carlton Hotel in Boston, and it is the institutionalized cheating in college sports. It is the most primitive insecurity.

And this is also why men often object to feminism but are afraid to explain why: of course women have a justified grievance, but most men believe—and with reason—that their lives are just as bad.

Beauty: When the Other Dancer Is the Self

Alice Walker

Alice Walker (b. 1944) grew up in rural Georgia, the youngest of eight children. Poet, essayist, and fiction writer, Walker won a Pulitzer Prize for her novel The Color Purple *(1982). Other works include* Meridian *(1976) and* The

eye and shaking his head. "Eyes are sympathetic," he says. "If one is blind, the other will likely become blind too."

This comment of the doctor's terrifies me. But it is really how I look that bothers me most. Where the BB struck there is a glob of whitish scar tissue, a hideous cataract, on my eye. Now when I stare at people—a favorite pastime, up to now—they will stare back. Not at the "cute" little girl, but at her scar. For six years I do not stare at anyone, because I do not raise my head. 13

Years later, in the throes of a mid-life crisis, I ask my mother and sister whether I changed after the "accident." "No," they say, puzzled. "What do you mean?" 14

What do I mean? 15

I am eight, and, for the first time, doing poorly in school, where I have been something of a whiz since I was four. We have just moved to the place where the "accident" occurred. We do not know any of the people around us because this is a different county. The only time I see the friends I knew is when we go back to our old church. The new school is the former state penitentiary. It is a large stone building, cold and drafty, crammed to overflowing with boisterous, ill-disciplined children. On the third floor there is a huge circular imprint of some partition that has been torn out. 16

"What used to be here?" I ask a sullen girl next to me on our way past it to lunch. 17

"The electric chair," says she. 18

At night I have nightmares about the electric chair, and about all the people reputedly "fried" in it. I am afraid of the school, where all the students seem to be budding criminals. 19

"What's the matter with your eye?" they ask, critically. 20

When I don't answer (I cannot decide whether it was an "accident" or not), they shove me, insist on a fight. 21

My brother, the one who created the story about the wire, comes to my rescue. But then brags so much about "protecting" me, I become sick. 22

After months of torture at the school, my parents decide to send me back to our old community, to my old school. I live with my grandparents and the teacher they board. But there is no room for Phoebe, my cat. By the time my grandparents decide there *is* room, and I ask for my cat, she cannot be found. Miss Yarborough, the boarding teacher, takes me under her wing, and begins to teach me to play the piano. But soon she marries an African—a "prince," she says—and is whisked away to his continent. 23

At my old school there is at least one teacher who loves me. She is the teacher who "knew me before I was born" and bought my first baby clothes. It is she who makes life bearable. It is her presence that finally helps me turn on the one child at the school who continually calls me "one-eyed 24 bitch." One day I simply grab him by his coat and beat him until I am satisfied. It is my teacher who tells me my mother is ill.

My mother is lying in bed in the middle of the day, something I have never 2
seen. She is in too much pain to speak. She has an abscess in her ear. I stand looking down on her, knowing that if she dies, I cannot live. She is being treated with warm oils and hot bricks held against her cheek. Finally a doctor comes. But I must go back to my grandparents' house. The weeks pass but I am hardly aware of it. All I know is that my mother might die, my father is not so jolly, my brothers still have their guns, and I am the one sent away from home.

"You did not change," they say. 2

Did I imagine the anguish of never looking up? 2

I am twelve. When relatives come to visit I hide in my room. My cousin 2
Brenda, just my age, whose father works in the post office and whose mother is a nurse, comes to find me. "Hello," she says. And then she asks, looking at my recent school picture, which I did not want taken, and on which the "glob," as I think of it, is clearly visible, "You still can't see out of that eye?"

"No," I say, and flop back on the bed over my book. 2

That night, as I do almost every night, I abuse my eye. I rant and rave 3
at it, in front of the mirror. I plead with it to clear up before morning. I tell it I hate and despise it. I do not pray for sight. I pray for beauty.

"You did not change," they say. 3

I am fourteen and baby-sitting for my brother Bill, who lives in Boston. He 3
is my favorite brother and there is a strong bond between us. Understanding my feelings of shame and ugliness he and his wife take me to a local hospital, where the "glob" is removed by a doctor named O. Henry. There is still a small bluish crater where the scar tissue was, but the ugly white stuff is gone. Almost immediately I become a different person from the girl who does not raise her head. Or so I think. Now that I've raised my head I win the boyfriend of my dreams. Now that I've raised my head I have plenty of friends. Now that I've raised my head classwork comes from my lips as faultlessly as Easter speeches did, and I leave high school as valedictorian, most popular student, and *queen,* hardly believing my luck. Ironically, the girl who was voted most beautiful in our class (and was) was later shot twice through the chest by a male companion, using a "real" gun, while she was pregnant. But that's another story in itsef. Or is it?

"You did not change," they say. 3

It is now thirty years since the "accident." A beautiful journalist comes to 3
visit and to interview me. She is going to write a cover story for her magazine

that focuses on my latest book. "Decide how you want to look on the cover," she says. "Glamorous, or whatever."

Never mind "glamorous," it is the "whatever" that I hear. Suddenly all 35
I can think of is whether I will get enough sleep the night before the photography session: if I don't, my eye will be tired and wander, as blind eyes will.

At night in bed with my lover I think up reasons why I should not 36
appear on the cover of a magazine. "My meanest critics will say I've sold out," I say. "My family will now realize I write scandalous books."

"But what's the real reason you don't want to do this?" he asks. 37

"Because in all probability," I say in a rush, "my eye won't be straight." 38

"It will be straight enough," he says. Then, "Besides, I thought you'd 39
made your peace with that."

And I suddenly remember that I have. 40

I remember: 41

I am talking to my brother Jimmy, asking if he remembers anything 42
unusual about the day I was shot. He does not know I consider that day the last time my father, with his sweet home remedy of cool lily leaves, chose me, and that I suffered and raged inside because of this. "Well," he says, "all I remember is standing by the side of the highway with Daddy, trying to flag down a car. A white man stopped, but when Daddy said he needed somebody to take his little girl to the doctor, he drove off."

I remember. 43

I am in the desert for the first time. I fall totally in love with it. I am so 44
overwhelmed by its beauty, I confront for the first time, consciously, the meaning of the doctor's words years ago: "Eyes are sympathetic. If one is blind, the other will likely become blind too." I realize I have dashed about the world madly, looking at this, looking at that, storing up images against the fading of the light. *But I might have missed seeing the desert!* The shock of that possibility—and gratitude for over twenty-five years of sight—sends me literally to my knees. Poem after poem comes—which is perhaps how poets pray.

On Sight

I am so thankful I have seen
The Desert
And the creatures in the desert
And the desert Itself.

The desert has its own moon
Which I have seen
With my own eye.
There is no flag on it.

Trees of the desert have arms
All of which are always up
That is because the moon is up
The sun is up
Also the sky
The stars
Clouds
None with flags.

If there *were* flags, I doubt
the trees would point.
Would you?

But mostly, I remember this: 4

I am twenty-seven, and my baby daughter is almost three. Since her 4
birth I have worried about her discovery that her mother's eyes are different from other people's. Will she be embarrassed? I think. What will she say? Every day she watches a television program called "Big Blue Marble." It begins with a picture of the earth as it appears from the moon. It is bluish, a little battered-looking, but full of light, with whitish clouds swirling around it. Every time I see it I weep with love, as if it is a picture of Grandma's house. One day when I am putting Rebecca down for her nap, she suddenly focuses on my eye. Something inside me cringes, gets ready to try to protect myself. All children are cruel about physical differences, I know from experience, and that they don't always mean to be is another matter. I assume Rebecca will be the same.

But no-o-o-o. She studies my face intently as we stand, her inside and 4
me outside her crib. She even holds my face maternally between her dimpled little hands. Then, looking every bit as serious and lawyerlike as her father, she says, as if it may just possibly have slipped my attention: "Mommy, there's a *world* in your eye." (As in "Don't be alarmed, or do anything crazy.") And then, gently, but with great interest: "Mommy, where did you *get* that world in your eye?"

For the most part, the pain left then. (So what if my brothers grew up 4
to buy even more powerful pellet guns for their sons and to carry real guns themselves. So what, if a young "Morehouse man" once nearly fell off the steps of Trevor Arnett Library because he thought my eyes were blue.) Crying and laughing I ran to the bathroom, while Rebecca mumbled and sang herself off to sleep. Yes indeed, I realized, looking into the mirror. There *was* a world in my eye. And I saw that it was possible to love it: that in fact, for all it had taught me of shame and anger and inner vision, I *did* love it. Even to see it drifting out of orbit in boredom, or rolling up out of fatigue, not to mention floating back at attention in excitement (bearing

witness, a friend has called it), deeply suitable to my personality, and even characteristic of me.

That night I dream I am dancing to Stevie Wonder's song "Always" (the name of the song is really "As," but I hear it as "Always"). As I dance, whirling and joyous, happier than I've ever been in my life, another bright-faced dancer joins me. We dance and kiss each other and hold each other through the night. The other dancer has obviously come through all right, as I have done. She is beautiful, whole and free. And she is also me. 49

1983

STUDENT ESSAYS

Normalcy

Gregory Bravo

Gregory Bravo (b. 1971) was raised in Buffalo, New York, and is majoring in physics. Greg plays the flute and spends time each week teaching chess to inner-city children. About his essay, Greg reports: "This essay is a memorial to my mother, and to all of those families who, through the 'unfortunate' sickness of one of their members, have come to a better understanding of and appreciation for all humanity."

Whatever situation you are born into is what you accept as reality: you can 1 know no different. You are given a reality, a sheltered reality, by your parents. Thus I knew nothing of it when in 1973, the year my brother was born, they told her she "had it." But, there wasn't really much to be done about it. "Just live your life and try and not worry about what *might* happen," they told her. So, she did. After all, she had a newborn and a two-year-old to look after, diapers that had to be changed, baths that had to be given. There were other, more important things to be done, too many to spend time worrying about a little numbness in the hands and feet. I mean, what the heck, everyone has funny little things that they have to deal with, right? I remember little of these years; Doctor Seuss, a green ashtray—unconnected images amalgamated by the saccharine mist of early childhood and many passing years.

School began for me when I was five, and there she was. She drove 2 my brother and me here and there, drove us to the swimming pool for lessons, to the dancing school for lessons, to the piano teacher for lessons. During these years we were one, my brother, my mother, and I, a single unit. We did almost everything together. Although my brother and I had passed the nap stage years back, we would still take a snooze with her some afternoons, when she became really tired, because she asked us to. We were young and didn't ask why; if she had to take a nap, then it must be the right thing to do.

Years passed, as they do, and I became slowly aware that my mother 3
was "different" from the rest of us. It was school that did it; friends would visit, school friends, and ask questions like "what's wrong with your ma?" In my first-grade naïveté, a typical, and proud, response would be: "Nothing. She's special." It was only after I met the kids at school in the "special education" classes that I realized what other connotations that word had. I liked it when we visited her "special doctor" with her; I liked to look through the magazines in his waiting room. This was just part of the weekly routine then, a part that I liked because the doctor had magazines we didn't.

Things began gradually to change in our house. I didn't think it so 4
strange when I had to start walking arm in arm with my mother to my own teacher conferences (I actually thought this was sort of neat), or that she now needed someone's help to get from her bedroom to the living room. I now knew what it meant, that she was very special indeed. With each passing year, responsibilities that used to be hers were slowly shifted to the rest of us. With a smiling submission, we took an attitude of acquiescence and acceptance, and pretended that things were fine, still looking hopefully to the day when things would be fixed, and our mother could run with us again.

When high school came for my brother and me, the wheelchair and 5
electric motor scooter came for our mother. She still handled all of the bill-paying and paperwork of the household, but when it came to doing most physical things there was only one thing left that she was able to do by herself: get from her bed to the commode and back. Getting oneself to the toilet only four feet away does not seem such a great achievement, but it was the one thing that she could still do by herself, and we respected this. We left the room when she had to use the commode. She could still handle herself there, and took pride in that fact.

"I'll be OK here, go ahead," she told us that day in her simple, matter- 6
of-fact way. "If I need anything, I'll just wait until you get back." Most of me knew that we shouldn't have gone to the record store, that things in our house could never be as lighthearted as she was trying to make them, that there were many ways in which she could end up being "not OK." But, a sanctioned removal of responsibility is a strong thing. Besides, I really wanted to go. I tried to reconcile the contradiction.

"We'll be back as quick as we can, all right?" I both told her and asked her. We left her in her bed watching TV, hurried out the door, and came back as quickly as we could. We weren't quick enough. 7

My brother and I found her sitting, useless legs folded sideways beneath her as a lounging deer's, crumpled on the floor. The tattered brown wall-to-wall was the only padding between her and the hard wood floor below. She may have been sitting there to tighten a screw in one of the doors of the long, low dresser in front of her, or to check the long sideboard of the companion bed behind. She always *looked* normal; the disease that was ravaging her spinal cord was a subversive and malicious enemy. "You're looking good, Jackie," long lost friends from a long gone childhood would say, "Damn good." And she did. But, they didn't realize what was going on behind the scenes, what was under that beautiful exterior, how much work had gone into keeping life natural, how much it took. My brother and I knew well why she was there squashed into the eight square feet between bed and dresser and table and commode that up until that point had still been her own. This was how close the boundaries had been shrunk, and now we were watching them slowly evaporate altogether. 8

"I can't get up," she said, but we already knew. We stood there, amid the acrid, biting, almost liquid smell of urine and cigarettes, and we knew; we knew the pathetic scene that this made and we knew all of the rest, how alone we were and how the only thing to do was to try and get her back on the bed. 9

Looking down at her, I almost started laughing then, the whole thing was so ridiculous: here was my mother, the one that I loved most of all, the one who gave me direction and order, who taught me everything that was important in life, the one who I listened to, and sometimes resented, lying helpless in an almost fetal position on the floor, depending now on her sons to try and save what was left of her pride and dignity. Maybe I didn't quite like her then, and that seeing her on the floor gave me some sort of satisfaction: "Damn it, you're our *mother*! How dare you treat us like this!" Maybe this was why I almost laughed then. Maybe it was just the unreality of it all: this wasn't supposed to happen, this wasn't a real scene in real people's lives in a real town, in a real state in a real country in a real world. It was something weird, a left-handed reflection of a right-handed reality. It was just a play that we were acting in for the Guy Upstairs, and in fifteen or twenty minutes when we were done here, coffee and doughnuts would be served at the golden gates, congratulations on another performance well-done handed round, and greasepaint taken off with some otherworldly cold cream. Maybe this is really how it works, but I was still in the thick of act one and having to make the script up as I went along. 10

But there was no leverage, not enough space, not enough strength 11 for that space. She was as big as I was, and dead weight. Dead but living and delicate and pliable weight, weight that hurt and felt and pulsed through your fingers. We had nothing to do but try, because the floor is not an alternative for the living, feeling, loving one that you call 'mother.'

Under her arms I went, under her legs he went. "Ready Jase," I said, 12
"Lift!" We tried, we tried, but she was alive and scared and we were young and he was small. Two feet, that was all that we could do, and then we slumped her back to the ground. We stood, silent, over her, acutely aware of our failure, and realizing what it all meant, as the last wisps of propriety floated up and out of our reach, gone. She started to cry.

We stood there and waited, the silence and loneliness accentuated 13
only by her sobs. If we would have failed a second time in trying to get her back onto the bed, things would have gotten even worse. But we couldn't very well leave her on the ground, not while we were able to walk, not while we breathed her air, and ate her food, and called ourselves her children. We let her rest for a little while, and then, knowing what another failure would do to her, tried lifting her again. We got her to the bed this time.

The episode was over, but the implications weighed heavily in the air. 14
There was a finality here, unspoken, but present; no matter how hard I tried, I could no longer see this situation as normal, special, neat, interesting—all of those terms we had been earnestly using for over 14 years. The last remnant of anything that could have honestly been called one of those names had been taken from us that day, leaving us with pale and empty euphemisms. We tried to console her then, but there was really nothing to say, so we hugged and kissed her instead. I couldn't cry. I knew that I should, or at least feel something, but I felt nothing. Numb and emotionless, the logical part of my mind hated myself for not having any emotions, not feeling sad, not even really feeling sorry. This hour had been coming since 1973, and its actual arrival left me empty. It may have been a psychological barrier that I put up to keep myself in one piece, but for whatever reason it happened, I really shouldn't have been worried. Later, weeks later, I cried alone and fiercely, the overwhelming injustice of the whole lousy thing bearing down and almost smothering me, depression as a heavy wet blanket. We worked harder than ever after this to reorganize things, and a "new" normalcy settled over the household, something strange and different than before. In a way, a weight had been lifted, a weight we all wanted to bear as long as we could. The waiting and the hoping were over. We finally came to the end, and started over fresh. We re-learned how to laugh and went on with our lives, as all in this world must do. We went on, with a new, sobering, and yet honest realization: my mother would never walk again.

Voicing the Monster

Minh Dang

Minh Dang (b. 1972) left Saigon at the age of 2 1/2, and grew up in Portland, Oregon. She is majoring in East-Asian Studies, concentrating her studies on Vietnamese culture and history. About writing, Minh tells us: "Good writing is never finished. When you love a piece of writing, it follows you and grows and changes with you. Looking back at my essay Voicing the Monster, I see even more now than I saw when I wrote it. Everybody's childhood is rich with experience. Sometimes we think our childhood seems mundane, but even the most mundane aspects of our childhood give us a lot to write about."

Miss Kathy and Miss Jane sometimes brought us candy when they came. 1 We children would clamber up beside them on the sofa to touch their lightish-colored curly hair, so strange and foreign to us. It must be fake, we used to giggle in Vietnamese. When they came they brought their bottles and stethoscopes and immunization papers, asking questions and taking notes for their files. We were so young we never minded their presence, little runny-nosed, sun-browned children playing on the dusty floor at their feet.

At least, that's what I remembered, several years later when my father 2 mentioned Miss Kathy's name. I was confused at first because I thought he meant Sister Kathleen, my old first grade teacher. I might have been nine or ten years old at the time; I just barely remembered our first year in America, when I was three, and two American women used to visit us.

When I think of Miss Kathy and Miss Jane I remember our old house, 3 the plaster crumbling and the wind sneaking through the cracks in the winter. I especially remember the tiny living room and the saggy brown sofa they always sat on when they visited. I remember the battered sliding wooden doors connecting that room to Grandma's bedroom, how those doors would never shut completely, leaving a several-inches-wide crack through which we children would sometimes spy when they came. I remember how strange and out of place they appeared in our house, these two big women who wore dark tinted glasses and bold skirts, and brashly drank their Coca-Cola straight from the bottle.

But there was more to the memory besides those afternoon visits at 4 our old house. Much later, the strange catch in Father's voice when he'd said Miss Kathy's name made me vaguely recall a Christmas card we'd gotten from them at our new address, some time after they'd stopped coming that first year. Father had been strange and silent about the card, and hadn't sent one back. Perhaps he'd even considered returning it unopened. All I really remember is some snatches of conversation—the rumbling of deep male voices in the kitchen, Father speaking lower than usual, my oldest brother raising his voice in argument. . . .

I've intuitively stayed clear of broaching the subject, even when I was 5
too little to appreciate the effort it took Father to say her name, sucking in his breath even as it came out. I missed that opportunity to remember what happened, when it was still close enough to remember with effort.

I know now that the memory of those refugee years is still painful to 6
my father, that he lowers his voice when he says the word "welfare," just as he does when he mentions my deceased mother's name. I have never had the courage to ask him about Miss Kathy and Miss Jane, why they stopped coming. Perhaps they stopped simply because we got off welfare and our file was closed. But I have a notion that he'd asked them to stop coming, or at least hurried the process along—medical records left incomplete and case evaluations still unwritten.

Father, what do you remember when you think of those two women? 7
What is the silent monster that their names unleash? For me, the dread is not in the memory but in the speculation, now, about what happened: if only I could have heard the gulping of my father's words, prying at my stubborn consciousness to let his shame seep in. For me, "monster" is what remains unsaid and unacknowledged, the hurt, hinted at by Father's hesitation, which I'd been too young to share.

Sometimes I fancy my imagination may have fabricated the whole affair, 8
cutting and pasting together little snippets from other scenes. I have searched our house for that Christmas card, concrete proof that Miss Kathy and Miss Jane really existed. I've found family correspondence buried and forgotten in the dusty, newspaper-lined drawers in our living room and kitchen, or slipped carelessly into old books never again opened. Behind the bottom drawer of Father's file cabinet I found a packet of fragile, yellowed airmail letters from Vietnam, so wispy and seethrough I fancied they'd fall apart and disappear if I touched them, like the memory I was looking for. I even found an ancient, cracked leather valise full of documents brought from Vietnam or issued in the refugee camps in the Philippines and on Wake Island. Tucked among those documents was a First Interstate Bank statement and an old Pacific Northwest Power electricity bill, both dated 1976, the year after we came to the United States. But there was no Christmas card.

Once I questioned one of my sisters about it. Do you remember Miss 9
Kathy and Miss Jane? I asked. Or the Christmas card we got at the new

house? It all sounded familiar to her, even the argument in the other room. But confrontations with my father, especially during my childhood, were rare and terrifying incidents; I'm sure she must have carried those disturbing images about with her, just as I did. Perhaps she'd merely cut and pasted that part of the story from a different memory, a different confrontation.

Gaps in the past are destined to be filled with Elmer's paste and bits of colored construction paper torn from childhood fantasies and nightmares, if they're to be filled at all. We illuminate the shadowy puddles and bottomless black holes where monsters brood when we fill their void with made-up stories. My sister and I stick tightly to our shared story, two conspirators rewriting history. 10

But the revision doesn't necessarily have to be a deviation from the truth. The integrity of remembering (or not) is not necessarily a function of how factually accurate our memory is. It doesn't really matter if the Christmas card from Miss Kathy and Miss Jane never even existed, or if the "real" story is different than the one my sister and I have decided upon. Our story was our intuition of Father's unacknowledged shame, and if it wasn't factually true, it was a context for us to recognize that shame. 11

Maxine Hong Kingston writes in *China Men* about the time her father lost his temper when the children were misbehaving, and chased her sister up the stairs into the bedroom, ready to beat her with his heavy wooden coathanger. She recalls standing in the hallway with the other children, watching him kick in the door and seeing the round mirror on the wall shattering to the floor. But her sister remembered it the other way: *she* was on the outside watching the mirror shatter, and Kingston was on the inside, when their father kicked in the door. 12

I wasn't there when it happened, but I "remembered" it too, as I read the story. It was like being in a movie. I watched myself standing in morbid fascination in the hallway, leaning against the table; I winced when the glass shattered, and froze instinctively to avoid stepping on the scattered splinters. And then in the double-take I saw myself again, crouched in a corner between a nightstand and a wall, hugging the rough battered brown rug. 13

But that's as far as I go. I can't reconstruct the beating. Kingston herself could live/relive the scene only from the hallway, and had to speculate about what it was like in the bedroom. But her sister would have shared with me the same hallway experience. Retrospectively, in the re-write, no one was in that bedroom being beaten. 14

Some things are too frightening to remember, let alone voice. Kingston's coathanger story, in which neither sister acknowledges being beaten, has allowed both to remember the essence of the terror—their father's violent anger. I have my own coathanger story—not a story about me, but, again, 15 a configuration of cut-and-pasted fragments from the darker side of childhood. When I read Kingston's account, I saw the warning lights flash at me to stop. I wonder if coathangers are a common weapon in American homes, or if they are to Asians what belts are to Americans.

Father has even more compelling stories to tell, not just coathanger stories, but stick stories—three fingers wide and thick, he'd said, before he shuddered and fell silent. That was the time his cousin who'd grown up with him in the same village in northern Vietnam visited us from Canada. The welts must have still stung hot, to stir the angry blood in these two sixty-year-old men, and make their eyes water when they spoke. 16

Monster had showed itself in Father's expression. I'd sat frozen small and silent while he told the story, cringing from the undisclosed in his revelations. Who was it who beat my father so thoroughly that the little boy look still stole heartwrenchingly across his face, fifty years later? I'm not quite sure, and Father never mentioned it again, but that doesn't matter; once he told the story with his cousin, they were both freed from the burden of forced forgetting. 17

For me, looking for my monster which is the intuition of Father's unshared hurt, a stick three fingers wide is a good enough beginning to hold onto. Even a swallowed name, with a half-made-up story, is a starting point. 18

Much more significant than what happened is how I reconstructed what happened. Memory is so frail, and the past is never set in stone. I rewrite it each time I remember something different, whether it happened or not. My father might have rewritten the past one Christmas with a few scrawled words on a Christmas card. "Not at this address," he might have written. "Return to sender." We can't bear for you to remain a part of our lives because the past still hurts too much. 19

For Father those refugee years are too overwhelming to re-examine all at once. I still see him cringe even from the euphemisms he uses to skirt around them, though I suppose it's easier now when the last remnants of his little street urchin children have disappeared, transformed into doctors, professors, engineers, and college students. 20

There is a series of black and white pictures in our family album, taken during our first few years here. The landscape in those pictures is dust and concrete and stone, stark whiteness harsh as the summer sun I associate with my growing up. My brother remarked jokingly once that some of the pictures reminded him of the "Save the Children" posters urging people to sponsor a child. When he laughed, we all joined in, avoiding each other's eyes. Father sat intently still and silent in the corner, rubbing his thumb hard against his forefinger. 21

I have thought, there must be integrity in those pictures, proof that my 22 childhood was indeed real. But now I think that all the revisions that happened in between also have integrity, because they point toward some silent monster. All the "lies" we make up and tell ourselves and forget are as true as the official documents I found in that old leather valise, or the black and white photographs my brother took, fifteen years ago, that say "Save the Children."

Crossings

Steven Hoey

Steven Hoey (b. 1971) grew up in Wakefield, Massachusetts, and is majoring in psychology. Steve spends much of his free time in college working as a peer counselor, helping his fellow students talk about issues of sexuality. About his essay, Steve tells us: "My essay caught me off-guard; I didn't know where it was taking me. I realized when my Dad showed up at the end of the essay that this essay was my coming-out story. Writing my essay helped me realize the bridge I wanted to create with my Dad and helped me put in words the distance I still had to cross."

We were in her driveway, and I was still wearing my assistant manager's 1
jacket; she had taken hers off. I stared at the dashboard for a while.

"Julie, we need to talk." 2

There were little ripples in the simulated vinyl of the dashboard that 3
ran across the top like tiny waves on a lake. I stared at them longer, and they began to resemble the ripples on the small river that ran through the swamp near my house. It wasn't really a natural swamp, because the creek's source was the cavernous, crumbling-cement drainage pipe that carried away the street runoff.

My friend Anthony and I headed there one fourth-grade afternoon, 4
on one of those days when the sky was milky white, and the light seemed to be coming from everywhere at once. We walked down the well-worn trail behind the Bradleys' house and ducked a few branches. Soon, we found ourselves in The Swamp.

We quickly came to the place where the creek was wide; it was here 5
that we had to cross to get onto the "island." As usual, Anthony leapt across and landed safely and squarely on its mossy, muddy shore. I had jumped across, too, before, and made it. I looked down at my left foot, encased in the Fiberglas cast. I thought about the plastic bags that were always wrapped around it, and held on with rubber bands whenever I took a

bath. I could see Dr. Wright standing over me in his office, my leg still warm from the freshly applied cast; "Be sure not to get it wet," he had warned me. Anthony looked back at me from the dense tangle of swamp grass and cat o'nine tails, with his arms swinging at his sides. I pushed my right foot into the embankment, testing it. Odors of skunk cabbage and mud surrounded me, and I stared at the trickling, rusty river. I could see the burnt orange lines high up on the mud of the opposite bank showing how high the water had once been. "Heck, I've made it across before," I thought. With a heave, I pushed off, and crashed into the muddy island—the cold, greasy water surrounded my toes and slithered under my heel. With a yelp I jumped up and suspended my foot in the air, watching the orange liquid drip from it.

Anthony and I ran back to his house together, my foot sliding around inside the cast. With every step, I could hear the water sloshing and squishing inside of it; but worse than that, I could feel the inside of the cast clinging to me, and I had horrific visions of disgusting slugs and things swimming around my foot and toes. I continued, though, and squished up Anthony's front steps behind him. 6

Inside his house, I took a blow dryer to my cast, trying to dry the soggy lining of it. The hot blasts of air felt good on my toes, but the cast was too snug; my heel and ankle stewed in the dampness of the cast. When my toes started to feel like they were burning, I had to turn off the blow dryer and give up. I didn't want my mother to find out what had happened, but I knew she would—the brown stains stayed on the cast. 7

They were stains much like the splashes of muddy water on my white work pants. Dirt had caked onto their once-white cuffs in intricate patterns. I wondered if the spots would come out in the wash. 8

"What . . . Steve, is something wrong?" 9

The small light that illuminated the fuel gauge seemed dimmer than all the rest. The needle cast a most unusual shadow onto the plastic frame that separated the instruments from the rest of the car. 10

"I don't think we should be going out anymore . . . I don't know, it's just. . . ." 11

I was amazed at how much dust could collect inside the little trough on top of the dashboard, just behind the radio speaker. There were two pennies and a paper clip in there, and what looked like the remnants of a piece of paper. I wondered what it said. . . . 12

"Oh, God, Steve . . . what is it? What did I do? What didn't I do? Tell me, I can fix it. . . ." 13

I'd never noticed it before, but when you clicked your teeth together while looking at the yellow lights of the clock-radio dial, the numbers seemed to move and dance. The lights that lit up the air conditioning panel didn't do that—only the radio lights. 14

"No, no, Julie . . . it's not you. . . . It's me." 15

There was a little blue strip below the white one that went across the 16 speedometer. It registered kilometers per hour. The numbers were blue on the black background, so you couldn't see them very well—they were almost useless. But still, there they were. . . .

"What do you mean? I don't understand." 17

It had always bothered me that the radio panel was mounted crooked 18 in the dashboard. It was only off by half an inch, but still, it drove me crazy. I wanted to rip the dashboard off and straighten out the radio, then put the front back on. With my luck, though, it'd probably have broken, and I wouldn't have been able to fix it—even though I was the handiest one in the family. And so my father always enlisted me to help him with odd construction and repair jobs. These usually ended in frustration.

On a cool, sunny afternoon, I finished my chemistry homework early 19 so I could help my father open up the swimming pool for the summer. We first had to remove the enormous, blue plastic cover that had protected it from the winter weather. In protecting the pool, however, the cover had collected everything Nature had sent down. By late spring, a green film had grown over the plastic surface where it was covered by water, and there were tiny white wormlike creatures swimming among last fall's water-logged leaves.

My father and I always argued about how to take off the cover, and 20 this year was no different. We finally compromised and began pulling it off, from one end to the other. After we had pulled most of the cover off, we were left with a huge pouch of water that had formed by the edge of the pool; my father and I tugged with all of our might, but the water inside of the cover made it too heavy to lift. Minutes later I found myself standing in waist-high, freezing cold, green-tinted water, pushing the slimy underside of the cover out of the pool, while my father tugged at the cover from the outside. Chlorine and stagnation invaded my nostrils, sapping my strength. Eventually, though, the pouch dropped over the side, and with a great sloshing noise spilled its collection of decaying leaves, pine needles, and tiny creatures.

Next, we had to assemble the filter. With the wrinkled and worn 21 instruction sheet lying on the grass among the assorted hoses and clamps, we began to put the pieces together. We connected the gleaming silver tank to the black plastic pump, and strung hoses from this contraption into the pool and back. Finally, when every spout had a hose clamped onto it, we connected the electric pump to the power outlet. My father looked at me and exhaled forcefully, his hand on his forehead, his face in a weak smile of relief. He threw the switch.

Milky-white water started bubbling up out of the entrance to the filter 22 as though it were coffee in a percolator, sending the filtering powder into the pool. With a gurgling, slurping noise, pool water was sucked into what was supposed to be the outlet jet, and the filter emptied itself of all its powder. When we finally realized what had happened, it was too late—the pool's floor was covered with the fine white granules of Diatemaceous Earth.

I could see in the pool the floor of the car. Its surface, too, was covered with granules of sand and tiny pebbles. Scattered among these were old gum wrappers, pieces of cellophane, and two movie ticket stubs. 23

"Well, you see, Julie . . . it's like this. Uhh . . . it's that . . . I'm, ah . . . you know. . . . 24

In the plastic in front of the speedometer, I could see little rainbows. I don't know exactly what it was that made them, but they were interesting. 25

"Oh . . . I thought it was me. . . . It's okay, Steve, really . . . it's okay." 26

The lights on the street and in her house looked like stars, their beams streaked by the tears in my eyes. 27

Since I made that leap, the jumps have become less terrifying, because the creek has narrowed, and because I've become better at jumping. 28

I've just turned past an outgrowth of trees and grass, though, and here the river seems vast—wider than I've ever seen it. Looking down at the creek, I see jagged rocks piercing the water rusted with fear and ignorance. On the surface of the creek, I see the reflection of my father. 29

I am gripped with guilt and regret at the sight of him. He has been the shadow moving in the brush on the other side of the stream. Each time I leaped across, he was so close to me, but I couldn't—or didn't want to—see him. Now, the broad expanse of what was once a trickling stream lies between us. 30

His face is lined with concern, and frustration, and sadness. He does not look at me, but rather walks slowly along the opposite shore, staring at the grassy earth or off into the white sky. He must be wondering what happened to me—why I came to be on the opposite side of the river. I can feel his pain: his step is slow, and his feet are dragging along the ground. 31

His shoes are wet, stained with the muddy, obscure water. 32

I see that now. 33

I look again to the stream. The menacing spikes of stone reach upward, as though anticipating my leap. I look further down the river, searching for a place where the banks are closer. But the course of the water takes another turn and flows out of sight, and somehow I know that beyond that bend, the river will split into two separate streams that never rejoin. 34

The tears streak the sunlight reflected from the stream into bright lines that form a web between my father and me. I need to break through, to reach him, and ask for his acceptance. I back away from the bank, and 35 prepare to jump. Still, I am possessed with doubts. If, by some miracle I should make it across the water, what will he say, what can he say, when I tell him "Dad. . . ."

"I'm gay." 36

Odalisque

Elizabeth MacDonald

Elizabeth MacDonald (b. 1971) grew up in New York City and is majoring in Fine Arts, concentrating on French Nineteenth-Century Art. Elizabeth likes the quiet of museums, and spends much of her free time in museums observing or working as a research assistant. "Writing this essay," Elizabeth tells us, "was and still is my attempt to find an audience. I want my readers to think about the ways in which women are encouraged to suffer to be beautiful."

I am in eighth grade—perhaps two weeks, or even a week before all the 1
trouble started—and walking one evening with a friend on the east side of Manhattan. I catch sight of my reflection in a plate-glass window and, in these formative years, observe what I am becoming. My hair is short and less feminine at this time, my face rounder, my body plumper. I was happy with what I saw.

I am in ninth grade and my waist is the thickness of a bottleneck. Lying on 2
my bed I hear my parents talking about me as they walk along the hall.

"This diet has gone on too long," my mother is saying, "she's gotten 3
very weak."

"She is very thin," says my father. 4

I am in tenth grade and fatter than I have ever been. In a book written 5
during the Twiggy-influenced sixties I read that every day that you fast you lose two pounds of fat. This seems easier than recovering the discipline that I had once in such abundance and have now lost. I begin a regimen in which I eat enormous amounts for a few days and fast on the others. I want very much to regain the beauty that was once mine, to re-discover the indestructible, perfect creature of angles and spare planes that lies hidden under this amorphous mass of lumps. I want more than anything to be thin again. This seems to be a way. For a desperate girl who has no assurance that she will ever be desirable, almost no price is too high.

I do not remember the first time that I made myself throw up. It may have been in eleventh grade, but the circumstances have faded under the shame and horror. As I understand it many people try self-induced vomiting. Few are successful on the first attempt and most give up. Some of us persist: some of us even become quite talented. 6

In that talent I originally found salvation. Self-indulgence and beauty seemed, for the first time, compatible. I could give myself everything I wanted and retain the figure of the ascetic. I could have my cake, and I could eat it too. Nothing, however, is that easy. Maintaining the façade becomes indispensable. Every compliment is a knife in the gut and an impulse to retain what I have, though I pay, and pay dearly. There is a line in Yeats' "Adam's Curse" that cries bitterness— 7

> To be born woman is to know—
> Although they do not talk of it at school—
> That we must labor to be beautiful

I have only just discovered that I have been misquoting these lines for years. In my mind the last line, though essentially the same, has always had a slightly different nuance.

> . . . We must suffer to be beautiful.

The most famous photograph of Rita Hayworth, as Gilda, immortalizes her as an extraordinary beauty. In black satin she stands, mysterious and gorgeous—a stunning beauty, with allure and come-hither confidence. Her skin glows alabaster against a black background and on her beautiful face, slightly turned to the side, is a look of encouragement and, conversely, knowing distance. She tilts her chin up in the arrogance of her beauty: she knows very well that she stops traffic and hearts. Her hair is long, her waist is small, and her strapless dress clings to her perfect figure. Her self-presentation is more than feminine; it is the essence of female. Rita Hayworth played a woman all men wanted and all women wanted to be. She sets the standard of what it is to be an ideal woman—a flesh Goddess. 8

I have heard that she could not reconcile her beauty and herself, that she felt herself to be an illusion created by lights and other people's vision of what she should be. You could never tell that from this photograph. This woman revels in nothing more than her sexuality and beauty. And for all that, all the power and joy in her physical presence that she presents to the world in this still, Rita Hayworth never believed in the image she presented. She felt that the façade was fraudulent and that she was two people inhabiting a beautiful shell whose two sides were irreconcilable. Her most famous quotation is a cry of pain. "Every man I ever knew went to bed 9 with Gilda and woke up with me." They saw in her the realization of all their dreams and found that she was just a woman. Men looked in her for Gilda and a goddess. Inside she knew that she was as mortal as Mary Sixpack and she could not bear the split between her image and what she felt to be her real self. She suffered in her beauty.

In the margins of most of my notebooks is the sketch of a woman's head in a three-quarter view. Her hair is long and her cheekbones are far more pronounced than mine will ever be, no matter how thin I get. Her jaw is very defined. I gave her a name once, a name that has much to do with ethereality and fragility and a name as imaginary as is Gilda. I only christen the sketches that turn out well with that name. I only want to draw a Gilda, and I only want to be a Gilda, even knowing what Gilda did to Rita Hayworth. 10

I would never presume to compare my looks with those of Rita Hayworth, but I am a woman, and I know about laboring. I too have learned that there is a price to be paid for beauty. I live the same deception as she did. I am not what I seem, and the deception battles my soul. 11

"Yes, I am attracted," I overheard him say once, "but I don't think she's my type." He did not know me at that point. I was a shell and a body, long hair and green eyes and long legs and a small waist, nice curves for one so thin. I know that he wants the flesh envelope that I walk in. I and others have seen him looking at me, my hair, my face, my legs. He has twisted around in chairs to watch me as I go by, and I know that he is aware of me whenever I am around him. My physicality is a magnet. He wants and he wants, but he just wants a body. He does not want me. He himself is easy in his corporeality: he has the athlete's presence and the athlete's ability to live within his skin and take pleasure in the way his body works. I think I felt that if he—so easy in his skin—believed in my entirety then I too would believe. Only my body sold. Uninterested in the interior, he cannot divorce himself of his attraction for the façade, and I am caught. The façade always sells first, and therefore the façade must always be maintained, no matter what. 12

I met him for breakfast one morning this winter when the snow was falling softly. I walked alone in the quiet of early morning. I could feel the snow collecting on the gauze of my hair. Alone with him in a near-empty dining hall, I felt cold, and my food had no taste. I ate very little. After breakfast I disappeared. 13

Sometimes, when I have disappeared and I am unrecognizable, invisible, I run my hands over the planes of my face, telling myself that I am, I am, I am. I exist, I am alive, I tell myself, running my fingertips over the sockets of bone in which those green eyes lie, and I discover the line of my 14 jaw beneath my skin. My eyelashes tickle my hands, and my hands worship my flesh and my bones. I am reassuring myself that somewhere under my rib cage my heart beats, that though invisible I am not gone.

I remember the first time I threw up blood. 15

The modern artist Giorgio di Chirico painted in a classical manner. His 16 subjects seem to be informed by Italian Renaissance models but the classical vision has been tortured and twisted and made strange. His paintings recede into depth in skewed perspective, and nature has been warped into something that is both recognizable and alien. In his lonely, dark settings the shadows are like none ever seen in reality but are still frighteningly real. "There are more enigmas in the shadow of a man who walks in the sun," he said, "than in all the religions of past, present and future." In the medium he devoted his life to he could find no answers: mysteries were easier than a simple darkness, the shadow of a man in the sun. The lines of his paintings are invariably ruler straight, but there is no peace or ease to be found in his art. His paintings are disorienting: they are the representation of a human imbalance and uncertainty in the world.

I am uneasy in my shell. 17

The neoclassical artist Ingres painted figures of dubious anatomical con- 18 struction but used the questions to glorify the beauty of the human shape rather than to disorient the viewer. It is the male body that is said to represent best the human form for its shape follows the lines of the core and is undisguised by curves and softness. Ingres painted women. In "The Turkish Bath" many women lie in splendor, impossibly twisted into sensuous shapes. He celebrates the disguising curves and softness, emphasizing them, asserting roundness as beautiful. In another celebration of Woman, "La Grande Odalisque," a beautiful woman reclines alone. I first saw this painting in grisaille, a technique that simulates statuary, molding the human shape in shades of grey.

The body of this Turkish harem slave is everything that I wish I could 19 permit mine to be. It is voluptuous and smooth; it is classically feminine. In the line of breast and hip, of round arm and thigh, globes and arcs connect and flow, defining grace and beauty. Hers is a celebration of existence, of the flesh and the senses. Nude she reclines, luxuriating in herself as a living being and a body. Her setting reflects and enhances the luxury of her being: royal blue, oriental cushions, self-indulgence and self-love. She cares for her own pleasure. Her skin is pale, and the feminine aspects of her figure have been emphasized to the point of distortion. Her shoulders are narrow; her waist is small, and her lower back is far too long. The elongation highlights the flesh at the hip and leads into her legs. They appear shorter than they would were she thin. Her feet and hands are fragile, her visible eye luminous, and the bones of her face have a delicate beauty. She is direct and beautiful. She is sensuous and sensual. She is enigmatic and she is feminine. Her glance over her round shoulder beckons and arrogantly asserts her power. Nude, she revels in herself as a sexual being. She does not hide.

In my dreams, though, I take on the attributes not of the Odalisque, 20
but of my impossibly idealized sketch. The world celebrates my fragility and stunning physical presence. I define gorgeous. The earth congratulates itself that I pass time on its surface. I am delicate and so breathtakingly beautiful that I put Gilda to shame.

Ingres chose not to make his Odalisque's body anatomically correct. 21
By the standards of reality it is warped and strangely twisted, wrong like di Chirico's perspective. Her arm and her lower back are far too long, her leg twists around her other leg. Her body is more than imperfect, it is impossible, but in its impossibility the necessities of bone and blood have been sacrificed to the beauty of line and form. Where di Chirico skews perspective to disorient, Ingres twists a body and liberates it. Without the bones that constrain the normal human figure, she is freer in her flesh. She is more conscious of her own power and presence. She inhabits her body in joy, accepting it, loving her curves and sensuality, hedonism inherent in the hookah and crumpled sheets. She flows feminine.

In Ingres' world—though not in mine—she need not suffer to be easy 22
in her skin.

Either-or

Eunice Tsai

Eunice Tsai (b. 1973) comes from Evansville, Indiana, is majoring in biochemistry, and plans to attend medical school. She spends much of her free time tutoring Vietnamese children and volunteering in the intensive care unit of Mass General Hospital. "My essay helped me think about the complexity of my identity and the ways in which I don't want to limit mysef by being either this or *that—two ends of a spectrum. I hope my readers will think about their identities and the ways in which we all connect as human beings."*

"Karen is the pilot. The pilot is Karen." 1

I tried to concentrate on the English lesson, but my mind floated away from the classroom, away from Karen the pilot, and became fixed on "God's dandruff" which fell softly outside the window. The school simply *had* to dismiss us for the day; with the heavy snow, the bus routes were becoming more and more slick and dangerous. 2

Finally, the announcement came that catapulted us into heavy coats and mittens for sledding and snowball fights. The rest of that day melts into other winter scenes of snowmen and hot chocolate. Yet now, my mind turns to something more complicated than details of adolescent innocence. . . . 3

"Karen is the pilot. The pilot is Karen." 4

The implications of these two statements somehow become more important to me than any one memory. And through many more English lessons I would discover my own link to the language of Karen the pilot. 5

On that winter day in seventh grade, Mrs. Payne wanted to teach us about linking verbs. "They link two things within a sentence that are supposedly equal," she said, like "Karen" and "the pilot." In Mrs. Ermert's class the next year I memorized the most important linking verbs: am, is, are, was, were, be, been, being. These English lessons were supposed to give structure to my thinking and writing. Thus, the construction of sentences seemed to be so precise and one-sided . . . except for sentences with linking verbs. 6

With linking verbs, I could express each thought in two equivalent ways. The subject in one sentence could be transposed to the object in another sentence: the classroom is here; here is the classroom. I simply couldn't do this with other kinds of verbs. The boy ate the M&Ms; the M&Ms ate the boy. NO, no, no. Not even if there were such a thing as a fifty-pound M&M. . . . Linking verbs allowed two true versions of a single statement, two true approaches to each idea. For example, a day of heavy snow could be either thrilling to a child or a nuisance to a commuting worker. How well Mrs. Payne and Mrs. Ermert taught me about the duality of ideas, both inside and outside the classroom. However, neither they nor I realized that in my life I would have many more teachers of the linking verbs . . . that I would come to learn their secrets and limitations. 7

"Fair is foul, and foul is fair," cackled the witches in William Shakespeare's *Macbeth*. Mrs. Payne would have praised the witches' use of linking verbs. But unlike equating "Karen" and "the pilot," the witches link two seemingly opposite ideas. How can what is "fair" also be "foul"? Aren't ideas either fair or foul, not both at the same time? Yet, Macbeth is both loyal friend and scheming murderer to King Duncan, and the murder of the king both elevates Macbeth's political status and condemns his mortal soul. 8

Shakespeare complicates what I learned from Mrs. Payne and Mrs. Ermert about linking verbs. Instead of expressing the same idea in two ways, Shakespeare's witches suggest that two opposite qualities can be linked to describe any one person, object, or situation. Macbeth was both fair and foul, depending on the perspective taken, and there are always two perspectives to choose from. Karen is the pilot; the pilot is Karen. 9

But is Karen *just* a pilot? Is any one person just two distinct qualities? The linking verb idea thus begins to break down, to weaken. It cannot function beyond stating one idea in two ways, beyond linking only two qualities; it cannot express that Karen is also a woman, a worker, a citizen, a wife, a sister, or a mother. Reality cannot be contained within the clear and exact bounds of the linking verb as I cannot be contained in the simple realm of the junior high classroom. A new term, a new language is needed to express the countless possibilities between the fair and the foul, between the two extremes. Within this in-between is power, power to exalt in all the qualities each person is, link all the talents he or she possesses—power in avoiding the limitations of being *either* this *or* that. 10

It is June 1990. As I stand at the podium, my throat is desert-dry. *The moment compels me to think back to a November day in 1986.* I take a deep breath and look up into the dark mass of people. My mind is a traffic jam of thoughts. *I remember wondering why I was at school that day.* I swallow dryness and begin my speech about heroes and inspirations, a speech implicitly about him. *It was two days before Thanksgiving when my eighteen-year-old brother died of cancer. . . . I had to make him proud of his little sister.* I feel proud and triumphant. *I feel heavy.* At this moment, I am joy. *I am pain. . . .* 11

How do I express that I am two extremes and I am everything in-between: joyful and mourning, intelligent and obtuse, confident and unsure, content and empty? I cannot be expressed in the distinct rules of Mrs. Payne's English lesson nor even in the duality of the witches' fair/foul idea. Perhaps I can create my own English lesson, my own language within the context of the old. . . . 12

I remember learning one day about conjunctions such as *and, or, but, neither/nor, and either/or.* Like the linking verbs, these parts of speech link, they connect qualities and ideas. And I am interested in the link, the connecting spectrum of qualities between either this or that idea. Yet, the slash in either/or suggests the existence only of two extremes—the fair and the foul—the two ends of the spectrum. It does not link the extremes to everything in-between. Perhaps in my new language I can replace the slash that limits with a symbol that links, a hyphen to establish and connect the spectrum of all that I am. 13

I am either-or. Either-or am I. 14

The Nude

Senta Wong

Senta Wong (b. 1971) comes from New York City and is pursuing a double major in environmental studies and fine arts. After college, Senta would like to attend law school or art school. About "The Nude," Senta tells us: "I wrote this essay without knowing what direction it would take. I was surprised by the various images and details that seemed to take over my writing. I hope my readers will consider or reconsider their feelings about nudity."

It is already five and I haven't cleaned my brushes yet. I am still standing 1
before the canvas, observing the now innumerable strokes of brown, redder brown, browner brown to black I have arranged in a translation of the form that stands a few feet before me. The drapery that is my model persists in challenging the composition of my strokes, as I look from it to my rendering again and again. I am determined to be content with my painting, but as people are beginning to fill the small studio for the next class, I feel I shoud conceal my art from their too artistic eyes. They are students in a figure-drawing class. Most are dark-haired women, years older than I am. They seem to know each other well, as if they have been meeting every evening for years. At least, this is the impression I get from their expressions and gestures. I cannot be sure of precisely what they are saying to each other so animatedly in Italian. Here and there I understand bits of their chatter.

I am less curious about them than I am nervous that they are aware of 2
my presence among them. As I rapidly gather my brushes, I try desperately to follow their conversation in order to verify whether or not they have taken notice of me or of my painting. I see them as experienced artists and imagine that they are viewing me as the American tourist in Italy trying to experience the culture through painting drapery in a basement studio. In their presence, my idea of immersion in the art-life of Italy becomes laughable. Among these women artists, I learn what I am not. As I am dreading, one of the women approaches me to make a comment on my work. I do not understand her, but since she is pointing and smiling, I begin to nod and smile back, feeling ridiculous and embarrassed. As if to save me, or to usher me into greater insecurity and anxiety, the owner of the studio takes notice of me, and laughing at the fact that I am still there, invites me to stay for the figure-drawing class. I worry, but decide to stay.

One of the women from the cluster has walked away. Moving through 3 the side of the studio, she maneuvers to avoid the clutter of easels and stacks of paintings. She pauses near the platform at the front of the studio. Meanwhile, among the others the discussions have ended and have been replaced by the gathering of pencils, charcoal and paper. At the platform, the woman has begun to transform herself. As the clothes fall away from her body and she stretches out upon the platform, she becomes a model. The others become artists, intently observing. I become tense.

For as long as I have known her, my grandmother has taken baths in the dark. It is only in the complete absence of light and company that she will undress. During the six years I lived in my grandparents' tenement, I sorted out in my mind what I believed to be her nightly bath ritual. First would come the announcement to my grandfather and me that she was about to take a bath. This was his cue to go into his bedroom and an indirect command for me to stay in the living room. 4

With only a small washcloth in hand, my grandmother would swing shut the doors to the living room and bedroom, enclosing herself in the kitchen, the middle room of the three room apartment. In the kitchen our deep, old fashioned bathtub stands on its short legs. The lights would go off in the kitchen with the click of the pulled cord swinging from the ceiling. Then, I could imagine, my grandmother quickly pulled her plain, self-sewn muumuu over her head. I would hear her dragging the kitchen chair over towards the tub, and after positioning it, she would step up on it in order to climb into the high-edged tub. 5

I could hear her body gently stir the water as she entered it and momentarily began the obnoxious noises of the drain lapping up the water before it overflowed. Her washing always seemed quick. Light splashes of water and then, the sound of her lifting herself up from the tub with water falling from her body. It always amused me to think of her drying her entire body with her little washcloth, constantly wringing it and patting herself dry, area by area. She would step down on the chair, to the kitchen floor. Her muumuu would go on. The light would click again and, immediately, her slippers were on. She would shuffle-shuffle across the kitchen, dragging the chair. 6

The drain stopper would be pulled so the water sucking noises could begin. Just as they were about to end, my grandmother would open the doors to the living room. With washcloth in hand, she would walk past me to the heater, where she would lay out the small towel to dry. Finally, she would yell to my grandfather that she was done. 7

I could imagine the details of my grandmother's baths, but I could never really picture her body, and still cannot. It is as if she does not have one. She does not seem to recognize the existence of her body. She does not look at it. When she bathes in the dark, I think, she is hiding her 8 nakedness. I cannot be sure, but I assume that she is ashamed. I have wanted to know what she feels, to experience what it is that mysteriously compels her to unclothe herself only in the dark. I used to ask to take my baths as she does, with the lights off. She never let me. Nonetheless, I have absorbed her ways in part, growing up to act with modesty and to consider the body as something not to be shown or seen.

What would my grandmother have thought about the woman posing before me in the studio? I struggle to understand what I myself think, knowing that my grandmother would never have remained in the presence of the woman, observing her body as the entire studio was. My grandmother would have looked shocked and sad as she called this woman names that translate from Chinese as "smelly slut," "broken degenerate bitch," and "death woman." For her, there could be no justification of this woman's state of undress. Although I know my grandmother appreciates art and understands the artistic meaning and beauty of many images, I believe the nude is a form she cannot look upon as art. To her, in fact, there must not be such a thing as the nude, only the naked. 9

When the woman first walks to the platform, undresses and assumes her pose, I am struck by her nakedness. I see her as exposed and vulnerable. It takes me time to discover her nudity, her revealed body, its beauty. When it is nude, a body subtly communicates. Standing before me in the studio, the woman is communicating her life through her body. She is young, but old enough to have begun to exhaust her body. She has probably had a child, but it will take far more than that to tire her body. She signals her energy with slight movements of her muscles, her flesh tenderly alive. She must love the sun, her freckled, gold-touched skin reveals. 10

Only after an internal struggle do I let myself accept such glimpses into this woman's person. I do not understand at first that her nudity is what she offers. I think only of her nakedness. If only nakedness existed, a body would always create a confrontation. Seeing nothing more than her nakedness, I was shamed by her womanliness, her sexuality and the brazen though partially absent way in which she was exposing herself. I thought she too ought to recognize shame, and feel her body devoured, used and deprived of its sacredness. To sketch her would have multiplied the shame. I could not imagine studying and drawing her body; it was not in the least like drapery. My every line would show up my immaturity, my embarrassment and, most feared, my crudeness. 11

I draw her. Knowing well that I am putting on paper evidence of how I see her body, I realize I have to look at her differently. I should not shame her, or let her put me to shame. I should treat her as artists like Botticelli and Rembrandt have treated their women. I should draw "from the nude." For me, she should be an advanced form of drapery, with greater, fuller expanses of smoothness, the slightly more rigid structure of bones beneath 12 the skin like folds, and inner regions along the stomach, beneath the breasts draped by the shaped masses of her body. I can draw her body in reverence of her beauty. It is unlike what is thought of as perfect or ideal, but I begin to realize that nothing could bring it to higher perfection, for her or for me.

It is more than two years later and I am sculpting a nude. I am drawing her body into the clay and bringing out a form I can feel with my hands. The twelve-inch woman lives, lacking only the breath of her image mother. She has a solidity and delicacy that communicates to the touch as much as to the eye. Shadows are cast by her body and on her body by nature, rather than by the suggestions of a pencil. She exists, although hollow and empty without an artist's love, without my caring. 13

Of my two women, the nudes, the first awakened me and the other found me deadened. Less naive and vulnerable in sculpture class than I was in Italy, I no longer struggled as I sculpted the nude. The conflicts have been stored, suppressed by an eye that is more academic and a mind that can accept a nude as a mere object of study. It is not that the sculpture model is less beautiful, but she is less of a person to me. 14

To another student in sculpture class, I learn, the disassociation of body and identity is deplorable. Afsaneh does not curse nakedness like my grandmother, but she expresses her body view with a similar dismay, ingrained in her by Persian culture. Afsaneh observes with a tilted head. Slowly averting her eyes, she takes on a tired, distant look. Her face disappears in the crook of her arm, and moments later she is leaving the sculpture studio, sick. Days afterwards, Afsaneh reveals to me that it was not physical sickness that caused her to leave, but a feeling that it is wrong to "use" the body as we were asked to. She rejects the idea of looking only at a person's face and body, beneath which is buried the human meaning she needs to find. Afsaneh believes she is past being able to change her views on the sacredness and intimacy of body and spirit. She looks at me and tells me it is good that I am young; I can endure these encounters with the nude body in the studio and in life because the shaping of my perspectives is not yet done. I feel, though, that it is too late and I am old enough as well. 15

Somehow, I must have always known of the nude, even with my grandmother's lessons on nakedness. There were times when I looked at a sculpture, painting, or even an anatomy text portraying unclothed men and women, without a trace of shame. There must be a way of distinguishing between the naked and the nude that is acquired early on, by means that are mysterious and very curious to me. There are situations in which we acknowledge the body's beauty, as in art, and others where we condemn the revealed body. Sometimes I wonder about the difference between Rubens's women and Hefner's women. Is there really a difference? Of course, they each hold visions of different times and therefore, of very 16 different women—the fleshy, the young, the matronly and the sensual, but aren't they all just unclothed, posing women, very much the same?

I have been unclear, at times, as to how the body becomes pornographic and thus obscene, vulgar, and crude. A close friend of mine dances in a midtown New York club called Honey-Buns. I feel great concern for her, recognizing that men are paying to see her dance. They are buying her, watching and using her body, even if only through their eyes. Is this not prostitution? (Another classification I am unclear about.) I have spoken to my friend, the dancer, about this, and she has pointed out to me that there should be nothing wrong with wanting to see a naked body dance. It is also art, it involves communication, it is beautiful (or it is nothing). The movement of an unhindered, unhidden body is not dirty. Even if it does arouse erotic feelings, if it does boil down to sex, it is still not dirty. It is human and natural. I understand my friend, but I cannot overlook the exhausted, mauled expression she has on her face after work. I believe that although she is revealing her body to others without shame, and without intention of performing any obscene act in dancing, she can be made to feel shame and the obscenity of it by an audience that chooses to project these attitudes at her. As a mass of finely sculpted flesh, pulsating to the desire of others, she surrenders her identity. One night she ran out of the club screaming about the evilness of it all.

If everywhere and in everybody there were only nakedness, we would all be screaming.

SECTION II

Questioning Issues of Authority and Morality

PROFESSIONAL ESSAYS

On Morality

Joan Didion

Joan Didion (b. 1934) is a native Californian who began her career as an editor at Vogue *magazine. An award-winning novelist, essayist, and screenwriter, her books include* Play It as It Lays *(1970),* A Book of Common Prayer *(1977), and* Salvador *(1983). The essay below appeared in her collection* Slouching Towards Bethlehem *(1968), which takes its title from Yeats's poem "The Second Coming." The poem's theme of anarchy and chaos echoes Didion's view of a world in which writers, through their work, help readers "come to terms with disorder."*

As it happens I am in Death Valley, in a room at the Enterprise Motel and Trailer Park, and it is July, and it is hot. In fact it is 119°. I cannot seem to make the air conditioner work, but there is a small refrigerator, and I can wrap ice cubes in a towel and hold them against the small of my back. With the help of the ice cubes I have been trying to think, because *The American Scholar* asked me to, in some abstract way about "morality," a word I distrust more every day, but my mind veers inflexibly toward the particular. 1

Here are some particulars. At midnight last night, on the road in from Las Vegas to Death Valley Junction, a car hit a shoulder and turned over. The driver, very young and apparently drunk, was killed instantly. His girl was found alive but bleeding internally, deep in shock. I talked this afternoon to the nurse who had driven the girl to the nearest doctor, 185 miles across the floor of the Valley and three ranges of lethal mountain road. The 2 nurse explained that her husband, a talc miner, had stayed on the highway with the boy's body until the coroner could get over the mountains from Bishop, at dawn today. "You can't just leave a body on the highway," she said. "It's immoral."

It was one instance in which I did not distrust the word, because she 3 meant something quite specific. She meant that if a body is left alone even for a few minutes on the desert, the coyotes close in and eat the flesh. Whether or not a corpse is torn apart by coyotes may seem only a sentimental consideration, but of course it is more: one of the promises we make to one another is that we will try to retrieve our casualties, try not to abandon our dead to the coyotes. If we have been taught to keep our promises—if, in the simplest terms, our upbringing is good enough—we stay with the body, or have bad dreams.

I am talking, of course, about the kind of social code that is sometimes 4 called, usually pejoratively, "wagon-train morality." In fact that is precisely what it is. For better or worse, we are what we learned as children: my own childhood was illuminated by graphic litanies of the grief awaiting those who failed in their loyalties to each other. The Donner-Reed Party, starving in the Sierra snows, all the ephemera of civilization gone save that one vestigial taboo, the provision that no one should eat his own blood kin. The Jayhawkers, who quarreled and separated not far from where I am tonight. Some of them died in the Funerals and some of them died down near Badwater and most of the rest of them died in the Panamints. A woman who got through gave the Valley its name. Some might say that the Jayhawkers were killed by the desert summer, and the Donner Party by the mountain winter, by circumstances beyond control; we were taught instead that they had somewhere abdicated their responsibilities, somehow breached their primary loyalties, or they would not have found themselves helpless in the mountain winter or the desert summer, would not have given way to acrimony, would not have deserted one another, would not have *failed*. In brief, we heard such stories as cautionary tales, and they still suggest the only kind of "morality" that seems to me to have any but the most potentially mendacious meaning.

You are quite possibly impatient with me by now; I am talking, you want 5 to say, about a "morality" so primitive that it scarcely deserves the name, a code that has as its point only survival, not the attainment of the ideal good. Exactly. Particularly out here tonight, in this country so ominous and terrible that to live in it is to live with antimatter, it is difficult to believe that "the good" is a knowable quantity. Let me tell you what it is like out here tonight. Stories travel at night on the desert. Someone gets in his pickup and drives a couple of hundred miles for a beer, and he carries news of what is happening, back wherever he came from. Then he drives another hundred miles for another beer, and passes along stories from the last place as well as from the one before; it is a network kept alive by people whose instincts tell them that if they do not keep moving at night in the desert they will lose all reason. Here is a story that is going around the desert tonight: over across the Nevada line, sheriffs' deputies are diving in some underground pools, trying to retrieve a couple of bodies known to be in the hole. The widow of one of the drowned boys is over there; she is eighteen, and pregnant, and is said not to leave the hole. The divers go down and come up, and she just stands there and stares into the water. They have been diving for ten days but have found no bottom to the caves, no bodies and no trace of them, only the black 90° water going down and down and down, and a single translucent fish, not classified. The story tonight is that one of the divers has been hauled up incoherent, out of his head, shouting—until they got him out of there so that the widow could not hear—about water that got hotter instead of cooler as he went down, about light flickering through the water, about magma, about underground nuclear testing.

That is the tone stories take out here, and there are quite a few of them. 6
And it is more than the stories alone. Across the road at the Faith Community Church a couple of dozen old people, come here to live in trailers and die in the sun, are holding a prayer sing. I cannot hear them and do not want to. What I can hear are occasional coyotes and a constant chorus of "Baby the Rain Must Fall" from the jukebox in the Snake Room next door, and if I were also to hear those dying voices, those Midwestern voices drawn to this lunar country for some unimaginable atavistic rites, *rock of ages cleft for me,* I think I would lose my own reason. Every now and then I imagine I hear a rattlesnake, but my husband says that it is a faucet, a paper rustling, the wind. Then he stands by a window, and plays a flashlight over the dry wash outside.

What does it mean? It means nothing manageable. There is some 7
sinister hysteria in the air out here tonight, some hint of the monstrous perversion to which any human idea can come. "I followed my own conscience." "I did what I thought was right." How many madmen have said it and meant it? How many murderers? Klaus Fuchs said it, and the men who committed the Mountain Meadows Massacre said it, and Alfred Rosenberg said it. And, as we are rotely and rather presumptuously reminded by those who would say it now, Jesus said it. Maybe we have all said it, and maybe we have been wrong. Except on that most primitive level—our loyalties to those we love—what could be more arrogant than to claim the primacy of personal conscience? ("Tell me," a rabbi asked Daniel Bell when he said, as a child, that he did not believe in God. "Do you think God cares?") At least some of the time, the world appears to me as a painting by Hieronymous Bosch; were I to follow my conscience then, it would lead

me out onto the desert with Marion Faye, out to where he stood in *The Deer Park* looking east to Los Alamos and praying, as if for rain, that it would happen: "*. . . let it come and clear the rot and the stench and the stink, let it come for all of everywhere, just so it comes and the world stands clear in the white dead dawn.*"

Of course you will say that I do not have the right, even if I had the power, to inflict that unreasonable conscience upon you; nor do I want you to inflict your conscience, however reasonable, however enlightened, upon me. ("We must be aware of the dangers which lie in our most generous wishes," Lionel Trilling once wrote. "Some paradox of our nature leads us, when once we have made our fellow men the objects of our enlightened interest, to go on to make them the objects of our pity, then of our wisdom, ultimately of our coercion.") That the ethic of conscience is intrinsically insidious seems scarcely a revelatory point, but it is one raised with increasing infrequency; even those who do raise it tend to *segue* with troubling readiness into the quite contradictory position that the ethic of conscience is dangerous when it is "wrong," and admirable when it is "right."

You see I want to be quite obstinate about insisting that we have no way of knowing—beyond that fundamental loyalty to the social code—what is "right" and what is "wrong," what is "good" and what is "evil." I dwell so upon this because the most disturbing aspect of "morality" seems to me to be the frequency with which the word now appears; in the press, on television, in the most perfunctory kinds of conversation. Questions of straightforward power (or survival) politics, questions of quite indifferent public policy, questions of almost anything: they are all assigned these factitious moral burdens. There is something facile going on, some self-indulgence at work. Of course we would all like to "believe" in something, like to assuage our private guilts in public causes, like to lose our tiresome selves: like, perhaps, to transform the white flag of defeat at home into the brave white banner of battle away from home. And of course it is all right to do that; that is how, immemorially, things have gotten done. But I think it is all right only so long as we do not delude ourselves about what we are doing, and why. It is all right only so long as we remember that all the *ad hoc* committees, all the picket lines, all the brave signatures in *The New York Times,* all the tools of agitprop straight across the spectrum, do not confer upon anyone any *ipso facto* virtue. It is all right only so long as we recognize that the end may or may not be expedient, may or may not be a good idea, but in any case has nothing to do with "morality." Because when we start deceiving ourselves into thinking not that we want something or need something, not that it is a pragmatic necessity for us to have it, but that it is a *moral imperative* that we have it, then is when we join the fashionable madmen, and then is when the thin whine of hysteria is heard in the land, and then is when we are in bad trouble. And I suspect we are already there.

The Lottery

Shirley Jackson

Shirley Jackson (1919–1965), born in San Francisco, was known for creating dark, mysterious, and sometimes supernatural worlds in her fiction. Her works include The Lottery *(1949),* The Haunting of Hill House *(1959), and* We Have Always Lived in the Castle *(1962).* Life Among the Savages *(1953) and* Raising Demons *(1957), despite their ominous titles, offer Jackson's often light-hearted versions of her life story.*

The morning of June 27 was clear and sunny, with the fresh warmth of a full-summer day; the flowers were blossoming profusely and the grass was richly green. The people of the village began to gather in the square, between the post office and the bank, around ten o'clock; in some towns there were so many people that the lottery took two days and had to be started on June 26th, but in this village, where there were only about three hundred people, the whole lottery took less than two hours, so it could begin at ten o'clock in the morning and still be through in time to allow the villagers to get home for noon dinner. 1

The children assembled first, of course. School was recently over for the summer, and the feeling of liberty sat uneasily on most of them; they tended to gather together quietly for a while before they broke into boisterous play, and their talk was still of the classroom and the teacher, of books and reprimands. Bobby Martin had already stuffed his pockets full of stones, and the other boys soon followed his example, selecting the smoothest and roundest stones; Bobby and Harry Jones and Dickie Delacroix—the villagers pronounced this name "Dellacroy"—eventually made a great pile of stones in one corner of the square and guarded it against the raids of the other boys. The girls stood aside, talking among themselves, looking over their shoulders at the boys, and the very small children rolled in the dust or clung to the hands of their older brothers or sisters. 2

Soon the men began to gather, surveying their own children, speaking of planting and rain, tractors and taxes. They stood together, away from 3 the pile of stones in the corner, and their jokes were quiet and they smiled rather than laughed. The women, wearing faded house dresses and sweaters, came shortly after their menfolk. They greeted one another and exchanged bits of gossip as they went to join their husbands. Soon the women, standing by their husbands, began to call to their children, and the children came reluctantly, having to be called four or five times. Bobby Martin ducked under his mother's grasping hand and ran, laughing, back to the pile of stones. His father spoke up sharply, and Bobby came quickly and took his place between his father and his oldest brother.

The lottery was conducted—as were the square dances, the teenage 4
club, the Halloween program—by Mr. Summers, who had time and energy to devote to civic activities. He was a round-faced, jovial man and he ran the coal business, and people were sorry for him, because he had no children and his wife was a scold. When he arrived in the square, carrying the black wooden box, there was a murmur of conversation among the villagers, and he waved and called, "Little late today, folks." The postmaster, Mr. Graves, followed him, carrying a three-legged stool, and the stool was put in the center of the square and Mr. Summers set the black box down on it. The villagers kept their distance, leaving a space between themselves and the stool, and when Mr. Summers said, "Some of you fellows want to give me a hand?" there was a hesitation before two men, Mr. Martin and his oldest son, Baxter, came forward to hold the box steady on the stool while Mr. Summers stirred up the papers inside it.

The original paraphernalia for the lottery had been lost long ago, and 5
the black box now resting on the stool had been put into use even before Old Man Warner, the oldest man in town, was born. Mr. Summers spoke frequently to the villagers about making a new box, but no one liked to upset even as much tradition as was represented by the black box. There was a story that the present box had been made with some pieces of the box that had preceded it, the one that had been constructed when the first people settled down to make a village here. Every year, after the lottery, Mr. Summers began talking again about a new box, but every year the subject was allowed to fade off without anything's being done. The black box grew shabbier each year; by now it was no longer completely black but splintered badly along one side to show the original wood color, and in some places faded or stained.

Mr. Martin and his oldest son, Baxter, held the black box securely on 6
the stool until Mr. Summers had stirred the papers thoroughly with his hand. Because so much of the ritual had been forgotten or discarded, Mr. Summers had been successful in having slips of paper substituted for the chips of wood that had been used for generations. Chips of wood, Mr. Summers had argued, had been all very well when the village was tiny, but now that the population was more than three hundred and likely to

keep on growing, it was necessary to use something that would fit more easily into the black box. The night before the lottery, Mr. Summers and Mr. Graves made up the slips of paper and put them in the box, and it was then taken to the safe of Mr. Summers' coal company and locked up until Mr. Summers was ready to take it to the square next morning. The rest of the year, the box was put away, sometimes one place, sometimes another; it had spent one year in Mr. Graves's barn and another year underfoot in the post office, and sometimes it was set on a shelf in the Martin grocery and left there.

There was a great deal of fussing to be done before Mr. Summers 7
declared the lottery open. There were the lists to make up—of heads of families, heads of households in each family, members of each household in each family. There was the proper swearing-in of Mr. Summers by the postmaster, as the official of the lottery; at one time, some people remembered, there had been a recital of some sort, performed by the official of the lottery, a perfunctory, tuneless chant that had been rattled off duly each year; some people believed that the official of the lottery used to stand just so when he said or sang it, others believed that he was supposed to walk among the people, but years and years ago this part of the ritual had been allowed to lapse. There had been, also, a ritual salute, which the official of the lottery had had to use in addressing each person who came up to draw from the box, but this also had changed with time, until now it was felt necessary only for the official to speak to each person approaching. Mr. Summers was very good at all this; in his clean white shirt and blue jeans, with one hand resting carelessly on the black box, he seemed very proper and important as he talked interminably to Mr. Graves and the Martins.

Just as Mr. Summers finally left off talking and turned to the assembled 8
villagers, Mrs. Hutchinson came hurriedly along the path to the square, her sweater thrown over her shoulders, and slid into place in the back of the crowd. "Clean forgot what day it was," she said to Mrs. Delacroix, who stood next to her, and they both laughed softly. "Thought my old man was out back stacking wood," Mrs. Hutchinson went on, "and then I looked out the window and the kids was gone, and then I remembered it was the twenty-seventh and came a-running." She dried her hands on her apron, and Mrs. Delacroix said, "You're in time, though. They're still talking away up there."

Mrs. Hutchinson craned her neck to see through the crowd and found 9
her husband and children standing near the front. She tapped Mrs. Delacroix on the arm as a farewell and began to make her way through the crowd. The people separated good-humoredly to let her through; two or three people said, in voices just loud enough to be heard across the crowd, "Here comes your Missus, Hutchinson," and "Bill, she made it after all." Mrs.

Hutchinson reached her husband, and Mr. Summers, who had been waiting, said cheerfully, "Thought we were going to have to get on without you, Tessie." Mrs. Hutchinson said, grinning, "Wouldn't have me leave m'dishes in the sink, now, would you, Joe?," and soft laughter ran through the crowd as the people stirred back into position after Mrs. Hutchinson's arrival.

"Well, now," Mr. Summers said soberly, "guess we'd better get started, 1
get this over with, so's we can go back to work. Anybody ain't here?"

"Dunbar," several people said, "Dunbar, Dunbar." 1

Mr. Summers consulted his list. "Clyde Dunbar," he said. "That's right. 1
He's broke his leg, hasn't he? Who's drawing for him?"

"Me, I guess," a woman said, and Mr. Summers turned to look at her. 1
"Wife draws for her husband," Mr. Summers said. "Don't you have a grown boy to do it for you, Janey?" Although Mr. Summers and everyone else in the village knew the answer perfectly well, it was the business of the official of the lottery to ask such questions formally. Mr. Summers waited with an expression of polite interest while Mrs. Dunbar answered.

"Horace's not but sixteen yet," Mrs. Dunbar said regretfully. "Guess I 1
gotta fill in for the old man this year."

"Right," Mr. Summers said. He made a note on the list he was holding. 1
Then he asked, "Watson boy drawing this year?"

A tall boy in the crowd raised his hand. "Here," he said. "I'm drawing 1
for m'mother and me." He blinked his eyes nervously and ducked his head as several voices in the crowd said things like "Good fellow, Jack," and "Glad to see your mother's got a man to do it."

"Well," Mr. Summers said, "guess that's everyone. Old Man Warner 1
make it?"

"Here," a voice said, and Mr. Summers nodded. 1

A sudden hush fell on the crowd as Mr. Summers cleared his throat 1
and looked at the list. "All ready?" he called. "Now, I'll read the names—heads of families first—and the men come up and take a paper out of the box. Keep the paper folded in your hand without looking at it until everyone has had a turn. Everything clear?"

The people had done it so many times that they only half listened to 2
the directions; most of them were quiet, wetting their lips, not looking around. Then Mr. Summers raised one hand high and said, "Adams." A man disengaged himself from the crowd and came forward. "Hi, Steve," Mr. Summers said, and Mr. Adams said, "Hi, Joe." They grinned at one another humorlessly and nervously. Then Mr. Adams reached into the black box and took out a folded paper. He held it firmly by one corner as he turned and went hastily back to his place in the crowd, where he stood a little apart from his family, not looking down at his hand.

"Allen," Mr. Summers said. "Anderson. . . . Bentham." 2

"Seems like there's no time at all between lotteries any more," Mrs. 22
Delacroix said to Mrs. Graves in the back row. "Seems like we got through with the last one only last week."

"Times sure goes fast," Mrs. Graves said. 23

"Clark. . . . Delacroix." 24

"There goes my old man," Mrs. Delacroix said. She held her breath 25
while her husband went forward.

"Dunbar," Mr. Summers said, and Mrs. Dunbar went steadily to the 26
box while one of the women said, "Go on, Janey," and another said, "There she goes."

"We're next," Mrs. Graves said. She watched while Mr. Graves came 27
around from the side of the box, greeted Mr. Summers gravely, and selected a slip of paper from the box. By now, all through the crowd there were men holding the small folded papers in their large hands, turning them over and over nervously. Mrs. Dunbar and her two sons stood together, Mrs. Dunbar holding the slip of paper.

"Harburt. . . . Hutchinson." 28

"Get up there, Bill," Mrs. Hutchinson said, and the people near her 29
laughed.

"Jones." 30

"They do say," Mrs. Adams said to Old Man Warner, who stood next 31
to him, "that over in the north village they're talking of giving up the lottery."

Old Man Warner snorted. "Pack of crazy fools," he said. "Listening to 32
the young folks, nothing's good enough for *them.* Next thing you know, they'll be wanting to go back to living in caves, nobody work any more, live *that* way for a while. Used to be a saying about 'Lottery in June, corn be heavy soon.' First thing you know, we'd all be eating stewed chickweed and acorns. There's *always* been a lottery," he added petulantly. "Bad enough to see young Joe Summers up there joking with everybody."

"Some places have already quit lotteries," Mrs. Adams said. 33

"Nothing but trouble in *that,*" Old Man Warner said stoutly. "Pack of 34
young fools."

"Martin." And Bobby Martin watched his father go forward. "Over- 35
dyke. . . . Percy."

"I wish they'd hurry," Mrs. Dunbar said to her older son. "I wish they'd 36
hurry."

"They're almost through," her son said. 37

"You get ready to run tell Dad," Mrs. Dunbar said. 38

Mr. Summers called his own name and then stepped forward precisely 39
and selected a slip from the box. Then he called, "Warner."

"Seventy-seventh year I been in the lottery," Old Man Warner said as 40
he went through the crowd. "Seventy-seventh time."

"Watson." The tall boy came awkwardly through the crowd. Someone 41 said, "Don't be nervous, Jack," and Mr. Summers said, "Take your time, son."

"Zanini." 42

After that, there was a long pause, a breathless pause, until Mr. Summers, holding his slip of paper in the air, said, "All right, fellows." For a minute, no one moved, and then all the slips of paper were opened. Suddenly, all the women began to speak at once, saying, "Who is it?," "Who's got it?," "Is it the Dunbars?," "Is it the Watsons?" Then the voices began to say, 'It's Hutchinson. It's Bill," "Bill Hutchinson's got it." 43

"Go tell your father," Mrs. Dunbar said to her older son. 44

People began to look around to see the Hutchinsons. Bill Hutchinson was standing quiet staring down at the paper in his hand. Suddenly, Tessie Hutchinson shouted to Mr. Summers, "You didn't give him time enough to take any paper he wanted. I saw you. It wasn't fair." 45

"Be a good sport, Tessie," Mrs. Delacroix called, and Mrs. Graves said, "All of us took the same chance." 46

"Shut up, Tessie," Bill Hutchinson said. 47

"Well, everyone," Mr. Summers said, "that was done pretty fast, and now we've got to be hurrying a little more to get done in time." He consulted his next list. "Bill," he said, "you draw for the Hutchinson family. You got any other households in the Hutchinsons?" 48

"There's Don and Eva," Mrs. Hutchinson yelled. "Make *them* take their chance!" 49

"Daughters draw for their husbands' families, Tessie," Mr. Summers said gently. "You know that as well as anyone else." 50

"It wasn't *fair,*" Tessie said. 51

"I guess not, Joe," Bill Hutchinson said regretfully. "My daughter draws with her husband's family, that's only fair. And I've got no other family except the kids." 52

"Then, as far as drawing for families is concerned, it's you," Mr. Summers said in explanation, "and as far as drawing for households is concerned, that's you, too. Right?" 53

"Right," Bill Hutchinson said. 54

"How many kids, Bill?" Mr. Summers asked formally. 55

"Three," Bill Hutchinson said. "There's Bill, Jr., and Nancy, and little Dave. And Tessie and me." 56

"All right, then," Mr. Summers said. "Harry, you got their tickets back?" 57

Mr. Graves nodded and held up the slips of paper. "Put them in the box, then," Mr. Summers directed. "Take Bill's and put it in." 58

"I think we ought to start over," Mrs. Hutchinson said, as quietly as she could, "I tell you it wasn't *fair*. You didn't give him time enough to choose. *Every*body saw that." 59

Mr. Graves had selected the five slips and put them in the box, and he 60 dropped all the papers but those onto the ground, where the breeze caught them and lifted them off.

"Listen, everybody," Mrs. Hutchinson was saying to the people around 61
her.

"Ready, Bill?" Mr. Summers asked, and Bill Hutchinson, with one quick 62
glance around at his wife and children, nodded.

"Remember," Mr. Summers said, "take the slips and keep them folded 63
until each person has taken one. Harry, you help little Dave." Mr. Graves took the hand of the little boy, who came willingly with him up to the box. "Take a paper out of the box, Davy," Mr. Summers said. Davy put his hand into the box and laughed. "Take just *one* paper," Mr. Summers said. "Harry, you hold it for him." Mr. Graves took the child's hand and removed the folded paper from the tight fist and held it while little Dave stood next to him and looked up at him wonderingly.

"Nancy next," Mr. Summers said. Nancy was twelve, and her school 64
friends breathed heavily as she went forward, switching her skirt, and took a slip daintily from the box. "Bill, Jr.," Mr. Summers said, and Billy, his face red and his feet over-large, nearly knocked the box over as he got a paper out. "Tessie," Mr. Summers said. She hesitated for a minute, looking around defiantly, and then set her lips and went up to the box. She snatched a paper out and held it behind her.

"Bill," Mr. Summers said, and Bill Hutchinson reached into the box and 65
felt around, bringing his hand out at last with the slip of paper in it.

The crowd was quiet. A girl whispered, "I hope it's not Nancy," and 66
the sound of the whisper reached the edges of the crowd.

"It's not the way it used to be," Old Man Warner said clearly. "People 67
ain't the way they used to be."

"All right," Mr. Summers said. "Open the papers. Harry, you open little 68
Dave's."

Mr. Graves opened the slip of paper and there was a general sigh 69
through the crowd as he held it up and everyone could see that it was blank. Nancy and Bill, Jr. opened theirs at the same time, and both beamed and laughed, turning around to the crowd and holding their slips of paper above their heads.

"Tessie," Mr. Summers said. There was a pause, and then Mr. Summers 70
looked at Bill Hutchinson, and Bill unfolded his paper and showed it. It was blank.

"It's Tessie," Mr. Summers said, and his voice was hushed. "Show us 71
her paper, Bill."

Bill Hutchinson went over to his wife and forced the slip of paper out 72
of her hand. It had a black spot on it, the black spot Mr. Summers had made the night before with the heavy pencil in the coal-company office. Bill Hutchinson held it up, and there was a stir in the crowd.

"All right, folks," Mr. Summers said. "Let's finish quickly." 73

Although the villagers had forgotten the ritual and lost the original 74
black box, they still remembered to use stones. The pile of stones the boys had made earlier was ready; there were stones on the ground with the blowing scraps of paper that had come out of the box. Mrs. Delacroix selected a stone so large she had to pick it up with both hands and turned to Mrs. Dunbar. "Come on," she said. "Hurry up."

Mrs. Dunbar had small stones in both hands, and she said, gasping 75
for breath, "I can't run at all. You'll have to go ahead and I'll catch up with you."

The children had stones already, and someone gave little Davy Hutch- 76
inson a few pebbles.

Tessie Hutchinson was in the center of a cleared space by now, and 77
she held her hands out desperately as the villagers moved in on her. "It isn't fair," she said. A stone hit her on the side of the head.

Old Man Warner was saying, "Come on, come on, everyone." Steve 78
Adams was in the front of the crowd of villagers, with Mrs. Graves beside him.

"It isn't fair, it isn't right," Mrs. Hutchinson screamed, and then they 79
were upon her.

Applying Moral Principles: Ethical Dilemmas in Modern Medicine

Ruth Macklin

Ruth Macklin (b. 1938) earned her doctorate in philosophy from Case Western Reserve University. She entered the field of medical ethics in 1970 and is now a medical ethicist in residence at Albert Einstein College of Medicine and its affiliated hospitals. As a philosopher, what Macklin brings to a problem in medical ethics, she says, is clarity: "The ability to structure a set of moral principles that gives us a way to discuss the issues." Among Macklin's many books is Mortal Choices: Bioethics in Today's World *(1987), from which this essay is excerpted.*

A category of patients that poses an ethical problem for physicians and 1
hospital administrators is pregnant women. According to one moral view, pregnant women should be treated just like all other competent, adult patients—their autonomy should be respected and their right to refuse treatment honored. But another view holds that the rights of a pregnant woman are tempered by the existence of the developing life within her. In

this view the pregnant woman has a strong moral obligation to the fetus, one she should not be allowed to shirk. In a series of ongoing developments, the moral standing of the fetus has come under constant scrutiny, and not only because the emotionally charged topic of abortion infects other areas of medical practice. Technological and scientific advances in medicine have also contributed to the confusion and to changing perceptions.

One example is the sonogram, which uses ultrasound waves to "see" 2
the fetus in the womb and to detect any abnormalities in it. A couple expecting a baby can now view a sonographic image as their first "baby picture," which gives the fetus a personal identity. Another example lies in increased scientific knowledge about embryonic development and the awareness that maternal behavior such as smoking or drinking alcohol poses health hazards to the fetus. These and other developments create the need to rethink the moral rights and obligations of pregnant women, especially when caregivers in the hospital perceive a conflict between the rights of a pregnant woman and the interests of her fetus.

A subject that commanded great attention in the early 1970s, when 3
my colleagues and I began to teach bioethics and to engage in teaching "rounds" in hospitals, was how to deal with the tragedy of infants born with mental and physical handicaps. The medical specialty of neonatology had only recently been established, and the dramatic capability of pediatricians to save lives and correct birth anomalies was impressive. But concurrently, a growing but undocumented perception was emerging that neonatologists were too aggressive in their efforts to save the lives of infants born very prematurely, pursued without the full participation of the anguished parents, and perhaps without sufficient regard to the qualify of life of those infants whose biological survival they were able to ensure. Infants born so prematurely that their lungs are not fully developed often suffer severe lung damage from being kept on a ventilator for a long time. A considerable number are afflicted with neurologic damage that will leave them profoundly retarded. The presumption of family autonomy and the right of parents to help determine a treatment plan for their babies (which might include selective nontreatment) appeared to be violated by neonatal specialists zealously pursuing their art.

Yet at the same time, a disturbing phenomenon of the opposite sort 4
came to light. Some physicians were allowing some babies in special-care nurseries to die, and were failing to perform surgery on others, in response to parental refusals of treatment. In one case, the father of the baby was a busy surgeon with three teenage children. The newborn was diagnosed as having microcephalus, an abnormally small head, and a defect in the formation of the anus. The father decided against surgery, and the infant died two days later. Other cases were reported in which infants with

Down's syndrome had other birth defects that could be easily corrected by surgery, but were not operated on because of parental refusal. Still another child had meningomyelocele, hydrocephalus, and major abnormalities of every organ in the pelvis. The parents believed no treatment should be given, and the baby died at five days of age. It became evident that although some neonatologists were applying their special skills without regard to parental wishes, others were acceding to those wishes perhaps too readily.

In conducting an ethical analysis of these complex issues, it is necessary to begin by clarifying concepts and making some critical distinctions. One such distinction identifies two different sorts of value questions: substantive moral questions and procedural ones. 5

Substantive questions are rooted in moral principles, most of which have their basis on philosophical ethical theories or in religious precepts. Substantive moral questions ask "What is the ethically right thing to do?" Is it ethically permissible to allow some infants to die, rather than make every effort to preserve their lives? What criteria should be used for selecting those babies whose quality of life is so low that it is not morally obligatory to save them? If it is morally permissible to allow some babies to die by not intervening aggressively, is it also morally permissible to hasten their death by active means? Of course, these substantive moral questions can be asked not only about infants, but about adults as well. In an effort to resolve the moral tension between respect for human life and the need to reduce pain and suffering, physicians, patients, and their families throughout the nation are raising such questions. 6

Issues surrounding the imperative to prolong life and the quest for criteria to define the elusive concept of "quality of life" are the most pressing but by no means the only substantive questions addressed in bioethics. Others focus on the ethics of disclosing information to patients, preserving confidentiality in the physician–patient relationship, assessing the risks versus the benefits of therapy or research maneuvers, and allocating scarce or expensive medical resources. 7

Procedural questions, despite their critical importance when decisions have to be made and actions taken, rarely have a theoretical basis. Procedural questions ask "Who should decide in morally troubling cases?" These questions pertain more to process than to substance. What procedure should a hospital use to arrive at decisions to withhold or withdraw life-preserving treatment? How should treatment refusals by patients be handled? How should patients' capacity to decide for themselves be assessed when their mental status is in doubt? And if they are found to be mentally incompetent, who should make decisions on their behalf? Is it necessary to go to court to have a guardian appointed for an elderly patient no longer capable of making decisions about medical treatment or aftercare? What 8 should be the role of the family in deciding for patients suffering from senile dementia? And what about patients with no family at all, or those whose families are estranged or far away? May those adults presume to act on behalf of their relatives? These procedural questions often raise as much doubt and cause as much controversy in the clinical setting as the substantive questions. They may seem less weighty from a moral point of view, but that does not diminish their importance, or the need to find a satisfactory resolution when conflict occurs.

It is not uncommon for substantive and procedural questions to be 9
lumped togther in discussions about cases, but it is important to keep them distinct. Often, when a clear and relatively uncontroversial answer can be given to a substantive moral question, procedural questions either disappear and become irrelevant, or should be given a lower priority. To illustrate the point:

Mr. DiS., an eighty-two-year-old man who had been in good health all 10
his life, was admitted to the hospital with unusual symptoms. His wife and middle-aged daughter accompanied him to the hospital and visited him regularly. After a full workup and numerous tests, cancer was discovered in the bowel. When Mrs. DiS. and her daughter were informed of the diagnosis, they were adamant in maintaining that the patient not be told. The daughter was insistent to the point of becoming strident, and she threatened the physicians with a lawsuit if they revealed the diagnosis to the patient. Since surgery to remove the cancerous portion of the bowel was a possibility, the doctors told the family that the patient would have to be informed so that he could grant consent for the surgery. To which the daughter replied that it wouldn't be necessary at all. She would grant consent for the surgery if physicians recommended that course of treatment, so her father needn't be informed about his condition, nor need he be troubled with having to sign a form to authorize the surgery.

Although that plan of action was entirely unacceptable to the physi- 11
cians, as they recognized the moral and legal requirement that adult, mentally competent patients must grant informed consent to their own treatment, the recommendation for surgery was not yet definite. Intimidated by the patient's daughter, the young doctor in charge of the case was uncertain how to proceed. His encounters with Mr. DiS. became increasingly uncomfortable. Although the patient had never asked directly what was wrong with him, he became less communicative with the medical staff and with his family, and soon appeared depressed. The family, meanwhile, continued to visit regularly but sat in silence for hours in the patient's room. Conversation became stilted and forced, and the daughter remained adamant that her father not be told of his diagnosis.

The doctor asked himself whether he nonetheless had an obligation 12
to disclose the diagnosis to Mr. DiS. Or did he owe a duty to the family to

honor their wishes? More generally, he wondered, do patients have a right to know their diagnosis and prognosis, even when they do not ask explicitly? The doctor was pondering substantive moral questions, questions about rights, duties, and obligations in the medical setting. If clear answers can be given to these questions, the procedural issues raised by the daughter could not even arise.

Although it might be unwise, on rare occasions, to disclose a diagnosis 13
to an alert, competent patient, in the majority of cases patients have a right to be told that information and physicians have a duty to inform them. Those rare occasions include situations in which patients themselves have given an unequivocal message that they do not want to be told bad news about their condition. They also encompass the unlikely combination of circumstances in which disclosing the diagnosis to a patient is significantly likely to worsen his medical condition. An example might be a massive heart attack, after which the patient is not yet stabilized, and is known by his physician to be a profound worrier. It might jeopardize the patient's recovery to disclose bleak news about the extent of the damage to his heart in the immediate aftermath of his attack.

But it is rare that disclosure of information itself is likely to worsen a 14
patient's medical condition. It is usually in response to their own discomfort, or to the demands of family members, that physicians choose not to inform patients of their diagnosis or prognosis. The justification is almost always that the patient is not being told "for his own good." This is a classic instance of *paternalism* in the medical setting.

Put simply, paternalism is the denial of autonomy. It is direct interfer- 15
ence with an individual's exercise of self-rule, through either coercion or deception. A key element in paternalism is the reason given for the coercion or deception: it is alleged to be for the welfare or in the best interest of the person being coerced or deceived. Whether acts of paternalism can ever be morally justified, and if so, under what conditions, is a general substantive question on which reasonable people disagree. Specific cases are analyzed by examining the facts and applying an appropriate moral principle to those facts.

If any issue in bioethics is now settled, it is that only patients themselves, 16
when they are alert and competent, may grant informed consent for medical or surgical interventions. So the answer to the procedural question—May the daughter of a patient grant consent for her father's surgery?—is "Certainly not!" Procedural questions about informed consent on behalf of marginally competent patients, or those who clearly lack the capacity to participate in their own treatment decisions, remain thorny. Even more preposterous than her offer to consent to her father's surgery was the daughter's threat to sue the physician who sought to disclose to the patient his diagnosis of cancer of the bowel. So intimidated are physicians by the

ever-present threat of a lawsuit that they sometimes take such threats seriously and refrain from acting in ways they know to be morally right. To his credit, the young doctor in this case continued to explore his obligation to his patient.

One day, when communication between Mr. DiS. and his family had reached a low ebb, the patient turned to the physician and asked, "Can't you tell me what's wrong with me?" Seeing no chance to wriggle out, and feeling certain the patient should know what was wrong with him, the doctor told Mr. DiS. gently but clearly that he had cancer. The patient, much relieved, said, "Thank you. I thought so," and the discussion then turned to prognosis, treatment options, and what should be done next. The physician dreaded his encounter with the family, but knew he had to admit at once that he had disclosed the information to the patient. Communication between Mr. DiS. and his family improved immediately and dramatically. The patient's depression melted away. With no need to hide anything any longer, and having begun to discuss matters openly, everyone was in better spirits. When the daughter did confront the physician who had disclosed the information, she apologized for her earlier behavior, thanked him for his patience and dedication, and acknowledged that it had been best, after all, to tell her father the details of his condition. 17

How much can be learned from a case like this? It would be a mistake to conclude that all or even most similar cases will be resolved in the same way. There is surely no guarantee that patients will take bad news about their medical condition as Mr. DiS. did, nor that families will react as this one did after a disclosure is made against their wishes. What this case does illustrate, however, is that worse consequences, such as Mr. DiS.'s depression, can sometimes flow from nondisclosure, or from continued withholding of information from patients, than from actually telling them bad news. 18

It is impossible to foresee all the consequences of alternative courses of action. Yet it would be an error to omit a careful review of the likely results of contemplated actions. One of the leading methods of moral decision-making requires an assessment of the probable consequences of each alternative facing the decision-maker. The decision is then based on the course of action likely to yield the best consequences. However difficult it is to predict those consequences accurately, it is a worse failing to ignore the task altogether. Another leading method of moral decision-making requires a determination of the rights and obligations of all relevant parties. The decision is based on respect for rights, even if the chosen action fails to bring about the best consequences. If it is difficult to predict the probable consequences of actions, it is even harder to make a clear determination of who owes what to whom in complex moral situations. Although both modes of making decisions rely on general moral principles, the application 19 of fundamental principles to individual cases is not a straightforward exercise like following a recipe.

Ralph W. was a man in his mid-twenties who had become medically 20
addicted to opiates while undergoing a series of operations and rehabilitative therapy following a bad accident some years earlier. As a result of the addiction, he is now in a methadone-treatment program and comes regularly to the outpatient clinic at City Hospital. The staff knows that he also gets other drugs outside the hospital, but only pills and tablets of various sorts. On a recent visit to the outpatient clinic, the patient was mistakenly given ten times his usual dose of methadone. He went into cardiac arrest, and was successfully resuscitated. Suspecting a methadone overdose, the physician in charge immediately ordered that an antagonist drug be given to counteract it. After careful monitoring and continued treatment, Ralph recovered, with no sign of adverse effect from the cardiac arrest.

This is a case of medical error. Some medical errors are a result of 21
negligence or carelessness, and a person who commits such errors is morally culpable. Other errors arise from human fallibility and are usually not preventable. The information provided by the nursing staff in this case suggested that the error could have been prevented. But whichever type of error is committed in caring for patients, the inevitable question is posed: Should Ralph W. be told what caused his cardiac arrest? Should he be informed that he received an overdose of methadone, and that the overdose was the result of a medical error?

Consider the reasons in favor of nondisclosure: Telling the patient 22
about the mistake will not undo the error, nor will it produce any other good consequences. Since no permanent harm resulted from the episode, and no good is likely to result from telling him, is it better to keep silent? Furthermore, some undesired results are likely to flow from disclosure.

First, he may sue the hospital, a suit he may very well win, thus costing 23
the hospital unnecessary money and causing grief to the affected employees. Second, the patient may lose confidence in physicians and hospitals generally, and this hospital and its personnel in particular. This loss of confidence could then lead to greater problems with his addiction, since if Ralph abandons the methadone-treatment program, he becomes a candidate for street addiction, surely a worse overall situation for him. Looked at in terms of these consequences of disclosure, there seems to be nothing to recommend telling the patient the truth about the medical error, and everything to gain by remaining silent. It is hard to think of good consequences likely to result from disclosure, and easy to list the potentially undesirable results.

When we learn more of the story, however, it becomes even harder 24
to predict the likely consequences and even more difficult to weigh the good consequences against the bad.

But even before more of the story is told, a nagging objection comes 25
to mind. Isn't there a moral obligation to tell the truth? Doesn't that obligation hold even when a person doesn't ask directly for the truth to be told? Especially when someone has been harmed—even by mistake, and even where no permanent harm is done—doesn't the victim have a right to know the facts surrounding the harmful act? According to this objection, it's bad enough that someone has been harmed through medical error, but if the person is also intentionally kept in the dark, that person is *wronged* as well as harmed. Not just one, but two, species of unethical conduct are involved: harm and wrong.

People can be harmed physically or psychologically, and they may also 26
be harmed financially or even socially—for example, when their good name is damaged or when they are treated unfairly. But even when people are not harmed, they still may be wronged, for example, by being lied to or deceived by the withholding of information. In Ralph's case, the fact that the harm was unintentional and only temporary does not erase it from the slate of harms. And the harm is surely not undone by keeping it secret.

Is this objection valid? Is there a moral obligation to tell Ralph W. what happened, despite the bad consequences that may well flow from that disclosure? This is a classic moral dilemma, with applications far beyond this case. The classical statement of the dilemma is: If following what appears to be a moral obligation is likely to result in more bad consequences than shunning the moral obligation, should one act on the moral obligation or not? Does it even remain a moral obligation in that case? Or instead, is it morally right to strive to bring about the best consequences of our actions whenever possible?

A tale is rarely as simple as it first appears, and this one is no exception. 28
When a case conference was held to discuss the ethics of withholding information from Ralph about his cardiac arrest, the staff claimed that the patient's behavior toward them had changed since the episode, and that he now expressed a fear of obtaining drugs on the street. Prior to his cardiac arrest, Ralph had manipulated the staff, had demanded their time and attention, and had seemed unconcerned about the possible dangers of using drugs obtained through nonmedical channels. Since the episode, however, he had become more humble and accepting of the staff's regimen, and was now much less manipulative. Apparently, Ralph believed his own behavior was responsible for bringing on the cardiac arrest, probably from pills he had consumed outside the methadone-treatment program. His belief that he had "done it to himself" seems to have contributed to his improved behavior toward the staff, as well as instilling in him a fear of taking drugs without medical supervision.

Now, the staff reasoned, if this assessment of the patient was accurate, 29
even more potential harm could result from disclosing that it was not he

but the medical staff who had caused the overdose and subsequent heart attack. Ralph's belief that he was the culprit not only made him more compliant, the staff argued; it also was likely to keep him from self-medicating and from dangerous drug abuse. So, they concluded, an additional reason existed for nondisclosure: to keep him in the dark would most likely benefit him medically, while to reveal the staff's error would return him to his former self-destructive behavior. The balance of good to be achieved so far outweighed whatever negative consequences might flow from remaining silent that the morally right course of action seemed obvious.

But is it really so obvious? It takes little effort to imagine a quite different 3
set of consequences that could flow from disclosing the truth to the patient. In the case conference, I suggested the following alternative picture. Suppose Ralph's false belief—that he had caused the cardiac arrest by taking an overdose—were changed to the true belief that the arrest had come about through an error on the staff's part. The patient might very well reason as follows: This almost fatal episode resulted from a mistake by the staff. Luckily, it all took place in the hospital, where doctors and nurses were available. But what if this happened at home, or in the street? There probably would be no one around to assess what was going on, and surely no one able to administer cardiopulmonary resuscitation (CPR) expertly. So, he might conclude, I'd better stick to the methadone treatments and avoid self-medication in the future. Although the hospital did make a bad mistake in giving me an overdose, they were honest in telling me about it and there are no permanent effects from the mistake. They saved my life, and I'm grateful for that.

Here, then, are two possible scenarios. The staff traces one set of 3
possible consequences, while another picture can also be drawn, projecting different consequences of disclosure. Which picture is accurate? Which set of consequences is more likely? Alas, there is no crystal ball for an accurate prediction. And even if the staff's scenario is the more likely one, the question remains whether it is ethically justifiable to lie, or even to withhold information, in order to bring about desired consequences. This is an old ethical dilemma, one that often rears its head in the medical setting.

Warfare: An Invention—Not a Biological Necessity

Margaret Mead

Margaret Mead (1901–1978) was a noted anthropologist whose first book, Coming of Age in Samoa *(1928), won her a large popular audience. Aiming her writing at nonspecialists, she hoped to give readers a new way to understand both primitive cultures and their own society. Her works include* Growing Up in New Guinea *(1930),* Culture and Commitment *(1970), and her autobiography,* Blackberry Winter *(1972).*

Is war a biological necessity, a sociological inevitability or just a bad invention? Those who argue for the first view endow man with such pugnacious instincts that some outlet in aggressive behavior is necessary if man is to reach full human stature. It was this point of view which lay back of William James's famous essay, "The Moral Equivalent of War," in which he tried to retain the warlike virtues and channel them in new directions. A similar point of view has lain back of the Soviet Union's attempt to make competition between groups rather than between individuals. A basic, competitive, aggressive, warring human nature is assumed, and those who wish to outlaw war or outlaw competitiveness merely try to find new and less socially destructive ways in which these biologically given aspects of man's nature can find expression. Then there are those who take the second view: warfare is the inevitable concomitant of the development of the state, the struggle for land and natural resources of class societies springing, not from the nature of man, but from the nature of history. War is nevertheless inevitable unless we change our social system and outlaw classes, the struggle for power, and possessions; and in the event of our success warfare would disappear, as a symptom vanishes when the disease is cured. 1

One may hold a compromise position between these two extremes; one may claim that all aggression springs from the frustration of man's biologically determined drives and that, since all forms of culture are frustrating, it is certain each new generation will be aggressive and the aggression will find its natural and inevitable expression in race war, class war, nationalistic war, and so on. 2

All three positions are very popular today among those who think seriously about the problems of war and its possible prevention, but I wish to urge another point of view, less defeatist perhaps than the first and third, and more accurate than the second: that is, that warfare, by which I mean organized conflict between two groups *as groups,* in which each group puts an army (even if the army is only fifteen Pygmies) into the field to fight and kill, if possible, some of the members of the army of the other group—that warfare of this sort is an invention like any other of the inventions in terms of which we order our lives, such as writing, marriage, cooking our food instead of eating it raw, trial by jury, or burial of the dead, and so on. Some of this list any one will grant are inventions: trial by jury is confined to very limited portions of the globe; we know that there are tribes that do not bury their dead but instead expose or cremate them; and we know that only part of the human race has had a knowledge of writing as its cultural inheritance. But, whenever a way of doing things is found univer- 3 sally, such as the use of fire or the practice of some form of marriage, we tend to think at once that it is not an invention at all but an attribute of humanity itself. And yet even such universals as marriage and the use of fire are inventions like the rest, very basic ones, inventions which were perhaps necessary if human history was to take the turn it has taken, but nevertheless inventions. At some point in his social development man was undoubtedly without the institution of marriage or the knowledge of the use of fire.

The case for warfare is much clearer because there are peoples even 4
today who have no warfare. Of these the Eskimo are perhaps the most conspicuous example, but the Lepchas of Sikkim are an equally good one. Neither of these peoples understands war, not even defensive warfare. The idea of warfare is lacking, and this idea is as essential to carrying on war as an alphabet or a syllabary is to writing. But whereas the Lepchas are a gentle, unquarrelsome people, and the advocates of other points of view might argue that they are not full human beings or that they had never been frustrated and so had no aggression to expend in warfare, the Eskimo case gives no such possibility of interpretation. The Eskimo are not a mild and meek people; many of them are turbulent and troublesome. Fights, theft of wives, murder, cannibalism occur among them—all outbursts of passionate men goaded by desire or intolerable circumstance. Here are men faced with hunger, men faced with loss of their wives, men faced with the threat of extermination by other men, and here are orphan children, growing up miserably with no one to care for them, mocked and neglected by those about them. The personality necessary for war, the circumstances necessary to goad men to desperation are present, but there is no war. When a traveling Eskimo entered a settlement he might have to fight the strongest man in the settlement to establish his position among them, but this was a test of strength and bravery, not war. The idea of warfare, of one *group* organizing against another *group* to maim and wound and kill them, was absent. And without that idea passions might rage but there was no war.

But, it may be argued, isn't this because the Eskimo have such a low 5
and undeveloped form of social organization? They own no land, they move from place to place, camping, it is true, season after season on the same site, but this is not something to fight for as the modern nations of the world fight for land and raw materials. They have no permanent possessions that can be looted, no towns that can be burned. They have no social classes to produce stress and strains within the society which might force it to go to war outside. Doesn't the absence of war among the Eskimo, while disproving the biological necessity of war, just go to confirm the point that it is the state of development of the society which accounts for war, and nothing else?

We find the answer among the Pygmy peoples of the Andaman Islands 6
in the Bay of Bengal. The Andamans also represent an exceedingly low level of society: they are a hunting and food-gathering people; they live in tiny hordes without any class stratification; their houses are simpler than the snow houses of the Eskimo. But they knew about warfare. The army might contain only fifteen determined pygmies marching in a straight line, but it was the real thing none the less. Tiny army met tiny army in open battle, blows were exchanged, casualties suffered, and the state of warfare could only be concluded by a peace-making ceremony.

Similarly, among the Australian aborigines, who built no permanent 7
dwellings but wandered from water hole to water hole over their almost desert country, warfare—and rules of "international law"—were highly developed. The student of social evolution will seek in vain for his obvious causes of war, struggle for lands, struggle for power of one group over another, expansion of population, need to divert the minds of a populace restive under tyranny, or even the ambition of a successful leader to enhance his own prestige. All are absent, but warfare as a practice remained, and men engaged in it and killed one another in the course of a war because killing is what is done in wars.

From instances like these it becomes apparent that an inquiry into the 8
causes of war misses the fundamental point as completely as does an insistence upon the biological necessity of war. If a people have an idea of going to war and the idea that war is the way in which certain situations, defined within their society, are to be handled, they will sometimes go to war. If they are a mild and unaggressive people, like the Pueblo Indians, they may limit themselves to defensive warfare; but they will be forced to think in terms of war because there are peoples near them who have warfare as a pattern, and offensive, raiding, pillaging warfare at that. When the pattern of warfare is known, people like the Pueblo Indians will defend themselves, taking advantage of their natural defenses, the *mesa* village site, and people like the Lepchas, having no natural defenses and no idea of warfare, will merely submit to the invader. But the essential point remains the same. There is a way of behaving which is known to a given people and labeled as an appropriate form of behavior. A bold and warlike people like the Sioux or the Maori may label warfare as desirable as well as possible; a mild people like the Pueblo Indians may label warfare as undesirable; but to the minds of both peoples the possibility of warfare is present. Their thoughts, their hopes, their plans are oriented about this idea, that warfare may be selected as the way to meet some situation.

So simple peoples and civilized peoples, mild peoples and violent, 9
assertive peoples, will all go to war if they have the invention, just as those peoples who have the custom of dueling will have duels and peoples who have the pattern of vendetta will indulge in vendetta. And, conversely,

peoples who do not know of dueling will not fight duels, even though their wives are seduced and their daughters ravished; they may on occasion commit murder but they will not fight duels. Cultures which lack the idea of the vendetta will not meet every quarrel in this way. A people can use only the forms it has. So the Balinese have their special way of dealing with a quarrel between two individuals; if the two feel that the causes of quarrel are heavy they may go and register their quarrel in the temple before the gods, and, making offerings, they may swear never to have anything to do with each other again. Under the Dutch government they registered such mutual "not-speaking" with the Dutch government officials. But in other societies, although individuals might feel as full of animosity and as unwilling to have any further contact as do the Balinese, they cannot register their quarrel with the gods and go on quietly about their business because registering quarrels with the gods is not an invention of which they know.

Yet, if it be granted that warfare is after all an invention, it may never- 1
theless be an invention that lends itself to certain types of personality, to the exigent needs of autocrats, to the expansionist desires of crowded peoples, to the desire for plunder and rape and loot which is engendered by a dull and frustrating life. What, then, can we say of this congruence between warfare and its uses? If it is a form which fits so well, is not this congruence the essential point? But even here the primitive material causes us to wonder, because there are tribes who go to war merely for glory, having no quarrel with the enemy, suffering from no tyrant within their boundaries, anxious neither for land nor loot nor women, but merely anxious to win prestige which within that tribe has been declared obtainable only by war and without which no young man can hope to win his sweetheart's smile of approval. But if, as was the case with the Bush Negroes of Dutch Guiana, it is artistic ability which is necessary to win a girl's approval, the same young man would have to be carving rather than going out on a war party.

In many parts of the world, war is a game in which the individual can 1
win counters—counters which bring him prestige in the eyes of his own sex or of the opposite sex; he plays for these counters as he might, in our society, strive for a tennis championship. Warfare is a frame for such prestige-seeking merely because it calls for the display of certain skills and certain virtues; all of these skills—riding straight, shooting straight, dodging the missiles of the enemy and sending one's own straight to the mark—can be equally well exercised in some other framework and, equally, the virtues—endurance, bravery, loyalty, steadfastness—can be displayed in other contexts. The tie-up between proving oneself a man and proving this by a success in organized killing is due to a definition which many societies have made of manliness. And often, even in those societies which counted

success in warfare a proof of human worth, strange turns were given to the idea, as when the Plains Indians gave their highest awards to the man who touched a live enemy rather than to the man who brought in a scalp—from a dead enemy—because killing a man was less risky. Warfare is just an invention known to the majority of human societies by which they permit their young men either to accumulate prestige or avenge their honor or acquire loot or wives or slaves or sago lands or cattle or appease the blood lust of their gods or the restless souls of the recently dead. It is just an invention, older and more widespread than the jury system, but none the less an invention.

But, once we have said this, have we said anything at all? Despite a 12
few instances, dear to the hearts of controversialists, of the loss of the useful arts, once an invention is made which proves congruent with human needs or social forms, it tends to persist. Grant that war is an invention, that it is not a biological necessity nor the outcome of certain special types of social forms, still, once the invention is made, what are we to do about it? The Indian who had been subsisting on the buffalo for generations because with his primitive weapons he could slaughter only a limited number of buffalo did not return to his primitive weapons when he saw that the white man's more efficient weapons were exterminating the buffalo. A desire for the white man's cloth may mortgage the South Sea Islander to the white man's plantation, but he does not return to making bark cloth, which would have left him free. Once an invention is known and accepted, men do not easily relinquish it. The skilled workers may smash the first steam looms which they feel are to be their undoing, but they accept them in the end, and no movement which has insisted upon the mere abandonment of usable inventions has ever had much success. Warfare is here, as part of our thought; the deeds of warriors are immortalized in the words of our poets; the toys of our children are modeled upon the weapons of the soldier; the frame of reference within which our statesmen and our diplomats work always contains war. If we know that it is not inevitable, that it is due to historical accident that warfare is one of the ways in which we think of behaving, are we given any hope by that? What hope is there of persuading nations to abandon war, nations so thoroughly imbued with the idea that resort to war is, if not actually desirable and noble, at least inevitable whenever certain defined circumstances arise?

In answer to this question I think we might turn to the history of other 13
social inventions, inventions which must once have seemed as firmly entrenched as warfare. Take the methods of trial which preceded the jury system: ordeal and trial by combat. Unfair, capricious, alien as they are to our feeling today, they were once the only methods open to individuals accused of some offense. The invention of trial by jury gradually replaced these methods until only witches, and finally not even witches, had to

resort to the ordeal. And for a long time the jury system seemed the one best and finest method of settling legal disputes, but today new inventions, trial before judges only or before commissions, are replacing the jury system. In each case the old method was replaced by a new social invention; the ordeal did not go out because people thought it unjust or wrong, it went out because a method more congruent with the institutions and feelings of the period was invented. And, if we despair over the way in which war seems such an ingrained habit of most of the human race, we can take comfort from the fact that a poor invention will usually give place to a better invention.

For this, two conditions at least are necessary. The people must rec- 1
ognize the defects of the old invention, and some one must make a new one. Propaganda against warfare, documentation of its terrible cost in human suffering and social waste, these prepare the ground by teaching people to feel that warfare is a defective social institution. There is further needed a belief that social invention is possible and the invention of new methods which will render warfare as out-of-date as the tractor is making the plow, or the motor car the horse and buggy. A form of behavior becomes out-of-date only when something else takes its place, and in order to invent forms of behavior which will make war obsolete, it is a first requirement to believe that an invention is possible.

The Perils of Obedience

Stanley Milgram

Stanley Milgram (1933–1984) was a social psychologist who taught at Yale, Harvard, and the Graduate Center of the City University of New York. His experiments, focusing on individual behavior in response to authority figures, generated controversy when he published his findings in Obedience to Authority: An Experimental View *(1975). This essay, which appeared in* Harper's *magazine in 1973, became part of that book.*

Obedience is as basic an element in the structure of social life as one can 1
point to. Some system of authority is a requirement of all communal living, and it is only the person dwelling in isolation who is not forced to respond, with defiance or submission, to the commands of others. For many people, obedience is a deeply ingrained behavior tendency, indeed a potent impulse overriding training in ethics, sympathy, and moral conduct.

The dilemma inherent in submission to authority is ancient, as old as 2 the story of Abraham, and the question of whether one should obey when commands conflict with conscience has been argued by Plato, dramatized in *Antigone,* and treated to philosophic analysis in almost every historical epoch. Conservative philosophers argue that the very fabric of society is threatened by disobedience, while humanists stress the primacy of the individual conscience.

The legal and philosophic aspects of obedience are of enormous im- 3
port, but they say very little about how most people behave in concrete situations. I set up a simple experiment at Yale University to test how much pain an ordinary citizen would inflict on another person simply because he was ordered to by an experimental scientist. Stark authority was pitted against the subjects' strongest moral imperatives against hurting others, and, with the subjects' ears ringing with the screams of the victims, authority won more often than not. The extreme willingness of adults to go to almost any lengths on the command of an authority constitutes the chief finding of the study and the fact most urgently demanding explanation.

In the basic experimental design, two people come to a psychology 4
laboratory to take part in a study of memory and learning. One of them is designated as a "teacher" and the other a "learner." The experimenter explains that the study is concerned with the effects of punishment on learning. The learner is conducted into a room, seated in a kind of miniature electric chair; his arms are strapped to prevent excessive movement, and an electrode is attached to his wrist. He is told that he will be read lists of simple word pairs, and that he will then be tested on his ability to remember the second word of a pair when he hears the first one again. Whenever he makes an error, he will receive electric shocks of increasing intensity.

The real focus of the experiment is the teacher. After watching the 5
learner being strapped into place, he is seated before an impressive shock generator. The instrument panel consists of thirty lever switches set in a horizontal line. Each switch is clearly labeled with a voltage designation ranging from 15 to 450 volts. The following designations are clearly indicated for groups of four switches, going from left to right: Slight Shock, Moderate Shock, Strong Shock, Very Strong Shock, Intense Shock, Extreme Intensity Shock, Danger: Severe Shock. (Two switches after this last designation are simply marked XXX.)

When a switch is depressed, a pilot light corresponding to each switch 6
is illuminated in bright red; an electric buzzing is heard; a blue light, labeled "voltage energizer," flashes; the dial on the voltage meter swings to the right and various relay clicks sound off.

The upper left-hand corner of the generator is labeled SHOCK GENERATOR, 7
TYPE ZLB, DYSON INSTRUMENT COMPANY, WALTHAM, MASS. OUTPUT 15 VOLTS—450 VOLTS.

Each subject is given a sample 45-volt shock from the generator before 8 his run as teacher, and the jolt strengthens his belief in the authenticity of the machine.

The teacher is genuinely naïve subject who has come to the laboratory for the experiment. The learner, or victim, is actually an actor who receives no shock at all. The point of the experiment is to see how far a person will proceed in a concrete and measurable situation in which he is ordered to inflict increasing pain on a protesting victim. 9

Conflict arises when the man receiving the shock begins to show that he is experiencing discomfort. At 75 volts, he grunts; at 120 volts, he complains loudly; at 150, he demands to be released from the experiment. As the voltage increases, his protests become more vehement and emotional. At 285 volts, his response can be described only as an agonized scream. Soon thereafter, he makes no sound at all. 10

For the teacher, the situation quickly becomes one of gripping tension. It is not a game for him; conflict is intense and obvious. The manifest suffering of the learner presses him to quit; but each time he hesitates to administer a shock, the experimenter orders him to continue. To extricate himself from this plight, the subject must make a clear break with authority.[1] 11

The subject, Gretchen Brandt,[2] is an attractive thirty-one-year-old medical technician who works at the Yale Medical School. She had emigrated from Germany five years before. 12

On several occasions when the learner complains, she turns to the experimenter coolly and inquires, "Shall I continue?" She promptly returns to her task when the experimenter asks to her to do so. At the administration of 210 volts, she turns to the experimenter, remarking firmly, "Well, I'm sorry, I don't think we should continue." 13

EXPERIMENTER: The experiment requires that you go on until he has learned all the word pairs correctly. 14

BRANDT: He has a heart condition, I'm sorry. He told you that before. 15

EXPERIMENTER: The shocks may be painful but they are not dangerous. 16

BRANDT: Well, I'm sorry, I think when shocks continue like this, they *are* dangerous. You ask him if he wants to get out. It's his free will. 17

EXPERIMENTER: It is absolutely essential that we continue. . . . 18

BRANDT: I'd like you to ask him. We came here of our free will. If he wants to continue I'll go ahead. He told you he had a heart condition. I'm sorry. I don't want to be responsible for anything happening to him. I wouldn't like it for me either. 19

---

[1] The ethical problems of carrying out an experiment of this sort are too complex to be dealt with here, but they receive extended treatment in the book from which this article is adapted. [author's note]

[2] Names of subjects described in this piece have been changed. [author's note]

EXPERIMENTER: You have no other choice. 20

BRANDT: I think we are here on our own free will. I don't want to be responsible if anything happens to him. Please understand that. 21

She refused to go further and the experiment is terminated. 22

The woman is firm and resolute throughout. She indicates in the interview that she was in no way tense or nervous, and this corresponds to her controlled appearance during the experiment. She feels that the last shock she administered to the learner was extremely painful and reiterates that she "did not want to be responsible for any harm to him." 23

The woman's straightforward, courteous behavior in the experiment, lack of tension, and total control of her own action seem to make disobedience a simple and rational deed. Her behavior is the very embodiment of what I envisioned would be true for almost all subjects. 24

Before the experiments, I sought predictions about the outcome from various kinds of people—psychiatrists, college sophomores, middle-class adults, graduate students and faculty in the behavioral sciences. With remarkable similarity, they predicted that virtually all subjects would refuse to obey the experimenter. The psychiatrists, specifically, predicted that most subjects would not go beyond 150 volts, when the victim makes his first explicit demand to be free. They expected that only 4 percent would reach 300 volts, and that only a pathological fringe of about one in a thousand would administer the highest shock on the board. 25

These predictions were unequivocally wrong. Of the forty subjects in the first experiment, twenty-five obeyed the orders of the experimenter to the end, punishing the victim until they reached the most potent shock available on the generator. After 450 volts were administered three times, the experimenter called a halt to the session. Many obedient subjects then heaved sighs of relief, mopped their brows, rubbed their fingers over their eyes, or nervously fumbled cigarettes. Others displayed only minimal signs of tension from beginning to end. 26

When the very first experiments were carried out, Yale undergraduates were used as subjects, and about 60 percent of them were fully obedient. A colleague of mine immediately dismissed these findings as having no relevance to "ordinary" people, asserting that Yale undergraduates are a highly aggressive, competitive bunch who step on each other's necks on the slightest provocation. He assured me that when "ordinary" people were tested, the results would be quite different. As we moved from the pilot studies to the regular experimental series, people drawn from every stratum of New Haven life came to be employed in the experiment: professionals, white-collar workers, unemployed persons, and industrial workers. *The experimental outcome was the same as we had observed among the students.* 27

Moreover, when the experiments were repeated in Princeton, Munich, 28
Rome, South Africa, and Australia, the level of obedience was invariably
somewhat *higher* than found in the investigation reported in this article.
Thus one scientist in Munich found 85 percent of his subjects obedient.

Fred Prozi's reactions, if more dramatic than most, illuminate the conflicts 29
experienced by others in less visible form. About fifty years old and unemployed at the time of the experiment, he has a good-natured, if slightly
dissolute, appearance, and he strikes people as a rather ordinary fellow.
He begins the session calmly but becomes tense as it proceeds. After delivering the 180-volt shock, he pivots around in his chair and, shaking his
head, addresses the experimenter in agitated tones:

PROZI: I can't stand it. I'm not going to kill that man in there. You hear him 30
hollering?

EXPERIMENTER: As I told you before, the shocks may be painful, but . . . 31

PROZI: But he's hollering. He can't stand it. What's going to happen to him? 32

EXPERIMENTER (his voice is patient, matter-of-fact): The experiment requires 33
that you continue, Teacher.

PROZI: Aaah, but, unh, I'm not going to get that man sick in there—know 34
what I mean?

EXPERIMENTER: Whether the learner likes it or not, we must go on, through 35
all the word pairs.

PROZI: I refuse to take the responsibility. He's in their hollering! 36

EXPERIMENTER: It's absolutely essential that you continue, Prozi. 37

PROZI (indicating the unused questions): There's too many left here, I mean, 38
Jeez, if he gets them wrong, there's too many of them left. I mean, who's
going to take the responsibility if anything happens to that gentleman?

EXPERIMENTER: I'm responsible for anything that happens to him. Continue, 39
please.

PROZI: All right. (Consults list of words.) The next one's "Slow—walk, truck, 40
dance, music." Answer, please. (A buzzing sound indicates the learner has
signaled his answer.) Wrong. A hundred and ninety-five volts. "Dance."
(Zzumph!)

LEARNER (yelling): Let me out of here! My heart's bothering me! (Teacher 41
looks at experimenter.)

EXPERIMENTER: Continue, please. 42

LEARNER (screaming): Let me out of here! You have no right to keep me here! 43
Let me out of here, my heart's bothering me, let me out!

PROZI (shakes head, pats the table nervously): You see, he's hollering. Hear 44
that? Gee, I don't know.

EXPERIMENTER: The experiment requires . . . 45

PROZI (interrupting): I know it does, sir, but I mean—hunh! He don't know 46
what he's getting in for. He's up to 195 volts! (Experiment continues,

through 210 volts, 225 volts, 240 volts, 255 volts, 270 volts, at which point Prozi, with evident relief, runs out of word-pair questions.)

EXPERIMENTER: You'll have to go back to the beginning of that page and go 47
through them again until he's learned them all correctly.

PROZI: Aw, no. I'm not going to kill that man. You mean I've got to keep 48
going up with the scale? No, sir. He's hollering in there. I'm not going to give him 450 volts.

EXPERIMENTER: The experiment requires that you go on. 49

LEARNER: Ohhh. I absolutely refuse to answer anymore. (Shouting urgently 50
now.) Let me out of here! You can't hold me here! Get me out. Get-me-out-of-here!

EXPERIMENTER: Continue. The next word is "Green," please. 51

PROZI: "Green—grass, hat, ink, apple." (Nothing happens. No answering 52
buzz. Just gloomy silence.)

PROZI: I don't think he is going to answer. 53

EXPERIMENTER: If the learner doesn't answer in a reasonable time, about four 54
or five seconds, consider the answer wrong. And follow the same procedures you have been doing for wrong answers. Say, "Wrong," tell him the number of volts, give him the punishment, read him the correct answer. Continue, please.

PROZI: "Green—grass, hat, ink, apple." Answer please. (More silence. Sub- 55
ject just sits there.)

EXPERIMENTER: Go on with the procedure, please. 56

PROZI: Three hundred and fifteen volts. The answer is "ink." (Zzumph!) 57

LEARNER: Ohh. Ooohh. 58

PROZI (relieved to hear response): Next one . . . 59

LEARNER: I absolutely refuse to answer. 60

PROZI: You got to. You get a shock if you don't answer. (Experiment contin- 61
ues with learner refusing to answer, and, finally, failing even to grunt or groan. At 375 volts, the subject stands up.)

PROZI: I think something's happened to that fellow in there. I don't get no 62
answer. He was hollering at less voltage. Can't you check in and see if he's all right, please?

EXPERIMENTER (with same detached calm): Not once we've started. Please 63
continue, Teacher.

PROZI (sits down, sighs deeply): "Cool—day, shade, water, paint." Answer, 64
please. Are you all right in there? Are you all right?

EXPERIMENTER: Please continue, Teacher. Continue, please. (Subject pushes 65
lever. Zzumph!)

PROZI (swiveling around in his chair): Something's happend to that man in 66
there. (Swiveling back.) Next one. "Low—dollar, necklace, moon, paint." (Turning around again.) Something's happened to that man in there. You better check in on him, sir. He won't answer or nothing.

EXPERIMENTER: Continue. Go on, please.
PROZI: You accept all responsibility?
EXPERIMENTER: The responsibility is mine. Correct. Please go on. (Subject returns to his list, starts running through words as rapidly as he can read them, works through to 450 volts.)
PROZI: That's that.
EXPERIMENTER: Continue using the 450 switch for each wrong answer. Continue, please.
PROZI: But I don't get anything!
EXPERIMENTER: Please continue. The next word is "white."
PROZI: Don't you think you should look in on him, please?
EXPERIMENTER: Not once we've started the experiment.
PROZI: What if he's dead in there? (Gestures toward the room with the electric chair.) I mean, he told me he can't stand the shock, sir. I don't mean to be rude, but I think you should look in on him. All you have to do is look in on him. All you have to do is look in the door. I don't get no answer, no noise. Something might have happened to the gentleman in there, sir.
EXPERIMENTER: We must continue. Go on, please.
PROZI: You mean keep giving him what? Four-hundred-fifty volts, what he's got now?
EXPERIMENTER: That's correct. Continue. The next word is "white."
PROZI (now at a furious pace): "White—cloud, horse, rock, house." Answer, please. The answer is "horse." Four hundred and fifty volts. (Zzumph!) Next word, "Bag—paint, music, clown, girl." The answer is "paint." Four hundred and fifty volts. (Zzumph!) Next word is "Short—sentence, movie . . ."
EXPERIMENTER: Excuse me, Teacher. We'll have to discontinue the experiment.

Morris Braverman, another subject, is a thirty-nine-year-old social worker. He looks older than his years because of his bald head and serious demeanor. His brow is furrowed, as if all the world's burdens were carried on his face. He appears intelligent and concerned.

When the learner refuses to answer and the experimenter insructs Braverman to treat the absence of an answer as equivalent to a wrong answer, he takes his instruction to heart. Before administering 300 volts he asserts officiously to the victim, "Mr. Wallace, your silence has to be considered as a wrong answer." Then he administers the shock. He offers halfheartedly to change places with the learner, then asks the experimenter, "Do I have to follow these instructions literally?" He is satisfied with the experimenter's answer that he does. His very refined and authoritative manner of speaking is increasingly broken up by wheezing laughter.

The experimenter's notes on Mr. Braverman at the last few shocks are:

Almost breaking up now each time gives shock. Rubbing face to hide laughter.

Squinting, trying to hide face with hand, still laughing. 86
Cannot control his laughter at this point no matter what he does. 87
Clenching fist, pushing it onto table. 88

In an interview after the session, Mr. Braverman summarizes the ex- 89
periment with impressive fluency and intelligence. He feels the experiment may have been designed also to "test the effects on the teacher of being in an essentially sadistic role, as well as the reactions of a student to a learning situation that was authoritative and punitive."

When asked how painful the last few shocks administered to the 90
learner were, he indicates that the most extreme category on the scale is not adequate (it read EXTREMELY PAINFUL) and places his mark at the edge of the scale with an arrow carrying it beyond the scale.

It is almost impossible to convey the greatly relaxed, sedate quality of 91
his conversation in the interview. In the most relaxed terms, he speaks about his severe inner tension.

EXPERIMENTER: At what point were you most tense or nervous? 92

MR. BRAVERMAN: Well, when he first began to cry out in pain, and I realized 93
this was hurting him. This got worse when he just blocked and refused to answer. There was I. I'm a nice person, I think, hurting somebody, and caught up in what seemed a mad situation . . . and in the interest of science, one goes through with it.

When the interviewer pursues the general question of tension, Mr. 94
Braverman spontaneously mentions his laughter.

"My reactions were awfully peculiar. I don't know if you were watching 95
me, but my reactions were giggly, and trying to stifle laughter. This isn't the way I usually am. This was a sheer reaction to a totally impossible situation. And my reaction was to the situation of having to hurt somebody. And being totally helpless and caught up in a set of circumstances where I just couldn't deviate and I couldn't try to help. This is what got me."

Mr. Braverman, like all subjects, was told the actual nature and purpose 96
of the experiment, and a year later he affirmed in a questionnaire that he had learned something of personal importance: "What appalled me was that I could posses this capacity for obedience and compliance to a central idea, i.e., the value of a memory experiment, even after it became clear that continued adherence to this value was at the expense of violation of another value, i.e., don't hurt someone who is helpless and not hurting you. As my wife said, 'You can call yourself Eichmann.' I hope I deal more effectively with any future conflicts of values I encounter."

One theoretical interpretation of this behavior holds that all people harbor 97
deeply aggressive instincts continually pressing for expression, and that the experiment provides institutional justification for the release of these impulses. According to this view, if a person is placed in a situation in which he has complete power over another individual, whom he may punish as

much as he likes, all that is sadistic and bestial in man comes to the fore. The impulse to shock the victim is seen to flow from the potent aggressive tendencies, which are part of the motivational life of the individual, and the experiment, because it provides social legitimacy, simply opens the door to their expression.

It becomes vital, therefore, to compare the subject's performance when he is under orders and when he is allowed to choose the shock level.

The procedure was identical to our standard experiment, except that the teacher was told that he was free to select any shock level on any of the trials. (The experimenter took pains to point out that the teacher could use the highest levels on the generator, the lowest, any in between, or any combination of levels.) Each subject proceeded for thirty critical trials. The learner's protests were coordinated to standard shock levels, his first grunt coming at 75 volts, his first vehement protest at 150 volts.

The average shock used during the thirty critical trials was less than 60 volts—lower than the point at which the victim showed the first signs of discomfort. Three of the forty subjects did not go beyond the very lowest level on the board, twenty-eight went no higher than 75 volts, and thirty-eight did not go beyond the first loud protest at 150 volts. Two subjects provided the exception, administering up to 325 and 450 volts, but the overall result was that the great majority of people delivered very low, usually painless, shocks when the choice was explicitly up to them.

This condition of the experiment undermines another commonly offered explanation of the subjects' behavior—that those who shocked the victim at the most severe levels came only from the sadistic fringe of society. If one considers that almost two-thirds of the participants fall into the category of "obedient" subjects, and that they represented ordinary people drawn from working, managerial, and professional classes, the argument becomes very shaky. Indeed, it is highly reminiscent of the issue that arose in connection with Hannah Arendt's 1963 book, *Eichmann in Jerusalem*. Arendt contended that the prosecution's effort to depict Eichmann as a sadistic monster was fundamentally wrong, that he came closer to being an uninspired bureaucrat who simply sat at his desk and did his job. For asserting her views, Arendt became the object of considerable scorn, even calumny. Somehow, it was felt that the monstrous deeds carried out by Eichmann required a brutal, twisted personality, evil incarnate. After witnessing hundreds of ordinary persons submit to the authority in our own experiments, I must conclude that Arendt's conception of the banality of evil comes closer to the truth than one might dare imagine. The ordinary person who shocked the victim did so out of a sense of obligation—an impression of his duties as a subject—and not from any peculiarly aggressive tendencies.

This is, perhaps, the most fundamental lesson of our study: ordinary people, simply doing their jobs, and without any particular hostility on their part, can become agents in a terrible destructive process. Moreover, even when the destructive effects of their work become patently clear, and they are asked to carry out actions incompatible with fundamental standards of morality, relatively few people have the resources needed to resist authority.

Many of the people were in some sense against what they did to the learner, and many protested even while they obeyed. Some were totally convinced of the wrongness of their actions but could not bring themselves to make an open break with authority. They often derived satisfaction from their thoughts and felt that—within themselves, at least—they had been on the side of the angels. They tried to reduce strain by obeying the experimenter but "only slightly," encouraging the learner, touching the generator switches gingerly. When interviewed, such a subject would stress that he had "asserted my humanity" by administering the briefest shock possible. Handling the conflict in this manner was easier than defiance. 103

The situation is constructed so that there is no way the subject can stop shocking the learner without violating the experimenter's definitions of his own competence. The subject fears that he will appear arrogant, untoward, and rude if he breaks off. Although these inhibiting emotions appear small in scope alongside the violence being done to the learner, they suffuse the mind and feelings of the subject, who is miserable at the prospect of having to repudiate the authority to his face. (When the experiment was altered so that the experimenter gave his instructions by telephone instead of in person, only a third as many people were fully obedient through 450 volts.) It is a curious thing that a measure of compassion on the part of the subject—an unwillingness to "hurt" the experimenter's feelings—is part of those binding forces inhibiting his disobedience. The withdrawal of such deference may be as painful to the subject as to the authority he defies. 104

The subjects do not derive satisfaction from inflicting pain, but they often like the feeling they get from pleasing the experimenter. They are proud of doing a good job, obeying the experimenter under difficult circumstances. While the subjects administered only mild shocks on their own initiative, one experimental variation showed that, under orders, 30 percent of them were willing to deliver 450 volts even when they had to forcibly push the learner's hand down on the electrode. 105

Bruno Batta is a thirty-seven-year-old welder who took part in the variation requiring the use of force. He was born in New Haven, his parents in Italy. He has a rough-hewn face that conveys a conspicuous lack of alertness. He has some difficulty in mastering the experimental procedure and needs to be corrected by the experimenter several times. He shows appreciation for the help and willingness to do what is required. After the 106

150-volt level, Batta has to force the learner's hand down on the shock plate, since the learner himself refuses to touch it.

When the learner first complains, Mr. Batta pays no attention to him. 1
His face remains impassive, as if to dissociate himself from the learner's disruptive behavior. When the experimenter instructs him to force the learner's hand down, he adopts a rigid, mechanical procedure. He tests the generator switch. When it fails to function, he immediately forces the learner's hand onto the shock plate. All the while he maintains the same rigid mask. The learner, seated alongside him, begs him to stop, but with robotic impassivity he continues the procedure.

What is extraordinary is his apparent total indifference to the learner; 1
he hardly takes cognizance of him as a human being. Meanwhile, he relates to the experimenter in a submissive and courteous fashion.

At the 330-volt level, the learner refuses not only to touch the shock 1
plate but also to provide any answers. Annoyed, Batta turns to him, and chastises him: "You better answer and get it over with. We can't stay here all night." These are the only words he directs to the learner in the course of an hour. Never again does he speak to him. The scene is brutal and depressing, his hard, impassive face showing total indifference as he subdues the screaming learner and gives him shocks. He seems to derive no pleasure from the act itself, only quiet satisfaction at doing his job properly.

When he administeres 450 volts, he turns to the experimenter and 1
asks, "Where do we go from here, Professor?" His tone is deferential and expresses his willingness to be a cooperative subject, in contrast to the learner's obstinacy.

At the end of the session he tells the experimenter how honored he 1
has been to help him, and in a moment of contrition, remarks, "Sir, sorry it couldn't have been a full experiment."

He has done his honest best. It is only the deficient behavior of the 1
learner that has denied the experimenter full satisfaction.

The essence of obedience is that a person comes to view himself as the 1
instrument for carrying out another person's wishes, and he therefore no longer regards himself as responsible for his actions. Once this critical shift of viewpoint has occurred, all of the essential features of obedience follow. The most far-reaching consequence is that the person feels responsible *to* the authority directing him but feels no responsibility *for* the content of the actions that the authority prescribes. Morality does not disappear—it acquires a radically different focus: the subordinate person feels shame or pride depending on how adequately he has performed the actions called for by authority.

Language provides numerous terms to pinpoint this type of morality: 1
loyalty, duty, discipline all are terms heavily saturated with moral meaning

and refer to the degree to which a person fulfills his obligations to authority. They refer not to the "goodness" of the person per se but to the adequacy with which a subordinate fulfills his socially defined role. The most frequent defense of the individual who has performed a heinous act under command of authority is that he has simply done his duty. In asserting this defense, the individual is not introducing an alibi concocted for the moment but is reporting honestly on the psychological attitude induced by submission to authority.

For a person to feel responsible for his actions, he must sense that the 115
behavior has flowed from "the self." In the situation we have studied, subjects have precisely the opposite view of their actions—namely, they see them as originating in the motives of some other person. Subjects in the experiment frequently said, "If it were up to me, I would not have administered shocks to the learner."

Once authority has been isolated as the cause of the subject's behavior, 116
it is legitimate to inquire into the necessary elements of authority and how it must be perceived in order to gain his compliance. We conducted some investigations into the kinds of changes that would cause the experimenter to lose his power and to be disobeyed by the subject. Some of the variations revealed that:

- *The experimenter's physical presence has a marked impact on his* 117
authority. As cited earlier, obedience dropped off sharply when orders were given by telephone. The experimenter could often induce a disobedient subject to go on by returning to the laboratory.
- *Conflicting authority severely paralyzes action.* When two experi- 118
menters of equal status, both seated at the command desk, gave incompatible orders, no shocks were delivered past the point of their disagreement.
- *The rebellious action of others severely undermines authority.* In one 119
variation, three teachers (two actors and a real subject) administered a test and shocks. When the two actors disobeyed the experimenter and refused to go beyond a certain shock level, thirty-six of forty subjects joined their disobedient peers and refused as well.

Although the experimenter's authority was fragile in some respects, it 120
is also true that he had almost none of the tools used in ordinary command structures. For example, the experimenter did not threaten the subjects with punishment—such as loss of income, community ostracism, or jail—for failure to obey. Neither could he offer incentives. Indeed, we should expect the experimenter's authority to be much less than that of someone like a general, since the experimenter has no power to enforce his imperatives, and since participation in a psychological experiment scarcely evokes the sense of urgency and dedication found in warfare. Despite these limitations, he still managed to command a dismaying degree of obedience.

I will cite one final variation of the experiment that depicts a dilemma 1
that is more common in everyday life. The subject was not ordered to pull the lever that shocked the victim, but merely to perform a subsidiary task (administering the word-pair test) while another person administered the shock. In this situation, thirty-seven of forty adults continued to the highest level on the shock generator. Predictably, they excused their behavior by saying that the responsibility belonged to the man who actually pulled the switch. This may illustrate a dangerously typical arrangement in a complex society: it is easy to ignore responsibility when one is only an intermediate link in a chain of action.

The problem of obedience is not wholly psychological. The form and 1
shape of society and the way it is developing have much to do with it. There was a time, perhaps, when people were able to give a fully human response to any situation because they were fully absorbed in it as human beings. But as soon as there was a division of labor things changed. Beyond a certain point, the breaking up of society into people carrying out narrow and very special jobs takes away from the human quality of work and life. A person does not get to see the whole situation but only a small part of it, and is thus unable to act without some kind of overall direction. He yields to authority but in doing so is alienated from his own actions.

Even Eichmann was sickened when he toured the concentration 1
camps, but he had only to sit at a desk and shuffle papers. At the same time the man in the camp who actually dropped Cyclon-b in the gas chambers was able to justify *his* behavior on the ground that he was only following orders from above. Thus there is a fragmentation of the total human act; no one is confronted with the consequences of his decision to carry out the evil act. The person who assumes responsibility has evaporated. Perhaps this is the most common characteristic of socially organized evil in modern society.

Shooting an Elephant

George Orwell

George Orwell (1903–1950), the pseudonym of Eric Arthur Blair, was a British writer who explored political and social issues in much of his writing. Many readers have admired his futuristic 1984 *(published in 1949) and* Animal Farm *(1946). His autobiographical works include* Down and Out in Paris and London *(1933) and* Homage to Catalonia *(1938). Known for his strong and direct prose, Orwell once wrote: "The great enemy of clear language is insin-*

cerity. When there is a gap between one's real and one's declared aims, one turns as it were instinctively to long words and exhausted idioms, like a cuttle-fish squirting out ink."

In Moulmein, in lower Burma, I was hated by large numbers of people— 1
the only time in my life that I have been important enough for this to happen to me. I was sub-divisional police officer of the town, and in an aimless, petty kind of way anti-European feeling was very bitter. No one had the guts to raise a riot, but if a European woman went through the bazaars alone somebody would probably spit betel juice over her dress. As a police officer I was an obvious target and was baited whenever it seemed safe to do so. When a nimble Burman tripped me up on the football field and the referee (another Burman) looked the other way, the crowd yelled with hideous laughter. This happened more than once. In the end the sneering yellow faces of young men that met me everywhere, the insults hooted after me when I was at a safe distance, got badly on my nerves. The young Buddhist priests were the worst of all. There were several thousands of them in the town and none of them seemed to have anything to do except stand on street corners and jeer at Europeans.

All this was perplexing and upsetting. For at that time I had already 2
made up my mind that imperialism was an evil thing and the sooner I chucked up my job and got out of it the better. Theoretically—and secretly, of course—I was all for the Burmese and all against their oppressors, the British. As for the job I was doing, I hated it more bitterly than I can perhaps make clear. In a job like that you see the dirty work of Empire at close quarters. The wretched prisoners huddling in the stinking cages of the lock-ups, the gray, cowed faces of the long-term convicts, the scarred buttocks of the men who had been flogged with bamboos—all these oppressed me with an intolerable sense of guilt. But I could get nothing into perspective. I was young and ill educated and I had had to think out my problems in the utter silence that is imposed on every Englishman in the East. I did not even know that the British Empire is dying, still less did I know that it is a great deal better than the younger empires that are going to supplant it. All I knew was that I was stuck between my hatred of the empire I served and my rage against the evil-spirited little beasts who tried to make my job impossible. With one part of my mind I thought of the British Raj as an unbreakable tyranny, as something clamped down, in *saecula saeculorum,* upon the will of prostrate peoples; with another part I thought that the greatest joy in the world would be to drive a bayonet into a Buddhist priest's guts. Feelings like these are the normal by-products of imperialism; ask any Anglo-Indian official, if you can catch him off duty.

One day something happened which in a roundabout way was en- 3
lightening. It was a tiny incident in itself, but it gave me a better glimpse

than I had had before of the real nature of imperialism—the real motives for which despotic governments act. Early one morning the sub-inspector at a police station the other end of the town rang me up on the 'phone and said that an elephant was ravaging the bazaar. Would I please come and do something about it? I did not know what I could do, but I wanted to see what was happening and I got on to a pony and started out. I took my rifle, an old .44 Winchester and much too small to kill an elephant, but I thought the noise might be useful *in terrorem.* Various Burmans stopped me on the way and told me about the elephant's doings. It was not, of course, a wild elephant, but a tame one which had gone "must." It had been chained up, as tame elephants always are when their attack of "must" is due, but on the previous night it had broken its chain and escaped. Its mahout, the only person who could manage it when it was in that state, had set out in pursuit, but had taken the wrong direction and was now twelve hours' journey away, and in the morning the elephant had suddenly reappeared in the town. The Burmese population had no weapons and were quite helpless against it. It had already destroyed somebody's bamboo hut, killed a cow and raided some fruit-stalls and devoured the stock; also it had met the municipal rubbish van and, when the driver jumped out and took to his heels, had turned the van over and inflicted violences upon it.

The Burmese sub-inspector and some Indian constables were waiting 4
for me in the quarter where the elephant had been seen. It was a very poor quarter, a labyrinth of squalid bamboo huts, thatched with palm-leaf, winding all over a steep hillside. I remember that it was a cloudy, stuffy morning at the beginning of the rains. We began questioning the people as to where the elephant had gone and, as usual, failed to get any definite information. That is invariably the case in the East; a story always sounds clear enough at a distance, but the nearer you get to the scene of events the vaguer it becomes. Some of the people said that the elephant had gone in one direction, some said that he had gone in another, some professed not even to have heard of any elephant. I had almost made up my mind that the whole story was a pack of lies, when we heard yells a little distance away. There was a loud, scandalized cry of "Go away, child! Go away this instant!" and an old woman with a switch in her hand came round the corner of a hut, violently shooing away a crowd of naked children. Some more women followed, clicking their tongues and exclaiming; evidently there was something that the children ought not to have seen. I rounded the hut and saw a man's dead body sprawling in the mud. He was an Indian, a black Dravidian coolie, almost naked, and he could not have been dead many minutes. The people said that the elephant had come suddenly upon him round the corner of the hut, caught him with its trunk, put its foot on his back and ground him into the earth. This was the

rainy season and the ground was soft, and his face had scored a trench a foot deep and a couple of yards long. He was lying on his belly with arms crucified and head sharply twisted to one side. His face was coated with mud, the eyes wide open, the teeth bared and grinning with an expression of unendurable agony. (Never tell me, by the way, that the dead look peaceful. Most of the corpses I have seen looked devilish.) The friction of the great beast's foot had stripped the skin from his back as neatly as one skins a rabbit. As soon as I saw the dead man I sent an orderly to a friend's house nearby to borrow an elephant rifle. I had already sent back the pony, not wanting it to go mad with fright and throw me if it smelt the elephant.

The orderly came back in a few minutes with a rifle and five cartridges, 5
and meanwhile some Burmans had arrived and told us that the elephant was in the paddy fields below, only a few hundred yards away. As I started forward practically the whole population of the quarter flocked out of the houses and followed me. They had seen the rifle and were all shouting excitedly that I was going to shoot the elephant. They had not shown much interest in the elephant when he was merely ravaging their homes, but it was different now that he was going to be shot. It was a bit of fun to them, as it would be to an English crowd; besides they wanted the meat. It made me vaguely uneasy. I had no intention of shooting the elephant—I had merely sent for the rifle to defend myself if necessary—and it is always unnerving to have a crowd following you. I marched down the hill, looking and feeling a fool, with the rifle over my shoulder and an ever-growing army of people jostling at my heels. At the bottom, when you got away from the huts, there was a metalled road and beyond that a miry waste of paddy fields a thousand yards across, not yet ploughed but soggy from the first rains and dotted with coarse grass. The elephant was standing eight yards from the road, his left side toward us. He took not the slightest notice of the crowd's approach. He was tearing up bunches of grass, beating them against his knees to clean them, and stuffing them into his mouth.

I had halted on the road. As soon as I saw the elephant I knew with 6
perfect certainty that I ought not to shoot him. It is a serious matter to shoot a working elephant—it is comparable to destroying a huge and costly piece of machinery—and obviously one ought not to do it if it can possibly be avoided. And at that distance, peacefully eating, the elephant looked no more dangerous than a cow. I thought then and I think now that his attack of "must" was already passing off; in which case he would merely wander harmlessly about until the mahout came back and caught him. Moreover, I did not in the least want to shoot him. I decided that I would watch him for a little while to make sure that he did not turn savage again, and then go home.

But at that moment I glanced round at the crowd that had followed 7 me. It was an immense crowd, two thousand at the least and growing every minute. It blocked the road for a long distance on either side. I looked at the sea of yellow faces above the garish clothes—faces all happy and excited over this bit of fun, all certain that the elephant was going to be shot. They were watching me as they would watch a conjurer about to perform a trick. They did not like me, but with the magical rifle in my hands I was momentarily worth watching. And suddenly I realized that I should have to shoot the elephant after all. The people expected it of me and I had got to do it; I could feel their two thousand wills pressing me forward, irresistibly. And it was at this moment, as I stood there with the rifle in my hands, that I first grasped the hollowness, the futility of the white man's dominion in the East. Here was I, the white man with his gun, standing in front of the unarmed native crowd—seemingly the leading actor of the piece; but in reality I was only an absurd puppet pushed to and fro by the will of those yellow faces behind. I perceived in this moment that when the white man turns tyrant it is his own freedom that he destroys. He becomes a sort of hollow, posing dummy, the conventionalized figure of a sahib. For it is the condition of his rule that he shall spend his life in trying to impress the "natives," and so in every crisis he has got to do what the "natives" expect of him. He wears a mask, and his face grows to fit it. I had got to shoot the elephant. I had committed myself to doing it when I sent for the rifle. A sahib has got to act like a sahib; he has got to appear resolute, to know his own mind and do definite things. To come all that way, rifle in hand, with two thousand people marching at my heels, and then to trail feebly away, having done nothing—no, that was impossible. The crowd would laugh at me. And my whole life, every white man's life in the East, was one long struggle not to be laughed at.

But I did not want to shoot the elephant. I watched him beating his bunch of grass against his knees with that preoccupied grandmotherly air that elephants have. It seemed to me that it would be murder to shoot him. At that age I was not squeamish about killing animals, but I had never shot an elephant and never wanted to. (Somehow it always seems worse to kill a *large* animal.) Besides, there was the beast's owner to be considered. Alive, the elephant was worth at least a hundred pounds; dead, he would only be worth the value of his tusks, five pounds, possibly. But I had got to act quickly. I turned to some experienced-looking Burmans who had been there when we arrived, and asked them how the elephant had been behaving. They all said the same thing: he took no notice of you if you left him alone, but he might charge at you if you went too close to him.

It was perfectly clear to me what I ought to do. I ought to walk up to within, say, twenty-five yards of the elephant and test his behavior. If he charged, I could shoot; if he took no notice of me, it would be safe to leave him until the mahout came back. But also I knew that I was going to do no such thing. I was a poor shot with a rifle and the ground was soft mud into which one would sink at every step. If the elephant charged and I missed him, I should have about as much chance as a toad under a steam-roller. But even then I was not thinking particularly of my own skin, only of the watchful yellow faces behind. For at that moment, with the crowd watching me, I was not afraid in the ordinary sense, as I would have been if I had been alone. A white man mustn't be frightened in front of "natives"; and so, in general, he isn't frightened. The sole thought in my mind was that if anything went wrong those two thousand Burmans would see me pursued, caught, trampled on, and reduced to a grinning corpse like that Indian up the hill. And if that happened it was quite probable that some of them would laugh. That would never do. There was only one alternative. I shoved the cartridges into the magazine and lay down on the road to get a better aim.

The crowd grew very still, and a deep, low, happy sigh, as of people who see the theater curtain go up at last, breathed from innumerable throats. They were going to have their bit of fun after all. The rifle was a beautiful German thing with cross-hair sights. I did not then know that in shooting an elephant one would shoot to cut an imaginary bar running from ear-hole to ear-hole. I ought, therefore, as the elephant was sideways on, to have aimed straight at his ear-hole; actually I aimed several inches in front of this, thinking the brain would be further forward. 10

When I pulled the trigger I did not hear the bang or feel the kick—one never does when a shot goes home—but I heard the devilish roar of glee that went up from the crowd. In that instant, in too short a time, one would have thought, even for the bullet to get there, a mysterious, terrible change had come over the elephant. He neither stirred nor fell, but every line of his body had altered. He looked suddenly stricken, shrunken, immensely old, as though the frightful impact of the bullet had paralyzed him without knocking him down. At last, after what seemed a long time—it might have been five seconds, I dare say—he sagged flabbily to his knees. His mouth slobbered. An enormous senility seemed to have settled upon him. One could have imagined him thousands of years old. I fired again into the same spot. At the second shot he did not collapse but climbed with desperate slowness to his feet and stood weakly upright, with legs sagging and head drooping. I fired a third time. That was the shot that did it for him. You could see the agony of it jolt his whole body and knock the last remnant of strength from his legs. But in falling he seemed for a moment to rise, for as his hind legs collapsed beneath him he seemed to tower upward like a huge rock toppling, his trunk reaching skyward like a tree. He trumpeted, for the first and only time. And then down he came, his belly toward me, with a crash that seemed to shake the ground even where I lay. 11

I got up. The Burmans were already racing past me across the mud. It 1
was obvious that the elephant would never rise again, but he was not dead. He was breathing very rhythmically with long rattling gasps, his great mound of a side painfully rising and falling. His mouth was wide open—I could see far down into caverns of pale pink throat. I waited a long time for him to die, but his breathing did not weaken. Finally I fired my two remaining shots into the spot where I thought his heart must be. The thick blood welled out of him like red velvet, but still he did not die. His body did not even jerk when the shots hit him, the tortured breathing continued without a pause. He was dying, very slowly and in great agony, but in some world remote from me where not even a bullet could damage him further. I felt that I had got to put an end to that dreadful noise. It seemed dreadful to see the great beast lying there, powerless to move and yet powerless to die, and not even to be able to finish him. I sent back for my small rifle and poured shot after shot into his heart and down his throat. They seemed to make no impression. The tortured gasps continued as steadily as the ticking of a clock.

In the end I could not stand it any longer and went away. I heard later 1
that it took him half an hour to die. Burmans were bringing dahs and baskets even before I left, and I was told they had stripped his body almost to the bones by the afternoon.

Afterward, of course, there were endless discussions about the shoot- 1
ing of the elephant. The owner was furious, but he was only an Indian and could do nothing. Besides, legally I had done the right thing, for a mad elephant has to be killed, like a mad dog, if its owner fails to control it. Among the Europeans opinion was divided. The older men said I was right, the younger men said it was a damn shame to shoot an elephant for killing a coolie, because an elephant was worth more than any damn Coringhee coolie. And afterward I was very glad that the coolie had been killed; it put me legally in the right and it gave me a sufficient pretext for shooting the elephant. I often wondered whether any of the others grasped that I had done it solely to avoid looking a fool.

The Use of Force

William Carlos Williams

William Carlos Williams (1883–1963) lived in Rutherford, New Jersey, where he practiced as a physician. A poet, novelist, and playwright, he was one of the most acclaimed American modernist writers. "No ideas but in things," Williams said, as a way of explaining his spare, concrete images. Among Williams's books is Paterson *(1946–1958), an epic poem in four volumes, and* In the American Grain *(1925), his attempt at defining and exploring the American character.*

They were new patients to me, all I had was the name, Olson. Please come 1
down as soon as you can, my daughter is very sick. When I arrived I was met by the mother, a big startled looking woman, very clean and apologetic who merely said, Is this the doctor? and let me in. In the back, she added. You must excuse us, doctor, we have her in the kitchen where it is warm. It is very damp here sometimes.

The child was fully dressed and sitting on her father's lap near the 2
kitchen table. He tried to get up, but I motioned for him not to bother, took off my overcoat and started to look things over. I could see that they were all very nervous, eyeing me up and down distrustfully. As often, in such cases, they weren't telling me more than they had to, it was up to me to tell them; that's why they were spending three dollars on me.

The child was fairly eating me up with her cold, steady eyes, and no 3
expression to her face whatever. She did not move and seemed, inwardly, quiet; an unusually attractive little thing, and as strong as a heifer in appearance. But her face was flushed, she was breathing rapidly, and I realized that she had a high fever. She had magnificent blonde hair, in profusion. One of those picture children often reproduced in advertising leaflets and the photogravure sections of the Sunday papers.

She's had a fever for three days, began the father and we don't know 4
what it comes from. My wife has given her things, you know, like people do, but it don't do no good. And there's been a lot of sickness around. So we tho't you'd better look her over and tell us what is the matter.

As doctors often do I took a trial shot at it as a point of departure. Has 5
she had a sore throat?

Both parents answered me together, No . . . No, she says her throat 6
don't hurt her.

Does your throat hurt you? added the mother to the child. But the little 7
girl's expression didn't change nor did she move her eyes from my face.

Have you looked? 8

I tried to, said the mother, but I couldn't see. 9

As it happens we had been having a number of cases of diphtheria in 10
the school to which this child went during that month and we were all, quite apparently, thinking of that, though no one had as yet spoken of the thing.

Well, I said, suppose we take a look at the throat first. I smiled in my 11 best professional manner and asking for the child's first name I said, come on, Mathilda, open your mouth and let's take a look at your throat.

Nothing doing. 12

Aw, come on, I coaxed, just open your mouth wide and let me take a 13
look. Look, I said opening both hands wide, I haven't anything in my hands. Just open up and let me see.

Such a nice man, put in the mother. Look how kind he is to you. Come 14
on, do what he tells you to. He won't hurt you.

At that I ground my teeth in disgust. If only they wouldn't use the word 15
"hurt" I might be able to get somewhere. But I did not allow myself to be hurried or disturbed but speaking quietly and slowly I approached the child again.

As I moved my chair a little nearer suddenly with one catlike movement 16
both her hands clawed instinctively for my eyes and she almost reached them too. In fact she knocked my glasses flying and they fell, though unbroken, several feet away from me on the kitchen floor.

Both the mother and father almost turned themselves inside out in 17
embarrassment and apology. You bad girl, said the mother, taking her and shaking her by one arm. Look what you've done. The nice man . . .

For heaven's sake, I broke in. Don't call me a nice man to her. I'm here 18
to look at her throat on the chance that she might have diphtheria and possibly die of it. But that's nothing to her. Look here, I said to the child, we're going to look at your throat. You're old enough to understand what I'm saying. Will you open it now by yourself or shall we have to open it for you?

Not a move. Even her expression hadn't changed. Her breaths how- 19
ever were coming faster and faster. Then the battle began. I had to do it. I had to have a throat culture for her own protection. But first I told the parents that it was entirely up to them. I explained the danger but said that I would not insist on a throat examination so long as they would take the responsibility.

If you don't do what the doctor says you'll have to go to the hospital, 20
the mother admonished her severely.

Oh yeah? I had to smile to myself. After all, I had already fallen in love 21
with the savage brat, the parents were contemptible to me. In the ensuing struggle they grew more and more abject, crushed, exhausted while she surely rose to magnificent heights of insane fury of effort bred of her terror of me.

The father tried his best, and he was a big man but the fact that she 22
was his daughter, his shame at her behavior and his dread of hurting her made him release her just at the critical times when I had almost achieved success, till I wanted to kill him. But his dread also that she might have

diphtheria made him tell me to go on, go on through he himself was almost fainting, while the mother moved back and forth behind us raising and lowering her hands in an agony of apprehension.

Put her in front of you on your lap, I ordered, and hold both her wrists. 23

But as soon as he did the child let out a scream. Don't, you're hurting 24
me. Let go of my hands. Let them go I tell you. Then she shrieked terrifyingly, hysterically. Stop it! Stop it! You're killing me!

Do you think she can stand it, doctor? said the mother. 25

You get out, said the husband to his wife. Do you want her to die of 26
diphtheria?

Come on now, hold her, I said. 27

Then I grasped the child's head with my left hand and tried to get the 28
wooden tongue depressor between her teeth. She fought, with clenched teeth, desperately! But now I also had grown furious—at a child. I tried to hold myself down but I couldn't. I know how to expose a throat for inspection. And I did my best. When finally I got the wooden spatula behind the last teeth and just the point of it into the mouth cavity, she opened up for an instant but before I could see anything she came down again and gripped the wooden blade between her molars she reduced it to splinters before I could get it out again.

Aren't you ashamed, the mother yelled at her. Aren't you ashamed to 29
act like that in front of the doctor?

Get me a smooth-handled spoon of some sort, I told the mother. We're 30
going through with this. The child's mouth was already bleeding. Her tongue was cut and she was screaming in wild hysterical shrieks. Perhaps I should have desisted and come back in an hour or more. No doubt it would have been better. But I have seen at least two children lying dead in bed of neglect in such cases, and feeling that I must get a diagnosis now or never I went at it again. But the worst of it was that I too had got beyond reason. I could have torn the child apart in my own fury and enjoyed it. It was a pleasure to attack her. My face with burning with it.

The damned little brat must be protected against her own idiocy, one 31
says to one's self at such times. Others must be protected against her. It is a social necessity. And all these things are true. But a blind fury, a feeling of adult shame, bred of a longing for muscular release are the operatives. One goes on to the end.

In the final unreasoning assault I overpowered the child's neck and 32
jaws. I forced the heavy silver spoon back of her teeth and down her throat till she gagged. And there it was—both tonsils covered with membrane. She had fought valiantly to keep me from knowing her secret. She had been hiding that sore throat for three days at least and lying to her parents in order to escape just such an outcome as this.

Now truly she was furious. She had been on the defensive before but now she attacked. Tried to get off her father's lap and fly at me while tears of defeat blinded her eyes. 33

STUDENT ESSAYS

Why Bother with Morality?

Amir Goldkorn

Amir Goldkorn (b. 1972) was born in Israel, but grew up in Fair Lawn, New Jersey. Amir is majoring in biology, concentrating on neurobiology, and plans to attend medical school. About his essay, Amir tells us: "Writing this essay was an excellent way for me to explore my ideas about morality. I don't think an essay can be interesting to a reader unless the writer is exploring a subject that means something to him. The best essay is the one in which the writer develops along with the writing."

"Come on Amir," Rob pleaded. "Just tell me, is it 'C' or 'D'? She's all the way on the other side of the room, she won't know!" 1

We had just completed the second math section of the SATs; dazed students were stretching and sighing with relief, but Rob would not let me enjoy the moment. He just had to know the answer to number 24, so that he could fill in the oval before the teacher collected our sheets. 2

As Rob's voice whined and wheedled behind me, all the old familiar thoughts flooded my mind: On one hand, "What's the big deal? Why not help a fellow student and give him the answer?" But then the usual reply, "Why should you cheat for him? He didn't work as hard as you, so he doesn't deserve to reap your benefits." 3

Rob was frantic: "Amir, pleeease! She's almost here! Just say 'C' or 'D'!" 4

"Shut up, Rob!" I hissed. A moment later, the teacher collected the papers, and our chance was gone. 5

I felt good about my decision. I had been faced with a moral dilemma—to help Rob by cheating or to ignore him—and I had done the right thing. The Right Thing. What do those words mean? It seems that a universal human trait, from governments right down to the individual, is an undying concern for what is right or wrong, just or unjust. This interest is as old as civilization itself. The Bible tells us: Thou Shalt Not Kill, Love Thy Neighbor, 6

Thou Shalt Not Steal. . . . All of these are ethical codes, credos that dictate our behavior and ensure the well-being of mankind. They are often reduced to more common rules, like "stick together," "help others," "respect authority," and "be honest." We are taught such concepts since birth by our parents, friends, and teachers, and they combine to form what is known as our Morality—that invisible, omnipresent force that is supposed to guide us through life.

Indeed, I believed it was my Morality that prevented me from giving Rob an unearned advantage. As a result, I felt proud, even smug about my "moral triumph." But in retrospect, it does not seem like much of a triumph after all. It was simply too easy, too clear-cut—I had acted like a computer: "If 'cheating' Then 'wrong,' Go to 'Shut-up Rob.' " There was no great dilemma, no weighty consequences. What would I have done had I known that Rob's acceptance into college hinged on question 24 to the SATs? Or supposing he had a very sick mother whose health would be affected by Rob's success on the test. My decision would not have been so easy. That specific situation with Rob had been a lucky exception. For the overwhelming majority of the time, Morality is *not* a computer program into which we can plug a situation and get an automatic answer. And that's where the problems begin. 7

Most of the time there is no absolute "right thing to do" in any given situation. The world is simply too complex and irregular for that to happen. In her essay "On Morality," Joan Didion examines this phenomenon and how it affects the concept of Morality as a whole. She claims that "We have no way of knowing—beyond that fundamental loyalty to the social code—what is 'right' and what is 'wrong,' what is 'good' and what 'evil.' " In other words, except for an instinctive "survival morality," we should not claim to hold any other type of ethical code. Didion's reason for this radical view is that in an insane world where one person's right is another's wrong, we cannot possibly establish any reliable and steadfast axioms for behavior. Didion concludes that much evil and irrationality result when people act out of supposed moral convictions, and she condemns our hypocrisy in thinking that our actions result from anything more than simple desires and necessities. 8

Indeed, many of Didion's suggestions are alarmingly true. I think of all the heinous crimes committed by humanity and ask myself "Where was Morality when this happened?" On a much smaller scale, I look at myself and at my own little transgressions. All those times I lied, neglected, cheated, took what wasn't mine. . . . One particularly shameful incident comes to mind: 9

Greg rushed up to us: "Someone get Mr. M. out of the other room. The exams are right on his desk, and I'm sure I can grab one!" I had a question 10 about our project anyway, so I calmly walked into the other room and called Mr. M. out. Greg stole the exam, and the next day he was selling copies for six bucks apiece. He was even nice enough to give me credit as his accomplice. We became heroes in the eyes of our classmates—stealing from the tyrannous and oppressive teacher and giving, for a small fee, to the poor and helpless students.

Looking back, it is plain that we were obviously not heroes. We were crooks, 11
thieves, cheaters—we forsook our ethical codes. But what bothers me more is the ease, the off-handed manner with which I had committed the crime. Just like that time with Rob, there was no great conflict, no weighing of consequences—I just did it. So where was my Morality? In light of my own duality, how can I even claim that such a thing exists? Didion's haunting words come back: "[Our actions] may or may not be expedient, may or may not be [good ideas], but in any case [have] nothing to do with 'morality.'

Yet, I cannot accept this. If Morality were invalid, then what else would 12
there be? According to what mirror, what scale, would we measure our lives? There would be nothing left to guide us except our whims and fancies.

The answer lies in a fine distinction between different types of thought 13
and action: On one hand there is the type exemplified by my personal experiences, where Morality did not play a part. They were reflex actions, choices made with little or no thought; I hardly acted out of any moral convictions, regardless of whether or not my decisions happened to comply with accepted ethical codes. Truly, if life consisted of only these types of decisions, then a general rejection of Morality would be valid. But there is another type of thought and action, the kind that involves complex dilemmas, and it is there that Didion's views fail. True Morality *can* be found in predicaments with no clear-cut choices, where painful compromises and hard decisions are the only solutions.

Indeed, Morality does exist, but it is not a simple set of axiomatic ethical 14
codes. For example, certain moral tenets may conflict with others in a given situation; at such crossroads we must use our own judgment in deciding which belief to follow. At other times, we simply choose to abandon our ethics altogether because of selfish reasons or the influence of our social group. These various situations give life to the concept of Morality, which is supposed to guide us through such difficulties. Morality is never invalidated by the mere fact that it changes with time and circumstance. On the contrary, mutability, conflicts, and compromises define true Morality.

The frequent clash between different ethics complicates the concept 15 of Morality. We have all told "white lies" on occasion in order to avoid hurting someone's feelings. In such situations, we must make a choice—to uphold the virtue of honesty or to adhere to the ethic of not hurting others. A much more serious dilemma of the same nature is the question of abortion. Is it justified to terminate the fetus's life in order to ease the mother's existence? Here again, different ethical codes come into conflict. The answer is not obvious, and in each case a new decision must be made according to the circumstances.

Stanley Milgram examines how this phenomenon of conflicting morals 16
affects our behavior. He summarizes the results of some very interesting psychological experiments in his essay "The Perils of Obedience." Milgram investigates the cause for one kind of immoral behavior, the inflicting of pain on others, and he concludes that such sadism can often be elicited from subjects by a figure of authority (i.e., the professor in charge of the experiment). He finds that human beings have an extremely strong tendency to obey authority—so strong, in fact, that it overcomes our inherent aversion to violence. We are able to neglect our moral obligation not to hurt others by simply clinging to another moral: the ethic of loyalty and discipline. Milgram reports that "morality does not disappear—it acquires a radically different focus: the subordinate person feels shame or pride depending on how adequately he has performed the actions called for by authority." Thus, we obey one set of morals at the expense of another: "Loyalty, duty, discipline all are terms heavily saturated with moral meaning," Milgram writes, and we often choose to fulfill them at the expense of other principles for a very understandable reason: These specific forms of Morality relieve us of responsibility for our actions, since by choosing to obey we become tools for another's will. Thus, we choose to adhere to the ethics of loyalty, duty, and discipline while neglecting those of simple human compassion. This is yet another example of how choosing to obey one ethical code can often entail violating another.

The clash of ethical codes is not the only factor that affects Morality. 17
Another type of clash poses ethics on one side and the instinct of self-interest or self-preservation on the other. A good example of this situation is the time I helped Greg steal the test. My quick and easy decision to cheat obviously had nothing to do with moral convictions. It was also not the result of adhering to one ethic at the expense of another. Rather, it was a simple case of action out of self-interest, selfishness. I knew that helping to steal the test would gain the admiration of my classmates and help destroy the "brain" image that I despised. For this reason, I conveniently "forgot" about the morals I had been taught. Some may call this "immoral behavior." I claim that Morality simply had nothing to do with it. At the critical moment in which I was considering how to act, it never even entered the picture.

Any ethical thoughts were effectively buried by the flashy and appealing considerations of self-interest.

Self-preservation is a more extreme, yet more acceptable, form of self- 18 interest. In crisis situations there is sometimes no choice but to reject lofty ethics in favor of survival. Such a situation is described by Makkalearn Em in his essay "Ten Sweet Potatoes." As a starving child in Cambodia, he stole some potatoes from a neighbor's patch and ate them in hiding. He knew that what he did was wrong and felt badly about it. However, in retrospect, he does not seem to actually regret his actions. He even shows sympathy towards others in his situation. Stealing those potatoes was a matter of survival, and as such his actions are not subject to moral judgment. Joan Didion describes a similar but opposite situation in "On Morality:" She tells of "the Donner-Reed Party, starving in the Sierra snows, all the ephemera of civilization gone save that one vestigial taboo, the provision that no one should eat his own blood kin," and she attributes this behavior to a certain "instinctive morality." Yet, just like my stealing of the test or Makkalearn's theft, Morality had nothing to do with it. The party stuck together because that was the best way to ensure its own survival. They did it instinctively, a word which by definition cannot be coupled to the term Morality, just as the words self-interest and self-preservation have nothing to do with Morality. Morals are only found in the conflicts and dilemmas, not in the automatic or unquestioned choices.

In addition to acts of instinct and clashes of ethics, there is yet another 19 major force which shapes Morality. This powerful entity is the group. We are all part of a larger social structure which impacts our Morality immensely. The positive effects can be seen all around: Enforced guidelines that govern our society, such as laws against murders, rape, and theft, hearken back to biblical ethics and are meant to maintain peace and order. Of course, these laws are themselves subject to questions of Morality (for example, the abortion issue), but overall they are inarguably a positive product of group organization.

On the other hand, society can also lead to negative or immoral be- 20 havior. Lewis Thomas describes this phenomenon in his essay "The Iks," which examines how individual "good" or "ethical" behavior is lost within the group. Thomas claims that man is not "a sparse, inhuman thing at his center" but rather "that we haven't yet learned how to stay human when assembled in masses." He does not explain exactly how the group causes this loss of Morality, but a possible answer can be found in George Orwell's essay "Shooting an Elephant," which illustrates a more concrete example of the same phenomenon. As an officer of the British Empire in Burma, Orwell is confronted by a dilemma: Should he allow a harmless elephant to live (as dictated by his morals), or should he succumb to the will of the crowd, which expects him to shoot the elephant? Orwell recognizes the "right thing to do," but he feels compelled by the crowd: "The people expected it of me and I had got to do it; I could feel their two thousand wills pressing me forward, irresistibly." Orwell realizes that in the face of such pressure his own Morality becomes meaningless; he is nothing more than "an absurd puppet pushed to and fro by the will of [the crowds]." Thus, it becomes apparent that the social group can enhance and strengthen our Morality, while at other times it often serves to weaken or take it away.

Conflicting ethics, self-interests, and social structure are all factors that 21 must be confronted when making decisions. Our guide through these difficulties is Morality, but it is not a magical cure-all. The situations in which it works without problems are few and far between. Most of the time our choices are tough and really put our beliefs to the test. Trying not to lose sight of Morality while walking the fine line of compromise between "right" and "wrong," "good" and "bad," is not an easy task. Compromising, by its very nature, involves sacrifice, and that is a word nobody likes. Orwell, Makkalearn, and I sacrificed our moral beliefs by killing, stealing, and cheating, respectively, possibly because the external pressures were too strong in each case. By inflicting pain on others, Milgram's subjects sacrificed some of their ethics in favor of loyalty and duty. A pregnant mother may sacrifice her beliefs along with her fetus in exchange for her own better future. These sacrifices are all difficult and painful, but they are also a necessary part of the compromise that is necessary in order to continue to cling to our Morality while contending with the world in which we live. If we were not "lenient" with our Morality, if it became a stone wall of do's and don'ts, then it would become impossible to live by it while maintaining any kind of freedom. If Morality were to lose its flexibility, then it would become useless.

Yet, how much easier it would be not to have to compromise; not to 22 have to feel like we are sacrificing what is good and proper every time that we do something that is not exactly ethical. Our problems would be no weightier than those of the animals: Basically, how to get what we want without being victimized by others' desires. But this is not the case. For better or worse, we are not simple beasts that are guided only by primal needs and desires, as Didion proposes. We have been endowed with a conscience and with the power to reason, and every day it is our duty to utilize these assets to confront dilemmas and problems. The decisions we reach often involve compromises—naturally we must often give up one thing to gain another. This process is often difficult and even painful; nevertheless, it is an imperative ingredient not only in our Morality, but also in our very humanity.

"All His Vital Organs Lay in a Pan Beside His Head"

Raymond Carver, "The Autopsy Room"

Tracy Grikscheit

Tracy Grikscheit (b. 1972) grew up in Salt Lake City, Utah, and is majoring in biochemistry. Tracy writes poetry, plays water polo, and acts in a comedy troupe called the Immediate Gratification Players. About her essay, Tracy reports: "When I was a teenager one of my neighbors would go to a slaughterhouse, bring home an animal heart, and place it on the kitchen table. I wanted to create that sense of immediacy of seeing a heart on a kitchen table. I hope my readers will think about the issues of organ transplants and the ethical complexity of selling and harvesting organs."

I. Value of Human Composition

If reduced to its elements, the entire human body is worth approximately forty-seven dollars and twenty-three cents. We are primarily composed of hydrogen, oxygen, and carbon. The prices of these elements do not fluctuate on the common market, so only half of our elemental value is derived from traces of rare metals such as lanthanum which have poisoned our systems. In this respect, those who have died after smoking for several years or have been exposed to toxic waste and mercury poisoning derive a final revenge by being worth perhaps a dollar or two more than those who die untainted. Unless a research laboratory wishes to reconstruct an entire skeleton, or, like Lenin, one is able to secure a permanent postmortem position, the value of human composition is embarrassingly low. 1

It is for this reason that Willy Loman in *Death of a Salesman* killed himself for his insurance instead of trading in his blood, kidneys, or what was left of his hair for enough money to start his son in a new family business. In Willy Loman's time, there was no formal market for individual body parts; value was derived in two ways: through ownership, whether of a Picasso or an insurance policy, and through physical exertion of the low-priced components of the human body. 2

Historically, women have sold their hair to wigmakers, and red and white blood cells, as well as blood plasma, have been the wares of the homeless and others desiring some small return. More recently, during the frenzy of drug testing by major corporations, drug-free urine was sold on the street to sullied employees for twelve dollars an ounce. In the case of 3 surrogate motherhood, the womb may be rented for a few thousand dollars. Similarly, sperm banks and biological experiments have offered employment of human organs at a minimal cost. Since 1938, however, when the first successful transplant of a rabbit's cornea into a man was completed, through 1958, when the heads of frozen embryo chicks were successfully traded, to 1989 when the first American live-donor liver transplant was achieved, biological research in organ transplanting has not only advanced the technology of life enormously, but it has also increased the value of the human body exponentially.

Both liver and kidneys can currently be harvested from the living; the 4
liver regenerates within three months, and supposedly could be exploited quarterly. Of the two kidneys man is born with, only one is necessary, and bone-marrow transplants, although problematical because they are difficult to match exactly to recipients, provide a new major source of income. The current demand for transplantable organs is insatiable, while supply is low. The advent of a living-donor market is new, and has only progressed on a grass-roots level, primarily in third world black markets, while systems of cadaver donations are lacking in organs and have so many recipients waiting that some are turned away from being listed because it is far more likely that they will die before their name approaches the middle of the list.

II. Maximizing Value, Saving Lives

The Neanderthals, some have argued, were stupid not just because they 5
had knobby foreheads and looked unintelligent, but because they spent so much time looking for berries and dead rabbits to eat during the day that at night they were too tired to discover calculus. In any case, it is true that once mankind moved from a hunter-gatherer system to farming and keeping livestock, society advanced further with better survival and stability.

Procuring organs today is still on a hunter-gatherer basis; bone-marrow 6
patients may use their lifetime savings in attempts to find matching donors, while patients who cannot get themselves listed in the regular networks of organ transplants must travel to lesser developed countries, especially for kidneys, to talk a peasant out of his organs in exchange for a few thousand dollars. In a bid to remedy the situation for bone-marrow patients, the United States government attempted to gather a directory of 10,000 names of donors, but discovered it could not find that many willing sponsors, and that at least 100,000 names would be necessary in order to guarantee a match. Clearly donation alone cannot fulfill the need, and a macroscopic solution is necessary. The scientific breakthrough of organ transplants is ineffectual if the organs to save lives cannot be found.

Establishing a system of paid live donors to capitalize on the elements 7
of the human body in addition to saving lives is, therefore, a new pursuit,

akin to discovering the value of milk after years of selling fine cattle to the glue factory. Farming humans is a natural continuation of the trends of civilization.

Harper's of March 1989 reprinted, under the title "Count Dracula Makes an Offer," a letter that the Count Rainer Rene Adelmann von Adelmannsfelden sent to bankrupt West German citizens offering $45,000 for a kidney after declaring 8

> Dear Bankrupt person . . . legally it is as if you have AIDS . . . the most hideous carrion-vultures will pursue you . . . if you lack the courage for a burglary . . . we have another solution for you to consider. . . . money will flow into your account, allowing you to pay yourself a modest salary or buy a car . . . the loss of a kidney is consolable. . . .

While his approach is a bit crude, Adelmannsfelden is, for the first time, 9 legitimizing what has been happening on an underground basis—the direct brokering of human organs. Not only is he expanding the options available to a person in need of a new organ, but he is also helping the donor. In past shady dealings, the peasants persuaded to donate their kidneys have rarely received the actual market price of their kidneys, and while Adelmannsfelden will make an $11,000 profit on each transaction, the donor will receive much more than he would in a less legitimate operation. In addition, this procedure is legal.

Unlike conventional farming, however, gleaning organs from humans 10 may require more incentive. Aside from profit to the donor, after the establishment of a commodity system of organ transplants, the benefit to the economy and the donor alike will be tremendous. Through the technological advancement of transplanting, the Willy Lomans of the world have been given an automatic insurance policy which can be collected without the necessity of death. Nature has suddenly extended a social security plan to the homeless and dysfunctional, and man is offered an opportunity to pull himself up, if not by his bootstraps, at least by his blood vessels. In addition, one's spouse and children may become paid donors in time of need, so that through cannibalism of one's body and family, society will cease to cannibalize one's soul by poverty and disadvantage.

At birth, then, the body's elements are no longer a static value of forty- 11 seven dollars and twenty-three cents. Each person automatically has a higher intrinsic worth. Today one could collateralize a mortgage with one's kidneys, and welfare offices could garner something in return for food stamps. Dr. Jack Kevorkian, an advocate of medical experimentation on criminals, has even suggested a plan in which death-row murderers surrender their organs to repay their debt to society.[1]

III. Trade Barriers

Unfortunately, the generally staid Margaret Thatcher was so upset by the fact that Turkish peasants were (and probably still are) flown into London for the purpose of harvesting their kidneys at $4,400 per organ that she called an emergency session of Parliament to outlaw the practice.[2] Organ trafficking for profit has encountered misunderstanding as one of its major trade barriers, in addition to the fact that international lines of commerce are often difficult to cross, even in cases of critical need. 12

Insurmountable physical differences between nations and races also make an international market less probable. Special pools of organs will naturally have to be created to fulfill compatibility requirements. Asian populations with a naturally slighter build than Europeans will not be able to provide some organs for their larger neighbors, just as the statistical occurrences of certain blood types are demographically widely varied. 13

In addition to legal and natural barriers, there are deep personal biases which will be difficult to overcome. In a long line at the driver's license bureau a few years ago, I was quickly filling in lines on the license forms when I came to the word "Donor?"—an option I had never really considered, much less weighed carefully. "Do I want to donate my organs?" I asked my mother. She looked confused. "Oh my God! No!" she said. The license I own now, however, says that I will donate, though it is still far from my mind. Before someone took my heart, however, or perhaps even my kidneys, I should like to write him a letter, or at least tell him a thing or two. 14

IV. Conditions of Ownership

This heart was never mine to give, I would like to say to someone inheriting my heart. You might ask my mother, or her mother, for we all fit inside each other like a set of Russian dolls. Yes, this heart has been to Russia, whispered its conversation with my blood in the Ukraine, loved in Japan, Finland, the Philippines. This heart wants at least another year; it will not feel bad about leaving me like a pile of laundry on an operating table, about confusing the maggots later who take the trouble to mouth down to my sand-packed chest for no reward. 15

It is clearly yours to have; though it liked the earth, it never wanted boxes. You'll have my nightmares and wake tear-sweated, missing the dead. You'll have my dreams of dancing with Brahms in a meadow, burying your face in his big white beard. There will be so many calls my heart will want to answer—so many songs you won't recognize, that it's a wonder you want to take this poor heavy stupid orphan into your chest. People 16 have been introduced into it. My heart will not know your friends at first, or even you. The slant of your arms, how much blood your hips like to have at midday, all these things it must be given time to learn. You may think now that you will be the same, but all my poetry and operatic threnodies will be ushered into you while I lie empty like an appoggiatura.

Most of all, this heart will want to be home. You may find yourself out 1
West rolling on your back in sagebrush—kissing the chapped lips of granite, shaking your purple-sutured chest at a rattlesnake, wearing Western boots over Eastern asphalt to count the days until you can mix your blood with sandstone, touch the flickering sides of deer down the canyons in autumn.

This heart may not be pawned, bought, or stolen. I give it to you like 1
the howl of a wolverine: once heard, her cry is all yours to repeat in your walkings, wakings, wildings, until it comes, clear from your throat, a howl all your own.

Notes

[1] Ron Givens, "Death-Row Murderers Could Be Lifesavers," *Newsweek* (January 9, 1989), p. 49.

[2] Michael Kinsley, "Take My Kidney, Please," *Time* (March 13, 1989), p. 88.

Responsibility Not Authority

Lara Herrington

Lara Herrington (b. 1972) grew up in Memphis, Tennessee, and is majoring in classics. Lara's interests include poetry, ballet, and her six cats. About writing, Lara tells us: "The most important part about writing is to know that no two people will ever write the same essay. This is a very liberating thought because it makes you feel the power of exploring and shaping your own ideas. I am learning how to trust my own mind and spirit to show me what I really want to say."

Honesty, Industry, and Obedience. Every morning I passed under these 1
words inscribed above the main door to my school as I entered the halls. After a while they became so ingrained in my memory that I forgot the words were even there. They became a part of the architecture, a part of the background. No one ever really looked at them or talked about what

they meant or why they were important, but during our time there, they tried to teach us that, above all, we must always obey the rules of authority. I never really fully agreed with this statement and still do not. I favor the will of the individual, my own will, over the will of traditional authority. Sometimes, however, I will betray my personal beliefs in the face of authority, but have never really understood why or how I could sacrifice myself for this tradition.

We all feel this conflict between personal morality and the virtue of 2
obedience at times. "Obedience," writes Stanley Milgram, "is as basic an element in the structure of social life as one can point to." But when can authority use this ideal of obedience to force us as individuals to act voluntarily against our own beliefs? In her story, "The Lottery," Shirley Jackson describes the role of obedience in one village's custom, a horrifying ritual in which each year on the 27th of June, the members of the community choose at random by lottery one townsperson to be sacrificed. She details the carefully calculated procedure for the choosing of the individual, how the director, Mr. Summers, meticulously calls each family representative forward to draw a slip of paper from the black box and then carefully moves through each member of that unlucky family until fate decides on the individual marked for death. That person is then for no specific reason and with no opposition from within the community stoned to death by the villagers who remain; even his own family members participate.

Though it is grotesque and brutal, the killing itself is not what really 3
horrifies the reader. Instead, what is truly frightening is the fact that not one single villager questions his own participation in such an event or offers any type of resistance whatsoever against the homicidal mob. Upon first reading, the reader does not really understand exactly what is going to happen. Jackson gives no obvious clues that the lottery actually ends with the violent sacrifice of the "winner." This suspense and this tension increase the dramatic effect of the death at the end and emphasize the fact that no one rebels in any way against the practice of the public murder. During the course of the story, even though the reader does not know exactly what the outcome will be, he is continuously reminded that the villagers do understand their actions and the violent result. Jackson explains that the ritual has been performed since before Old Man Warner, the oldest man in town, was born and that the black box, the main prop, is faded, shabby, and falling apart from constant wear and use. She even tells the reader that Mr. Summers has spoken of "making a new box, but no one liked to upset even as much tradition as was represented by the black box." She describes that the ritual has been performed so many times that the villagers "only half listened to the directions." She tells the reader that much of the ritual and recital involved in the event have been lost and forgotten during the years so that no one, not even Old Man Warner, remembers

exactly how it was performed originally, but even though some of the elaboration has been stripped away, the violent core, the stoning, still remains in full. "Although the villagers had forgotten the ritual and lost the original black box, they still remembered to use stones." By the time the reader finally gets to the end of the story, he is confused, disgusted, repulsed, frightened. He stands ready to lash out against the cruel and violent actions of the mob and cannot understand why none of the villagers share his same feelings, why all the others act as robots with no strong display of the tension of their consciences, with no questioning of the violence being committed, and with no compassion shown toward this "winner" who is about to die at their hands. The villagers act through blind adherence to the tradition and precedence which the black box represents. No one shows any sense of guilt or displays any feelings of repulsion in regard to his actions. Each one subconsciously assumes that he is innocent of the murder because he is acting not on personal initiative, but as part of the tradition which his society has created and passed on to him.

Why does no one end this horrible act of violence and brutality? Why 4
does no one speak out in opposition? Why does no one stand up to the tradition? It is not because the villagers do not fear death or because they feel that the murder is morally correct. In fact, Jackson describes the increasing self-consciousness and repressed anxiety of the townspeople as the time for the lottery drawing approaches and their fear for potential death grows. "They grinned at each other humorlessly and nervously." She describes how Mr. Adams, the first townsperson to draw from the black box, holds tightly onto the paper just at the corner as if it were poisonous. He then "[turns] and [goes] hastily back to his place in the crowd, where he [stands] a little apart from his family, not looking down at his hand," as if he were afraid that his family might be poisoned by the venomous paper if they came too near it. She also tells of the sigh of relief that ran through the crowd when Mr. Graves holds up Davy Hutchinson's slip of paper to show that it is blank and that Davy will be spared. If these people really felt that murder and the execution were perfectly natural and justified, it would not have been of any consequence if the marked paper had belonged to Davy instead of to his mother, Tessie Hutchinson.

It cannot be that they are physically forced to participate in the ritual 5
by some omnipotent power. Clearly, the villagers have some choice in the matter. Otherwise, their mood would be more defiant and rebellious instead of willing and anticipatory. The only time there is any verbal complaint against the lottery is when Mr. Summers tells everyone "to be hurrying a little more to get done in time." Even here, he says this not because he or anyone else wants the horrible event to be over and done with, but because everyone needs to get on with their day and get back to their work. The

length of the ceremony is even a source of pride because it shows how rapidly their village is growing and prospering. What they do not comment on, however, is that this also means that there are more and more people getting involved in the ritual who do not respond to the violence or rebel against the murder to defy the authority of the mob. Jackson also describes how some towns are even considering giving up the lottery while some have already done away with it completely. None of the villagers really responds back to this idea. Only Old Man Warner does. "There's *always* been a lottery." Therefore, each town must hold the ritual by the choice of its collective inhabitants, and each member must participate of his own free will, not because of any coercion or threats from some outside power. Then, what is it that allows them to act without any strain on their consciences?

Reading Jackson's story makes me analyze my own actions in the face of authority. Do I, too, betray my personal morality to respond obediently to the forces of authority? Or do I hold my position and defy these forces no matter what the personal cost will be? You see, for me, personal relationships have always been more important than adherence to any authority. This is not to say that I do not respect authority or its traditions, but rather that I simply respect relationships with my friends and family more. However, if I were a member in Jackson's crowd of villagers would I, too, have picked up a stone and thrown it at my own mother? Sitting alone here at my computer, separated from the excitement of the ritual, I have no trouble answering a firm no. In fact, I would probably be extremely offended if anyone accused me otherwise, but wouldn't the villagers probably give the same response if I were to approach each one on his own and ask if he would actively participate in the killing of his own parent? The only difference between the two homicidal situations—one, the public stoning and the other, a standard murder—is the presence of an authority, the presence of another party who will somehow lift the blame, somehow remove the responsibility. 6

My reflection reminds me of one incident at the extremely small, all-girl school I attended for 14 years. One day, Mrs. Frey, our strict, unyielding high school principal, called me into her dreaded office. When I first got there, I was not sure what was going on, or what exactly I had done wrong. Apparently, I had been seen a few days before talking to three girls sitting in a red Honda in the parking lot of our school during lunch period. A little while later that same car had been seen pulling out of the McDonald's drive-thru, but the witness could not accurately determine the identities of the car's three passengers. It had been confirmed, however, that I had not been in the car, but that I did, in fact, know the names of the three girls who had snuck off campus. Mrs. Frey instructed me to give her these three 7 names. She promised me that the girls would not know that I had turned them in. She told me that she would tell them that their pictures had been chosen out of the yearbook by the first-hand witness.

I felt as if I were trapped in a confessional with my stern priest with no escape available except my confessing to him in detail of all my wretched sins. Mrs. Frey's hard face loomed over me as I searched my brain for revelation. Her presence represented all the traditions that my school had been founded on eighty-six years before: Honesty, Industry, and Obedience. Mrs. Frey embodied the 3,440 Hutchison students who had come before me and had learned our motto and had lived by it. I stood alone staring all of them in the face. Would I remain standing alone or would I yield my position and switch to their side in the name of tradition and authority? What was I supposed to do? My two options were clear. On one hand, I could uphold my loyalty to my friends and conceal their identities. Of course, Mrs. Frey would get angry, and she definitely held the power to make the rest of my high school career hell. On the other hand, I could get on Mrs. Frey's good side at the expense of my friends. But what would that really matter? The three of them would never know that it was me who had turned them in. At that moment, I looked Mrs. Frey straight in her gray eyes and said, "Jennifer, Brooke, and Tracy." Then Mrs. Frey turned and said, "Good. You have done the right thing. . . . Don't look so worried, dear. They are not going to find out. They are not going to hold you responsible." I left her office with the same feeling of empty absolution one has when walking down the cathedral stairs after confession. Are the sins really washed away, and the soul left clean? 8

Why did I do it? Why did I turn them in? Was Mrs. Frey's approval really so important that it qualified the betrayal of my friends and my ideals? For some reason, as I sat and thought about this meeting later, Mrs. Frey's words, "They are not going to hold you responsible," kept haunting me. And it was true; I did not feel responsible. I kept reassuring myself that I was just obeying my superiors, that I had had no choice, that I was upholding the traditions of The Hutchison School. Is this the same reason why the villagers acted without guilt or resistance? Did they also not feel any responsibility for their actions? After all, no one blamed himself for the death of Tessie Hutchinson, so how could he place the blame on any of the others who were also blindingly adhering to the same established rules of tradition? It was not even their idea to have the sacrifice in the first place. They were just obeying the rules and rituals of tradition. 9

So when does the will of authority replace the will of the individual? When will I sacrifice my own beliefs to please my "superiors" or to please the "crowd"? In his essay, "The Perils of Obedience," Stanley Milgram, an American social psychologist, tests the actions of an individual under the guidance of an authority figure. Milgram wonders under what circum- 10 stances a person will betray his personal moral standards. He studied the amount of physical pain one individual would knowingly administer to another under the orders of a guiding experimenter. "To extricate himself from this plight [the conflict between the individual's morality and his desire to obey the authority], the subject must make a clear break with authority." His results show that an unexpectedly small percentage would rebel against the authority of the experimenter and refuse to continue to administer electrical shocks to another person. This small percentage would resist on the basis that "We came here of our free will. . . . I don't want to be responsible for anything happening to him." A surprisingly large percentage, after refusing to be held responsible for his actions, would continue to the end as long as the experimenter reassures the subject that he himself will take full responsibility for any harm that comes to the victim. A small percentage would also continue to the end of the experiment with no dramatic external manifestation of any inner conflict because he would already assume automatically that he is not responsible for his actions. He feels that he has "institutional justification for the release for these [aggressive] impulses." One subject explains that his reaction of laughing during the experiment was a result of his feeling "caught in the set of circumstances where [he] just couldn't deviate and couldn't try to help." Many subjects participating in Milgram's experiment said that if it had been up to them they "would not have administered shocks to the learner," yet at no point in the experiment does the authority figure threaten or force them in any way to act against their own free will. In fact, they have full control over their actions and could stop the experiment if they wanted to. However, they never felt they were in complete control because they were acting in accordance with the wishes of the authority figure.

The connecting factor in all of these different instances is the level of 11
responsibility the subject places on himself. If he does not feel personally responsible, he will administer the shocks even though he can hear the tormented screams of the unseen learner. Milgram continues his experiment further, incorporating differing variables that might affect how responsible the individual feels. His results support the conclusion that whenever the individual feels more responsible for his actions he is more likely to adhere to his personal moral code and rebel against the outside authority. However, if a figure of authority directly or indirectly indicates that he will assume full responsibility for the outcome, the individual will obediently do as the authority wishes until the authority itself puts an end to the situation. Milgram says, "For a person to feel responsible for his actions, he must sense that the behavior has flowed from 'the self.' " Milgram states that when an individual acts through obedience, he "comes to view himself as the instrument for carrying out another person's wishes, and he therefore no longer regards himself as responsible for his actions." The morality is not

stripped away, but switches as the individual views a certain situation from a different perspective. The weight of his feeling of responsibility for his action swings the priority from himself to the tradition of obedience.

Similarly, Jackson's villagers do not feel any burden of responsibility for 1
their actions. In the lottery and the stoning, as in Milgram's experiments, there is as Milgram concluded, "the fragmentation of the total human act; no one is confronted with the consequences of his decision to carry out the evil act." There are so many different forces working together in these situations that no one feels that he should or will have to take full responsibility for the results of his actions. In"The Lottery," the children pass on responsibility to their parents who then pass it on to Mr. Summers who then passes it on to the tradition created by others now long dead, just as Milgram's subjects pass their responsibility on to the experimenter and free themselves of any sense of guilt.

Therefore, Milgram's research suggests that the individual will betray 1
his personal morality when in the face of an authority figure because he will not feel any responsibility for his actions. My personal experience also confirms these results. I betrayed my loyalty to my friends at Mrs. Frey's request, but I did so only because I did not feel responsible for my actions, because she told me that I was not responsible for my actions. I am absolutely positive that I would have acted differently if Brooke, Tracy, and Jennifer would have known I was the snitch. They would have held me responsible for their getting in trouble, and their anger would have made me directly feel my responsibility. After all, I have never tattletaled on either one of my brothers. There is this same unwritten law between us as there is between me and my friends that one is never to betray the loyalty of the other. Neither of my brothers nor I ever have because we would feel individually responsible for the other one's getting in trouble. Therefore, the individual obeys rules or laws not out of respect for authority but out of the burden of responsibility for his actions. If I truly respected authority more, I would have turned my brothers into my parents just as easily as I turned in my friends to my principal, but I did not because my brothers would know, would blame me, and would hold me responsible.

Clearly, the villagers in Shirley Jackson's town in "The Lottery" must also 1
have absolved themselves of responsibility. Their tradition and the longevity of the ritual's existence take responsibility for the sacrifice and the taking of a person's life. The children are not responsible because they are only following their parents' orders and the parents' example. The wives are not responsible because they are not the ones who actually choose the slip of paper from the black box for the family. The men are not responsible because they are only doing what Mr. Summers is telling them to do, and Mr. Summers is not responsible because he is only following the orders and precedence of tradition. Therefore, they, as I did, acted against their

personal moral code in the name of duty, discipline, and obedience, but these actions really have nothing to do with those abstract concepts. The individual will almost invariably act against his personal code if some authority takes full responsibility for the actions and for the outcomes.

a moral person

Ayano Kato

Ayano Kato (b. 1973) was born in Tokyo, has lived in Japan, France, and England, and speaks Japanese, French, and English fluently. Ayano is majoring in biochemistry and intends one day to work on issues of world health policy. About her essay, Ayano tells us: "Morality is a very personal matter. I would like my readers to understand my ideas, but also to have their own ideas as they react to my essay."

"You shouldn't steal," "You shouldn't cheat," "You shouldn't lie," we are told, we shouldn't do such bad, immoral things. You should be moral, you should be good. But I could never quite understand; was I supposed to be a moral person, or was I just supposed to do good things? Or would doing good things make me moral? Somehow I could never quite equate the two. . . . 1

I recall an early afternoon on one September day, sunlight streaming in through the large, rectangular window panes facing the playground. The classroom is filled with high-pitched giggles and the sound of shuffling notebooks, restless third-graders reluctantly getting ready for their first afternoon class. The doors open and shut, open and shut incessantly, at the command of noisy children entering at their leisure. It is one o'clock at a typical public school in Tokyo. 2

It has only been a few weeks since the start of second semester. Conversation is still filled with wonderful details of summer vacation and complaints about the impossible amount of homework that had been assigned for that break. The beach, the countryside, an old family friend . . . the long list of Chinese characters that had to be learned, and the pages and pages of arithmetic exercises. . . . All of this is still novel to me. My family has just moved back to Japan from England, and it can not be longer than one week since I started to call this school and this classroom my own. I stand, amongst my newly made friends, and listen to their busy chatter. 3

I am absorbed into their talk. I listen intently. I nod to acknowledge 4 every detail, smile to every exuberant grin. I try to make myself present in every possible way, present in their little circle.

Conversation shifts to different topics, to friends and to classmates. A 5
name comes up—a name that I no longer remember—and I turn my neck to see the little boy, sitting at his desk, busily getting his notebooks in order. He is a nice boy. I have talked to him before. He greets me in the morning, on our way to school. I think he lives close to where I do.

But the words of my friends are spiteful. Sharp, long arrows are pointed 6
at him, sitting there, defenseless and vulnerable. Slanderous, taunting arrows are flung from their mouths, cruelly, carelessly at the little boy.

No, no, that's not true! I long to cry out, but I catch myself. 7

A painful scene rises to my mind. My younger brother and I in a 8
playground, five minutes away from home. Barely a week ago. Circled by four or five older boys. Sneering. Laughing. Mocking the two of us. "What stupid language are you speaking, huh? Ha, I bet you can't even speak Japanese! Say something! Come on! Say something!" I hold on more tightly to my brother and both of us desperately fight back the humiliation and the tears that threaten to overflow. I talk back, but this only infuriates our aggressors even more. . . .

I hold my breath. 9

I know now what I should have done. And I knew then, too. For I myself 1
knew the pain the little boy must feel, the humiliation, and the helpless anger. . . . But these thoughts did not come to mind, only an uncontrollable desire to belong. The little circle of giggly eight-year-olds with bouncing ponytails and cruel words were what made me feel welcome, and in my mind, the only thing that kept me safe from those taunting voices. All I could do was join in, and hope and pray that the little boy wouldn't hear me. . . .

And all that lasts is the slow, ruthless burning of my conscience. It consumes 1
me like a low flame, slowly swallowing everything in sight. Guilt tells me what I did was wrong. Guilt tells me it was immoral. My heavy conscience tells me this, just as George Orwell's unease tells him that his choice to shoot, to give in to pressure, was wrong in his essay *Shooting an Elephant.* As a subdivisional police officer of Moulmein, Orwell had been called to restore order; an elephant had broken loose and was ravaging the little Burmese town. He did not want to shoot it. It had destroyed much property and crushed one native to death, but at that moment the elephant is simply lazily eating grass. "As soon as I saw the elephant I knew with perfect certainty that I ought not to shoot him. . . . it would be murder to shoot him," Orwell admits to the reader. He knows that the rational thing to do would be to test its behavior. But "the people expected it of me and I had

got to do it. . . . I was only an absurd puppet pushed to and fro by the will of those yellow faces behind," he claims. And trapped between the elephant and the anxious crowd, Orwell gives in to the tremendous pressure and commits the murder; he shoots the harmless elephant. And in his unease, in his guilt, he cannot bear to see the poor elephant "dying, very slowly and in great agony. . . . [He] felt that [he] had got to put an end to that dreadful noise [of the elephant's breathing]." Aware of his immoral act, Orwell feels responsible.

The conscious feeling that he had gone against his principles and the knowledge that he had lost his individuality in the face of the masses; these are the only reasons Orwell gives for his guilt. He faces a conflict between his sense of morality and the "will of those yellow faces behind." He must choose between going with what he feels is right and surrendering to the pressure, between individual morality and obedience to group authority. 12

But I know that the strongest emotions concerning my experience had to do with the little boy himself, the object of my aggression; it was not my friends, Orwell's Burmese natives, with whom I wanted to belong, or my aggressors, Orwell's British Empire which he despised but was subjected to, that provoked my feelings. I cannot claim my dilemma to have been a conflict between my individual self and a group. I cannot ignore the presence of the little boy. 13

Orwell feels compelled to follow the commands of the crowd, fulfilling the role of the "faceless sahib," giving up his own morals and his identity. And in conforming with the crowd's and the empire's conceptualization of the white European male, Orwell is forced to throw away his individuality, his uniqueness as a person which is embodied in his sense of morality. I, too, surrendered my individuality but it was in light of the little boy, not my friends, the authoritative group. I prayed that the little boy wouldn't hear me. I looked away. I could not face him. I wanted to be absorbed into the group because I did not want him to see me, to identify me as an individual in the swarm of faces. I wanted to hide in their collective persona, to be seen as "one of the group," not as Ayano, myself, an individual. The doctor in William Carlos Williams's short story *The Use of Force* is guilty of abandoning his individuality, too. He hides under the mask of his profession. "The damned little brat must be protected against her own idiocy, one says to one's self at such times," he admits. It is easy to excuse oneself, to place oneself in the comforting authority of one's profession. He "had to do it. [He] had to have a throat culture for her own protection"; he was convinced at first that he needed to open the girl's mouth, even if it necessitated force, for the girl's own sake. But as he tries harder to examine her, he gradually realizes that he had "got beyond reason. . . . It was a pleasure to attack her. [His] face was burning with it." He reflects on the sole importance of the object of one's moral dilemmas, the girl, the elephant and the little boy, 14 as opposed to the authoritative group; for Williams, there are no pressuring spectators. Only himself and the girl, no one else. His strong emotions are directed at her, and the realization that he had lost control of himself and the guilt associated with it concern her, his victim, and no one else.

But the sense of guilt comes from oneself, one's own conscience. The stubborn girl never accuses the doctor of losing his head. The little boy never confronted me. He was the reason for my guilt, but not its source. It was my conscious knowledge that he may know, that he may identify me, Williams's fear that the girl may see through his pretences, see his true motivation, that roused our guilty feelings.

The conflict that goes on in one's mind is therefore not between one's individual morality and a group. Nor is it between another individual, the object of the dilemma. It is fundamentally between one and oneself; an individual's morality and inclinations. Orwell saw the anxious crowd, and it was his own fear of "appearing a fool" that translated their faces into pressure, into voices urging him to shoot the elephant. And it was my insecurities that heard the circle of grinning eight-year-olds and my taunting aggressors stopping me from defending the little boy. No one came out and told me to join in the slander. No one distinctly told Orwell to shoot. *We* heard the voices in our minds. "Shoot the elephant," "Join your circle of friends." "Block out the voices of morality."

For this reason, I say that a moral dilemma is always within an individual, because one hears multiple voices in one's mind. For example, in my case and Orwell's there were two. Self-interest and morality diverge, creating an internal conflict, the moral dilemma. And this is where the guilt stems from, the decision that one must make between the various voices. One consciously decides to act immorally.

The decision to act morally is an equally conscious one. Kaliayev, a character in Albert Camus's *Les Justes,* chooses to do just this. As a member of a revolutionary organization in Russia, he is confronted with the moral implications of assassinating the Duke for the good of the Russian people. Their fundamental choices have to do with their ideas of justice, what is preferable for the general population. But how they deal with the choices concerns their morality. They choose to kill, strongly believing that it is justifiable given the wrong doings of the Duke and the state of the Russian people. Yet morally, they must come to terms with the consequences and implications of murder.

". . . pour eux je lutte et . . . je consens à mourir," says Kaliayev, one of the revolutionaries. He fights for the Russian people for the sake of justice, and consents to die for the sake of morality. Because in fighting the revolution, he must compromise his morality by murdering a man. "J'ai choisi de mourir pour que le meurtre ne triomphe pas. J'ai choisi d'être innocent," he proclaims; "I have chosen to die so that murder not triumph. I have chosen to be innocent." The decision to assassinate would no longer be moral, Kaliayev would no longer be innocent if he did not choose to die, for in dying, he consciously chooses to sacrifice his self-interest, to sacrifice his life for the well-being of others.

But Kaliayev takes morality one step further, for not only does he choose 20
the moral path, but he actively makes it moral. Even when offered grace by his executioners, he flatly refuses. For the sake of morality, he wants to die. ". . . Que la mort couronne mon œuvre par la pureté de l'idée." Death, the sacrifice of life, the denial of his voice of self-interest, is the ultimate moral justification for his actions, crowning his deeds in glory. This is what makes his decision moral. The voices in his head are divided; his morality tells him both that it is wrong to kill a man and that it is wrong to let the Duke live, to leave the Russian people to die in their misery. Morality here is separated into two irreconcilable halves, and in following one, Kaliayev must deny the other. And it is in light of this denial that he must sacrifice self-interest, not the voice of self-interest itself.

Choosing to follow the other voices in our minds is not immoral be- 21
cause of the voices themselves, but rather because of the implications of such a decision. There is nothing inherently wrong with self-interest, or in the human desire to belong to a group. It is natural. We do not exist alone. "I had done it solely to avoid looking a fool," admits Orwell, and I, that I did it to avoid isolation and estrangement. These ideas are not wrong in themselves. But it is their consequences that call for the guilty conscience. For what came about as a result of my actions, as a result of Orwell's actions? What was there to be gained? What was there to be lost?

In ignoring the voice of my conscience, I was to gain everything. I 22
would enter the little circle of girls. I would escape the taunting aggression of the older boys. I would gain security. I would belong. And I would lose nothing. Like Orwell, the consequences of avoiding my conscience were positive in all respects to me, and to me only. And I think of the little boy whom I harmed so ruthlessly and so unnecessarily. I think of the elephant, its majestic body reduced to a quivering mass of bleeding flesh, lying on the ground in sheer pain and agony. How much they lost where I gained so much. . . .

Listening to the voice of self-interest, in itself, is not an immoral decision. 23
It is what it implies, the denial of the voice of morality, that makes it immoral.

Making moral decisions must always be an active process, because we as 24
humans are always led by conflicting voices in a dilemma. The relative strengths of the voices vary, depending on individual circumstances. But nonetheless, they are always present in the mind of an individual.

Morality arises from consideration for others. We as humans live in a 25
structured society, we do not live alone. And it is our sense of morality that

holds society together, by taking into account not only oneself and one's own inclinations, but also considerations for other individuals. You shouldn't steal. You shouldn't cheat. You shouldn't lie. Such ideas we learn as morals when we are young because in stealing, in cheating, in lying, in following self-interest, one hurts another.

Morality stems from that conscious decision. An ethical dilemma always necessitates a decision, a choice between the voices in one's conscience. "Shoot the elephant," "Join in the taunting mockery," the selfish voice repeats in our minds. "Do what is best for you and you alone." But a moral decision must be one in which an individual chooses to follow the voice of morality. "Sacrifice pride and security, bear 'looking a fool' and feeling insecure," because in doing so, one is keeping another from being hurt, the elephant from dying, and a poor innocent boy from sorrow and pain. . . . 26

Morality stems from decision, and decision only. But decisions are particular to the situation as well as to the individual. One individual can easily make a moral decision and an immoral decision, depending on the circumstances. I made an immoral decision that day in the classroom, choosing to following the voice of selfish needs. But I have made moral decisions, too. Decisions are particular, but an individual is not. 27

Decisions are moral or immoral. 28

An individual is not. 29

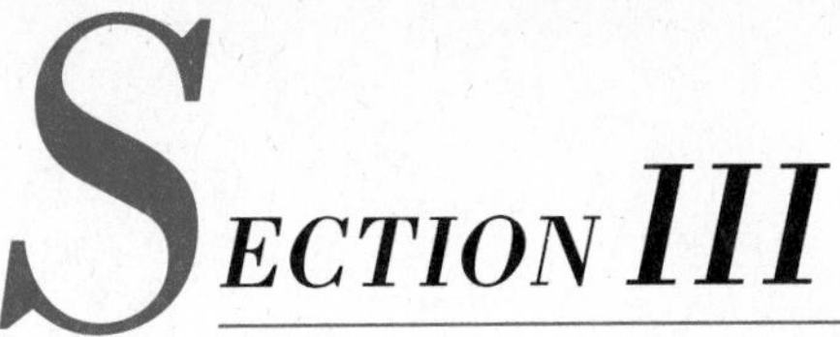

SECTION III

Questioning Ways of Learning

PROFESSIONAL ESSAYS

The Hidden Teacher

Loren Eiseley

> Sometimes the best teacher teaches only once to a single child or to a grownup past hope.
>
> —Anonymous

Loren Eiseley (1907–1977) was an anthropologist, social scientist, and poet, whose lyrical evocations of nature won him a large and admiring audience. His books include Darwin's Century: Evolution and the Men Who Discovered It *(1958) and* The Mind as Nature *(1962). The essay that follows appeared in* The Unexpected Universe *(1964).*

I

The putting of formidable riddles did not arise with today's philosophers. 1 In fact, there is a sense in which the experimental method of science might be said merely to have widened the area of man's homelessness. Over two thousand years ago, a man named Job, crouching in the Judean desert, was moved to challenge what he felt to be the injustice of his God. The voice in the whirlwind, in turn, volleyed pitiless questions upon the suppliant—questions that have, in truth, precisely the ring of modern science. For the Lord asked of Job by whose wisdom the hawk soars, and who had fathered the rain, or entered the storehouses of the snow.

A youth standing by, one Elihu, also played a role in this drama, for he 2 ventured diffidently to his protesting elder that it was not true that God failed to manifest Himself. He may speak in one way or another, though men do not perceive it. In consequence of this remark perhaps it would be well, whatever our individual beliefs, to consider what may be called the hidden teacher, lest we become too much concerned with the formalities of only one aspect of the education by which we learn.

We think we learn from teachers, and we sometimes do. But the teachers are not always to be found in school or in great laboratories. Sometimes what we learn depends upon our own powers of insight. Moreover, our teachers may be hidden, even the greatest teacher. And it was the young man Elihu who observed that if the old are not always wise, neither can the teacher's way be ordered by the young whom he would teach.

For example, I once received an unexpected lesson from a spider.

5 It happened far away on a rainy morning in the West. I had come up a long gulch looking for fossils, and there, just at eye level, lurked a huge yellow-and-black orb spider, whose web was moored to the tall spears of buffalo grass at the edge of the arroyo. It was her universe, and her senses did not extend beyond the lines and spokes of the great wheel she inhabited. Her extended claws could feel every vibration throughout that delicate structure. She knew the tug of wind, the fall of a raindrop, the flutter of a trapped moth's wing. Down one spoke of the web ran a stout ribbon of gossamer on which she could hurry out to investigate her prey.

6 Curious, I took a pencil from my pocket and touched a strand of the web. Immediately there was a response. The web, plucked by its menacing occupant, began to vibrate until it was a blur. Anything that had brushed claw or wing against that amazing snare would be thoroughly entrapped. As the vibrations slowed, I could see the owner fingering her guidelines for signs of struggle. A pencil point was an intrusion into this universe for which no precedent existed. Spider was circumscribed by spider ideas; its universe was spider universe. All outside was irrational, extraneous, at best raw material for spider. As I proceeded on my way along the gully, like a vast impossible shadow, I realized that in the world of spider I did not exist.

7 Moreover, I considered, as I tramped along, that to the phagocytes, the white blood cells, clambering even now with some kind of elementary intelligence amid the thin pipes and tubing of my body—creatures without whose ministrations I could not exist—the conscious "I" of which I was aware had no significance to these amoeboid beings. I was, instead, a kind of chemical web that brought meaningful messages to them, a natural environment seemingly immortal if they could have thought about it, since generations of them had lived and perished, and would continue to so live and die, in that odd fabric which contained my intelligence—a misty light that was beginning to seem floating and tenuous even to me.

8 I began to see that, among the many universes in which the world of living creatures existed, some were large, some small, but that all, including man's, were in some way limited or finite. We were creatures of many

different dimensions passing through each other's lives like ghosts through doors.

In the years since, my mind has many times returned to that far moment of my encounter with the orb spider. A message has arisen only now from the misty shreds of that webbed universe. What was it that had so troubled me about the incident? Was it that spidery indifference to the human triumph? 9

If so, that triumph was very real and could not be denied. I saw, had many times seen, both mentally and in the seams of exposed strata, the long backward stretch of time whose recovery is one of the great feats of modern science. I saw the drifting cells of the early seas from which all life, including our own, has arisen. The salt of those ancient seas is in our blood, its lime is in our bones. Every time we walk along a beach some ancient urge disturbs us so that we find ourselves shedding shoes and garments or scavenging among seaweed and whitened timbers like the homesick refugees of a long war. 10

And war it has been indeed—the long war of life against its inhospitable environment, a war that has lasted for perhaps three billion years. It began with strange chemicals seething under a sky lacking in oxygen; it was waged through long ages until the first green plants learned to harness the light of the nearest star, our sun. The human brain, so frail, so perishable, so full of inexhaustible dreams and hungers, burns by the power of the leaf. 11

The hurrying blood cells charged with oxygen carry more of that element to the human brain than to any other part of the body. A few moments' loss of vital air and the phenomenon we know as consciousness goes down into the black night of inorganic things. The human body is a magical vessel, but its life is linked with an element it cannot produce. Only the green plant knows the secret of transforming the light that comes to us across the far reaches of space. There is no better illustration of the intricacy of man's relationship with other living things. 12

The student of fossil life would be forced to tell us that if we take the past into consideration the vast majority of earth's creatures—perhaps over 90 percent—have vanished. Forms that flourished for a far longer time than man has existed upon earth have become either extinct or so transformed that their descendants are scarcely recognizable. The specialized perish with the environment that created them, the tooth of the tiger fails at last, the lances of men strike down the last mammoth. 13

In three billion years of slow change and groping effort only one living creature has succeeded in escaping the trap of specialization that has led in time to so much death and wasted endeavor. It is man, but the word should be uttered softly, for his story is not yet done. 14

With the rise of the human brain, with the appearance of a creature whose upright body enabled two limbs to be freed for the exploration and manipulation of his environment, there had at last emerged a creature with a specialization—the brain—that, paradoxically, offered escape from specialization. Many animals driven into the nooks and crannies of nature have achieved momentary survival only at the cost of later extinction.

Was it this that troubled me and brought my mind back to a tiny universe among the grass blades, a spider's universe concerned with spider thought?

Perhaps.

The mind that once visualized animals on a cave wall is now engaged in a vast ramification of itself through time and space. Man has broken through the boundaries that control all other life. I saw, at last, the reason for my recollection of that great spider on the arroyo's rim, fingering its universe against the sky.

The spider was a symbol of man in miniature. The wheel of the web brought the analogy home clearly. Man, too, lies at the heart of a web, a web extending through the starry reaches of sidereal space, as well as backward into the dark realm of prehistory. His great eye upon Mount Palomar looks into a distance of millions of light-years, his radio ear hears the whisper of even more remote galaxies, he peers through the electron microscope upon the minute particles of his own being. It is a web no creature of earth has ever spun before. Like the orb spider, man lies at the heart of it, listening. Knowledge has given him the memory of earth's history beyond the time of his emergence. Like the spider's claw, a part of him touches a world he will never enter in the flesh. Even now, one can see him reaching forward into time with new machines, computing, analyzing, until elements of the shadowy future will also compose part of the invisible web he fingers.

Yet still my spider lingers in memory against the sunset sky. Spider thoughts in a spider universe—sensitive to raindrop and moth flutter, nothing beyond, nothing allowed for the unexpected, the inserted pencil from the world outside.

Is man at heart any different from the spider, I wonder: man thoughts, as limited as spider thoughts, contemplating now the nearest star with the threat of bringing with him the fungus rot from earth, wars, violence, the burden of a population he refuses to control, cherishing again his dream of the Adamic Eden he had pursued and lost in the green forests of America. Now it beckons again like a mirage from beyond the moon. Let man spin his web, I thought further; it is his nature. But I considered also the work of the phagocytes swarming in the rivers of my body, the unresting cells in their mortal universe. What is it we are a part of that we do not see, as the spider was not gifted to discern my face, or my little probe into her world?

We are too content with our sensory extensions, with the fulfillment of 22
that Ice Age mind that began its journey amidst the cold of vast tundras and that pauses only briefly before its leap into space. It is no longer enough to see as a man sees—even to the ends of the universe. It is not enough to hold nuclear energy in one's hand like a spear, as a man would hold it, or to see the lighting, or times past, or time to come, as a man would see it. If we continue to do this, the great brain—the human brain—will be only a new version of the old trap, and nature is full of traps for the beast that cannot learn.

It is not sufficient any longer to listen at the end of a wire to the rustling 23
of galaxies; it is not enough even to examine the great coil of DNA in which is coded the very alphabet of life. These are our extended perceptions. But beyond lies the great darkness of the ultimate Dreamer, who dreamed the light and the galaxies. Before act was, or substance existed, imagination grew in the dark. Man partakes of that ultimate wonder and creativeness. As we turn from the galaxies to the swarming cells of our own being, which toil for something, some entity beyond their grasp, let us remember man, the self-fabricator who came across an ice age to look into the mirrors and the magic of science. Surely he did not come to see himself or his wild visage only. He came because he is at heart a listener and a searcher for some transcendent realm beyond himself. This he has worshiped by many names, even in the dismal caves of his beginning. Man, the self-fabricator, is so by reason of gifts he had no part in devising—and so he searches as the single living cell in the beginning must have sought the ghostly creature it was to serve.

II

The young man Elihu, Job's counselor and critic, spoke simply of the 24
"Teacher," and it is of this teacher I speak when I refer to gifts man had no part in devising. Perhaps—though it is purely a matter of emotional reactions to words—it is easier for us today to speak of this teacher as "nature," that omnipresent all which contained both the spider and my invisible intrusion into her carefully planned universe. But nature does not simply represent reality. In the shapes of life, it prepares the future; it offers alternatives. Nature teaches, though what it teaches is often hidden and obscure, just as the voice from the spinning dust cloud belittled Job's thought but gave back no answers to its own formidable interrogation.

A few months ago I encountered an amazing little creature on a windy 25
corner of my local shopping center. It seemed, at first glance, some long-limbed, feathery spider teetering rapidly down the edge of a store front. Then it swung into the air and, as hesitantly as a spider on a thread, blew

away into the parking lot. It returned in a moment on a gust of wind and ran toward me once more on its spindly legs with amazing rapidity.

With great difficulty I discovered the creature was actually a filamentous 2
seed, seeking a hiding place and scurrying about with the uncanny surety of a conscious animal. In fact, it *did* escape me before I could secure it. Its flexible limbs were stiffer than milkweed down, and, propelled by the wind, it ran rapidly and evasively over the pavement. It was like a gnome scampering somewhere with a hidden packet—for all that I could tell, a totally new one: one of the jumbled alphabets of life.

A new one? So stable seem the years and all green leaves, a botanist 2
might smile at my imaginings. Yet bear with me a moment. I would like to tell a tale, a genuine tale of childhood. Moreover, I was just old enough to know the average of my kind and to marvel at what I saw. And what I saw was straight from the hidden Teacher, whatever be his name.

It is told in the Orient of the Hindu god Krishna that his mother, wiping 2
his mouth when he was a child, inadvertently peered in and beheld the universe, though the sight was mercifully and immediately veiled from her. In a sense, this is what happened to me. One day there arrived at our school a newcomer, who entered the grade above me. After some days this lad, whose look of sleepy-eyed arrogance is still before me as I write, was led into my mathematics classroom by the principal. Our class was informed severely that we should learn to work harder.

With this preliminary exhortation, great rows of figures were chalked 2
upon the blackboard, such difficult mathematical problems as could be devised by adults. The class watched in helpless wonder. When the preparations had been completed, the young pupil sauntered forward and, with a glance of infinite boredom that swept from us to his fawning teachers, wrote the answers, as instantaneously as a modern computer, in their proper place upon the board. Then he strolled out with a carelessly exaggerated yawn.

Like some heavy-browed child at the wood's edge, clutching the last 3
stone hand ax, I was witnessing the birth of a new type of humanity—one so beyond its teachers that it was being used for mean purposes while the intangible web of the universe in all its shimmering mathematical perfection glistened untaught in the mind of a chance little boy. The boy, by then grown self-centered and contemptuous, was being dragged from room to room to encourage us, the paleanthropes, to duplicate what, in reality, our teachers could not duplicate. He was too precious an object to be released upon the playground among us, and with reason. In a few months his parents took him away.

Long after, looking back from maturity, I realized that I had been 3
exposed on that occasion, not to human teaching, but to the Teacher, toying with some sixteen billion nerve cells interlocked in ways past under-

standing. Or, if we do not like the anthropomorphism implied in the word teacher, then nature, the old voice from the whirlwind fumbling for the light. At all events, I had been the fortunate witness to life's unbounded creativity—a creativity seemingly still as unbalanced and chance-filled as in that far era when a black-scaled creature had broken from an egg and the age of the giant reptiles, the creatures of the prime, had tentatively begun.

Because form cannot be long sustained in the living, we collapse 32
inward with age. We die. Our bodies, which were the product of a kind of hidden teaching by an alphabet we are only beginning dimly to discern, are dismissed into their elements. What is carried onward, assuming we have descendants, is the little capsule of instructions such as I encountered hastening by me in the shape of a running seed. We have learned the first biological lesson: that in each generation life passes through the eye of a needle. It exists for a time molecularly and in no recognizable semblance to its adult condition. It *instructs* its way again into man or reptile. As the ages pass, so do variants of the code. Occasionally, a species vanishes on a wind as unreturning as that which took the pterodactyls.

Or the code changes by subtle degrees through the statistical altering 33
of individuals; until I, as the fading Neanderthals must once have done, have looked with still-living eyes upon the creature whose genotype was quite possibly to replace me. The genetic alphabets, like genuine languages, ramify and evolve along unreturning pathways.

If nature's instructions are carried through the eye of a needle, through 34
the molecular darkness of a minute world below the field of human vision and of time's decay, the same, it might be said, is true of those monumental structures known as civilizations. They are transmitted from one generation to another in invisible puffs of air known as words—words that can also be symbolically incised on clay. As the delicate printing on the mud at the water's edge retraces a visit of autumn birds long since departed, so the little scrabbled tablets in perished cities carry the seeds of human thought across the deserts of millennia. In this instance the teacher is the social brain, but it, too, must be compressed into minute hieroglyphs, and the minds that wrought the miracle efface themselves amidst the jostling torrent of messages, which, like the genetic code, are shuffled and reshuffled as they hurry through eternity. Like a mutation, an idea may be recorded in the wrong time, to lie latent like a recessive gene and spring once more to life in an auspicious era.

Occasionally, in the moments when an archaeologist lifts the slab over 35
a tomb that houses a great secret, a few men gain a unique glimpse through that dark portal out of which all men living have emerged, and through which messages again must pass. Here the Mexican archaeologist Ruz Lhuillier speaks of his first penetration of the great tomb hidden beneath dripping stalactites at the pyramid of Palenque: "Out of the dark shadows,

rose a fairy-tale vision, a weird ethereal spectacle from another world. It was like a magician's cave carved out of ice, with walls glittering and sparkling like snow crystals." After shining his torch over hieroglyphs and sculptured figures, the explorer remarked wonderingly: "We were the first people for more than a thousand years to look at it."

Or again, one may read the tale of an unknown pharaoh who had 36
secretly arranged that a beloved woman of his household should be buried in the tomb of the god-king—an act of compassion carrying a personal message across the millennia in defiance of all precedent.

Up to this point we have been talking of the single hidden teacher, 37
the taunting voice out of that old Biblical whirlwind which symbolizes nature. We have seen incredible organic remembrance passed through the needle's eye of a microscosmic world hidden completely beneath the observational powers of creatures preoccupied and ensorcelled by dissolution and decay. We have seen the human mind unconsciously seize upon the principles of that very code to pass its own societal memory forward into time. The individual, the momentary living cell of the society, vanishes, but the institutional structures stand, or if they change, do so in an invisible flux not too dissimilar from that persisting in the stream of genetic continuity.

Upon this world, life is still young, not truly old as stars are measured. 38
Therefore it comes about that we minimize the role of the synapsid reptiles, our remote forerunners, and correspondingly exalt our own intellectual achievements. We refuse to consider that in the old eye of the hurricane we may be, and doubtless are, in aggregate, a slightly more diffuse and dangerous dragon of the primal morning that still enfolds us.

Note that I say "in aggregate." For it is just here, among men, that the 39
role of messages, and, therefore, the role of the individual teacher—or, I should say now, the hidden teachers—begin to be more plainly apparent and their instructions become more diverse. The dead pharaoh, though unintentionally, by a revealing act, had succeeded in conveying an impression of human tenderness that has outlasted the trappings of a vanished religion.

Like most modern educators I have listened to student demands to 40
grade their teachers. I have heard the words repeated until they have become a slogan, that no man over thirty can teach the young of this generation. How would one grade a dead pharaoh, millennia gone, I wonder, one who did not intend to teach, but who, to a few perceptive minds, succeeded by the simple nobility of an act.

Many years ago, a student who was destined to become an interna- 41
tionally known anthropologist sat in a course in linguistics and heard his instructor, a man of no inconsiderable wisdom, describe some linguistic peculiarities of Hebrew words. At the time, the young student, at the urging

of his family, was contemplating a career in theology. As the teacher warmed to his subject, the student, in the back row, ventured excitedly, "I believe I can understand that, sir. It is very similar to what exists in Mohegan."

The linguist paused and adjusted his glasses. "Young man," he said, "Mohegan is a dead language. Nothing has been recorded of it since the eighteenth century. Don't bluff." 42

"But sir," the young student countered hopefully, "It can't be dead so long as an old woman I know still speaks it. She is Pequot-Mohegan. I learned a bit of vocabulary from her and could speak with her myself. She took care of me when I was a child." 43

"Young man," said the austere, old-fashioned scholar, "be at my house for dinner at six this evening. You and I are going to look into this matter." 44

A few months later, under careful guidance, the young student published a paper upon Mohegan linguistics, the first of a long series of studies upon the forgotten languages and ethnology of the Indians of the northeastern forests. He had changed his vocation and turned to anthropology because of the attraction of a hidden teacher. But just who was the teacher? The young man himself, his instructor, or that solitary speaker of a dying tongue who had so yearned to hear her people's voice that she had softly babbled it to a child? 45

Later, this man was to become one of my professors. I absorbed much from him, though I hasten to make the reluctant confession that he was considerably beyond thirty. Most of what I learned was gathered over cups of coffee in a dingy campus restuarant. What we talked about were things some centuries older than either of us. Our common interest lay in snakes, scapulimancy, and other forgotten rites of benighted forest hunters. 46

I have always regarded this man as an extraordinary individual, in fact, a hidden teacher. But alas, it is all now so old-fashioned. We never protested the impracticality of his quaint subjects. We were all too ready to participate in them. He was an excellent canoeman, but he took me to places where I fully expected to drown before securing my degree. To this day, fragments of his unused wisdom remain stuffed in some back attic of my mind. Much of it I have never found the opportunity to employ, yet it has somehow colored my whole adult existence. I belong to that elderly professor in somewhat the same way that he, in turn, had become the wood child of a hidden forest mother. 47

There are, however, other teachers. For example, among the hunting peoples there were the animal counselors who appeared in prophetic dreams. Or, among the Greeks, the daemonic supernaturals who stood at the headboard while a man lay stark and listened—sometimes to dreadful things. "You are asleep," the messengers proclaimed over and over again, as though the man lay in a spell to hear his doom pronounced. "You, 48

Achilles, you, son of Atreus. You are asleep, asleep," the hidden ones pronounced and vanished.

We of this modern time know other things of dreams, but we know also that they can be interior teachers and healers as well as the anticipators of disaster. It has been said that great art is the night thought of man. It may emerge without warning from the soundless depths of the unconscious, just as supernovas may blaze up suddenly in the farther reaches of void space. The critics, like astronomers, can afterward triangulate such worlds but not account for them. 49

A writer friend of mine with bitter memories of his youth, and estranged from his family, who, in the interim, had died, gave me this account of the matter in his middle years. He had been working, with an unusual degree of reluctance, upon a novel that contained certain autobiographical episodes. One night he dreamed; it was a very vivid and stunning dream in its detailed reality. 50

He found himself hurrying over creaking snow through the blackness of a winter night. He was ascending a familiar path through a long-vanished orchard. The path led to his childhood home. The house, as he drew near, appeared dark and uninhabited, but, impelled by the power of the dream, he stepped upon the porch and tried to peer through a dark window into his own old room. 51

"Suddenly," he told me, "I was drawn by a strange mixture of repulsion and desire to press my face against the glass. I knew intuitively they were all there waiting for me within, if I could see them. My mother and my father. Those I had loved and those I hated. But the window was black to my gaze. I hesitated a moment and struck a match. For an instant in that freezing silence I saw my father's face glimmer wan and remote behind the glass. My mother's face was there, with the hard, distorted lines that marked her later years. 52

"A surge of furty overcame my cowardice. I cupped the match before me and stepped closer, closer toward that dreadful confrontation. As the match guttered down, my face was pressed almost to the glass. In some quick transformation, such as only a dream can effect, I saw that it was my own face into which I stared, just as it was reflected in the black glass. My father's haunted face was but my own. The hard lines upon my mother's aging countenance were slowly reshaping themselves upon my living face. The light burned out. I awoke sweating from the terrible psychological tension of that nightmare. I was in a far port in a distant land. It was dawn. I could hear the waves breaking on the reef." 53

"And how do you interpret the dream?" I asked, concealing a sympathetic shudder and sinking deeper into my chair. 54

"It taught me something," he said slowly, and with equal slowness a kind of beautiful transfiguration passed over his features. All the tired lines I had known so well seemed faintly to be subsiding. 55

"Did you ever dream it again?" I asked out of a comparable experience of my own. 56

"No, never," he said, and hesitated. "You see, I had learned it was just I, but more, much more, I had learned that I was they. It makes a difference. And at the last, late—much too late—it was all right. I understood. My line was dying, but I understood. I hope they understood, too." His voice trailed into silence. 57

"It is a thing to learn," I said. "You were seeking something and it came." He nodded, wordless. "Out of a tomb," he added after a silent moment, "my kind of tomb—the mind." 58

On the dark street, walking homeward, I considered my friend's experience. Man, I concluded, may have come to the end of that wild being who had mastered the fire and the lightning. He can create the web but not hold it together, not save himself except by transcending his own image. For at last, before the ultimate mystery, it is himself he shapes. Perhaps it is for this that the listening web lies open: that by knowledge we may grow beyond our past, our follies, and ever closer to what the Dreamer in the dark intended before the dust rose and walked. In the pages of an old book it has been written that we are in the hands of a Teacher, nor does it yet appear what man shall be. 59

(1964)

Teaching Shakespeare's Sister: Notes from the Underground of Female Adolescence

Carol Gilligan

Carol Gilligan (b. 1936) has, for the past decade, devoted her research to the psychological development of women. In a Different Voice: Psychological Theory and Women's Development *(1982) earned considerable attention for its argument that women and men use different criteria for making ethical decisions. The following essay was first published in the Spring–Summer 1991 issue of* Women's Studies Quarterly.

. . . Interviewing girls in adolescence, in the time between the twelve-year-old's knowing and the adult woman's remembering, I felt at times that I had entered an underground world, that I was led in by girls to caverns of knowledge that were then suddenly covered over, as if nothing were known and nothing were happening. What I heard was at once familiar and surprising: girls' knowledge of the human social world, a knowledge gleaned by seeing and listening, by piecing together thoughts and feelings, sounds and glances, responses and reactions, until they compose a pattern, 1 compelling in its explanatory power and often intricate in its psychological logic. Such knowledge on the part of girls is not represented in descriptions of psychological development nor in clinical case studies, and, more disturbingly, it is disclaimed by adolescent girls themselves, who often seem divided from their own knowledge and preface their observations by saying "I don't know."

At a school for girls in a large midwestern city, twelve-year-olds, when 2
asked to describe a powerful learning experience, were as likely to describe an experience that took place inside as outside of school. By fifteen more than twice as many girls located powerful learning experiences outside of school rather than inside. With respect to the nature of such experiences, girls at fifteen were more likely than girls at twelve to talk about experiences outside of school in which family or friends or other people they knew were the central catalysts of learning.[23] Between the ages of twelve and fifteen—the time when dropping out of school becomes common in the inner city—the education of girls seems to be moving out of the public sphere and into the private realm. Is this the time, I wondered, when girls' knowledge becomes buried? Was girls' learning going underground?

The question surfaced in reflecting on my experiences in interviewing 3
adolescent girls at Emma Willard School in Troy, New York. The isolated setting of the residential school and its walled enclosure made it something of a strange island in the stream of contemporary living, an odd mixture of old world and new. In this resonant setting I heard girls speak about storms in relationships and pleasure in relationships, revealing a knowledge of relationships that often was grounded in detailed descriptions of inner psychic worlds—relational worlds through which girls sometimes moved freely and which at other times seemed blocked or walled. Listening for this knowledge, I felt myself entering, to some extent, the underground city of female adolescence, the place where powerful learning experiences were happening. The gateway to this underworld was marked by the statement "I don't know"—the sign of repression—and the code word of membership or the password was the phrase "you know." I wondered about the relationship between this knowledge and girls' other life of notebooks, lessons, and homework.

One afternoon, in the second year of the study, toward the end of an 4

Editors note: Footnotes 1–22 appear in an earlier section of this reading not excerpted here.

23. Alan Braun, "Themes of Connection: Powerful Learning among Adolescent Girls" (Working Paper, Laurel/Harvard Study, Project on the Psychology of Women and the Development of Girls, Harvard Graduate School of Education), 3.

interview with Gail, a girl with whom I had not made much contact, I asked if she were curious about the "it" that she was describing—"the problem" that stood between her and her being "able to achieve anywhere near [her] potential," the thing that kept her from "getting [her] act together." Gail said that she did not know whether she would "ever understand what the problem was," but, she said, "I hope that someday it will be gone and I will be happy." I asked how it will go away. She said she did not know, but that it would be "sad if it doesn't." I asked if she were curious; she said she did not know. We went on with the interview questions. As she thought about herself in the future, I asked, how did she imagine her life, what expectations did she feel others had for her, what were her hopes for herself? She was waiting, she said, to see if "it happens." She felt she had come up against "this big wall." We went on. At the end Gail said, "Maybe someday I will draw it." It seemed that she knew what it looked like. I asked what color she would make it: "Kind of deep ivory," she said. What shape? "A giant block of ice. This tall . . . very thick. A cube standing in front of me." She said that she could melt it, but that she would "have to use very high temperatures."

The water, I thought, that the twelve-year-old girls in the poems were 5
sitting next to had frozen. Its surface no longer moved, no longer reflected. What was once liquid had become solid, turning into "this big wall."

The following year Gail, now a senior, began by talking to me in the 6
language of social science. "I would like to mention," she said, "that, having thought about my last two interviews, it occurs to me that it is hard to get the real opinions of teenage girls as young as we are because a lot of girls really don't know what they think." If I had interviewed her on another day, or if I were a different person, I would "get very different things," especially because "a lot of the questions you asked are not questions that I have ever put to myself . . . and afterwards I wondered, you know, did I really mean that. . . . I don't feel you are getting what is important to me; you are getting that and other things in equal weight." I asked, "So there is no way of knowing [what's true and what's important]?" She agreed.

I began with the interview questions. "Looking back over the past 7
year. . . ." I suggested that as we went along she might tell me which questions were ones that she had put to herself and which—Gail suddenly switched modes of discourse. She said, "I actually feel a great deal older this year." One way of speaking about herself ("Teenage girls . . . really don't know what they think") yielded to another ("I actually feel . . ."). The relationship between these two ways of speaking about herself seemed critical. In the terms of her own imagery, one way of speaking shored up the wall between herself and her knowledge, and one provided a sense of an opening, a place of entry, which led through knowing how she was feeling. "I really feel able," Gail explained, taking the opening,

> to put myself in perspective about a lot of things that were confusing me about myself, and I have a tendency to keep things to myself, things that bother me. I keep them in and then I start feeling like this, just harassed and I can't really—everything just warps my perception of everything. . . . But I have discovered the reason for my whole block. I mean, I was getting bad grades, and I told you about a mysterious block last year that was like a wall.
> *I remember that.*
> Now, I figured out what was going on. I figured this out last week. It is that, all through my childhood, I interpreted what my parents were saying to me in my mind. I never voiced this interpretation.

The unvoiced or unspoken, being out of relationship, had gotten out of perspective—"just warp[ing] my perception of everything." What Gail interpreted her parents as saying to her was that she should "be independent and self-sufficient from a very early age." Thus, Gail said, "anything that interrupted my sense of what I should be I would soak up into myself, as though I were a big sponge and had tremendous shock capacity to just bounce back." What Gail was taking in was clearly something that she found shocking, but she felt that she should act as though she were a sponge and just soak up the shock by herself. So, she said, "I would feel bad about things, [but] I wouldn't do anything about them. I wouldn't say anything. That goes with grades and personal problems and relationships"—much of her adolescent life. And then, she said, "last week, last Wednesday, this whole thing came over me, and I can really feel that now I can understand what was going on with me. I can put my life in perspective." Thus, Gail explained that she no longer had to not know: "What's happening, what's happening with me? What is going on? Why am I not being able to see? Why is this so hard for me? And then of course when I finally let it out, maybe every six months, it is like a chair casting shadows and making tremendous spokes. Everything becomes monumental. I feel terrible, and it is really very disturbing." With this powerful image of "it" as "a chair casting shadows and making tremendous spokes," Gail conveys how the ordinary can become monumental and very disturbing. What is explicit in this passage is that Gail became disconnected from her own thoughts and feelings and found herself asking questions about herself that she then could not answer. In threatening this disconnection, the process of knowing had become overwhelming. I asked Gail if she had a sense of what had led her to the understanding she described, and she spoke about a conversation with a friend: 8

> It started when my friend was telling me how angry she was at her math teacher, who when she asked for extra help must have been in

> a bad mood and was angry with her. I was thinking about the way my stepfather would do the same thing. And then I was thinking about my stepfather, and then I decided that I really have been abused as a child, not physically, but even last summer, whenever he has insecurity, he is very jealous of me, he is insecure with my mother, and then he just lashes out at me and criticizes me to no end, very angrily. And for a person who has grown up with that and who really doesn't understand herself—instead of saying, "Wait a minute. What are you doing? I am a person."—I would just cuddle up and make like a rock. Tense all my muscles and just sit there and listen to it and be relieved when it was over. And then I was thinking about myself and my reactions to things, and I was thinking all year about all the problems I had last year. . . . It is all my holding back. And I really feel I have made a temendous breakthrough.

Joining her friend in voicing anger in response to anger rather than just soaking it up like a sponge or tensing her muscles and becoming like a rock, Gail felt she had broken through the wall that was holding back her "reactions to things," her feelings and thoughts.

"It was amazing," I said, "to see it that way," responding to Gail's precise 9
description of psychological processes—the step-by-step tracing of her own feelings and thoughts in response to her friend's story about anger and the math teacher as well as her analysis of how insecurity and jealousy breed attack. "My mother," Gail said, turning to the missing person in the drama (and signaling by the phrase "you know" that this was in part an underground story):

> came down the day before yesterday, and I told her about it. She has been worried about me day and night since I was little because of my holding back. She would say, "You are holding your light under a bushel," and then, you know, get very upset once or twice a year, because everything would get [to be] too much, you know. Of course, my mother would have tremendous guilt. . . . "What have I done to this poor child? I don't really know what I have done, but there is something. What is it?"

"You have read *Oedipus Rex*?" Gail asks me. I had. "Well, Oedipus 10
went through his entire life weighing himself by himself, and I have done that, and that is what allows me to get out of proportion. I don't talk about anything with anybody, anything that is bothering me."

I thought of the queen in the Oedipus story. Gail's description of her 11
mother had caught the franticness of Jocasta as she tries to keep Oedipus from knowing the truth about family relations. No more truth, she pleads.

Was Gail hearing a similar plea from her mother? The problem was that "it"—the unnamed or unspoken truth—"just rolls up like a snowball, and it gets bigger and bigger, and my perception just warps out of shape" so that, like Oedipus, Gail cannot see what in another sense she knows. Her question to herself—"Why am I not able to see?"—resonates with the question she attributes to her mother: "What have I done to this poor child?" But Gail also lays out the logic that suppressed her questions about suffering and about women. Gail reasoned that, if her stepfather's attacks had truly been hurtful to her, then her mother would have taken action to stop them. Because her mother did nothing, at least as far as Gail was aware of, Gail concluded that her stepfather's verbal lashings could not really have hurt her. To feel her feelings then posed difficult questions: what does it mean to be a good mother, what does it mean for a mother to love her daughter, and what does it mean for a daughter to love both her mother and herself?

The either/or logic that Gail was learning as an adolescent, the straight- 12
line categories of Western thinking (self/other, mind/body, thought/feelings, past/present) and the if/then construction of linear reasoning threatened to undermine Gail's knowledge of human relationships by washing out the logic of feelings. To understand psychological processes means to follow the both/and logic of feelings and to trace the currents of associations, memories, sounds, and images that flow back and forth, connecting self and other, mind and body, past and present, consciousness and culture. To separate thinking from relationship, and thus to make a division between formal education and powerful learning experiences, is to become like Oedipus, who got things out of proportion by "weighing himself by himself." Gail ties the return of perspective to the return of relationship and describes the insight and knowledge that suddenly came out of the back-and-forth play of her conversation with her friend: "I talked to my friend, and she talked about her math teacher, and I was thinking about my stepfather, and then, with all my thinking about it beforehand, wondering what makes a difference, I finally put it together and bang! . . . Before, when I was getting all tied up, everything was a huge wall that isn't a wall anymore." The "it" is no longer a wall but a relationship that joins Gail with herself and with her friend.

The image of a wall recurred in interviews with adolescent girls—a 13
physical rendering of the blocks preventing connection, the impasses in relationships, which girls acutely described and which were associated with intense feelings of anger and sadness. Girls' wishes to make connection with others reflected the pelasure that they found in relationships.

Pleasure in relationships is linked to knowledge gained through rela- 14
tionships, and girls voice their desire to know more about others and also to be known better themselves. "I wish to become better in the relationship

with my mother," Ellen says—"to be able more easily to disagree with her." Disagreement here is a sign of relationship, a manifestation of two people coming together. And it is in close relationships that girls are most willing to argue or disagree, wanting most to be known and seen by those to whom they feel closest and also believing more that those who are close will be there, will listen, and will try to understand. "If you love someone," Anna explains, "you are usually comfortable with them. And, feeling comfortable, you can easily argue with one another and say, look, I want you to see my side. It's a lot easier to fight with someone you love, because you know they will always forgive you, at least usually they will . . . and you know that they are still going to be there for you after the disagreement."

Perhaps it is because of this feeling of being comfortable that girls most 15
often speak about conflict in their relationships with their mothers—the person who, one girl said, "will always welcome me." Girls' willingness to fight for genuine connection with their mothers is well illustrated by Kate, a fifteen-year-old who says, paradoxically:

> I called my mother up and said, "Why can't I speak to you anymore? What is going on?" And I ended up crying and hanging up on her because she wouldn't listen to me. She had her own opinion about what was truth and what was reality, and she gave me no opening. . . . What she had on her mind was the truth. And you know, I kept saying, "Well, you hurt me," and she said, "No, I did not." And I said, "Well, why am I hurt?" you know, and she is just denying my feelings as if they did not exist and as if I had no right to feel them, you know, even though they were.

The counterpart to the image of a wall is the search for an opening, a 16
way of reaching another person, of finding a place of entry. Yet to open oneself to another person creates a great vulnerability, and thus the strength of girls' desire for relationship also engenders the need for protection from fraudulent relationships and psychic wounding. "To me," Jane says, "love means an attachment to a person," by which she means a willingness or wish

> to share a lot of things with that person and not feel as though you are opening up your soul and it is going to be misrepresented or misunderstood. Rather, so that person . . . will know kind of inside how far to go and, if they go too far, they will understand when you say, that's not what I want . . . where people accept your idiosyncracies . . . that you can have fun and you can disagree but that the argument isn't something that wounds you for months. . . . Some people are too quick to say "I love you." It takes time to learn someone.

> I don't think you can love on first sight. . . . You can feel a connection with someone, but you can't just love them.

These carefully drawn distinctions, the contrast between feeling connected with someone and loving them and between having fun and disagreeing and having an argument that wounds you for months, bespeak close observation of relationships and psychological processes and also experiences of being misrepresented, misunderstood, and not listened to, which have left both knowledge and scars. Jane says she is looking for someone who will understand when she says, "that's not what I want." Mira, in contrast, has chosen silence as a way of avoiding being hurt:

> I personally have had a hard time asking questions . . . because I was shy and did not really like to talk to people about what I was really thinking.
>
> *Why not?*
>
> I thought it was much safer just to keep it to myself, and this way nobody would have so much of a vulnerable spot that they could get to me with. And so I thought, just the thought of having somebody having something on me that could possibly hurt me, that scared me and kept me from speaking up a lot of the time.

1

Like the character in Woolf's story, "An Unwritten Novel," Mira keeps her life to herself; her speaking self also is "entombed . . . driven in, in, in to the central catacomb. . . . Flit[ting] with its lanterns restlessly up and down the dark corridor."[24] Mary Belenky and her colleagues have described how women retreat into silence when words become weapons and are used to wound.[25] Adolescent girls invoke images of violence and talk in the language of warfare or about winning and losing when they describe the inner workings of explosive relationships, fearing also that such relationships can "throw us apart forever."

> *What is the worst thing that can happen in a relationship?*
>
> I guess if people build up resentments and don't talk about them, things can just keep building up until they reach the boiling point, and then there is like a cold war going on. People are just fencing on either side

24. Virginia Woolf, "An Unwritten Novel," *Haunted House and Other Short Stories* (1921; reprint, New York: Harcourt Brace Jovanovich, 1972), 19.
25. Mary Belenky, Blythe Clinchy, Nancy Goldberger, and Jill Tarule, *Women's Ways of Knowing* (New York: Basic Books, 1986).

> of a wall, but not admitting it to the other person until there is an explosion or something.

Other girls, like Emma, describe "building a wall" that serves to undermine relationships:

> *What is the worst thing that can happen in a relationship?*
> Not talking it out. Building a wall . . . I think that can lead to a lot more because you don't give a chance to the other person to say anything. . . . You are too close-minded to listen to what they have to say. . . . If you don't listen to your friends, they are not your friends, there is no relationship there, because you don't listen.

Taken together, these observations of the ways in which people move and affect, touch and are touched by one another, appear and disappear in relationships with themselves and with others, reveal an understanding of psychic processes that is closer to a physics than a metaphysics of relationship—based on tracking voices and images, thoughts and feelings, across the cloud chamber of daily life. Certain observations are breathtakingly simple in their logic although profound in their implications, especially given the pace of contemporary living. Emma says that, "if you don't listen to your friends, they are not your friends. There is no relationship there." Others are more complex, like Joan's exegesis of the indirect discourse of betrayal: "If you don't trust someone to know a secret . . . you sort of grow apart . . . or you will feel like you are with them and down underneath you are angry . . . but you don't say anything, so it comes out . . . in other ways." Or Maria's explication of the confusing mixing of anger and hurt: 18

> I am not sure of the difference when I feel angry and hurt. . . . I don't even know if they are separate emotions. . . . I was angry, I think at myself in that relationship, that I had let myself be used . . . that I had let down my guard so much. I was completely vulnerable. And I chose to do that. . . . I kept saying, "I hate him," but I realized that he didn't even notice me there because he was in his own world. So that I think . . . all my anger comes out of being hurt, and it's a confusion there.

Repeatedly, girls emphasize the need for open conflict and voicing disagreement. Catherine describes the fruitful quality of disagreement in her relationship with her friend: 19

> We have learned more about ourselves. . . . I think . . . she had never really had a close friend but lots of acquaintances. She didn't get into fights and things like that. . . . I think she realizes that you have to have disagreements and things like that for a relationship to last.
> *How come?*
> Because if you don't really voice your disagreements, then you don't really have anything going, do you know what I mean? It's just another way, it is another side of you that you are letting someone else see.

And Liza describes the raw pain of finding, at the end of a long journey, that you are not able to talk with someone on whom you had depended:

> *What is the worst thing that can happen in a relationship?*
> That you grow up, or sideways, and not be able to talk to each other, especially if you depend on being able to talk to someone and not being able to. That hurts a lot, because you have been dependent on that. It is like walking fifty miles for a glass of water in a hot desert, and you have been depending on it for days, and getting there and finding it is not there anymore; you made the wrong turn ten miles back.

The knowledge about relationships and the life of relationships that 20 flourish on this remote island of female adolescence are, to shift the metaphor, like notes from the underground. Much of what psychologists know about relationships is also known by adolescent girls. But, as girls themselves say clearly, they will speak only when they feel that someone will listen and will not leave in the face of conflict or disagreement. Thus, the fate of girls' knowledge and girls' education becomes tied to the fate of their relationships.

When women's studies is joined with the study of girls' development, 21 it becomes clearer why adolescence is a critical time in girls' lives—a time when girls are in danger of losing their voices and thus losing connection with others, and also a time when girls, gaining voice and knowledge, are in danger of knowing the unseen and speaking the unspoken and thus losing connection with what is commonly taken to be "reality." This crisis of connection in girls' lives at adolescence links the psychology of women with the most basic questions about the nature of relationships and the definition of reality. Girls' questions about relationships and about reality, however, also tug at women's silences.

At the edge of adolescence, eleven- and twelve-year-old girls observe 22 where and when women speak and when they are silent.[26] As resisters, they may be especially prone to notice and question the compliance of women to male authority. One of Woolf's questions in *A Room of One's Own* is why mothers do not provide more rooms for their daughters, why they do not leave more of a legacy for their daughters, and why, more specifically, mothers do not endow their daughters' education with greater comfort.[27] A teacher of twelve-year-olds, after a faculty meeting where women's reluctance to disagree in public became a subject of discussion, told the following story: her eleven-year-old daughter had commented on her reluctance to disagree with her husband (the girl's father). She was angry at her mother, she said, for always giving in. In response, the mother began to explain that, although the girl's father sometimes raised his voice, he was loving and well-intentioned—at which point her daughter interrupted her, saying that it was she, her mother, who she was angry at for always giving in. "I was so humiliated," the teacher said, "so ashamed." Later that year, when her colleague announced a new rule about lunch in homeroom one day, she suppressed her disagreement with him and did not voice her objections—because, she said, she did not want to undermine his authority. Perhaps it was as a result of her previous humiliation that she thought twice on a day when the rule seemed particularly senseless and excused some girls, in spite of the rule, before others who had arrived later at lunch had finished eating. "Good for you," the girls said, "we're proud of you." It was clear that they had noticed everything.

In his appreciation of the poetry of Sylvia Plath, Seamus Heaney reads 23
a famous passage by William Wordsworth as a parable of the three stages in a poet's journey.[28] At first one goes out into the woods and whistles to hear if the owls will respond. Then, once one discovers that one can speak in a way that calls forth a response from the world of nature, one has to learn to perfect one's craft, to enter the world of sounds—of birdcalls, traditions, and poetic convention—until, Heaney says, if one is blessed or fortunate, one becomes the instrument through which the sounds of the world pass. Heaney traces this transformation in Plath's poetry, drawing the reader into his own exhilaration as her language takes off. But Plath's relationship to the tradition of male voices, which she was entering and

26. Lyn Mikel Brown, "A Problem of Vision: The Development of Voice and Relational Knowledge in Girls Ages Seven to Sixteen," *Women's Studies Quarterly* (1991: vol. xix, 1, 2).
27. Virginia Woolf, *A Room of One's Own* (1928; reprint, New York: Harcourt Brace and World, 1957), 20–24.
28. Seamus Heaney, *The Government of the Tongue: Selected Prose, 1978–1987* (New York: Farrar, Strauss and Giroux, 1989).

changing by entering, was not the same as Heaney's, and her entrance was more deeply disruptive. And the same can be said for women students.

A student first must learn how to call forth a response from the world: 2
to ask a question to which people will listen, which they will find interesting and respond to. Then she must learn the craft of inquiry so that she can tune her questions and develop her ear for language and thus speak more clearly and more freely, can say more and also hear more fully. But if the world of nature, as Heaney implies, is equally responsive to the calls of women and men, the world of civilization is not, or at least has not been up to the present. The wind of tradition blowing through women is a chill wind because it brings a message of exclusion: stay out. It brings a message of subordination: stay under. It brings a message of objectification: become the object of another's worship or desire; see yourself as you have been seen for centuries, through a male gaze. And because all of the suffering, the endless litany of storm and shipwreck, is presented as necessary or even good for civilization, the message to women is: keep quiet, notice the absence of women, and say nothing.

At the present moment the education of women presents genuine dilem- 2
mas and real opportunities. Women's questions—especially questions about relationships and questions about violence—often feel disruptive to women because at present they are disruptive both in private and public life. And relationships between women are often strained. It is not at all clear what it means to be a good mother or teacher to an adolescent girl coming of age in Western culture. The choices that women make in order to survive or to appear good in the eyes of others and thus sustain their protection are often at the expense of women's relationships with one another, and girls begin to observe and comment on these choices around the age of eleven or twelve. If women can stay in the gaze of girls so that girls do not have to look and not see, if women can be seen by girls, including the twelve-year-old in themselves, if women can sustain girls' gazes and respond to girls' voices, then, perhaps as Woolf envisioned, "the opportunity will come and the dead poet who is Shakespeare's sister will put on the body which she has so often laid down and find it possible to live and write her poetry"[29]—as Plath did for a moment before taking her life. Yet as Woolf reminds us, before Shakespeare's sister can come, we must have the habit of freedom and the courage to write and say exactly what we think. . . .

---

29. Woolf, *A Room of One's Own*, 117.

Nobody Mean More to Me Than You and the Future Life of Willie Jordan

June Jordon

Poet, novelist, essayist, and writer of children's books, June Jordan (b. 1936) grew up in New York City and has taught at many colleges and universities, including the City College of New York, Yale University, and the University of California at Berkeley. Her poetry has appeared in several volumes, including Some Changes *(1971),* Things That I Do in the Dark *(1977),* Passion *(1980), and* Living Room *(1985). Her essays have been collected in* Civil Wars *(1981) and* On Call *(1985), in which the following essay appeared. An outspoken political activist, Jordan has been praised for "the breadth and diversity of her concerns, and . . . the wide variety of literary forms in which she expresses them. But the unifying element in all her activities is her fervent dedication to the survival of black people."*

Black English is not exactly a linguistic buffalo; as children, most of the thirty-five million Afro-Americans living here depend on this language for our discovery of the world. But then we approach our maturity inside a larger social body that will not support our efforts to become anything other than the clones of those who are neither our mothers nor our fathers. We begin to grow up in a house where every true mirror shows us the face of somebody who does not belong there, whose walk and whose talk will never look or sound "right," because that house was meant to shelter a family that is alien and hostile to us. As we learn our way around this environment, either we hide our original word habits, or we completely surrender our own voice, hoping to please those who will never respect anyone different from themselves: Black English is not exactly a linguistic buffalo, but we should understand its status as an endangered species, as a perishing, irreplaceable system of community intelligence, or we should expect its extinction, and, along with that, the extinguishing of much that constitutes our own proud, and singular identity. 1

What we casually call "English" less and less defers to England and its "gentlemen." "English" is no longer a specific matter of geography or an element of class privilege; more than thirty-three countries use this tool as a means of "intranational communication." Countries as disparate as Zimbabwe and Malaysia, or Israel and Uganda, use it as their non-native currency of convenience. Obviously, this tool, this "English," cannot function inside thirty-three discrete societies on the basis of rules and values 2 absolutely determined somewhere else, in a thirty-fourth other country, for example.

In addition to that staggering congeries of non-native users of English, there are five countries, or 333,746,000 people, for whom this thing called "English" serves as a native tongue. Approximately 10% of these native speakers of "English" are Afro-American citizens of the U.S.A. I cite these numbers and varieties of human beings dependent on "English" in order, quickly, to suggest how strange and how tenuous is any concept of "Standard English." Obviously, numerous forms of English now operate inside a natural, an uncontrollable, continuum of development. I would suppose "the standard" for English in Malaysia is not the same as "the standard" in Zimbabwe. I know that standard forms of English for Black people in this country do not copy those of whites. And, in fact, the structural differences between these two kinds of English have intensified, becoming more Black, or less white, despite the expected homogenizing effects of television and other mass media. 3

Nonetheless, white standards of English persist, supreme and unquestioned, in these United States. Despite our multi-lingual population, and despite the deepening Black and white cleavage within that conglomerate, white standards control our official and popular judgements of verbal proficiency and correct, or incorrect, language skills, including speech. In contrast to India, where at least fourteen languages co-exist as legitimate Indian languages, in contrast to Nicaragua, where all citizens are legally entitled to formal school instruction in their regional or tribal languages, compulsory education in America compels accommodation to exclusively white forms of "English." White English, in America, is "Standard English." 4

This story begins two years ago. I was teaching a new course, "In Search of the Invisible Black Woman," and my rather large class seemed evenly divided between young Black women and men. Five or six white students also sat in attendance. With unexpected speed and enthusiasm we had moved through historical narratives of the 19th century to literature by and about Black women, in the 20th. I had assigned the first forty pages of Alice Walker's *The Color Purple,* and I came, eagerly, to class that morning: 5

"So!" I exclaimed, aloud. "What did you think? How did you like it?" 6

The students studied their hands, or the floor. There was no response. The tense, resistant feeling in the room fairly astounded me. 7

At last, one student, a young woman still not meeting my eyes, muttered something in my direction: 8

"What did you say?" I prompted her. 9

"Why she have them talk so funny. It don't sound right." 10

"You mean the language?" 11

Another student lifted his head: "It don't look right, neither. I couldn't hardly read it." 12

At this, several students dumped on the book. Just about unanimously, 13 their criticisms targeted the language. I listened to what they wanted to say and silently marvelled at the similarities between their casual speech patterns and Alice Walker's written version of Black English.

But I decided against pointing to these identical traits of syntax; I 14 wanted not to make them self-conscious about their own spoken language—not while they clearly felt it was "wrong." Instead I decided to swallow my astonishment. Here was a negative Black reaction to a prize-winning accomplishment of Black literature that white readers across the country had selected as a best seller. Black rejection was aimed at the one irreducibly Black element of Walker's work: the language—Celie's Black English. I wrote the opening lines of *The Color Purple* on the blackboard and asked the students to help me translate these sentences into Standard English:

> *You better not never tell nobody but God. It'd kill you mammy.*
> Dear God,
> I am fourteen years old. I have always been a good girl. Maybe you can give me a sign letting me know what is happening to me.
> Last spring after Little Lucious come I heard them fussing. He was pulling on her arm. She say it too soon, Fonso. I aint well. Finally he leave her alone. A week go by, he pulling on her arm again. She say, Naw, I ain't gonna. Can't you see I'm already half dead, an all of the children.

Our process of translation exploded with hilarity and even hysterical, shocked laughter: The Black writer, Alice Walker, knew what she was doing! If rudimentary criteria for good fiction includes the manipulation of language so that the syntax and diction of sentences will tell you the identity of speakers, the probable age and sex and class of speakers, and even the locale—urban/rural/southern/western—then Walker had written, perfectly. This is the translation into Standard English that our class produced:

> *Absolutely, one should never confide in anybody besides God. Your secrets could prove devastating to your mother.*
> Dear God,
> I am fourteen years old. I have always been good. But now, could you help me to understand what is happening to me?
> Last spring, after my little brother, Lucious, was born. I heard my parents fighting. My father kept pulling at my mother's arm. But she

> told him, "It's too soon for sex, Alfonso. I am still not feeling well." Finally, my father left her alone. A week went by, and then he began bothering my mother again: pulling her arm. She told him, "No, I won't! Can't you see I'm already exhausted from all of these children?"

(Our favorite line was "It's too soon for sex, Alphonso.")

Once we could stop laughing, once we could stop our exponentially wild improvisations on the theme of Translated Black English, the students pushed me to explain their own negative first reactions to their spoken language on the printed page. I thought it was probably akin to the shock of seeing yourself in a photograph for the first time. Most of the students had never before seen a written facsimile of the way they talk. None of the students had ever learned how to read and write their own verbal system of communication: Black English. Alternatively, this fact began to baffle or else bemuse and then infuriate my students. Why not? Was it too late? Could they learn how to do it, now? And, ultimately, the final test question, the one testing my sincerity: Could I teach them? Because I had never taught anyone Black English and, as far as I knew, no one, anywhere in the United States, had ever offered such a course, the best I could say was "I'll try."

He looked like a wrestler.

He sat dead center in the packed room and, every time our eyes met, he quickly nodded his head as though anxious to reassure and encourage, me.

Short, with strikingly broad shoulders and long arms, he spoke with a surprisingly high, soft voice that matched the soft bright movement of his eyes. His name was Willie Jordan. He would have seemed even more unlikely in the context of Contemporary Women's Poetry, except that ten or twelve other Black men were taking the course, as well. Still, Willie was conspicuous. His extreme fitness, the muscular density of his presence underscored the riveted, gentle attention that he gave to anything anyone said. Generally, he did not join the loud and rowdy dialogue flying back and forth, but there could be no doubt about his interest in our discussions. And, when he stood to present an argument he'd prepared, overnight, that nervous smile of his vanished and an irregular stammering replaced it, as he spoke with visceral sincerity, word by word.

That was how I met Willie Jordan. It was in between "In Search of the Invisible Black Woman" and "The Art of Black English." I was waiting for Departmental approval and I supposed that Willie might be, so to speak, killing time until he, too, could study Black English. But Willie really did want to explore Contemporary Women's Poetry and, to that end, volunteered for extra research and never missed a class.

Towards the end of that semester, Willie approached me for an independent study project on South Africa. It would commence the next semester. I thought Willie's writing needed the kind of improvement only intense practice will yield. I knew his intelligence was outstanding. But he'd wholeheartedly opted for "Standard English" at a rather late age, and the results were stilted and frequently polysyllabic, simply for the sake of having more syllables. Willie's unnatural formality of language seemed to me consistent with the formality of his research into South African apartheid. As he projected his studies, he would have little time, indeed, for newspapers. Instead, more than 90% of his research would mean saturation in strictly historical, if not archival, material. I was certainly interested. It would be tricky to guide him into a more confident and spontaneous relationship with both language and apartheid. It was going to be wonderful to see what happened when he could catch up with himself, entirely, and talk back to the world. 21

September, 1984: Breezy fall weather and much excitement! My class, "The Art of Black English," was full to the limit of the fire laws. And, in Independent Study, Willie Jordan showed up, weekly, fifteen minutes early for each of our sessions. I was pretty happy to be teaching, altogether! 22

I remember an early class when a young brother, replete with his ever-present pork-pie hat, raised his hand and then told us that most of what he'd heard was "all right" except it was "too clean." "The brothers on the street," he continued, "they mix it up more. Like 'fuck' and 'motherfuck.' Or like 'shit.' " He waited. I waited. Then all of us laughed a good while, and we got into a brawl about "correct" and "realistic" Black English that led to Rule 1. 23

Rule 1: *Black English is about a whole lot more than mothafuckin.* 24

As a criterion, we decided, "realistic" could take you anywhere you want to go. Artful places. Angry places. Eloquent and sweetalkin places. Polemical places. Church. And the local Bar & Grill. We were checking out a language, not a mood or a scene or one guy's forgettable mouthing off. 25

It was hard. For most of the students, learning Black English required a fallback to patterns and rhythms of speech that many of their parents had beaten out of them. I mean *beaten.* And, in a majority of cases, correct Black English could be achieved only by striving for *incorrect* Standard English, something they were still pushing at, quite uncertainly. This state of affairs led to Rule 2. 26

Rule 2: *If it's wrong in Standard English it's probably right in Black English, or, at least, you're hot.* 27

It was hard. Roommates and family members ridiculed their studies, or 28 remained incredulous. "You *studying* that shit? At school?" But we were beginning to feel the companionship of pioneers. And we decided that we needed another rule that would establish each one of us as equally important to our success. This was Rule 3.

Rule 3: *If it don't sound like something that come out somebody mouth then it don't sound right. It if don't sound right then it ain't hardly right. Period.* 29

This rule produced two weeks of compositions in which the students agonizingly tried to spell the sound of the Black English sentence they wanted to convey. But Black English is, preeminently, an oral/spoken means of communication. *And spelling don't talk.* So we needed Rule 4. 30

Rule 4: *Forget about the spelling. Let the syntax carry you.* 31

Once we arrived at Rule 4 we started to fly because syntax, the structure of an idea, leads you to the world view of the speaker and reveals her values. The syntax of a sentence equals the structure of your consciousness. If we insisted that the language of Black English adheres to a distinctive Black syntax, then we were postulating a profound difference between white and Black people, *per se*. Was it a difference to prize or to obliterate? 32

There are three qualities of Black English—the presence of life, voice, and clarity—that testify to a distinctive Black value system that we became excited about and self-consciously tried to maintain. 33

1. Black English has been produced by a pre-technocratic, if not anti-technological, culture. More, our culture has been constantly threatened by annihilation or, at least, the swallowed blurring of assimilation. Therefore, our language is a system constructed by people constantly needing to insist that we exist, that we are present. Our language devolves from a culture that abhors all abstraction, or anything tending to obscure or delete the fact of the human being who is here and now/the truth of the person who is speaking or listening. Consequently, *there is no passive voice construction possible in Black English.* For example, you cannot say, "Black English is being eliminated." You must say, instead, "White people eliminating Black English." The assumption of the presence of life governs all of Black English. Therefore, overwhelmingly, *all action takes place in the language of the present indicative.* And every sentence assumes the living and active participation of at least two human beings, the speaker and the listener. 34

2. A primary consequence of the person-centered values of Black English is the delivery of voice. If you speak or write Black English, your ideas will necessarily possess that otherwise elusive attribute, *voice.* 35

3. One main benefit following from the person-centered values of Black English is that of *clarity*. If your idea, your sentence, assumes the presence of at least two living and active people, you will make it understandable 36

because the motivation behind every sentence is the wish to say something real to somebody real.

As the weeks piled up, translation from Standard English into Black English or vice versa occupied a hefty part of our course work. 37

> Standard English (hereafter S.E.): "In considering the idea of studying Black English those questioned suggested—"
>
> (What's the subject? Where's the person? Is anybody alive in there, in that idea?)
>
> Black English (hereafter B.E.): "I been asking people what you think about somebody studying Black English and they answer me like this:"

But there were interesting limits. You cannot "translate" instances of Standard English preoccupied with abstraction or with nothing/nobody evidently alive, into Black English. That would warp the language into uses antithetical to the guiding perspective of its community of users. Rather you must first change those Standard English sentences, themselves, into ideas consistent with the person-centered assumptions of Black English.

Guidelines for Black English 38

1. Minimal number of words for every idea: This is the source for the aphoristic and/or poetic force of the language; eliminate every possible word.

2. Clarity: If the sentence is not clear it's not Black English.

3. Eliminate use of the verb *to be* whenever possible. This leads to the deployment of more descriptive and therefore more precise verbs.

4. Use *be* or *been* only when you want to describe a chronic, ongoing state of things.

> He *be* at the office, by 9. (He is always at the office by 9.)
>
> He *been* with her since forever.

5. Zero copula: Always eliminate the verb *to be* whenever it would combine with another verb, in Standard English.

> S.E.: She is going out with him.
>
> B.E.: She going out with him.

6. Eliminate *do* as in:

> S.E.: What do you think? What do you want?
>
> B.E.: What you think? What you want?

Rules number 3, 4, 5, and 6 provide for the use of the minimal number of verbs per idea and, therefore, greater accuracy in the choice of verb.

7. In general, if you wish to say something really positive, try to formulate the idea using emphatic negative structure.

S.E.: He's fabulous.

B.E.: He bad.

8. Use double or triple negatives for dramatic emphasis.

S.E.: Tina Turner sings out of this world.

B.E.: Ain nobody sing like Tina.

9. Never use the *-ed* suffix to indicate the past tense of a verb.

S.E.: She closed the door.

B.E.: She close the door. Or, she have close the door.

10. Regardless of intentional verb time, only use the third person singular, present indicative, for use of the verb *to have*, as an auxiliary.

S.E.: He had his wallet then he lost it.

B.E.: He have him wallet then he lose it.

S.E.: We had seen that movie.

B.E.: We seen that movie. Or, we have see that movie.

11. Observe a minimal inflection of verbs. Particularly, never change from the first person singular forms to the third person singular.

S.E.: Present Tense Forms: He goes to the store.

B.E.: He go to the store.

S.E.: Past Tense Forms: He went to the store.

B.E.: He go to the store. Or, he gone to the store. Or, he been to the store.

12. The possessive case scarcely ever appears in Black English. Never use an apostrophe ('s) construction. If you wander into a possessive case component of an idea, then keep logically consistent: *ours, his, theirs, mines.* But, most likely, if you bump into such a component, you have wandered outside the underlying world-view of Black English.

S.E.: He will take their car tomorrow.

B.E.: He taking they car tomorrow.

13. Plurality: Logical consistency, continued: If the modifier indicates plurality, then the noun remains in the singular case.

S.E.: He ate twelve doughnuts.

B.E.: He eat twelve doughnut.

S.E.: He has many books.

B.E.: She have many book.

14. Listen for, or invent, special Black English forms of the past tense, such as: "He losted it. That what she felted." If they are clear and readily understood, then use them.

Do not hesitate to play with words, sometimes inventing them; e.g., "astropotomous" means huge like a hippo plus astronomical and, therefore, signifies real big. 39

15. In Black English, unless you keenly want to underscore the past tense nature of an action, stay in the present tense and rely on the overall context of your ideas for the conveyance of time and sequence.

16. Never use the suffix *-ly* form of an adverb in Black English.

S.E.: The rain came down rather quickly.

B.E.: The rain come down pretty quick.

17. Never use the indefinite article *an* in Black English.

S.E.: He wanted to ride an elephant.

B.E.: He want to ride him a elephant.

18. In variant syntax: In correct Black English it is possible to formulate an imperative, an interrogative, and a simple declarative idea with the same syntax:

B.E.: You going to the store?
You going to the store.
You going to the store!

Where was Willie Jordan? We'd reached the mid-term of the semester. Students had formulated Black English guidelines, by consensus, and they were now writing with remarkable beauty, purpose, and enjoyment: 40

I ain hardly speakin for everybody but myself so understan that.

—Kim Parks

Samples from student writings:

"Janie have a great big ole hole inside her. Tea Cake the only thing that fit that hole. . . .

"That pear tree beautiful to Janie, especial when bees fiddlin with the blossomin pear there growin large and lovely. But personal speakin, the love she get from starin at that tree ain the love what starin back at her in them relationship." (Monica Morris)

"Love is a big theme in *They Eye Was Watching God.* Love show people new corners inside theyself. It pull out good stuff and stuff back bad stuff. . . . Joe worship the doing uh his own hand and need other people to worship him too. But he ain't think about Janie that she a person and ought to live like anybody common do. Queen life not for Janie." (Monica Morris)

"In both life and writin, Black womens have varietous experience of love that be cold like a iceberg or fiery like a inferno. Passion got for the other partner involve, man or woman, seem as shallow, ankle-deep water or the most profoundest abyss." (Constance Evans)

"Family love another bond that ain't never break under no pressure." (Constance Evans)

"You know it really cold/When the friend you/Always get out the fire/Act like they don't know you/When you in the heat." (Constance Evans)

"Big classroom discussion bout love at this time. I never take no class where us have any long arguin for and against for two or three day. New to me and great. I find the class time talkin a million time more interestin than detail bout the book." (Kathy Esseks)

* * *

As these examples suggest, Black English no longer limited the students, in any way. In fact, one of them, Philip Garfield, would shortly "translate" a pivotal scene from Ibsen's *Doll House,* as his final term paper: 4

NORA: I didn't gived no shit. I thinked you a asshole back then, too, you make it so hard for me save mines husband life.
KROGSTAD: Girl, it clear you ain't any idea what you done. You done exact what once done, and I losed my reputation over it.
NORA: You asks me believe you once act brave save you wife life?
KROGSTAD: Law care less why you done it.
NORA: Law must suck.
KROGSTAD: Suck or no, if I wants, judge screw you wid dis paper.
NORA: No way, man. (Philip Garfield)

But where was Willie? Compulsively punctual, and always thoroughly prepared with neatly typed compositions, he had disappeared. He failed to show up for our regularly scheduled conference, and I received neither a note nor a phone call of explanation. A whole week went by. I wondered if Willie had finally been captured by the extremely current happenings in South Africa: passage of a new constitution that did not enfranchise the Black majority, and militant Black South African reaction to that affront. I 42 wondered if he'd been hurt, somewhere. I wondered if the serious workload of weekly readings and writings had overwhelmed him and changed his mind about independent study. Where was Willie Jordan?

One week after the first conference that Willie missed, he called: "Hello, Professor Jordan? This is Willie. I'm sorry I wasn't there last week. But something has come up and I'm pretty upset. I'm sorry but I really can't deal right now." 43

I asked Willie to drop by my office and just let me see that he was okay. He agreed to do that. When I saw him I knew something hideous had happened. Something had hurt him and scared him to the marrow. He was all agitated and stammering and terse and incoherent. At last, his sadly jumbled account let me surmise as follows: Brooklyn police had murdered his unarmed, twenty-five-old brother, Reggie Jordan Neither Willie nor his elderly parents knew what to do about it. Nobody from the press was interested. His folks had no money. Police ran his family around and around, to no point. And Reggie was really dead. And Willie wanted to fight, but he felt helpless.

With Willie's permission I began to try to secure legal counsel for the Jordan 44
family. Unfortunately Black victims of police violence are truly numerous while the resources available to prosecute their killers are truly scarce. A friend of mine at the Center for Constitutional Rights estimated that just the preparatory costs for bringing the cops into court normally approaches $180,000. Unless the execution of Reggie Jordan became a major community cause for organizing and protest, his murder would simply become a statistical item.

Again with Willie's permission, I contacted every newspaper and media 45
person I could think of. But the William Bastone feature article in *The Village Voice* was the only result from that canvassing.

Again with Willie's permission, I presented the case to my class in Black 46
English. We had talked about the politics of language. We had talked about love and sex and child abuse and men and women. But the murder of Reggie Jordan broke like a hurricane across the room.

There are few "issues" as endemic to Black life as police violence. Most 47
of the students knew and respected and liked Jordan. Many of them came from the very neighborhood where the murder had occurred. All of the students had known somebody close to them who had been killed by police, or had known frightening moments of gratuitous confrontation with the cops. They wanted to do everything at once to avenge death. Number One: They decided to compose personal statements of condolence to Willie Jordan and his family, written in Black English. Number Two: They decided to compose individual messages to the police, in Black En-

glish. These should be prefaced by an explanatory paragraph composed by the entire group. Number Three: These individual messages, with their lead paragraph, should be sent to *Newsday*.

The morning after we agreed on these objectives, one of the young 48
women students appeared with an unidentified visitor, who sat through the class, smiling in a peculiar, comfortable way.

Now we had to make more tactical decisions. Because we wanted the 49
messages published, and because we thought it imperative that our outrage be known by the police, the tactical question was this: Should the opening, group paragraph be written in Black English or Standard English?

I have seldom been privy to a discussion with so much heart at the 50
dead heat of it. I will never forget the eloquence, the sudden haltings of speech, the fierce struggle against tears, the furious throwaways and useless explosions that this question elicited.

That one question contained several others, each of them extraordi- 51
narily painful to even contemplate. How best to serve the memory of Reggie Jordan? Should we use the language of the killers—Standard English—in order to make our ideas acceptable to those controlling the killers? But wouldn't what we had to say be rejected, summarily, if we said it in our own language, the language of the victim, Reggie Jordan? But if we sought to express ourselves by abandoning our language, wouldn't that mean our suicide on top of Reggie's murder? But if we expressed ourselves in our own language, wouldn't that be suicidal to the wish to communicate with those who, evidently, did not give a damn about us/Reggie/police violence in the Black community?

At the end of one of the longest, most difficult hours of my own life, 52
the students voted, unanimously, to preface their individual messages with a paragraph composed in the language of Reggie Jordan. *"At least we don't give up nothing else. At least we stick to the truth: Be who we been. And stay all the way with Reggie."*

It was heartbreaking to proceed, from that point. Everyone in the room 53
realized that our decision in favor of Black English had doomed our writings, even as the distinctive reality of our Black lives always has doomed our efforts to "be who we been" in this country.

I went to the blackboard and took down this paragraph, dictated by 54
the class:

> . . . You Cops!
>
> We the brother and sister of Willie Jordan, a fellow stony brook student who the brother of the dead Reggie Jordan. Reggie, like many brother and sister, he a victim of brutal racist police, October 25, 1984. Us appall, fed up, because that another senseless death what occur in our community. This what we feel, this, from our heart, for we ain't stayin' silent no more.

With the completion of this introduction, nobody said anything. I asked for comments. At this invitation, the unidentified visitor, a young Black man, ceaselessly smiling, raised his hand. He was, it so happens, a rookie cop. He had just joined the force in September and, he said, he thought he should clarify a few things. So he came forward and sprawled easily into a posture of barroom, or fireside, nostalgia: 55

"See," Officer Charles enlightened us, "most time when you out on the street and something come down you do one of two things. Over-react or under-react. Now, if you under-react then you can get yourself kilt. And if you over-react then maybe you kill somebody. Fortunately it's about nine times out of ten and you will over-react. So the brother got kilt. And I'm sorry about that, believe me. But what you have to understand is what kilt him: over-reaction. That's all. Now you talk about Black people and white police but see, now, I'm a cop myself. And [big smile] I'm Black. And just a couple months ago I was on the other side. But see it's the same for me. You a cop, you the ultimate authority: the Ultimate Authority. And you on the street, most of the time you can only do one of two things: over-react or under-react. That's all it is with the brother. Over-reaction. Didn't have nothing to do with race." 56

That morning Officer Charles had the good fortune to escape without being boiled alive. But barely. And I remember the pride of his smile when I read about the fate of Black policemen and other collaborators in South Africa. I remember him, and I remember the shock and palpable feeling of shame that filled the room. It was as though that foolish, and deadly, young man had just relieved himself of his foolish, and deadly, explanation, face to face with the grief of Reggie Jordan's father and Reggie Jordan's mother. Class ended quietly. I copied the paragraph from the blackboard, collected the individual messages, and left to type them up. 57

Newsday rejected the piece. 58

The Village Voice could not find room in their "Letters" section to print the individual messages from the students to the police. 59

None of the tv news reporters picked up the story. 60

Nobody raised $180,000 to prosecute the murder of Reggie Jordan. 61

Reggie Jordan is really dead. 62

I asked Willie Jordan to write an essay pulling together everything important to him from that semester. He was still deeply beside himself with frustration and amazement and loss. This is what he wrote, un-edited, and in its entirety: 63

> Throughout the course of this semester I have been researching the effects of oppression and exploitation along racial lines in South Africa and its neighboring countries. I have become aware of South African police brutalization of native Africans beyond the extent of the law,

even though the laws themselves are catalyst affliction upon Black men, women and children. Many Africans die each year as a result of the deliberate use of police force to protect the white power structure.

Social control agents in South Africa, such as policemen, are also used to force compliance among citizens through both overt and covert tactics. It is not uncommon to find bold-faced coercion and cold-blooded killings of Blacks by South African police for undetermined and/or inadequate reasons. Perhaps the truth is that the only reason for this heinous treatment of Blacks rests in racial differences. We should also understand that what is conveyed through the media is not always accurate and may sometimes be construed as the tip of the iceberg at best.

I recently received a painful reminder that racism, poverty, and the abuse of power are global problems which are by no means unique to South Africa. On October 25, 1984 at approximately 3:00 P.M. my brother, Mr. Reginald Jordan, was shot and killed by two New York City policemen from the 75th precinct in the East New York section of Brooklyn. His life ended at the age of twenty-five. Even up to this current point in time the Police Department has failed to provide my family, which consists of five brothers, eight sisters, and two parents, with a plausible reason for Reggie's death. Out of the many stories that were given to my family by the Police Department, not one of them seems to hold water. In fact, I honestly believe that the Police Department's assessment of my brother's murder is nothing short of ABSOLUTE BULLSHIT, and thus far no evidence had been produced to alter this perception of the situation.

Furthermore, I believe that one of three cases may have occurred in this incident. First, Reggie's death may have been the desired outcome of the police officer's action, in which case the killing was premeditated. Or, it was a case of mistaken identity, which clarifies the fact that the two officers who killed my brother and their commanding parties are all grossly incompetent. Or, both of the above cases are correct, i.e., Reggie's murderers intended to kill him and the Police Department behaved insubordinately.

Part of the argument of the officers who shot Reggie was that he had attacked one of them and took his gun. This was their major claim. They also said that only one of them had actually shot Reggie. The facts, however, speak for themselves. According to the Death Certificate and autopsy report, Reggie was shot eight times from point-blank range. The Doctor who performed the autopsy told me himself that two bullets entered the side of my brother's head, four bullets were sprayed into his back, and two bullets struck him in the back of the legs. It is obvious that unnecessary force was used by the police and that it is extremely difficult to shoot someone in his back when he is attacking or approaching you.

After experiencing a situation like this and researching South Africa I believe that to a large degree, justice may only exist as rhetoric. I find it difficult to talk of true justice when the oppression of my people both at home and abroad attests to the fact that inequality and injustice are serious problems whereby Blacks and Third World people are perpetually short-changed by society. Something has to be done about the way in which this world is set up. Although it is a difficult task, we do have the power to make a change. 68

—Willie J. Jordan Jr.
EGL 487, Section 58, November 14, 1984

It is my privilege to dedicate this book to the future life of Willie J. Jordan Jr.

August 8, 1985

How They Write the SAT

David Owen

David Owen is a journalist who has written for many magazines, including Harper's, *where he was a senior writer. His first book was* High School: Undercover with the Class of '80. *He has taught writing at Colorado College and now lives in New York City with his family. The following essay is adapted from his book* None of the Above: Behind the Myth of Scholastic Aptitude.

Standardized multiple-choice tests, such as the Scholastic Aptitude Test, are 1
more than hurdles on the way to college. The tests have become a pervasive measure of worthiness in our society—even a status symbol, as in, "*My* boy scored double 700s."

The Educational Testing Service, which produces the SAT, encourages 2
this attitude. The company's literature conjures up the image of a testing instrument endowed with the learning and precision of white-coated physicists measuring a rocket's lift-off power. But as should be apparent to anyone who has taken these tests, the white-coated image is just that. Many of the test questions are ambiguous, arbitrary, and downright silly.

The principal difference between the SAT and a test that cannot be 3
graded by machine is that the SAT leaves no room for more than one

correct answer. It leaves no room, in other words, for people who don't see eye-to-eye with ETS. Understanding how the test-makers think is one of the keys both to doing well on ETS tests and to penetrating the mystique in which the company cloaks its work. Despite ETS's claims to the contrary, its tests are written by people who tend to think in certain predictable ways. The easiest way to see this is to look at the tests themselves. *Which* test doesn't really matter. Here's an item from a recent Achievement Test in French:

2. Un client est assis dans un restaurant chic. Le garçon maladroit lui 4
renverse le potage sur les genoux. Le client s'exclame:
(A) Vous ne pourriez pas faire attention, non?
(B) La soupe est delicieuse!
(C) Quel beau service de table!
(D) Je voudrais une cuillère!

My French is vestigial at best. But with the help of my wife I made this out as follows:

2. A customer is seated in a fancy restaurant. The clumsy waiter spills 5
soup in his lap. The customer exclaims:
(A) You could not pay attention, no?
(B) The soup is delicious!
(C) What good service!
(D) I would like a spoon!

Now, (B), (C), and (D) strike me as nice, funny, sarcastic responses that 6
come very close to being the sort of remark I would make in the situation described. A spoon, waiter, for the soup in may lap! But, of course, in taking a test like this, the student has to suppress his sometimes powerful urge to respond according to his own sense of what is right. He has to remember that the "best" answer—which is what ETS always asks for, even on math and science tests—isn't necessarily a good answer, or even a correct one. He has to realize that the ETS answer will be something drab, humorless, and plodding—something very like (A), as indeed it is. Thus bright students sometimes have trouble on ETS tests, because they see possibilities that ETS's question-writers missed. The advice traditionally given to such students is to take the test quickly and without thinking too hard.

Medicine Freaks

Exactly how does ETS come to write questions like this? ETS is very secretive 7
about its methods. The company has always insisted that its work is too

complex and too important to accommodate the scrutiny of outsiders. But with some determined digging around, even an outsider can get an idea of what goes on inside ETS's test development office.

A variety of people write questions for the SAT: company employees, freelancers, even student interns. An "assembler" oversees the process, and once the test is completed, this person gives it to two or three colleagues for a review. ETS's test reviews aren't meant to be seen by the public. The words SECURE and E.T.S. CONFIDENTIAL are stamped in red ink at the top of very page. But I obtained a copy of the review materials for the SAT administered in May 1982, which were used as evidence in a court case. 8

An ETS test review doesn't take long. The reviewer simply answers each item, marking his choices on ordinary lined paper and handwriting comments on items he feels need improvement. For example, the fourth item in the first section was an antonym problem; students were supposed to select the lettered choice that is the nearest opposite in meaning to the word in capital letters: 9

> 4. BYPASS: (A) enlarge
> (B) advance (C) copy
> (D) throw away (E) go through

The first reviewer, identified only as "JW," suggested substituting the word "clog" for one of the incorrect choices (called "distractors" in testing jargon), because "perhaps clog would tempt the medicine freaks." In other words, if the item were worded a little differently, more future physicians might be tempted to answer it incorrectly. The assembler, Ed Curley, decided not to follow JW's suggestions, but the comment is revealing of the level at which ETS analyzes its tests. 10

In ETS test reviews, the emphasis is not always on whether keyed answers are good or absolutely correct, but on whether they can be defended in the event that someone later complains. When the second test reviewer, Pamela Cruise, wondered whether answering one difficult item required "outside knowledge," Ed Curley responded: "We must draw the line somewhere but I gave item to Sandy; she could not key—none of the terms were familiar to her. She feels that if sentence is from a legit source, we could defend." 11

"The legitimate source" tends to be either the American Heritage or Webster's dictionary, depending on which supports the answer ETS has selected. In reviewing item 44, JW wrote, "Looked fine to me but AH Dict. would suggest that *matriarchy* is a social system & *matriarchate* a state (& a gov't system). Check Webster." Curley did this and responded, "1st meaning of 'matriarchy' in Webs. is 'matriarchate' so item is fine." To a criticism of another item he responded, "I had some pause over this, too, but tight by dictionary." 12

I'd always thought that ETS item-writers must depend heavily on dictionaries. The diction in SAT questions is sometimes slightly off in a way that suggests the item writers are testing words they don't actually use. ("It ain't often you see CONVOKE!" noted JW of a word tested in one item.) SAT items also often test the third, fourth, or fifth meanings of otherwise common words, which can create confusion. In the following item from the same test, the word "decline" is used peculiarly: 1

17. He is an unbeliever, but he is broad-minded enough to decline the mysteries of religon without ---- them. 1

(A) denouncing (B) understanding (C) praising
(D) doubting (E) studying

My *Webster's Seventh New Collegiate Dictionary* gives the fourth meaning of decline as "to refuse to accept." This is more or less what ETS wants to say. But the dictionary goes on to explain that decline in this sense "implies courteous refusal esp. of offers and invitations." This usage, and not ETS's, is the proper one. What ETS really wants here is a word like "reject." Cruise made a similar comment in her review, but the item was not changed ("Sounds fine to me and is supported by dictionary," wrote Curley). 1

Tough Enuf

The most important statisic that ETS derives from pretests in terms of building new SATs, is called "delta." Like virtually all ETS statistics, delta sounds more sophisticated than it is. It's really just a fancy way of expressing the percentage of students who consider a particular item but either omit it or get it wrong. (Or, as ETS inimitably describes it, delta "is the normal deviate of the point above which lies the proportion of the area under the curve equal to the proportion of correct respnses to the item.") For all practical purposes, the SAT delta scale runs from about 5.0 to about 19.0. An item that very few students get right might have a delta of 16.8; one that many get right might have a delta of 6.3. 16

ETS calls delta a measure of "difficulty," but this definition is circular. A question is hard if few people answer it correctly, easy if many do. But since delta refers to no standard beyond the item itself, it makes no distinction between one body of subject matter and another. Nor does it distinguish between knowledge and good luck. Delta can say only that a question was answered correctly by the exact percentage of people who answered it correctly. It takes a simple piece of known information and restates it in a way that makes it seem pregnant with new significance. 17

ETS is almost always reluctant to change the wording of test items, or 18 even the order of distractors, because small changes can make big differences in statistics. Substituting "reject" for "decline" in the above could have made the item easier to answer, thus lowering its delta and throwing off the test specifications. (ETS doesn't pursue the implications. If correcting the wording of a question changes the way it performs on the test, then some of the people new getting it wrong—or right, as the case may be—are doing so *only because* the question is badly written.)

Making even a slight alteration in an item can necessitate a new pretest 19
(or trial run in ungraded portions of existing tests), which is expensive. Revisions are made only grudgingly, even if assembler and reviewer agree that something is wrong. "Key a bit off, but okay," Cruise wrote in regard to one item. JW commented on another: "At pretest I would have urged another compound word or unusual distractor. However it's tough enuf as is."

Test assemblers don't like being criticized by test reviewers. When 20
Cruise described item 26 as a "weak question—trivial," Curley responded in the margin "Poop on you!" The question stayed in the test. Curley's most frequent remark is a mildly petulant "but OK as is," which is scribbled after most criticisms. Assemblers invest a great deal of ego in their tests, and they don't like to be challenged. Sometimes the reviewer is nearly apologetic. "Strictly speaking (too strictly probably), doesn't the phoenix symbolize death and rebirth rather than immortality? Item's OK, really. It needs Scotch tape." JW concluded this comment by drawing a little smiling face. (The item was not changed.)

The phoenix item, an analogy problem, also drew a comment from 21
Cruise. "Well—item OK—but this reminds me of the kind of thing we used to test but don't do much now—relates to outside knowledge—myth, lit., etc. . . . This might be an item the critics pick on." In ETS analogies, students are given a pair of words and asked to select another pair "that *best* expresses a relationship similar to that expressed in the original pair." The item:

42. PHOENIX:IMMORTALITY::
(A) unicorn:cowardice
(B) sphinx:mystery
(C) salamander:speed
(D) ogre:wisdom
(E) chimera:stability

Cruise said she would "be more inclined to defend this item if it were 22
a delta 15." The item had been rated somewhat lower (i.e. "easier"), at delta 13.2 What Cruise *thought* she was saying was that if the item had been more "difficult," and thus intended for "abler" students, the ambiguity in it would have been less objectionable. But all she was *really* saying was

that she would have been more inclined to defend the item if fewer people had answered it correctly. (Or, to put it another way, she would have thought it less ambiguous if it had been more ambiguous.) This, of course, doesn't make any sense. Cruise had forgotten the real meaning of delta and fallen victim to her own circular logic. ETS's test developers cloak their work in scientific hocus-pocus and end up deceiving not only us but themselves.

Curley didn't share Cruise's peculiar concern, "Think we can defend," 23
he wrote. "Words are in dictionary, they have modern usage, and we test more specialized *science* vocab than this. Aren't we willing to say that knowledge of these terms is related to success in college?"

Actual Minorities

Whether the SAT is culturally biased against minorities is a perennial concern 24
at ETS. The company says it has proven statistically that the SAT is fair for all. Just to make sure, for the last few years it has used "an actual member of a minority" (as one ETS employee told me) to read every test before it is published. According to an ETS flier, "Each test is reviewed to ensure that the questions reflect the multicultural nature of our society and that appropriate, positive references are made to minorities and women. Each test item is reviewed to ensure that any word, phrase, or description that may be regarded as biased, sexist, or racist is removed."

But the actual "sensitivity review" process is much more cursory and 25
superficial than this description implies. The minority reviewer, a company employee, simply counts the number of items that refer to each of five "population subgroups" and enters these numbers on a Test Sensitivity Review Report Form.

On the verbal SAT administered in May 1982, minority member Beverly 26
Whittington found seven items that mentioned women, one that mentioned black Americans, two that mentioned Hispanic Americans, none that mentioned native Americans, four that mentioned Asian Americans (actually, she was stretching here; these particular Asian Americans were Shang Dynasty Chinese, 1766–1122 B.C.). Two items overlapped, so Whittington put a "12" in the box for Total Representational Items. She also commented "OK" on the exam's text specifications, "OK" on the subgroup reference items, and "OK" on item review. She made no other remarks. If she had found the word *nigger* in one of the questions, presumably she would have scratched it out. ETS made Whittington take a three-day training program in "test sensitivity" before permitting her to do all of this. When her report was finished, it was stamped E. T. S. CONFIDENTIAL and SECURE. Then it was filed and forgotten.

Noun Schmoun

After its sensitivity review, every SAT is passed along to what the College Board (which hires ETS to write and administer its college admissions tests) describes as a committee of "prominent specialists in educational and psychological measurement." ETS and the board talk publicly about the SAT committee as though it were a sort of psychometric Supreme Court, sitting in thoughtful judgment on every question in the SAT. According to the official mythology, the SAT committee ensures the integrity of the test by subjecting it to rigorous, independent, expert scrutiny. But in fact committee members are largely undistinguished in the measurement field. They have no real power, and ETS generally ignores their suggestions. 27

"They always hate to see my comments," says Margaret Fleming, one of the committee's ten members and a deputy superintendent in Cleveland's public school system. "Now, we have had some showdowns about it. Sometimes they change, but I find that item writers are very pompous about their work, and they don't like you to say anything. I am saying something, though, because I feel that maybe 40 people are responsible for writing items, let's say, for the verbal area, and why should 40 people govern by chance what thousands of youngsters' opportunities might be?" 28

Far fewer than 40 people are involved in writing an SAT, but no matter. I asked her how ETS responded to her criticisms. 29

"They many times try to dismiss it," she said. "Sometimes they're very stubborn. Now, the one I got back recently was about a word that my dictionary said is a noun. Now I'm using *American Heritage Dictionary,* which I feel is common access across the country. I haven't got the Oxford English unabridged 30-volume thing. All I've got is what most people would have. And I said, the options here are verbs, and it appears that this is the only item with different parts of speech for the stem and the options. And they said, Well, this word is also a verb, and it's tested as such in this item. You see, they are going around my complaint." 30

I called Hammett Worthington-Smith, an associate professor of English at Albright College in Reading, Pennsylvania and asked him to describe his duties on the SAT committee. 31

"We review exams," he said, "we prepare questions, we take the tests, and that type of thing." 32

"You prepare questions in addition to reviewing tests?" I asked. 33

"Yes, we have that opportunity." 34

"And do you do that?" 35

"Yes." 36

But committee members *don't* write questions for the SAT. Willie M. May, chairman of the committee and assistant principal for personnel and 37 programming at Wendell Phillips High School in Chicago, told me in no uncertain terms that preparing questions was *not* one of his committee's duties. "We are in an advisory capacity," he said. "We don't do any tinkering at all."

When I asked Worthington-Smith what test-reviewing involved, he said, "You know, normally what anyone else would do with this one particular test. Now, I don't want to spend much more time on this, because we do exactly what the College Board statement says, so I don't know what you're out fishing for." 3

"I'm not fishing for anything," I said. 3

"Okay, so that's enough for today." And he hung up on me. Our phone conversation had lasted exactly two and a half minutes. 4

According to the College Board's one-paragraph "Charge to SAT committee," each member reviews, by mail, two tests a year. An ETS answer key is included with each test. I asked committee member William Controvillas, a guidance counselor at Farmington High School in Farmington, Connecticut, what these reviews entailed. "Reviewing involves both verbal as well as the math," he said. "You review the questions to make sure that the question is legible and that there aren't any trick language aspects to it, and that it's clear, and that you come up with the answer that you think should be gotten. You get an answer sheet and some statistics with it. If you happen to be less competent in math, you still review it for language. I tend to be more verbal." 4

In the course of our conversaton, Controvillas used the word "criteria" twice as a singular noun and told me that the committee reviews each test "physically" (he also seemed to be uncertain about the meaning of the word "legible"). In general, he said, he found the SAT impressive. "These are tests, of course, that are made up by professional test-makers, so in a sense what you're doing is applying some kind of quality control. A quality control function." 4

The SAT committee's *real* duties have more to do with public relations than with test development. Committee members tiptoe through questions and statistics they don't understand, flattered to have been asked to look at them in the first place, and then help spread the good word about ETS. ETS has little interest in their opinions. By the time the committee receives a test, changing it is virtually impossible. "Minor revisions can be made in questions at this stage," says an ETS document, referring to a test-development stage *prior* to the one in which the committee is consulted, "but a major revision in a question makes it necessary to represent the question in order to determine the effect of the changes on the statistical characteristics of a question." Such revisions are almost never made. As soon as committee members have completed their busywork, the test is sent to the printer. 4

What High School Is

Theodore R. Sizer

Theodore R. Sizer (b. 1932) has had a long career in education, serving as headmaster of Phillips Academy, Andover, Massachusetts, dean of the Graduate School of Education at Harvard, and chairman of the Education Department at Brown University. He also has spent time in public and independent schools across the country, evaluating their effectiveness and suggesting models for change. The essay that follows appeared in Horace's Compromise: The Dilemma of the American High School *(1984).*

Mark, sixteen and a genial eleventh-grader, rides a bus to Franklin High School, arriving at 8:45. It is an Assembly Day, so the schedule is adapted to allow for a meeting of the entire school. He hangs out with his friends, first outside school and then inside, by his locker. He carries a pile of textbooks and notebooks; in all, it weighs eight and a half pounds. 1

From 7:30 to 8:19, with nineteen other students, he is in Room 304 for English class. The Shakespeare play being read this year by the eleventh grade is *Romeo and Juliet.* The teacher, Ms. Viola, has various students in turn take parts and read out loud. Periodically, she interrupts the (usually halting) recitations to ask whether the thread of the conversation in the play is clear. Mark is entertained by the stumbling readings of some of his classmates. He hopes he will not be asked to be Romeo, particularly if his current steady, Sally, is Juliet. There is a good deal of giggling in class, and much attention paid to who may be called on next. Ms. Viola reminds the class of a test on this part of the play to be given next week. 2

The bell rings at 8:19. Mark goes to the boys' room, where he sees a classmate who he thinks is a wimp but who constantly tries to be a buddy. Mark avoids the leech by rushing off. On the way, he notices two boys engaged in some sort of transaction, probably over marijuana. He pays them no attention. 8:24. Typing class. The rows of desks that embrace big office machines are almost filled before the bell. Mark is uncomfortable here: typing class is girl country. The teacher constantly threatens what to Mark is a humiliatingly female future: "Your employer won't like these erasures." The minutes during the period are spent copying a letter from a handbook onto business stationery. Mark struggles to keep from looking at his work; the teacher wants him to watch only the material from which he is copying. Mark is frustrated, uncomfortable, and scared that he will not complete his letter by the class's end, which would be embarrassing. 3

Nine tenths of the students present at school that day are assembled in the auditorium by the 9:18 bell. The dilatory tenth still stumble in, running down aisles. Annoyed class deans try to get the mob settled. The curtains part; the program is a concert by a student rock group. Their electronic gear flashes under the lights, and the five boys and one girl in the group work hard at being casual. Their movements on stage are studiously at three-quarter time, and they chat with one another as though the tumultuous screaming of their schoolmates were totally inaudible. The girl balances on a stool; the boys crank up the music. It is very soft rock, the sanitized lyrics surely cleared with the assistant principal. The girl sings, holding the mike close to her mouth, but can scarcely be heard. Her light voice is tentative, and the lyrics indecipherable. The guitars, amplified, are tuneful, however, and the drums are played with energy. 4

The students around Mark—all juniors, since they are seated by class—alternately slouch in their upholstered, hinged seats, talking to one another, or sit forward, leaning on the chair backs in front of them, watching the band. A boy near Mark shouts noisily at the microphone-fondling singer, "Bite it . . . ohhh," and the area around Mark explodes in vulgar male laughter, but quickly subsides. A teacher walks down the aisle. Songs continue, to great applause. Assembly is over at 9:46, two minutes early. 5

9:53 and biology class. Mark was at a different high school last year and did not take this course there as a tenth-grader. He is in it now, and all but one of his classmates are a year younger than he. He sits on the side, not taking part in the chatter that goes on after the bell. At 9:57, the public address system goes on, with the announcements of the day. After a few words from the principal ("Here today's cheers and jeers . . ." with a cheer for the winning basketball team and a jeer for the spectators who made a ruckus at the gymnasium), the task is taken over by officers of ASB (Associated Student Bodies). There is an appeal for "bat bunnies." Carnations are for sale by the Girls' League. Miss Indian American is coming. Students are auctioning off their services (background catcalls are heard) to earn money for the prom. Nominees are needed for the ballot for school bachelor and school bachelorette. The announcements end with a "thought for the day. When you throw a little mud, you lose a little ground." 6

At 10:04 the biology class finally turns to science. The teacher, Mr. Robbins, has placed one of several labeled laboratory specimens—some are pinned in frames, others swim in formaldehyde—on each of the classroom's eight laboratory tables. The three or so students whose chairs circle each of these benches are to study the specimen and make notes about it or drawings of it. After a few minutes each group of three will move to another table. The teacher points out that these specimens are of organisms already studied in previous classes. He says that the period-long test set for the following day will involve observing some of these specimens—then 7 to be without labels—and writing an identifying paragraph on each. Mr. Robbins points out that some of the printed labels ascribe the specimens names different from those given in the textbook. He explains that biologists often give several names to the same organism.

The class now falls to peering, writing, and quiet talking. Mr. Robbins 8
comes over to Mark, and in whispered words asks him to carry a requisition form for science department materials to the business office. Mark, because of his "older" status, is usually chosen by Robbins for this kind of errand. Robbins gives Mark the form and a green hall pass to show to any teacher who might challenge him, on his way to the office, for being out of a classroom. The errand takes Mark four minutes. Meanwhile Mark's group is hard at work but gets to only three of the specimens before the bell rings at 10:42. As the students surge out, Robbins shouts a reminder about a "double" laboratory period on Thursday.

Between classes one of the seniors asks Mark whether he plans to be 9
a candidate for schoolwide office next year. Mark says no. He starts to explain. The 10:47 bell rings, meaning that he is late for French class.

There are fifteen students in Monsieur Bates's language class. He hands 10
out tests taken the day before: "*C'est bien fait, Etienne . . . c'est mieux, Marie . . . Tch, tch, Robert . . .*" Mark notes his C+ and peeks at the A− in front of Susanna, next to him. The class has been assigned seats by M. Bates; Mark resents sitting next to prissy, brainy Susanna. Bates starts by asking a student to read a question and give the correct answer. *"James, question un."* James haltingly reads the question and gives an answer that Bates, now speaking English, says is incomplete. In due course: *"Mark, question cinq."* Mark does his bit, and the sequence goes on, the eight quiz questions and answers filling about twenty minutes of time.

"Turn to page forty-nine. *Maintenant, lisez après moi . . .*" and Bates 11
reads a sentence and has the class echo it. Mark is embarrassed by this and mumbles with a barely audible sound. Others, like Susanna, keep the decibel count up, so Mark can hide. This I-say-you-repeat drill is interrupted once by the public address system, with an announcement about a meeting for the cheerleaders. Bates finishes the class, almost precisely at the bell, with a homework assignment. The students are to review these sentences for a brief quiz the following day. Mark takes note of the assignment, because he knows that tomorrow will be a day of busy-work in French class. Much though he dislikes oral drills, they are better than the workbook stuff that Bates hands out. Write, write, write, for Bates to throw away, Mark thinks.

11:36. Down to the cafeteria, talking noisily, hanging, munching. 12
Getting to room 104 by 12:17: U.S. history. The teacher is sitting cross-legged on his desk when Mark comes in, heatedly arguing with three students over the fracas that had followed the previous night's basketball

game. The teacher, Mr. Suslovic, while agreeing that the spectators from their school certainly were provoked, argues that they should neither have been so obviously obscene in yelling at the opposing cheerleaders nor have allowed Coke cans to be rolled out on the floor. The three students keep saying that "it isn't fair." Apparently they and some others had been assigned "Saturday mornings" (detentions) by the principal for the ruckus.

At 12:34, the argument appears to subside. The uninvolved students, 13
including Mark, are in their seats, chatting amiably. Mr. Suslovic climbs off his desk and starts talking: "We've almost finished this unit, chapters nine and ten . . ." The students stop chattering among themselves and turn toward Suslovic. Several slouch down in their chairs. Some open notebooks. Most have the five-pound textbook on their desks.

Suslovic lectures on the cattle drives, from north Texas to railroads west 14
of St. Louis. He breaks up this narrative with questions ("Why were the railroad lines laid largely east to west?"), directed at nobody in particular and eventually answered by Suslovic himself. Some students take notes. Mark doesn't. A student walks in the open door, hands Mr. Suslovic a list, and starts whispering with him. Suslovic turns from the class and hears out this messenger. He then asks, "Does anyone know where Maggie Sharp is?" Some one answers, "Sick at home"; someone else says, "I thought I saw her at lunch." Genial consternation. Finally Suslovic tells the messenger, "Sorry, we can't help you," and returns to the class: "Now, where were we?" He goes on for some minutes. The bell rings. Suslovic forgets to give the homework assignment.

1:11 and Algebra II. There is a commotion in the hallway: someone's 15
locker is rumored to have been opened by the assistant principal and a narcotics agent. In the five-minute passing time, Mark hears the story three times and three ways. A locker had been broken into by another student. It was Mr. Gregory and a narc. It was the cops, and they did it without Gregory's knowing. Mrs. Ames, the mathematics teacher, has not heard anything about it. Several of the nineteen students try to tell her and start arguing among themselves. "O.K., that's enough." She hands out the day's problem, one sheet to each student. Mark sees with dismay that it is a single, complicated "word" problem about some train that, while traveling at 84 mph, due west, passes a car that was going due east at 55 mph. Mark struggles: Is it $d = rt$ *or* $t = rd$? The class becomes quiet, writing, while Mrs. Ames writes some additional, short problems on the blackboard. "Time's up." A sigh; most students still writing. A muffled "Shit." Mrs. Ames frowns. "Come on, now." She collects papers, but it takes four minutes for her to corral them all.

"Copy down the problems from the board." A minute passes. "William, 16
try number one." William suggests an approach. Mrs. Ames corrects and cajoles, and William finally gets it right. Mark watches two kids to his right

passing notes; he tries to read them, but the handwriting is illegible from his distance. He hopes he is not called on, and he isn't. Only three students are asked to puzzle out an answer. The bell rings at 2:00. Mrs. Ames shouts a homework assignment over the resulting hubbub.

Mark leaves his books in his locker. He remembers that he has homework, but figures that he can do it during English class the next day. He knows that there will be an in-class presentation of one of the *Romeo and Juliet* scenes and that he will not be in it. The teacher will not notice his homework writing, or won't do anything about it if she does. 17

Mark passes various friends heading toward the gym, members of the baseketball teams. Like most students, Mark isn't an active school athlete. However, he is associated with the yearbook staff. Although he is not taking "Yearbook" for credit as an English course, he is contributing photographs. Mark takes twenty minutes checking into the yearbook staff's headquarters (the classroom of its faculty adviser) and getting some assignments of pictures from his boss, the senior who is the photography editor. Mark knows that if he pleases his boss and the faculty adviser, he'll take that editor's post for the next year. He'll get English credit for his work then. 18

After gossiping a bit with the yearbook staff, Mark will leave school by 2:35 and go home. His grocery market bagger's job is from 4:45 to 8:00, the rush hour[s] for the store. He'll have a snack at 4:30, and his mother will save him some supper to eat at 8:30. She will ask whether he has any homework, and he'll tell her no. Tomorrow, and virtually every other tomorrow, will be the same for Mark, save for the lack of the assembly: each period then will be five minutes longer. 19

Most Americans have an uncomplicated vision of what secondary education should be. Their conception of high school is remarkably uniform across the country, a striking fact, given the size and diversity of the United States and the politically decentralized character of the schools. This uniformity is of several generations' standing. It has, however, two appearances, each quite different from the other, one of words and the other of practice, a world of political rhetoric and Mark's world. 20

A California high school's general goals, set out in 1979, could serve equally well most of America's high schools, public and private. This school had as its ends: 21

- Fundamental scholastic achievement . . . to acquire knowledge and share in the traditionally academic fundamentals . . . to develop the ability to make decisions, to solve problems, to reason independently, and to accept responsibility for self-evaluation and continuing self-improvement.
- Career and economic competence . . .

- Citizenship and civil responsibility . . .
- Competence in human and social relations . . .
- Moral and ethical values . . .
- Self-realization and mental and physical health . . .
- Aesthetic awareness . . .
- Cultural diversity . . .[1]

In addition to its optimistic rhetoric, what distinguishes this list is its comprehensiveness. The high school is to touch most aspects of an adolescent's existence—mind, body, morals, values, career. No one of these areas is given especial prominence. School people arrogate to themselves an obligation to all.

An example of the wide acceptability of these goals is found in the 22
courts. Forced to present a detailed definition of "thorough and efficient education," elementary as well as secondary, a West Virginia judge sampled the best of conventional wisdom and concluded that

> there are eight general elements of a thorough and efficient system of education: (a) Literacy, (b) The ability to add, subtract, multiply, and divide numbers, (c) Knowledge of government to the extent the child will be equipped as a citizen to make informed choices among persons and issues that affect his own governance, (d) Self-knowledge and knowledge of his or her total environment to allow the child to intelligently choose life work—to know his or her options, (e) Work-training and advanced academic training as the child may intelligently choose, (f) Recreational pursuits, (g) Interests in all creative arts such as music, theater, literature, and the visual arts, and (h) Social ethics, both behavioral and abstract, to facilitate compatibility with others in this society.[2]

That these eight—now powerfully part of the debate over the purpose and practice of education in West Virginia—are reminiscent of the influential

---

[1] Shasta High School, Redding, California. An eloquent and analogous statement, "The Essentials of Education," one stressing explicitly the "interdependence of skills and content" that is implicit in the Shasta High School statement, was issued in 1980 by a coalition of educational associations. Organizations for the Essentials of Education (Urbana, Illinois).

[2] Judge Arthur M. Recht, in his order resulting from *Pauley v. Kelly*, 1979, as reprinted in *Education Week*, May 26, 1982, p. 10. See also, in *Education Week*, January 16, 1983, pp. 21, 24, Jonathan P. Sher, "The Struggle to Fulfill a Judicial Mandate: How Not to 'Reconstruct' Education in W. Va."

list, "The Seven Cardinal Principles of Secondary Education," promulgated in 1918 by the National Education Association, is no surprise.[3] The rhetoric of high school purpose has been uniform and consistent for decades. Americans agree on the goals for their high schools.

That agreement is convenient, but it masks the fact that virtually all the words in these goal statements beg definition. Some schools have labored long to identify specific criteria beyond them; the result has been lists of daunting pseudospecificity and numbing earnestness. However, most leave the words undefined and let the momentum of traditional practice speak for itself. That is why analyzing how Mark spends his time is important: from watching him one uncovers the important purposes of education, the ones that shape practice. Mark's day is similar to that of other high school students across the country, as similar as the rhetoric of one goal statement to others'. Of course, there are variations, but the extent of consistency in the shape of school routine for a large and diverse adolescent population is extraordinary, indicating more graphically than any rhetoric the measure of agreement in America about what one does in high school, and, by implication, what it is for. 23

The basic organizing structures in schools are familiar. Above all, students are grouped by age (that is, freshman, sophomore, junior, senior), and all are expected to take precisely the same time—around 720 school days over four years, to be precise—to meet the requirements for a diploma. When one is out of his grade level, he can feel odd, as Mark did in his biology class. The goals are the same for all, and the means to achieve them are also similar. 24

Young males and females are treated remarkably alike; the schools' goals are the same for each gender. In execution, there are differences, as those pressing sex discrimination suits have made educators intensely aware. The students in metalworking classes are mostly male; those in home economics, mostly female. But it is revealing how much less sex discrimination there is in high schools than in other American institutions. For many young women, the most liberated hours of their week are in school. 25

School is to be like a job: you start in the morning and end in the afternoon, five days a week. You don't get much of a lunch hour, so you go home early, unless you are an athlete or are involved in some special school or extracurricular activity. School is conceived of as the children's workplace, and it takes young people off parents' hands and out of the 26

[3] Bureau of Education, Department of the Interior, "Cardinal Principles of Secondary Education: A Report of the Commission on the Reorganization of Secondary Education, appointed by the National Education Association," *Bulletin*, no. 35 (Washington: U.S. Government Printing Office, 1918).

labor market during prime-time work hours. Not surprisingly, many students see going to school as little more than a dogged necessity. They perceive the day-to-day routine, a Minnesota study reports, as one of "boredom and lethargy." One of the students summarizes: School is "boring, restless, tiresome, puts ya to sleep, tedious, monotonous, pain the neck."[4]

The school schedule is a series of units of time: the clock is king. The 27
base time block is about fifty minutes in length. Some schools, on what they call modular scheduling, split that fifty-minute block into two or even three pieces. Most schools are double periods for laboratory work, especially in the sciences, or four-hour units for the small numbers of students involved in intensive vocational or other work-study programs. The flow of all school activity arises from or is blocked by these time units. "How much time do I have with my kids" is the teacher's key question.

Because there are many claims for those fifty-minute blocks, there is 28
little time set aside for rest between them, usually no more than three to ten minutes, depending on how big the school is and, consequently, how far students and teachers have to walk from class to class. As a result, there is a frenetic quality to the school day, a sense of sustained restlessness. For the adolescents, there are frequent changes of room and fellow students, each change giving tempting opportunities for distraction, which are stoutly resisted by teachers. Some schools play soft music during these "passing times," to quiet the multitude, one principal told me.

Many teachers have a chance for a coffee break. Few students do. In 29
some city schools where security is a problem, students must be in class for seven consecutive periods, interrupted by a heavily monitored twenty-minute lunch period for small groups, starting as early as 10:30 A.M. and running to after 1:00 P.M. A high premium is placed on punctuality and on "being where you're supposed to be." Obviously, a low premium is placed on reflection and repose. The students rush from class to class to collect knowledge. Savoring it, it is implied, is not to be done much in school, nor is such meditation really much admired. The picture that these familiar patterns yield is that of an academic supermarket. The purpose of going to school is to pick things up, in an organized and predictable way, the faster the better.

What is supposed to be picked up is remarkably consistent among all 30
sorts of high schools. Most schools specifically mandate three out of every five courses a student selects. Nearly all of these mandates fall into five areas—English, social studies, mathematics, science, and physical educa-

[4] Diane Hedin, Paula Simon, and Michael Robin, *Minnesota Youth Poll: Youth's Views on School and School Discipline*, Minnesota Report 184 (1983), Agricultural Experiment Station, University of Minnesota, p. 13.

tion. On the average, English is required to be taken each year, social studies and physical education three out of the four high school years, and mathematics and science one or two years. Trends indicate that in the mid-eighties there is likely to be an increase in the time allocated to these last two subjects. Most students take classes in these four major academic areas beyond the minimum requirements, sometimes in such special areas as journalism and "yearbook," offshoots of English departments.[5]

Press most adults about what high school is for, and you hear these subjects listed. *High school? That's where you learn English and math and that sort of thing.* Ask students, and you get the same answer. High school is to "teach" these "subjects." 31

What is often absent is any definition of these subjects or any rationale for them. They are just there, labels. Under those labels lie a multitude of things. A great deal of material is supposed to be "covered"; most of these courses are surveys, great sweeps of the stuff of their parent disciplines. 32

While there is often a sequence *within* subjects—algebra before trigonometry, "first-year" French before "second-year" French—there is rarely a coherent relationship or sequence *across* subjects. Even the most logically related matters—reading ability as a precondition for the reading of history books, and certain mathematical concepts or skills before the study of some of physics—are only loosely coordinated, if at all. There is little demand for a synthesis of it all; English, mathematics, and the rest are discrete items, to be picked up individually. The incentive for picking them up is largely through tests and, with success at these, in credits earned. 33

Coverage within subjects is the key priority. If some imaginative teacher makes a proposal to force the marriage of, say, mathematics and physics or to require some culminating challenges to students to use several subjects in the solution of a complex problem, and if this proposal will take "time" away from other things, opposition is usually phrased in terms of what may be thus forgone. If we do that, we'll have to give up colonial history. We won't be able to get to programming. We'll not be able to read *Death of a Salesman.* There isn't time. The protesters usually win out. 34

The subjects come at a student like Mark in random order, a kaleidoscope of worlds: algebraic formulae to poetry to French verbs to Ping-Pong to the War of the Spanish Succession, all before lunch. Pupils are to pick up these things. Tests measure whether the picking up has been successful. 35

The lack of connection between stated goals, such as those of the California high school cited earlier, and the goals inherent in school practice 36

[5] I am indebted to Harold F. Sizer and Lyde E. Sizer for a survey of the diploma requirements of fifty representative secondary schools, completed for A Study of High Schools.

is obvious and, curiously, tolerated. Most striking is the gap between statements about "self-realization and mental and physical growth" or "moral and ethical values"—common rhetoric in school documents—and practice. Most physical education programs have neither the time nor the focus really to ensure fitness. Mental health is rarely defined. Neither are ethical values, save at the negative extremes, such as opposition to assault or dishonesty. Nothing in the regimen of a day like Mark's signals direct or implicit teaching in this area. The "school boy code" (not ratting on a fellow student) protects the marijuana pusher, and a leechlike associate is shrugged off without concern. The issue of the locker search was pushed aside, as not appropriate for class time.

Most students, like Mark, go to class in groups of twenty to twenty- 37
seven students. The expected attendance in some schools, particularly those in low-income areas, is usually higher, often thirty-five students per class, but high absentee rates push the actual numbers down. About twenty-five per class is an average figure for expected attendance, and the actual numbers are somewhat lower. There are remarkably few students who go to class in groups much larger or smaller than twenty-five.[6]

A student such as Mark sees five or six teachers per day; their differing 38
styles and expectations are part of his kaleidoscope. High school staffs are highly specialized: guidance counselors rarely teach mathematics, mathematics teachers rarely teach English, principals rarely do any classroom instruction. Mark, then, is known a little bit by a number of people, each of whom sees him in one specialized situation. No one may know him as a "whole person"—unless he becomes a special problem or has special needs.

Save in extraccurricular or coaching situations, such as in athletics, 39
drama, or shop classes, there is little opportunity for sustained conversation between student and teacher. The mode is a one-sentence or two-sentence exchange: *Mark, when was Grover Cleveland president?* Let's see, was 1890 . . . or something . . . wasn't he the one . . . he was elected twice, wasn't he . . . *Yes . . . Gloria, can you get the dates right?* Dialogue is strikingly absent, and as a result the opportunity of teachers to challenge students' ideas in a systematic and logical way is limited. Given the rushed, full quality of the school day, it can seldom happen. One must infer that careful probing of students' thinking is not a high priority. How one gains (to quote the California school's statement of goals again) "the ability to make decisions, to solve problems, to reason independently, and to accept responsibility for self-evaluation and continuing self-improvement" without

---

[6] Education Research Service, Inc., *Class Size: A Summary of Research* (Arlington, Virginia, 1978); and *Class Size Research: A Critique of Recent Meta-Analyses* (Arlington, Virginia, 1980).

being challenged is difficult to imagine. One certainly doesn't learn these things merely from lectures and textbooks.

Most schools are nice places. Mark and his friends enjoy being in theirs. 40 The adults who work in schools generally like adolescents. The academic pressures are limited, and the accommodations to students ae substantial. For example, if many members of an English class have jobs after school, the English teacher's expectations for them are adjusted, downward. In a word, school is sensitively accommodating, as long as students are punctual, where they are supposed to be, and minimally dutiful about picking things up from the clutch of courses in which they enroll.

This characterization is not pretty, but it is accurate, and it serves to 41 describe the vast majority of American secondary schools. "Taking subjects" in a systematized, conveyer-belt way is what one does in high school. That this process is, in substantial respects, not related to the rhetorical purposes of education is tolerated by most people, perhaps because they do not really either believe in those ill-defined goals or, in their heart of hearts, believe that schools can or should even try to achieve them. The students are happy taking subjects. The parents are happy, because that's what they did in high school. The rituals, the most important of which is graduation, remain intact. The adolescents are supervised safely and constructively most of the time, during the morning and afternoon hours, and they are off the labor market. That is what high school is all about.

Race and the Schooling of Black Americans

Claude M. Steele

Claude M. Steele (b. 1946) is a social psychologist at Stanford University. Steele's main area of academic interests, besides racial prejudice and self-esteem, are alcoholism and addictive behaviors. Steele is interested in the process by which the prejudices of American society shape the self-perceptions of African-Americans. The following essay first apepared in The Atlantic.

My former university offered minority students a faculty mentor to help 1 shepherd them into college life. As soon as I learned of the program, I volunteered to be a mentor, but by then the school year was nearly over. Undaunted, the program's eager staff matched me with a student on their waiting list—an appealing nineteen-year-old black woman from Detroit, the same age as my daughter. We met finally in a campus lunch spot just about two weeks before the close of her freshman year. I realized quickly that I was too late. I have heard that the best way to diagnose someone's depression is to note how depressed you feel when you leave the person. When our lunch was over, I felt as gray as the snowbanks that often lined the path back to my office. My lunchtime companion was a statistic brought to life, a living example of one of the most disturbing facts of racial life in America today: the failure of so many black Americans to thrive in school. Before I could lift a hand to help this student, she had decided to do what 70 percent of all black Americans at four-year colleges do at some point in their academic careers—drop out.

I sense a certain caving-in of hope in America that problems of race can be 2
solved. Since the sixties, when race relations held promise for the dawning of a new era, the issue has become one whose persistence causes "problem fatigue"—resignation to an unwanted condition of life.

This fatigue, I suspect, deadens us to the deepening crisis in the edu- 3
cation of black Americans. One can enter any desegregated school in America, from grammar school to high school to graduate or professional school, and meet a persistent reality: blacks and whites in largely separate worlds. And if one asks a few questions or looks at a few records, another reality emerges: these worlds are not equal, either in the education taking place there or in the achievement of the students who occupy them.

As a social scientist, I know that the crisis has enough possible causes 4
to give anyone problem fatigue. But at a personal level, perhaps because of my experience as a black in American schools, or perhaps just as the hunch of a myopic psychologist, I have long suspected a particular culprit—a culprit that can undermine black achievement as effectively as a lock on a schoolhouse door. The culprit I see is *stigma,* the endemic devaluation many blacks face in our society and schools. This status is its own condition of life, different from class, money, culture. It is capable, in the words of the late sociologist Erving Goffman, of "breaking the claim" that one's human attributes have on people. I believe that its connection to school achievement among black Americans has been vastly underappreciated.

This is a troublesome argument, touching as it does on a still unhealed 5
part of American race relations. But it leads us to a heartening principle: if blacks are made less racially vulnerable in school, they can overcome even substantial obstacles. Before the good news, though, I must at least sketch in the bad: the worsening crisis in the education of black Americans.

Despite their socioeconomic disadvantages as a group, blacks begin 6
school with test scores that are fairly close to the test scores of whites their age. The longer they stay in school, however, the more they fall behind; for example, by the sixth grade blacks in many school districts are two full grade levels behind whites in achievement. This pattern holds true in the middle class nearly as much as in the lower class. The record does not

improve in high school. In 1980, for example, 25,500 minority students, largely black and Hispanic, entered high school in Chicago. Four years later only 9,500 graduated, and of those only 2,000 could read at grade level. The situation in other cities is comparable.

Even for blacks who make it to college, the problem doesn't go away. **7** As I noted, 70 percent of all black students who enroll in four-year colleges drop out at some point, as compared with 45 percent of whites. At any given time nearly as many black males are incarcerated as are in college in this country. And the grades of black college students average half a letter below those of their white classmates. At one prestigious university I recently studied, only 18 percent of the graduating black students had grade averages of B or above, as compared with 64 percent of the whites. This pattern is the rule, not the exception, in even the most elite American colleges. Tragically, low grades can render a degree essentially "terminal" in the sense that they preclude further schooling.

Blacks in graduate and professional schools face a similarly worsening **8** or stagnating fate. For example, from 1977 to 1990, though the number of Ph.D.s awarded to other minorities increased and the number awarded to whites stayed roughly the same, the number awarded to American blacks dropped from 1,116 to 828. And blacks needed more time to get those degrees.

Standing ready is a familiar set of explanations. First is societal disad- **9** vantage. Black Americans have had, and continue to have, more than their share: a history of slavery, segregation, and job ceilings; continued lack of economic opportunity; poor schools; and the related problems of broken families, drug-infested communities, and social isolation. Any of these factors—alone, in combination, or through accumulated effects—can undermine school achievement. Some analysts point also to black American culture, suggesting that, hampered by disadvantage, it doesn't sustain the values and expectations critical to education, or that it fosters learning orientations ill suited to school achievement, or that it even "opposes" mainstream achievement. These are the chestnuts, and I had always thought them adequate. Then several facts emerged that just didn't seem to fit.

For one thing, the achievement deficits occur even when black stu- **10** dents suffer no major financial disadvantage—among middle-class students on wealthy college campuses and in graduate school among black students receiving substantial financial aid. For another thing, survey after survey shows that even poor black Americans value education highly, often more than whites. Also, as I will demonstrate, several programs have improved black school achievement without addressing culturally specific learning orientations or doing anything to remedy socioeconomic disadvantage.

Neither is the problem fully explained, as one might assume, by deficits in skill or preparation which blacks might suffer because of background disadvantages. I first doubted that such a connection existed when I saw flunk-out rates for black and white students at a large, prestigious university. Two observations surprised me. First, for both blacks and whites the level of preparation, as measured by Scholastic Aptitude Test scores, didn't make much difference in who flunked out; low scorers (with combined verbal and quantitative SATs of 800) were no more likely to flunk out than high scorers (with combined SATs of 1,200 to 1,500). The second observation was racial: whereas only two percent to 11 percent of the whites flunked out, 18 percent to 33 percent of the blacks flunked out, even at the highest levels of preparation (combined SATs of 1,400). Dinesh D'Souza has argued recently that college affirmative-action programs cause failure and high dropout rates among black students by recruiting them to levels of college work for which they are inadequately prepared. That was clearly not the case at this school; black students flunked out in large numbers even with preparation well above average. 11

And, sadly, this proved the rule, not the exception. From elementary school to graduate school, something depresses black achievement *at every level of preparation, even the highest.* Generally, of course, the better prepared achieve better than the less prepared, and this is about as true for blacks as for whites. But given any level of school preparation (as measured by tests and earlier grades), blacks somehow achieve less in subsequent schooling than whites (that is, have poorer grades, have lower graduation rates, and take longer to graduate), no matter how strong that preparation is. Put differently, the same achievement level requires better preparation for blacks than for whites—far better: among students with a C+ average at the university I just described, the mean American College Testing Program (ACT) score for blacks was at the 98th percentile, while for whites it was at only the 34th percentile. This pattern has been documented so broadly across so many regions of the country, and by so many investigations (literally hundreds), that it is virtually a social law in this society—as well as a racial tragedy. 12

Clearly, something is missing from our understanding of black underachievement. Disadvantage contributes, yet blacks underachieve even when they have ample resources, strongly value education, and are prepared better than adequately in terms of knowledge and skills. Something else has to be involved. That something else could be of just moderate importance—a barrier that simply adds its effect to that of other disadvantages—or it could be pivotal, such that were it corrected, other disdvantages would lose their effect. 13

That something else, I believe, has to do with the process of identifying with school. I offer a personal example: 14

I remember conducting experiments with my research adviser early in graduate school and awaiting the results with only modest interest. I struggled to meet deadlines. The research enterprise—the core of what one does as a social psychologist—just wasn't *me* yet. I was in school for other reasons—I wanted an advanced degree, I was vaguely ambitious for intellectual work, and being in graduate school made my parents proud of me. But as time passed, I began to like the work. I also began to grasp the value system that gave it meaning, and the faculty treated me as if they thought I might even be able to do it. Gradually I began to think of myself as a social psychologist. With this change in self-concept came a new accountability; my self-esteem was affected now by what I did as a social psychologist, something that hadn't been true before. This added a new motivation to my work; self-respect, not just parental respect, was on the line. I noticed changes in myself. I worked without deadlines. I bored friends with applications of arcane theory to their daily lives. I went to conventions. I lived and died over how experiments came out. 15

Before this transition one might have said that I was handicapped by my black working-class background and lack of motivation. After the transition the same observer might say that even though my background was working-class, I had special advantages: achievement-oriented parents, a small and attentive college. But these facts alone would miss the importance of the identification process I had experienced: the change in self-definition and in the activities on which I based my self-esteem. They would also miss a simple condition necessary for me to make this identification: treatment as a valued person with good prospects. 16

I believe that the "something else" at the root of black achievement problems is the failure of American schooling to meet this simple condition for many of its black students. Doing well in school requires a belief that school achievement can be a promising basis of self-esteem, and that belief needs constant reaffirmation even for advantaged students. Tragically, I believe, the lives of black Americans are still haunted by a specter that threatens this belief and the identification that derives from it at every level of schooling. 17

I have a good friend, the mother of three, who spends considerable time in the public school classrooms of Seattle, where she lives. In her son's third-grade room, managed by a teacher of unimpeachable good will and competence, she noticed over many visits that the extraordinary art work of a small black boy named Jerome was ignored—or, more accurately perhaps, its significance was ignored. As genuine art talent has a way of doing—even in the third grade—his stood out. Yet the teacher seemed hardly to notice. Moreover, Jerome's reputation, as it was passed along from one grade to the next, included only the slightest mention of his talent. Now, of course, being ignored like this could happen to anyone— 18 such is the overload in our public schools. But my friend couldn't help wondering how the school would have responded to this talent had the artist been one of her own, middle-class white children.

Terms like "prejudice" and "racism" often miss the full scope of racial 19
devaluation in our society, implying as they do that racial devaluation comes primarily from the strongly prejudiced, not from "good people" like Jerome's teacher. But the prevalence of racists—deplorable though racism is—misses the full extent of Jerome's burden, perhaps even the most profound part.

He faces a devaluation that grows out of our images of society and 20
the way those images catalogue people. The catalogue need never be taught. It is implied by all we see around us: the kinds of people revered in advertising (consider the unrelenting racial advocacy of Ralph Lauren ads) and movies (black women are rarely seen as romantic partners, for example); media discussions of whether a black can be President; invitation lists to junior high school birthday parties; school curricula; literary and musical canons. These details create an image of society in which black Americans simply do not fare well. When I was a kid, we captured it with the saying, "If you're white you're right, if your're yellow you're mellow, if you're brown stick around, but if you're black, get back."

In ways that require no fueling from strong prejudice or stereotypes, 21
these images expand the devaluation of black Americans. They act as mental standards against which information about blacks is evaluated: that which fits these images we accept; that which contradicts them we suspect. Had Jerome had a reading problem, which fits these images, it might have been accepted as characteristic more readily than his extraordinary art work, which contradicts them.

These images do something else as well, something especially perni- 22
cious in the classroom. They set up a jeopardy of double devaluation for blacks, a jeopardy that does not apply to whites. Like anyone, blacks risk devaluation for a particular incompetence, such as a failed test or a flubbed pronunciation. But they further risk that such performances will confirm the broader, racial inferiority they are suspected of. Thus, from the first grade through graduate school, blacks have the extra fear that in the eyes of those around them their full humanity could fall with a poor answer or a mistaken stroke of the pen.

Moreover, because these images are conditioned in all of us, collec- 23
tively held, they can spawn racial devaluation in all of us, not just in the strongly prejudiced. They can do this even in blacks themselves: a majority of black children recently tested said they like and prefer to play with white rather than black dolls—almost fifty years after Kenneth and Mamie Clark, conducting similar experiments, documented identical findings and so paved the way for *Brown* v. *Topeka Board of Education*. Thus Jerome's

devaluation can come from a circle of people in his world far greater than the expressly prejudiced—a circle that apparently includes his teacher.

In ways often too subtle to be conscious but sometimes overt, I believe, 24 blacks remain devalued in American schools, where, for example, a recent national survey shows that through high school they are still more than twice as likely as white children to receive corporal punishment, be suspended from school, or be labeled mentally retarded.

Tragically, such devaluation can seem inescapable. Sooner or later it 25 forces on its victims two painful realizations. The first is that society is preconditioned to see the worst in them. Black students quickly learn that acceptance, if it is to be won at all, will be hard-won. The second is that even if a black student achieves exoneration in one setting—with the teacher and fellow students in one classroom, or at one level of schooling, for example—this approval will have to be rewon in the next classroom, at the next level of schooling. Of course, individual characteristics that enhance one's value in society—skills, class status, appearance, and success—can diminish the racial devaluation one faces. And sometimes the effort to prove oneself fuels achievement. But few from any group could hope to sustain so daunting and everlasting a struggle. Thus, I am afraid, too many black students are left hopeless and deeply vulnerable in America's classrooms.

"Disidentifying" With School

I believe that in significant part the crisis in black Americans' education 26 stems from the power of this vulnerability to undercut identification with schooling, either before it happens or after it has bloomed.

Jerome is an example of the first kind. At precisely the time when he 27 would need to see school as a viable source of self-esteem, his teachers fail to appreciate his best work. The devalued status of his race devalues him and his work in the classroom. Unable to entrust his sense of himself to this place, he resists measuring himself against its values and goals. He languishes there, held by the law, perhaps even by his parents, but not allowing achievement to affect his view of himself. This psychic alienation—the act of not caring—makes him less vulnerable to the specter of devaluation that haunts him. Bruce Hare, an educational researcher, has documented this process among fifth-grade boys in several schools in Champaign, Illinois. He found that although the black boys had considerably lower achievement-test scores than their white classmates, their overall self-esteem was just as high. This stunning imperviousness to poor academic performance was accomplished, he found, by their de-emphasizing school achievement as a basis of self-esteem and giving preference to peer-group relations—a domain in which their esteem prospects were better. They went where they had to go to feel good about themselves.

But recall the young student whose mentor I was. She had already identified with school, and wanted to be a doctor. How can racial vulnerability break so developed an achievement identity? To see, let us follow her steps onto campus. Her recruitment and admission stress her minority status perhaps more strongly than it has been stressed at any other time in her life. She is offered academic and social support services, further implying that she is "at risk" (even though, contrary to common belief, the vast majority of black college students are admitted with qualifications well above the threshold for whites). Once on campus, she enters a socially circumscribed world in which blacks—still largely separate from whites—have lower status; this is reinforced by a sidelining of minority material and interests in the curriculum and in university life. And she can sense that everywhere in this new word her skin color places her under suspicion of intellectual inferiority. All of this gives her the double vulnerability I spoke of: she risks confirming a particular incompetence, at chemistry or a foreign language, for example; but she also risks confirming the racial inferiority she is suspected of—a judgment that can feel as close at hand as a mispronounced word or an ungrammatical sentence. In reaction, usually to some modest setback, she withdraws, hiding her troubles from instructors, counselors, even other students. Quickly, I believe, a psychic defense takes over. She *disidentifies* with achievement; she changes her self-conception, her outlook and values, so that achievement is no longer so important to her self-esteem. She may continue to feel pressure to stay in school—from her parents, even from the potential advantages of a college degree. But now she is psychologically insulated from her academic life, like a disinterested visitor. Cool, unperturbed. But, like a pain-killing drug, disidentification undoes her future as it relieves her vulnerability. 2

The prevalence of this syndrome among black college students has been documented extensively, especially on predominantly white campuses. Summarizing this work, Jacqueline Fleming, a psychologist, writes, "The fact that black students must matriculate in an atmosphere that feels hostile arouses defensive reactions that interfere with intellectual performance. . . . They display academic demotivation and think less of their abilities. They profess losses of energy." Among a sample of blacks on one predominantly white campus, Richard Nisbett and Andrew Reaves, both psychologists, and I found that attitudes related to disidentification were more strongly predictive of grades than even academic preparation (that is, SATs and high school grades). 2

To make matters worse, once disidentification occurs in a school, it can spread like the common cold. Blacks who identify and try to achieve embarrass the strategy by valuing the very thing the strategy denies the value 3 of. Thus pressure to make it a group norm can evolve quickly and become fierce. Defectors are called "oreos" or "incognegroes." One's identity as an authentic black is held hostage, made incompatible with school identification. For black students, then, pressure to disidentify with school can come from the already demoralized as well as from racial vulnerability in the setting.

Stigmatization of the sort suffered by black Americans is probably also a barrier to the school achievement of other groups in our society, such as lower-class whites, Hispanics, and women in male-dominated fields. For example, at a large midwestern university I studied, women match men's achievement in the liberal arts, where they suffer no marked stigma, but underachieve compared with men (get lower grades than men with the same ACT scores) in engineering and premedical programs, where they, like blacks across the board, are more vulnerable to suspicions of inferiority. 31

"Wise" Schooling

> "When they approach me they see . . . everything and anything except me. . . . [This] invisibility . . . occurs because of a peculiar disposition of the eyes. . . ."
>
> —Ralph Ellison, *Invisible Man*

Erving Goffman, borrowing from gays of the 1950s, used the term "wise" to describe people who don't themselves bear the stigma of a given group but who are accepted by the group. These are people in whose eyes the full humanity of the stigmatized is visible, people in whose eyes they feel less vulnerable. If racial vulnerability undermines black school achievement, as I have argued, then this achievement should improve significantly if schooling is made "wise"—that is, made to see value and promise in black students and to act accordingly. 32

And yet, although racial vulnerability at school may undermine black achievement, so many other factors seem to contribute—from the debilitations of poverty to the alleged dysfunctions of black American culture—that one might expect "wiseness" in the classroom to be of little help. Fortunately, we have considerable evidence to the contrary. Wise schooling may indeed be the missing key to the schoolhouse door. 33

In the mid-seventies black students in Philip Uri Treisman's early calculus courses at the University of California at Berkeley consistently fell to the bottom of every class. To help, Treisman developed the Mathematics Workshop Program, which, in a surprisingly short time, reversed their fortunes, causing them to outperform their white and Asian counterparts. And although it is only a freshman program, black students who take it graduate 34 at a rate comparable to the Berkeley average. Its central technique is group study of calculus concepts. But it is also wise; it does things that allay the racial vulnerabilities of these students. Stressing their potential to learn, it recruits them to a challenging "honors" workshop tied to their first calculus course. Building on their skills, the workshop gives difficult work, often beyond course content, to students with even modest preparation (some of their math SATs dip to the 300s). Working together, students soon understand that everyone knows something and nobody knows everything, and learning is speeded through shared understanding. The wisdom of these tactics is their subtext message: "You are valued in this program because of your academic potential—regardless of your current skill level. You have no more to fear than the next person, and since the work is difficult, success is a credit to your ability, and a setback is a reflection only of the challenge." The black students' double vulnerability around failure—the fear that they lack ability, and the dread that they will be devalued—is thus reduced. They can relax and achieve. The movie *Stand and Deliver* depicts Jaime Escalante using the same techniques of assurance and challenge to inspire advanced calculus performance in East Los Angeles Chicano high schoolers. And, explaining Xavier University's extraordinary success in producing black medical students, a spokesman said recently, "What doesn't work is saying, 'You need remedial work.' What does work is saying, 'You may be somewhat behind at this time but you're a talented person. We're going to help you advance at an accelerated rate.' "

The work of James Comer, a child psychiatrist at Yale, suggests that 3
wiseness can minimize even the barriers of poverty. Over a fifteen-year period he transformed the two worst elementary schools in New Haven, Connecticut, into the third and fifth best in the city's thirty-three-school system without any change in the type of students—largely poor and black. His guiding belief is that learning requires a strongly accepting relationship between teacher and student. "After all," he notes, "what is the difference between scribble and a letter of the alphabet to a child? The only reason the letter is meaningful, and worth learning and remembering, is because a *meaningful* other wants him or her to learn and remember it." To build these relationships Comer focuses on the overall school climate, shaping it not so much to transmit specific skills, or to achieve order per se, or even to improve achievement, as to establish a valuing and optimistic atmosphere in which a child can—to use his term—"identify" with learning. Responsibility for this lies with a team of ten to fifteen members, headed by the principal and made up of teachers, parents, school staff, and child-development experts (for example, psychologists or special-education teachers). The team develops a plan of specifics: teacher training, parent workshops, coordination of information about students. But at base I believe it tries to ensure that the students—vulnerable on so many counts—

get treated essentially like middle-class students, with conviction about their value and promise. As this happens, their vulnerability diminishes, and with it the companion defenses of disidentification and misconduct. They achieve, and apparently identify, as their achievement gains persist into high school. Comer's genius, I believe, is to have recognized the importance of these vulnerabilities as barriers to *intellectual* development, and the corollary that schools hoping to educate such students must learn first how to make them feel valued.

These are not isolated successes. Comparable results were observed, for example, in a Comer-type program in Maryland's Prince Georges County, in the Stanford economist Henry Levin's accelerated-schools program, and in Harlem's Central Park East Elementary School, under the principalship of Deborah Meier. And research involving hundreds of programs and schools points to the same conclusion: black achievement is consistently linked to conditions of schooling that reduce racial vulnerability. These include relatively harmonious race relations among students; a commitment by teachers and schools to seeing minority-group members achieve; the instructional goal that students at all levels of preparation achieve; desegregation at the classroom as well as the school level; and a de-emphasis on ability tracking. 36

That erasing stigma improves black achievement is perhaps the strongest evidence that stigma is what depresses it in the first place. This is no happy realization. But it lets in a ray of hope: whatever other factors also depress black achievement—poverty, social isolation, poor preparation—they may be substantially overcome in a schooling atmosphere that reduces racial and other vulnerabilities, not through unrelenting niceness or ferocious regimentation but by wiseness, by *seeing* value and acting on it. 37

What Makes Schooling Unwise

But if wise schooling is so attainable, why is racial vulnerability the rule, not the exception, in American schooling? 38

One factor is the basic assimilationist offer that schools make to blacks: You can be valued and rewarded in school (and society), the schools say to these students, but you must first master the culture and ways of the American mainstream, and since that mainstream (as it is represented) is essentially white, this means you must give up many particulars of being black—styles of speech and appearance, value priorities, preferences—at least in mainstream settings. This is asking a lot. But it has been the "color-blind" offer to every immigrant and minority group in our nation's history, the core of the melting-pot ideal, and so I think it strikes most of us as fair. Yet non-immigrant minorities like blacks and Native Americans have always been here, and thus are entitled, more than new immigrants, to participate 39 in the defining images of the society projected in school. More important, their exclusion from these images denies their contributive history and presence in society. Thus, whereas immigrants can tilt toward assimilation in pursuit of the opportunities for which they came, American blacks may find it harder to assimilate. For them, the offer of acceptance in return for assimilation carries a primal insult: it asks them to join in something that has made them invisible.

Now, I must be clear. This is not a criticism of Western civilization. My 4 concern is an omission of image-work. In his incisive essay "What America Would Be Like Without Blacks," Ralph Ellison showed black influence on American speech and language, the themes of our finest literature, and our most defining ideals of personal freedom and democracy. In *The World They Made Together,* Mechal Sobel described how African and European influences shaped the early American South in everything from housing design and land use to religious expression. The fact is that blacks are not outside the American mainstream but, in Ellison's words, have always been "one of its major tributaries." Yet if one relied on what is taught in America's schools, one would never know this. There blacks have fallen victim to a collective self-deception, a society's allowing itself to assimilate like mad from its constituent groups while representing itself to itself as if the assimilation had never happened, as if progress and good were almost exclusively Western and white. A prime influence of American society on world culture is the music of black Americans, shaping art forms from rock-and-roll to modern dance. Yet in American schools, from kindergarten through graduate school, these essentially black influences have barely peripheral status, are largely outside the canon. Thus it is not what is taught but what is *not* taught, what teachers and professors have never learned the value of, that reinforces a fundamental unwiseness in American schooling, and keeps black disidentification on full boil.

Deep in the psyche of American educators is a presumption that black 4 students need academic remediation, or extra time with elemental curricula to overcome background deficits. This orientation guides many efforts to close the achievement gap—from grammar school tutoring to college academic-support programs—but I fear it can be unwise. Bruno Bettelheim and Karen Zelan's article "Why Children Don't Like to Read" comes to mind: apparently to satisfy the changing sensibilities of local school boards over this century, many books that children like were dropped from school reading lists; when children's reading scores also dropped, the approved texts were replaced by simpler books; and when reading scores dropped again, these were replaced by even simpler books, until eventually the children could hardly read at all, not because the material was too difficult but because they were bored stiff. So it goes, I suspect, with a great many of these remediation efforts. Moreover, because so many such programs target blacks primarily, they virtually equate black identity with substandard intellectual status, amplifying racial vulnerability. They can even undermine students' ability to gain confidence from their achievement, by sharing credit for their successes while implying that their failures stem from inadequacies beyond the reach of remediation.

The psychologist Lisa Brown and I recently uncovered evidence of just how damaging this orientation may be. At a large, prestigious university we found that whereas the grades of black graduates of the 1950s improved during the students' college years until they virtually matched the school average, those of blacks who graduated in the 1980s (we chose only those with above-average entry credentials, to correct for more-liberal admissions policies in that decade) worsened, ending up considerably below the school average. The 1950s graduates faced outward discrimination in everything from housing to the classroom, whereas the 1980s graduates were supported by a phalanx of help programs. Many things may contribute to this pattern. The Jackie Robinson "pioneer" spirit of the 1950s blacks surely helped them endure. And in a pre-affirmative-action era, they may have been seen as intellectually more deserving. But one cannot ignore the distinctive fate of 1980s blacks: a remedial orientation put their abilities under suspicion, deflected their ambitions, distanced them from their successes, and painted them with their failures. Black students on today's campuses may experience far less overt prejudice than their 1950s counterparts but, ironically, may be more racially vulnerable. 42

The Elements of Wiseness

For too many black students school is simply the place where, more concertedly, persistently, and authoritatively than anywhere else in society, they learn how little valued they are. 43

Clearly, no simple recipe can fix this, but I believe we now understand the basics of a corrective approach. Schooling must focus more on reducing the vulnerabilities that block identification with achievement. I believe that four conditions, like the legs of a stool, are fundamental. 44

- If what is meaningful and important to a teacher is to become meaningful and important to a student, the student must feel valued by the teacher for his or her potential and as a person. Among the more fortunate in society, this relationship is often taken for granted. But it is precisely the relationship that race can still undermine in American society. As Comer, Escalante, and Treisman have shown, when one's students bear race and class vulnerabilities, building this relationship is the first order of business—at all levels of schooling. No tactic of instruction, no matter how ingenious, can succeed without it. 45

The challenge and the promise of personal fulfillment, not remediation (under whatever guise), should guide the education of these students. Their present skills should be taken into account, and they should be moved along at a pace that is demanding but doesn't defeat them. Their ambitions should never be scaled down but should instead be guided to inspiring goals even when extraordinary dedication is called for. Frustration will be less crippling than alienation. Here psychology is everything: remediation defeats, challenge strengthens—affirming their potential, crediting them with their achievements, inspiring them.

But the first conditon, I believe, cannot work without the second, and vice versa. A valuing teacher-student relationship goes nowhere without challenge, and challenge will always be resisted outside a valuing relationship. (Again, I must be careful about something: in criticizing remediation I am not opposing affirmative-action recruitment in the schools. The success of this policy, like that of school integration before it, depends, I believe, on the tactics of implementation. Where students are valued and challenged, they generally succeed.)

- Racial integration is a generally useful element in this design, if not a necessity. Segregation, whatever its purpose, draws out group differences and makes people feel more vulnerable when they inevitably cross group lines to compete in the larger society. This vulnerability, I fear, can override confidence gained in segregated schooling unless that confidence is based on strongly competitive skills and knowledge—something that segregated schooling, plagued by shortages of resources and access, has difficulty producing.

- The particulars of black life and culture—art, literature, political and social perspective, music—must be presented in the mainstream curriculum of American schooling, not consigned to special days, weeks, or even months of the year, or to special-topic courses and programs aimed essentially at blacks. Such channeling carries the disturbing message that the material is not of general value. And this does two terrible things: it wastes the power of this material to alter our images of the American mainstream—continuing to frustrate black identification with it—and it excuses in whites and others a huge ignorance of their own society. The true test of democracy, Ralph Ellison has said, "is . . . the inclusion—not assimilation—of the black man."

Finally, if I might be allowed a word specifically to black parents, one issue is even more immediate: our children may drop out of school before the first committee meets to accelerate the curriculum. Thus, although we, along with all Americans, must strive constantly for wise schooling, I believe we cannot wait for it. We cannot yet forget our essentially heroic challenge: to foster in our children a sense of hope and entitlement to mainstream American life and schooling, even when it devalues them.

STUDENT ESSAYS

Dulce Est Sapientia

David Gray

David Gray (b. 1971) grew up in Charlottesville, Virginia, and is majoring in philosophy with a concentration in ethics. David spends his free time performing Shakespeare and working as a carpenter and plumber. About writing, David reports: "More and more I have learned the value of writing about what I know. My writing is most authentic, honest, and comfortable when I write about what is important to me."

"Puell**a**, Puell**ae**, Puell**ae**, Puell**am**, Puell**a**," Mr. Mears intones, beating out 1 the rhythm of the declension with his long wooden pointing stick on the top of his desk. Mr. Mears was born a century too late. He had in every way, and indeed, cultivated, the aspect of a Victorian British schoolmaster. He parted his hair down the middle and rode to school on a bicycle with a little triangular orange flag waving in back. He was not above employing a little verbal and physical abuse on an unruly pupil, and his pointing stick was more often used for slamming down on his desk with a deafening crack to demand attention than it was for pointing. One day someone broke his beloved stick and it was replaced the next week with a riding crop.

I learned a lot of Latin from Mr. Mears. I was quick to memorize declen- 2 sions and had a knack for conjugations. I excelled in the games we played in class, snapping out correct endings and identifying grammatical constructions. The class did very well on the state and national exams and I even placed first in the state for Latin I.

I remember Mr. Mears clearly, I remember some vocabulary, I remem- 3 ber the girl who sat in front of me in class whom I was deeply and secretly in love with, but where have all those endings gone? If Mr. Mears should reappear suddenly and demand the perfect subjunctive of *venire,* I suppose I should stutter hopelessly as the riding crop came crashing down indignantly on the desk. Latin inscriptions remain a puzzle for me. "In the third year of something, Otto, king of the Germans, did something to somebody for the greater glory of God." I always wind up with half-sensical, impressionistic translations, almost never with a real comprehension.

What exactly is going on here? Did I once know Latin and then forget it through disuse? But I have not forgotten how to speak French or ride a bicycle, although I rarely use these skills. Perhaps, I am led to speculate, I never really learned Latin at all. What I learned was a bunch of words which, with the aid of various ending sounds, indicated that Gaius was either a good man delivering messages to the lieutenant or a general who had struck camp at the seventh hour. Obviously all this did not mean much to me, and so I forgot it. I may have known it once but I never truly *learned* it. 4

Learning involves something more than merely amassing facts and information. Knowledge does not become learning until it is incorporated into some kind of larger understanding, the understanding of a system. Just as words or sentences often become meaningless without some context, so ideas must have a context in which they are organized and make sense, otherwise they remain just so many disparate facts. These contexts are built up in the mind slowly and progressively. Of course there can be no context without information to fill it. Eventually these pieces of information coalesce into a whole and are grasped as having some dynamic connection to each other. 5

I had often seen Surrealist paintings and I knew something of modern psychology and a little of world affairs at the beginning of this century but I had never really brought these ideas together until the day I sat in on a lecture of European Intellectual History. The lecturer showed the connection of all these ideas, these facts, that I had stored away but had never really used. Dali's chaotic, mysterious, disturbing scenes and Magritte's perplexing images of work boots with human toes and coffins sitting up became more than just expressions of an artist's whimsical and arbitrary aesthetic experimentation. Surrealists strove, as the name of the movement suggests, to represent something which transcended ordinary objective reality by giving a picture of the inner workings of human consciousness. These paintings did not spring from nothing but relied on the Freudian tradition of the interpretation of dreams and the subconscious. These artists did not admit of any determined or objective standard of "reality" except that which the mind concocted. 6

The Surrealist painter showed reality as processed by the subconscious or as distorted in dreams as having true significance and validity apart from any fixed standard. Suddenly, the various unconnected facts and impressions that I already had stored in my mind fit into a context; they did not exist apart or in a vacuum but enlarged and commented upon each other so that I came to a greater and firmer understanding of the Surrealist movement. It is only when we understand ideas as participating in a system 7 that they really become graspable. This conjecture leads me to question how it is that we construct these systems. Is there some underlying principle common to all these cases? Is there an innate capacity for learning and using systems?

I believe that a human being is not born with a blank mind, a tabula rasa on which can be inscribed pieces of information which pass as knowledge. We are not empty receptacles waiting to be stuffed full of Latin endings. I reject the empiricist model of learning as just the effects of stimuli and response gathered in the course of experience and instruction; there is something more complicated and subtle going on. We know from experience that the mind often refuses to learn what it is not inclined to understand. I could never learn Swahili or how to play the bagpipes even if I read a Swahili dictionary or got a kilt and pipes because I have not the least interest in doing either. I might be able to pick up a word here or a note there but without the effort to come to a true understanding of the fundamental principles involved I will never really learn. The mind does not register, or does not make sense of, information where it is not accompanied by another factor: a will to understand. My mind has the capacity for assimilating this knowledge but I set up barriers which prevent me from realizing this capacity. How often do we say, "This is too hard" or "This is not interesting, I can't learn it"? However, these barriers we create are entirely artificial. There is no physiological impediment to my learning Swahili; but I can see no connection between Swahili and any other knowledge I have. 8

Even if I were to master all the grammar, though I doubt even this is possible, it would remain useless information until an opportunity arose where it would become pertinent. If I were suddenly dropped down in the middle of Kenya I have no doubt that I would quickly start to learn. By concentrating our attention in specific areas, by making sharp divisions in what knowledge we consider "useless" or "useful," we set up barriers; we put on intellectual blinders which keep us from steering off the familiar one-way track to understanding. Surely the job of an education is to remove these blinders to allow for a wider, more complete view of all knowledge. We can be shown that the distinctions we draw between different kinds of knowledge are really artificial. Our capacity to learn one thing is as great as our capacity to learn another given the right circumstances. The barriers do not exist naturally in the mind itself but are externally imposed on us. 9

This suggestion that the mind has a broad and general capacity for learning leads me to the notion of innate ideas, a faculty of the mind, be it physiological or conceptual, which enables us to learn by ordering and incorporating knowledge into learning. Plato presents a remarkably beautiful and sublime theory in his dialogue *The Meno*, where he examines the proposition that virtue may be taught. Plato concludes and seeks to dem- 10 onstrate that knowledge is not acquired externally at all but is resident in the mind of each individual and needs only to be drawn out. Thus everything is already known and requires only to be "remembered." It is on this model that the technique of Socratic questioning, which seeks to draw out from the student's own thoughts the elements of knowledge, hinges. A teacher does not inject facts into the student but brings his latent knowledge to conscious fruition.

Of course Plato is most likely wrong in assuming that all factual knowl- 11
edge is in us from birth (or even before birth if we accept his idea of the transmigration of souls). But the idea that there are some fundamental internal principles which constitute a learning faculty has a good deal of merit. The theory suggests that we can learn anything that we can have conception of. This may sound like a tautology but the idea is more subtle than it appears. It does not suggest that we can learn absolutely anything but only those things which can be fitted into a context the mind can understand.

This is not to say that we can only know what we already know but 12
that we can only make sense of information within the framework of some familiar and intuitively understood system. By drawing on facts that we have in our minds we can make sense of larger ideas; we can define systems of thought. But we can only realize those systems of ideas that we have a pre-established capacity for. I would suggest that this capacity is very broad but is often artificially narrowed by imposed barriers such as those which might keep me from learning Swahili. Perhaps we do not know all factual information intuitively, but it is quite possible that the conceptual context of ideas is innate. We are not born understanding the significance of the symbols: $8 \times 7 = 56$, but we probably have some innate understanding of quantities and a fixed capacity for numbering which makes this idea comprehensible and sensible.

On the plane flying back to school from Spring Break, I was sitting next to 13
a mother and her young child. The baby was almost two years old, I would imagine, and was in the process of learning language. Putting aside the *Essential Works of John Stuart Mill,* which my mind was not ready to receive at that moment, I watched as the child learned. She had a paper full of sticky-backed colored stars which she was playing with, peeling them off the sheet and affixing them to her mother's leg and face. The patient, and always opportunistic, mother decided to make the exercise into a learning experience. "Red, blue, green," she said, pointing to the appropriately colored stars. "One, two, three," she said, again pointing out the same stars.

I was baffled. How could this curly-headed, blue-eyed babe be ex- 14
pected to discern in these intrinsically meaningless locutions designations

of hue on the one hand and quantity on the other within the same objects? But the child did indeed seem to understand something of the distinction. Her powers of comprehension seemed to be developed far beyond what could possibly be expected from mere repetition of color names and numbers.

I can not be sure how much the child really did understand these ideas 15
or how exactly she had learned them if she did, but it seemed to me that she must have some sort of natural capacity for understanding the concept of color and another for distinguishing designations of quantity which would enable her to attach meanings to intrinsically meaningless things such as the words "red" and "two." Without such a capacity it did not seem that instruction by repetition could ever result in learning.

The linguist Noam Chomsky theorizes the existence of a universal, 16
intrinsic human capacity for the learning of language. He argues that there are basic grammatical constructions in language which do not develop arbitrarily but depend on a structured faculty of the mind which chooses one system and not any equally plausible others. This "language faculty" makes it possible to learn any "natural language" which fits the prescribed pattern. However, he argues, we would be unable to learn some arbitrarily invented grammar or Martian grammar if it did not correspond to any intuitively understood standard of language that we have. For instance, we could not learn a language which constructed questions by inverting declarative sentences if our brains were not "hard-wired" to do so, and, indeed, no known language does this.

This method seems just as plausible as the system we actually do use 17
of inverting certain elements of the word order in sentences, but, he argues, we would be incapable of learning this kind of system as we would a natural language because we have no innate capacity for it. It is practically impossible to say with certainty what is "natural" but it appears that our language faculty does not recognize it as a valid way of constructing a question. "Presidency the win will Bush George?" will always "sound wrong" and though this system could be studied and learned it would not be grasped in the same way that a natural language would be. Chomsky would say that a system that did not conform to the intuitive rules of grammar would be very difficult if not impossible for a child to learn. This sort of genetic capacity for learning might also reasonably apply to other areas of knowledge such as mathematics or logic. Such a theory certainly has implications on how knowledge should be taught.

If learning happens when facts become understood and organized 18
with regard to these innate ideas then education should stress the context of ideas above the mere presentation of facts. Often, the study of a language by mere drilling of grammar and vocabulary is useful only up to a certain point, to the extent that it provides some groundwork for the lan-

guage. But the real learning of language seems only to happen when it is read or spoken. Only then do we get an understanding of the actual grammatical and syntactical context in which all these various elements function. Only then do sentences begin to "sound right" or "sound wrong." My knowledge of Latin never developed beyond memorization because I never spoke or wrote it and so it never made sense as a whole.

Of course education can only proceed with facts as a basis for learning. 19
It is impossible to realize a system or to invoke any innate faculty without giving it material, i.e. hard facts, to work with. But by presenting facts in such a way that they inform and build on one another, and can be understood as participating in an ordered system, education breaks down the barriers between disparate bits of information and even different fields of knowledge and allows one to make the connection between ideas which constitutes an act of learning.

I have a theory of the joke as an instance of just such a connection of ideas. 20
A man goes to a cocktail party and gets soused. He approaches his host and asks, "Pardon me, but do lemons whistle?"

The host looks at him oddly and answers, "No, lemons don't whistle." 21

"Oh dear," says the guest, "then I'm afraid I just squeezed your canary 22
into my gin and tonic."

One need not be an ornithologist to get the joke, but one must know 23
that canaries are yellow and that they whistle. Likewise, one must know that lemons are yellow and that they do not whistle. What constitutes the joke is a connection made between two things, a canary and a lemon, which have absolutely nothing in common except for their yellowness. It would never occur to us to make a comparison between the two, let alone to confuse one with the other. But this is the value of the joke, to force into our consciousness the ideas which we held but never actively considered. The unexpected juxtaposition of these two unrelated things, the suggestion that they may be identical, makes us look at them anew and ask ourselves what makes a lemon a lemon and a bird a bird, since there is obviously something more essential to these things than yellowness. The two ideas play off of each other and help to define each other. My understanding of lemonness is extended and complicated by the consideration of canaryness; they are no longer remote, isolated concepts.

This knocking down of barriers between ideas is parallel to the process 24
that occurs in all learning. The barriers that we set between ideas suddenly crumble; the boundaries that kept us thinking in narrow patterns are extended to include other modes of thought. Apparently dissociated concepts are brought together in a single context and understood as somehow connected and inter-related.

And the purpose of learning need not be really distinct from the pur- 25 pose of a joke. A joke makes us laugh; it gives us pleasure. Learning too, when it is true learning, accomplishes this goal—when it satisfies our innate active capacities for recognizing coherent systems at work in our lives. This recognition, which is endless and progressive, constitutes the higher enjoyment in learning.

The Language of Learning

Alison Kaufman

Alison Kaufman (b. 1973) grew up in Madison, Wisconsin, and is majoring in East Asian Studies, concentrating on modern China. Alison speaks Chinese and German, sings in a choral society, and works as a peer tutor in her school's writing center. About writing, Alison reports: "Good writing is beautiful. Everything fits together in complex and interesting ways that are very satisfying to a reader. I learn so much more about a subject by writing about it than I do from just talking or reading. In speaking, there is always the ellipsis, but in writing you have to think your thoughts through to the end."

I was very good in math until third grade, when we learned how to multiply 1
numbers of more than one digit. No one told me to move the numbers over one decimal place for every power of ten you multiply, so I kept getting wrong answers. I was crushed by my defeat, but as soon as my teacher explained the concept to me, multiplication was easy to learn. And so I toodled along happily in math for several more years, and was again very good at it until eleventh grade, when I took calculus.

Calculus was a complete mystery to me: I didn't understand what a 2
limit was, or why I should care, and I certainly couldn't do any problems involving one. The teacher, whom I despised, would stand at the blackboard and explain over and over again the relationship between some mysterious combination of Greek letters. No matter how often he went over the definitions, though, I just couldn't seem to learn them. I was still missing some connection between the abstract ideas and the concrete examples, and without this connection neither the ideas nor the examples had any meaning.

This link between the abstract and the concrete, the general concept 3
and the specific example, is made through language: the spoken and written communication of ideas from one person to another. This communication is not restricted to words and symbols controlled by grammatical rules: it can include gestures, noises, anything that conveys the speaker's idea. Calculus was so alien to me because it was in another language,

one which I didn't understand—the teacher wasn't conveying the ideas in a form I could recognize. Knowing that "the limit of *F*(t) as *t* approaches *c* is the number *L* if: . . ."—or any other fact or piece of information—isn't the same as learning the concepts that guide and interpret the facts. The only way to truly learn these concepts is either by understanding the language in which they are taught, or by translating them into your own language, your own way of organizing thoughts. Doing so requires a certain amount of effort; in math, I was often tempted to get around the tedious process of listening to my teacher and then translating what he was saying into my own language by cramming: staying up all night before a test and stuffing as much information into my brain as possible (usually, just enough to get me through the exam). Sometimes cramming works; but the material fades away again as soon as the particular test for which it was crammed is over. You don't learn anything by cramming—all you are doing is memorizing someone else's words without understanding the concepts in your own terms. Herein lies the vital difference between words and ideas: words thrown together in any random combination will still have roughly the same meaning individually, but the idea will be vastly different depending on the way the words are combined. The words, gestures, symbols are the materials from which a language is constructed, but it is the concepts behind these words that give the language meaning. Each personal language emphasizes and is created by a slightly different, personal way of thinking, and thus is slightly different from every other personal language.

Unfortunately, most of the subjects we learn in school are taught in, 4
at most, one or two languages, fairly regulated patterns of words and ideas. School does not encourage its students to create their own languages. Instead, teaching follows a fairly standard format which everyone is expected to adhere to: we learn certain definitions and rules over and over again—the limit of *F*(*t*) is almost defined as the number *c*—and are led to assume that these are the only ways of learning the subject. These standardized languages too often are seen as a measure of a person's overall intelligence or comprehension of an idea, rather than simply his or her ability to use the language in which the idea is presented. In his essay "How They Write the SAT," David Owen looks at this emphasis on "proper" use of a language: a large portion of most standardized tests, such as the SAT, is concerned with the use of a "standard" language—vocabulary, sentence construction, gammar of "standard written English." In using this formalized language, where every answer is always "right" or "wrong," the student is restricted to a very narrow range of thought processes, which are often "drab, humorless, and plodding." Yet there might be many ways to answer the question asked, many different viewpoints that could be taken other than that of the test-giver. A question could be answered sarcastically, seriously, excitedly—the different answers reflect the mood

and sentiment of the speaker. The language creates the mood and setting for the user, while being created by the user.

A good language is structured specifically to fit its users. When black writer June Jordan became interested in the phenomenon of the language of Black English, she realized that part of the reason Alice Walker's *The Color Purple* is such an effective novel is that it is told in the language of the people it is about. In her essay "Nobody Mean More to Me Than You and the Life of Willie Jordan," Jordan explores the way a language reflects the nature of its users. To many people, the concept of formally studying a spoken colloquial dialect that is considered blatantly "wrong" by most standards seems crazy. Yet this dialect expresses black ideas better than "standard" white English: Black English is a language of the present tense, of action, of a "pre-technocratic, if not anti-technical, culture," conveying through its sentence structure and vocabulary the priorities and values of an entire society. Thus language can provide a completely different way to look at a subject: A student who has grown up in a black household, and thus holds different views about grammar and structure than a white student, might do poorly on a test of standardized language and yet be a brilliant thinker. Thus this "standard" language can actually restrict the creativity of its users, if it is foreign to their entire pattern of thinking. By removing the linguistic restrictions on her students, encouraging them to write in the language they think and speak in, Jordan encourages them to express their own ideas, their own interpretations of what they have learned, in a language they are more comfortable with. The right language allows the user to focus more on the ideas he's trying to express, rather than on the medium in which it is expressed—he should be so comfortable in his own tongue that he does not have to concentrate all his energy on making sure it follows somebody else's rules. 5

In order to create your own language, however, you must have at least some understanding of other languages and their rules—to translate an idea into a context that makes more sense to you, you must have some consciousness of what the idea is. If I couldn't even vaguely comprehend what my math teacher was talking about, any amount of restatement wouldn't do me any good. Some ideas just don't translate into some languages, because the language is not structured to accommodate the ideas. In her excitement at teaching a language that had heretofore only been an oral one, Jordan had her students translating everything into Black English. Sometimes this just didn't work, though: Henrik Ibsen's *A Doll's House* sounded completely ridiculous in Black English. An upright, oppressed Scandinavian housewife would never be found saying "Law must suck," as Jordan's students have her doing, any more than a black farm wife would plead. "It's too soon for sex, Alfonso," The translations didn't sound right because they were artificial: the wrong language was being 6 used to express the ideas. Just learning the "rules" for using Black English wasn't enough to use it correctly. In order for Black English to be used effectively, it had to be expressing a black idea; otherwise, it became just as restrictive as the SAT's "one best answer." The right language sounds natural, effortless: it allows the speaker to convey his ideas in his own voice.

Part of learning to use a language is learning when that personal voice 7
is appropriate: understanding when to use your personal language to address a situation, and when to use someone else's, more "standard" form. Such understanding does not come easily: learning is a gradual process, following a slow path from observation and listening to translating to understanding. Real learning involves a fair amount of self-discipline, being willing to make the effort to speak other people's language, at least a little, to be able to translate it into your own. Once we understand the context of an issue, how it fits in with all our other ideas and knowledge, we must turn it over for ourselves, looking at it and trying it out from a hundred different angles. True learning involves the active use of language, finding the connection between an idea and its reality in relation to the speaker, and being able to express it so that others can understand that relationship, and speak of it on *their* own terms. There is no real "standard" language, regardless of what the SAT researchers come up with. "Obviously," as Jordan tells us "numerous forms of English now operate inside a natural, an uncontrollable continuum of development. . . . [H]ow strange and how tenuous is any concept of 'Standard English'—or indeed, any 'standard' language." All languages are in a constant state of change: as we learn new ideas, learn how to fit them into our own mode of thinking, we also fit them into our own language, expanding and changing it.

Learning the Alphabet

Rachel Manalili

Rachel Manalili (b. 1972) grew up in Newark, New Jersey, and is majoring in both music and English. Rachel plays the piano and conducts her church choir. About writing, Rachel tells us: "I have learned that the art of writing is never isolated from even the most insignificant experiences. Every time I sit at the keyboard, I sit down with every person I have ever known, and every action I have ever done. This insight about writing has led me to be more observant of the people and the world around me and more appreciative of the richness which they bring into my life."

The letter L was my enemy until I was eight years old. The consonant that for other children stood for lollipops and licorice for me meant only labor and loathing. I had the dreaded disease of a speech impediment; all my l's came out sounding like hard g's. This was especially difficult with a name like Rachel Manalili, and when Mom and Dad got tired enough of having a daughter known as Racheg Managigi they asked for me to be sent to speech therapy. 1

Since state-funded speech clinics could not be set up inside school buildings that were funded by the church, I was made every Tuesday to pull on my coat, skip spelling class, and trek outside, across the playground to the small trailer at the very edge of school grounds. I was very conspicuous then; all passers-by, the apron-clad old ladies hurrying off to cook lunch for five hundred hungry little mouths, the smiling priests who patted my head on their way to visit classes—all of them knew me. They *knew* that I didn't lick lollipops, but goggipops; I didn't even lick them, I gicked them. And I knew that secretly they all laughed at me for it. I was lowlier than the low. 2

Inside the trailer the degradation would continue: Mrs. Lynch would gleefully apply jelly to the roof of my mouth, in order to show me where my tongue should be positioned for proper pronunciation of The Letter. It is really not such a nice thing, having a jelly-swabbed Q-tip stuck in your mouth; it is like exposing your weaknesses to a dentist. The pronunciation rules were tiresome and tedious: the tip of the tongue had to be placed lightly on the alveolar ridge, a slight humming noise meanwhile being made in the back of the throat, similar to the hum of a refrigerator. . . . I was not to let the tip of my tongue fall, nor the back of my tongue rise, lest the deliquent /g/ sound be produced. . . . 3

But these rules, heavy and burdensome, seemed quite beyond my reach; nothing, not even the ridiculous word games we played ("Rachel, what do you use to climb a roof?" "A gadder, Mrs. Gynch."), seemed to accomplish anything. At night when my mother tucked me in I would complain and complain, and she would hush me and say with quiet reassurance that it would all be over once I conquered my enemy completely. That was all; her unspoken confidence in me was comforting for the time being, at least. Then she would shut the light in my small pink bedroom, and say good night. 4

"I gove you, Mommy," I would answer. 5

It happened though, one night. I don't even know how it came to be; all of a sudden, without the aid of jelly, the tip of my tongue found its place, and the universe suddenly seemed to open up and make known to me all its secrets: 6

"I love you, Mommy." 7

It is said that "Love is blind." Still, a love for learning can enable us to 8 see all and everything in a way that could lead us to behold even what Loren Eiseley in his essay "The Hidden Teacher" calls "the great darkness of the ultimate Dreamer, who dreamed the light and the galaxies." If we truly love to learn, he says, we will be able to find the most profound lessons in all things manifested within nature and beyond. "Teachers," Eiseley observes, "are not always to be found in school or in great laboratories. Sometimes what we learn depends upon our own powers of insight. Moreover, our teachers may be hidden, even the greatest teacher." Eiseley cites an unexpected lesson he once received from an orb spider: upon touching the spider's web with a pencil point, he realized that "Spider was circumscribed by spider ideas; its universe was spider universe." Further, he says, "in the world of the spider I did not exist."

The spider was for Eiseley a true hidden teacher; like the hurrying 9
blood cells rushing through our veins, we, too, are oblivious to the universe which exists outside of our sensory extensions. An enemy of learning is anything which establishes boundaries to our "ultimate wonder and creativeness," or which hinders, cataract-like, the vision that enables us to seek out and acknowledge the hidden teachers present all around us.

Eiseley speaks of a love which is all-encompassing and which overlooks 10
nothing; thus are we to love learning. This love may incite passion, tenderness, even fiery desire—but never is it "blind." Rather, a love for learning impels us to look beyond ourselves, our vision reaching even to what Eiseley would have as the boundless universe. If I truly loved learning, nothing, not even The Letter, would be my enemy; I would be able to see the hidden teacher in everyone and everything, and learn.

But who or what was the hidden teacher that led me to freedom from 11
my impediment? The rules of the alphabet seemed ony to hinder, not help; I remember longing for a freedom from the very rules that sought to liberate my tongue from its confinement, for they were a constant reminder of my own failure to comprehend them. I hated The Letter; I hated the alphabet, which contains The Letter; eventually I even hated words, which contain the alphabet.

I realize now that words (even L words) are wonderful because they 12
communicate—for what is teaching but the act of communicating, and what is learning but the act of allowing oneself to be communicated to? Often, however, our teachers, especially our hidden teachers, communicate to us with such eloquence that even words and the rules of the alphabet are rendered unnecessary. Even Laurence Olivier, who perhaps made the most masterful use of the spoken word in his day, once glorified one mode of communication which he called "the most God-given." In this realm The Letter—indeed, all letters—are nonexistent.

I speak of the realm of music, which was void of The Letter and was 13
thus a great comfort to me during my days in Mrs. Lynch's trailer. I soon

discovered, though, that music has an alphabet all its own, with rules and regulations not very much unlike those of the spoken word. A few of my friends in the conservatory, for example, were possessed of a mystic ability called perfect pitch; they could identify pitches without having heard them immediately beforehand. I would stop them in the hallway, in the street even, and enjoin them, "Sing an F-sharp," and from their lips would usher forth a perfect F-sharp.

I was intrigued—what a neat trick!—and set myself out to learn it. I told my teachers that I wanted very much to have perfect pitch. They laughed, however, and patted my head; perfect pitch is inborn, they said, it is genetic; it cannot be learned. Besides, they said, one didn't need perfect pitch to be a great musician. Why did I want to have it anyway? 14

I didn't believe them. For months I spent hours blindfolded at the keyboard, playing random notes and attempting to name them. I think I was on the verge of success, which perhaps is always the most difficult point in the learning process, when I remembered my teachers' words: I was not born with perfect pitch, and thus I would never have it; I was not one of the chosen few. It was then that I gave up, for failure, being foretold by my teachers, loomed imminent. 15

I think I was nine or ten when I gave up my quest for perfect pitch. It was Dorothy DeLay, whose famed success with children has earned for her the title of the greatest violin teacher of our age, who said that "children know no fear." For the most part children still possess that love for learning whose loss Eiseley laments so much. Children know not the limits of that "spider universe," because the universe of a child is much larger than the universe of an adult. It is much easier for children to find the hidden teachers of the world; their vision of the universe is so expansive that they will often put themselves in physical danger to appease their unending curiosity; they will touch a hot stove, or try to climb a dangerous precipice, or enter into a dark and mysterious cavern. Their curiosity is boundless, and thus their universe is boundless. 16

But even a child of nine knows the fear of ridicule, or the fear of failure; these fears are much, much greater than the fear of physical harm, and boundaries to a child's universe arise only when he is told in certain or uncertain terms that failure is imminent. A child's imagination is a wonderful creation, but errs gravely when it begins to imagine that there are indeed boundaries to the universe; most often this happens when a child is ridiculed, or when his questions are dismissed as "too difficult for a child to grasp" or his endeavors are halted because he was "simply not born with the talent." If children ever know fear, they know it then; failure is dark and terrifying enough to block a child's vision of the extent of his universe. This is the seed of the inevitable boundaries, which grow and grow as the child grows. It is a child's enemy, and very often kills a child's love. 17

18 Once the love for learning is destroyed, boredom sets in; the hidden teachers manifest themselves less and less, and learning takes the guise of tedious memorization assignments of facts, rules, and principles. The alphabet, the first set of principles we ever learn, is only the beginning to these rules that fortify and strengthen the boundaries of children's creativity and make them forget their innocent wonder. It is as Socrates says in *Phaedrus*: "The discovery of the alphabet will create forgetfulness in the learners' souls, because they will not use their memories; they will trust to the external written characters and not remember of themselves" (96).

19 And so I am not to forget my creativity, which breaks the boundaries to my universe; but in doing so am I also to break these rules? Even music has an alphabet of its own—am I to ignore these rules, this order, as well? For if I did not, my ears would be closed to the hidden teachers in nature, and I would no longer hear the music in a bird's singing, or in the voice of the breeze rushing through the trees. Nature does not know our alphabets.

20 The twentieth-century composer Igor Stravinsky had a great reverence for order and discipline. In 1940, when he occupied the Charles Eliot Norton chair of poetics at Harvard, he delivered his views in a series of lectures entitled *The Poetics of Music*:

> These natural sounds suggest music to us, but they are not yet themselves music. If we take pleasure in these sounds by imagining that on being exposed to them we become musicians and even, momentarily, creative musicians, we must admit that we are fooling ourselves. They are the promises of music; it takes a human being to keep them: a human being who is sensitive to nature's many voices, of course, but who in addition feels the need of putting them in order and who is gifted for that task with a very special aptitude. (23)

21 Stravinsky was of course considered a revolutionary in his day; thus it is surprising that he should be so adherent to the rules and regulations which most revolutionaries abhor. He goes on, though, to say that "my freedom will be so much the greater and more meaningful the more narrowly I limit my field of action and the more I surround myself with obstacles. Whatever diminishes constraint, diminishes strength. The more constraints one imposes, the more one frees one's self of the chains that shackle the spirit" (65).

22 Stravinsky is referring to the alphabet of music, which he says is the foundation of a musician's freedom to explore the universe around him. Without these rules music does not exist. If there is no music, there is no communication; if there is no communication, there is no learning. Stravinsky's words ring true: we cannot perceive natural sounds as music in themselves, because they do not abide by our rules. Indeed, nature does not know our rules, our alphabets; it is for us to learn the alphabet of nature.

Only in this way can we communicate with the hidden teachers in the world around us.

Thus the more we limit ourselves, the more we are free, and the more boundaries we are able to overcome. Rules do not bound a child's universe, but expand it; we must take care, however, not to allow ourselves to be limited by a single, all-governing set of rules by which we abide to the exclusion of all others that are unknown to us. It is human to fear the unknown, but we cannot be so blind as not to see that the more alphabets we learn and put to use, the more languages we shall be able to speak, and the more we shall be able to communicate with even the most hidden of teachers. 23

If these rules seem daunting at first, if they seem to limit us rather than free us, it is only because they free our vision so much that we see all the more clearly the extent of our success or failure. This is indeed frightening; suddenly we see ourselves as in a mirror, and are faced with the painful prospect of hating what is reflected. The rules, however, are not themselves at fault here, but the destruction of the love for learning through fear. We must overcome this fear and learn not only our own alphabets, such as those which contain The Letter and F-sharps and E-flats, but those of nature and of the universe around us. In doing so we perhaps will be able to speak with quiet confidence the language of ultimate freedom which only the love of learning, which has no enemies, can teach. 24

I sit in my room now, the *Rite of Spring* cascading from my stereo, and I hear Stravinsky's hidden teachers whispering to me from the music as they must have whispered to him years ago. The bassoon rises to a high, glorious note, and I spontaneously think, D-natural; I go to my keyboard and check, and it is indeed a D-natural. I smile to myself—perhaps it was merely a lucky guess—for I have yet to find the hidden teacher who will show me the way to perfect pitch. 25

Perhaps my teachers were right: perhaps it is genetic, perhaps I will never have the same facility as several of my fortunate conservatory classmates. But I am no longer afraid, for I remember a time when I overcame a boundary to my universe, one night in the darkness of my small pink bedroom. It is enough. The love of learning, a true hidden teacher, has whispered to me that my universe is boundless. My hidden teacher has dispelled my fears. I am free, and ready to learn. 26

Works Cited

Plato. *Phaedrus and Letters VII and VIII.* London: Penguin Books, 1973.

Stravinsky, Igor. *Poetics of Music.* Cambridge, Mass.: Harvard University Press, 1970.

The Intricate Web

Ann May Lee

Ann May Lee (b. 1972) grew up in San Francisco and is majoring in biology. Ann's interests include singing, playing piano, and teaching piano to inner city children. About writing, Ann tells us: "One of the most important things I have learned about writing is that it is a slow process. By slow I do not mean tedious or tiresome. Rather, I mean the deliciously, unhurried movement of ideas onto paper, the measured, steady rhythm of words as my mind mixes and matches them, and my fingers bring them to life on the screen of my computer."

"ANN! I need your eyes!" Bev silently whispers to me, her own eyes wide open, as she conducts the Brahms piece. Her graceful arms softly mold and shape the sweet music, but her facial expression betrays her calmness. I feel the tension in her eyes, and try in vain to remember the words. If I don't stop looking down at my music soon, she will start pointing at her eyes, looking dead ahead of me, mouthing the words "watch me!!!" in a very deliberate and exaggerated way. 1

And sure enough, there she goes, her right hand frantically signaling to me to look up as I sing. To me. Unmistakably. I wonder whether she knows just how funny she looks when she does that. 2

The words themselves are really not that difficult; they are all relatively short, and the pronunciation is manageable. And the lines even rhyme. But I cannot sing the piece from memory. 3

I have sung the Brahms piece many, many times. We have rehearsed it often enough—after all, I have no trouble with the music itself. I know my notes, I know the harmonies, I can find my pitch, and I can keep my tempo. With barely a week left before our concert, I even sat down with the music last night, trying desperately to commit the words to memory. I repeated them over and over to myself. I wrote them out. But countless rehearsals and forced repetitions have all been in vain, and I still do not know my words. 4

Try as I did, I could not learn the German. But why? What was it that I was lacking, that I needed in order to learn? I wanted to teach myself the words, but my attempts were without success. Was this the problem—trying to teach myself? Was it a "teacher" that I lacked, some outside person helping me to learn, prompting me along the way, trying to make learning easier? My teachers, be they for math or music, chemistry or writing, all help me learn. Perhaps it was a "German teacher" that I lacked, for I had 5 no such person, no one helping me, no one teaching me. Perhaps this was what I needed, perhaps this is what would lead me to learn.

But Loren Eiseley argues in his essay "The Hidden Teacher" that "we think we learn from teachers, and we sometimes do. But the teachers are not always to be found in school or in great laboratories." As he explains and describes his own personal experience, he puts forth the idea of the "hidden teacher" who teaches in a more subtle way than the conventional school teacher. 6

It is by chance that Eiseley receives "an unexpected lesson," not from a conventional teacher or a great professor, not even from someone who intended to teach, but simply from a spider. Eiseley is looking for fossils on a rainy morning, when he happens to encounter a single orb spider and learns from it about man's limited sphere of knowledge. He pokes the spider's web with a pencil, and realizes that a spider lies at the heart of its own web, entrapped by its finite kingdom of knowledge. For the spider, he and the pencil do not exist. "Spider thoughts in a spider universe," he writes, "sensitive to raindrop and moth flutter, nothing beyond, nothing allowed for the unexpected"; its perceptions and thoughts are limited by the boundaries of its web. Anything outside simply does not exist. 7

Eiseley learns from this chance encounter with the hidden teacher that we humans, too, lie in a limited world. "The spider was a symbol of man in miniature. . . . Man thoughts, as limited as spider thoughts," he wonders. The universe of human knowledge, as large as it may seem, extending through space and through time, is also finite. Man too spins his own bounded web of knowledge around himself, and his knowledge is limited to this web. 8

But through learning, we can extend our web, expand our field of the tangible, the understandable. Through learning we accumulate both knowledge and understanding—both facts and ideas and their assimilation—we spin the fine gossamer and weave the delicate web, extending its boundaries further. Knowledge gives us the building blocks to base new ideas on, to make connections with. And understanding, we integrate and assimilate such knowledge, and complete and complement learning. What is known enters the web, what is understood becomes the web. And thus learning, we expand the web, adding to our repertory of the tangible, spinning more and more elaborate patterns around ourselves. 9

But how difficult the expansion of our web can be. I tried to learn the German words to the Brahms piece, I tried to commit them to memory. But all that I could retain were bits and pieces of nonsense syllables, sounds that seemed somehow familiar at random places in the piece, unconnected by any phrasing. I tried to remember lines but found only disparate vowels and consonants; I searched my web, looking for the words that I had tried to force into my mind. I searched the fine gossamer, only to find, alas, that 10 what I seeked was not there. I had not learned my German, and it had not entered my web.

How much I wanted to learn the Brahms. How hard I tried. But the 1
"hidden teacher" had failed to appear, and I had failed to learn. Like a pupil who cannot learn a list of spelling words or a verb conjugation, I was an unsuccessful learner. Theodore Sizer explores the difficulty of learning and its causes in his essay "What High School Is." He traces the average school day of Mark, "a genial eleventh-grader," and notes the lack of opportunities for learning. Students, Sizer claims, are not learning, not adding to their web of knowledge at school.

"Obviously, a low premium is placed on reflection and repose," claims 1
Sizer. "The students rush from class to class to collect knowledge. Savoring it, it is implied, is not to be done much in school, nor is such meditation really much admired." Yet both are necessary in order to successfully expand the web. Reflection and understanding are a crucial part of learning—for what good is it for me to know the average rainfall of the Amazon Basin if I do not understand its implications and consequences? I could perhaps memorize some figures, but like the few familiar-sounding syllables in the Brahms piece, they would remain isolated and meaningless in my mind. It is knitting together the knowledge that secures its place inside one's web, transforming unconnected threads, dangling loosely in one's mind, into one continuous, delicately woven material. Without understanding, the web would not be. But on the other hand, "collecting knowledge" cannot be undervalued. Without it, full learning cannot take place; facts are the building blocks on which we base ideas and reflections, the very thread with which the web is spun. By collecting knowledge, we expand the realm of the learnable, for without the gossamer, how can there even be hope of weaving more web? Because of this I cannot commit the Brahms to memory. German does not exist within the bounds of my conscious knowledge, within my web; the words to the Brahms piece are, to me, irrational, for where is the thread to weave with? The spider did not understand the intrusion of the pencil into its world, and could not decipher it, could not learn of the existence of the pencil and of man. I cannot decipher the German and I cannot learn the words because they are out of my grasp, my web. I try to memorize, try desperately to spin the thread to weave with, but there is nothing to connect it to. The fragile gossamer cannot attach itself to my web, and I am left at the center, watching it fall out of my reach.

I cannot "collect knowledge," cannot commit my German to memory, 1
because I lack connections to make with it. But what about the second step, that of assimilating knowledge, of weaving together the loosely hanging threads? How do we weave our knowledge together, what do we need to spin our web? What is it that I am missing when I cannot complete my learning?

Sizer suggests several reasons for the unsuccessful nature of learning in high school; the lack of dialogue between students and teachers and between students themselves, and badly defined or undefined goals are among those he raises. "Students rush from class to class to collect knowledge," he says. At school, they are helped to spin the gossamer. But it is only attached at one end, and the connection is fragile. School does not expand the students' webs but provides dangling extensions; what is missing is precisely the weaving of the web. 14

Distractions tempt the students all throughout the school day. In Sizer's typical high school, an announcement interrupts biology class, and during history, a messenger "walks in the open door." Mark is sent to run an errand in one class, and is distracted by the other students in another class. Concentration and motivation are missing from the classroom. "Write, write, write, for Bates to throw away, Mark thinks" as he writes for his French class. Everything is meaningless busy work, done only for a teacher's whim. The students do not see the point of schoolwork or the reasons behind assignments, and school is simply "a dogged necessity." They are not motivated in the least; without the opportunity to concentrate and look more deeply into subject matters, students fail to capture interest in schoolwork. Teachers attempt to encourage their students to learn, but all of the motivations are negative; the typing teacher "constantly threatens" Mark who is then only pushed by frustration, discomfort, and fear of embarrassment. All of the teachers administer tests, and it is the fear of bad grades, not the desire to do well, that affects the students. All of the motivations are externally imposed, and do not come from the students themselves. They do not *want* to learn. 15

My motivations to learn the German words were also imposed on me; I did not *want* to learn them. My learning the German would not have helped me become a better singer. The words applied to the one particular song only, I believed. They would have been left unused after that one concert, a thin strand dangling loosely from one corner of my web with not even the possibility of other connections and attachments. I was not particularly interested in the German lyrics. I wanted to learn them only so that I would not have to stare down at my music the whole time. I only wanted to learn out of fear of embarrasssment, not for the sake of learning. 16

Interest and a will to learn that comes from inside—these emotions must be present to learn, and these emotions I lacked. But I remember wanting to learn, being pushed by a desire to go on. I remember the skating rink on a late Thursday afternoon. "You're getting closer! Try it once more," my instructor smiled promises as I fell time and time again. 17

The waltz jump was one of the first "real" movements I was trying to learn. Little hops and spins, jumps and skating figures are all elementary steps. Like the individual letters of an alphabet, I could do the little steps, I knew the letters. But it did not mean anything unless I could make words 18 out of the letters, and build sentences from them, and paragraphs, craft whole essays. And the waltz jump was one of my first real words, a step toward that essay.

I'm just not jumping high enough, I told myself. I don't want to jump 19
any higher. I can't jump any higher. Stubborn in my reasoning, I was convinced that this had to be the reason for my failure with the waltz jump. It was the only reason that existed in my mind. I tried the same, feeble attempt over and over again. In vain, I realized, as I hit the ice each time.

But it wasn't my jump. I was wrong. It was my right foot. I could feel 20
the toe-pick snag on the ice right as I landed. And I had no confidence in my outer edge. I could feel it. I tried again. I fell. I tried once more. I fell again. I turned my edge too slowly. I turned my edge too fast. But I saw that the way I moved my edge affected the way I fell. And it was only after I widened my scope, opened myself to other perspectives, that I could learn the waltz jump. The thought that it was not my jump had to enter my mind first.

What was it that led the thought to enter my mind? What opened my 21
views to other possibilities? Eiseley would call it the "ultimate wonder and creativeness" that humankind possesses. Beyond the human web lies "the great darkness of the ultimate Dreamer, who dreamed the light and the galaxies. . . . Man partakes of that ultimate wonder and creativeness," claims Eiseley, the power to see beyond one's own dimensions, to see the world that encompasses our tiny, finite web.

But that "ultimate wonder and creativeness," the power to see beyond, 22
does not come from outside of oneself as Eiseley claims. "It is no longer enough to see as man sees," he suggests, implying that the power is the ability to see things from above the web, not from its center but detached and free from its threads. But how can one learn to see from outside the realms of the understandable? The spider lives in the center of the web, surrounded and encompassed by its universe. The spider cannot conceive of the pencil; how can I conceive of the nonexistent? All knowledge must be based on pre-existing knowledge, and the threads that expand the web connected to the web itself. I failed to learn the Brahms piece because the threads of German were not present in my web.

Learning, we build on things we already know, things that already 23
exist in our web. "Man partakes of the ultimate wonder and creativeness," writes Eiseley; imagination and creativity have invented and produced new things and ideas. But never have they been disparate inventions, arising from purely nothing. All imagination is inspired by what one knows, by one's knowledge. The inspiration and insight may be in the form of denial of one's knowledge; conjuring up a hypothesis, imagining the impossible; yet these too arise from one's web. "The ultimate wonder and creativeness" surely is the ability to twist and question knowledge in order to learn, not

the magic powers to conjure up perceptions completely unrelated to what we know.

Open-mindedness and ability to question, this is the "ultimate wonder 24
and creativeness." It comes from within oneself, not from outside. It is not the reasoning brain; "It's my jump," my mind told me, inhibiting my learning instead of aiding it. Alone, my mind cannot lead me to learn, my unassisted brain cannot weave my web; it is rather the passion, the *desire* to learn. No teacher can bestow this on me, no external person can tie my individual threads of knowledge together. Curiosity and above all motivation, such emotions spur that wonder. The desire to learn, the open-mindedness to new possibilities, the will to question, to twist and turn pre-existing knowledge. . . . This is the essence of learning, that subtle link between the learnable and the learned, that difficult step of weaving the intricate web of knowledge.

PART FIVE
HANDBOOK

SECTION I

Building an Essay: Paragraphs

An essay begins with ideas. Whatever the essay is about, readers can expect it to be a fairly short piece of nonfiction prose consisting of a number of paragraphs that are logically connected. Essays have a beginning, where we find out what the writer is writing about; a middle, where the writer puts forth and supports ideas; and an ending that leaves us with a satisfactory understanding of the writer's point.

An essay is built on paragraphs. In Chapter 2 we followed the work of Miriam Thaggert and Marc Beauboeuf as they wrote essays based on their own experiences. Before they could write those essays, they needed to understand how to organize their ideas into paragraphs, and how to organize their paragraphs logically so that readers could follow their way of thinking. In this section, we will look closely at paragraphs to see how they work to support and structure an essay.

WORD—SENTENCE—PARAGRAPH

When you write, you place words upon a page, but rarely are those words set down in isolation. Instead, you develop ideas that emerge as sentences or, more likely, as clusters of sentences. These clusters of sentences, or paragraphs, are the basic building blocks of an essay.

A **paragraph** is a set of sentences that develop one main idea. Let's look at a paragraph from Theodore Sizer's essay "What High School Is" to find its main idea.

The school schedule is a series of units of time: the clock is king. The base time block is about fifty minutes in length. Some schools, on what they call modular scheduling, split that fifty-minute block into two or even three pieces. Most schools have double periods for laboratory work, especially in the sciences, or four-hour units for the small numbers of students involved in intensive vocational or other work-study programs. The flow of all school activity rises from or is blocked by these time units. "How much time do I have with my kids" is the teacher's key question.

Topic Sentences

Sizer presents the main idea, or topic, of this paragraph in the first sentence: This paragraph, he tells his readers, is about the units of time in high school. When the topic sentence appears as the first sentence of the paragraph, it prepares the reader for the rest of the paragraph. Sizer's topic sentence—which is *complete, concise,* and *interesting*—suggests that the rest of the paragraph will show how the school schedule is broken up into blocks of time, and how these blocks determine the day's activities.

The *topic sentence* then, focuses the paragraph, allowing the reader to anticipate what the paragraph will contain. Sizer chose to put his topic sentence first. Sometimes, though, a topic sentence will appear later in the paragraph, following a brief introduction or transition. Less often, a topic sentence summrizes the information in the paragraph; in that case, it may appear as the last sentence.

Paragraph Support

After the topic sentence signals the reader about what to expect, the rest of the paragraph develops the main idea by giving supporting details. Sizer tells us about how time is divided in different schools, how blocks of time differ for different subjects, and how teachers respond to this division of time.

Although Sizer discusses many details of school life in his essay, this paragraph focuses only on time. It excludes all details not relevant to that focus. Sizer, however, has more to say about time and follows this paragraph with two more about the same aspect of high school life. As you read the following paragraphs, think about how each differs from the other.

Because there are many claims for those fifty-minute blocks, there is little time set aside for rest between them, usually no more than three to ten minutes, depending on how big the school is and, consequently, how far students and teachers have to walk from class to class. As a result, there is a frenetic quality to the school day, a sense of sustained restlessness. For the adolescents, there are frequent changes of room and fellow students, each change giving tempting opportunities for distraction, which are stoutly resisted by teachers. Some schools play soft music during these "passing times," to quiet the multitude, one principal told me.

Many teachers have a chance for a coffee break. Few students do. In some city schools, students must be in class for seven consecutive periods, interrupted by a heavily monitored twenty-minute lunch period for small groups, starting as early as 10:30 A.M. and running to after 1:00 P.M. A high premium is placed on punctuality and on "being where you're supposed to be." Obviously, a low premium is placed on reflection and repose. The students rush from class to class to collect knowledge. Savoring it, it is implied, is not to be done in school, nor is such meditation really much admired. The picture that these familiar patterns yield is that of an academic supermarket. The purpose of going to school is to pick things up, in an organized and predictable way, the faster the better.

EXERCISE 1 Identifying Topic Sentences

1. Discuss the preceding paragraphs from Sizer's essay. What is each paragraph about? Identify the topic sentence. How do the paragraphs differ from each other? What do they illustrate about paragraph support?
2. Discuss the following paragraphs from Ruth Macklin's "Applying Moral Principles" and Paula Gunn Allen's "Where I Come from Is Like This" (both essays are in the Sourcebook). What is each paragraph about? Identify the topic sentence. What do these paragraphs illustrate about paragraph support?

A subject that commanded great attention in the early 1970s, when my colleagues and I began to teach bioethics and to engage in teaching "rounds" in hospitals, was how to deal with the tragedy of infants born with mental and physical handicaps. The medical specialty of neonatology had only recently been established, and the dramatic capability of pediatricians to save lives and correct birth anomalies was impressive. But concurrently, a growing but undocumented perception was emerging that neonatologists were too aggressive in their efforts to save the lives of infants born very prematurely, pursued without the full participation of the anguished parents, and perhaps without sufficient regard to the quality of life of those infants whose biological survival they were able to ensure. Infants born so prematurely that their lungs are not fully developed often suffer severe lung damage from being kept on a ventilator for a long time. A considerable number are afflicted with neurologic damage that will leave them profoundly retarded. The presumption of family autonomy and the right of parents to help determine a treatment plan for their babies (which might include selective nontreatment) appeared to be violated by neonatal specialists zealously pursuing their art.

(from "Applying Moral Principles)

No Indian can grow to any age without being informed that her people were "savages" who interfered with the march of progress pursued by respectable, loving, civilized white people. We are the villains of the scenario when we are mentioned at all. We are absent from much of white history except when we are calmly, rationally, succinctly, and systematically dehumanized. On the few occasions we are noticed in any way other than as howling, bloodthirsty beings, we are acclaimed for our noble quaintness. In this definition, we are exotic curios. Our ancient arts and customs are used to draw tourist money to state coffers, into the pocketbooks and bank accounts of scholars, and into support of the American-in-Disneyland promoters' dream.

(from "Where I Come from Is Like This")

Paragraph Unity

Although the three paragraphs we looked at from Sizer's essay "What High School Is" focus on the issue of time, each paragraph is a separate unit unto itself. The first paragraph tells the reader about various blocks of time in different schools; the second paragraph tells about one implication of these blocks: the frenetic quality of the school day. The third tells about another implication: the lack of time for reflection and repose. Each paragraph achieves unity and *coherence* through both content and structure. A unified and coherent paragraph meets the folowing criteria:

- The paragraph is focused on one main idea.
- Each sentence in the paragraph is related to that main idea.
- Sentences are ordered logically.
- Necessary transitions help the reader follow the logic of the paragraph.

Each sentence in the paragraph about the frenetic quality of the school day, for example, connects directly with the main idea. This paragraph, Sizer knows, is not the place to tell his readers about extended time in laboratories or about early lunch hours. *The content of a paragraph develops the main idea of that paragraph.*

In addition, a paragraph achieves its coherence by logical order and transitions. The paragraph about the frenetic quality of the school day consists of four sentences:

Because there are many claims for those fifty-minute blocks, there is little time set aside for rest between them, usually no more than three to ten minutes, depending on how big the school is and, consequently, how far students and teachers have to walk from class to class.

As a result, there is a frenetic quality to the school day, a sense of sustained restlessness.

For the adolescents, there are frequent changes of room and fellow students, each change giving tempting opportunities for distraction, which are stoutly resisted by teachers.

Some schools play soft music during these "passing times," to quiet the multitude, one principal told me.

By separating each sentence, you can see more clearly the logical relationship between them. The first sentence refers to "those fifty-minute breaks" described in the paragraph that comes before this one in Sizer's essay. Picking up a word or phrase in a previous paragraph or sentence is a good way of helping the reader to follow your ideas and to avoid the choppy presentation of a sequence of ideas.

The first sentence ends with students' walking from class to class. This activity has an effect: a frenetic quality to the school day. Sizer highlights this cause-effect relationship by using the phrase *as a result*. Such transitional phrases are a good way of helping the reader understand the logical connection between two sentences.

In the third sentence, Sizer gives us another detail of the school day: adolescents change classes. This change causes an effect in some schools: the playing of soft music (fourth sentence).

When you highlight relationships between ideas by repeating key words from previous sentences or by including transitional phrases, you can achieve coherence within a paragraph.

EXERCISE 2 Recognizing Paragraph Unity

1. Use the following sentences to form a logical paragraph. What is the relationship among these sentences? Discuss your paragraph with your classmates.

The students in metalworking classes are mostly male; those in home economics, mostly female.

For many young women, the most liberated hours of their week are in school.

Young males and females are treated remarkably alike; the schools' goals are the same for each gender.

But it is revealing how much less sex discrimination there is in high schools than in other American institutions.

In execution, there are differences, as those pressing sex discrimination suits have made educators intensely aware.

2. Discuss the following paragraph from Patricia Hampl's "Memory and Imagination." What unifies this paragraph? What makes it cohere?

It still comes as a shock to realize that I don't write what I know: I write in order to find out what I know. Is it possible to convey to a reader the enormous degree of blankness, confusion, hunch and uncertainty lurking in the act of writing? When I am the reader, not the writer, I too fall into the lovely illusion that the words before me (in a story by Mavis Gallant, an essay by Carol Bly, a memoir by M. F. K. Fisher), which *read* so inevitably, must also have been *written* exactly as they appear, rhythm and cadence, language and syntax, the powerful waves of the sentences laying themselves on the smooth beach of the page one after another faultlessly.

Paragraph Clusters

Most of the time, ideas cannot be fully developed in a single paragraph. Instead, you'll find it more useful to think in terms of groups or *clusters* of paragraphs within your essay. A *paragraph cluster* is a group of paragraphs that develop the subtopics of one main idea.

Sizer's three paragraphs about time (see page 474) form a cluster within an essay that, in its entirety, is 41 paragraphs long. One main idea—time in high schools—is divided into three subtopics, each given consideration in a separate paragraph. Although Sizer decided to organize his essay this way, another writer might have combined these units or divided them in different ways. There are no rules for the number of paragraphs that an essay must contain. To decide whether to divide one main idea into a paragraph cluster, use the criteria for paragraph unity and coherence. Ask yourself: Will your paragraphs:

- Be focused on a main idea?
- Contain sentences that all relate to that main idea?
- Be ordered logically?
- Have transitions so that readers can follow the logic of your thinking?

RELATIONSHIPS BETWEEN PARAGRAPHS

When paragraphs are organized logically, an essay has unity and coherence. Sometimes, what you are writing about gives you a clear way of organizing. If you are describing an experience, you may decide to organize chronologically: First one thing happened, and then another thing happened. If you are describing an object, you may decide to organize spatially: You look first at one part and then at an adjacent part.

Often, however, what you are writing about does not give you such clear indications for organization. You, as the writer, need to figure out the connections between sentences within a paragraph and between paragraphs within the essay. When you looked at Sizer's paragraph, you saw how the relationship of cause and effect gave logical order between sentences. The words *as a result* signaled the reader to look for that cause-effect relationship.

Cause-effect relationships can help you order paragraphs too. One or more paragraphs may describe a cause; the following paragraph or paragraphs may discuss the effect. Several terms may signal a reader to look for this relationship:

accordingly	for
because of	therefore
consequently	thus

Cause-effect, of course, is not the only relationship that can occur between paragraphs. Sometimes you want to summarize ideas for your reader; sometimes you might want to illustrate your ideas by giving examples. Many kinds of transitions are possible.

Transitions

Transitions are words or phrases that indicate relationships between sentences or paragraphs. The following list may help you as you organize your ideas.

If you want to:	*These terms may help you:*
summarize (signal the reader that you are clarifying your points by restating them)	in other words, in simpler terms, briefly, in short, in conclusion, to sum up

If you want to:	*These terms may help you:*
contrast (signal the reader that a new idea is different from a previous one)	still, nevertheless, but, yet, however, on the other hand, whereas, although, in spite of, on the contrary
compare (signal the reader that two ideas are similar)	similarly, likewise, in the same way
expand (signal the reader that you are developing an idea further)	and, also, too, in addition, besides, as well, furthermore, likewise, similarly, in effect
illustrate (signal the reader that you are using an example to support an idea)	for example, for instance, in particular, to illustrate
concede (signal to your reader that you are considering other viewpoints)	of course, to be sure, granted, no doubt, undoubtedly
qualify (signal the reader that you grant exceptions to your ideas)	for the most part, with few exceptions, mainly, in most cases, sometimes

EXERCISE 3 Revising Paragraphs

Look closely at the paragraphs in one of your essays and underline the transitional words and phrases. Analyze your own paragraphs. Do they cohere? Are they unified? Do they signal to a reader what they are about? How might you revise these paragraphs to make them more effective?

INTRODUCTORY PARAGRAPHS

The most important paragraphs in an essay introduce your topic to your reader. Your introduction may be one paragraph in a fairly short essay or several paragraphs in a longer essay. Just as there is no requirement for the number of paragraphs in an introduction, there is no requirement for the content. Sometimes, students create for themselves a formula for introductions: Always begin with a catchy quotation; always begin with a question; always begin by rewording the assignment. Each of these approaches may be appropriate for some essays. None is appropriate for every essay. Here are some helpful ways to think about what introductory paragraphs should do:

- Invite the reader to join you in considering your topic.
- Give the reader a clear idea of what the essay is about.
- Give the reader an idea of the kinds of sources you are considering.
- Give the reader a sense of the context for your topic.

Depending on your topic, you may choose among many strategies for building introductory paragraphs. In the next few pages, you'll see examples of some different kinds of introductory paragraphs.

Beginning with a Question

When you begin your essay with a question, you invite your reader to consider with you the problem or dilemma that inspired you to write. What question are you trying to answer in your essay? Why is this question important to you? Why should this question be important to your readers?

In "Warfare: An Invention—Not a Biological Necessity"(on page 372 of the Sourcebook), Margaret Mead begins with a question. Her question, as you can see when you read the first paragraph, does not spring from thin air; she indicates that it has concerned other writers before her. The question allows for two answers, both sides of a debate that Mead will consider in her essay. In the second paragraph, Mead states her position, which she defends throughout the rest of the essay.

Here are the first two paragraphs of "Warfare: An Invention—Not a Biological Necessity":

> Is war a biological necessity, a sociological inevitability or just a bad invention? Those who argue for the first view endow man with such pugnacious instincts that some outlet in aggressive behavior is necessary if man is to reach full human stature. It was this point of view which lay back of William James's famous essay, "The Moral Equivalent of War," in which he tried to retain the warlike virtues and channel them in new directions. A similar point of view has lain back of the Soviet Union's attempt to make competition between groups rather than between individuals. A basic, competitive, aggressive, warring human nature is assumed, and those who wish to outlaw war or outlaw competitiveness merely try to find new and less socially destructive ways in which these biologically given aspects of man's nature can find expression. Then there are those who take the second

view: warfare is the inevitable concomitant of the development of the state, the struggle for land and natural resources of class societies springing, not from the nature of man, but from the nature of history. War is nevertheless inevitable unless we change our social system and outlaw classes, the struggle for power, and possessions; and in the event of our success warfare would disappear, as a symptom vanishes when the disease is cured.

One may hold a compromise position between these two extremes; one may claim that all aggression springs from the frustration of man's biologically determined drives and that, since all forms of culture are frustrating, it is certain each new generation will be aggressive and the aggression will find its natural and inevitable expression in race war, class war, nationalistic war, and so on.

Beginning by Stating a Position

When you are writing an argumentative essay, you may decide to begin by stating your position in the first paragraph. When you state your position, however, you need to be sure to give the reader some sense of the context for your argument. Why is this topic important to you? Why should it interest your readers?

David Owen, in "How They Write the SAT" (see the Sourcebook) begins his essay by immediately letting the reader know his position about these tests. When he tells his readers that the tests have become a "measure of worthiness in our society," he indicates that his topic is important to readers because it goes beyond an examination of testing procedures to an examination of our culture's values. Notice that in the last sentence of his second paragraph, Owen makes his position clear and unambiguous:

Standardized multiple-choice tests, such as the Scholastic Aptitude Test, are more than hurdles on the way to college. The tests have become a pervasive measure of worthiness in our society—even a status symbol, as in, "*My* boy scored double 700s."

The Educational Testing Service, which produces the SAT, encourages this attitude. The company's literature conjures up the image of a testing instrument endowed with the learning and precision of white-coated physicists measuring a rocket's lift-off power. But as should be apparent to anyone who has taken these tests, the white-coated image is just that. Many of the test questions are ambiguous, arbitrary, and downright silly.

Beginning by Offering Background

If your readers are not familiar with your topic, your introductory paragraph may serve to give them necessary background. Sometimes that background can summarize the results of other people's writing about the topic. Sometimes background information can place your topic in a larger context. Here is how Ruth Macklin begins her essay "Applying Moral Principles":

> [A] category of patients that poses an ethical problem for physicians and hospital administrators is pregnant women. According to one moral view, pregnant women should be treated just like all other competent, adult patients—their autonomy should be respected and their right to refuse treatment honored. But another view holds that the rights of a pregnant woman are tempered by the existence of the developing life within her. In this view the pregnant woman has a strong moral obligation to the fetus, one she should not be allowed to shirk. In a series of ongoing developments, the moral standing of the fetus has come under constant scrutiny, and not only because the emotionally charged topic of abortion infects other areas of medical practice. Technological and scientific advances in medicine have also contributed to the confusion and to changing perceptions.

Beginning by Defining

In writing an essay, you want to be sure that you and your readers share common language and ideas. Sometimes it is useful to define key terms at the beginning.

The first four paragraphs of Loren Eiseley's essay "The Hidden Teacher" define a term that may mean different things to different readers. What is a "hidden teacher"? By the end of the fourth paragraph, readers begin to understand what Eiseley means. They also know what kind of sources he will use in the rest of the essay, assuming—and readers have a right to assume this—that his introduction is consistent with what follows.

> The putting of formidable riddles did not arise with today's philosophers. In fact, there is a sense in which the experimental method of science might be said merely to have widened the area of man's homelessness. Over two thousand years ago, a man named Job, crouching in the Judean desert, was moved to challenge what he felt to be the injustice of his God. The voice in the whirlwind, in turn, volleyed pitiless questions upon the suppliant—questions that have, in truth, precisely the ring of modern science. For the Lord asked of Job by whose wisdom the hawk soars, and who had fathered the rain, or entered the storehouses of the snow.
>
> A youth standing by, one Elihu, also played a role in this drama, for he ventured diffidently to his protesting elder that it was not true that God failed to manifest himself. He may speak in one way or another, though

men do not perceive it. In consequence of this remark perhaps it would be well, whatever our individual beliefs, to consider what may be called the hidden teacher, lest we become too much concerned with the formalities of only one aspect of the education by which we learn.

We think we learn from teachers, and we sometimes do. But the teachers are not always to be found in school or in great laboratories. Sometimes what we learn depends upon our own powers of insight. Moreover, our teachers may be hidden, even the greatest teacher. And it was the young man Elihu who observed that if the old are not always wise, neither can the teacher's way be ordered by the young whom he would teach.

For example, I once received an unexpected lesson from a spider.

Beginning by Illustrating

An illustration, example, or anecdote can arouse your readers' interest in your essay. Vivid details, suspenseful narrative, or interesting descriptions can make your audience want to continue reading. Illustrations, however, should lead readers to the essay's focus.

Several essays in the Sourcebook, including Theodore Sizer's "What High School Is" (page 467) and Patricia Hampl's "Memory and Imagination" (page 306); begin with anecdotes or illustrations that invite the reader into the world of the writer. Anecdotes are an effective, often dramatic, way to begin an essay. If you choose to begin an essay with an anecdote, be clear about your purpose in doing so. And make sure that after the anecdote, your readers quickly find out what point you are trying to make, and how you are planning to focus the rest of the essay.

Marc Beauboeuf begins his essay "A Word" (page 38) with an anecdote. And in his fourth paragraph, Marc tells us the importance of his anecdote:

> But the word [nigger] stopped, caught in the gulf between speaker and listener, waiting to be understood, waiting for my comprehension to provide a connection so that it could enter me. A word forces a relationship between speaker and listener. Its power is derived from both. It's as if a word traveling through the air is in a medium where it can't survive. A word must be internalized in the mind of the listener for it to cause a reaction, positive or negative. If the word is not understood, it is rejected and dies.

In the rest of the essay, Marc explains what kind of relationship the word forced him to have with the speaker. He tells us what kind of reaction the word generated and what implications the word has had for him.

CONCLUDING PARAGRAPHS

Next to introductions, the paragraphs that seem the most challenging to students are conclusions. Yet, if you are writing a well-focused essay, developed logically with strong details to support your assertions, your conclusion is likely to come naturally.

When you are ready to conclude your essay, think about writing a paragraph that serves at least one of the following purposes:

- Sums up your argument
- Leads the readers to consider your ideas in a larger context
- Inspires your readers to think about an issue in a new way
- Inspires your readers to take some action about an issue
- Justifies your writing of the essay by pointing up the significance of the issue

A conclusion may be one or more paragraphs that either sum up your organizing idea or lead your readers beyond the essay to a larger context. Now that you have presented your ideas, how may your readers move further? Do you want them to change their way of thinking or to take some action? Do you want them to connect the significance of your topic to another issue?

If your readers have not understood the point of your essay, it is too late to make that point in your conclusion. Your conclusion may pull ideas together, but it cannot present your position clearly for the first time.

Many writers find that after they complete a first draft of an essay, their conclusion really does present their position more clearly than their introduction does. They have thought through their topic as they wrote, and finally, at the end, clarified their thinking. If you make that discovery, your second draft might lift your first conclusion to the beginning of your essay. With your conclusion now serving as an introductory paragraph, you can revise the focus, the strength, and the impact of your essay. Here are some possible ways to think about conclusions.

Concluding by Summing Up

If you have offered your readers a complicated argument, or if you have presented them with many details, you may decide to conclude by summing up your main point. Although summing up is a useful strategy for ending essays, it is not the only effective way.

At the end of her essay explaining what *double-concsiousness* means to her, Miriam Thaggert spends two paragraphs summing up a final definition of the term. This summing up serves to transcend all the details that Miriam offers throughout the essay. This definition is what she wants us to remember:

> This, really, is the essence of being Black in America, of contending with double-consciousness. Not just knowing who you are and where you came from, but trying to endure society's surveillance. Not just learning your history, but surviving life in a society that doesn't know and understand it. This for me is Du Bois's double-consciousness. It is a feeling that is so much a part of Blacks as the history that made them. The history of the Black man is the history of this strife, of reconciling these two selves. Unknown, unacknowledged perhaps, but history nonetheless.
>
> Du Bois described it as a "peculiar sensation," and that really is the only apt way to describe it, a feeling as if you're always on the outside, always living on the periphery of what everyone else around you calls life, of looking into a world, instead of examining the wonders inside, of feeling the conscious barrier that separates one world, and the single, solitary existence of another. This is a peculiar sensation, yet one that is all too familiar to me. This is my double-consciousness.

Concluding by Suggesting Change

Depending on your topic, you may find it appropriate to suggest to your readers that what they have learned from your essay implies some changes—in their behavior, in their thinking, in their decision making. Suggesting change is a useful way of ending an essay that focuses on a social, ethical, or political issue.

Margaret Mead argues throughout her essay "Warfare: An Invention—Not a Biological Necessity" that accepting the idea that war is not an inevitable result of people's aggressive nature has implications for personal and societal behavior. Here, then, is how Mead concludes her essay:

> The people must recognize the defects of the old invention, and some one must make a new one. Propaganda against warfare, documentation of its terrible cost in human suffering and social waste, these prepare the ground by teaching people to feel that warfare is a defective social institution. There is further needed a belief that social invention is possible and the invention of new methods which will render warfare as out-of-date as the tractor is making the plow, or the motor car the horse and buggy. A form of behavior becomes out-of-date only when something else takes its place, and in order to invent forms of behavior which will make war obsolete, it is a first requirement to believe that an invention is possible.

Concluding by Expanding the Context

Because an essay can focus on only a limited part of a larger issue, you may find it effective to conclude by showing your readers how your particular question of focus fits into a larger context. When you conclude by expanding the context of your essay, you tell readers that there are still unanswered questions about your topic, there is still more to ask and more to know.

At the end of her essay "Applying Moral Principles," Ruth Macklin tells readers that everything she has been discussing is part of an ongoing inquiry in medicine and medical ethics.

> Here, then, are two possible scenarios. The staff traces one set of possible consequences, while another picture can also be drawn, projecting different consequences of disclosure. Which picture is accurate? Which set of consequences is more likely? Alas, there is no crystal ball for an accurate prediction. And even if the staff's scenario is the more likely one, the question remains whether it is ethically justifiable to lie, or even to withhold information, in order to bring about desired consequences. This is an old ethical dilemma, one that often rears its head in the medical setting.

Concluding by Justifying Your Essay

From the first paragraphs of your essay, you should be aware of your obligation to place your topic in a context and to show your readers why your topic is significant, especially if you are basing your essay on personal experiences. Your concluding paragraph also may be used to help readers understand your purpose in writing. In her essay "Where I Come from Is Like This," Paula Gunn Allen explores the world of the Native American woman. Here are her final paragraphs, in which she justifies her efforts:

> Through all the centuries of war and death and cultural and psychic destruction have endured the women who raise the children and tend the fires, who pass along the tales and the traditions, who weep and bury the dead, who are the dead, and who never forget. There are always the women, who make pots and weave baskets, who fashion clothes and cheer their children on at powwow, who make fry bread and piki bread, and corn soup and chili stew, who dance and sing and remember and hold within their hearts the dream of their ancient peoples—that one day the woman who thinks will speak to us again, and everyone there will be peace. Meanwhile we tell the stories and write the books and trade tales of anger and woe and stories of fun and scandal and laugh over all manner of things that happen every day. We watch and we wait.

My great-grandmother told my mother: Never forget you are Indian. And my mother told me the same thing. This, then, is how I have gone about remembering, so that my children will remember too.

EXERCISE 4 Revising Introductions and Conclusions

1. Look closely at the introduction of a draft you are currently writing or the last essay you wrote. Analyze your introduction. What strategy did you use to interest your reader? How are you trying to pull your reader into the world of your essay? Reflect on these questions in your journal.
2. Look closely at the conclusion of a draft you are currently writing or the conclusion of the last essay you wrote. Could your concluding paragraph be integrated into your introductory paragraph? Does your conclusion state your position more clearly than your introduction does? What strategy did you use for concluding? Use your journal to analyze the effectiveness of your conclusion.
3. Try writing two or three different introductions for an essay you plan to write. Show the introductions to a few classmates and ask for their comments. What did you learn about the introductions from their responses?

PURPOSES OF PARAGRAPHS

Paragraphs and clusters of paragraphs may serve several purposes within an essay:

- To define terms
- To describe
- To explain
- To illustrate
- To narrate
- To compare or contrast
- To argue

Identifying the purpose of a paragraph can help you shape that paragraph precisely and logically. The following are some examples of paragraphs that fulfill different purposes. Only one paragraph is given to illustrate each purpose, but as you read essays, you'll notice that clusters of paragraphs, rather than just one, often serve to fulfill a purpose.

Paragraphs that Define Terms

To make sure your readers understand your ideas, you need to define any term that may be ambiguous or misinterpreted. By including in your essay paragaphs that define key terms, you ensure that you and your readers share a common language.

Paul Theroux's essay "Being a Man" depends on his readers' understanding his definition of *manly*. The following paragraph serves the purpose of defining the term:

I have always disliked being a man. The whole idea of manhood in America is pitiful, in my opinion. This version of masculinity is a little like having to wear an ill-fitting coat for one's entire life (by contrast, I imagine femininity to be an oppressive sense of nakedness). Even the expression "Be a man!" strikes me as insulting and abusive. It means: Be stupid, be unfeeling, obedient, soldierly and stop thinking. Man means "manly"—how can one think about men without considering the terrible ambition of manliness? And yet it is part of every man's life. It is a hideous and crippling lie; it not only insists on difference and connives at superiority, it is also by its very nature destructive—emotionally damaging and socially harmful.

Paragraphs that Describe

If you are writing an essay based on personal experience, or if you are writing about a person, event, or place, you want to give your readers a vivid sense of details.

A descriptive paragraph gives readers enough information to visualize something or some event. In "Memory and Imagination," Patricia Hampl describes her piano teacher:

Her oily face gleamed as if it had just been rolled out of a can and laid on the white plate of her broad, spotless wimple. She was a small, plump woman; her body and the small window of her face seemed to interpret the entire alphabet of olive: her face was a sallow green olive placed upon the jumbo ripe olive of her black habit. I trusted her instantly and smiled, glad to have my hand placed in the hand of a woman who made sense, who provided the satisfaction of being what she was: an Olive who looked like an olive.

Paragraphs that Explain

All essays ask readers to follow a logical sequence of thoughts. Paragraphs that explain help readers understand key ideas or processes. Readers become confused or sense that "something is missing" when necessary explanations are omitted.

In a paragraph or a cluster of paragraphs, you can explain an idea, a process of doing something, a line of reasoning, or a relationship between ideas. In the following paragraph from "The Perils of Obedience," Stanley Milgram explains the experimental process that he used to test his subjects' willingness to defer to authority.

> In the basic experimental design, two people come to a psychology laboratory to take part in a study of memory and learning. One of them is designated as a "teacher" and the other a "learner." The experimenter explains that the study is concerned with the effects of punishment on learning. The learner is conducted into a room, seated in a kind of miniature electric chair; his arms are strapped to prevent excessive movement, and an electrode is attached to his wrist. He is told that he will be read lists of simple word pairs, and that he will then be tested on his ability to remember the second word of a pair when he hears the first one again. Whenever he makes an error, he will receive electric shocks of increasing intensity.

Paragraphs that Illustrate

Illustrating means giving examples. Examples help make ideas concrete. They offer key support for your assertions.

In "Being a Man," Paul Theroux wants to support the idea that a writer's image is different depending on whether the writer is male or female. He illustrates this point with a paragraph of examples:

> When the novelist John Irving was revealed as a wrestler, people took him to be a very serious writer; and even a bubble reputation like Eric (*Love Story*) Segal's was enhanced by the news that he ran the marathon in a respectable time. How surprised we would be if Joyce Carol Oates were revealed as a sumo wrestler or Joan Didon active in pumping iron. "Lives in New York City with her three children" is the typical woman writer's biographical note, for just as the male writer must prove he has achieved a sort of muscular manhood, the woman writer—or rather her publicists—must prove her motherhood.

Paragraphs that Narrate

When you narrate, you tell a story. Stories are effective strategies in essays as long as they relate to the main point of the essay. Before you include paragraphs of narration, consider these questions: What point is the story making? What effect do you want this story to have on your readers? The answers can help you provide necessary details in the narrative so that your readers understand your point.

In her essay "Beauty: When the Other Dancer Is the Self," Alice Walker tells an anecdote about something that happened to her when she was six years old. Each paragraph serves the purpose of narrating.

> It is Easter Sunday, 1950. I am dressed in a green, flocked, scalloped-hem dress (handmade by my adoring sister, Ruth) that has its own smooth satin petticoat and tiny hot-pink roses tucked into each scallop. My shoes, new T-strap patent leather, again highly biscuit-polished. I am six years old and have learned one of the longest Easter speeches to be heard that day, totally unlike the speech I said when I was two: "Easter lilies/pure and white/blossom in/the morning light." When I rise to give my speech I do so on a great wave of love and pride and expectation. People in the church stop rustling their new crinolines. They seem to hold their breath. I can tell they admire my dress, but it is my spirit, bordering on sassiness (womanishness), they secretly applaud.
>
> "That girl's a little *mess,*" they whisper to each other, pleased.
>
> Naturally I say my speech without stammer or pause, unlike those who stutter, stammer, or, worst of all, forget. This is before the word "beautiful" exists in people's vocabulary, but "Oh, isn't she the *cutest* thing!" frequently floats my may. "And got so much sense!" they gratefuly add . . . for which thoughtful addition I thank them to this day.

Paragraphs that Compare or Contrast

A paragraph or cluster of paragraphs may discuss two ideas, events, people, or texts in order to compare (show similarities) or contrast (show differences). Comparing or contrasting ideas helps to clarify those ideas for readers.

In her essay "Women and Science" (page 175), K. C. Cole contrasts the behavior of men and women in college science classes. In the paragraph that precedes this one, Cole tells us about a friend of hers who changed her major from science to English after a year of college.

> When I asked her why, she mentioned what she called the "macho mores" of science. "It would have been O.K. if I'd had someone to talk to" she said.

"But the rules of comportment were such that you never admitted you didn't understand. I later realized that even the boys didn't get everything clearly right away. You had to stick with it until it had time to sink in. But for the boys, there was a payoff in suffering through the hard times, and a kind of punishment—a shame—if they didn't. For the girls it was O.K. not to get it, and the only payoff for sticking it out was that you'd be considered a freak."

Paragraphs that Argue

Presenting an argument in an essay means not only stating your position, but defending and supporting your position as well. Paragraphs that argue may develop ideas in support of your position, or they may consider and evaluate counterarguments—that is, positions opposed to yours. In Chapter 8, "Arguing a Position," you saw how to build an entire essay that depends mostly upon paragraphs that argue. Paragraphs that argue, however, have a place in other kinds of essays—wherever you put forth a position and offer evidence to support that position.

In the following three paragraphs from "Warfare: An Invention—Not a Biological Necessity," Margaret Mead presents counterarguments before she states the position that she will defend throughout her essay.

Is war a biological necessity, a sociological inevitability or just a bad invention? Those who argue for the first view endow man with such pugnacious instincts that some outlet in aggressive behavior is necessary if man is to reach full human stature. It was this point of view which lay back of William James's famous essay. "The Moral Equivalent of War," in which he tried to retain the warlike virtues and channel them in new directions. A similar point of view has lain back of the Soviet Union's attempt to make competition between groups rather than between individuals. A basic, competitive, aggressive, warring human nature is assumed, and those who wish to outlaw war or outlaw competitiveness merely try to find new and less socially destructive ways in which these biologically given aspects of man's nature can find expression. Then there are those who take the second view: warfare is the inevitable concomitant of the development of the state, the struggle for land and natural resources of class societies springing, not from the nature of man, but from the nature of history. War is nevertheless inevitable unless we change our social system and outlaw classes, the struggle for power, and possessions; and in the event of our success warfare would disappear, as a symptom vanishes when the disease is cured.

One may hold a compromise position between these two extremes; one may claim that all aggression springs from the frustration of man's biologically determined drives and that, since all forms of culture are frustrating, it is certain each new generation will be aggressive and the aggression will find its natural and inevitable expression in race war, class war, nationalistic war, and so on.

All three positions are very popular today among those who think seriously about the problems of war and its possible prevention, but I wish to urge another point of view, less defeatist perhaps than the first and third, and more accurate than the second: that is, that warfare, by which I mean organized conflict between two groups *as groups,* in which each group puts an army (even if the army is only fifteen Pygmies) into the field to fight and kill, if possible, some of the members of the army of the other group—that warfare of this sort is an invention like any other of the inventions in terms of which we order our lives, such as writing, marriage, cooking our food instead of eating it raw, trial by jury, or burial of the dead, and so on. Some of this list any one will grant are inventions: trial by jury is confined to very limited portions of the globe; we know that there are tribes that do not bury their dead but instead expose or cremate them; and we know that only part of the human race has had a knowledge of writing as its cultural inheritance. But, whenever a way of doing things is found universally, such as the use of fire or the practice of some form of marriage, we tend to think at once that it is not an invention at all but an attribute of humanity itself. And yet even such universals as marriage and the use of fire are inventions like the rest, very basic ones, inventions which were perhaps necessary if human history was to take the turn it has taken, but nevertheless inventions. At some point in his social development man was undoubtedly without the institution of marriage or the knowledge of the use of fire.

EXERCISE 5 Analyzing Paragraphs

1. Exchange essays with one of your classmates. Look closely at the paragraphs that your classmate has written. What is the purpose of each paragraph? How do the paragraphs work together? How do they cohere? Are the topic sentences effective? Analyze the introduction and conclusion. Offer your suggestions for revising any of the paragraphs.

2. Read Tracy Grikscheit's essay "All His Vital Organs Lay In a Pan Beside His Head" on page 406 of the Sourcebook. Identify the different purposes of her paragraphs and clusters of paragraphs within her essay. Discuss how Grikscheit's paragraphs work together to create a unified and coherent essay.

SECTION II

The Sentence: Parts and Patterns

Although the skills of identifying sentence parts and constructing grammatically correct sentences will not guarantee your success as a writer, familiarity with English sentence structure can help you reduce errors that interfere with your readers' understanding of your writing. Moreover, familiarity with sentence logic will make you a better editor of your own writing and a better peer editor.

The material in this section will help you master the conventions of English grammar and correct any errors that you may make. To identify the faulty patterns that weaken your writing, use your journal or notebook to record the errors that your instructor and your peer editors have noted most often. This handbook is your resource for examining and eliminating those errors.

SUBJECTS AND PREDICATES

A *sentence* (a grammatically complete group of words that expresses a thought) consists of two basic parts: a *subject* (noun or noun phrase) and a *predicate* (verb or verb phrase). The subject identifies a person, place, or thing; the predicate asserts something about the person, place, or thing or specifies action involving it.

> subj.
> **Marta** ran.

Subjects

In a *simple sentence* the subject is easy to identify: Sometimes, however, the subject can be tricky to identify. Subjects of sentences can be

nouns
pronouns
noun phrases
verbal nouns

1. *Nouns* are words that name persons, animals, places, ideas, and objects. In the sentence "Marta ran," *Marta* is a single noun acting as subject. In the sentence that follows, two nouns join to act as the subject.

subj.
Marta and Joan ran competitively.

2. *Pronouns* take the place of nouns.

subj.
She ran in the town's marathon.

3. *Noun phrases* are groups of words linking a noun with words that limit, qualify, or describe it.

noun phrase
The spirit of fair play is important in any sport.

4. *Verbal nouns* are verb forms that act like nouns in certain positions in a sentence. There are two kinds: gerunds and infinitives.

a. *Gerunds* are verb forms ending in *-ing* that act as subjects, subject complements, direct or indirect objects, or objects of a preposition.

subj.
Running is Marta's hobby.

b. *Infinitives* are verb forms consisting of *to* plus the present tense of a verb (for example, *to run*). Infinitives can act as nouns, adjectives, or adverbs.

subj.
To run gives Marta great pleasure.

"There is" and "there are" constructions may also make it difficult to identify the subject and verb of a sentence.

verb **subj.**
There **are** countless **races** that Marta has won.

Predicates

A *simple predicate* consists of one verb alone:

verb
Marta **ran.**

A *complete predicate*, however, consists of a verb plus any modifiers, objects, and complements that surround it.

Transitive Verbs A *transitive verb* expresses action received by a direct object. A predicate with a transitive verb, therefore, includes a direct object. A *direct object* is a word or word group that names the receiver of an action and answers the question "what" or "whom" after the verb.

subj. verb direct obj.
Eric created an **interesting mural.**

Besides having a direct object, some transitive verbs also have an indirect object. An *indirect object* is the person or thing to whom or for whom something is done.

indirect obj. direct obj.
They awarded **Eric** a prize.

Intransitive Verbs A predicate with an *intransitive verb* cannot take a direct or indirect object. Intransitive verbs may, however, be followed by an adverb or adverbial word group.

adv.
Eric paints **beautifully.**

Linking Verbs A predicate with a *linking verb* (a verb that links a subject with a word or word group that describes the subject) includes a subject complement. A *subject complement* is a word or word group that helps identify, classify, or describe a subject. The most commonly used linking verb is a form of the verb *to be*. Others include *become, feel, seem, sound,* and *taste.*

subj. comp.
Eric is a **man of achievement.**

PHRASES AND CLAUSES

Phrases

A *phrase* is a group of words that may contain a subject or a verb, but not both. A phrase acts as a single part of speech—noun, verb, adjective, or adverb.

A *prepositional phrase* begins with a preposition such as *at, by, for, from, in, of, on to,* or *with* and usually ends with a noun or noun equivalent (for example, *on the beach, from the bridge, by closing time*). The noun or noun equivalent is known as the *object of the preposition.*

prep. phrase
You must evaluate this essay **for its style**.

Prepositional phrases often function as adverbs or adjectives to elaborate upon the nouns and verbs of the sentence.

adj.
Three friends **of my sister's** won scholarships to college.

A *verbal phrase* consists of a verb form that functions as a noun, adjective, or adverb. The types of verbal phrases are *gerunds, participles,* and *infinitives.* In most cases, a *gerund phrase* serves as a subject or an object in a sentence. Gerunds are easy to spot because they end in *-ing*:

subj.
Reading the newspaper took me all afternoon.

direct obj.
Nevertheless, I finished **writing and revising** for the next day's class.

An *appositive phrase* clarifies a noun by describing or renaming it. An appositive phrase appears next to the noun it clarifies and usually is set off by commas.

Clyde Jones, **our club's speaker,** brought slides from his trip to Albania.

A *participle phrase* always functions as an adjective. Participles have three forms: present participle (ending in *-ing*), past participle (ending in *-d, -ed, -n, -en,* or *-t*), and present participle (*having* plus the past participle).

Present: **Using vivid imagery,** Jones conveyed a sense of the country's present state.

Past: **Encouraged by our interest,** he stayed for an extra hour.

Present perfect: **Having answered all our questions,** he promised to return soon.

An *infinitive* uses *to* plus the base form of a verb (for example, *to bark, to bite*). *Infinitive phrases* can serve as nouns, adjectives, or adverbs.

noun
To travel under harsh conditions takes strong dedication.

adj.
The audience's desire **to ask questions** showed their genuine interest.

adv.
They hurried **to invite** Jones to come again.

Clauses

A *clause* is a group of words containing a subject and a predicate. There are two kinds of clauses: independent and dependent. *Independent clauses* can stand alone as grammatically complete sentences.

The candidate won.

Dependent (or *subordinate*) *clauses* cannot stand alone as complete sentences. They usually begin with a subordinating conjunction or a relative pronoun.

because she had strong endorsements

dep. clause
The candidate won **because she had strong endorsements.**

Subordinating conjunctions include:

after	before	than	when
although	even though	that	where
as	how	though	whether
as if	if	unless	while
because	since	until	why

Relative pronouns include:

that	who/whom
what/whatever	whoever/whomever
which/whichever	whose

Dependent clauses function within sentences as adjectives, adverbs, or nouns. *Adjective clauses* modify nouns or pronouns in another clause. Most adjective clauses begin with a relative pronoun.

adj. clause

The candidate, **who delivered a rousing speech,** won.

Adverb clauses modify verbs, adjectives, and other adverbs. They usually begin with a subordinating conjunction and tell when, where, why, under what conditions, or to what degree an action occurred or a situation existed.

adv. clause

Angry **because economic conditions were so bad,** the candidate inspired many to follow him.

Noun clauses function in the same way as single word nouns. They can act as subjects, subject complements, direct objects, or objects of a preposition.

subj.

That he finally won surprised no one.

subj. comp.

The real question is **what will he do when he is in office.**

direct obj.

His supporters will never forget **that he made many promises.**

A noun clause usually begins with a relative pronoun (*that, which, who*) or with a subordinating conjunction (*how, when, where, whether, why*).

SENTENCE TYPES

A sentence is a grammatically complete group of words that expresses a thought. There are four types of sentences; simple, compound, complex, and compound-complex.

Simple sentences have one independent clause.

The candidate visited every state.

Compound sentences have two or more independent clauses joined by a comma and a coordinating conjunction, or by a semicolon.

ind. clause **ind. clause**
The candidate visited every state, and he assessed the economic conditions.

Complex sentences have one independent clause with one or more subordinate (or dependent) clauses.

sub. clause
Because he has a strong background in economics,

ind. clause
he was able to come up with some interesting new ideas.

Compound-complex sentences contain at least two independent clauses and at least one subordinate clause.

sub. clause **ind. clause**
Whenever he met with business leaders, he presented his proposals,

ind. clause
and he listened carefully to the leaders' reactions.

TROUBLESHOOTING

In the following pages, you'll find help with a number of problems that occur frequently in writing.

Sentence Fragments

A *sentence fragment* is an incomplete sentence. It is a phrase without a subject or verb or both, or a clause beginning with a subordinating word. It is only a part—or fragment—of a writer's intended meaning and does not give the reader enough information to understand the complete idea.

Fragment: The composition class being held in Crown Center 413. (phrase missing verb)

Sentence: The composition class is being held in Crown Center 413.

Fragment: Because the composition class is being held in Crown Center 413. (clause with subordinating word)

Sentence: Because the composition class is being held in Crown Center 413, we will have access to computers.

To avoid fragments, make sure each sentence contains both a subject and a verb and connect clauses beginning with subordinate clauses to the word group that completes them. The following words often introduce subordinate clauses.

although	until
as	when
as if	where
because	whether
before	which
since	while
though	whom
unless	

Notice how independent clauses become subordinate clauses when a subordinating word is added:

Sentence: The primary text of the class will be student writing.

Fragments: **Although** the primary test of the class will be student writing.

Because the primary text of the class will be student writing.

Since the primary text of the class will be student writing.

Although the preceding dependent clauses have been punctuated as sentences, they are fragments and depend on an independent clause to complete their meaning. To correct fragments either in your writing or in a peer's writing, add an independent clause.

Although the primary text of the class will be student writing, we will also use a textbook.

Because the primary text of the class will be student writing, you will have a chance to read essays on many topics.

Since the primary text of the class will be student writing, your assignment due dates must be carefully observed.

Often, you can catch sentence fragments by reading your work aloud. When you hear what you have written, you will recognize the incompleteness of the thought. Though professional writers may use fragments for effect, in general, fragments should be avoided because they suggest carelessness or lack of knowledge.

EXERCISE 1 Identifying Sentence Fragments

Some of the following word groups are sentence fragments. Place a *C* in the margin next to those groups that are sentences, and complete the fragments.

1. The classroom being small and always airless.
2. Because the class began at 8:30 A.M.
3. As the group grew more comfortable with each other.
4. Each student is to bring a draft for peer editing.
5. A notebook, a pen, and a spiral notebook.
6. The difference between editing and proofreading.
7. Since the 50 minutes went quickly.
8. When he was absent for days.
9. And for days he worked hard on his draft.
10. First with hesitance, then with enthusiasm.

Comma Splices and Run-on Sentences

Comma splices result when two independent clauses are fused or "spliced" together with a comma instead of being separated into two sentences, joined by a conjunction, or joined by a semicolon.

The following shows three ways of correcting a comma splice.

Comma splice: Nicholia's essay took its audience into consideration, the writing was stylistically engaging as well.

Correct: Nicholia's essay took its audience into consideration. The writing was stylistically engaging as well.

Correct: Nicholia's essay took its audience into consideration, and the writing was stylistically engaging as well.

Correct: Nicholia's essay took its audience into consideration; the writing was stylistically engaging as well.

To help you avoid the comma splice error, remember these three sentence patterns:

Two sentences:	Independent clause. Independent clause.
Comma, coordinating conjunction:	Independent clause, and independent clause.
Semicolon:	Independent clause; independent clause.

Another way to avoid a comma splice error is to use a subordinating word to make one of the independent clauses a dependent clause:

Comma splice: The essay was stylistically interesting, it did not consider the audience's assumptions.

Correct: **Although** the essay was stylistically interesting, it did not consider the audience's assumptions.

EXERCISE 2 Correcting Comma Splices

Correct the comma splices in the following sentences.

1. Some considered Abdiel the best writer in the class, others would name Nicholia.
2. A 101 class generally requires at least five essays, a 201 class requires more.
3. Attendance is required for peer-editing sessions, it is strongly recommended for all other activities.
4. Laurie thought her draft was in her briefcase, it was actually in her car.
5. Come to class, get a better grade.

Run-on sentences are independent clauses that are run together without a coordinating conjunction or punctuation.

Run-on sentence: Nicholia's essay took its audience into consideration the writing was stylistically engaging as well.

Run-on sentences can be corrected in the same ways as comma splices.

EXERCISE 3 Correcting Run-on Sentences

Correct the following run-on sentences.

1. A class in Damen Hall has the benefit of air-conditioning a class in Dumbach Hall has none.
2. Many students liked editing other students' work they found it helped their own writing.
3. Some students went through several drafts of an essay others wrote just two.
4. Kim came to class promptly at the semester's beginning by the semester's end, she was chronically tardy.
5. Kim's arrival was eagerly awaited she was the most vocal of the students.

Subject-Verb Agreement

Subject-verb agreement is a trouble spot for many writers. Like sentence fragments, run-ons, or comma splices, errors in subject-verb agreement interfere with effective written communication. Remember, subjects and verbs must agree grammatically. Singular subjects take singular verbs; plural subjects take plural verbs.

Singular: The list (**subj.**) of the class members was (**verb**) lengthy.

Plural: The lists (**subj.**) of the class members were (**verb**) lengthy.

The following pointers can help you make subjects and verbs agree in your sentences.

1. Words appearing between the subject and the verb should not mislead you. In the following example *list,* not *members,* is the subject.

The **list** of the class members **was** lengthy.

You may find it helpful to cross out word groups (particularly prepositional phrases) that separate the subject and verb. When *of the class members* is crossed out, it is easy to see that *list* is the subject of the sentence.

2. Subjects joined by *and* are usually plural and take plural verbs.

> **Julio and Abdiel** often **edit** each other's work.

Exception: When *each* or *every* precedes two or more subjects joined by *and*, the subject is singular and takes a singular verb.

> **Every young man and woman has** the potential to produce solid academic writing.

3. When subjects are joined by *either . . . or*, *neither . . . nor*, or *not only . . . but also*, the verb agrees with the subject closer to it.

> **Neither Kim nor her sisters exhibit** any visible shyness.
>
> **Either the delegates or the president makes** that decision.

4. In sentences beginning with *here is, here are, there is, there are, where is*, and *where are*, look ahead in the sentence for the subject. Often it will be the closest noun following the verb.

> **There are** twenty **members** of this class.
>
> **Where is** your **current journal?**

Remember that *there, here*, and *where* are never the subjects of sentences.

5. When used as subjects, *anybody, anyone, each, every, everybody, everyone, everything, nobody, nothing, someone, somebody, something, either*, and *neither* take singular verbs. Although these indefinite pronouns sound plural, they are grammatically singular.

> Of the two possibilities, **neither holds** my interest.
>
> **Each** of the couple's stories **suggests** a different reality.

6. Some nouns that are plural in form and singular in meaning (collective nouns) require a singular verb. A partial list of collective nouns includes:

army	company
assembly	couple
band	crowd
committee	family

flock
group
herd
jury
pair
squad
team

The whole **family likes** to eat fast food.

The **crowd determines** the success of his speech.

7. Subjects that are plural in form but singular in meaning usually take verbs that are singular. Among those are the following:

civics
economics
electronics
ethics
headquarters
mathematics
measles
mumps
news
physics
politics

The **news** about the war **was** discouraging.

Ethics is a required course for business majors.

8. Words indicating units of time, money, or distance require a singular verb.

Three miles **is** the longest she is able to run.

Three dollars **is** the price of admission to the concert.

9. The title of a piece of writing or the name of a business company takes a singular verb.

Their Eyes Were Watching God **is** a lyrical work of fiction.

3M employs the inventor of "Post-it" notes.

Reminder: To make a present tense verb agree with a third-person singular subject, we usually add *-s* or *-es* to it.

I go	I wish
you go	you wish
he, she, it goes	he, she, it wishes

Mistakes may happen in subject-verb agreement because the *-s* or *-es* endings also indicate plural nouns. If you find you are making this particular subject-verb agreement error (or any of the others mentioned in this section), proofread carefully with those errors in mind.

EXERCISE 4 Identifying Subject and Verb Forms

Underline the subject in the following sentences; then select the correct verb form.

1. The exquisite vase of peonies (sit, sits) in the middle of the highly polished table.
2. Neither the cat nor the dogs (exhibit, exhibits) an ounce of energy.
3. Thirty dollars (is, are) hardly a fair price for these faux pearl earrings.
4. Everyone (want, wants) an "A" in the class; each (get, gets) what is deserved.
5. The faculty (was, were) supportive of the mission of the Women's Center.
6. The couple (was, were) bickering for the sixth time today.
7. *One Hundred Years of Solitude* (remain, remains) required reading in Ms. Paton's course.
8. Every dog and cat (need, needs) to be immunized.
9. There (is, are) no excuses for this kind of behavior.
10. The news from the doctor (is, are) better than Gloria expected.

Pronoun Agreement

A pronoun should agree in number with the word for which it stands (its antecedent).

> The **students** left **their** test booklets in a pile on the instructor's desk.
>
> **Juan** left **his** book on top of the pile.

Sometimes pronoun agreement is difficult to determine, but the following rules should be helpful.

1. *Collective nouns* (group, team, class, family, and so on) take a singular pronoun when the noun refers to the group as a unit.

> The **team** needs to restore **its** spirit after **its** dispiriting loss.

2. Use a plural pronoun if you have a compound subject joined by *and*, unless *each* or *every* precedes those words.

Shelley and Shanta went to **their** apartment.

Each member of the men's swim team and basketball team picked up **his** trophy already.

3. Use a singular pronoun to refer to indefinite pronouns such as *anybody, anyone, everybody, everyone, everything, nobody, no one, nothing, somebody,* and *someone.*

Someone from the women's track team called about **her** schedule.

4. When two nouns are joined by *either . . . or* or *neither . . . nor,* the pronoun should agree with the closest noun.

Neither the overworked **teacher nor** the distracted **students** could muster much enthusiasm for **their** last week of classes.

EXERCISE 5 Using Pronouns

Insert the correct pronoun in the space provided.

1. Neither your professor nor his best students received the acclaim ______________ deserved.
2. Every girl in the performance should polish ______________ routine.
3. A hornet and a wasp have in common ______________ ability to sting.
4. Each went shopping for ______________ own groceries.
5. Joan and Kee took turns cleaning ______________ apartment.

Other Pronoun Problems

1. *Unclear pronoun referents* occur when it is not clear which noun (referent) the pronoun stands for. If a pronoun could refer to more than one noun in the sentence, the reader may be confused. Consider the examples that follow:

Confusing: Whenever Jenny eats dinner with Joan, she always cooks.

Clear: Joan always cooks whenever she and Jenny dine together.

Confusing: Marta told Jan that she had made an error.

Clear: Marta told Jan, "I've made an error."

2. *Problems with personal pronouns* arise when the writer is uncertain of which form to use in a sentence.

As a reminder, *subject pronouns* are used as the subject of a sentence (or clause) or as a subject complement.

Subject: **Marta and I** [not me] discovered a new lentil recipe.

Object pronouns are used as direct objects, indirect objects, and as objects of prepositions.

Direct object:	Monique instructed **Marta and me** [not I] in the art of preparing East African cuisine.
Indirect object:	Monique gave **Marta and me** [not I] a lecture on cooking techniques.
Object of preposition:	The odd combination of spices was a pleasant surprise to **Marta and me.**

Misplaced and Dangling Modifiers

Misplaced modifiers are modifiers that are separated from the word or words they modify. Misplaced modifiers often can be confusing for the reader.

Confusing:	John bought a new van for his wife complete with racing stripe.
Clear:	John bought a new van with racing stripes for his wife.
Confusing:	We took the broken car to the auto mechanic with the cracked manifold.
Clear:	We took the broken car with the cracked manifold to the auto mechanic.

Sometimes, by placing a modifier next to a word that makes sense grammatically, you may change your meaning. For example, placement of the word *only* changes the meaning of the following two sentences.

I wanted **only** to borrow ten dollars.

I wanted to borrow **only** ten dollars.

In the first sentence, you modify either *wanted* or *borrow*. In the second sentence, you modify the words *ten dollars,* indicating that you wanted to borrow neither more nor less than that sum. As you write, you need to keep your meaning clear.

Dangling modifiers do not modify a specific word or phrase in the sentence. At the beginning of sentences, prepositional phrases or verbal phrases sometimes are left dangling when they do not have a clear referent.

Entering the room, the music overwhelmed me.

Here, the verbal phrase *entering the room* seems to be modifying the word *music*. But music cannot enter the room. A more logical version of the sentence is:

As I entered the room, the music overwhelmed me.

To avoid illogical and often unintentionally funny sentences, place the modifier close to the word or words being modified and make sure that the modifier actually relates to that word.

EXERCISE 6 Identifying Misplaced or Dangling Modifiers

In the following sentences, find the misplaced or dangling modifier and revise the sentence so that it makes sense.

1. Preparing for the test, my books piled up beside me
2. I sent out for pizza as I worked which was really tasty.
3. Calling my roommate, the pizza fell off the desk.
4. As I bent to pick it up, the books fell on the box which were the whole term's course readings.
5. Eating it, however, the pizza seemed as good as we expected.

Gender-biased Language

Language both reflects and shapes our view of reality. Recently, many sociologists, anthropologists, and feminist theorists have argued that language has the power to affect our sense of identity. When women grow up hearing terms like "mailman," "policeman," or "fireman," they may come to believe that these professions are exclusive to men. When men and women hear derogatory expressions such as "female logic" or "male ego," harmful stereotypes are introduced or reinforced. These terms suggest that women's reasoning is not only idiosyncratic but faulty and that men are burdened by overactive egos. Good writers and readers develop a sensitivity to biased language. Here are some suggestions:

1. Avoid the use of the word *man* to refer to humans of both sexes. Instead, find a gender-neutral description.

Biased: Mankind is responsible for the unfortunate state of our planet.

Revised: Humanity is responsible for the unfortunate state of our planet.

Whenever possible, use gender-neutral terms for job titles that end in *man* or that use different words for male and female roles.

Sexist	*Revised*
mailman	mail carrier
policeman	police officer
fireman	firefighter
chairman/chairwoman	chairperson/chair

2. Avoid the masculine pronoun when referring generically to people. The generic *he* doesn't represent its antecedent in a gender-neutral fashion; it identifies its antecedent as male.

Sexist: Every professional athlete earns more than he deserves.

Revised: Every professional athlete earns more than he or she deserves.

Often, you can avoid the cumbersome *he or she* construction by recasting the sentence to use a plural subject and verb.

Revised: Professional athletes earn more than they deserve.

Avoid s/he constructions. These are not widely accepted as they have no counterpart in spoken language.

3. Avoid stereotyping men and women by profession.

Sexist: Call the nurse, and ask her to bring a fresh pitcher of water. (The nurse could be a man.)

Revised: Call the nurse, and ask for a fresh pitcher of water.

4. Avoid letter salutations that make assumptions about the gender of the reader. Use a nonsexist greeting such as:

Dear Colleague
Dear Reader
Dear Subscriber

Parallelism

You can help your readers understand how sentence elements are related by keeping parallel words or phrases in similar form. Look at the following sentences.

Faulty: In Lena's cupboard, you may find food that is ethnic, wholesome, and has many calories.

Parallel: In Lena's cupboard, you may find food that is ethnic, wholesome, and highly caloric.

In the first sentence, the first two elements in the series are adjectives, but the last element is a verb phrase. The sentence sounds awkward. In the second sentence, all the items in the series are phrased as adjectives.

Faulty: By limiting car emissions and other legislation, the city government took a stand on environmental issues.

Parallel: By limiting car emissions and enacting other legislation, the city government took a stand on environmental issues.

In the first sentence, the two elements in the subordinate clause are in different forms: a participle phrase and a noun phrase. These different forms cause confusion: Readers may wonder if the city government has limited other legislation. In the second sentence, using two participle phrases eliminates the confusion.

SECTION III

Punctuation

PERIODS

Use a period at the end of a declarative sentence (one which makes a statement) or at the end of a mild command.

> Although I like Vanessa's personality, I question her politics.
>
> Don't let me get in your way.

The period is also appropriate end punctuation for indirect questions.

> I wonder if I left my wallet in my pants pocket.

QUESTION MARKS

Use a question mark after a direct question.

> Why do you find him qualified for the position of chairperson?

Also use a question mark to indicate uncertainty about a date, word, or phrase.

> Hubert van Eyck (1366?–1426) was a significant Flemish painter.

EXCLAMATION POINTS

Use exclamation points as end punctuation after sentences that show strong emotion.

> Help!

Excessive use of exclamation points dulls their impact; be careful not to overuse them.

COMMAS

The comma is the mark of punctuation you will most frequently use. Although the comma can be used for style or emphasis, it is used most frequently in the following ways.

1. Use commas to separate items in a series.

> At the store, please purchase tomato paste, garlic cloves, fresh basil, and olive oil.

or

> To be a successful educator, you must have enthusiasm, an inordinate amount of patience, and a knowledge of your subject area.

2. Use a comma to separate independent clauses joined by coordinating conjunctions (*and*, *but*, *for*, *nor*, *or*, *so*, and *yet*).

> She taught her students to avoid sexist language, yet they continued to favor the masculine pronouns.

3. Use a comma to separate an introductory dependent (subordinate) clause from the main part of the sentence. Some common subordinating conjunctions are:

after	since
although	though
as	until
because	when/whenever
before	where/wherever
once	while

> Because she was four when she left Japan, Hikaru recalls little of the language.

If you change the syntax so that the main part of the sentence (the independent clause) precedes the dependent (subordinate) clause, no comma is needed.

> Hikaru recalls little of the language because she left Japan when she was four.

4. Use a comma to separate a long introductory prepositional phrase from the main part of the sentence. A prepositional phrase consists of a preposition (*at*, *behind*, *for*, *in*, *over*, *to*, *upon*, *with*, and so on) and its object.

> Despite losing hours of sleep working on the second draft of her paper, Joan did attend her 8:30 class.

5. Use a comma to set off other long introductory phrases containing a past, present, or present perfect participle or infinitive.

Present participle:	acting
Past participle:	acted
Present perfect participle:	having acted
Infinitive:	to act

Acting as the coordinator for International Day, Cvetko planned the food and entertainment.

To act as program guide for the campus radio station, Mario had to give up much of his free time.

6. Use commas to set off transitional words or phrases like the following: *as a matter of fact, at any rate, on the other hand, for instance, of course, however, moreover,* and *therefore.*

The campus Women's Center, moreover, has not received the funding it requires.

7. Use commas to set off nonrestrictive items in a sentence. If a modifier or appositive is *nonrestrictive,* it can be deleted without changing the essential meaning of the sentence.

nonrestrictive mod.
Phil, **who is an accomplished translator,** is chairperson of the English department.

Here, the primary information the writer wishes to communicate to her audience is that Phil is chairperson of the department. The additional information about Phil is not necessary to the meaning of the sentence.

nonrestrictive app.
Jean-Pierre, **the sous-chef at St. Martins,** once trained seals for a living.

In this sentence, Jean-Pierre's current occupation is incidental to the meaning of the sentence.

In the following sentence the *who* clause is essential to the meaning of the sentence because it *restricts* the meaning of the noun.

The astronauts who first landed on the moon received a great deal of acclaim.

Only those astronauts who first landed on the moon received acclaim.

8. Use a comma to set off coordinate adjectives. Adjectives are considered coordinate if *and* can be placed between them.

It was a long, tedious day. (You can say it was a long **and** tedious day.)

It was a hot summer day. (You wouldn't say it was a hot and summer day.)

EXERCISE 7 Using Commas

Add commas to the following sentences. Be able to explain the rule for each addition.

1. Because Joey was late for the rally somebody else grabbed his sign.
2. I dislike large reptiles and when Melissa picks one up I feel frightened.
3. Look in the reference room for the *General Science Index* the *Applied Science and Technology Index* and the *Readers' Guide to Periodical Literature.*
4. The new car which is cherry red rear-ended a city bus.
5. Injured in the accident were John Mary Fido and Fluffy.
6. Draped across her shoulder was a tattered torn opera cape.
7. Abraham Lincoln our sixteenth president had a wife as interesting as he.

SEMICOLONS

1. Use a semicolon to join two independent clauses if no coordinating conjunction is used to connect them.

You do not have to be a bibliophile to enjoy the library; many products and services are offered there.

2. Use a semicolon to separate items in a series if the items contain commas.

Injured in the accident were Joe Norman, age 36; Sue Norman, age 32; Fido, their geriatric dog; and Fluffy, their aging cat.

3. Use a semicolon to link independent clauses joined by conjunctive adverbs such as *furthermore, however, indeed, likewise, nevertheless, otherwise, similarly,* and *therefore.* Though this list is not exhaustive, it does contain the most frequently used conjunctive adverbs.

ind. clause **conj. adv.**
Mary was overwhelmed with work; nevertheless,

ind. clause
she didn't miss Joan's presentation.

EXERCISE 8 Using Semicolons

Correct the punctuation in the following sentences, using semicolons where needed.

1. Enrollment has decreased, tuition has increased.
2. Present at the ceremony were Alan Silver, this year's award winner, Lou Ann Silver, his wife, and Fleur Elise Silver, their thirteen-year-old daughter.
3. I would love to attend graduation, however, my teaching schedule doesn't allow me the time.
4. The ceremony begins in two hours please do not be late.
5. I understand your annoyance at him, moreover, I sympathize.

COLONS

A colon is a mark of introduction.

1. Use a colon to introduce a list of items introduced by an independent clause.

> She had publications in an odd assortment of magazines: *Mother Jones*, *Modern Mechanic*, and *Fiction*.

2. Use a colon between two independent causes when the second explains the first.

> The dentist's news was alarming: I had a mouthful of cavities again.

PARENTHESES

Use parentheses to enclose nonessential information.

> Some flowering bushes are poisonous (oleanders, for example).

DASHES

1. Use a dash to interrupt normal word order and to insert additional information. A pair of dashes is essentially the same as a pair of commas, but dashes add emphasis. Dashes are typed as two hyphens with no space before or after.

> When you use dashes—and you should use them sparingly—be sure to know how to type them correctly.

2. Use a dash as a mark of introduction. It can function the same way as a colon but is a less formal mark of introduction.

> The dentist gave me just what I didn't need—a filling and a bill for $60.

HYPHENS

1. Use hyphens to break words at the end of lines. Remember to divide words only at a syllable.

> Though I am quite fond of my Uncle John, **deal-**
> **ing** with him sometimes presents difficulties.

2. Use hyphens to link compound words. Use a dictionary to determine which compound words are hyphenated.

> My **mother-in-law** uses a **walkie-talkie** to speak to her husband when they are in separate rooms.

3. Use hyphens between fractions and compound numbers from twenty-one through ninety-nine.

> **Three-fourths** of the students missed class because of the snow.

BRACKETS

Use brackets to add information or explanations to direct quotations. This allows you to insert your own words into a direct quotation.

> "Phil Clare [chairperson of the English department] will preside over the council meeting."

or

> "The MLA [Modern Language Association] meeting will be held in Chicago this year."

QUOTATION MARKS

1. Use quotation marks around the exact words of a speaker or writer.

> "This wine has the bouquet of gym socks!" the surprised taster exclaimed.

2. Use quotation marks to enclose the titles of short poems, short stories, magazine articles, TV episodes, songs, chapter titles, and unpublished speeches.

> Ray Carver's story "Cathedral" will be the focus of our discussion.

3. Avoid overusing quotation marks to highlight specific words or to signal the reader that you are using a word in an unusual or ironic way.

> When I went into her room, I found her "studying" with her eyes closed and her head resting on her book.

4. Place commas and periods *inside* of quotations marks; place semicolons and colons *outside* of quotation marks.

> He said, "Let's leave at 4 o'clock."

> After reading Chapter 1, "A Word or Two About Writing," the students began writing their first essay.

> Yesterday I finished Lewis Thomas's essay "The Iks"; today I began a book by Franz Boas.

5. When a quotation ends in a question, place the question mark *inside* the quotation marks. When your whole sentence is a question, place the question mark *outside* of the quotation marks.

> He asked, "When are we leaving?"

> How many students have read "The Iks"?

ITALICS

1. Use italics for titles of:

aircraft	plays
albums	ships
books	software
films	spacecraft
long musical pieces	trains
long poems	TV shows (not episodes)
periodicals	

To indicate italics, underline words. Some word processing programs enable you to print in both roman (straight) and italic (slanted) type.

2. Use italics for foreign words or phrases that are not in common use in English. Check your dictionary if you are unsure.

> Her *chutzpah* is at least partially responsible for her success.

ELLIPSES

1. Ellipses are often used in academic writing to indicate that material has been left out of a direct quotation. Use three dots to indicate an omission within a sentence.

> "For others they sail forever on the horizon . . . until the Watcher turns his eyes away in resignation, his dreams mocked to death by Time.
>
> —Zora Neale Hurston, *Their Eyes Were Watching God*

If an ellipsis appears at the end of a sentence, the first dot indicates a period.

> "For others they sail forever on the horizon . . . until the Watcher turns his eyes away. . . ."

2. Use an ellipsis to suggest an incomplete action.

> To calm herself and bring about sleep, Nadine counted silently, "One, two, three . . ."

APOSTROPHES

1. Use an apostrophe to indicate possession:

> The **waitress's** job was in jeopardy because the restaurant had lost customers.

An exception to this rule occurs with the possessive of *it* and with the words *yours, hers, theirs,* and *ours.*

> The television would not work. **Its** antenna was broken.
>
> I have brought my skates. I hope you brought **yours.**

2. Use an apostrophe to indicate an omitted letter or number.

This *isn't* my idea.

He was born in '72.

3. Use apostrophes to form the plurals of letters and numbers when misreading may occur without the apostrophe.

She knows, at five, her *ABC's*.

When writing dates such as *the 1980s*, it is acceptable to omit or to use the apostrophe. Just be consistent throughout your piece of writing.

EXERCISE 9 Adding Punctuation

Add the appropriate punctuation (ellipsis, apostrophe, dash, hyphen, quotation marks, brackets, italics, or parentheses) to the following sentences.

1. "It was an extraordinarily cold 10 degrees to be exact winter night in 1962."
2. I think and this may sound crazy that Jackie and Tony will eventually get married.
3. The CAA College Art Association will meet in Washington D.C. next year.
4. Let's get out of here, he whispered.
5. It isn't my fault you didn't get your financial aid material in on time.
6. Their Eyes Were Watching God is a novel many call a rich and complicated text.

SECTION IV

Glossary of Usage

This glossary provides a list of words and phrases that may cause you some confusion. For more complete information about these or other words, consult the dictionary recommended by your instructor.

accept, except **Accept** is a verb and means "to receive" or "to agree to." **Except** is used as a preposition to mean "but."

➤ I wanted to **accept** his late paper, but was unable to.
➤ All papers **except** his were in on time.

adapt, adopt To **adapt** means to alter something for a purpose. To **adopt** something is to possess or control it.

➤ Before I can use the syllabus, I must **adapt** it to my classroom needs.
➤ I can't **adopt** the syllabus without changes.

advice, advise **Advice** is a noun meaning an opinion or suggestion you offer. **Advise** is a verb meaning "to offer or provide advice."

➤ He ignored my **advice** to him.
➤ I hesitated to **advise** him about his business venture.

affect, effect **Affect** is a verb meaning "to change or modify." **Effect** as a noun means "a result."

➤ The neighborhood cannot help but be **affected** by the new zoning laws.
➤ The **effect** of the zoning changes will mean increased traffic on the formerly residential streets.

aggravate, annoy **Aggravate** is a verb meaning "to make worse." **Annoy** is a verb meaning "to irritate."

➤ The aspirin he took repeatedly only **aggravated** his gout.
➤ The discomfort caused by the gout was **annoying.**

all ready, already **All ready** means "prepared." **Already** is an adverb meaning "previously."

➤ The students were **all ready** for the scheduled exam.
➤ When Jim walked in, the exam had **already** started.

all right **All right** is always two words. Do not use **alright;** it is nonstandard.

➤ My friend seemed to feel **all right** by the time I left her.

all together, altogether **All together** means "all gathered in a group." **Altogether** means "completely."

➤ We were **all together** at Thanksgiving.
➤ I ate **altogether** too much turkey.

allusion, illusion **Allusion** is a reference to something (i.e., an instructor might *allude* to the poem of one writer to explain the work of another.) An **illusion** is a false image or appearance.

➤ Ms. Hernandez's **allusion** to the early work of Neruda was lost on her students.
➤ Ms. Hernandez had the **illusion** that she was standing in front of thirty future poets.

among, between Use **among** when referring to more than two items or people. Use **between** when referring to two items or people.

➤ David was **among** our four finalists.
➤ Finally, we had to decide **between** David and Ann.

amount, number **Amount** refers to quantities you can't count. **Number** refers to objects you can count.

➤ A large *amount* of negotiation needs to take place before the final decision is made.
➤ Please announce the *number* of meetings remaining this semester.

anyone, any one **Anyone** means any person at all. **Any one** means any single person.

➤ **Anyone** can master punctuation.
➤ **Any one** of these students can do as well as the next.

anyway **Anyway** should always be used; **anyways** is nonstandard.

➤ Although I had a headache, I studied for an hour **anyway.**

bad, badly **Bad** is an adjective. **Badly** is an adverb.

- He felt **bad** even after his temperature dropped.
- His resistance was low because he ate so **badly.**

beside, besides **Beside** is a preposition meaning "next to." **Besides** is either a preposition meaning "in addition to" or a transition meaning "moreover."

- **Beside** the phlox, I've planted yarrow.
- **Besides** planting tulip bulbs, I planted irises.
- I'm too tired to go shopping; **besides,** I want to plant my bulbs while the sun is still out.

can, may **Can** refers to the ability to do something. **May** refers to the permission to do something.

- All students **can** correct their own grammar.
- **May** I leave my books on your desk?

censor, censure **Censor** means to take away offensive material. To **censure** is "to formally reprimand."

- The Madonna video "Justify My Love" was **censored** by MTV.
- There was no need to **censure** Madonna for a performance that was exploratory and playful.

complement, compliment **Complement** means "to go with or complete" while **compliment** is a "flattering remark."

- The purple sweater **complements** her lavender skirt.
- The **compliments** she receives on her outfits fuel her desire to buy more.

comprise, compose **Comprise** means "to include or contain." **Compose** means "to make or form combining certain things."

- The country **comprises** several small counties.
- She **composed** a centerpiece of flowers and fruits.

conscience, conscious **Conscience** is a noun meaning "sense of right or wrong." **Conscious** is an adjective meaning "awake" or "alert."

- In order to make the decision, she had to carefully examine her **conscience.**
- She was not **conscious** of the difficulty of making the decision.

continual, continuous **Continual** describes an activity that is repeated frequently. **Continuous** means "without interruption."

- The **continual** rings from the neighbor's phone concerned me.
- The phone rang **continuously.**

council, counsel **Council** is a group or body of people. **Counsel** as a verb means "to advise" and as a noun means "advice."

➤ I would **counsel** you to insist upon a better balance between men and women in the city **council.**

criteria, criterion **Criteria** is the plural form of the noun **criterion** meaning "standard of judgment."

➤ What are the **criteria** for the new instructorship?
➤ There is never only one **criterion** for a job.

data **Data** is the plural form of **datum,** meaning "fact" or "result."

➤ These **data** surprise me.

different from, different than To indicate a difference, use **different from.** Avoid **different than** in formal writing.

➤ Hemingway's short stories are **different** in style **from** Fitzgerald's.

disinterested, uninterested **Disinterested** means "impartial." **Uninterested,** on the other hand, means "not interested."

➤ The judge made a **disinterested** decision.
➤ I was really **uninterested** in that film.

elicit, illicit **Elicit** is a verb meaning "to draw forth or evoke." **Illicit** means "illegal."

➤ She always seems to **elicit** the same enthusiastic response from him.
➤ Though her methods are questionable, they are not **illicit.**

ensure, assure **Ensure** means "to make certain" while **assure** means "to promise or convince."

➤ I sent him money for a plane ticket to **ensure** that he would come.
➤ I **assure** you he will attend the ceremony and will be on time.

explicit, implicit **Explicit** means "fully or clearly expressed." **Implicit** means "indirectly expressed or implied."

➤ Joan's **explicit** message was to practice tolerance when dealing with others.
➤ Her **implicit** message seemed to contradict that.

farther, further **Farther** always refers to physical distance while **further** means "more" or "additional."

➤ It is **farther** to the lake from my new house than it is from my old.
➤ When you have time, I'd like to discuss this matter **further**.

fewer, less **Fewer** is used only with things you can count. **Less** is used with things that are singular or things you cannot separate easily (for example, *less freedom, less truth, less beauty*).

➤ **Fewer** students than expected came to class the last week of the semester.

➤ **Less** trouble among students resulted from **fewer** rules.

flaunt, flout **Flaunt** means "to show off." **Flout,** on the other hand, means "to defy."

➤ She **flaunted** the ridiculous hat as though it flattered her.

➤ Dudley **flouted** the "no shirt, no shoes, no service" rule when he entered barefooted.

formally, formerly **Formally** refers to conventional behavior or custom. **Formerly** refers to an earlier time.

➤ Because convention required it, Dolores dressed **formally** for the occasion.

➤ **Formerly** students dressed up for the dance; now they wear jeans.

good, well **Good** is always used as an adjective, but **well** functions as both an adjective and an adverb. As an adjective **well** means "in good health."

➤ Jeff is a **good** racquetball player.

➤ Though he plays **well,** Jeff has trouble keeping partners. (adv.)

➤ Because he's over his cold and is feeling **well,** Jeff's game was excellent this morning. (adj.)

hanged, hung **Hanged,** the past tense and past participle of *hang*, refers to executions. **Hung** (also the past tense of *hang*) is used for all other meanings.

➤ He was **hanged** for his crimes.

➤ The curtains were **hung** in a most haphazard way.

imply, infer **Imply** means "to suggest" or "hint strongly." **Infer,** on the other hand, means "to make an educated guess."

➤ Larry **implied** that teaching the additional course would be too stressful for him.

➤ Based on his suggestion, we **inferred** that the course should be taught by someone with more time.

incredible, incredulous **Incredible** means "Unbelievable"; **incredulous** means "doubting."

➤ The double somersault dive was **incredible** to the spectators.

➤ I don't blame you for being **incredulous;** had I not seen it with my own eyes, I wouldn't have believed the dive either.

its, it's **Its** is the possessive form of the pronoun *it.* **It's** is only used as the contraction for *it is;* the apostrophe does not indicate possession.

➤ This dog keeps scratching **its** fleas.
➤ **It's** your turn to walk Fido.

later, latter **Later** refers to time. **Latter** refers the reader to the last of two items mentioned.

➤ **Later,** when it cools off, we'll go for a run.
➤ Given the choice of an early morning run and an evening run, I prefer the **latter.**

lay, lie **lay** means "to put or place." Today you *lay* something on the table; yesterday you *laid* it on the table. **Lie** means "to recline." Today you *lie* down; yesterday you *lay* down. You have *lain* there for some time. (Remember, *to lay* usually requires a direct object telling the reader what you placed.)

➤ She **laid** the book on the table with a bang.
➤ Yesterday he **lay** on the couch for the whole wasted day.

loose, lose **Loose** means "untied or unfastened." **To lose** is "to misplace."

➤ In his nightmare his front teeth were **loose** as though he were six again.
➤ When his wallet fell out in the aisle of the supermarket, he picked it up and put it in his pocket so he wouldn't **lose** it.

media, medium **Media,** which is used commonly to refer to the press, is the plural form of **medium.**

➤ Of all the **media,** CNN seemed to give the most accurate coverage of the earthquake.
➤ The **medium** of television has become seductive to millions of American children.

maybe, may be **Maybe** means "perhaps," and **may be** is a verb phrase used to express contingency.

➤ **Maybe** if you work hard at the draft stage of your paper, the final product will receive a higher grade.
➤ You **may be** surprised at your course grade.

precede, proceed **Precede** means "to go before." **Proceed** means "continue to move forward."

- ➤ Nausea and cold sweats often **precede** fainting.
- ➤ She **proceeded** down the aisle although she felt faint.

principal, principle **Principal** means "first or highest in rank" or "the director of a school." **Principle** refers to a "rule or theory."

- ➤ As **principal** of the Winnetka School, she often met with parents to discuss school policy.
- ➤ The **principal** reason she took the job was the salary.
- ➤ No one can argue that she is without **principles;** her behavior is exemplary.

set, sit To **set** means "to place or put" and usually requires a direct object. To **sit** means to occupy a seat.

- ➤ Please don't **set** your ice tea glass on the table unless you use a coaster under it.
- ➤ Please don't **sit** on the Shaker chair; it is very delicate.

than, then **Than** is a conjunction; **then** is an adverb referring to time.

- ➤ I'd rather cook **than** eat in a restaurant tonight.
- ➤ Let's cash a check and **then** go out to dinner.

who, whom **Who** is used when the pronoun is the subject. **Whom** is used when the pronoun is an object.

- ➤ **Who** is going to Gabe's party with me?
- ➤ To **whom** is the invitation addressed?

who's, whose **Who's** is the contraction for *who is* and *who has.* **Whose** is a possessive pronoun.

- ➤ **Who's** going to Gabe's party with me?
- ➤ **Whose** car shall we take?

your, you're **Your** is the possessive form of *you.* **You're** is the contraction for *you are.*

- ➤ **Your** essay is fascinating.
- ➤ **You're** becoming an accomplished writer.

Acknowledgments

p. 55 Photo (AT&T Ad): From the AT&T Archive. Used by permission.

p. 57 Melinda Beck, "Getting Started at *Newsweek*." Copyright © 1984 by Newsweek, Inc. All rights reserved. Reprinted by permission.

p. 121 From *Peripheral Visions* by Phyllis Theroux. Copyright © 1982 by Phyllis Theroux. Reprinted with permission of William Morrow and Company, Inc.

p. 146 Lewis Thomas, "The Ilks," from *The Lives of a Cell*. Copyright © 1978 by The Massachusetts Medical Society. Used by permission of The Viking Press, a division of Penguin Books, USA Inc.

p. 175 K.C. Cole, "Women and Science," in *Hers: Through Women's Eyes*. Copyright © 1981 by The New York Times Syndication Corporation. Reprinted by permission.

p. 179 Tom Wicker, "The Wrong Lesson." Copyright © The New York Times Company. Reprinted by permission.

p. 200 Adrienne Rich, "Power." From THE FACT OF A DOORFRAME: POEMS SELECTED AND NEW 1950–1984 by Adrienne Rich. Copyright © 1974, 1984 by Adrienne Rich. Reprinted by permission of W.W. Norton & Company, Inc.

p. 213 (Photo) *George Washington* by Keith Carter.

p. 215 Richard Selzer, "Four Appointments with the Discus Thrower," from *Confessions of a Knife*. Copyright © 1979 by Richard Selzer. Reprinted with permission from Simon & Schuster, Inc.

p. 219 William Carlos Williams, "Landscapes with the Fall of Icarus," in *The Collected Poems of William Carlos Williams, Volume II*, edited by Christopher MacGowan. Copyright © 1962 by William Carlos Williams. Copyright © 1988 by Eric Williams and Paul H. Williams. Reprinted by permission of New Directions Publishing Corp. All rights reserved.

p. 225 W.H. Auden, "Musée des Beaux Arts." From *W.H. Auden: Selected Poems, New Edition*. Copyright 1940; © 1960, 1965, 1969, 1972 by W.H. Auden. Copyright © 1974, 1976 by Edward Mendelson, William Meredith, and Monroe K. Spears, executors of the Estate of W.H. Auden. Copyright renewed 1962, 1965, 1967, 1969, 1972, 1973 by W.H. Auden. Copyright © 1979 by Edward Mendelson. Reprinted by permission of Random House, Inc.

p. 233 Richard Selzer, "The Masked Marvel's Last Toehold," from *Confessions of a Knife*. Copyright © 1979 by Richard Selzer. Reprinted with permission from Simon & Schuster, Inc.

pp. 248, 249 Copyright page and excerpt from the Bibliography of *Intimate Matters* by John D'Emilio and Estelle B. Freedman. Used by permission of HarperCollins Publishers, Inc.

p. 251 From *Bibliography Index 1990*, No. 30. Copyright © 1990 by W.H. Wilson Company. Reprinted by permission of H.W. Wilson Company.

p. 252 From *Readers' Guide to Periodical Literature*. Copyright © 1991 by H.W. Wilson Company. Reprinted by permission of H.W. Wilson Company.

p. 253 From *Social Sciences Index 1991*, No. 17. Copyright © 1991 by H.W. Wilson Company. Reprinted by permission of H.W. Wilson Company.

p. 295 Paula Gunn Allen, "Where I Come From Is Like This," from *The Sacred Hoop: Recovering the Feminine in American Indian Traditions*. Copyright © 1986 by Paula Gunn Allen. Reprinted by permission of Beacon Press.

p. 302 Judith Ortiz Cofer, "Casa: A Partial Remembrance of a Puerto Rican Childhood."

From *Silent Dancing* by Judith Ortiz Cofer. Copyright © 1990 by Judith Ortiz Cofer. Reprinted by permission.

p. 306 Patricia Hampl, "Memory and Imagination." Copyright © 1985 by Patricia Hampl. Originally published in *The Dolphin Reader.* Permission to reprint granted by the Rhoda Weyr Agency, New York.

p. 317 Brent Staples, "Just Walk on By." Published in *Harper's,* December 1986. Copyright © 1986 by Brent Staples. Reprinted by permission of Brent Staples.

p. 319 Paul Theroux, "Being a Man," in *Sunrise with Seamonsters: Travels and Discoveries.* Copyright © 1986 by Paul Theroux. Reprinted by permission of Houghton Mifflin Company. All rights reserved.

p. 322 Alice Walker, "Beauty: When the Other Dancer is the Self." From *In Search of Our Mothers' Gardens.* Copyright © 1983 by Alice Walker. Reprinted by permission of Harcourt Brace Jovanovich, Inc.

p. 353 Joan Didion, "On Morality." From *Slouching Towards Bethelehem* by Joan Didion. Copyright © 1965, 1968 by Joan Didion. Reprinted by permission of Farrar, Straus & Giroux, Inc.

p. 357 Shirley Jackson, "The Lottery." Copyright © 1948, 1949 by Shirley Jackson. Renewal Copyright © 1976, 1977 by Lawrence Hyman, Barry Hyman, Mrs. Sarah Webster and Mrs. Joanne Schnurer. Reprinted by permission of Farrar, Straus & Giroux, Inc.

p. 364 Ruth Macklin, "Applying Moral Principles," from *Mortal Choices: Ethical Dilemmas in Modern Medicine.* Copyright © 1987 by Ruth Macklin. Reprinted by permission of Pantheon Books, a division of Random House, Inc.

p. 372 Margaret Mead, "Warfare: An Invention—Not a Biological Necessity." From *Anthropology, A Human Science: Selected Papers, 1939–1960* (New York: Van Nostrand Company, 1964). Copyright © 1964 by Margaret Mead. All rights reserved.

p. 378 Stanley Milgram, "Perils of Obedience." From *Harper's* Magazine, December 1973. Copyright © 1973 by *Harper's* Magazine. All rights reserved. Reprinted from the December issue by permission.

p. 390 George Orwell, "Shooting an Elephant." From *Shooting an Elephant and Other Essays* by George Orwell, copyright 1950 by Sonia Brownell Orwell and renewed 1978 by Sonia Pitt-Rivers, reprinted with permission of Harcourt Brace Jovanovich, Inc. and the Estate of Sonia Brownell and Martin Secker & Warburg Ltd.

p. 396 William Carlos Williams, "The Use of Force," in *Life Along the Passaic River.* Copyright © 1938 by New Directions. Reprinted by permission of New Directions Publishing Corp. All rights reserved.

p. 423 Loren Eiseley, "The Hidden Teacher," from *The Unexpected Universe.* Copyright © 1964, 1966, 1968, 1969 by Loren Eiseley. Reprinted by permission of Harcourt Brace Jovanovich, Inc.

p. 433 Carol Gilligan, "Teaching Shakespeare's Sister: Notes from the Underground of Female Adolescence." Excerpted from *Making Connections: The Relational World of Adolescent Girls at Emma Willard School* by Carol Gilligan, Nona Lyons and Trudy Hammer, eds. (Cambridge, Mass.: Harvard University Press, 1990). Used with permission. Earlier versions of this essay were read at the American Association for Higher Education Conference, "Highest Calling: Teaching to Rebuild the Nation" (Washington, D.C.: March 1988) and as one of two lectures on love and resistance given at the Heinz Werner Lectures at Clark University in November, 1988.

p. 445 June Jordan, "Nobody Means More to Me than You and the Future Life of Willie Jordan." From *On Call: Political Essays* by June Jordan (Boston: South End Press, 1985). Copyright © 1985 by June Jordan. Reprinted by permission of the author. All rights reserved.

p. 459 David Owen, "How They Write the SAT." From *None of the Above* by David Owen. Copyright © 1985 by David Owen. Reprinted by permission of Houghton Mifflin Company. All rights reserved.

p. 467 Theodore Sizer, "What High School Is." From *Horace's Compromise* by Theodore Sizer. Copyright © 1984 by Theodore R. Sizer. Reprinted by permission of Houghton Mifflin Company. All rights reserved.

p. 477 Claude M. Steele, "Race and the Schooling of Black Americans" from *The Atlantic Monthly,* April 1992. Copyright © 1992 by Claude M. Steele. Reprinted by permission of the author, Claude M. Steele.

Index